The Military Order of the Loyal Legion of the United States

Special Limited Edition
No. _____ of 500

PORTRAIT OF PRESIDENT ABRAHAM LINCOLN

Part of the collection of the commandery of Wisconsin, this portrait was painted in Rome by the Austrian artist Anton Romako (1832–1889) for Major General Rufus King, Minister to the Papal States, and displayed in the American Legation for the courtesy visit of diplomatic personnel, following the assassination of President Lincoln in 1865. The portrait was based on a *carte d'visite* in the possession of General King and was painted two days after word reached Rome of the assassination of the president. General King brought the portrait to Wisconsin and it was presented by his son, Captain Charles King, to the Wisconsin commandery.

Photograph courtesy of the Wisconsin Commandery MOLLUS

UNION BLUE

THE HISTORY OF THE MILITARY ORDER OF THE LOYAL LEGION OF THE UNITED STATES

By
Robert Girard Carroon
and
Dana B. Shoaf

With a Preface by Steven James Wright

WHITE MANE BOOKS
SHIPPENSBURG, PENNSYLVANIA

Copyright © 2001 by the Military Order of the Loyal Legion of the United States

ALL RIGHTS RESERVED—No part of this book may be reproduced in any form without permission in writing from the publisher, except by a reviewer who wishes to quote brief passages in connection with a review.

This White Mane Books publication
was printed by
Beidel Printing House, Inc.
63 West Burd Street
Shippensburg, PA 17257-0152 USA

The acid-free paper used in this book meets the guidelines for permanence and durability of the Committee on Production Guidelines for Book Longevity of the Council on Library Resources.

For a complete list of available publications
please write
White Mane Books
Division of White Mane Publishing Company, Inc.
P.O. Box 152
Shippensburg, PA 17257-0152 USA

Library of Congress Cataloging-in-Publication Data

Carroon, Robert G. (Robert Girard), 1937-
  Union blue : the history of the Military Order of the Loyal Legion of the United States / by Robert Girard Carroon and Dana B. Shoaf ; with a preface by Steven James Wright.
    p. cm.
  Includes bibliographical references (p.   ).
  ISBN 1-57249-190-6 (alk. paper)
  1. Military Order of the Loyal Legion of the United States--History. 2. Military Order of the Loyal Legion of the United States--Biography. 3. United States--History--Civil War, 1861-1865--Biography. I. Shoaf, Dana B., 1962- II. Title.

E462.2.A7 C37 2000
369'.15--dc21

00-049955

PRINTED IN THE UNITED STATES OF AMERICA

**DEDICATED TO THE MEMORY OF
JOHN PAGE NICHOLSON
AND
WILLIAM AUGUSTUS HAMANN, III**

Contents

List of Illustrations ix
Preface xi
Acknowledgments xiii
History of the Military Order of the Loyal Legion 1
Biographical Sketches
    George Cadwalader 31
    Winfield Scott Hancock 34
    Rutherford Birchard Hayes 40
    Philip Henry Sheridan 45
    John Jay Almy 49
    Lucius Fairchild 54
    John Gibbon 60
    Bancroft Gherardi 65
    John McAllister Schofield 69
    David McMurtrie Gregg 74
    John Rutter Brooke 78
    Grenville Mellen Dodge 84
    John Coalter Bates 90
    George Wallace Melville 93
    Arthur MacArthur 97
    Arnold Augustus Rand 102
    Thomas Hamlin Hubbard 106
    Louis Kempff 110
    Samuel Baldwin Marks Young 113
    Nelson Appleton Miles 118
    Purnell Frederick Harrington 124
    Robert Means Thompson 127
    Samuel Warren Fountain 131
    George Mason 135
    William Parkinson Wright 139
    John Page Nicholson 142

Commanders in Chief Who Did Not See Service in the Civil War 145
Roster of the Original Companions in the MOLLUS 147
Bibliography 403

ILLUSTRATIONS

President Abraham Lincoln .... frontispiece
Loyal Legion medal 5
Coat of arms 6
Honorary membership to President Hoover 19
Seal of the Loyal Legion 19
The Union League Building 20
The Lincoln Museum 20
Loyal Legion march sheet music 21–24
Meeting of the Loyal Legion, October 24, 1934 25
Major General George Cadwalader 31
Major General Winfield Scott Hancock 34
Major General Rutherford Birchard Hayes 40
General Philip H. Sheridan 45
Rear Admiral John J. Almy 49
Brigadier General Lucius Fairchild 54
Major General John Gibbon 60
Rear Admiral Bancroft Gherardi 65
Lieutenant General John M. Schofield 69
Major General David M. Gregg 74
Major General John Rutter Brooke 78
Major General Grenville M. Dodge 84
Lieutenant General John C. Bates 90
Rear Admiral George W. Melville 93
Lieutenant General Arthur MacArthur 97
Colonel Arnold A. Rand 102
Brigadier General Thomas H. Hubbard 106

Rear Admiral Louis Kempff	110
Lieutenant General Samuel B. M. Young	113
Lieutenant General Nelson Appleton Miles	118
Rear Admiral Purnell F. Harrington	124
Master Robert M. Thompson	127
Brigadier General Samuel Warren Fountain	131
Major George Mason	135
Captain William P. Wright	139
Lieutenant Colonel John Page Nicholson	142

PREFACE

As any reader of this volume will discover, the historic membership of the Military Order of the Loyal Legion of the United States comprised some of the most influential and significant men of late-19th- and early-20th-century America. Several presidents of the United States, physicians, attorneys, clergymen, business moguls, as well as thousands of everyday gentlemen with equally distinguished war records, all comprised the membership of MOLLUS. This volume is respectfully dedicated to two individuals who typify everything positive about the order. One was responsible for carrying the organization from the 19th to the 20th century, while the other brought it to the brink of the 21st century. Both served tirelessly as recorder in chief.

John Page Nicholson, insignia number 1870, enlisted as a private in the Twenty-eighth Pennsylvania Infantry, but quickly rose to the rank of first lieutenant and regimental quartermaster. Promoted to captain, Nicholson served as quartermaster of the First Brigade, Second Division, XII Corps, and was advanced to the grades of brevet major and brevet lieutenant colonel for services in the Savannah and Carolina campaigns. Upon returning to civilian life, Nicholson took up the family business of bookbinding and immersed himself in veteran's affairs and early battlefield preservation. A member of numerous societies, Nicholson also served as president of the Valley Forge Park Commission and chairman of the Gettysburg National Military Park Commission, established by the act of Congress in March 1894. In addition to his steadfast efforts as recorder in chief of the Military Order of the Loyal Legion of the United States, Nicholson translated and edited the four-volume *History of the Civil War in America*, by the Comte de Paris, and edited the landmark *Pennsylvania at Gettysburg*. At the time of his death in 1922, he had held the office of recorder in chief for 37 years.

William Augustus Hamann, III, insignia number 21248, was a United States Navy veteran of World War II, and an hereditary member of MOLLUS through his great-grandfather, Lieutenant Colonel Horace Kellogg, of the 123rd Ohio Infantry. An engineer by profession, Hamann was as much as a Renaissance man as Nicholson, with interests ranging from theater and music, to historic preservation and quantum physics. At the time of his death, in October 1998, Hamann had been serving as recorder in chief for 12 years.

As with every group, the character of the organization was with its membership; and so it was, and is with the Military Order of the Loyal Legion of the United States. John Page Nicholson and William Augustus Hamann, III, exemplify the spirit and intent of the order. One postwar dedication to John Page Nicholson could speak equally as well of William Augustus Hamann, "…from the first to the last of his service he was constant and remitting in his attentions to his duty."

Steven James Wright, #22225
Recorder in Chief

Acknowledgments

The authors would like to thank all those who were of assistance in making this publication possible. Past Commanders in Chief Lowell Varner Hammer, Michael Patrick Sullivan, IV, and William Henry Upham for suggesting and encouraging the idea of this book. We would also like to thank Companions Thomas Pelham Curtis, Harry H. Anderson, the late William A. Hamann, III, and the late Frederick Talley Drum Hunt for their enthusiastic advice and support. Thanks also to Lee Allen Tryon, treasurer in chief of MOLLUS; Douglas Reed Niermeyer, junior vice commander in chief; Stephen James Wright, recorder in chief; Benjamin Charles Frick, judge advocate in chief; Karl Frederick Schaeffer, past commander of the Ohio commandery; and companions Richard Holmes Knight and John William Spaeth, III, for their expertise, contributions, and willingness to help whenever called upon.

The staff at the United States Military History Institute (USMHI), Carlisle, Pennsylvania, and most particularly Dr. Richard J. Sommers, Michael J. Winey, Randy Hackenburg, Pamela Cheyney, and David Keough assisted us far beyond the call of duty; their maintenance of the collections and records of MOLLUS and care for all who are privileged to do research at the USMHI is second to none. James Mundy at the Union League, Philadelphia, Pennsylvania, and Dr. Jerry Bishop, Dr. Charles Hubbard, and Martha Wiley of Lincoln Memorial University, Harrodsgate, Tennessee, were very kind in providing any reference material and photographs we needed. Of considerable assistance, always most cheerfully given, were the staffs of the U.S. Naval Historical Center and E. C. Finney, Jr., the U.S. Naval Institute, the Library of Congress, the National Archives, the Arizona Historical Society, the Missouri Historical Society, the State Historical Society of Wisconsin, the Milwaukee County Historical Society, and the Rutherford B. Hayes Center.

Last but by no means least, we wish to thank the editors and publishers at White Mane, especially Dr. Martin Gordon, Harold Collier, Beverly Kuhn, and Vicki Stouffer for enabling us to tell the story of the great veterans' organization which was central in the lives of so many officers of the armed forces of the United States in the Civil War.

History of the Military Order of the Loyal Legion of the United States

HISTORY OF THE MILITARY ORDER OF THE LOYAL LEGION OF THE UNITED STATES

BY DANA B. SHOAF

April 15, 1865, was a day of mourning in Philadelphia, Pennsylvania, despite the fact the Civil War had recently ended. Workers hung black drapery from buildings throughout the city as citizens anxiously scanned the latest newspaper headlines for more distressing news of President Abraham Lincoln's assassination the previous day. In the midst of the sober atmosphere, three men met in Thomas Ellwood Zell's office on Sixth Street. At that meeting, Zell, a former lieutenant colonel in a Pennsylvania regiment; Samuel Brown Wylie Mitchell, still commissioned as the Eighth Pennsylvania Cavalry's surgeon; and Peter Dirck Keyser, who had soldiered as an officer and a doctor in the Ninety-first Pennsylvania Infantry, decided to form an honor guard for Lincoln's body.[1]

It is likely that Zell, Mitchell, and Keyser had little idea the organization that would develop out of their remorse-motivated decision would be the first Union veterans' group to form; ultimately growing to become the North's second-largest veterans' organization—the Military Order of the Loyal Legion of the United States, more commonly known by its acronym, MOLLUS. Despite the fact the legion became sizeable, counted some of the North's greatest military leaders as members, and developed a strong organization that still exists, modern historians have generally ignored MOLLUS.

Scholars have tended to focus on and examine the larger Grand Army of the Republic and have glossed over the Loyal Legion as a mere fraternal organization, given to lavish dinners and self-congratulatory prose. It is true companions did eat well. The menu for one meeting included an appetizer of soft-shell crabs and main courses of filet mignon and squab—hominy grits was included as a side dish, presumably to evoke harsher and less-refined rations eaten about a smoky fire. It is also true that legionnaires could get a bit verbose in their war recollections, and at least one member realized that many saw the Loyal Legion merely as a platform that allowed the veterans to continue "blowin' about" their wartime adventures. It is equally true, however, that MOLLUS was an organization of influence in Gilded Age America (for example, beginning with President William McKinley, almost the entire military and civil leadership during the Spanish-American War and Boxer Rebellion Era was composed of MOLLUS companions), and one that has a rich, diverse history that deserves to be studied.[2]

Following Lincoln's funeral, the three founders met regularly and quickly came to the decision that they wanted their creation to continue to exist, and to be one with all the trappings of an organized fraternal order: a constitution, members known as "companions" whose actions would be governed by rules and requirements, formal meetings, and regalia. In late May 1865, the first public meeting was held in Constitution Hall in Philadelphia, after which the order slowly took shape.[3]

Though the Loyal Legion's constitution has undergone numerous revisions during the order's existence, most of the tenets expressed in the 1866 edition, the order's first, have remained consistent with some slight changes. Initially, it was decreed that each state would have a "grand commandery" to which smaller "district commanderies" within a given state would answer. That feature was eventually modified so that officer veterans in each state would be permitted to organize one "state commandery" per state. A commandery in chief oversaw all the state chapters, a task the Pennsylvania commandery undertook for the first 19 years of the legion's existence.

Each commandery had a staff of officers to administer the chapter and to officiate at meetings. A commander, assisted by a senior and junior vice commander, was charged with maintaining parliamentary procedure at functions and making sure his chapter followed a "strict observance of the Constitution and By-Laws." A recorder kept the commandery's minutes and collected the ever-important membership dues; a registrar assisted the recorder by maintaining a list of companions and their membership status. A treasurer kept a balance sheet for the commandery.

Like most fraternal orders, MOLLUS had its own regalia and rules for the wearing of such insignia, and a chancellor was in charge of ensuring new members received the required items. A chaplain watched over the spiritual well-being of a commandery and opened each meeting with a prayer, while a five-member council, known as a board of officers, was empowered to audit a commandery's records and fill officer vacancies caused by emergencies or unforeseen circumstances.

The regalia of the order doled out by the chancellor consisted of a "Badge pendent," a medal suspended from a watered silk ribbon. Variations in the ribbon's color scheme denoted whether a member was a veteran or a descendent of one. The badge was an enameled azure and white, eight-pointed star, with rays of gold inserted between each arm of the star. In the center of the star, a gold American eagle was displayed, surrounded by the legion's Latin motto: *Lex Regent, Arma Tuentur*—Laws Rule, Arms Defend.

The reverse side of the medal contained a gold relief that included crossed sabers and a fasces surmounted by a phyrgian cap, over which was an arch of 13 stars. A legend encircled the relief stating "M.O. Loyal Legion, U.S., MDCCCLXV." A companion's membership number was stamped on the backside of the link that connected the ribbon to the badge.

OBVERSE SIDE OF MEDAL   **REVERSE SIDE OF MEDAL**

Massachusetts Commandery Military Order of the Loyal Legion

While the badge was to be worn only on "occasions of ceremony"—officers wore the item on a neck ribbon, while other members wore it upon their left breast—a rosette was designed to be worn in the left lapel of a jacket while companions went about their daily business. The rosette was circular, a half inch in diameter, and was also color-keyed to indicate the status of a companion.

The founding companions designed the legion's coat of arms as an impressive collection of images and symbolism pertaining to the Civil War. A shield formed the center of the coat of arms and was emblazoned with 34 rays that represented the "loyal" states. In the center of the shield was a pillar, a symbol of unity and strength. Above the shield was a crest, a hemisphere on which "AMERICA" was written and that was topped by an eagle and surmounted by 13 stars. To the left stood a Union soldier, his left hand on the shield while his right clutched a flag with the U.S. coat of arms. A sailor supported the opposite side of the shield, grasping it with his right hand while he gripped a billowing American flag with his left. Beneath the soldiers, a banner displayed the legion's motto, once again in Latin.

COAT OF ARMS

From the beginning, two factors made the Loyal Legion distinct—and more controversial, as it would turn out—from the Grand Army and other Union veteran societies. The legion, in accordance with the vision of its founding triumvirate, followed the example of the Revolutionary War Society of Cincinnati, and allowed only veterans who had been "honorably discharged commissioned officers of the United States Army, Navy and Marine Corps, Regular or Volunteer," who had served during the Civil War to join as "First Class" members. Additionally, the order's constitution allowed for primogeniture, the principle whereby the first-born sons of the officers could belong as "Second Class" members. Non-commissioned veterans were excluded from joining.

The constitution also made allowances for "First Class Hereditary Companions," who were direct male descendents of deceased veterans, and a "Third Class" of "gentlemen" who had remained in civil occupations during the conflict, but who had made measurable contributions toward the Union war effort. Andrew Curtin, the wartime governor of Pennsylvania, was an example of such a member.

Two "Principles" and one "Object" were outlined in the constitution as guiding merits of the Loyal Legion. The first principle espoused a "firm belief and trust in almighty God...." The second smacked more of wartime sentiment, as the legionnaires were required to a "True allegiance to the United States of America, based upon paramount respect for and fidelity to the National constitution and Laws...." That principle also included text that decried "insurrection, treason, or rebellion...," and any nefarious practices that would "weaken loyalty" to the federal government.

The stated "Object" of the legion was more expressly fraternal, as members determined to keep alive the memories and friendships forged during their service in the national calamity, and help provide relief to "widows and children" of fallen comrades in arms. Companions were also expected to support the advancement of military technology.[4]

Why Zell and his two brethren chose to follow the example of the Cincinnati might hinge on two distinct factors. Firstly, in the initial weeks following Lincoln's death, the fear spread through the North that rebellion might reawaken in a celebration of the president's demise. Though that concept seems farfetched to modern students who are plainly aware of the state of the Confederacy's armies at the close of the war, such a thought was real enough to cause concern in the "loyal" states. MOLLUS, in part, was therefore conceived as a pool of experienced officers that could quickly reform and lead troops into battle against any new threats to the Union.

The second reason is more pragmatic and self-interested. The men wanted to continue to bond and associate with fellows of similar status and achievement. In other words, the legion was an organization that might allow the ex-officers to maintain their wartime status in peacetime. That was a potentially inflammatory concept in a country inculcated in the values of democracy and the ingrained mistrust of standing armies with their built-in, and potentially dictatorial, officer class. Because of the Loyal Legion's membership policies, it had a homogeneous, Caucasian middle- to upper-middle-class membership. There were a few Hispanic companions in the Colorado and California commanderies. Seventy percent of the companions of the Massachusetts commandery, for example, were considered "high-status white collar"—doctors, lawyers, and the like.[5]

MOLLUS, however, was far from capable of causing much controversy. The first dozen years of its existence, it was a small, disorganized and poorly run group that just barely survived. It foundered for several reasons, including the fact that for over a decade after the war ended veterans of all stripes, North and South, wanted to disassociate themselves from things military. The reasons are obvious: The urge to get started in civilian careers, reacquaint themselves with loved ones and comfortable homes, and the desire to let memories of gore subside dominated the actions of veterans immediately after the conflict. All veteran organizations experienced lean times during the 1870s.[6]

The Loyal Legion was also on shaky ground, however, because Mitchell, a member of the Philadelphia commandery, which was also the national commandery, held the post of the legion's first recorder in chief. Mitchell, it turned out, was a very poor administrator. That was an unfortunate circumstance for the legion, for the recorder in chief was the heartbeat of the organization. Despite the fact the various officers described above were to share in the duties of running the organization, in practice the recorders ended up with most of the responsibility for promulgating and developing official legion communications, and seeing to the myriad of other tasks that kept the various commanderies functioning smoothly.

Mitchell, it seems, was unable to meet most of those obligations. Members carped about the fact they heard little from the order until they received a dues notice, while others complained they never received dues notices. Meetings were poorly organized and attended, and little surrounding the Loyal Legion bespoke esprit or an evolving order. Members drifted away, spoke ill of the legion, and in general seemed to care little if the order succeeded or failed.[7]

In fairness to the surgeon, it must be noted that he was trying to tackle running a nascent veterans' order while handling the demands of a full-time medical practice, and was likely stretched too thin. Nonetheless, evidence points to the fact that if things had not changed, the Loyal Legion would have ceased to exist past the 1880s. A bittersweet turn of events, however, brought life to the struggling organization. In 1879, Mitchell died, and a most remarkable veteran—John Page Nicholson—replaced him in the post of recorder in chief.

If one were to scrutinize all the administrators and officers of Civil War veterans' organizations, it is doubtful one would find a more influential person than Nicholson. It is no exaggeration to say that he not only reinvigorated MOLLUS, but he saved it from imminent collapse. He deserves more attention than can be given him in this introduction, and one will read more of him in other sections of this book, but an additional mention of his accomplishments here is warranted due to the immense impact he had on the Loyal Legion and Union veterans' affairs in general.

Nicholson claimed membership in the Loyal Legion based on his service as an officer with the Twenty-eighth Pennsylvania Infantry. Enlisting as a private in 1861, he fought in many major battles of the eastern theater, including Gettysburg, before his command was transferred west in 1863, where he soldiered on through the Chattanooga and Atlanta campaigns. He then made the famous March to the Sea, and also took part in the Carolina's campaign that brought the Army of Tennessee to heel. By the time the war ended, he had earned a first lieutenant's commission and a brevet to lieutenant colonel.

After his 1865 discharge, Nicholson worked for a bookbinding firm that he co-owned, but his life changed drastically when he took over the position of recorder of the Pennsylvania commandery in 1879. From that point until his death on March 8, 1922, at age 79, he was in reality a professional veteran who devoted all of his time to the affairs of former soldiers. A brief listing of the organizations Nicholson was involved with includes: chairman of the Gettysburg National Park Commission, president of the Valley Forge Park Commission, and vice president of the Soldiers' and Sailors' Home in Erie, Pennsylvania. In addition, he was also a member of the GAR and at least seven other veterans' and hereditary societies.

But Nicholson unquestionably saved his greatest efforts for MOLLUS. A fellow companion remembered that when Nicholson became recorder in chief, he did so "when the treasury was empty, and the Commandery embarrassed by debt...." To rectify those problems, Nicholson embarked on a massive correspondence campaign, writing companions across the country and urging them to become active in the order. To ensure the state recorders took their jobs seriously, Nicholson carefully watched over their performance, making sure they turned in the twice-annual reports required of them by the constitution.[8]

If such a report was late to Nicholson, there had better have been a good reason. In one amusing instance in 1889, Hoyt Sherman, the recorder of the Iowa commandery, went to New York to recuperate from an illness. In his absence, he relied on his son, Frank, to keep his Loyal Legion paperwork "well up." In a case that will ring familiar with fathers and sons everywhere, Frank was remiss, and failed to send in the material. Hoyt explained to Nicholson he was sure he had "instructed [Frank] in the matter of Monthly Reports." Frank, however, claimed not to remember his father's assignment, and therefore, said his father, "missed your [Nicholson's] first call for them." The elder Sherman was "much mortified" by the gaff, and hoped that his recorder in chief would "understand fully for the delay."[9]

When Nicholson took over as recorder in 1879, the Loyal Legion consisted of eight active chapters: Pennsylvania, Tennessee, New York, Maine, Massachusetts, California, Wisconsin, and Illinois. From 1879 to 1904, thanks in part to Nicholson's efforts, 14 more commanderies were chartered: District of Columbia, Ohio, Michigan, Minnesota, Oregon, Missouri, Nebraska, Kansas, Iowa, Colorado, Indiana, Washington, Vermont, and Maryland.

By 1885, in large measure due to Nicholson's exertions, the Loyal Legion had grown to the point where it needed a commandery in chief that functioned independently from the Pennsylvania chapter to oversee the nationwide collection of commanderies and their approximately nine thousand members. The commandery in chief was, naturally enough, based in the legion's birth city of Philadelphia. The officers of the commandery in chief were to mirror those of the state commanderies, and the eminent Nicholson was naturally maintained as the recorder in chief. Happy legionnaires celebrated their hard-working administrator as the "rarest of recorders," and one who was most "able and efficient," and fully realized that to "state the services rendered by him in connection with the building up...of the...Commanderies which compose the Loyal Legion...would be in effect to write their history." Another companion stated more succinctly that Nicholson was the "Chief Power of the Order."[10]

All that "building up," however, had a problematic side, for as the Loyal Legion expanded in size throughout the 1880s and 1890s, it went through a series of growing pains—internal controversies that generally pitted a state commandery against the views of the commandery in chief. These cases can also aptly be described as struggles between the wants of a state chapter and that of John Nicholson's beliefs as to how the legion should be run, as he was generally in the center of such frays.

One such controversy erupted between the Ohio commandery and the overseeing body in Philadelphia in the opening months of 1886 and continued throughout the year, turning out to be one of the first tests of the power of the commandery in chief. The incident was over proxy votes—Ohio companions that were living outside the bounds of the Buckeye State used proxy ballots to elect members to their commandery, even though such a voting procedure was forbidden by the legion's constitution. Absalom H. Mattox, the Ohio recorder and a former artilleryman, sent a letter to Nicholson from Cincinnati on February 24, 1886, explaining that new members had been elected by a "suspension of the rules" due to the exigencies of having many members out of state. Mattox assured Nicholson that the matter would be made whole and proper at the chapter's next meeting on March 3, when the ballots would be cast in a manner that conformed with the MOLLUS constitution.[11]

Nicholson, however, was not appeased by Mattox's letter, and remained displeased with the actions of his Ohio brethren. In Nicholson's view, the Loyal Legion had been created with one of its guiding principles being "respect and fidelity" for the U.S. Constitution, and companions should hold the rules of their order's constitution no less sacrosanct. In the rhetoric of the controversy can be heard the echoes of the crisis of 1861, though on a much smaller scale, of course, as the Ohioans argued a "state's rights" interpretation of the MOLLUS constitution, while Nicholson held firm to a "central government" view of the proceedings.

The recorder in chief wrote Mattox to tell him of his disappointment with the actions of the Ohio companions, and chastised them for not at least bringing a resolution forward to change the constitution concerning proxy voting. He continued that while the constitution did allow for members to live in another state from the one that contained the chapter to which they belonged, it did not permit the casting of proxy ballots. The prohibition on proxy voting could be viewed as a "good or bad law," admitted Nicholson, but he quickly added that it was the "duty" of all legionnaires to continue to "abide by it...." To

Nicholson, the rules of the constitution were to be held with all the respect due legal precedents.[12]

Mattox gamely rejoined in an April 14 letter that some understanding of the condition of the Ohio commandery was needed. Mattox explained that many of the men that belonged to the Buckeye chapter lived out of state, for while they were residents of Ohio when they joined, due to job requirements and other such factors they had since moved away. Others lived in state, but were often absent while traveling on business. The Ohioan estimated that some one hundred of his members were "scattered through 12 states & several territories," and try as those men might, they could not be "present at meetings oftener than once each year." In light of such conditions, Mattox found it reasonable that the Ohio companions should be allowed to make use of proxy voting procedures.[13]

Nicholson then sent Mattox a copy of the minutes from the May 5, 1869, meeting at which the constitutional ruling against proxy votes had been made. Mattox wrote back to thank his superior for the missive, and admitted that the ruling was clear. Recorder Mattox then went on to state, however, "I believe though & know that it would be for the good of the Ohio Comdy to allow non-resident members to send their ballot by mail & have it cast." The issue seemed to be wearing on Mattox, for in a marginal note he scrawled, "I had almost made up my mind a week ago to decline a renomination for Recorder."[14]

In early May, Mattox again penned his chief once more, and the tone of the letter seemed to indicate that while he was ready to acquiesce to the writ of the legion's constitution, other companions would not let the matter rest. Mattox agreed with Nicholson that the order's "laws must be sustained," and claimed he would henceforth "decline to receive [proxy] ballots. ...I have been so much annoyed lately by the peculiar 'cranky' actions of some of our companions...because I insist upon enforcing the Constitution that I am heartsick and about ready to step down & out & take a much needed rest."[15]

The beleaguered Ohio recorder stuck it out, however, and throughout the rest of the month of May, he exchanged two more letters with Nicholson that reiterated he was holding the line in favor of the MOLLUS constitution even though he was under internal pressure to accept the dreaded proxy votes. For the remainder of the spring and the summer of 1886, the issue seemed to calm, at least as far as the extant records of the commandery in chief indicate. But in October, Mattox once again wrote to Nicholson concerning proxy votes.[16]

In the October letter, Mattox had once again taken up the banner of defending proxy voting, claiming that "Out of a membership of over 400, more than 300 are non residents and they feel that in not being allowed to send their votes, they are being disenfranchised and absolutely without a voice in the affairs of the Comdy." The letter went on for four pages, revealing that the current commander of the Ohio chapter, Rutherford B. Hayes, and Jacob D. Cox, also a former general of some note, were arguing for the use of proxy balloting based on "Section 4 Article 21 of the Constitution," which stated that a state commandery had the right "to make its own rules about voting." It appeared Hayes and Cox had a valid point, for that section of the MOLLUS constitution did allow the state chapters to "adopt whatever rules and regulations may be deemed necessary for its own peculiar government."[17]

The nettlesome issue became a matter of debate at the 1886 annual meeting of the commandery in chief, during which the board of officers of the commandery in chief, who had been studying the controversy, presented their conclusion that the voting change proposed by Ohio was "contrary to the spirit" of the legion constitution, and should not be "sustained." Nicholson, as was his duty, then brought forward the Midwesterners' proposed amendment that would permit proxy voting. The proposal was tabled, however, and the commandery in chief formally adopted the recommendation of its board of officers—proxy voting would not be permitted.[18]

Though the debate over proxy voting can seem trite on the surface, it says much about how highly Nicholson and the governing body of MOLLUS viewed the structure of the constitution, and how predominant the belief in strong, centralized control was within the Loyal Legion. Albert Ordway, a member of the Washington, D.C., commandery, wrote to Nicholson to express his support of the defeat of the Ohioans proposal. "It looks," said Ordway, "very much as if the Ohio Commd'y needs disciplining." He continued by expressing his displeasure over the idea of a "State Commd'y assuming to interpret the Constitution—or...worse, suspending its provisions." In the view of the majority of MOLLUS companions, they had fought to defeat concepts launched by the idea of state's rights, and they were not about to let such a notion flourish in their order.[19]

As the organization grew throughout the last two decades of the 19th century, MOLLUS was also beset by negativity from non-members, particularly over its officers-only membership requirements and its acceptance and use of primogeniture. Such criticisms had plagued the legion since its beginnings, but the attacks intensified as MOLLUS grew and became a larger organization during Nicholson's reign.

For example, the *Army and Navy Journal*, a publication primarily read by active-duty military personnel and veterans, critiqued MOLLUS on several occasions as "essentially an Aristocracy" and "one of the most aristocratic organizations of the day." The editors of the *Journal* stated that the legion's hereditary principles were of "doubtful utility" in a democracy, and considered its membership policy to be a "dangerous innovation."[20]

In reaction to such comments, the legionnaires found comfort by comparing themselves to the Society of Cincinnati, another officers-only organization that had been accused of elitism, but one that had proven over time to be no threat to American ideals. Rutherford B. Hayes poetically stated that, like the men who belonged to the Cincinnati, MOLLUS members would be no more disruptive to society than would "snow flakes upon water." Nonetheless, companions soon came to realize that they would have to prove through their actions and behavior that the legion was a useful organization dedicated to the celebration and preservation of democratic ideals. As one member put it, MOLLUS needed to "give to the world...an acceptable reason for its existence."[21]

To that end, the Loyal Legion developed an ideology that was designed to prove to the public at large that the organization filled an important place in American society by functioning as a "role model" for the values of patriotism. The ex-officers also argued that although enlisted men could not join, MOLLUS represented the patriotic sacrifices of every Federal soldier, no matter what rank they held during the war. Coupled with the above ideals, legionnaires also acknowledged that their order did have an aristocratic air about it, but they stressed that it was not a European-style "aristocracy of blood,...birth, or wealth." Instead they considered MOLLUS a peculiarly American aristocracy "born of gallant and heroic...patriotic service." Ephraim C. Dawes, a very active member of the Ohio commandery who often corresponded with Nicholson, coined a phrase that described precisely how members of the Loyal Legion viewed their order, and how they wanted it to be viewed, when he stated that MOLLUS was an "Aristocracy of Patriotism."[22]

Members of the legion pointed out dozens of ways the order was American in nature and representative and respectful of democratic ideals. Companions often pointed out that many of them had started their military careers as enlisted men that had served in the ranks carrying "the musket and the knapsack," and had often advanced in rank by very democratic officer elections, wherein the "votes of fellow soldiers" had earned them their shoulder straps.[23]

Companions also began to place wreaths on the graves of enlisted men in 1884, a very visible means of recognizing the contributions and sacrifices of those in the ranks. Initially, legionnaires had only decorated the resting places of deceased members, and the departure from that policy was designed to "take away from public opinion [the] sharp edge [of] criticisms" leveled at the legion's supposedly haughty nature. To make it clear that the wreaths had been placed by MOLLUS companions, it was decided that "Loyal Legion" would be the only acceptable version of the order's name used on such commemorative items.[24]

Companions took seriously their function as role models of patriotic sacrifice, as they were concerned that the youth of the Gilded Age, a time of great prosperity for the middle and upper classes, were becoming softened by the abundance of new material possessions and diversions. Legionnaire Carl Adae, who had soldiered as a captain in the Fourth Ohio Cavalry, spoke for many when he stated that he was proud MOLLUS was helping to present the "martial spirit...[to] youths who had grown up without the knowledge of war." That same belief justified, companions believed, the legion's hereditary qualities, for the sons of the officers would be inculcated with patriotic values. They, in turn, could continue passing such values on to Americans, allowing the order to function as a "school of patriotism" after the veterans themselves had passed away. One companion even celebrated the sons as patriotic "Videttes of the Republic."[25]

The legionnaires embarked on several campaigns to ensure that the Loyal Legion's patriotic nature received public exposure. They considered it important that the rosette be viewed as more than a "mere badge of hereditary aristocracy." To achieve that end, companions pushed for regulations that would allow MOLLUS members still in the military to wear the rosette, arguing that to do so would allow "younger officers" to easily identify the Civil War veterans, and hence benefit from their example. John Nicholson considered the matter serious enough to write and state the legion's case directly to W. C. Endicott, secretary of war, in 1886. MOLLUS was successful in its effort, for in 1898 the Senate Military Committee formalized a regulation that permitted military officers to wear the rosette during ceremonial functions.[26]

The treatment of the American flag was another issue in which companions were actively involved. Considering the flag to be "sacred," the members of MOLLUS were dismayed by the fact the banner was used increasingly for advertising purposes during the late-19th century. To stop the use of the flag for "private gain," MOLLUS sent petitions to the U.S. government to enact laws governing its use. No such law was put into place, but the organization continued to work internally regarding matters pertaining to the American flag. In 1887, each commandery was ordered to form a "Flag Committee" to "foster public sentiment in favor of honoring the flag." In 1898, the legion became a member of the "American Flag Association," a congress of organizations dedicated to developing legislation that ensured the "proper" use of the flag.[27]

MOLLUS also claimed to be the organization that started the practice of standing for "The Star-Spangled Banner," tracing the beginnings of that expression of respect to Companion Rossell G. O'Brien, a member of the Washington commandery, who supposedly originated the practice in 1893. An 1895 legion circular made the practice of standing for the national anthem a standard procedure in the organization.[28]

Another component of the aristocracy of patriotism identity focused on commemoration of the Civil War, as companions considered it to be their duty to present the story of the conflict to the American public. Their efforts in that regard were very productive and successful, and it is likely that most students of the conflict have used at some point during their research a resource compiled by MOLLUS. One of the first accomplishments of the Loyal Legion in that regard was the compilation and publication of speeches and essays regarding the Civil War—the famous collection of "War Papers" published by each commandery. Many of the speeches were initially put in print as essays in the *Republic Magazine*. That fact that the essays are often found cited in the bibliographies of modern studies of the conflict would undoubtedly make the veterans smile, for they designed the series to reach a wide audience. It was their hope that the recollections would inform future generations about the war while also developing a favorable "public sentiment" about the North's fight to preserve the Union.[29]

The Loyal Legion also played a role in ensuring that the invaluable multivolume *The War of the Rebellion: A Compilation of the Official Records of the Union and Confederate Armies* came to be published. In 1888, the D.C. commandery sent a resolution to the congressional sub-committee involved with the project that urged "increased appropriations" be applied to expand and hasten the completion of the *Official Records*. The commandery continued to keep a sharp eye on the progress of the volumes until they were completed.[30]

In order to provide a repository for artifacts and books related to the Civil War, the Massachusetts commandery instituted the order's first "War Library and Museum," a facility that was open to public view. At one point, every commandery had its own museum, but they were eventually phased out. The Pennsylvania commandery's is the last remaining, and it houses a fine collection of Civil War items.

The Massachusetts commandery, more particularly Arnold Rand, the chapter's longtime recorder, is also responsible for saving hundreds of photographic plates that were taken by Mathew Brady and his assistants during the war. Rand began the campaign to acquire the photographs for his commandery in 1883. Albert Ordway of the D.C. commandery, who fielded Rand's requests and discussed them directly with Brady, immeasurably helped him in the matter. Ordway also negotiated prices with Brady, and made sure he was paid accordingly.

Numerous letters survive that document the process, which was oftentimes very frustrating for Rand and Ordway. At the time, Brady was poverty-stricken and concerned for the care of his ill wife. He wrote Ordway on one occasion that he was in the "Valley of dispair," and sick with worry over the condition of his "poor dear wife, paralysed and bed ridden." Ever the spendthrift, Brady appealed to Ordway and Rand for advances that he quickly used up without producing any photographs. His images were scattered in dozens of locations in the D.C. area, and though it caused Rand and Ordway a great deal of work, they doggedly kept after Brady to retrieve the plates for them to purchase.[31]

Over time, the photographer sold hundreds of plates and prints to the Massachusetts commandery, images that have since been transferred to the photo archives at the United States Army Military History Institute at Carlisle, Pennsylvania. The photographs have appeared in dozens of books about the Civil War, and are truly a priceless resource. It is entirely plausible that had MOLLUS not gotten involved in collecting these unique images, they would have been lost or destroyed.[32]

By 1900, the aristocracy of patriotism and its attendant values of war commemoration and setting a patriotic example to the American populace were well ingrained in the Loyal Legion. Legionnaires were comfortable with the role of their order and its purpose, and felt they had adequately addressed and disproved MOLLUS' critics. Companions viewed the United States quick victory in the Spanish-American War as proof of the worth of their order. Irving Bean of the Wisconsin commandery summarized that view when he contended that America's triumph over Spain proved that MOLLUS had served as an influence "to all of those brave men who were ready to serve their country in its hour of need."[33]

From the turn of the century onward, the legion began to change in character as the original veterans died off. As early as 1897 a concerned companion wrote John Nicholson, "The veterans are going fast." Indeed they were. In 1905, the legion abolished primogeniture out of necessity, for even the first-born sons were beginning to pass, and any male descendent of a veteran was welcome to join. The same year, the constitution was amended to allow the most direct descendent of an officer to join as a first-class member. The organization weathered those changes, surviving through depressions, world wars, and civil unrest. The Loyal Legion enters the 21st century as an active order of approximately nine hundred companions in 17 commanderies, and it is still involved in Civil War commemorative activities. Mitchell, Zell, Keyser, and Nicholson would no doubt be happy to hear that.[34]

This brief introduction is intended to provide the reader with a snapshot of the Loyal Legion's activities and mindset from its formation until the turn of the century. Obviously, further research needs to be done. How, for example, did the order function, and what were its goals after the veterans began to die off and leave the organization to their progeny? What role did the women's auxiliary—the Dames of the Loyal Legion, chartered in 1899—play in the organization? At the very least, however, it is hoped that the preceding facts illustrate the complexity of the organization, and that the information will provide some background for the biographies that follow.

The legionnaires, and in particular John Page Nicholson, were meticulous record-keepers, as the voluminous MOLLUS papers held at the United States Army Military History Institute attest. Such wealth

Left to right: **President Herbert Hoover, Colonel Walter Hopper, commander in chief of the Loyal Legion, and General Douglas MacArthur, senior vice commander of Wisconsin commandery**

The occasion was the presentation of an honorary membership to President Hoover. General MacArthur in his remarks called the Military Order of the Loyal Legion the "Noblest of all the American Orders." The photograph was taken in New York in 1964.

Walter Hopper

Official seal of the MOLLUS

The Union League, c. 1883, in Philadelphia where meetings of the Military Order of the Loyal Legion have been held from 1865 to the present.
Courtesy of the Union League of Philadelphia

The Lincoln Museum at Lincoln Memorial University, Harrodsgate, Tennessee, which houses MOLLUS material, much of it from the Ohio commandery.
Courtesy Lincoln Memorial University

Office of the Recorder in Chief, MOLLUS

THE LOYAL LEGION.
MARCH.

SOUSA.

23

24

A meeting of the Commandery in Chief of MOLLUS was held on October 24, 1934, in front of the War Library and Museum, 1805 Pine Street, Philadelphia, Pennsylvania. Seated in front is Albert L. Woodworth who served as second lieutenant in the Twenty-ninth Connecticut Infantry (D.C. commandery insignia number 7798). The tall gentleman standing to Lieutenant Woodworth's immediate left is Colonel Hugh Means of the Kansas commandery who was commander in chief. Second gentleman from the right is Major General U. S. Grant, III.

Courtesy of the Office of the Recorder in Chief, MOLLUS

can be a blessing and a curse, and I have spent hours reading the letters and circulars of the legion. I am grateful to Robert G. Carroon for his asking me to write this text and allowing me to share some of what I have uncovered during my research.

I would also like to express my thanks to William A. Hamann, III, the recently deceased recorder in chief of the Loyal Legion. When I first began my research on MOLLUS, "Bill" welcomed me to Philadelphia, had me to his home for coffee, and did what he could to facilitate my research and encourage my efforts. I will always be grateful for this thoughtfulness.

NOTES

Abbreviations

JPN—John Page Nicholson
USAMHI—United States Army Military History Institute, Carlisle, Pennsylvania

1. J. Harris Aubin, *Register of the Military Order of the Loyal Legion of the United States: Compiled from the Registers and Circulars of the Various Commanderies* (Boston: Commandery of the State of Massachusetts, 1906), 3–9.
2. *The Military Order of the Loyal Legion of the United States: A Stenographic Report of After-Dinner Speeches at the Seventeenth Annual Dinner of the Commandery of Ohio,*

Cincinnati, May 2, 1900 (Cincinnati: Published by the Commandery, 1900), 2; Orlando Poe, untitled speech delivered June 1, 1887, contained in *War Papers Read Before the Michigan Commandery of the Military Order of the Loyal Legion of the United States, October 6, 1886 to April 6, 1893,* vol. 1 (Detroit: Winn and Hammond, Printers, 1893), 8.

3. Aubin, *Register,* 3–9.
4. Military Order of the Loyal Legion of the United States, *Constitution and By-Laws* (Philadelphia: 1866); The Military Order of the Loyal Legion of the United States, *Constitution and By-Laws* (Philadelphia: 1889). The legion's constitution underwent numerous revisions during the 19th century, and it is possible that the tenets contained in the constitution used by the modern order differ from those described here. For the purposes of simplicity, examples were drawn from the 1866 and 1889 constitutions for this introduction. The USAMHI holds copies of all of the various revisions.
5. George M. Frederickson's *The Inner Civil War: Northern Intellectuals and the Crisis of the Union* (New York: Harper & Row, 1965) contains a good discussion of how wealthy Americans viewed the military and its related organizations as a means to "cluster" with their social equals. The conclusion regarding the membership of the Massachusetts commandery was drawn from data collected from the membership applications of that chapter from 1868–1900. The applications are held at the USAMHI.

Jacqueline Dorgan Meketa, *Legacy of Honor, the Life of Rafael Chacon—A Nineteenth Century New Mexican* (Las Cruces, New Mexico: University of New Mexico Press); (Reprint Albuquerque, New Mexico: Yucca Tree Press, 2000).

6. Gerald Linderman's "Epilogue" in *Embattled Courage: The Experience of Combat in the American Civil War* (New York: The Free Press, 1987), discusses the lethargy of veterans' orders in the 1870s.
7. Numerous letters in the MOLLUS papers at the USAMHI attest to the malaise of the order from 1866–1879.
8. *John Page Nicholson Memoriam,* circular #3, series of 1922, whole #892, USAMHI; Aubin, *Register,* 5–9.
9. Hoyt Sherman to JPN, March 11, 1889, *Recorder in Chief Letter File,* 1890, USAMHI. No reply from Nicholson to Sherman's letter has been found.
10. John S. Cunningham to JPN, January 29, 1884, *National Commandery Letter File, 1882–1884,* USAMHI; *In Memoriam* circular; John S. Cunninghman to Senator John L. Miller, no date, USAMHI.
11. A. H. Mattox to JPN, February 24, 1886, *Commandery in Chief Letter File, 1882–1885,* USAMHI. The entire series of letters pertaining to the incident were apparently misfiled in the wrong binder.
12. JPN to A. H. Mattox, April 20, 1886, *Commandery in Chief Letter File, 1882–1885,* USAMHI.
13. A. H. Mattox to JPN, April 14, 1886, *Commandery in Chief Letter File, 1882–1885,* USAMHI.
14. A. H. Mattox to JPN, April 26, 1886, *Commandery in Chief Letter File, 1882–1885,* USAMHI.
15. A. H. Mattox to JPN, May 2, 1886, *Commandery in Chief Letter File, 1882–1885,* USAMHI.
16. Mattox wrote to Nicholson on May 12 and May 25, 1886, basically reiterating the statements already mentioned in the text. Both of the letters are in the *Commandery in Chief Letter File, 1882–1885,* at the USAMHI.

17. A. H. Mattox to JPN, October 14, 1886, *Commandery in Chief Letter File, 1882–1885,* USAMHI; *1866 Constitution,* 36.
18. *Commandery in Chief Journal* (no publisher, 1886), 85, USAMHI.
19. Albert Ordway to JPN, October 13, 1886, *Commandery in Chief Letter File, 1882–1885,* USAMHI.
20. *The United States Army and Navy Journal and Gazette of the Regular and Volunteer Armed Forces,* February 14, 1885, 525, and March 29, 1890, 589–90.
21. *Personal Recollections of the War of the Rebellion: Addresses Delivered Before the New York Commandery of the Loyal Legion of the United States, 1883–1891,* vol. 1 (New York: Published by the Commandery, 1891), 376–77; Orlando Poe (untitled speech), *War Papers Read Before the Michigan Commandery of the Military Order of the Loyal Legion of the United States, October 6, 1886 to April 6, 1893,* vol. 1 (Detroit: Winn and Hammond, Printers, 1893), 8.
22. J. P. Morton speech (Kansas commandery), printed in *Army and Navy Journal,* June 2, 1898, 904; Ephraim C. Dawes to JPN, December 31, 1887, *Recorder in Chief Letter File,* 1887, USAMHI.
23. Charles Devens, untitled speech in *The Military Order of the Loyal Legion of the United States: Ceremonies at the Twenty-fifth Anniversary, Held at the American Academy of Music, Philadelphia, April 15, 1890* (Philadelphia: 1890), 12–13.
24. Albert Ordway to JPN, February 10, May 10, 1884, *National Commandery Letter File,* 1882–1884, USAMHI.
25. *Sketches of War History, 1861–1865: Papers Read Before the Ohio Commandery of the Military Order of the Loyal Legion of the United States, 1883–1886,* vol. 1 (Cincinnati: Robert Clarke and Co., 1888), 314–27; *The Military Order of the Loyal Legion of the United States: A Stenographic Report of After-Dinner Speeches at the Fourteenth Annual Dinner of Commandery of Ohio, May 5, 1897* (Cincinnati: published by the commandery), 30; *War Papers Read Before the Michigan Commandery,* vol. 1, 23.
26. *After-Dinner Speeches...Commandery of Ohio,* 30; JPN to Secretary of War W. C. Endicott, December 20, 1886; *Army and Navy Journal,* June 16, 1898, 929.
27. *Journal of the Proceedings of the Eleventh Annual Meeting of the Commandery in Chief, Held in the City of Washington, D.C., October 16, 1895* (Philadelphia: no publisher, 1895), 460–61; Commandery in Chief Circular Book, 1896–1902, circular #12, series of 1897, USAMHI.
28. *Journal...Eleventh Annual Meeting,* 460–61; *The American Legion Magazine* (January 17, 1976), 12.
29. *After-Dinner Speeches...Commandery of Ohio,* 25.
30. Rueben D. Mussey to JPN, December 3, 1888, *Recorder in Chief Letter File,* 1888; Alan C. and Barbara A. Aimone, *A User's Guide to the Official Records of the American Civil War* (Shippensburg: White Mane Publishing Co., 1993), vii.
31. Mathew Brady to Albert Ordway, January 20, 1884, *Massachusetts Commandery Letter File,* 1884, USAMHI.
32. Numerous letters held in the Massachusetts commandery papers at the USAMHI document Ordway's and Rand's travails in dealing with Brady and obtaining the photographs.
33. *War Papers Read Before the Commandery of the State of Wisconsin Military Order of the Loyal Legion of the United States,* vol. 3 (Reprint, Wilmington: Broadfoot Publishing Co., 1993), 336.
34. [Illegible] to JPN, *Recorder in Chief Letter File,* April 6, 1897, USAMHI.

Biographical Sketches of Those Commanders in Chief Who Served in the Civil War

By Robert G. Carroon

George Cadwalader

MAJOR GENERAL GEORGE CADWALADER
Massachusetts Commandery Military Order of the Loyal Legion
and the U.S. Army Military History Institute

Major General George Cadwalader was the first commander in chief of the Military Order of the Loyal Legion of the United States and served from 1865 to 1879, longer than any other companion in that office. He was born on May 16, 1806, to Thomas and Mary (Biddle) Cadwalader in Philadelphia, Pennsylvania. He graduated from the University of Pennsylvania, read law, and was admitted to the bar.

In 1826, he became a member of the First Troop Philadelphia City Cavalry, and in 1832 Cadwalader was elected captain of the Philadelphia Grays. Ten years later he was commissioned brigadier general of the First Brigade, First Division, Pennsylvania Militia. He commanded the forces which quelled the Native American, or Know-Nothing Party, riots of 1844.

On March 3, 1847, at the beginning of the Mexican War, he was commissioned brigadier general of volunteers, and participated in every general engagement from the landing at Vera Cruz to the taking of the city of Mexico. He was brevetted major general on September 13, 1847, for gallant conduct at Chapultepec. On his return to Philadelphia he was accorded a public reception at Independence Hall. He resumed the practice of law and was involved in a number of business ventures in Philadelphia until the outbreak of the Civil War.

General Cadwalader's first assignment was as commander of United States forces at Baltimore and Annapolis. In June 1861, he was sent as a divisional commander to the Shenandoah Valley. It was reported that he urged a movement of the forces in the Valley toward General Irwin McDowell's main force at Manassas that would have prevented Johnston's reinforcement at Bull Run, but his advice was not acted upon. Transferred to the western theater of war, General Cadwalader, who was commissioned a major general on April 25, 1862, commanded the Second and Sixth Divisions of the Army of the Western Tennessee at Corinth, Mississippi. He participated in the severe fighting about that post and in the successive Western campaigns under Generals Grant, Sherman, and Thomas. He served throughout the war and returned to Philadelphia in April 1865 just in time to assume the chief command of the ceremonies surrounding the death of President Abraham Lincoln.

General Cadwalader was elected a member of MOLLUS at the organizational meeting on April 17, 1865, and officially became a member on May 1, 1865, when he was assigned Pennsylvania commandery membership number 60. As there was only one commandery in existence at that time his national insignia number was also 60. General Cadwalader served as commander in chief for the remainder of his life and at the time of his death was also commander of the Pennsylvania commandery. He died in Philadelphia on February 3, 1879. He was married in 1830 to Frances Butler Mease; they had three sons, Thomas, Henry, and William, and one daughter, Frances. General Cadwalader was a member of the Society of the Cincinnati and the Aztec Club of 1847 as well as the MOLLUS, and is represented in all of these organizations in 1996. General Cadwalader's long tenure as commander in chief was a major factor in shaping the traditions of the MOLLUS and many of its institutions, such as the design of the insignia, are attributed to him. At his death General Cadwalader was succeeded as commander in chief by Major General Winfield Scott Hancock.

Winfield Scott Hancock

Major General Winfield Scott Hancock
Massachusetts Commandery Military Order of the Loyal Legion
and the U.S. Army Military History Institute

Major General Winfield Scott Hancock was the second commander in chief of the Military Order of the Loyal Legion of the United States and served from 1879 through 1886. A native of Montgomery Square, Pennsylvania (north of Norristown), Winfield Scott Hancock was the son of Benjamin Franklin Hancock and Elizabeth Hoxworth; Winfield Scott Hancock (named for the hero of the War of 1812) was born on February 14, 1824. He attended the Norristown Academy and entered West Point on July 1, 1840, at the age of 16. Among his contemporaries at the U.S. Military Academy were a number who later became generals in the Civil War, including Grant, McClellan, Franklin, Armisted, W. F. Smith, Reynolds, Rosecrans, Longstreet, Pickett and "Stonewall" Jackson. Ulysses S. Grant described him as "tall, well-formed...young and fresh looking—he presented an appearance that would attract attention of an army as he passed."

Upon his graduation from West Point, Hancock was brevetted a second lieutenant in the Sixth U.S. Infantry. In the Mexican War he was brevetted first lieutenant for "gallant and meritorious conduct in the battles of Contreras and Churubusco, Mexico." Hancock also took part in the assaults upon Molino Del Rey and Chapultepec. Following the Mexican War he took part in operations against the Seminoles in the Kansas War, and in the Utah expedition against the Mormons. He was then assigned to duty in Los Angeles. He was promoted to the rank of Captain on November 7, 1855. In 1850 he married Almira Russell of St. Louis, Missouri. At the outbreak of the Civil War, Hancock was still stationed in California, but immediately left for Washington, D.C., where he was made a brigadier general of volunteers on November 29, 1861.

Hancock was given command of a brigade in the II Corps consisting of the Forty-ninth Pennsylvania, Forty-third New York, Fifth Wisconsin, and 9th Maine Regiments. He served with his brigade in the Peninsular campaign (where he was termed "the Superb"), at Crampton's Pass, South Mountain, and Antietam. At Antietam he succeeded to command of the First Division of the II Corps and was promoted major general on November 29, 1862. His leadership at the Battle of Chancellorsville, May 1–4, 1863, was so outstanding that he was promoted to the then vacant command of the II Corps, with whom he was forever after associated in Civil War history.

At Gettysburg, June 30–July 4, 1863, Hancock showed the qualities which made him the hero of that great battle and established his reputation as the finest corps commander in the Civil War. On July 1 he selected, in concert with General Oliver Otis Howard, the position on Cemetery Hill which consolidated the Union position. On the second day of the battle, he commanded the left wing and frustrated the Confederate attempt to turn the flank of the Army of the Potomac. On July 3 it was Hancock, despite his being wounded, who, with the II Corps, repulsed the charge of Pickett and Pettigrew in Lee's attempt to break the center of the Union line. After partially recovering from his wound he again assumed command of the II Corps and led it in action at Wilderness and Spotsylvania. His wound continued to trouble him and he was assigned to staff duty in Washington, D.C., on November 26, 1864.

On July 26, 1866, he was appointed a major general in the Regular Army. The following year, while serving as commander of the Central Military Department he led an expedition against the Indians. In 1867 he was made commander of the Department of Louisiana and Texas. From 1870 to 1872 Hancock commanded the Department of Dakota, and from 1872 to 1886 the Department of the Atlantic. His final assignment was the command of the Department of the East with headquarters at Governor's Island, New York. A member of the "War Democrat" wing of the Democratic Party during the Civil War, General Hancock was nominated for the presidency of the United States in 1880 as the Democratic standard bearer. He lost the election to James A. Garfield by a small plurality of the popular vote and 59 votes in the electoral college.

On February 4, 1866, Winfield Scott Hancock wrote to S. B. Wylie Mitchell, recorder of the Pennsylvania commandery, applying for membership in the MOLLUS. Recorder Wylie replied at once that he would be happy to present the general's name for consideration and Hancock was elected a companion of the first class on February 12, 1866. He was assigned national insignia number 161. He was elected to the council of the Pennsylvania commandery on May 2, 1866, and served for three years. On June 5, 1879, Hancock was elected commander of the Pennsylvania commandery and also commander in chief of the order to succeed Major General George Cadwalader. General Hancock remained as commander in chief until his death at Governor's Island, New York, on February 9, 1886. Funeral services took place at Trinity Church, New York City, on February 13, 1886, and internment was in the cemetery at Norristown, Pennsylvania, on the same day. Hancock was succeeded by Rutherford Birchard Hayes as commander in chief of the MOLLUS.

There are two letters in General Hancock's file in the papers of the commandery in chief, which are of historical interest and are quoted here:

The first letter is from General Hanock to his father, Benjamin F. Hancock, in Norristown. It is interesting in that it suggests the possibility of the secession of California and other western territories from the Union. Hancock's use of the term "Revolution" for the secession of the Southern states is also of interest as that was a term often used by the Confederates themselves.

Los Angeles, Cal.
February 28, 1861

Dear Father:

We have to-day heard, by Poney, that a Southern Confederacy has been formed, and that Jefferson Davis is the President and Mr. Stevens the Vice President. That looks to me that they do not intend to come back under any circumstances. Mr. Stevens may not lend himself to that, but it is intended to make you acknowledge their right of entering themselves into another Government. It appears to complicate matters much.

If there is a separation between the whole North and South, the States on the Pacific will secede from both, you may rely on it. There is a strong Union feeling yet, but the Southern element, desire for novelty and self interest to avoid taxation, will inevitably bring about the result I predict.

I can but stand waiting for the future. I have Government property to protect and if there is any unlawful raid upon it, I intend to do my best to defend it. I am not free to go home now; I would not be permitted to do so if I desired it. If something is not done soon to sustain the Federal Union its defenders will become demoralized and the people too.

If Lincoln thinks more of his country than his party he may yet do something. He will have to offer the olive branch in one hand and hold the sword in the other. I think it most likely that the Southern Confederacy will be recognized by European Governments, if something is not done promptly to put down the Revolution. We can expect nothing else.

We are all pretty well. Allie, Russell and Ava send much love to you all.

        Truly and affectionately yours,
        Winfield S. Hanock
        Captain A.Q.M.

The second letter is from Lieutenant General Ulysses S. Grant to President Abraham Lincoln. This letter is of historical interest since it suggests that General Meade might be moved to a newly created command resulting from consolidation of four departments, and General Hancock would then be given command of the Army of the Potomac. The real purpose of the letter appears, despite the mention of Franklin as a candidate for the "military division," to be making a suggestion to President Lincoln that Meade be "kicked upstairs." Most historians have suggested that Grant was perfectly content with Meade as commander of the Army of the Potomac, but this letter suggests that the general commanding may have really felt otherwise and was seeing how the president would react to putting Hancock in command of the Army of the Potomac. In fact, of course, nothing came of Grant's suggestion (perhaps Lincoln did not like the idea of putting a Democrat such as Hancock in such a position) and Meade remained in command of the Army of the Potomac, but the letter raises an interesting point not previously mentioned by historians of the war or biographers of Meade, Grant, or Hanock, i.e., that Grant may have not been as accepting of Meade as commander of the Army of the Potomac as has been supposed.

City Point, Va., July 25th 1864
Grant to Lincoln
President A. Lincoln.

After the late raid into Maryland had extended itself, seeing the necessity of having the four Departments of the "Susquehanna," the "Middle," "Western Va," and "Washington" under one head, I recommended that they be merged into one and named Gen'l Franklin as a suitable person to command the whole. I still think it highly essential that these four Departments should be in one command—I do not insist that the Departments should be broken up, nor do I insist upon Gen'l Franklin Com'd'g. All I ask is that one general officer, in whom I and yourself have confidence, should command the whole. Gen'l Franklin was named because he was available and I know him to be capable and believe him to be trustworthy. It would suit me equally as well to call the four Departments referred to as a "Military Division" and to have placed in command of it Gen'l Meade. In this case I would suggest Gen'l Hanock for the command of the Army of the Potomac, and Gen'l Gibbon for the command of the 2nd Corps. With Gen'l Meade in command of such a division, I would have every confidence that all the troops within the Military Division would be used to the very best advantage, from a personal examination of the ground and would adopt means of getting the earliest information of any advance of the enemy and would prepare to meet it.

During the last raid the wires happened to be down between here and Fort Monroe and the cable broke between here and Cherrystone. This made it take from twelve to twenty four hours each way, for dispatches to pass. Under such circumstances it was difficult for me to give orders or directions because I could not tell how the conditions might change during the transit of dispatches. Many reasons might be assigned for the changes here suggested, some of which I would not care to commit to paper, but would not hesitate to give verbally.

I send this by Brig. Gen'l Rawlins, Chief of Staff, who will be able to give more information of the situation here than I could give you in a letter. Hoping that you will see this matter in the light I do, I have the honor of subscribing myself, etc.

U.S. Grant
Lieut-Gen'l

Rutherford Birchard Hayes

Major General Rutherford B. Hayes
Rutherford B. Hayes Presidential Center

Major General and President Rutherford Birchard Hayes was both the third and the fifth individual to serve as commander in chief of the Military Order of the Loyal Legion of the United States. He served his first term as commander in chief during the year 1886 and then was re-elected serving from 1888 to 1893.

A native of Ohio, Rutherford B. Hayes was born on October 4, 1822, in the town of Delaware, the son of Rutherford Hayes and Sarah Birchard. In 1842 he graduated from Kenyon College in Gambier, Ohio, and began to read law in the office of Sparrow and Matthew in Columbus. Following a year and a half at Harvard Law School he was admitted to the bar in 1845 and began the practice of his profession in Lower Sandusky, now Fremont, Ohio. In 1850 he opened a law office in Cincinnati.

Hayes became involved in the political arena and in 1858 was elected city solicitor. Initially a Whig he was attracted to the new Republican Party and actively supported John C. Fremont in the presidential election of 1856. In 1860 he made a few speeches on behalf of Abraham Lincoln. With the outbreak of the War of the Rebellion he made patriotic addresses and recruited soldiers for the Union army; however, he soon decided that he wished to embark on a military career himself. "I would prefer to go into it," he wrote, "if I knew that I was to die, or be killed in the course of it than to live through and after it without taking any part in it."

Rutherford was commissioned a major in the Twenty-third Ohio on June 27, 1861, under Colonel William S. Rosecrans. Rosecrans was soon promoted and by the end of the year Hayes was in command of the regiment. Hayes was identified both during and after the war with the Twenty-third Ohio. He and his regiment participated in action in West Virginia, serving under General Fremont in the Valley campaigns against "Stonewall" Jackson. Hayes was severely wounded at the Battle of South Mountain just prior to Antietam. Recovering from his wounds he aided in the capture of the rebel General John Hunt Morgan during Morgan's raid of Ohio. Appointed brigadier general commanding George Crook's First Brigade, he fought well in General Philip Sheridan's Shenandoah Valley campaign and took command of a division in the Army of West Virginia. In March 1865 Rutherford Hayes was brevetted major general of volunteers "for gallant and distinguished service" at the Battles of Fisher's Hill and Cedar Creek.

In October 1864, Hayes was elected to Congress representing the second district of Ohio, and in June 1865 he resigned his commission in order to take his seat in the House of Representatives. He was re-elected in 1866 but resigned in 1867 to run for governor of Ohio. He was elected and then re-elected in 1869. Hayes refused to run for a third term and retired to Fremont where he practiced law and promoted the establishment of public libraries, a special interest of his. He was persuaded by colleagues in the Republican Party to run again for governor in 1875 and was elected. The reform wing of the GOP supported his nomination for the presidency of the United States in 1876 and he secured the nomination. In what is still regarded as a controversial election he was chosen by an electoral commission over Samuel Tilden of New York. Hayes had promised to end the era of Reconstruction in the South and carried out his pledge following his inauguration. He called out federal troops to suppress the railroad riots of 1877. He also tried to introduce measures to reform the civil service, but failed to get his proposals adopted by Congress. His wife, known as "Lemonade Lucy," was an ardent champion of temperance causes. He had told the convention in 1876 that he would accept only one term as president and so refused to stand for re-election.

Hayes returned to his home, "Spiegel Grove," in March 1881. On May 17, 1881, he applied for membership in the MOLLUS through the commandery of the state of Illinois and was elected a companion of the first class on July 6, 1881. His membership certificate was issued on July 10, 1881, and he was assigned insignia number 2175. He transferred to the Ohio commandery and in 1883 was elected commander of that commandery, the first companion to serve as commander of a state commandery prior to being elected commander in chief. He was elected senior vice commander in chief in 1885, and in 1886, upon the death of then Commander in Chief Winfield Scott Hancock, General Hayes became commander in chief. He had served less than six months when Lieutenant General Philip H. Sheridan was elected commander in chief at the annual meeting of the commandery in chief. President Hayes was elected to the office of senior vice commander in chief. On the death of General Sheridan in 1888 Rutherford Hayes again became commander in chief serving until his own death on January 17, 1893.

President Hayes made several notable contributions to the order while serving as commander in chief, including the establishment of the Civil War Library and Museum in Philadelphia. He visited a number of commanderies and made addresses on the purpose and work of the Loyal Legion.

At a meeting of the New York commandery on October 7, 1891, he said, "The Military Order of the Loyal Legion of the United States is writing the history and biography of the war for the Union on such a scale that they will soon fill many volumes...The Loyal Legion is essentially the organic expression of our comradeship in a sacred war...we stood together as comrades on holy ground, fighting for the eternal right. Where is holy ground? If anywhere, it is where man freely dies for his fellow man. That sublime privilege was the crown of Lincoln's fame. And we of the Loyal Legion, and our comrades of the Grand Army, can reverently thank God that we were permitted to stand by Lincoln in the deadly crisis of our nation's history..."

Later, General Hayes remarked, "The Union of our fathers was imperiled by secession. Our faith is, that the American Republic, in the language of the Supreme Court, is 'an indestructible Union of indestructible States.' The general Government was threatened by the doctrine that the allegiance of the citizen was due only to his State. Our faith is, that the citizen's allegiance is to the United States, and that the United States in authority and duty, is in the fullest possible sense, a nation. The contention of our adversaries was that slavery was national, perpetual, and of divine origin. Our faith is, that no statute and no constitution can make valid the false and fatal fantasy that man can hold property in man...The cornerstone of the slave-holding system was the impious dogma that 'might makes right.'"

"Finally one of the mistakes of the Rebellion was unduly to exalt what they called 'sovereign States.' They thought each State should have its own flag for its people to gaze upon and to admire and love. They would have had thirty-four flags in 1861—forty-four in 1891—and at no distant day a hundred. Each would represent a separate government, a separate army and a separate navy, and all of them would wave helplessly and miserably over 'States discordant, dissevered, belligerent!' The faith of the Loyal Legion is the reverse of all this. We believe that the whole of the American Republic—every State and every acre in every State belongs to one flag—'the old flag,' the stars and stripes, the flag of Washington and of Lincoln, the flag of the United States."

"Their rabble of flags would have represented never-ending petty wars between the inhabitants of petty States. Our one flag represents a people great, prosperous and happy, whose heritage will be, as long as they are guided by wisdom and justice, the enjoyment of unbroken harmony and perpetual peace throughout a continental republic. These, companions and friends, are some of the lessons which the Loyal Legion would teach to our children and our children's children to the end of the chapter."

Philip Henry Sheridan

General Philip H. Sheridan
Massachusetts Commandery Military Order of the Loyal Legion
and the U.S. Army Military History Institute

Lieutenant General Philip Henry Sheridan was the fourth individual to serve as commander in chief of the Military Order of the Loyal Legion of the United States. His term of office covered the years 1886 to 1888. In 1886 on the death of Major General Winfield Scott Hancock, who was serving as commander in chief, the senior vice commander in chief, Major General and President Rutherford Birchard Hayes succeeded to the office of commander in chief. That same year at the annual congress of the Loyal Legion, President Hayes stepped aside and resumed his office of senior vice commander in chief in order that General Sheridan might be elected commander in chief. President Hayes made this generous gesture so that the Loyal Legion might have as its commander in chief one of the most popular and illustrious soldiers of the Civil War. Sheridan, the third Civil War officer to hold the rank of lieutenant general (the others being Ulysses S. Grant and William T. Sherman), was considered to be one of the "big three" who commanded the Union army and was the most celebrated army officer in the United States at the time of his election.

Philip Henry Sheridan was born on March 6, 1831, in Somerset, Ohio, the son of John Sheridan and Mary Meenagh, natives of County Cavan, Ireland. He was educated in the village school, and eventually secured an appointment, on the nomination of Congressman Thomas Ritchey, to the United States Military Academy at West Point, entering on July 1, 1848. Sheridan gave his age as 18 years and one month, which would have meant that he was born in 1830, but he was not pressed by the admitting officer. He passed his entrance examinations with the aid of his roommate, Henry Warner Slocum. Sheridan was an outstanding horseman at the academy and this would prove a harbinger of his future career. Unfortunately, his frequently hot temper got the better of him and, after chasing a cadet officer around the parade with a bayonet, Sheridan was suspended for a year. He re-entered and managed to graduate 34th out of 49 in the class of 1853, his low ranking was due to what he called "that odious column of demerits." He counted among his classmates John M. Schofield, John Bell Hood, and James B. McPherson.

On graduation, Phil Sheridan was assigned to the First Infantry as a brevet second lieutenant and found himself, after a brief stopover at Newport Barracks, Kentucky, in Texas fighting Indians. He was promoted to full second lieutenant in the Fourth Infantry and from 1853 to

1861 he continued on frontier duty in Texas, California, Washington, and Oregon territories with a very brief tour of duty as a recruiting officer at Fort Columbus in New York City. He was promoted to first lieutenant on March 1, 1861, and captain on May 14, 1861, in the Thirteenth Infantry, and was serving at Fort Yamhill, Oregon, when he was ordered east to St. Louis.

Sheridan's Civil War career began somewhat inauspiciously as president of the board for auditing claims at St. Louis and then as chief commissary of the Army of the Southwest in the Pea Ridge campaign from December 26 to March 12, 1862. He served as quartermaster of Major General Henry Wager Halleck's headquarters in the advance to Cornish, Mississippi, in April–May 1862. It began to appear to Sheridan and others that he was in line to be a staff officer for his entire career when he managed to wangle an appointment as colonel commanding the Second Michigan Cavalry.

It was Sheridan's appointment to the Second Michigan that set off one of the most meteoric rises in command in the history of the United States Army. He led his regiment in pursuit of Confederates all over northern Mississippi, capturing Booneville and engaging in skirmishes in Blackland, Donaldson's Cross Roads, and Baldwin. He was promoted to command of the Second Brigade, Cavalry Division, of the Army of the Mississippi on June 11 and continued with engagements at Guntown and Rienzi (where he acquired his famous horse). On July 1, 1862, he was brevetted brigadier general of U.S. Volunteers and given command of the Third Division, Army of Kentucky, leading the advance into Kentucky in September 1862. He commanded the Eleventh Division, III Corps, Army of the Ohio, at the Battle of Perryville. He then succeeded to the command of various divisions in the Army of the Cumberland in the Tennessee campaign from November 1862 to September 1863.

Sheridan commanded the Third Division of the XX Corps in the Battle of Murfreesboro at Stone's River, Tennessee, and was brevetted major general of U.S. Volunteers, November 8, 1864. He continued in command of his division at Chickamauga, and then changed to the Second Division, IV Corps, in the Battle of Missionary Ridge. From April 1864 to April 1865 he was in general command of the cavalry corps of the Army of the Potomac and as such participated in the Battles of the Wilderness, Spotsylvania Court-House, Yellow Tavern, Richmond, Cold Harbor, and Trevilian Station. From August 7, 1864, to May 22, 1865, he also commanded the Middle Military Division and for a good portion of that time also the Army of the Shenandoah in which he totally subdued the Shenandoah Valley fighting the Battles of Opequon, Fisher's Hill, Tom's Brook, Cedar Creek, and Winchester.

During the Richmond campaign of 1865 he commanded the cavalry corps and also several army corps and fought the Battles of Dinwiddie Court-House, Five Forks, Amelia Court-House, Jettersville, Sailor's Creek, and Appomattox Depot. He was in command of all of the cavalry at the collapse of the insurgent army at Appomattox Court-House and was present when General Robert E. Lee signed the surrender of the Army of Northern Virginia.

Following the Civil War, General Sheridan commanded the Military Division of the Southwest and the army in Louisiana, Texas, Florida, and Mississippi. He also commanded the army of observation on the Rio Grande during the Mexican War for independence against Maximilian. He then commanded the Department of the Gulf and the Fifth Military District to September 1867 when he succeeded to command of the Military Division of Missouri with headquarters in Chicago. On March 4, 1869, he was promoted to lieutenant general of the United States Army by President Ulysses S. Grant.

General Sheridan returned to the western and southwestern military divisions in 1878 and then succeeded General Sherman as commander in chief of the army in 1884. On June 1, 1884, he was promoted to general by the act of Congress. Like his friend Ulysses S. Grant, he wrote his memoirs (*Personal Memoirs*, 2 vols., 1888) and signed the preface only three days before his death on August 5, 1888, in Nonquitt, Massachusetts.

Philip Henry Sheridan was elected a companion of the first class by the commandery of Pennsylvania on May 12, 1868, and received insignia number 750. He was then transferred to the Illinois commandery as he was then resident in Chicago in command of the District of Missouri. He was actually at Fort Leavenworth, Kansas, at the time he signed his application on December 9, 1867, which was transmitted to Captain Kilbourn Knox who was, at that time, aide-de-camp to the president. The Loyal Legion was honored to have as its commander in chief such a great captain of arms as General Sheridan. General Sheridan is buried at Arlington National Cemetery in Arlington, Virginia.

JOHN JAY ALMY

REAR ADMIRAL JOHN J. ALMY, USN
Officers of the Army and Navy Who Served in the Civil War, 1892
U.S. Naval Historical Center

John Jay Almy was the first naval officer to serve as the commander in chief of the Military Order of the Loyal Legion. As senior vice commander in chief he succeeded Major General and President Rutherford Birchard Hayes upon the latter's death in January 1893, and served as commander in chief until his own death May 16, 1895.

Rear Admiral Almy's career was one of considerable length and he certainly had his share of excitement and thrilling experiences on the high seas in both the Mexican and Civil Wars. He was a blue water sailor who began his naval life at age 14 as a midshipman beginning as an apprentice on the USS *Concord* in 1830. Born in Newport, Rhode Island, on April 24, 1815, he lost his parents while still a boy and the navy was really the only home he ever knew for many years. He rose through the ranks becoming a passed midshipman in 1835 at the conclusion of his cruise on the USS *Ontario* in Brazilian waters. He then served on a receiving-ship at New York from 1836 to 1837 and then transferred to the USS *Cyane* serving in the Mediterranean as an acting master and navigator. Almy was promoted to lieutenant on March 8, 1841, and assigned to the USS *Bainbridge* serving in the Caribbean. From 1843 to 1845 Lieutenant Almy served on the USS *Macedonian* primarily on the African coast.

During the Mexican War he sailed on the USS *Ohio* and participated in the capture of Vera Cruz and Tuspan. Following the war he was assigned to the coast survey working for five years on the coasts of Virginia, North Carolina, and on the Chesapeake Bay. With the outbreak of William Walker's "filibustering" expedition against Nicaragua in 1857 he was given command of the USS *Fulton* in the squadron under Commodore Hiram Paulding. He continued in command of the *Fulton* in an expedition to Paraguay in 1858–59.

The beginning of the Civil War found John Almy on duty at the navy yard in New York. He was commissioned a commander U.S. Navy on April 24, 1861, and given command of the USS *South Carolina* serving on station with the South Atlantic Blockading Squadron. He then assumed command of the USS *Connecticut* on the same station and it was while on that duty that he had his most exciting encounters on the high seas with the enemy blockade runners. During the fourteen months he commanded the *Connecticut* he captured four steamers: *Juno, Scotia, Minnie,* and *Greyhound.* The admiralty court adjudged the value of these vessels and cargoes at $1,063,352.49. The *Connecticut* also drove ashore and destroyed four other blockade runners: *Phantom, Herald, Ceres,* and *Diamond*. The success of these operations made Commander Almy and the *Connecticut* heroes in the North and villains in the South.

Rear Admiral Almy, in an address to the commandery of the District of Columbia in 1882, described the action which resulted in the capture of the *Juno*, "It was a bright pleasant morning off shore, and out about 70 miles from Wilmington, when, at daylight, she was discovered. Chase was immediately given, and in three hours she was a prize. When the captain was brought on board he was greeted with the usual 'Good morning,' with the additional remark, 'Glad to see you,' to which he replied, 'D——d if I am glad to see you.' 'I suppose not,' I remarked. I didn't blame him at all, for to him it was becoming acquainted under very unpleasant conditions. A week before the *Juno* had safely run the blockade in—had discharged her English cargo, had taken on board the usual Confederate American cargo of cotton, tobacco, and turpentine, and was now bound to Nassau."

"Among other letters found on board of the *Juno* was one left open and unfinished, commenced at Wilmington and addressed to the owners in England, in which the captain described the successfully running in by the sleepy-headed Yankees at night, and that he expected to be lucky enough in running out of which he would inform them upon his arrival at Nassau, when he would close and send his letter. But the said letter never reached Nassau nor England." Almy also described a typical pursuit of a blockade runner, "We knew that blockade-runners were expected. The tides and the state of the moon were favorable to them. The moon went down early. Orders had been given that at that time every vessel should have her anchor up, with steam up and ready to start. The vessels, four in number—*Connecticut, Georgia, Emma,* and *Buckingham*—were swinging about, and a little steam used to keep them in their assigned positions. They were like restless race-horses awaiting the order to 'Go!'"

"The officer of the deck was lying down upon his stomach on the hurricane-deck sweeping the horizon with his glass when he reported that there was something moving upon the water like a blockade-runner. The commander looked, and confirmed the report. Orders were immediately given to start, and move with full speed. Two shotted guns were fired at her, when she changed her course, stood off under full speed and was lost sight of. In this move she met with the *Georgia*, which vessel started after her and drove her off. She was faster than most of our vessels, and in the dark, as it was, she could soon run out of sight. Continuing in her persistency to enter (the harbor), the *Emma* met her and drove her off. But she wasn't going to give it up. She had now stood pretty well over towards Smith's Island, thinking she might get in by running close along the land. And now the fourth time she attempted it, when the *Buckingham* espied her, opened her guns, and drove her off. As we didn't see nor hear anything more of her that night, we supposed that she had gone out to sea, to try it perhaps another night, which they frequently did."

"But at day-break the next morning, lo and behold! there was the steamer hard and fast ashore. She had been forced off and shoved over so many times that she was nearer the land than she had calculated, and had run badly ashore. Attempts were made by our vessels to get her off, which was found impossible. A few days after, a gale of wind came on, which broke the vessel to pieces. She was found to be the noted English blockade-runner *Herald*. The officers and crew had left in their boats, and landed on Smith's Island in the dark of the night. This steamer had been running between Bermuda and Charleston, had made ten or twelve successful trips, and had paid for herself several times over. She had now changed her blockade-running route to between Nassau and Wilmington, which proved bad luck to her, as she was wrecked on this her first trip."

John Almy's most publicized capture was that of the *Greyhound* on May 10, 1864. On board was the notorious Southern spy Belle Boyd. Belle, in her book *Belle Boyd in Camp and Prison*, described the pursuit and capture of the *Greyhound*. Commander Almy's report noted that they had stopped and boarded the *Greyhound* at 1:40 P.M. and found the cargo to be cotton, turpentine and tobacco. Among the passengers was the "famous rebel lady, Miss Belle Boyd, and her servant." A prize crew was put on board and the ship proceeded to Boston via Fortress Monroe and New York. Following several weeks' stay in Boston, Belle was escorted to the Canadian border and released.

Commander Almy was commissioned captain on March 3, 1865, and took command of the USS *Juanita*. He cruised along the coast of Brazil and then sailed to the southern coast of Africa where he remained on station for the next two years. Returning to the United States,

Captain Almy was assigned to ordnance duty at the navy yard in New York serving at that post through 1869. On December 30, 1869, he was commissioned commodore and became chief signal officer of the U.S. Navy. His promotion to rear admiral came on August 24, 1873, when he assumed command of the U.S. Pacific Squadron. Rear Admiral Almy was instrumental in suppressing a revolt in Panama in October 1873, protecting transportation across the isthmus, and saving the city of Panama. In 1875 he received the order of Kamehameha I from King Kalakua of Hawaii for services rendered to the king during a visit to the United States.

Rear Admiral Almy resigned from the naval service in April 1877, having reached retirement age as prescribed by law. At the time of his retirement he had served longer at sea than any other officer in the history of the U.S. Navy, 27 years and 10 months; his service ashore was 14 years and 8 months. It was a truly extraordinary career and he received many tributes in the nation's press.

Rear Admiral John Jay Almy was elected a companion of the MOLLUS on May 6, 1868, through the commandery of the state of New York and was assigned insignia number 740. On February 1, 1882, he transferred to the commandery of the District of Columbia as a charter member. He served on the council of the D.C. commandery during 1882–1883 and as senior vice commander during 1887–1888. He was elected senior vice commander in chief of the order on May 14, 1891, and served in that office until 1893 when he succeeded Rutherford Birchard Hayes as commander in chief. Rear Admiral Almy died on May 16, 1895, in Washington, D.C. He was succeeded as commander in chief by Brigadier General Lucius Fairchild. John Almy was married to Alida Gardner. They had three sons and two daughters. Lieutenant Augustus C. Almy followed his father in naval service and Lieutenant William E. Almy joined the army. Also surviving were Charles J. Almy, Ann E. Almy, and Sarah G. Almy. The funeral services for John Jay Almy were at the Church of the Epiphany in Washington, D.C., and he is interred at the Congressional Cemetery, Washington, D.C.

Lucius Fairchild

BRIGADIER GENERAL LUCIUS FAIRCHILD

State Historical Society of Wisconsin

Lucius Fairchild succeeded Rear Admiral John Jay Almy as the commander in chief of the Military Order of the Loyal Legion. Admiral Almy had served a portion of the year 1893, succeeding President Rutherford Birchard Hayes and being himself succeeded by Brigadier General Fairchild who was elected at the annual congress of the Loyal Legion that same year. Brigadier General Fairchild served a two-year term as commander in chief, from 1893 to 1895.

Brigadier General Fairchild was considered one of the heroes of the Civil War and particularly of the Battle of Gettysburg. He was the commanding officer of the Second Wisconsin Volunteer Infantry, one of the regiments forming the famed "Iron Brigade." General Fairchild was seriously wounded on the first day of the Battle of Gettysburg.

A native of Ohio, Lucius Fairchild was born in Franklin Mills (now Kent), Portage County, on December 27, 1831. After living in Cleveland for several years he moved with his parents to Madison, Wisconsin, in 1846. His father, Jairus, became the first mayor of Madison and the first treasurer of the state of Wisconsin; his mother was Sally Blair. After attending Carroll College in Waukesha, Wisconsin, Lucius departed for California in 1849, to participate in the gold rush. He was successful as a merchant and entrepreneur rather than as a gold miner. Returning to Wisconsin in 1855, young Fairchild decided to follow his father into politics. He was successful and in 1858 was elected clerk of the circuit court of Dane County on the Democratic ticket serving from January 1, 1859 to January 1, 1861. In 1860 Lucius successfully passed the required examinations and was admitted to the bar, and became a practicing attorney; he also became a member of the Republican Party. Lucius was active in the Wisconsin state militia, serving in the "Governor's Guard," eventually rising to the rank of first lieutenant.

In response to President Abraham Lincoln's call for volunteers to suppress the rebellion, Lucius enlisted as a private in the Wisconsin infantry on April 17, 1861, but only three days later he was elected captain of Company "K" of the First Wisconsin Volunteer Infantry which was a three-month regiment. Participating in the engagement at Falling Waters on July 2, 1861, Lucius with the First Wisconsin faced the famous "Stonewall" Brigade under the command of Colonel Thomas J. Jackson. Captain Fairchild later wrote, "The bullets whizzed around us thick and fast. The men were cool and easy to manage, only they wanted to go in and shoot, whether or no." On August 5 he was commissioned a captain in the Sixteenth Regiment of the U.S. Army with leave to serve with the volunteer forces, and four days later was transferred to the Second Wisconsin Volunteer Infantry with the rank of major. On August 20 he was commissioned as lieutenant colonel of the Second Wisconsin. Colonel Edgar O'Connor was the colonel of the regiment, but a throat infection prevented him from exercising many of his duties and Lieutenant Colonel Fairchild was, in effect, the commander of the regiment. In early October the Second Wisconsin became part of the brigade composed of the Second, Sixth, and Seventh Wisconsin, the Nineteenth Indiana, and, after Antietam, the Twenty-fourth Michigan which became known as the "Iron Brigade," one of the most famous units to serve in the Civil War.

After service at Chain Bridge under General William F. "Baldy" Smith, command of the Iron Brigade was assumed by General Rufus King and then by Brigadier General John Gibbon. As part of the famed brigade Lieutenant Colonel Fairchild participated in the Battle of Second Manassas. In that engagement Colonel O'Connor was mortally wounded and Lieutenant Colonel Fairchild assumed command of the regiment. On September 8 Fairchild received his commission as colonel as well as command of the Second Wisconsin to date from August 30, 1862. The next major battle in which the Second Wisconsin participated was that of South Mountain. Captain John B. Callis of the Seventh Wisconsin reported, "Colonel Fairchild, of the Second Wisconsin, seeing our perilous condition, brought his regiment forward on our left, and commenced a fire that relieved us from further annoyance on our left, this leaving us to contend against a direct fire from behind a stone wall in our front."

The Battle of Antietam was fought on September 17, and Fairchild, who had fallen ill, insisted in accompanying his regiment while lying in an ambulance. The action grew so intense that Colonel Fairchild was unable to restrain himself and insisted on mounting his horse and taking direct command of his regiment. An orderly carried a blanket so that whenever there was a lull in the action the commander might dismount and rest. Following Antietam, Fairchild and his regiment were engaged in the Battles of Fredericksburg, Fitzhugh's Crossing, and Chancellorsville. After the Battle of Chancellorsville, Colonel Fairchild participated in the pursuit of General Robert E. Lee and the Army of Northern Virginia, which resulted in the confrontation with the Army of the Potomac on July 1, 2, and 3 at Gettysburg, Pennsylvania.

The Iron Brigade was part of the I Corps of the Army of the Potomac which was commanded by Major General John F. Reynolds. As the head of his column approached Gettysburg, General Reynolds turned it across the fields to the left at the Codori House, toward the Cashtown Road, where Brigadier General John Buford's cavalry was heavily engaged. The Second Corps of the Army of Northern Virginia under Lieutenant General A. P. Hill was moving against Buford's troops and Archer and Davis's Brigades of Heth's Division were approaching through McPherson's Wood. General Reynolds ordered the Iron Brigade, commanded by Colonel Solomon Meredith, to expel the enemy from the wood. The Confederate forces could be seen in the wood and Colonel Fairchild and his staff at once dismounted and led the Second Wisconsin, which was the lead regiment of the brigade, in the attack. They received a heavy volley from Archer's brigade; General Reynolds was killed instantly and Colonel Fairchild, who was standing less than a hundred paces from his corps commander, was struck by a Minié ball which shattered his left arm just above the elbow.

Colonel Fairchild was taken to the house of Dr. Schaffer, president of the Pennsylvania (now Gettysburg) College. Dr. A. J. Ward was at the house and undertook to amputate Colonel Fairchild's arm just below the left shoulder. A few hours later, Colonel Fairchild was seen by members of Battery B of the Fourth United States Artillery on the porch of the Schaffer home, waving his remaining hand and calling out, "Stick to 'em boys! Stay with 'em! You'll fetch 'em finally!"

Colonel Fairchild was captured by the advancing Confederates, but as he was too ill to be moved they accepted his parole and he remained in Gettysburg for the remainder of the battle. Following the Battle of Gettysburg, Colonel Fairchild returned to Madison, Wisconsin, on sick leave and on October 20 the president commissioned him brigadier general of volunteers. His wound was so severe that it was obvious that he could not continue on active service, so he resigned his commission and was mustered out of service on November 2, 1863. General Fairchild had allowed his name to be placed in nomination for the office of secretary of state for Wisconsin by the Union Party, and he was elected on the day after his mustering out.

General Fairchild continued in the office of secretary of state until 1865 when he was elected to the first of three terms as governor of Wisconsin, serving in that office until 1872. At the conclusion of his third term, Governor Fairchild accepted an appointment as U.S. Consul in Liverpool, England, and four years later was promoted to the post of U.S. Consul General in Paris, France. In March 1880, he succeeded James Russell Lowell as minister and envoy plenipotentiary to Spain. While minister to Spain he participated in an international congress which had been assembled to settle problems in Morocco. His diplomatic career came to an end in December 1881 when he was succeeded as minister to Spain by former Vice President Hannibal Hamlin.

General Fairchild now turned from politics and diplomacy to veterans' affairs. He had served a term from 1869 to 1870 as senior vice commander in chief of the Grand Army of the Republic (GAR). In 1884 he became commander of the GAR post in Madison, Wisconsin, and in 1886 commander of the Department of Wisconsin of the GAR; that same year at the national encampment in San Francisco, he was elected commander in chief of the GAR. It was while serving as commander in chief of the GAR that Fairchild, campaigning for Republican candidates, became one of the more famous "wavers of the bloody shirt" against Southern Democrats and former Confederates. At a speech in Harlem, New York, before the GAR, he remarked, regarding President Grover Cleveland's executive order that the Confederate battle flags be returned to their respective states, "May God palsy the hand that wrote that order. May God palsy the brain that conceived it, and may God palsy the tongue that dictated it." So great was the resulting outcry in response to Fairchild's speech among the United States Civil War veterans that the president was forced to withdraw the order and it was not until the next century that Congress was able to secure the return of most of the Confederate battle flags to the South. President Benjamin Harrison, who defeated Cleveland in the presidential election partially on the basis of General Fairchild's electioneering, appointed General Fairchild to the Cherokee Claims Commission in Oklahoma.

Lucius Fairchild became a companion of the MOLLUS by election as a companion of the first class by the commandery of the state of Wisconsin on March 4, 1882, and was assigned insignia number 2387. On May 7, 1884, General Fairchild was elected commander of the Wisconsin commandery and served for three terms, through May of 1887. On October 11, 1893, General Fairchild was elected commander in chief of the MOLLUS. While commander in chief he made numerous visits to various state commanderies making speeches and taking greetings to the companions of the order. He wrote a number of articles including several published in the papers of the Wisconsin commandery. He served a two-year term, becoming past commander in chief in 1895 when Major General John Gibbon, who also was associated with the "Iron Brigade" as its most famous commander, succeeded him. General Fairchild died at Madison, Wisconsin, on May 23, 1896. At Fairchild's funeral, which was held from his home, one of the pallbearers was the Honorable William Henry Upham, governor of Wisconsin; Governor Upham's son, William Henry Upham, Jr., served as commander in chief of the MOLLUS from 1985 to 1989.

Governor Fairchild's brother, Colonel Cassius Fairchild, died during the Civil War as a result of wounds received at the Battle of Shiloh. Governor Fairchild was survived by his wife, Frances Bull, and three daughters: Mary Fairchild Morris, Sarah Fairchild Bacon, and Caryl Frances Fairchild. Governor Fairchild was buried in Forest Hill Cemetery, Madison. His nephews, Charles Fairchild and John Cummings Fairchild, succeeded him in the Loyal Legion.

John Gibbon

Major General John Gibbon
Massachusetts Commandery Military Order of the Loyal Legion
and the U.S. Army Military History Institute

John Gibbon succeeded his old comrade, Lucius Fairchild, as commander in chief of the Military Order of the Loyal Legion in 1895, upon the latter's retirement from office. Major General Gibbon was one of the most popular officers of the Union army in the Civil War. Next to General Henry Hunt, Gibbon, as author of *The Artillerist's Manual*, was, arguably, the best-known "cannoneer" of the United States Army in the Civil War.

A native of Pennsylvania, John Gibbon was born just outside of present-day Philadelphia on April 20, 1827. He moved almost immediately to Charlotte, North Carolina, with his parents, Dr. John Heysham Gibbon and Catherine Lardner. John and his three brothers were, consequently, raised in the South and it was from North Carolina that the young Gibbon was appointed to West Point in 1842.

Although John Gibbon graduated in 1847, he missed any meaningful participation in the Mexican War and did not see active service until the conflict with the Seminoles two years later. His specialty in artillery led to an appointment as instructor at West Point in 1852, where he published his treatise on gunnery. He was promoted first lieutenant in 1850 and captain on November 2, 1859. Captain Gibbon commanded the artillery in the expedition against the Mormons in Utah but returned to Fort Leavenworth at the news, brought in Gibbon's case by the "pony express," of outbreak of the Civil War.

Gibbon was appointed chief of artillery of the division commanded by General Irving McDowell in October 1861. Gibbon's three brothers joined the Confederate army, but John remained steadfastly loyal to the Union. Captain Gibbon manifested a particular aptitude in working with the volunteer soldiers who were coming into the army in great numbers in response to President Abraham Lincoln's call for 75,000 men to come to the defense of the Republic. In May 1862, Gibbon was promoted to brigadier general and assigned command of the brigade composed of the Second, Sixth, and Seventh Wisconsin and the Nineteenth Indiana (the Twenty-fourth Michigan was added at a later date) which was to go down in history as the famous "Iron Brigade." Lucius Fairchild commanded the Second Wisconsin in the brigade and when General Gibbon was promoted to the command of a division he recommended that Fairchild succeed him as brigade commander.

General Gibbon commanded the Iron Brigade at the Battles of Painesville, Second Bull Run, South Mountain, and Antietam. He was brevetted major in the Regular Army of the United States on September 17, 1862, and lieutenant colonel on December 13 for service at the Battle of Fredericksburg where he commanded a division in the I Corps. General Gibbon was wounded in the wrist at Fredericksburg and was invalided home for three months' recuperation. While in the hospital in Washington, D.C., he was visited by President Lincoln for whom he developed a great personal regard.

General Gibbon rejoined the army in time for the Battle of Gettysburg and was given command of the Second Division of the II Corps and succeeded General Winfield Scott Hancock (who was assigned by General George G. Meade to take over the III Corps from General Daniel Sickles) in command of the corps. As commanding officer of the II Corps, Gibbon participated in the famous council of war at Meade's headquarters on the night of July 2. As the junior officer present General Gibbon had to give his opinion first as to what tactics should be followed on the following day. When asked his opinion by General Daniel Butterfield, Meade's chief of staff, Gibbon replied, "Remain here, and make such corrections in our position as may be deemed necessary but take no step which even looks like retreat." The following day, while commanding the center in repulsing Pickett's Charge, General Gibbon was shot in the left shoulder.

Following his recovery from his wound at Gettysburg, General Gibbon rejoined the army and was brevetted major general of volunteers on June 7, 1864. He participated in the Battles of the Wilderness, Spotsylvania, and Cold Harbor. On January 15, 1865, he was given command of the XXIV Corps of the Army of the James and as such was the senior officer in charge of arrangements for the surrender of the Army of Northern Virginia at Appomattox Court-House where he supervised the printing of the parole forms. On January 15, 1866, he was mustered out of the volunteer service and the following July assumed command of the Thirty-sixth Infantry in the U.S. Army.

From 1869 to 1886 General Gibbon commanded the Seventh Infantry and was commanding officer of the Yellowstone Expedition in 1876 during which General Custer and units of the Seventh Cavalry were killed in action against the Sioux. The following year General Gibbon commanded the army in the fight on August 9, 1877, which resulted in the defeat of the Nes Percés at Big Hole Pass, Montana, where he was again wounded in action. General Gibbon commanded the Department of Dakota in 1878 and later that of Columbia in Washington Territory where he suppressed the riots against the Chinese in Seattle. On July 1, 1885, he was promoted brigadier general in the United States Army.

On July 11, 1888, General Gibbon was elected a companion of the first class of the MOLLUS through the commandery of the state of Oregon and, assigned insignia number 6388. Although his active service in the U.S. Army restricted his participation in the Loyal Legion, he did attend meetings when able. On October 8, 1890, General Gibbon gave a paper on the subject of pensions before the Oregon commandery in Portland. In advocating improvement in pensions for those who faithfully served in the War of the Rebellion, General Gibbon said, "When we look back on the dark days of 1862 and '63 and recall the sacrifices made by the patriots of this country, and the promises freely given on all hands in regard to what care should be extended to the widows and orphans and dependents of all kinds of those who, volunteering to take the field in support of the government, should fall or be crippled in the National cause, the very natural question arises now, 25 years after the close of the struggle, have those promises been kept? If called on suddenly to face our comrades who fell in the war, could we truthfully say that the promises made to them as they marched to the battle field had been faithfully kept?"

General Gibbon retired from the army on April 20, 1891, and moved to Baltimore, Maryland. He was elected commander in chief of the Loyal Legion on October 15, 1895, and died in Baltimore on February 6, 1896, just as he was to start on a trip west to visit the commanderies of Wisconsin and Minnesota. General Gibbon was buried in Arlington National Cemetery. His wife, Frances North Moale, a son, John Gibbon, and a daughter, Frances Moale Gibbon, survived him. In 1885 Gibbon wrote his memoirs, *Personal Recollections of the Civil War*, but it was not published until 1928 after being edited by his daughter. John Gibbon's memoirs are among the best by one of the important brigade and division commanders of the United States Army in the Civil War and, as one reviewer noted, "are written in a straightforward, frank and soldierly fashion and tell only what the writer himself saw." General Ulysses S. Grant said of General Gibbon, "I know that whatever John Gibbon is directed to do will be done and well done." General Gibbon was succeeded as commander in chief of the MOLLUS by Rear Admiral Bancroft Gherardi.

On his retirement John Gibbon wrote a poem which says, in part,

> Nations and horses and soldiers as well,
> Have their downs and their ups, their heaven, their hell:
> Nations and horses run their course, then expire;
> Soldiers run theirs, for a time, then retire.
> The bugle no longer shall call them to arms;
> No longer the "long roll" to them sounds alarms;
> Once bearded as pards and full of strong "damns"
> They peaceful become, yes as peaceful as lambs.
> To farewells I'm averse. I don't like "good byes"
> They make the voice tremble, they moisten the eyes;
> 'Tis better to flank them, it brings on no fight;
> So with a God bless you, I bid you "good night."

Bancroft Gherardi

Rear Admiral Bancroft Gherardi, USN
U.S. Naval Historical Center

Rear Admiral Bancroft Gherardi, United States Navy, became commander in chief of the Military Order of the Loyal Legion of the United States upon the unexpected death of Commander in Chief John Gibbon in February 1895. Rear Admiral Gherardi was serving as senior vice commander in chief to General Gibbon and had been elected to that office in October 16, 1895.

Bancroft Gherardi was a native of Louisiana, and was born in Jackson on November 10, 1832. His father, Donato Gherardi, emigrated from Italy and became an instructor in classics at the Round Hill School in Jackson. Donato Gherardi married Jane Bancroft, the sister of the historian George Bancroft, who was the principal of the school. Deciding on a naval career, young Bancroft secured an appointment in 1846 to the naval academy as an acting midshipman through the assistance of his uncle, who was, by that time, secretary of the navy. As the Mexican War was underway Bancroft left the academy and reported to the USS *Ohio,* on which he served to the end of the war. He wrote that his first action was at the bombardment of Vera Cruz. Also on board the *Ohio* was another future commander in chief of MOLLUS, John J. Almy. At the conclusion of the war Bancroft was assigned to the USS *Saranac* but returned to the naval academy in the fall of 1851. Gherardi who graduated from the naval academy in 1852 was warranted passed midshipman and assigned to the USS *St. Louis*, which was bound for duty in the Mediterranean.

On September 16, 1855, Midshipman Gherardi was commissioned a lieutenant (and master) and reported on board the USS *Saratoga.* He was serving with the Pacific Squadron on the USS *Lancaster* when the Civil War broke out. As a Southerner he was offered a commission by the Confederate government, but rejected the overtures of Secretary of the Navy Stephen Mallory and President Jefferson Davis. Returning to the eastern coast he became executive officer of the USS *Chippewa* and was at the bombardment and capture of Fort Macon. He was promoted to lieutenant commander on July 26, 1862, and ordered to the USS *Mohican.*

Gherardi's duty on the *Mohican* was the among his most memorable of the war, when, as executive officer, he participated in the hunt for the Confederate raiders *Alabama, Georgia,* and *Florida*. At one time only the *Mohican* was available to pursue the *Alabama, Georgia,* and *Florida* in the South Atlantic off the coast of Brazil where she missed the *Florida* by a week at Pernambuco and the *Alabama* at Bahia by three days.

In the fall of 1863 Lieutenant Commander Gherardi was appointed to the command of the USS *Chocura* in the West Gulf Blockading Squadron and the following May was transferred to the USS *Port Royal*. As captain of the *Port Royal* Gherardi participated in the Battle of Mobile Bay on August 5, 1864. While the fleet under Admiral Farragut ran past Fort Morgan and Fort Gaines into the bay, the *Port Royal* was lashed to the USS *Richmond* but then cast off to attack, in a running battle, several of the Confederate gunboats. In company with the USS *Metacomet*, Gherardi chased and either sank or drove off the rebel gunboats *Morgan, Gaines,* and *Selma*.

Following the Battle of Mobile Bay, Gherardi was given command of the USS *Pequot* in the North Atlantic Squadron, and he remained in command of her until the end of the Civil War. On July 26, 1866, he was promoted to commander, U.S. Navy, and assigned to duty at the Philadelphia Navy Yard, and then at the Mare Island yard on the receiving-ship USS *Independence*. On November 9, 1874, he was commissioned a captain and took command of the USS *Pensacola*, the flagship of the North Pacific Squadron. Two years later he was sentenced to be suspended for two years for "causing punishment forbidden by law to be inflicted on persons in the Navy." The sentence was remitted and he took command of the receiving ship USS *Colorado*. From 1881 to 1883 he commanded the USS *Lancaster* flagship of the European Station.

Promoted to commodore on November 3, 1884, he served as president of the Naval Examining Board, governor of the Naval Asylum in Philadelphia, and, upon promotion to rear admiral in August 1887, became commandant of the Brooklyn Navy Yard. From 1889 to 1892 Admiral Gherardi commanded the North Atlantic Squadron. When a revolution broke out in Haiti he arranged a diplomatic solution which was highly commended by the U.S. Government and the parties involved.

In 1893 he commanded a naval review fleet on the Hudson which consisted of 35 ships from 10 different nations. The review was part of the celebration of Columbus' discovery of America. Secretary of the Navy H. A. Herbert wrote that Admiral Gherardi commanded more ships on that occasion from "more different nations than any other Admiral in the history of the world." He was serving a second tour of duty as commandant of the navy yard in Brooklyn when he reached the mandatory retirement age of 62 years. Admiral Gherardi retired at impressive ceremonies, including a 13-gun salute from the USS *Vermont*, on November 10, 1894.

Bancroft Gherardi was an active participant in the the MOLLUS. He was elected as a companion of the first class on July 2, 1866, by the Pennsylvania commandery, while he was on duty in Philadelphia, and assigned insignia number 177. He served on the council of the commandery in 1886–1887 and then as senior vice commander from 1887 to 1888. On October 16, 1895, he was elected senior vice commander in chief and, as noted, became commander in chief on the death of General Gibbon. Admiral Gherardi was elected commander in chief in his own right on October 13, 1896, and served until the annual meeting of the commandery in chief in 1899 when General John M. Schofield succeeded him.

Admiral Gherardi had the privilege of leading the Loyal Legion during the Spanish-American War, when membership was at an all-time high and many companions were on active duty in senior positions in the U.S. military. As commander in chief he was frequently interviewed by the press regarding his analysis of various naval actions during the war. In commenting on Admiral Dewey and the Battle of Manila Bay, Admiral Gherardi said, "The greatest tribute to the courage and efficiency of the United States navy was paid when Manila fell and the Spanish fleet sunk beneath the guns of Commodore Dewey's squadron. That victory is a practical demonstration and an additional proof, if any be needed, that the great advantages in naval action are the things preeminently possessed by our navy…the high efficiency of the drill of our men; the constant training they have had in target practice, and the fact that they have been taught that the guns aboard ship are not to be looked at, but to be used, and that the deadly execution they are capable of doing is possible only by their own efforts. The victory of Manila was full and complete. It would have been impossible to exceed or add to it in any way."

Admiral Gherardi was married to Anna Talbot Rockwell, a native of San Francisco, in 1872. The Gherardis had two sons, Bancroft Gherardi, Jr., and Lieutenant Walter Gherardi, USN. After Admiral Gherardi's retirement in 1894 the family moved to Stratford, Connecticut, where the admiral died on December 10, 1903, from complications of diabetes. Admiral Gherardi was interred at the Naval Academy Cemetery, Annapolis, Maryland, on December 14, 1903.

John McAllister Schofield

LIEUTENANT GENERAL JOHN M. SCHOFIELD
Massachusetts Commandery Military Order of the Loyal Legion
and the U.S. Army Military History Institute

John McAllister Schofield became commander in chief of the Military Order of the Loyal Legion of the United States on October 18, 1899, succeeding Rear Admiral Bancroft Gherardi. A veteran of 46 years' service in the United States Army, Schofield retired with the rank of lieutenant general in September 1895.

John Schofield was one of the greatest serving officers in the history of the United States Army, holding virtually every military office his country could bestow. Born in Gerry, Chautauqua County, New York, on September 29, 1831, to The Reverend James and Caroline (McAllister) Schofield. John's father, a Baptist clergyman, was called to a parish in Freeport, Illinois, and the young Schofield graduated from the public schools in that area. Following a brief stint as a surveyor and schoolteacher in Wisconsin, John secured an appointment to West Point. He graduated seventh in the Class of 1853 and was commissioned a brevet second lieutenant and assigned to the Second Artillery at Fort Moultrie, South Carolina. After joining the First Artillery in Florida, Lieutenant Schofield returned to West Point in the capacity of professor of natural and experimental philosophy.

In 1860 he secured a leave of absence to accept a visiting professorship in physics at Washington University in St. Louis, Missouri, and it was there that he commenced his career in the Civil War. He was promoted to captain on May 14, 1861, and assisted General Nathaniel Lyon, whom he served as chief of staff, in organizing the forces of the Union army in Missouri. Captain Schofield commanded the First Missouri Volunteer Infantry at the Battle of Wilson's Creek with the rank of brevet major. Following General Lyon's death at Wilson's Creek, Schofield continued to serve in Missouri and on November 21, at age 31, was commissioned brigadier general of volunteers. Following the removal of General John C. Fremont as commander of Union forces in Missouri, General Schofield assumed command of the state militia and on June 1, 1862, he became commander of the District of Missouri. His aggressive action swept the Confederates into the southwestern corner of the state. General Schofield formed the "Army of the Frontier" which was the major Union army in the Trans-Mississippi area.

During his tenure in Missouri, General Schofield manifested administrative as well as military abilities dealing with many problems, particularly on the Missouri-Kansas border, in a very effective manner. Following a brief appointment as a division commander in the XIV

Corps, Schofield was assigned to St. Louis as commander of the Department of Missouri. His diplomatic skills continued to stand him in good stead, particularly with the powerful Blair family and with President Abraham Lincoln, with whom he had several interviews, who sustained General Schofield when he was criticized for what some considered to be harsh procedures involving pro-Southern elements in the state.

General Schofield took command of the XXIII Corps and the Department of the Ohio. He joined General William T. Sherman as one of three army commanders in the Atlanta campaign and was made a brigadier general in the Regular Army on November 30, 1864. It was in that capacity that he commanded the United States forces at the Battle of Franklin when he practically destroyed the Confederate army of Tennessee under Lieutenant General John Bell Hood. Although Schofield retreated to Nashville, pursued by Hood, the latter's army was in such a state of near collapse that the forces under the command of Major General George Thomas, assisted by Schofield, easily dispersed the rebel remnant. On March 13, 1865, John Schofield was commissioned a brevet major general for "gallant and meritorious services in the battle of Franklin, Tennessee." General Schofield closed his service in the War of the Rebellion by commanding the Department of North Carolina, occupying Wilmington, and leading his forces to a junction with those of General Sherman at Goldsboro, North Carolina, which effectively ended the war in the eastern theatre. Schofield accompanied Sherman to the meeting with Lieutenant General Joseph E. Johnston, who arranged the terms of surrender of the Confederate forces in the area. General Schofield was mustered out of the volunteer service on September 1, 1866.

General Schofield was immediately called upon by Secretary of War Edwin M. Stanton and Secretary of State William H. Seward to go to Paris on an unofficial diplomatic mission regarding the presence of French forces in Mexico. Schofield's diplomatic finesse enabled him to secure the withdrawal of the French army. Upon his return from France, General Schofield was assigned as commander of Military District Number 1 (Virginia) under Reconstruction. He remained in that position until 1868 when he briefly served as secretary of war, a post he resigned upon President Grant's inauguration. John Schofield was commissioned a major general in the Regular Army on March 4, 1869. General

Schofield then served as commander of the Department of Missouri and later of the Pacific. From 1876 to 1881 he was superintendent of the U.S. Military Academy at West Point and then returned to command once again the military Departments of Missouri, the Pacific, and the Atlantic. In 1888, upon the death of Lieutenant General Philip Sheridan, General Schofield became commander in chief of the army.

During his service in the period following the War of the Rebellion, General Schofield was responsible for establishing the U.S. Cavalry School at Fort Riley, Kansas, and selecting Pearl Harbor as the United States naval base in the Hawaiian Islands. He received the Medal of Honor "for conspicuous gallantry at the battle of Wilson's Creek, Missouri, August 10, 1861." On February 25, 1895, John Schofield was promoted to lieutenant general and retired on September 29, 1895. During the Spanish-American War, President McKinley asked that he return, to active service, but General Scofield's incompatibility with the views of the General in Chief Nelson A. Miles made that an impossibility.

General Schofield was an active and enthusiastic member of the Military Order of the Loyal Legion. He was elected to membership as a companion of the first class through the commandery of the state of Pennsylvania on April 12, 1871, and assigned insignia number 1274. He transferred to the commandery of the state of California as a charter member on May 3, 1871, and to the commandery of the state of New York, October 31, 1878. He returned to California on February 7, 1883, and then transferred to Illinois on May 5, 1884, returning to New York on October 16, 1886, and finally to the commandery of the District of Columbia on May 7, 1890. General Schofield served as commander of the commandery of the state of California from May 3, 1871 to May 1, 1876, and was thus its founding commander. He served two terms as commander of the commandery of the state of New York, May 7, 1879–May 4, 1881, and May 4, 1887 to May 1, 1889. He served as commander in chief from October 18, 1899 to October 21, 1903, when he was succeeded by Major General David McMurtrie Gregg.

General Schofield died in St. Augustine, Florida, on March 4, 1906. He was twice married, first to Harriet Bartlett by whom he had two sons and a daughter and, following the death of his first wife to Georgia Kilbourne by whom he had a daughter, Georgiana. He was survived by his wife and daughter. He was buried at Arlington National Cemetery. His memoirs, *Forty-six Years in the Army,* were controversial and also a best seller. General T. H. Ruger summed up General Schofield's career on the latter's death when he said of John McAlister Schofield, "The country has lost a great soldier, a great statesman, a great negotiator, a great patriot."

David McMurtrie Gregg

Major General David McMurtrie Gregg
Massachusetts Commandery Military Order of the Loyal Legion
and the U.S. Army Military History Institute

Major General David McMurtrie Gregg succeeded Lieutenant General John McAllister Schofield as commander in chief of the order by election on October 21, 1903. General Gregg had made his reputation during the Civil War as a dashing commander of cavalry and, after the war, had become a prominent figure in Pennsylvania politics.

A native of Huntingdon, Pennsylvania, where he was born to Matthew Duncan Gregg and Ellen McMurtrie, he was educated in private schools and then entered Lewisburg University, the predecessor of Bucknell. In July 1851 he entered West Point graduating four years later when he was commissioned a brevet second lieutenant of Dragoons. He was assigned to Jefferson Barracks in St. Louis and then, having been promoted to second lieutenant, he was sent to New Mexico. From New Mexico he went to Fort Tejon in California and from there to Fort Vancouver and Walla Walla in Washington. He was in combat at To-Hono-Nimme against the Indians and then returned to Fort Tejon where he was promoted to first lieutenant on March 21, 1861.

With the outbreak of the Civil War, Lieutenant Gregg was ordered to Washington, D.C., where, on May 14, he was commissioned a captain in the Sixth United States Cavalry. He remained on duty in Washington, D.C., until March 1862. On January 24 he was promoted to colonel of the Eighth Pennsylvania Cavalry and joined the Army of the Potomac. Serving under General George B. McClellan, he fought in the Peninsular campaign including the Battles of Seven Pines, Fair Oaks, Malvern Hill, and covered the retreat of the Federal troops from Harrison's Landing to Yorktown, Virginia.

David Gregg next participated in the Battles of South Mountain and Antietam and, as part of the cavalry of the Army of the Potomac pursued the rebel forces to Warrenton and Fredericksburg. On November 29, 1862, Colonel Gregg was promoted to brigadier general, United States Volunteers, and was assigned the command of the brigade of cavalry attached to the Left Grand Division under Major General William Franklin. In February 1863, he assumed command of the Third Division of the cavalry corps of the Army of the Potomac and continued in that position through May.

From June through February 1864 General Gregg commanded the Second Division of the cavalry corps. He was actively engaged in almost all of the military operations leading up to the Battle of Gettysburg. He commanded troops, and on occasion was in overall command at

Brandy Station, Beverly Ford, Aldie, and Upperville. At Gettysburg, with his Second Division comprising 14 regiments, he defeated General J. E. B. Stuart's Cavalry of the Army of Northern Virginia and, in the opinion of a number of scholars gained the most conspicuous cavalry victory of the war, saving the army from the disaster which would have resulted had the rebel cavalry gained the rear of the Union lines.

"Full justice has yet to be done to the services of General Gregg, and of his command, in the Battle of Gettysburg," wrote Companion William Brooke Rawle, a captain in the Third Pennsylvania Cavalry at Gettysburg. "That gallant and distinguished soldier; that upright and courteous gentleman; that modest and retiring man, was not given to writing glowing descriptions of what he had done, or what he thought or dreamed he had done, as was the case with some others. But the country is gradually and surely coming to a proper appreciation of those services. Had Stuart succeeded in his well-laid plan, and, with his large force of cavalry, struck the Army of the Potomac in the rear of its line of battle, directly toward which he was moving, simultaneously with Longstreet's magnificent and furious assault in its front, when our infantry had all it could do to hold on to the line of Cemetery Ridge, and but little more was needed to make the assault a success—the merest tyro in the art of war can readily tell what the result would have been."

It has often been said that Gregg's fight at Gettysburg was one of the finest cavalry fights of the war. As George Armstrong Custer said in his report of it: "I challenge the annals of warfare to produce a more brilliant or successful charge of cavalry than the one just recounted."

Pursuing the enemy, General Gregg was again in action at Rappahannock Station, Beverly Ford, Auburn, and New Hope Church. Actively engaged in Lieutenant General Ulysses S. Grant's campaigns, he was in command at Todd's Tavern, Trevelian Station, Boydton Plank Road, and in virtually every action during 1864. On August 1, 1864, he was promoted brevet major general "for highly meritorious and distinguished conduct throughout the campaign particularly in the reconnaissance on Charles City Road."

Major General Gregg continued his service with the Army of the Potomac until the acceptance of his resignation on February 8, 1865. No explanation has ever been given for his resignation and he did not offer one. At the time of his resignation Gregg had participated in more than 40 engagements. General Gregg returned to Washington, D.C., and then retired to his home in Reading, Pennsylvania.

In 1874 President Grant appointed General Gregg as U.S. Consul at Prague, but he remained at his post less than a year. After his return to Pennsylvania he became active in state politics (Pennsylvania's War Governor Andrew G. Curtin was a first cousin) and was elected auditor general of Pennsylvania serving a three-year term.

David McMurtrie Gregg was an active and hardworking participant in the Military Order of the Loyal Legion. He was elected a companion of the first class on August 29, 1866, by the commandery of the state of Pennsylvania and assigned insignia number 342. He served in various offices in the Pennsylvania commandery and was its commander from 1886 to 1904. On October 21, 1903, he was elected commander in chief, succeeding Lieutenant General John McAllister Schofield. General Gregg served a two-year term, retiring in 1905. He was honored with a statue in Reading and a memorial tablet in the Prince of Peace Church in Gettysburg, erected by the Pennsylvania commandery. In 1907 he published *The Second Cavalry Division of the Army of the Potomac in the Gettysburg Campaign.*

David McMurtrie Gregg died in Reading, Pennsylvania, on August 7, 1916, at age 83 "from general debility aggravated by the intense heat." He married Ellen Frances Sheaff in 1862 (she predeceased him in 1915). Two sons, David M. Gregg and George S. Gregg (the latter becoming a member of the Pennsylvania commandery with insignia number 8782), survived General Gregg. Major J. Edward Carpenter said of David McMurtrie Gregg, "To him the regiment owed everything. His modesty kept him from the notoriety that many gained through the newspapers, but in the army the testimony of all officers who knew him was the same. Brave, prudent, dashing when the occasion required dash, and firm as a rock he was looked upon, both as a regimental commander and afterwards as a Major General, as a man in whose hands any troops were safe."

JOHN RUTTER BROOKE

MAJOR GENERAL JOHN RUTTER BROOKE
Massachusetts Commandery Military Order of the Loyal Legion
and the U.S. Army Military History Institute

Major General John Rutter Brooke became commander in chief of the Military Order of the Loyal Legion of the United States in 1905 succeeding Major General David McMurtrie Gregg. He had served with distinction in both the War of the Rebellion and the Spanish-American War. General Brooke was a native of Montgomery County, Pennsylvania, and the son of William Brooke and Martha Rutter. Born July 21, 1838, he was educated at Freeland Seminary and Bolmars School in West Chester.

With the outbreak of the Civil War, John R. Brooke enlisted and was commissioned a captain in the Fourth Pennsylvania Infantry. He said his father's last words to him as he left his home in Pottstown, Pennsylvania, were, "Good by John. Don't get shot in the back." The Fourth Pennsylvania was a three-month regiment, which gained a bad reputation by disbanding and returning home just before the first Battle of Bull Run. Captain Brooke re-enlisted on November 7, 1861, and was commissioned colonel of the Fifty-third Pennsylvania Infantry. He remained in command of the Fifty-third Pennsylvania until May 12, 1864. His command of the Fifty-third placed him in the thick of action in many of the major battles of the Civil War. Brooke's regiment was part of the Third Brigade, First Division, II Corps. Originally stationed in Washington, D.C., in March 1862 the regiment joined the rest of the Army of the Potomac in the siege of Yorktown and the Peninsular campaign. Describing the action at Fair Oaks, Virginia, on June 1, 1862, Colonel Brooke wrote, "After standing for a long time in line without having been advised that the enemy was about to attack us, and the forest being so dense that nothing could be seen at a short distance, a desperate assault was made on our line by what appeared to me to be a large force. This was my first real battle during that war. My whole mind was concentrated on the question as to whether my men would stand. They did stand; they repulsed the assault, and not only that, but five successive assaults were made, all of which were repulsed, and the regiment then advanced, and, to use a very technical term "cleaned them out" in our front. You can well imagine a young man in command of a regiment, having present 900 men, feeling a thrill." Colonel Brooke was wounded in this engagement but not seriously.

From July 4 to August 18, 1862, Colonel Brooke commanded the Third Brigade, First Division, II Corps until relieved by Major General William H. French at Newport News. Returning to command of his regiment Colonel Brooke fought at the second Battle of Bull Run and then again assumed command of the Third Brigade, a position he held during the campaign and Battle of Antietam. Following the Battle of Antietam, Brooke led a special detachment of five regiments of infantry, three of cavalry, and two batteries of artillery, which served as the advance units in a reconnaissance commanded by Major General Winfield Scott Hancock, from Harpers Ferry to Charlestown, Virginia. Colonel Brooke then returned to the command of his regiment leading it and the Twenty-seventh Connecticut at the Battle of Fredericksburg. He participated in the Battle of Chancellorsville on May 1, 2, and 3, 1863, and was in action at the Battle of Gettysburg.

"At Gettysburg," Colonel Brooke, who was in command of the Fourth Brigade (consisting of the Twenty-seventh Connecticut, the Second Delaware, Sixty-fourth New York, Fifty-third Pennsylvania, and the 145th Pennsylvania) wrote, "When the Third Army Corps had been engaged for some time, and the enemy had succeeded in practically driving it back, the 1st division of the Second Corps was ordered to the left to stay the advance of the enemy in the vicinity of the wheat field which lay in front of Little Round Top. Three brigades of the division were in my front, my brigade then being the fourth of that division. The division commander ordered me forward. In fact from the time we left the position we had occupied to make this movement to the end of that day's battle, we were in rapid motion. Passing into the wheat field I found our line standing on a crest near the western edge of it fighting the enemy, who seemed strongly posted. My brigade pressed through this line and attacked the enemy in the rocks and timber driving them out of their position and off that part of the field. My brigade was not alone in this. Zook's [Brigadier General Samuel K. Zook], the 3rd brigade, was on my right, and went forward with mine, Zook having fallen dead before this period of the fight was reached. The passage through that wheat field, and through the rocks and timber beyond, you can well imagine was a most thrilling moment.

"All this occurred in the evening of July 2. On the third, after the rebel fire—which has been frequently spoken of—ceased, we expected the advance of their infantry to an assault. The movement forward of that column of about 16,000 men was very majestic. The plowing of lanes through the mass by our artillery was plainly seen, as was also the closing of these gaps by the contraction of their front, and when they came to close quarters with our infantry, their men dropped like leaves in Autumn. They pressed back a portion of our line and passed within to encounter a majority of Doubleday's division, who rose up from the ground and confronted them. Looking back they found that the line on either side of the gap made by their advance had closed in. They were actually and entirely surrounded. I was engaged during that assault, and, under the orders of General Hancock, I had moved forward and wheeled to the right to attack the advancing column on the flank. Before I could reach the point I observed a heavy column of troops moving out from our lines evidently with the intention of attacking this assaulting column. I immediately wheeled to the left and attacked the brigade of the enemy, which was deployed on the right of their assault, but I saw it all, and in all the histories of war I doubt whether there was any more thrilling moment than that which came under my observation during the assault made by General Longstreet on July 3rd 1863 at Gettysburg." Colonel Brooke sustained a wound at Gettysburg but it was not of such a nature as to prevent him from continuing to lead his troops.

Colonel Brooke and his brigade and the other units making up the Army of the Potomac took up the pursuit of General Robert E. Lee and his Army of Northern Virginia, participating in engagements at Banks' Ford and Thoroughfare Gap as well as Auburn Mills and Bristoe Station. In 1864 Colonel Brooke became active in the battle of the Wilderness, May 5, 6, and 7, and in skirmishes on the Po River on May 9 and 10. On May 12 he was commissioned brigadier general of volunteers. On June 3 he was severely wounded in the assault at Cold Harbor and carried from the field. His wounds were so severe (he was shot in the chest) that he was not able to return to full duty until March 11, 1865. He was given command of a provisional division of the Army of the Shenandoah (subsequently known as the Second Division, District of West Virginia) until August 10, 1865. He was then on leave and serving on court-martial duty at Annapolis, Maryland, to February 1, 1866, when he resigned from the Volunteer Army.

On July 28, 1867, John R. Brooke was commissioned lieutenant colonel of the Thirty-seventh Infantry in the Regular Army of the United States and transferred two years later to the Third Infantry whom he commanded until 1888. He was promoted colonel, March 20, 1879, brigadier general, April 6, 1888, and major general, May 22, 1897. He commanded the Department of the Platte from May 5, 1888 to May 16, 1895, and the Department of Dakota from May 18, 1895 to April 10, 1897.

During the next several years he commanded the Department of Missouri and the Department of the Lakes.

With the outbreak of the Spanish-American War, General Brooke assumed command of the Provisional Army Corps at Camp Thomas, Georgia, and on May 17, 1898, took command of the I Corps and the Department of the Gulf. He commanded the invasion of Puerto Rico on July 31, 1898, landing at Arroyo. He advanced to Guayama where he engaged units of the Spanish army, and proceeded to Cayey, which he was about to assault, when word came to him of the declaration of an armistice. After the departure of the Spanish he was appointed military governor of Puerto Rico and served from August 30, 1898, to December 5, 1898. General Brooke was then transferred to Cuba where he served as governor general from December 28, 1898 to December 20, 1899. Following his tour of duty in the Caribbean, General Brooke was detailed as commander of the Department of the East in the United States from May 10, 1900 to July 21, 1902 when he retired from the army.

On March 13, 1882, Brooke applied for membership as a companion of the first class in the Military Order of the Loyal Legion through the commandery of the state of Pennsylvania. On May 2, 1882, he was assigned insignia number 2434. General Brooke subsequently transferred to the commandery of Nebraska, then that of New York, and finally, on December 4, 1902 (with his retirement and move to Rosemont, Pennsylvania), he transferred back to the commandery of the state of Pennsylvania. On May 4, 1904, General Brooke was elected commander of the Pennsylvania commandery, succeeding General Gregg. His opponents in the election were Generals Galusha Pennypacker and James A. Beaver. The following year he again succeeded General Gregg by being elected commander in chief of the Loyal Legion. General Brooke served two years as commander in chief, retiring in 1907.

General Brooke was twice married, first to Louisa Roberts, who died in 1867, and, secondly, to Mary Stearns. By his first marriage he had two sons, William Brooke and Louis R. Brooke. His son William, later a colonel in the U.S. Army, was also a companion, belonging to the Illinois commandery with insignia number 10356. General Brooke died in Frankford, Pennsylvania, on September 5, 1926, and was buried in Arlington National Cemetery. G. C. Craig wrote of General Brooke, "He had the best voice for a commander I ever heard. In the spring of

1864 our brigade was encamped near Brandy Station, in the extreme front as a picket support. Whenever he had the brigade out on drill we could hear his commands from the picket line almost as distinctly as if we were on the drill ground a half-mile off. At the Wilderness I remember we could hear his commands above the din of battle when we could hear no one else except our company officers." General Brooke was succeeded at the conclusion of this term of office as commander in chief of the Loyal Legion by Major General Grenville Mellen Dodge.

Grenville Mellen Dodge

Major General Grenville M. Dodge
Massachusetts Commandery Military Order of the Loyal Legion
and the U.S. Army Military History Institute

One of the big players in the group of tycoons who made up the Gilded Age, Grenville M. Dodge was far more than a financier and builder of railroads. Major General Dodge was an important figure in the War of the Rebellion, rising eventually to command the XVI Corps at the Battle of Atlanta. Although a valiant and inspiring leader on the battlefield it was in the areas of engineering and military intelligence that General Dodge made his greatest contributions to the war effort.

A native of Danvers, Massachusetts, Grenville Mellen Dodge was born on April 12, 1831, the son of Sylvanus Dodge and Julia Theresa Phillips. The family was not well off financially, and Grenville worked at various jobs, clerking in stores, driving delivery carts, and selling fruits and vegetables. Eventually he was able to attend Durham Academy in New Hampshire and then Norwich University in Vermont. He graduated from the scientific department with a degree in civil and military engineering in 1851 and immediately became involved in the work that would concern him most of his life, railroad construction. His interest in railroad engineering and in all aspects of the real estate business that accompanied the westward expansion of the railroad system brought him to Peru, Illinois, where he secured a position with the Illinois Central Railroad. He soon became associated with the Mississippi and Missouri Railroad and undertook survey work from Davenport to Iowa City and from thence to Council Bluffs, Iowa, and Omaha, Nebraska.

It was in Council Bluffs that Dodge found a home. He became an established citizen, organizing the banking house of Baldwin and Dodge as well as continuing his work for the railroads. In 1856, together with other young men in the town, he organized a company of militia, the Council Bluff Guards. His military experience as a graduate of Norwich University led to his selection as captain of his company. At the outbreak of the rebellion Governor Kirkwood sent Dodge on a mission to Washington, D.C., to obtain arms and equipment for the Iowa regiments then being raised. He was successful in his mission and upon returning to Council Bluffs was given permission to raise a regiment, the Fourth Iowa Infantry, and also Dodge's Battery, Iowa Light Artillery. He was commissioned colonel of the Fourth and it was in that capacity that he attacked and defeated a large group of rebel infantry under Colonel John A. Poindexter. He then reported to Major General John C. Fremont in St. Louis. Given command of the Fourth Division of the Army of the Southwest under Major General Samuel R. Curtis he participated in the Battle of Pea Ridge where he had three horses killed under him and was wounded. Promoted brigadier general and recovering from his wound, he was assigned to command the District of Columbia, Missouri. He showed an unexpected aptitude for military intelligence. He soon recruited over one hundred operatives who spread themselves throughout the western Confederacy from Missouri through Tennessee and Alabama. He recruited African Americans who had escaped from slavery and formed the First Alabama Colored Infantry Regiment. Together with another of his creations, the First Alabama Cavalry, they did secret service work for General Dodge. It was his excellent intelligence reports that enabled Dodge to defeat in short order General John B. Villepigue on the Hatchie River, capture General Faulkner and his command near Island No. 10, and attacked General Earl Van Dorn at Tuscumbia, Tennessee.

In the spring of 1863 from his headquarters at Corinth, Mississippi, Dodge brilliantly opened the campaign with the defeat of the forces under Generals Nathan Bedford Forrest, Philip R. Roddy, and Samuel W. Ferguson. In July he was assigned to command the left wing of the XVI Corps and made a raid on Grenada which resulted in the capture of 55 locomotives and one thousand cars. He rebuilt railroads, organized, armed and equipped many thousands of colored troops, and continued to send his operatives into all areas of the Trans-Mississippi. Attached to General William T. Sherman's force at Vicksburg his intelligence agents penetrated the city with ease and provided General Ulysses S. Grant with up-to-the-minute reports on the conditions of the city under siege.

It was while he was stationed in Tennessee and directing the Bureau of Military Intelligence for General Grant that he captured Samuel Davis, the young spy often referred to as the "Nathan Hale of the Confederacy." Serving as a courier, Davis was captured in a Union army overcoat with incriminating documents which would have provided Confederate General Braxton Bragg with much needed information on Grant's movements. When Davis refused to identify his superior, the infamous Captain Henry B. Shaw, head of Bragg's scouts, who was, unknown to Dodge, already in his custody under the alias of Captain E. Coleman, General Dodge reluctantly ordered the boy's execution. Shaw, alias Coleman, could, of course, have saved Samuel by revealing his presence to Dodge, but chose not to do so. After the war General Dodge contributed to a monument erected to the memory of Samuel Davis.

In the spring of 1864 General Dodge joined General Sherman at the Battle of Chattanooga and participated in the opening of the Atlanta campaign. On the August 19, while leading units of the XVI Corps before Atlanta he was hit on the head and seriously wounded. Recovering from the wound he was ordered to relieve General William S. Rosecrans and take command of the Department of Missouri. Again his aptitude for intelligence work enabled him to train operatives to penetrate the various rebel guerilla forces in Missouri and Kansas, and soon he either killed or captured almost all the violent bushwhackers in the department. General Jeff C. Thompson surrendered eight thousand officers and men and General Kirby Smith surrendered approximately four thousand.

General Oliver Otis Howard wrote of Grenville, "General G. M. Dodge, was Sherman's special favorite on account of his work with bridge making and railway construction on marches or in battles. Dodge's capabilities and personality alike drew Sherman to him. I never knew an officer who on all occasions could talk so freely and frankly to Sherman as Dodge. One good reason for this was that Dodge's courage was always calm and his equanimity contagious no matter how great or trying the disturbing causes."

Following the end of the war, General Dodge, promoted major general for his work at Vicksburg, held a command embracing Kansas, Nebraska, Colorado, western Dakota, Montana, and Utah. While in command of this vast area he opened a major campaign against the Native American tribes, overseeing forces under Generals John B. Sanborn, Patrick E. Connor, and others. Treaties of peace were made with the Comanches, Apaches, southern Cheyennes, and other tribes in the area.

In June 1866 Grenville Dodge tendered his resignation and returned to Council Bluffs where he took up the duties of chief engineer of the Union Pacific Railroad. Hardly had he begun his interrupted career in railroading when he was elected to the 40th Congress. He served on the Military Affairs Committee assisting in the reorganization of the postwar army. He declined renomination and returned to his work on the transcontinental railroad. On May 10, 1869, he was one of those driving the golden spike at Promontory Point, Utah. His railroad work continued, chiefly in the West and Southwest on such roads as the Texas and Pacific, the Denver and Fort Worth, the Denver, Texas and Gulf and so on. He supervised the construction of the Mexican Oriental Railway in Mexico and served as an onsite consultant for the construction of the Trans-Siberian Railway. His railroad and military record resulted in the communities of Dodge City, Kansas, Dodge City, Nebraska, and Fort Dodge, Iowa, being named in his honor.

As he continued his railroad work he found it expedient, in view of his many business ventures, to move to New York City. While there he became active in many civic causes serving as vice president of the Grant Monument Association, and chairman of the Grant memorial in Washington, D.C.

General Dodge was involved with the Military Order of the Loyal Legion almost from its inception, becoming a member of the Pennsylvania commandery on May 1, 1867, with insignia number 484. He enjoyed his membership in the Loyal Legion a great deal, particularly relishing occasions when he could gather with old comrades, such as Generals Sherman and Howard and swap stories of their wartime experiences. He was instrumental in founding the New York commandery to which he was transferred in 1886. He served as commander of the New York commandery from May 5, 1897 to May 5, 1898. On October 16, 1907, he succeeded General John R. Brooke as commander in chief of the MOLLUS.

Commenting on the Loyal Legion, General Dodge said, "I look upon this organization as the most distinguished and useful of all patriotic societies. In its constitution and actions it has shown above and beyond any selfish or personal motives the greatest patriotism and interest in the welfare of our country. Since its organization it has been run so successfully that it is looked upon the world over as a great honor to become one of its members."

Grenville M. Dodge's last major service to the nation was to chair the commission appointed by President William McKinley to examine the conduct of the United States Armed Forces in the Spanish-American War. Known as the Dodge Commission and composed of 12 veterans of the Civil War, all but one of whom, a Confederate captain, were members of the Loyal Legion. The commission, while making some criticisms, which drew the umbrage of General Nelson A. Miles, determined that the armed forces had performed admirably. Not unexpectedly,

Dodge himself had a hand in postwar reconstruction in the Caribbean; he supervised the construction of the Cuban railways. President Theodore Roosevelt said that if General Dodge were 10 years younger he would have given him the supervision of the construction of the Panama Canal.

General Dodge was succeeded as commander in chief, after serving a two-year term, by Lieutenant General John C. Bates. Grenville Mellen Dodge died in Council Bluffs, Iowa, on January 13, 1916, and is interred in a magnificent mausoleum in Walnut Hill Cemetery overlooking the Missouri River. In 1854 he had married Ruth Anne Brown, a native of Peru, Illinois. The Dodges had three daughters: Lettie, Ella, and Anne. Lettie married Major Robert H. Montgomery of the U.S. Cavalry. Their son, Grenville Mellen Dodge Montgomery, became a member by inheritance of the Pennsylvania commandery with insignia number 16144.

John Coalter Bates

Lieutenant General John C. Bates

John Coalter Bates

John Coalter Bates was the 14th officer to serve as commander in chief of the Military Order of the Loyal Legion, and the first from the commandery of the state of Missouri. Born in 1842 he was the son of Edward Bates who was attorney general in the cabinet of President Abraham Lincoln. John C. Bates was a native of Charles County, Missouri, and, after graduating from public school, he entered Washington University at St. Louis. With the outbreak of the War of the Rebellion he enlisted and, at age 19, was commissioned a first lieutenant in the Eleventh United States Infantry on May 14, 1861, and with his regiment, joined the Army of the Potomac in October 1861. His regiment served with the Army of the Potomac throughout the entire war.

The Eleventh was in Major General George Sykes's Division and Bates served with it until April 27, 1863, when he joined the staff of General Joseph Hooker. Lieutenant Bates was promoted to captain on May 1, 1863. On June 27, 1863, when Hooker was relieved of command of the Army of the Potomac, Captain Bates was appointed aide-de-camp (ADC) to Major General George Meade with whom he served for the remainder of the war mustering out June 30, 1865. Captain Bates was brevetted major on August 1, 1864, and lieutenant colonel on April 9, 1865, the day of General Robert E. Lee's surrender to Lieutenant General Ulysses S. Grant at Appomattox "for gallant and meritorious services during the recent operations resulting in the fall of Richmond, Virginia, and the surrender of the insurgent army under General R.E.Lee."

During the Civil War John C. Bates participated in the Battles of Gaines Mill, Malvern Hill, Second Bull Run, Antietam, Fredericksburg, Chancellorsville, Gettysburg, Mine Run, Wilderness, Spotsylvania, North Anna, Bethesda Church, Cold Harbor, and the siege of Petersburg and the operations leading to the surrender of the Army of Northern Virginia at Appomattox. His distinguished career in the U.S. Army influenced his decision to continue in military service and he was assigned to the Twentieth U.S. Infantry as a captain on September 21, 1866. For almost the next 30 years Bates served with the forces in the West fighting the Indians in the Northwest and along the Mexican border. He was promoted major and transferred to the Fifth Infantry on May 6, 1882, and transferred back to the Twentieth Infantry on May 24, 1882. After three years' service with the Twentieth he was promoted lietenant colonel of the Thirteenth Infantry on October 19, 1886, and then returned to the Twentieth on December 10, 1890. With his promotion to colonel on April 25, 1892, he transferred to the Second U.S. Infantry.

During the Spanish-American War he was made a brigadier general of volunteers and later became major general of volunteers serving in Cuba. He participated in the Battles of El Caney and Santiago. In 1899 General Bates was assigned to the Philippines and was made brigadier general in the U.S. Army. He soon became commander of the First Division, succeeding General Henry W. Lawton who was killed in action. General Bates' area of command was southern Luzon.

While in command in Luzon he negotiated a treaty with the sultan of Sulu, known as the Bates Treaty, and also pacified Cavite and Mindanao. General Bates was promoted to major general in the Regular Army on July 15, 1902, and lieutenant general on February 1, 1906. Upon the retirement of Lieutenant General Adna R. Chaffee, General Bates became chief of staff of the U.S. Army until his retirement April 14, 1906, when he was succeeded by Brigadier General J. Franklin Bell.

John Coalter Bates was quite active in the Military Order of the Loyal Legion in the Missouri commandery. He was elected a companion of the first class in Missouri on October 8, 1887, and assigned insignia number 5704. He was senior vice commander of the Missouri commandery, 1904–1905, and commander, 1905–1906. He was elected junior vice commander in chief of the order on October 16, 1907, and was elected commander in chief on October 20, 1909, succeeding Major General Grenville Mellen Dodge. General Bates served a two-year term, retiring in 1911. He was succeeded by Rear Admiral George W. Melville. After completing his term as commander in chief, General Bates moved to San Diego, California, where he died on February 14, 1919. General Bates never married.

George Wallace Melville

Rear Admiral George W. Melville, USN

U.S. Naval Historical Center

George Wallace Melville was irascible, short-tempered, a near genius and to a great degree, as chief engineer, father of the modern United States Navy. Of Scottish descent he was born in New York City, the son of Alexander Melville and Sara Wallace, on January 10, 1841. He showed an early aptitude for mathematics and engineering, and following a high school education at the School of the Christian Brothers, he enrolled and graduated from the Brooklyn Collegiate and Polytechnic Institute. He began his career as an apprentice with the James Binns engineering works of East Brooklyn.

Melville's employment was abruptly terminated with the outbreak of the War of the Rebellion. On July 29, 1861, he was commissioned a third assistant engineer in the United States Navy. Barely 20 years of age at the time of his commissioning he was to lead an active and important life in the navy during the Civil War. His initial assignment was on the USS *Michigan* on the Great Lakes. He was then transferred to the sloop of war *Dacotah* on the North Atlantic Blockading Squadron. He participated in the attack on Lambert's Point, the capture of Norfolk, Virginia, and assisted in clearing the obstructions from the James River. He served with the fleet supporting General McClellan's forces at Harrison's Landing during the Peninsular campaign. He was appointed second assistant engineer with the rank of master on December 18, 1862.

His most heroic exploit during the war was his participation in the engagement between the USS *Wachusett* and the CSS *Florida* in the harbor of Bahia, Brazil, on October 6, 1864. Despite being in a neutral port the captain of the *Wachusett*, Commander Napoleon Collins, was determined to either seize the *Florida* or sink her. Dressed in civilian clothing Melville rowed around the Confederate vessel in broad daylight in order to make an assessment of her strength. Commander Collins decided to ram the *Florida*, but all the officers believed that there was a strong probability that the shock would dislodge the machinery and cause death to all in the boiler room by scalding. Melville volunteered to remain below to operate the machinery taking his chances. One enlisted man finally agreed to stay with him. Owing to some oversight, some part of the anchor gear remained overboard reducing the speed of the *Wachusett* so that the impact did not seriously damage the *Florida*. The rebel steamer was, however, boarded and captured and taken north where, after several misadventures in the harbor at Newport News, she sank.

George Melville was appointed chief engineer of the *Wachusett* remaining with her until he was transferred to *Torpedo Boat No. 6* serving in the fleet under the command of Admiral David Dixon Porter and, as such, was present at the capture of Fort Fisher. For his services at Fort Fisher he was promoted first assistant engineer (lieutenant) on January 30, 1865. At the close of the war he determined to make the navy his profession and continue in the engineering field. He served successively in the West Indies, Brazil, and the East Indian stations and at various United States Navy yards.

His interest in exploration came to a head with his participation in Arctic exploration. He made two voyages to the Arctic, all in attempts to rescue previous expeditions: the *Polaris* expedition, and the *Jeannette* expedition to relieve the Greely expedition. In the *Jeannette* expedition Melville commanded the whaleboat which managed to bring the entire crew out alive and then returned to bring out the bodies of Lieutenant George W. DeLong and his companions and the records of the expedition. In response to his heroic efforts Congress advanced him fifteen numbers in grade for promotion and awarded him a gold medal for heroism in the Arctic. He was appointed lieutenant commander on March 4, 1881.

On August 9, 1887, President Grover Cleveland advanced Melville over 44 senior officers, and appointed him chief engineer with the rank of commander. On January 16, 1892, he was appointed chief of the Bureau of Steam Engineering, and engineer in chief of the U.S. Navy with flag rank of commodore. On March 4, 1899, he was promoted to rear admiral. During his tenure in the navy he designed the machinery of about 60 percent (120 ships) of all vessels of the U.S. Navy. In the course of his career in naval engineering he invented the watertube boiler, the triple-screw system, vertical engines, and numerous other devices. He served as president of the American Society of Mechanical Engineers and of the American Society of Naval Engineers. He received honorary degrees from six universities, including Harvard and Columbia. He retired August 1, 1903, at the mandatory age for retirement from the U.S. Navy.

Admiral Melville's work was concentrated in the later years of his career at the Philadelphia Navy Yard, and he became a resident of Philadelphia for the last 25 years of his life. On May 5, 1886, George Wallace Melville was elected a companion of the first class of the Military Order of the Loyal Legion through the commandery of Pennsylvania. He served as senior vice commander of the commandery for the years 1892–1893 and as commander for the period 1908–1909. On October 18,

1911, Rear Admiral Melville was elected commander in chief of the order.

After serving only five months as commander in chief of MOLLUS, Rear Admiral Melville died at his home in Philadelphia on March 17, 1912. George Melville was married twice, first to Henriatte Beatty Waldron, from whom he was later divorced (and by whom he had four daughters, Estella, Maude, Elsie and Meta), and secondly, Estella Smith Polis by whom he had no issue. Meta married Herbert G. Stockwell, and their son, Melville Stockwell, was designated his grandfather's successor in MOLLUS. He was laid to rest in Laurel Hill Cemetery, Philadelphia. In his will he wrote, "I devise and bequest that all paintings, relics and articles of vertu relating to my military, naval and Arctic service, including all my medals, orders, swords, bronze bust and statuettes, and other articles contained in my dwelling house in the city of Philadelphia, all said articles to be selected by my literary executor, Walter M. McFarland, and delivered to the Recorder of the Loyal Legion of the United States, Commandery of the State of Pennsylvania, and I hereby allot $2,000 out of my estate to properly place them in the musuem of that Order." Previously, on December 13, 1905, Admiral Melville had donated to the War Library and Museum, in a letter to Colonel John Page Nicholson, the recorder in chief of MOLLUS, "two of the flags that were captured on the Confederate State Ship 'Florida' in the harbor of Bahia when the 'Wachusett' cut her out in the fall of 1864. These flags were taken from her signal chest by myself the day after the capture. I was serving on the 'Wachusett' at the time of the capture and was transferred to the 'Florida' to prepare her to make the voyage to the United States, and so secured the flags."

A large bronze statue of Admiral Melville is in the Philadelphia Navy Yard. In 1970 a 2,075-ton oceanographic research vessel was commissioned at the Nimitz Marine Facility, Scripps Institute of Oceanography, University of California in San Diego, and named the *Melville*.

Arthur MacArthur

Lieutenant General Arthur MacArthur
U.S. Army Military History Institute

Lieutenant General Arthur MacArthur had been elected senior vice commander in chief of the Military Order of the Loyal Legion of the United States on October 18, 1911, and, as such, succeeded the commander in chief, Rear Admiral George Wallace Melville, upon the latter's death on March 17, 1912. As commander in chief he held office for seven months when he died unexpectedly on September 5, 1912.

Arthur MacArthur was the son of Arthur MacArthur, a native of Glasgow, Scotland, and Aurelia Belcher of Massachusetts. The father was an attorney who opened a practice in Springfield, Massachusetts. It was while the family was living in Chicopee, Massachusetts, that young Arthur was born on June 2, 1845. Four years later the family moved to Milwaukee, Wisconsin, where Arthur pursued his legal and political career as an attorney, judge and, briefly, lieutenant governor of Wisconsin.

Young Arthur entered the public school system of Milwaukee and was graduating from the local high school when the Civil War broke out. On August 4, 1862, at the age of 17, he was commissioned first lieutenant and adjutant of the Twenty-fourth Wisconsin Volunteer Infantry. He served throughout the war and was mustered out as lieutenant colonel of the Twenty-fourth on June 10, 1865. The regiment formed part of the Army of the Cumberland, and with it he participated in the Perryville, Stone's River, Chickamauga, Chattanooga, Atlanta, and Franklin campaigns. He received the brevet rank of lieutenant colonel of volunteers, March 13, 1865, for gallant and meritorious service in action at Perryville, Kentucky, Stone's River, Missionary Ridge, and Dandridge, Tennessee, and of colonel of volunteers on the same day for gallant and meritorious service in action at Franklin, Tennessee, and in the Atlanta campaign. The Medal of Honor was awarded him on June 30, 1890, "for seizing the colors of his regiment at a critical moment and planting them on a captured work on the crest of Missionary Ridge." During that action he was grazed in the head and fell, clutching the colors. Arthur was more seriously wounded at Kenesaw Mountain and at Franklin, Tennessee, where, in a sword fight on the front steps of the Carter House he and a Confederate officer managed to bloody each other with their sabers. The event ended when MacArthur was severely wounded by a shot in the left knee and another in the shoulder.

At the close of the war Arthur was unsure of his future. His father who was about to be appointed a federal district judge in Washington, D.C., wanted his son to return home, attend college, and get his law degree. Arthur, however, had done well in the army and he finally decided to try and make it his career. He asked for letters of recommendation and received glowing endorsements from both Generals George H. Thomas and Philip Sheridan. Of course, at the close of the Civil War he was only 21 years old and so, giving up his eagles on his shoulder straps, he entered the Regular Army as a second lieutenant in the Seventeenth Infantry on February 23, 1866. The same day he was promoted to first lieutenant, and on September 21, was transferred to the Twenty-sixth Infantry. In the course of the expansion of the Regular Army during 1866 he became a captain in the Thirty-sixth Infantry; but in 1869 the army was again reduced and on May 19 he was placed on the list of officers unassigned and awaiting orders. A little over a year later he returned to active duty as captain in the Thirteenth Infantry. At that time Arthur applied for membership in the MOLLUS through the commandery of the state of Pennsylvania, was elected on February 5, 1868, and assigned insignia number 648. In this rank and regiment he served for nearly 20 years, chiefly in the West. It was during this period that he married, on May 19, 1875, in Norfolk, Virginia, Mary Pinkney Hardy. Three sons were born to the MacArthurs during the next five years, Arthur III in 1876, Malcolm in 1878, and Douglas on January 26, 1880. On October 21, 1886, Arthur transferred his membership in MOLLUS to the newly formed commandery of Wisconsin.

On July 1, 1889, Arthur was transferred to the adjutant general's department in Washington, D.C., as a major. After four years in Washington he returned to the West and served at the headquarters of the Departments of Texas and of Dakota. On May 26, 1896, as war loomed with Spain, Arthur was promoted to lieutenant colonel. During the Spanish-American War, Arthur served as adjutant general of the troops at Tampa, Florida, and, later, of the III Corps at Camp Chickamauga.

Following the victory of Admiral George Dewey at Manila Bay, an army of occupation for the Philippines was deemed necessary and Colonel MacArthur was appointed brigadier general of volunteers on May 27, 1898, and assigned to the expeditionary forces. His brigade sailed from San Francisco on June 25 and reached Manila on July 25, 1898. The brigade landed at once and took part in the advance upon and occupation of the city of Manila, August 13. After the occupation he was appointed provost marshal general and civil governor of Manila. Later he was promoted major general of volunteers and assumed command of the Second Division. He was promoted brigadier general in the Regular Army on January 2, 1900, and major general on February 18, 1901.

In the Philippine insurrection, which began February 4, 1899, he took a very prominent part. The first insurgent attack upon the city having been repulsed and order restored, his command led the advance upon the insurgent capital, Malolos, which was occupied on March 31. He was then given command of the Department of Northern Luzon, and directed the advances on the "north line" until the capture of Tarlac in November, after which the organized insurrection collapsed, the insurgent president, Aquinaldo, became a fugitive, and the operations passed into guerrilla warfare.

On the return of General Ewell S. Otis to the United States on May 5, 1900, General MacArthur became commander of the Division of the Philippines and military governor of the islands which post he held until July 4, 1901, when he was relieved by the establishment of a civilian government headed by William Howard Taft. General MacArthur returned to the United States and held various departmental commands. While commanding the Department of the Pacific he was sent as senior military observer with the Japanese forces during the Russo-Japanese War. His son, Douglas, who had recently graduated from West Point at the head of his class, was assigned as his aide. For almost two years the MacArthurs visited Japan, most of Southeast Asia, China, and India.

On September 15, 1906, Major General Arthur MacArthur was appointed lieutenant general and became the ranking officer in the United States Army. He continued to command the Department of the Pacific until his retirement on June 2, 1909, when he returned to Milwaukee, Wisconsin. General MacArthur was a very active member of the MOLLUS, always transferring to the commandery nearest to his place of residence; consequently, he was at various times a companion of the Pennsylvania commandery, the District of Columbia, California, and Wisconsin. He was elected commander of the Wisconsin commandery on May 6, 1908, and served until 1911 when he was elected senior vice commander in chief of order on October 18, 1911. On the death of Rear Admiral George Wallace Melville on March 17, 1912, General MacArthur became commander in chief.

General MacArthur held the office of commander in chief barely seven months, dying on September 5, 1912. On that evening he attended the 50th reunion of the Twenty-fourth Wisconsin held at Wolcott Hall in downtown Milwaukee. The hall was very warm and the general, who had been unwell, had not intended to be present, but could not resist being with his fellow veterans of the Twenty-fourth. He rose to speak, but after about 10 minutes said he was too weak to continue; he sank into his chair and his head fell forward on the table. Later, it was determined that he died of a brain aneurysm. The body was lowered to the floor and covered with an American flag as the 64 members of the Twenty-fourth Wisconsin who were present said the Lord's Prayer. At the service the pallbearers were members of the Wisconsin commandery of the Loyal Legion. Initially interred in Forest Lawn Cemetery in Milwaukee his body was later moved to Arlington National Cemetery by the direction of his son, Douglas MacArthur, who was, by that time, chief of staff of the army. General of the Army Douglas MacArthur was a hereditary companion of the Loyal Legion with insignia number 15317, and at one time served as senior vice commander of the Wisconsin commandery. General Arthur MacArthur was succeeded as commander in chief by the junior vice commander in chief, Colonel Arnold Augustus Rand, of the Massachusetts commandery.

Arnold Augustus Rand

Colonel Arnold A. Rand
Massachusetts Commandery Military Order of the Loyal Legion
and the U.S. Army Military History Institute

Arnold Augustus Rand was serving as junior vice commander in chief (actually senior vice commander in chief after the death of Rear Admiral Melville moved Lieutenant General Arthur MacArthur to the place of commander in chief) when the unexpected death of Lieutenant General Arthur MacArthur on September 5, 1912, resulted in his becoming the first officer not of general or flag rank to succeed to the office of commander in chief of the Military Order of the Loyal Legion of the United States.

Arnold Rand was born in Boston, Massachusetts, March 25, 1837, the son of Edward Sprague Rand and Elizabeth Arnold. He was educated at Mr. Dixwell's School in Boston and in Vevey, Switzerland. Upon his return from Europe he entered the employ of Blake, Howe and Company, Bankers, continuing with their successors, Blake Brothers and Company until the outbreak of the War of the Rebellion. The imminent outbreak of the war caused him to enlist as a private in the Fourth Battalion, Massachusetts Volunteer Militia, on April 14, 1861, but on October 30 of that same year he was commissioned second lieutenant of the First Massachusetts Cavalry. He was promoted to captain on February 4, 1862, and made assistant adjutant general, U.S. Volunteers, on June 3, 1863. His next advancement was to lieutenant colonel of the Fourth Massachusetts Cavalry on December 3, 1864, and this was followed by promotion to colonel of the regiment on January 22, 1864. He resigned his commission on February 3, 1865. Colonel Rand served in the X Corps and the Army of the James and in the Shenandoah Valley under Major General Philip Sheridan.

Major Edward T. Bouve in an article on the battle at High Bridge, Virginia, wrote, "The Fourth Regiment of Massachusetts Cavalry had been subjected to a training and discipline which caused it to develop rapidly into one of the finest cavalry regiments in the army. The officers were nearly all veteran soldiers, educated in the hard school of war. A large proportion of the men in the ranks had seen service, and the rank and file, as a whole, proved to be such as any officer might be proud to lead. The quality of the regiment is easily accounted for, when it is considered that its first colonel left the lasting impression of himself upon it: that colonel was Arnold A. Rand."

Following the end of the war Colonel Rand moved to California for three years, but returned to Massachusetts where he entered the law school at Boston University. He was admitted to the Suffolk bar in 1874 and entered law practice with his father. In 1885 in company with N. J. Bradlee he organized the Massachusetts Title Insurance Company. Ten years later he returned to the practice of law but then became vice president of the John Hancock Life Insurance Company, a member of the Board of Directors and chairman of the Finance Committee. He also served as vice president of the Real Estate Exchange and a trustee of the Massachusetts Soldiers' Home.

Colonel Rand became a companion of the Loyal Legion on June 7, 1871, when he was elected a companion of the first class of the commandery of Massachusetts with insignia number 1311. On May 4, 1881, he was elected recorder of the Massachusetts commandery and served in that office until 1906. As such, he was the executive officer in charge of the cadet armory and was the one most responsible for assembling the great collection of Civil War artifacts, flags, trophies, and medals as well as paintings, engravings, and an enormous number of records and photographs of Civil War soldiers both North and South. (Most of these items, including 37 volumes of portraits and 36,000 views, are now at the United States Military History Institute at Carlisle Barracks, Pennsylvania, where they form the basis of the great collections of the USMHI.)

Arnold Rand steadfastly refused to accept election as commander of the commandery of Massachusetts, but in 1911 he allowed his name to go forward for election as junior vice commander in chief, never intending to move beyond that position. The deaths of Rear Admiral George Wallace Melville and Lieutenant General Arthur MacArthur, however, raised Colonel Rand to the position of commander in chief. It was the intent of the national nominating committee that Colonel Rand be nominated to succeed to a full term as commander in chief, but he steadfastly refused, feeling that the position should be held by an officer of general or flag rank. On October 25, 1913, he wrote the recorder in chief, Lieutenant Colonel John Page Nicholson, "I should not be human if I did not feel proud of the honor which came to me, and that I have been the commander in chief of what I regard as the grandest organization of our country—representing a certain class of the men who put down the rebellion, established the Union and destroyed slavery—it is good reason for pride. But the special gratification which comes to me is that the Commandery of the State of Massachusetts will go down into history as having had a Commander-in-Chief when names will practically be forgotten and only the proud record remains. I heartily wish that all the Commanderies may receive like recognition. For all the courtesy which I have received, for all the kind words which have been said, I am profoundly grateful."

Colonel Rand remained an active member of the MOLLUS until his death at his home in Brookline, Massachusetts, on December 23, 1917. He and his wife, Anna Eliza Lebarron Brownell, had no children. Colonel Rand's brother, Captain Frederick H. Rand, who served in the Twenty-sixth New York Calvary and was a companion of the first class (insignia number 1451) of the Massachusetts commandery, survived him as did Frederick H. Rand, Jr. (insignia number 14755). Colonel Rand was succeeded as commander in chief by Brevet Brigadier General Thomas Hamlin Hubbard.

Thomas Hamlin Hubbard

By Karl Frederick Schaeffer
Past Commander of the Ohio Commandery

Brigadier General Thomas H. Hubbard

Massachusetts Commandery Military Order of the Loyal Legion
and the U.S. Army Military History Institute

Thomas Hamlin Hubbard was born in Hallowell, Maine, on December 20, 1838, the son of Governor John Hubbard and Sarah Hodge Barrett. Thomas prepared for college at the Hallowell Academy and entered Bowdin College at the age of 14 in the fall of 1853. He ranked high in his class and at the commencement exercises in 1857 he delivered the English oration. He was a member of Chi Psi, the Athenaean, and Phi Beta Kappa Fraternities. From 1859 to 1860 he was principal of the Hallowell Academy. In the fall of 1860 he entered law school in Albany, New York, and was admitted to the New York bar on May 4, 1861. He then was employed by the firm of Barney, Butler and Parsons in New York City, becoming the managing clerk.

On September 29, 1862, Thomas enlisted in the 25th Maine Volunteer Infantry with the rank of first lieutenant and adjutant. The regiment proceeded from Portland, Maine, to Washington, D.C., on October 16 and was attached to General Silas Casey's Division. The Twenty-fifth served on garrison duty in the defense of Washington from October 18, 1862 until March 24, 1863. The regiment then moved to Chantilly, Virginia, for picket duty until June 26. It was ordered home on June 30 and Thomas was mustered out on July 11, 1863.

Thomas was re-commissioned on December 19, 1863, as a lieutenant colonel in the Thirtieth Maine Volunteer Infantry as second in command to Colonel Francis Fessenden. The regiment left for New Orleans on January 8, 1864, and arrived on February 16. It was attached to the Third Brigade, First Division, XIX Corps, Department of the Gulf. On February 18, 1864, the regiment was on duty at Algiers and Franklin, Louisiana, until March 15 when it participated in the Red River campaign under Major General Nathaniel P. Banks. They advanced to Alexandria through March 26 and to Natchiotoches on March 29. They fought in the Battle of Sabine Cross Roads on April 8 and Pleasant Hill on April 9 followed by Cane River Crossing on April 23.

On April 30, 1864, a dam at Alexandria was started and completed on May 10. Lieutenant Colonel Hubbard received a citation from General Joseph Bailey for his superior engineering techniques in raising the water level by a series of wing dams, which enabled the forces of General Banks to complete its passage to safety. He also received a special commendation in Admiral David Dixon Porter's report for his conduct in aiding the construction of the Red River Dam at Alexandria for the passage of the Federal fleet. With Colonel Fessenden's promotion to brigade command Lieutenant Colonel Hubbard was promoted to colonel and given command of the Thirtieth Maine.

The Thirtieth Maine was moved to Fortress Monroe and Bermuda Hundred and from thence, via Washington, D.C., to Harpers Ferry, West Virginia. They participated in General Philip Sheridan's Shenandoah Valley campaign. After recovering from a bout of typhoid fever, Colonel Hubbard participated with his regiment through the remainder of the war with his last posting to Savannah, Georgia, on June 30, 1865, following his regiment's participation in the grand review in Washington, D.C., on May 23–24, 1865, where it served as the provost guard. Colonel Hubbard was promoted brevet brigadier general on July 13, 1865, for "meritorious service." He resigned his commission on July 23, 1865.

On Thomas' return to New York, he again took up the practice of law and on January 1, 1867, was made a partner in the firm of Barney, Butler and Parsons, with which firm he was associated for 20 years. The firm's name was changed in 1874 to Butler, Stillman and Hubbard. He and his partners were among the organizers of the Association of the Bar of the city of New York and of the New York County Lawyers Association. He was serving as president of the latter organization at the time of his death. He retired from active practice. His work had been largely corporate litigation and he tended naturally toward corporation management. He managed Mark Hopkins' estate and it was said that for managing that estate he received the largest salary ever paid to an administrator up to that time, $75,000. The estate owned one-fourth of the Southern Pacific Railroad Company of which General Hubbard was a director for 11 years and first vice president for five. He established the International Banking Corporation, the first American bank to gain and retain a foothold in the Orient.

General Hubbard was always interested in Bowdin College and contributed liberally to various projects including the library and the grandstand. In 1901 he endowed the chair of legal ethics in the law department of Union University, known as the Albany Law School, of which law school he was a trustee. He was president of the Peary Arctic Club in New York whose philanthropy was largely responsible for the success of the Peary expedition to the North Pole. Cape Thomas H. Hubbard in the Arctic was named for him by Admiral Peary as a tribute to his friend and helper.

On February 9, 1867, Hubbard was elected a companion of the first class of the Military Order of the Loyal Legion through the commandery of the state of Maine and assigned insignia number 2302. He transferred to the New York commandery on May 4, 1887. From May 6, 1891, to 1892 he served as junior vice commander of the New York commandery and as commander from May 6, 1903 to 1907. On October 15, 1913, he was elected commander in chief of the order serving until his death in New York City on May 19, 1915.

General Hubbard's death came as a great shock to his many friends and companions of the Loyal Legion whose 50th anniversary on April 15 he had attended a little over a month before being taken ill. His funeral was held on Saturday, May 22, 1915, at Madison Square Presbyterian Church and it is estimated that it was attended by the largest number of companions of the Loyal Legion ever assembled at a burial. Admiral Peary was one of the pallbearers. Thomas Hubbard was interred in Woodlawn Cemetery, New York, New York.

Thomas Hubbard had married Sibyl Amelia Fahnestock in Harrisburg, Pennsylvania, on January 28, 1868. He was survived by his widow, and son, John, and daughters: Sibyl Emma and Anna Weir. Two other children had predeceased their father. General Hubbard was succeeded as commander in chief by the senior vice commander in chief, Rear Admiral Louis Kempff, USN.

Louis Kempff

Rear Admiral Louis Kempff, USN

U.S. Naval Historical Center

A naval officer who gained a national reputation for his conduct during the Boxer Rebellion in China in 1900, Louis Kempff became commander in chief of the Military Order of the Loyal Legion of the United States on the death of Brevet Brigadier General Thomas Hamlin Hubbard on May 19, 1915. A native of Bellville, Illinois, Louis was the son of Friedrich and Henrietta Kempff. He was born on October 11, 1841, and, after education in local schools, successfully passed the entrance examinations entered the U.S. Naval Academy in 1857. In company with a number of his classmates he was detached from the academy and ordered to active service in May 1861 with the rank of midshipman. Cadet Kempff was first assigned to the USS *Vandalia*, which was part of the Charleston blockade.

He was commissioned acting master on October 25, 1861, assigned to the USS *Wabash,* and participated in the fight at Port Royal on November 7 of that year and at Port Royal Ferry, January 1, 1862. He was present at the capture of Fort Clinch, Fernandina, Florida, and also at St. Mary's, Georgia, and Jacksonville, Florida. Assigned to the USS *Susquehanna* he was at the bombardment of the Confederate batteries at Sewall's Point and the occupation of Norfolk, which resulted in the blowing up of the ironclad CSS *Virginia*. He was then commissioned lieutenant on August 1, 1862, and assigned to the USS *Connecticut* on duty with the North Atlantic Blockading Squadron. The close of the War of the Rebellion found Lieutenant Kempff on duty on the Pacific Station serving on board the USS *Sewanee.*

Louis Kempff's service during his remaining career in the navy was spent in the Pacific theatre of operations. His first assignment, on the USS *Sewanee* covered the years 1864 to 1867 and it was during that period, on July 25, 1866, that he was promoted to lieutenant commander. Louis was then assigned over the next 30 years to duty in such vessels as the *Portsmouth, Independence, Mohican, Saranac,* and *California.* He also drew duty on several occasions at Mare Island Navy Yard and later on the USS *Alert* of the Asiatic Squadron. On March 7, 1876, he was promoted to the rank of commander which was followed, during his service on the Naval Inspection Board, by a promotion to captain on March 19, 1891. On March 3, 1899, he made rear admiral and took command of the Asiatic Fleet, which he led from 1900 to 1902.

The outbreak in China, generally known as the Boxer Rebellion, found Rear Admiral Kempff as the senior American naval officer off

Taku where an international fleet had assembled to protect the foreigners in northern China. When other foreign ships and forces attacked the Chinese forts at Taku, Rear Admiral Kempff refused to take part, pointing out that the policy of the United States was not to engage in combat with the Imperial Chinese troops as the United States was not at war with the government of the dowager empress. Kempff did cooperate in later efforts to relieve the foreign legations at Peking, but he was highly commended for following the instructions of his government in not attacking the forts at Taku. Kempff received the thanks of the Chinese community in San Francisco at a complimentary banquet on his return to the United States. Rear Admiral Kempff closed his naval career as commandant of the Pacific Naval District, retiring on October 11, 1903.

Upon his retirement Rear Admiral Louis Kempff became very active in the California commandery of the MOLLUS. He joined as a companion of the first class of the California commandery on May 10, 1884, with insignia number 3236. He served as senior vice commander of the California commandery from 1904 to 1905. On October 15, 1913, he was elected senior vice commander in chief of MOLLUS and on the death of Brigadier General Hubbard he became commander in chief. Louis Kempff served as commander in chief until October 20, 1915. After his retirement from the navy, Rear Admiral Kempff lived at Santa Barbara, California, and he died there on July 29, 1920. In 1873 at Fair Oaks, California, he married Cornelia Reese. Their son was Captain Clarence S. Kempff, USN, a hereditary companion of the Loyal Legion with insignia number 12441. Lieutenant General Samuel B. M. Young succeeded Rear Admiral Kempff as commander in chief.

Samuel Baldwin Marks Young

By Richard Holmes Knight, Esquire
Commander of the Commandery of Tennessee (Provisional)

Lieutenant General Samuel B. M. Young
Massachusetts Commandery Military Order of the Loyal Legion
and the U.S. Army Military History Institute

Samuel Baldwin Marks Young enlisted in Company K, Twelfth Pennsylvania Infantry, on April 25, 1861, with the rank of private, and retired from the United States Army on January 9, 1904, with the rank of lieutenant general. In between S. B. M. Young commanded the Fourth Pennsylvania Cavalry and was breveted a brigadier general at the age of 25; was mustered out of service in 1865, only to return months later with the rank of second lieutenant; was assigned to the Eighth U.S. Cavalry and languished in the rank of captain for 17 years; was transferred to the Third U.S. Cavalry, to the Fourth U.S. Cavalry, and then back again to the Third U.S. Cavalry; was a veteran of the Indian Wars; was acting superintendent of both Yosemite and Yellowstone National Parks; was the hero of Las Guasimas in the Philippine insurrection and was responsible for Aguinaldo's defeat on Luzon; was the first president of the U.S. Army War College; and was the U.S. Army's last commanding general and its first chief of staff.

Sam Young was born on January 9, 1840, at Forest Grove, near Pittsburgh, Pennsylvania, the ninth of 11 children born to John Young, Jr., a colonel in the Pennsylvania militia, and Hanna Phillips (Scot) Young. Sam was raised on a farm, and, after graduating from Jefferson College in Cannonsburg, Pennsylvania, began a career in surveying and civil engineering. Upon the outbreak of the War of the Rebellion, he enlisted in the Twelfth Pennsylvania Infantry, a 90-day regiment, and was discharged on August 5, 1861. Returning home, Sam organized a company of cavalry, married Margaret Jane McFadden on September 2, 1861, and returned to active service on September 6, 1861, as captain of Company B, Fourth Pennsylvania Cavalry.

The first major engagement in which Captain Young participated was the Seven Days' campaign when Major General Fitz John Porter observed that Young had brilliantly handled two squadrons of cavalry in the repulse of an enemy charge at Gaines Mill. A few days later Major General George B. McClellan asked Captain Young to lead the advance to Harrison's Landing.

At Antietam, on September 17, 1862, Captain Young led two squadrons of cavalry across Antietam Creek at Rohrback Bridge, even though Confederate artillery had the exact range of the bridge. Crossing the bridge, the attacking party cut its way through a heavy skirmish line and climbed the hill overlooking Sharpsburg, where it was pinned down by the concentrated fire of two batteries. The little force lost eight horses and more than 20 men, killed or wounded, but Captain Young held his ground. On September 20, 1862, Captain Young was notified of his promotion to major by Governor Andrew Gregg Curtin of Pennsylvania, who congratulated him on his good work at "Burnside Bridge." During the Gettysburg campaign he was active in the cavalry force commanded by Brigadier General David McMurtrie Gregg and was in action against J. E. B. Stuart at Hanover, Pennsylvania. Later that year, on October 12, 1863, in action along the Rappahannock River, Major Young was struck by a Minié ball, which shattered his right elbow.

Returning to active duty after a six-month medical leave, Major Young was promoted lieutenant colonel on May 1, 1864, and seven weeks later to colonel on June 25, 1864. After action in the Shenandoah and Harpers Ferry, Colonel Young led a provisional brigade at the Second Battle of Kernstown, July 24, 1864. There he was wounded in the right arm a second time, resulting in two bone fractures. The arm was spared from amputation, and after a three-month medical leave, Colonel Young rejoined the replenished Fourth Pennsylvania Cavalry in front of Petersburg in October 1864.

Colonel Young particularly distinguished himself in the closing days of the War. On April 9, 1865, he led a brigade against Major General Thomas Rosser's command. In just four days, beginning on April 5, 1865, Colonel Young was brevetted twice for "gallant and meritorious services in action," and once for "the campaign terminating with the surrender of the insurgent army under General R. E. Lee." Following the surrender at Appomattox, Brevet Brigadier General Young petitioned the War Department for a commission in the Regular Army. A number of prominent officers endorsed his application. Nevertheless, he was mustered out of service with the Fourth Pennsylvania Cavalry on July 1, 1865. He had participated in 18 battles, 16 engagements, and 13 skirmishes.

Following the close of the Civil War, Samuel Young secured an appointment to the Regular Army with the rank of captain. For the next 15 years Captain Young was stationed in the Southwest primarily with the 8th U.S. Cavalry, where he saw action against hostile Indians on a number of occasions. After serving a term as a cavalry instructor at Fort Leavenworth, Kansas, the now Major Young (he was promoted on August 2, 1883) was transferred to the Third U.S. Cavalry where he saw service again in the Southwest for a further six years. In 1892 Major

Young was promoted to lieutenant colonel and transferred to the Fourth U.S. Cavalry in 1893. In 1896 Lieutenant Colonel Young commanded a squadron in Yosemite National Park, and for almost seven months served as acting superintendent. Upon his promotion and reassignment to the Third U.S. Cavalry in 1897, Colonel Young took command of the cavalry detachment at Yellowstone National Park, and during that time served as acting superintendent for almost five months. On May 4, 1898, Colonel Young was promoted to brigadier general of the U.S. Volunteers.

During the Spanish-American War, Brigadier General Young commanded a brigade in the Santiago campaign and "won the fight at Las Guasimas on the 24th of June 1898." (General Order No. 71, War Department, January 9, 1904.) He was promoted major general of U.S. Volunteers on July 8, 1898. He then served in the Philippine insurrection commanding the cavalry advance of Lawton's Division in its march through northern Luzon. Major General Young served as military governor of northwestern Luzon and afterward commanded the First District, Department of Northern Luzon for 10 months, until February 28, 1901. He had been discharged from the U.S. Volunteers and appointed a brigadier general in the Regular Army on January 2, 1900; on February 2, 1901, he was promoted major general. That year, he returned to California and took command of the Department of California. In 1902, strongly supported by his old comrade and friend, President Theodore Roosevelt, Major General Young became the first president of the U.S. Army War College.

With the mandatory retirement of Lieutenant General Nelson A. Miles, on August 3, 1903, Major General Young was appointed commanding general of the U.S. Army, a post he would hold for eight days. On August 15, 1903, Lieutenant General Young was appointed chief of staff of the army. He held this position until his own mandatory retirement on January 9, 1904.

Lieutenant General Young became a companion of the first class of the Military Order of the Loyal Legion on October 17, 1888, through the commandery of the state of Pennsylvania and was assigned insignia number 6477. He was transferred to the Missouri commandery in 1891 where he served as senior vice commander and from thence to the California commandery where he served as commander from May 13, 1896 to May 5, 1897. He then transferred to the D.C. commandery. Lieutenant

General Young was elected commander in chief of the Loyal Legion in 1915 and served until 1919 when he was succeeded by Lieutenant General Nelson Appleton Miles.

Following his military career Samuel Young engaged in a number of activities including serving as superintendent of Yellowstone National Park from 1907 to 1908, the only person to hold that position twice. From 1910 to 1920 General Young was governor of the Soldiers' Home in Washington, D.C. He retired to Helena, Montana, in 1920 and died there on September 1, 1924. He was buried in Arlington National Cemetery. The flag, which was used to drape his coffin and was then buried with him, was supplied by the MOLLUS.

General Young was first married to Margaret Jane McFadden in 1861 by whom he had five daughters. She died on April 25, 1892, and is buried at Jefferson Barracks National Cemetery, St. Louis, Missouri. He married Mrs. Anna Dean Huntley, of Helena, Montana, in 1908. The author of this article, Richard Holmes Knight, Esq., is General Young's great-great-grandson and commander of the commandery of Tennessee (Provisonal) of MOLLUS.

Nelson Appleton Miles

LIEUTENANT GENERAL NELSON APPLETON MILES

The Arizona Historical Society

Nelson Appleton Miles served as commander in chief of the Military Order of the Loyal Legion of the United States from 1919 to1925. His brilliance as a military commander who found himself at the center of American history for over a half century made him a major figure in the story of the United States. A man of little formal education when compared to his peers his natural ability in the field of military operations and real genius as a leader of men made him an individual whose destiny could not be denied.

Nelson Miles was born in Westminster, Massachusetts, on August 8, 1839, the son of Daniel Miles and Mary Curtis. He attended the local public schools and at age 16 went to Boston where he became a clerk in John Collamore's crockery store. With the outbreak of the War of the Rebellion young Miles, a popular figure with the local clerks and employees in the stores and markets of Boston, raised what became Company E of the Twenty-second Massachusetts Volunteer Infantry. Miles was elected captain; however, Governor John A. Andrew felt he was too young and asked him to exchange his captaincy for a commission as a first lieutenant. Nelson was not pleased with this arrangement but he agreed and accompanied the regiment to Washington, D.C. There, he was temporarily assigned to the staff of Brigadier General Silas Casey. While on Casey's staff he came to the notice of Brigadier General Oliver O. Howard who requested that he be permanently assigned to his staff as an aide-de-camp.

Towering six feet in height and with a soldierly bearing that set him apart even from veteran West Pointers, he made an immediate impression on those who met him. On meeting him on the western plains after the war, the artist Frederic Remington wrote of Miles, "I felt his presence before conscious of his identity, a good style of man. His personal looks I shall never forget." But it was not his looks but his determination and unflinching courage that was to make him, as one soldier put it, "the pride of the volunteer soldiers of the Union."

At the Battle of Fair Oaks, Lieutenant Miles led some reinforcements to the support of Colonel James Miller's Eighty-first Pennsylvania. Seeing Miller's body being carried to the rear, Miles assumed command of the regiment and led it in two brigade bayonet charges which drove the rebel forces from the field. During the close of the Peninsular campaign while serving as a staff officer to Brigadier General John C. Caldwell, at Malvern Hill, Miles led the Eighty-first to support Colonel Francis Barlow's Sixty-first New York. This resulted in his commission as lieutenant colonel of the Sixty-first. During the Battle of Antietam, when Barlow was wounded at the Sunken Road, Miles assumed command. Barlow was promoted to brigadier general and Miles was promoted to command of the Sixty-first New York. General Caldwell wrote of Miles, that he had "added to the laurels he has acquired on every battle-field where he has been present."

This was only the beginning of a career in the Army of the Potomac that saw Miles participate in every major battle in the eastern theatre except Gettysburg. He was still recovering from a serious wound received at Chancellorsville while commanding a successful rear guard action. (It was for this action that he later received the Medal of Honor.) He was temporarily paralyzed from the waist down and was furloughed home to Massachusetts where he soon made a complete recovery. Major General Winfield Scott Hancock said of Miles at Chancellorsville, "He was one of the bravest men in the army, a soldier by nature. Had we all such men in command of our troops we should never suffer disaster. He is one of that class of commanders who seeks the enemy and fights him—never hides his troops when the cannon sounds in his ears." Miles was successively promoted brigadier general of volunteers on May 12, 1864, and brevet major general of U.S. Volunteers on August 25, 1864. He participated in every major engagement, leading troops at Bristoe Station, Mine Run, Wilderness, Poe River, Spotsylvania, North Anna, Cold Harbor, Petersburg, Deep Bottoms, Hatcher's Run, Ream's Station, Fort Stedman, Five Forks, Welden Railroad, Farmville, and Appomattox Court-House. Brevet Major General Miles ended his Civil War career as commander of the First Division, II Corps. He was promoted to major general of volunteers on October 21, 1865; he was just 26 years of age.

Nelson Miles post–Civil War career began with the unenviable task of serving for almost a year as Jefferson Davis's jailer at Fort Monroe, Virginia. As a young officer he was bound to obey the directives of Secretary of War Stanton and Assistant Secretary of War Charles A. Dana. One of the directives, carried out only briefly, was putting leg irons on the ex-president of the Confederacy and for this Miles was criticized, particularly in the Southern press. Davis called the young major general "a heartless vulgarian" and also, "a damned ass." But, recalling the deaths suffered by Union soldiers in Andersonville, Miles was not too concerned about the opinion of his lone prisoner. Miles actually took a number of measures to ease Mr. Davis's situation, including getting him transferred from the damp casemate in the fort to a much more comfortable location in the officers' quarters at Carroll Hall. On July 28, 1866, Miles was appointed colonel of the Fortieth Infantry in the Regular Army. On March 15, 1869, he was transferred as colonel to the Fifth Infantry and began his 15-year career as an Indian fighter on the Great Plains.

Nelson Miles' career involved conflicts with the Cheyennes, Kiowas, Comanches, Sioux, and Apaches. In 1877, while in command of the Department of the Yellowstone, Colonel Miles in one of the great struggles in United States history succeeded in capturing Chief Joseph of the Nez Percé. In 1880, Miles was promoted to brigadier general in the U.S. Army. He successively commanded the Departments of the Columbia, the Missouri, Arizona, and the Pacific. On April 15, 1890, he was promoted to major general in the U.S. Army. It was while he was in command of an expedition to pacify an outbreak by the Sioux in 1890–91 that the Battle of Wounded Knee occurred. Miles was outraged by the conduct of the troops under Colonel Forsyth, and termed it "about the worst I have ever known." It was, he said, the result of "either blind indifference or criminal stupidity."

In 1894 he was in command of the troops ordered into Chicago to suppress the riots occasioned by the Pullman strike which did not endear him to the rising labor movement. From 1894 to 1895 General Miles commanded the Department of the East with headquarters at Governor's Island, New York. Following the retirement of John M. Schofield, Nelson A. Miles, then the senior major general became the commander in chief of the army, effective October 2, 1895. The Spanish-American War found him in charge of the organization and training of the volunteer forces with Major General William Shafter getting command of the expeditionary force. Miles was in at the finish in Cuba, however, and also in Puerto Rico. On February 11, 1901, President William McKinley promoted him to lieutenant general. General Miles' tendency to speak out on subjects without following military protocol got him into hot water, especially with the new president, Theodore Roosevelt. Roosevelt viewed Miles as a possible presidential rival and Miles felt that Roosevelt interfered in military matters about which he had no real understanding. Miles pointed out, somewhat indelicately, that Roosevelt had never charged up San Juan Hill, but up the neighboring Kettle Hill. While Miles was technically correct Roosevelt felt that the lieutenant general had humiliated him and was insubordinate.

President Roosevelt and Secretary of War Elihu Root felt the easiest way to silence Miles' statements to the press was to send him on a tour of the Philippines and the Far East. This strategy backfired when Miles criticized the relations between the U.S. Army and the Filipinos, but it did keep him out of the country. General Miles was mustered out of the army on August 8, 1903, when he had reached the mandatory retirement age of 64. Instead of the usual laudatory statement from the White House issued on such occasions, Miles was sent off with a perfunctory statement of his retirement signed by order of the secretary of war. There was a considerable amount of criticism of Roosevelt and Root in the press for what was seen as shabby treatment of the nation's greatest soldier.

General Miles was an enthusiastic companion of the MOLLUS. He was elected a companion of the first class through the commandery of Massachusetts on May 1, 1878, and was assigned insignia number 1818. During his lifetime he was very careful to transfer to the commandery nearest to where he was stationed so that he could attend meetings as a member of that commandery. He was a charter member of the Oregon commandery on May 6, 1885, and that of Kansas on April 22, 1886, and that of California on July 26, 1887. He was elected commander of the California commandery on May 31, 1889. He transferred back to Massachusetts when he was appointed adjutant general of the state militia in 1903 by Governor William A. Douglas. After his tour of duty during the Douglas administration in Massachusetts, General Miles returned to Washington, D.C. (and that commandery) where he lived the remainder of his life. In 1919 General Miles was elected commander in chief of the MOLLUS serving in that capacity until his death in 1925.

Nelson Miles wrote a number of articles and two autobiographies, *Personal Recollections and Observations of General Nelson A. Miles,* published in 1896, and *Serving the Republic: Memoirs of the Civil and Military Life of Nelson A. Miles, Lieutenant General,* published in 1911. No less than six biographies of Miles have been written, the most recent being *A Hero to His Fighting Men: Nelson A. Miles 1839–1925* by Peter R. DeMontravel, published in 1998.

On June 30, 1868, Nelson A. Miles married Mary Hoyt Sherman, daughter of Judge Charles Sherman and niece of General William T. Sherman. Mary Miles died on August 2, 1904, while Miles and their daughter, Cecilia Sherman Miles, were spending the summer at West Point, New York, where their son, Sherman, was a first classman at the U.S. Military Academy. General Miles died of a heart attack on May 15, 1925, while attending a circus in Washington, D.C., with several of his grandchildren. His full military funeral with his casket draped in a flag provided by the Loyal Legion was at St. John's Episcopal Church, Lafayette Square, in Washington, D.C., with internment in Arlington National Cemetery. His son, Colonel Sherman Appleton Miles, was a hereditary companion of the commandery of the District of Columbia with insignia number 14443. General Miles was succeeded as commander in chief by the senior vice commander in chief, Rear Admiral Purnell Frederick Harrington.

Purnell Frederick Harrington

Rear Admiral Purnell F. Harrington, USN

Harper's Weekly

Purnell Frederick Harrington was a career naval officer who served as commander in chief from 1925 to 1927. A graduate of the U.S. Naval Academy, he was both a scholar and a blue water sailor of uncommon ability. Purnell was born in Dover, Delaware, on June 6, 1844, the son of Samuel M. Harrington and Mary Lofland. Upon completion of high school he received an appointment to the U.S. Naval Academy and was mustered in as acting midshipman on September 20, 1861. On July 16, 1862, he was promoted to midshipman, and upon graduation was appointed acting ensign.

Acting Ensign Harrington's first assignment was service on the USS *Ticonderoga* on duty with the North Atlantic Blockading Squadron from October 1863 through January 1864. He then was transferred to the USS *Niagara* on special service from January to June 1864 when he was transferred to the USS *Monongahela* with the Western Gulf Blockading Squadron. It was while serving on the *Monongahela* that Ensign Harrington participated in the Battle of Mobile Bay in the naval force under the command of Rear Admiral David Glasgow Farragut.

After shore leave at the end of the War of the Rebellion, Acting Ensign Harrington returned to service on the *Monongahela* and was promoted ensign on December 21, 1865. After his appointment as master on May 10, 1866, Harrington was appointed lieutenant on February 21, 1867, and assigned to the U.S. Naval Academy. After a two-year tour of duty, during which he was promoted to lieutenant commander on March 12, 1868, he was assigned to temporary torpedo duty with the USS *California* on August 1870, followed by an appointment as executive officer on the USS *Pensacola*, flagship of the Pacific Fleet from December 1870 through August 1873. He returned to the U.S. Naval Academy in September 1873 serving on the faculty until September 1876 when he became the executive officer of the USS *Hartford* with the South Atlantic Squadron. He returned to the faculty of the U.S. Naval Academy in January 1880 and was promoted to the rank of commander on May 28, 1881. His next sea assignment was as captain of the USS *Juanita* on the Asiatic Station from March 1883 to January 1886 when he became commandant of cadets at the U.S. Naval Academy. While commanding the *Juanita* he was involved in United States affairs on Madagascar and the Comoro Islands, particularly the relationship between the sultan of Johanna and Dr. B. F. Wilson, an American citizen.

Purnell Harrington's next assignment was as inspector of the Fourth Lighthouse District in Philadelphia where he served until 1893 when he assumed command of the USS *Yorktown*. Following his service on the *Yorktown* he went on special duty at the Navy Department in Washington, D.C., and then assumed the presidency of the steel board of the U.S. Navy. Purnell Harrington was promoted to captain, United States Navy, on March 1, 1895. After commanding the USS *Terror* with the North Atlantic Squadron from April 1896 to July 1897, Captain Harrington found himself in command of the USS *Puritan* at the outbreak of the Spanish-American War. From November 1898 to October 1901 Captain Harrington was commandant of the navy yard at Portsmouth, New Hampshire. On March 21, 1903, Captain Harrington was promoted to rear admiral and became commandant of the U.S. Navy Yard at Norfolk, Virginia. On June 6, 1906, after an illustrious career of service in the United States Navy and to the Republic, Rear Admiral Harrington was placed on the retired list. His final military duty was in connection with the Jamestown exposition from July 1906 to January 1908.

A scholar in the area of nautical engineering he wrote a number of articles bearing such titles as "The Coefficient of Safety in Navigation" and "Notes of Navigation and the Determination of Meridian Distances for the Use of Naval Cadets at the U.S. Academy." He is listed among the "founding fathers" of the U.S. Naval Institute.

Rear Admiral Harrington was elected a companion of the first class of the Military Order of the Loyal Legion on December 7, 1910, by the commandery of the state of New York and assigned insignia number 16399. On May 1, 1912, he was elected senior vice commander of the New York commandery and on February 15, 1913, he became commander. In 1923 he was elected senior vice commander in chief. Rear Admiral Harrington succeeded Lieutenant General Nelson Appleton Miles as commander in chief upon the latter's death.

On August 5, 1868, Purnell Frederick Harrington was married to Mia N. Ruan of St. Croix, Danish West Indies, and they had four children including Colonel Samuel Milby Harrington, USMC, who was a hereditary companion of MOLLUS with insignia number 16527. Rear Admiral Harrington died at his home in Yonkers, New York, on October 20, 1937.

Robert Means Thompson

Master Robert M. Thompson

Library of Congress

Robert Means Thompson was a naval officer and graduate of the United States Naval Academy. He was born in Corsica, Pennsylvania, on March 2, 1849, the son of Judge John Jamison Thompson and Agnes Kennedy. He was commissioned a midshipman on July 30, 1864, while at the academy in Newport, Rhode Island, and graduated 10th out of 81 in the Class of 1868 at Annapolis, Maryland.

Robert Thompson was involved in no military engagements in the Civil War even though he saw some sea service as a midshipman. He spent most of the time from his enlistment and commissioning as a midshipman in 1864 to his graduation in 1868 at the naval academy. Upon his graduation he was assigned to the USS *Contooruck* of the North Atlantic Squadron and then was promoted to ensign on April 19, 1869. Sent to the Mediterranean Squadron he served on board the USS *Wachusett* and was promoted to master on July 12, 1870. He resigned his commission on July 12, 1870.

Immediately upon leaving the navy Thompson embarked on the study of law and graduated from the Harvard Law School in 1874. He then served as a reporter for the Massachusetts Supreme Court, and in 1876 and 1877 was elected a member of the Boston Common Council. He was retained as counsel in an investigation of titles of several Canadian mining firms, and this resulted his becoming manager of the Orford Copper Company and, later, a director of the International Nickel Company. He also served as a partner in Pell & Company in New York. All of these activities resulted in Robert Means Thompson becoming a very wealthy man. He essentially retired from business activities about 1910 and then devoted himself to his three major interests: the U.S. Navy, the United States Olympic Committee, and the Military Order of the Loyal Legion.

Robert Means Thompson was an active alumnus of the U.S. Naval Academy and first president of the New York Naval Academy Alumni Association. He founded the Navy Athletic Association and donated the bronze doors on the chapel at the naval academy at Annapolis, and the Thompson Trophy Cup. Thompson Athletic Field at the academy is named for him. He also served as head of the Navy League and was active in founding the United States Naval Institute. He never missed a June week at the academy for 55 years.

A large, vigorous, and athletic individual Robert was interested in the promotion of athletic competition and especially international athletic contests. This interest led him to becoming involved in the Olympic movement and he became the first president of the American Olympic Association. He served as chairman of the United States Committee at the games in Stockholm in 1912 and Paris in 1924 (The games made famous in the film *Chariots of Fire*).

Thompson was elected a companion of the first class through the commandery of the state of Massachusetts on November 4, 1874, and assigned insignia number 1599. He transferred to the commandery of the state of New York on December 2, 1885. He served on the council of the New York commandery in 1897 and 1898. On May 6, 1914, he transferred to the commandery of the District of Columbia. He served as junior vice commander of the District of Columbia commandery, November 9, 1925 to February 2, 1926. He served as senior vice commander from February 2 1926 to May 5, 1926, and commander for the remainder of 1926 until October 1927. On October 27, 1927, Thompson was elected commander in chief of MOLLUS, succeeding Rear Admiral Frederick Purnell Harrington. Commander in Chief Thompson was re-elected in 1929 and served until his death on September 5, 1930.

Commander in Chief Thompson was a gregarious individual known for his great good humor and boundless enthusiasm for projects involving every aspect of the Loyal Legion. He particularly enjoyed entertaining companions on board his yacht *The Everglades*. During his tenure as commander in chief he visited every one of the 21 commanderies then in existence. This trip, as described by companion Graham H. Powell, began in 1928 in Washington, D.C., and covered 14,000 miles extending to Los Angeles, Portland, Oregon, and Portland, Maine. All of this was at his own expense and he was "accompanied by a large party." This trip enabled him to become acquainted with every commandery in the nation. Not satisfied with this he personally paid the expenses of at least one companion of the first class to come to the annual congress in Philadelphia in 1928, so that every one of the state commanderies would be represented when the constitution was revised. It was at this meeting that measures were taken so that the distinction in ribbons and rosettes between original and hereditary companions was abolished. Lieutenant General Nelson Appleton Miles had advocated this change in 1924 and Commander in Chief Thompson felt it his duty to carry this through while there were enough companions of the first class present to enable it to be voted as a legitimate change in the constitution.

Thompson maintained, "...whether Original or Hereditary we are all Companions of one distinguished and world-known brotherhood, and than no distinction by class should be made." As Companion Powell also noted, "Only those intimately associated with Colonel Thompson (he was made a Colonel on the staff of the Governor of New Jersey during the Spanish-American War) can have any conception of the vast store of knowledge and wealth of experience ever at his instant call."

Robert Means Thompson was also a scholar of naval history during the War of the Rebellion. Together with his classmate from the academy (and fellow MOLLUS companion) Rear Admiral Richard Wainright, he edited for the Navy History Society, of which he was president, *Confidential Correspondence of Gustavus Vasa Fox, Assistant Secretary of the Navy, 1861–1865,* which was published in two volumes in 1920.

On April 30, 1873, Robert Thompson married Sarah Gibbs, daughter of William Channing Gibbs, governor of Rhode Island. Robert and Sarah had one daughter, Sarah Gibbs Thompson. Robert Means Thompson died on September 5, 1930, while visiting his daughter at Fort Ticonderoga, New York. He was interested in the restoration of the fort and had contributed liberally to its restoration. As Alexander Leo said of him, "...he amassed a great fortune which, however, he seemed to administer merely as a trustee for others. Money to him was merely a means whereby he could help and give enjoyment to others. He apparently cared nothing for it except as a means to this end." Companion C. Peter Clark of the Massachusetts commandery wrote, "...no companion of our Order, however obscure, or however exalted, exceeded Robert Means Thompson in his love for our Order, or in his devotion to the principles and ideals for which our Order stands." His memorial service, attended by hundreds of companions of the Loyal Legion, was at the chapel of the United States Military Academy at Annapolis, Maryland.

Samuel Warren Fountain

BRIGADIER GENERAL SAMUEL WARREN FOUNTAIN
Philadelphia *Public Ledger*

Samuel Warren Fountain was born in Parkersburg, West Virginia, on December 13, 1846. As he was only 15 years old at the outbreak of the War of the Rebellion, Samuel Fountain had to wait until 1864 to enlist in the Union army. On May 2, 1864, he enlisted as a private in the 140th Ohio Infantry. The 140th Ohio (one of the one hundred days' regiments) was part of the VIII Corps, Army of West Virginia. Private Fountain was stationed at Camp White and Camp Warren near Charleston, West Virginia, and at Meadow's Bluff. He participated in the attack on Lynchburg, Virginia, led by Major General David Hunter. Private Fountain was discharged on September 3, 1864, at Gallipolis, Ohio, by reason of expiration of term of service.

On July 1, 1866, Fountain was appointed to the United States Military Academy at West Point from the Fifteenth Congressional District of Ohio, and graduated on June 15, 1870, at which time he was commissioned a second lieutenant in the Eighth U.S. Cavalry. From September 1870 until December 1875 Fountain served in Colorado and New Mexico. He was then transferred to Texas where he served from January 1876 until June 1885. On October 22, 1878, he was promoted to first lieutenant. In 1885 Lieutenant Fountain returned to New Mexico where he was active in the campaigns against Geronimo and the Apache Indians commanding Troop C of the Eighth Cavalry. He led his troops in fights at Snow Creek on December 9, 1885, and at Dry Creek on December 19, 1886. On April 11, 1889, he was promoted to captain.

Captain Fountain assumed command of Troop H of the Eighth U.S. Cavalry and led that force in campaigns against the Sioux in Montana and North Dakota in 1890 and 1891. During the Spanish-American War he commanded a squadron of the Eighth Cavalry in Cuba. He was promoted to major and transferred to the Ninth Cavalry on February 2, 1901. From February 28, 1901 to August 26, 1903, he was assistant adjutant general of the Department of Mindanao and Jolo in the Philippines and at Zamboango until August 1903. One of the captains on his staff was John J. Pershing and the two men remained warm personal friends for the rest of their lives. Major Fountain was promoted to lieutenant colonel in the Thirteenth U.S. Cavalry on August 26, 1903, and two days later transferred to the Fourth U.S. Cavalry.

Lieutenant Colonel Fountain was then assigned to Jefferson Barracks, St. Louis, Missouri, where he commanded the Jefferson Guard at the World's Fair from September 1904 until March 1905. On April 10,

1905, Lieutenant Colonel Fountain was promoted to brigadier general and retired the next day. Newspapers reported that, "Under his direction the members of the Guard controlled the great mass of people on 'President's Day' so that not one incident occurred to mar the events of that memorable day. And on the last day of the Fair, when disorder and vandalism were feared, every officer and member of the Guard was on duty, and so placed that when the lights were out and the World's Fair at St. Louis had passed into history, not a disorderly act had occurred, or a dollars worth of property had been destroyed."

Brigadier General Fountain was elected a companion of the first class of the Military Order of the Loyal Legion through the commandery of the state of Ohio on October 7, 1885, and assigned insignia number 4207. On April 15, he transferred to the commandery of the District of Columbia on April 15, 1893, and to the commandery of the state of Pennsylvania on February 1, 1907. He served three different terms as commander of the Pennsylvania commandery, 1912–1913, 1924–1925, and 1926–1930. He served on the council of the commandery in chief from October 28, 1925, to 1927. He was elected senior vice commander in chief of MOLLUS on October 27, 1927, and served in that office until September 5, 1930, when he succeeded Commander in Chief Robert Means Thompson on his death.

In a speech at the Union League of Philadelphia on February 9, 1921, General Fountain said of Abraham Lincoln, "Not too often and never too reverently can Americans pause to honor the memory of Lincoln or express gratitude to the Almighty for his services to his Country. Other men have reunited a divided nation, or liberated an enslaved race, or carried to conclusion a fratricidal war, or swept immoral institutions from the earth by consummate Statesmanship; but no man ever combined and carried through, chiefly by the clarity of his mind and the purity of his character, several such gigantic enterprises in half a decade. Washington welded a handful of colonies into a Confederation of States; Lincoln fused them, after they had fallen apart, into a self-conscious Nation."

Samuel Warren Fountain only served a little over two months as commander in chief since he died on November 15, 1930, of heart failure at his home in Philadelphia, Pennsylvania. He and his wife, the former Katherine McGrath, had one child, Adele Fountain. Funeral services for General Fountain were at Our Lady of Lourdes Church in

Philadelphia and interment was in Arlington National Cemetery. A number of companions, including Major General John Clem, were pallbearers. Besides serving as commander in chief of the MOLLUS, General Fountain was past commander general of the Military Order of Foreign Wars.

George Mason

Major George Mason

MOLLUS, Portraits of the Companions

George Mason was the only commander in chief of the Military Order of the Loyal Legion not born in the United States; he was born on March 1, 1840, in Paisley, Scotland. His father, Carlisle Mason, brought him to America at the age of four when the family settled in Chicago in 1845. In 1857 George enrolled at the University of Michigan and remained there until his senior year when, in 1861, he enlisted in the Union army.

George initially enlisted as a private in Company C of the Twelfth Illinois Infantry, United States Volunteers, in September 1861. He was promoted to sergeant in February 1862. On May 24, 1862, he was promoted to first lieutenant and assigned as an adjutant on the staff of Generals Oglesby, McArthur (General John McArthur was his mother's brother), Chetlain, and Sweeny—always with the command known originally as the Second Brigade, Second Division, Army of the Tennessee.

Lieutenant Mason served with the Army of the Tennessee at the Battles of Fort Donelson, Pittsburgh Landing (Shiloh), Corinth, Iuka, Middle Tennessee, and part of the Atlanta campaign. Writing about his experience at Shiloh (published in *Military Essays and Recollections of the Illinois Commandery,* vol. 1, pp. 93–104), he wrote that having arrived on the battlefield he asked the question of all whom he met, "Do you think it will last long enough for us to get in?" After telling of the severe fighting on April 6, he turned to the events of April 7, writing, "...the morning of the 7th found us ready to take the aggressive. A new line had been formed, and a new army was ready to take the lead in an effort to recover the ground lost the day before. The main battle began about nine o'clock in the morning, and ended about four o'clock in the afternoon. On this field was to be seen the most splendid fighting ever seen on this continent. Our artillery was admirably worked and the infantry ably supported the artillery. The maneuvering was splendid. The enemy were driven inch by inch. They seldom regained anything they had lost; still they fought desperately at times, until by four o'clock they were in full retreat and the victory was ours. It was my good fortune to serve immediately on the left of the Eighteenth United States Regulars, and their perfect discipline and regular movements lifted a load from our breasts, and filled us with a confidence we had well nigh lost the day before. Every advance was stubbornly resisted; every charge was met by a counNtercharge; and though the lines shifted forward and back, yet every returning charge carried us farther along toward the camps we had lost, then through them and beyond, until McCook's division, that had marched twenty-two miles the day before and stood in the streets of Savannah all night of the 6th, was at nightfall beyond our farthest camp of Saturday night."

He served with distinction until July 28, 1864, when he was honorably discharged from the Union army. On March 13, 1865, he was commissioned captain and brevet major in recognition of his service with the Union forces and "for meritorious service April 6 and 7, at Pittsburgh, Tennessee."

On leaving the army, Major Mason returned to Chicago and, with T. K. Holden, established a general foundry business. In 1866, Mr. Holden retired and George Mason became the sole owner. The next year, he merged his business with his father, Carlisle Mason, and a new firm emerged, known as Carlisle Mason and Company. The company manufactured boilers, engines, and general machinery.

In 1877 the firm's name was changed to the Excelsior Iron Works, and Major Mason remained until 1905, serving successively as secretary, vice president, and for 10 years as president. In 1905 the stock was sold to the Miehle Printing Press and Manufacturing Company, and later Major Mason went with them as vice president, holding that position until September 10, 1910, when he became connected with the Wisconsin Granite Company and the Superior Construction Company.

George Mason was also involved in many civic activities during his lifetime. From 1874 to 1880 he served as a director of the Chicago Public Library. In 1880 he was elected director and a member of the Executive Committee of the Inter-State Industrial Exposition, serving until 1892 when the exposition was transformed into the Chicago World's Fair. On March 6, 1886, Governor Oglesby appointed him a member of the Board of West Chicago Park Commissioners, where he served until April 1893, part of the time as president.

In 1897 Governor Tanner made him a member of the Shiloh Battlefield Commission, of which he was secretary until the work of the body was completed. He was a member of the state commission, representing Illinois at the Paris Exposition, and in 1901 he was appointed a member of the Board of Inspectors for the House of Corrections at Chicago; he was chair of this board for 10 years.

On October 8, 1879, George Mason was made a companion of the first class of the MOLLUS through the commandery of the state of

Illinois and assigned insignia number 1935. He was became commander in chief of the MOLLUS on the death of Brigadier General Samuel Warren Fountain on November 15, 1930. George Mason's son, Carlisle Mason II, was elected an hereditary companion with insignia number 9394 and was a member of the Illinois and then the California commandery.

WILLIAM PARKINSON WRIGHT

Captain William P. Wright
Office of the Recorder in Chief MOLLUS

William Parkinson Wright was the last commander in chief to have served in the War of the Rebellion. He was born March 29, 1846, in Napierville, Dupage County, Illinois. He enlisted as a private in Company I, 132nd Illinois Volunteer Infantry Regiment, in May 1864 and was discharged as a corporal in the fall of the same year by reason of expiration of term of service (one hundred days). He re-enlisted as first sergeant of Company D, 156th Illinois Volunteer Infantry, on February 25, 1865. He was discharged by reason of promotion as second lieutenant effective June 2, 1865, and he was further commissioned a captain on July 26, 1865.

During his time of service with the 132nd Illinois he was on duty at Paducah, Kentucky, and Columbus, Kentucky. In the 156th he was on duty guarding the railroad between Chattanooga, Tennessee, and Dalton, Georgia. On July 5, 1865, he was ordered to Memphis, Tennessee, when his regiment did patrol duty until September 1865, when his unit was mustered out at Springfield, Illinois. After the war he worked in real estate in the Chicago area.

One of the early members of the Grand Army of the Republic, Captain Wright served as commander of the Walter Blanchard Post in Napierville, Illinois, and of the Abraham Lincoln Post in Chicago. He was commander of the Department of Illinois from May 1921 to May 1922, and also served as president of the Board of Directors of the Grand Army Hall and Memorial Association of Illinois.

William Parkinson Wright was elected a companion of the first class of the Military Order of the Loyal Legion of the United States through the Illinois commandery on July 24, 1894. He was assigned insignia number 10240. He was elected commander of the Illinois commandery and then treasurer in chief. He was elected commander in chief of MOLLUS on October 28, 1931. At the time of his election in Philadelphia, Captain Wright addressed the companions present as follows, "Companions, I have hardly any words to express my gratitude—perhaps it may be sympathy that I need in accepting this office. I thought when I was made treasurer of this organization that I had received all the honors that I was entitled to, and I have performed the duties that have been given me by my different Companions of the Order, in my own department, to the best of my ability. When we had in Illinois a very large Commandery, I was perfectly surprised when they elected me Commander of that organization. Twenty years later they re-elected me again to that position so that I would be a Commander when the Commandery-in-Chief met there last year, and I had no idea of ever having any greater honor given me by this Commandery-in-Chief. I am going to do the best I can, but I am going to ask each one of you individually and personally to be a right hand to your Commander-in-Chief. Without that assistance, this office will be a failure, and we must try the best we can to be present and to promote the interests of the organization throughout the United States. Let us all together put our shoulders to the wheel and make up our minds that during this administration the Military Order of the Loyal Legion shall not diminish any. I thank you."

Commander in Chief Wright died on June 15, 1933, in Pittsburgh, Pennsylvania, while still in office. His son, Henry Delco Wright, was a hereditary companion with insignia number 11547.

Recorder in Chief
John Page Nicholson

Lieutenant Colonel John Page Nicholson
Office of the Recorder in Chief MOLLUS

Although he never served as commander in chief John Page Nicholson, the recorder in chief of the Military Order of the Loyal Legion from 1879 to 1922, was the single most influential person in the development of the order. His long tenure of service and national stature in preserving the written and physical history of the Civil War makes him the quintessential MOLLUS companion.

John Page Nicholson was born in Philadelphia, Pennsylvania, on July 4, 1842. His birthdate almost seemed to guarantee his involvement in his country's history. He was in his third year at Princeton University when the War of the Rebellion commenced. He left college, returned home, and enlisted in Company K of the Twenty-eighth Pennsylvania Volunteer Infantry which was forming at Camp Coleman, Philadelphia. He became a sergeant within a month, a commissary sergeant at Point of Rocks, Maryland, and the next week was commissioned a first lieutenant in the Twenty-eighth Pennsylvania.

Lieutenant Nicholson's service in the Twenty-eighth Pennsylvania enabled him, as an officer in the XII Corps, to participate in the Battles of Cedar Mountain, Second Bull Run, Antietam, Chancellorsville, and Gettysburg with the Army of the Potomac. With the transfer of the XII Corps to the west after Gettysburg, Nicholson participated in the Battles of Lookout Mountain, Missionary Ridge, Peach Tree Creek, Atlanta, Sherman's March to the Sea, Savannah, and the final campaign through the Carolinas. In these campaigns he served with the Army of West Virginia, Bank's Corps, the Army of Virginia, the Army of the Potomac, the Army of the Cumberland, and the Army of Georgia. He was brevetted lieutenant colonel of the U.S. Volunteers "for gallant and meritorious services during the War, to date from March 13th, 1865." Lieutenant Colonel Nicholson was honorably discharged on July 28, 1865.

John Page Nicholson was elected a companion of the first class by the Pennsylvania commandery on May 7, 1879, and assigned insignia number 1870. On August 21, 1879, he was elected recorder of the Pennsylvania commandery and also became acting recorder in chief of the order. He became recorder in chief on the establishment of the commander in chief apart from the Pennsylvania commandery on October 21, 1885. He served as recorder of the Pennsylvania commandery and the commandery in chief until his death on March 8, 1922, in Philadelphia.

Following the war he was a member of the firm of Pawson and Nicholson, Bookbinders. As such he accumulated and bound more than

17,000 volumes on the Civil War and related topics. At the time of his death it was the largest collection of books on the Civil War in private hands. While his primary interest was the MOLLUS, he also served in many related organizations dedicated to the preservation of the history of the Civil War. He was chairman of the Gettysburg National Park Commission, president of the Valley Forge Park Commission, chairman of the General Wayne Monument Commission, chairman of the Hanover, Pennsylvania, Monument Commission, and trustee of the Soldiers' and Sailors' Home at Erie, Pennsylvania. The author of many scholarly works on the War of the Rebellion his greatest contribution was the translation from the French and editing of the *History of the Civil War in America* in four volumes by Louis d'Orleans, Comte de Paris. Colonel Nicholson's other major contribution was the compiling and editing of *Pennsylvania at Gettysburg* in two volumes.

John Page Nicholson, together with President Rutherford B. Hayes, was the founder of the War Library and Museum of the Military Order of the Loyal Legion, and Colonel Nicholson was the primary fundraiser which secured the money necessary to construct and furnish the library and museum. He was a member of the Society of the Cincinnati in the state of New Jersey. In recognition of his scholarly pursuits he received an A.M. from Marrietta College and the Litt.D from Pennsylvania College. At his death his widow, Gertrude M. Nicholson, and a daughter, Mrs. George R. Stull, as well as two grandchildren, survived him. The funeral service was at the Episcopal Church of the Saviour, Philadelphia, Pennsylvania, and internment was at Mount Peach Cemetery, Philadelphia, Pennsylvania.

COMMANDERS IN CHIEF WHO DID NOT SEE SERVICE IN THE CIVIL WAR

Colonel Hugh Means, Kansas, 1933–1935
Colonel William Innes, Forbes, Pennsylvania, 1935–1940
Major General Malvern Hill Barnum, Massachusetts, 1940–1941
James Vernon, Michigan, 1941–1947
Rear Admiral Reginald R. Belkap, New York, 1947–1951
Donald H. Whittemore, Massachusetts, 1951–1953
Commander William C. Duval, Ohio, 1953–1957
Major General Ulysses S. Grant, III, New York, 1958–1961
Lieutenant Colonel Donald M. Liddell, Jr., New York, 1961–1962
Lieutenant Colonel Durstan Saylor, II, Pennsylvania, 1962–1964
Major General Clayton B. Vogel, District of Columbia, 1964
Colonel Walter E. Hopper, New York, 1964–1966
Lieutenant Colonel Lenahan O'Connell, Massachusetts, 1966–1971
Colonel Brooke M. Lessig, Pennsylvania, 1971–1973
Charles Allen Brady, Jr., Illinois, 1973–1975
Colonel Joseph B. Dougherty, Indiana, 1975–1977
Thomas N. McCarter, III, New York, 1977–1981
Lieutenant Colonel Philip M. Watrous, Pennsylvania, 1981–1983
Alexander P. Hartnett, Pennsylvania, 1983–1985
William H. Upham, Jr., Wisconsin, 1985–1989
Lowell Varner Hammer, District of Columbia, 1989–1991
Henry Nathan Sawyer, Massachusetts, 1991–1993
Colonel Scott Wallace Stucky, District of Columbia, 1993–1995
Dr. Robert Girard Carroon, Connecticut, 1995–1997
The Honorable Michael Patrick Sullivan, IV, Wisconsin, 1997–1999
Major Robert James Bateman, District of Columbia, 1999–2001

THE ROSTER

COMPILED BY ROBERT G. CARROON

Introduction to the Roster

The roster consists of the names of the companions of the first and third class of Military Order of the Loyal Legion of the United States. Companions of the first class were those who served in the War of the Rebellion in the regular or volunteer forces of the United States. The companions of the third class were those men who were honored for their contribution to the war effort but who did not serve in a federal or federalized military capacity. Companions of the third class (we would call them today honorary companions) were elected by the individual state commanderies up until April 15, 1890, when such elections were no longer permitted under the constitution and bylaws of MOLLUS.

The portion of the roster of companions of the first class is arranged alphabetically by surname, followed by first name and middle name or initials. This is followed by the rank, brevet rank (if any) name of unit in which the officer served, the commandery which he initially joined or was his primary commandery of record, and his insignia number. The insignia number appeared on his application form (assigned upon his acceptance of membership) membership certificate and on his medal if he purchased one. The insignia numbers sometimes have the word "Dup" following which indicates that the same number was assigned to more than one companion, probably in error by the recorder in chief or the chancellor in chief whose responsibility it is to issue the insignia number. Occasionally, a companion will have two numbers assigned to him or no number.

The portion of the roster of companions of the third class is interspersed alphabetically with that of the first class, but indicates only the commandery which elected the individual and occasionally his office or contribution to the war effort if it is known and also his insignia number. As far as we have been able to determine all companions of the first and third class are included in the roster but there may be some who by oversight might have been omitted.

GLOSSARY

The various designations or abbreviations listed in the roster:

RANK OR DUTY ABBREVIATIONS

1st Lt.	First Lieutenant
2nd Lt.	Second Lieutenant
A	Assistant
AAG	Assistant Adjutant General
Act	Acting
Adj.	Adjutant
Adv	Advocate
AIG	Assistant Inspector General
Asst	Assistant
BG	Brigadier General
Bvt	Brevet
Capt.	Captain
Chap	Chaplain
Chief Eng.	Chief Engineer
Col.	Colonel
Commander	Commander
Commodore	Commodore
CS	Chief of Staff
Dept. Com. Gen.	Deputy Commissary General
DQM	Deputy Quartermaster
Eng.	Engineer
Ensign	Ensign
General	General
IG	Inspector General
Jdge	Judge
LG	Lieutenant General
Lt.	Lieutenant
Lt. Com.	Lieutenant Commander
LTC	Lieutenant Colonel
Maj	Major
Master	Master
Med. Director	Medical Director
MG	Major General
Midshipman	Midshipman
P	Passed

THE ROSTER

Passed Asst. Eng. .... Passed Assistant Engineer
Pay Inspector .... Pay Inspector
Paymaster .... Paymaster
QM .... Quartermaster
RAdm .... Rear Admiral
RCS .... Regimental Chief of Staff
RQM .... Regimental Quartermaster
Surg. .... Surgeon
VAdm .... Vice Admiral

UNIT ABBREVIATIONS

Arty .... Artillery
Batt .... Battery
Battn .... Battalion
Cav .... Cavalry
Ch.Bd. Trade Batt .... Chicago Board of Trade Battery
Comm. Gen. of Subst. ... Commissary General of Subsistence
Corps .... Corps
H Arty .... Heavy Artillery
Hosp .... Hospital
Ind .... Independent
Indpt .... Independent
Infy .... Infantry
L Arty .... Light Artillery
Mil .... Militia
Mtd. .... Mounted
Mount. .... Mountineer
Res .... Reserve
Rifles .... Rifles
Shpshtrs. .... Sharpshooters
Sig. Corps .... Signal Corps
Storekpr. .... Storekeeper
Trp. .... Troop
US .... United States
USA .... United States Army
USC .... United States Colored
USCT .... United States Colored Troops
USMC .... United States Marine Corps

USN .... United States Navy
USV .... United States Volunteers
Vet. .... Veteran
Vol .... Volunteers
VRC .... Veteran Reserve Corps

Commandery Abbreviations

CA	California
CO	Colorado
DC	District of Columbia
IA	Iowa
IL	Illinois
IN	Indiana
KS	Kansas
MA	Massachusetts
MD	Maryland
ME	Maine
MI	Michigan
MN	Minnesota
MO	Missouri
NE	Nebraska
NY	New York
OH	Ohio
OR	Oregon
PA	Pennsylvania
TN	Tennessee
VT	Vermont
WA	Washington
WI	Wisconsin

The Roster

Name	Rank	Commandery	Insignia No.
Abbey, Joseph N.	Capt. 2nd PA H Arty	PA	00829
Abbot, Henry L.	BG USA	NY	07448
Abbot, John C.	1st Lt. 13th CT Infy	CA	09045
Abbot, Walter	Lt. Com. USN	PA	00703
Abbott, Abial R.	1st Lt. 1st IL L Arty	IL	02789
Abbott, Charles P.	2nd Lt. 19th MA Infy	MA	01220
Abbott, Delon H.	Surg. 9th ME Infy	DC	13720
Abbott, Edward A.	Capt. 23rd OH Infy	OH	07035
Abbott, Horace R.	1st Lt. Adj. 180th OH Infy	MI	03045
Abbott, Hubbard M.	1st Lt. 37th MA Infy	MA	09329
Abbott, Ira C.	Col. 1st MI Infy BvtBG	DC	05598
Abbott, Joseph C.	Col. 1st NH Infy BvtBG	NY	01168
Abbott, Josiah	Surg. 119th USCT	MA	08851
Abbott, Lemuel A.	Maj USA	VT	14398
Abbott, Nathan B.	1st Lt. 20th CT Infy	OH	01266
Abbott, Othman A.	1st Lt. 9th IL Cav	NE	10180
Abbott, Robert A.	Capt. 132 PA Infy	PA	08449
Abbott, Robert O.	Bvt. LTC USA	PA	00245
Abbott, Samuel W.	Surg. 1st MA Cav	MA	12426
Abbott, Willard	Capt. 104th NY Infy	OH	12150
Abdill, Edward C.	1st Lt. Adj. 120th IN Infy	IL	12662
Abeel, William C.	Capt. 4th MI Cav	MI	16737
Abercrombie, John J.	BG USV	NY	0389-746
Abercrombie, John J.	1st Lt. 127th NY Infy	IL	06520
Abernathy, James L.	LTC 8th KS Infy	KS	04803
Abert, James W.	Maj Eng. BvtLTC USA	OH	05381
Able, Augustus H.	Chief Eng. USN	PA	10393
Acheson, William H.	1st Lt. 129th IN Infy	MI	12220
Achilles, Henry L.	Capt. 27th NY Infy	WA	07193
Ackerman, Thomas F.	Act 1st Asst Eng. USN	MO	08278
Ackley, Charles	Act Master USN	PA	00694
Ackley, John B.	Surg. USN	PA	00516
Ackley, Shreve	Capt. 27 PA Infy	PA	15300
Adae, Carl A.G.	Capt. 4th OH Cav	CA	02888
Adair, Addison A.	Capt. 78th OH Infy	IL	09349
Adair, John S.	1st. Lt. Adj. 97th OH Infy	OH	07948
Adam, Emil	Maj 6th Cav USA	CA	03541
Adams, Abbott L.	2nd Lt. Ch.Bd.Trade Batt IL Arty	IL	01937
Adams, Albert E.	Capt. 7th NY Cav	IL	04157
Adams, Archibald H.	1st Lt. 35th WI Infy	CA	04301
Adams, Axel S.	Capt. 2nd Cav USA	IL	10441
Adams, Charles Francis	Col. 5th MA Cav BvtBG	MA	06100
Adams, Charles W.	Act Master USN	IL	05540
Adams, Edgar E.	Bvt. LTC USV	OH	16396
Adams, Henry C.	2nd Lt. 26th IN Infy	IN	06576
Adams, Henry C.	Maj 11th ME Infy	NY	07979
Adams, Henry H.	BG USA	OH	12546
Adams, Henry J.	Capt. 118th NY Infy BvtMaj	CO	11014

Name	Rank	Commandery	Insignia No.
Adams, Hugh W.	Maj 7th KY Infy	NY	03185
Adams, J.F. Allyne	Act Asst Surg. USN	MA	10313
Adams, James W.	2nd Lt. 7th IN Infy	IA	12265
Adams, John G.B.	Capt. 19th MA Infy	MA	02362
Adams, John Q.	Capt. 1st Cav USA	IN	05846
Adams, John Q.	Capt. 30th USCT	MA	10509
Adams, John W.	Chap. 2nd NH Infy	MA	08049
Adams, John W.	Capt. 73rd OH Infy	CA	17610
Adams, Matthew	Capt. 4th NH Infy	CO	07164
Adams, Myron	2nd Lt. Sig. Corps USV	NY	09947
Adams, Nathaniel A.	Maj 11th KS Cav	KS	06864
Adams, Robert N.	Col. 81st OH Infy BvtBG	MN	10112
Adams, Robert, Jr.	Capt. AAG, USV	MO	06551
Adams, Samuel G.	Capt. 66th NY Infy	NY	03771
Adams, Samuel R.	Bvt. Maj USV	OH	16366
Adams, Seymour F.	Capt. 5th NY H Arty	OH	09593
Adams, Silas	1st Lt. 41st USCT	ME	12889
Adams, Stephen D.	2nd Lt. 18th NY H Arty	NY	01547
Adams, Z. Boylston	Surg. 32nd MA Infy	MA	01025
Adams, Zabdiel B.	Maj 5th MA Cav	CA	01805
Adamson, Alfred	Chief Eng. USN	MA	07970
Addison, William C.	1st Lt. 5th IL Cav	KS	15092
Admire, Jacob V.	Capt. 65th IN Infy	KS	09225
Ady, George	1st Lt. 14th USC H Arty	CO	05068
Agnew, Benjamin L.	Chap. 76th PA Infy	PA	11153
Agnew, Cornelius R.	3rd Class (Surg. Gen. NY Sanitary Com.)	NY	00165
Agnus, Felix	Maj 165th NY Infy BvtBG	DC	01194-2617
Ahl, George W.	Capt. Indpt Co. Del H Arty	MA	09879
Aid, Francis	2nd Lt.1st Regt. Miss. Marine Brigade	MO	11759
Aiken, John	1st Lt. 29th USCT	PA	09490
Aiken, William A.	Act Asst Paymaster USN	NY	01365
Aikman, Robert	Capt. 19th KS Cav	KS	14845
Ainsworth, Francis B.	2nd Lt. 6th NY H Arty	IN	12095
Aiten, Robert	Capt. 128th USCT	DC	14792
Akers, William G. J.	Capt. 3rd MN Infy	MO	15974
Albee, Eugene A.	Capt. 40th MA Infy	MA	02999
Alberger, Morris H.	BvtCol. USV	NY	01376
Alberger, William G.	LTC 49th NY Infy BvtCol.	NY	01154
Albers, Claus H.	1st Lt. RQM 1st IA Cav	MO	05089
Albers, William T.	Capt. 35th IA Infy	WI	12121
Albert, John S.	Chief Eng. USN	NY	00730
Albright, Charles	Col. 202nd PA Infy BvtBG	PA	00552
Alden, Charles H.	BG USA	MA	01227
Alden, George C.	BvtMaj AQM	MA	00955
Alden, Hiram C.	Capt. 4th MA Infy	MA	04553
Alden, James	RAdm USN	PA	00064
Aldrich, Charles	1st Lt. Adj 32nd IA Infy	IA	01147 (Dup)
Aldrich, Harrison	Capt. 21st MA Infy	MA	09802

Name	Rank	Commandery	Insignia No.
Aldrich, Horace	Capt. 106th NY Infy	MO	04279
Aleshire, Edward S.	Capt. 2nd OH H Arty	OH	11700
Alexander, George W.	Capt. 1st MI Cav	MI	07577
Alexander, Henry E.	Capt. Balt. Batt MD L Arty BvtMaj	NY	07449
Alexander, Isaac N.	LTC 46th OH Infy	OH	06886
Alexander, Jeremiah S.	Capt. 31st IA Infy	IA	06202
Alexander, John D.	Capt. 97th IN Infy	IN	11514
Alexander, John W.	1st Lt. RQM 1st NY Cav	OH	07711
Alexander, William L.	Col. Asst Com. Gen. USA	IA	07298
Alexander, William W.	2nd Lt. 1st NC Infy	CA	10064
Alford, Lore	Capt. 8th ME Infy	IA	07299
Alger, Amos B.	Capt. 22nd Batt Ohio L Arty	OH	09591
Alger, Russell A.	Col. 5th MI Cav BvtMG	MI	03572
Alkins, George Edwin	Midshipman, USN	OH	No Number
Allabach, Peter H.	Col. 131st PA Infy	DC	07896
Allaire, Anthony J.	LTC. 133rd NY Infy BvtBG	NY	06018
Allanson, George	Capt. 24th WI Infy	WI	03888
Allanson, John S.	1st Lt. 20th Infy USA	MN	01002
Allee, Abraham	Capt. 6th IL Cav	NE	04306
Alleman, Hiram C.	Col. 36th Infy PA Militia	NY	01404
Alleman, Levi J.	Asst Surg. 1st NY Cav	IA	05793
Allen, Abner J.	Capt. AQM USV	KS	07386
Allen, Amos D.	Act Asst Paymaster USN	CA	11527
Allen, Charles C.	Capt. 25th MO Infy	CA	06930
Allen, Charles J.	BG USA	DC	03495
Allen, Charles L.	1st Lt. 38th OH Infy	OH	16012
Allen, David F.	2nd Lt. 10th IN Infy	IN	07038
Allen, Edward J.	Col. 155th PA Infy	PA	03087
Allen, Edward P.	Capt. 29th MI Infy	MI	07282
Allen, Edward T.	Capt. 7th RI Infy	CA	03338
Allen, Edward W.	2nd Lt. 16th WI Infy	WI	10243 (Dup)
Allen, Edwin R.	1st Lt. 7th RI Infy	CA	17609
Allen, Ethel M.	Capt. 98th NY Infy	MI	12898
Allen, Francis B.	2nd Asst Eng. USN	NY	09417
Allen, Frank	1st Lt. 9th RI Infy	MA	13976
Allen, Gorton W.	1st Lt. Adj. 160th NY Infy	NY	05709
Allen, Harrison	Asst Surg. BvtMaj USA	PA	05237
Allen, Harrison	BvtBG USV	MN	04457
Allen, Henry F.	Act 3rd Asst Eng. USN	NY	03778
Allen, Horace R.	Surg. 123rd IL Infy	IN	06577
Allen, James P.	Capt. 1st MN H Arty	MN	09228
Allen, John H.	1st Lt. 14th VT Infy	VT	14102
Allen, Justin W.	2nd Lt. 50th WI Infy	KS	06979
Allen, Louis J.	RAdm USN	CA	12288
Allen, Lucius H.	3rd Class (MG CA Militia)	CA	03246
Allen, Orville C.	1st Lt. 1st MI Infy	MI	06537
Allen, Ralph W.P.	LTC 40th Infy PA Militia	PA	00279
Allen, Robert W.	Pay Inspector USN	DC	09379

Name	Rank	Commandery	Insignia No.
Allen, Samuel H.	Col. 1st ME Cav	ME	03708
Allen, Theodore F.	Capt. 7th OH Cav BvtCol.	OH	13026
Allen, Thomas O.	Maj 6th MA Infy	MA	14197 (Dup)
Allen, Thomas S.	Col. 5th WI Infy BvtBG	WI	01587-5220
Allen, Truman H.	Capt. 22nd NY Cav	CA	02864
Allen, Vanderbilt	BvtMaj USA	NY	04594
Allen, Walter	Act Asst Paymaster USN	MA	11585
Allen, William J.	1st Lt. 20th Batt Ind L Arty	IN	06578
Allen, William P.	1st Lt. Adj. 65th USCT BvtCapt.	MN	06352
Allison, James N.	LTC Dept. Com. Gen. USA	NY	00886
Allison, William B.	3rd Class (US Senator IA)	IA	07828
Allor, Louis A.	1st Lt. 22nd MI Infy	MI	12579
Allyn, Arthur W.	Capt. 16th Infy BvtMaj USA	OR	08135
Almond, Latham C.	Capt. 82nd IN Infy	CA	17608
Almy, John J.	RAdm USN	DC	04329
Alston, Theodore W.	2nd Lt. 2nd NJ Infy	NY	12129
Alvord, Austin W.	Capt. 109th NY Infy	MI	11554
Alvord, William	3rd Class (Mayor of San Francisco)	CA	06338
Ambrose, Mordecai J.W.	Chaplain 47th KY Infy	OH	13466
Ames, Adelbert	BG USV, BvtMG USV	NY	00729
Ames, Azel, Jr.	1st Lt. 96th USCT	MA	02527
Ames, John H.	2nd Asst Eng. USN	MN	10012
Ames, John W.	Col. 6th USCT BvtBG	CA	01475
Ames, Luther S.	Capt. 2nd Infy USA	NE	04987
Ames, Pelham W.	Act Asst Paymaster USN	CA	01438
Ames, Sullivan D.	Commander USN	MA	00912
Ames, T. Edward	BvtMaj USV	MA	01431
Ames, William	Col. 3rd RI H Arty BvtBG	MA	01666
Amidon, John R.	2nd Lt. 3rd WI Infy	IA	06443
Ammen, Daniel	RAdm USN	DC	00572
Ammon, John H.	LTC 16th NY H Arty	NY	01842
Amory, Charles B.	Capt. AAG, Bvt Maj USV	MA	06911
Amory, Charles W.	1st Lt. 2nd MA Cav	MA	03882
Amory, Copley	1st Lt. 4th Cav USA	MA	01616
Amory, Robert G.	2nd Lt. 2nd MA H Arty	MA	08050
Amory, William A.	Maj 2nd MA H Arty	IL	02317
Amsden, Fred. J.	2nd Lt. Sig. Corps, BvtCapt.USV	PA	08740
Anderson Thomas M.	BG USA, MG USV	OH	03642
Anderson, Andrew M.	1st Lt. RQM 189th OH Infy	OH	11811
Anderson, Charles	Col. 93rd OH Infy	OH	08162
Anderson, David M.	Asst Surg. 12th USCT	PA	10131
Anderson, Edward	Col. 22nd IN Cav	MA	02991
Anderson, Edward L.	Capt. 52nd OH Infy	OH	07323
Anderson, Frederick P.	1st Lt. Adj. 181st OH Infy BvtMaj	MI	09143
Anderson, George C.	LTC 53rd PA Infy	PA	14472
Anderson, Harry R.	LTC Arty USA	KS	08342
Anderson, Holman M.	Capt. 3rd ME Infy	IA	06688
Anderson, Hugh	Capt. 81st USCT BvtMaj	CA	04518

Name	Rank	Commandery	Insignia No.
Anderson, James	Capt. 21st USCT	CA	04517
Anderson, James W.	Capt. 10th IL Infy	CO	08371
Anderson, John	Maj USA	MA	05357
Anderson, John D.	1st Lt. 3rd Battn MD Infy	ME	09701
Anderson, John G.	Capt. 1st CO Vet. Cav	PA	00561
Anderson, Latham	Col. 8th CA Infy	OH	06348
Anderson, Marion T.	Capt. 51st IN Infy	DC	04775
Anderson, Nicholas L.	Col. 6th OH Infy BvtMG	DC	01133
Anderson, Robert	Bvt MG USA	NY	00120
Anderson, Thomas J.	Maj AAG BvtCol. USV	KS	04431
Anderson, Turner	Maj 28th KY Infy	OH	01543
Anderson, Wendall A.	Maj Surg. 3rd MD Infy	WI	16127
Anderson, William H.	Paymaster USN	ME	02391
Andrade, Cipriano	RAdm USN	PA	06759
Andreas, Alfred T.	1st Lt. RQM 12th IL Infy	IL	02412
Andres, Hiram	Capt. CS BvtMaj USV	PA	07854
Andrew, Abram P.	Capt. 21st Batt. IN L Arty	IN	11182
Andrew, John A.	3rd Class (Gov. MA)	PA	00051
Andrews Albert H.	Capt. 19th Infy BvtMaj USA	MA	12471
Andrews, Christopher G.	BG, BvtMG USV	MN	04250
Andrews, E. Benjamin	2nd Lt. 1st CT H Arty	NE	08639
Andrews, Edmund	Surg. 1st IL L Arty	IL	05805
Andrews, Geo. Leonard	BG, BvtMG USV	MA	01061
Andrews, Geol. Lippitt	BG USA	DC	03640
Andrews, James M.	1st Lt. 30th NY Infy	NY	02928
Andrews, John	2nd Lt. 1st CT Cav	MA	09666
Andrews, John N.	Col. 12th Infy USA, BvtBG USV	KS	10601
Andrews, John W.	Capt. 2nd USCT	DC	13795
Andrews, Judson B.	Capt. 77th NY Infy	NY	05007
Andrews, Martin M.	Capt. 85th OH Infy	MI	17458
Andrews, Robert R.	2nd Lt. 60th MA Infy	MA	11983
Andrews, Simon S.	Capt. 30 ME Infy	ME	11475
Andrews, William D.E.	Capt. 11th IL Infy	IL	06213 (Dup)
Andrews, William H.H.	1st Lt. RQM 11th ME Infy	MA	06510
Andrews, William J.	1st Lt. Asst Surg. 39th OH Infy	OH	15552
Andrews, William S.	Bvt Capt. USV	NY	02279
Andross, Dudley K.	Col. 9th VT Infy	VT	10665
Androus, Samuel N.	1st Lt. 44th IL Infy	CA	05684
Andrus, Charles H.	Surg. 176th NY Infy	NY	03903
Andrus, Wallace R.	1st Lt. 16th CT Infy	WA	15703
Andrus, William D.E.	Capt. 11th IL Infy	IL	06213 (Dup)
Andruss, E. Van Arsdale	BG USA	DC	13101
Angevine, William F.	Capt. 98th NY Infy	WI	01602
Ankeny, Henry G.	Capt. 4th IA Infy	IA	13801
Annable, E. Augustus	2nd Lt. MA H Arty	MA	10044
Annesley, Richard L.	Capt. 43rd NY Infy BvtMaj	NY	02270
Anson, Charles H.	1st Lt. Adj 1st VT H Arty BvtMaj	WI	05215
Anson, Frank A.	1st Lt. 1st VT H Arty	WI	02717 (Dup)

Name	Rank	Commandery	Insignia No.
Anthony, Edward J.	1st Lt. 88th USCT	MA	11823
Anthony, George T.	Cap. 17th Batt NY L Arty BvtMaj	KS	04437
Anthony, Henry B.	3rd Class (US Senator RI)	DC	02703
Anthony, Scott J.	Maj 1st CO Cav	CO	08957
Apgar, Allen S.	Act Asst Paymaster USN	NY	02366
Appel, Charles A.	Maj 9th PA Cav	DC	04883
Apperson, John B.	BvtCol. USV	MO	04366 (Dup)
Apperson, John T.	1st Lt. 1st OR Cav	OR	07585
Apple, Theodore L.	1st Lt. 1st WV Infy	OH	16009
Appleby, Charles	Capt. 80th USCT BvtMaj	NY	03605
Appleton, John F.	Col. 81st USCT BvtBG	ME	00264
Appleton, John W.M.	Maj 1st MA H Arty	DC	02247
Appleton, Nathan	2nd Lt. 5th Batt MA L Arty BvtCapt.	NY	00751
Appleton, Samuel	1st Lt. 12th MA Infy	MN	01943
Appleton, Thomas L.	Capt. 54th MA Infy	MA	05873
Appleton, William H.	Capt. 4th USCT BvtMaj	NY	06960
Armbrust, Bernhard	Capt. 4th MO Cav	CA	02032
Armitage, John E.	1st Lt. 24th WI Infy	WI	03686
Armor, William C.	Capt. 28th PA Infy BvtMaj	PA	08741
Armour, Robert	Capt. 79th NY Infy	DC	05228
Arms, Robert B.	Capt. 16th VT Infy	VT	09251
Armstrong, George	Maj 2nd NE Cav BvtCol	NE	07589
Armstrong, Julius	1st Lt. 52nd OH Infy	OH	10127
Armstrong, Leroy G.	Maj Surg. 48th WI Infy	WI	06494
Armstrong, Luther	1st Lt. 33rd MO Infy	MO	17418
Armstrong, Robert G.	Capt. 1st Infy USA	KS	02567
Armstrong, Samuel C.	Col. 8th USCT BvtBG	MA	08733
Armstrong, William H.	2nd Lt. 8th USC H Arty	IN	07039
Armstrong, William H.	2nd Lt. 1st NY Mntd Rifles	NY	17106
Arndt, Albert F.R.	Maj 1st MI L Arty	MI	04709
Arno, Philip	BvtMaj USV	IA	16982
Arnold, Abraham K.	Col. 1st Cav USA BvtBG USV	CA	03644
Arnold, Isaac, Jr.	LTC Ordnance USA	NY	10082
Arnold, Moses N.	Capt. 12th MA Infy	MA	02244
Arthur, Chester A.	3rd Class (BG QMG NY Militia:Pres US)	DC	02430
Arthur, Elliott J.	Lt. USN	NY	01711
Arthur, William	Maj Paymaster USA BvtLTC	MN	07246
Artman, William	Maj 213th PA Infy	PA	04937
Artsman, Gustavus	Capt. AQM USV	OH	09154
Asay, Jacob L.	Surg. 208th PA Infy	CA	03462
Asch, Morris	Asst Surg. BvtMaj USA	NY	01647
Asch, Myer	Capt. 1st NJ Cav BvtMaj	NY	01528 (Dup)
Ashbrook, Joseph	Capt. 118th PA Infy BvtMaj	PA	05714
Ashcroft, James E.	Capt. 3rd NY L. Arty	MO	08138
Ashcroft, James H.	Maj 29 KY Infy	OH	12600
Ashley, Albert B.	2nd Lt. 21st USCT	IL	08391
Ashmun, George C.	2nd Lt. 7th Ind Troop OH Cav	OH	03971
Ashton, Frank M.	Passed Asst. Eng. USN	PA	04161

Name	Rank	Commandery	Insignia No.
Ashton, James W.	1st Lt. 157th PA Infy	NY	14828
Ashton, Thomas J.	Capt. 44th Infy PA Militia	PA	01979
Ashurst, Richard L.	1st Lt. Adj 150th PA Infy BvtMaj	PA	02655
Ashworth, Thomas W.	1st Lt. 8th OH Cav	OH	09152
Askew, Frank	Col. 15th OH Infy BvtBG	MO	10895
Askin, Robert M.	Capt. 32nd MO Infy	MO	11565
Aspinwall, Lloyd	Col. 22nd Infy N.G.S. NY	NY	00229
Asserson, Peter C.	Civil Eng. USN	DC	10650
Aston, Howard	1st Lt. 13th OH Cav	OH	15139
Aston, Ralph	RAdm USN	NY	11039
Astor, John Jacob	Col. ADC BvtBG USV	NY	01909
Atherton, Arlon S.	Capt. 3rd NH Infy	MA	06499
Atherton, Bicknell B.	Lt. 141st PA Infy	PA	16326
Atkins, Alfred	Capt. 98th NY Infy	NY	10083
Atkins, Smith D.	Col. 92nd IL Infy BvtMG	IL	07755
Atkinson, George	Capt. 5th MN Infy	CA	02731
Atkinson, George H.	Act Chief Eng. USN	PA	14051
Atkinson, James J.	1st Lt. Adj. 3rd MI Infy	MI	10592
Atkinson, John	LTC 3rd MI Infy	MI	04008
Atkinson, Louis E.	Surg. 188th PA Infy	PA	01100
Atkinson, William F.	Capt. 3rd MI Infy	MI	06810
Atkinson, William L.	Capt. 1st MD Cav	PA	07629
Atlee, Charles H.	Capt. 121st PA Infy	PA	02337
Attwood, Cornelius G.	Maj 25th MA Infy BvtLTC	MA	00679
Atwell, Benjamin D.	1st Lt. 36th WI Infy	DC	16711
Atwell, Seager S.	Col. 7th CT Infy	MA	11773
Atwell, William P.	Capt. BvtMaj USA	DC	05002
Atwill, James W.	LTC 1st NC Infy	MA	00976
Atwood, Edwin B.	BG USA	OH	08163
Audenried, Joseph C.	Col. ADC USA	PA	01655
Auer, Michael	Maj 15th NY Cav	NY	17412
Augur, Christopher C.	MG USV, BG USA	DC	00167
Aulick, Richmond	Commander USN	PA	No Number
Auman, William	BG USA	CA	11660
Austin, Albert	1st Lt. 14th Infy USA	CA	04000
Austin, David R.	1st Lt. 100th OH Infy	OH	03152
Austin, Henry R.	1st Lt. 14th USCT	MI	10607
Austin, Horace	Capt. 1st MN Mntd Rangers	CA	09355
Austin, John H.	Asst Surg. USN	PA	00013
Austin, Samuel J.	Capt. 98th NY Infy	MN	11682
Averill, John T.	Col. 6th MN Infy BvtBG	MN	04046
Averill, William	MG USV	NY	00230-847
Avery, Charles N.	1st Lt. Adj. 117th USCT	OH	07434
Avery, George S.	Maj 3rd MO Cav	IL	10003
Avery, Irving M.	1st Lt. RQM 48th NY Infy	NY	12552
Avery, John H.	Capt. 9th IL Cav BvtMaj	IL	12997
Avery, Robert	LTC 102nd NY Infy BvtMG	NY	03121
Avery, William	LTC 95th IL Infy	IL	04971

Name	Rank	Commandery	Insignia No.
Awl, John W.	LTC 201st PA Infy	PA	04160
Ayer, Don C.	2nd Lt. 1st VT H Arty	NE	11691
Ayer, Edward E.	2nd Lt. 1st NM Infy	IL	05541
Ayers, Charles L.	2nd Lt. 4th MA H Arty	MA	03776 (Dup)
Ayers, David C.	Surg. 7th WI Infy	WI	06448
Ayers, Henry P.	1st Lt. Adj. 77th IL Infy	IL	06131
Ayers, Hugh A.	Capt. 78th PA Infy	PA	12228
Ayers, John H.	Surg. 34th OH Infy	OH	09026
Ayling, Augustus D.	1st Lt. Adj. 24th MA Infy	MA	02077
Ayres, Eben R.	Capt. 23rd MI Infy	MI	12083
Ayres, Robert	Capt. 19th Infy USA	PA	07326
Ayres, Romeyn B.	BvtBG USV, BvtMG USA	ME	00447
Ayres, Samuel L.P.	Chief Eng. USN	PA	08202
Ayres, Stephen C.	Asst Surg. BvtCapt. USV	OH	03300
Babb, Edward C.	Capt. 9th NH Infy	MN	04040
Babbitt, Albert T.	2nd Lt. 93rd OH Infy	OH	05935
Babbitt, Lawrence S.	Col. Ordnance USA	CA	03722
Babcock, Courtlandt G.	Maj 96th NY Infy	NY	07776
Babcock, Edwin F.	1st Lt. 2nd IL Cav	IL	10359
Babcock, Frelon J.	Capt. 41st USCT	OR	04185
Babcock, Heman P.	Passed Asst. Surg. USN	CA	00940
Babcock, John B.	BG USA	CA	05354
Babcock, Paul	Capt. 7th NJ Infy BvtMaj	NY	11999
Babcock, Simeon	1st Lt. 1st WI Infy	MI	06410
Babcock, Stephen H.	1st Lt. Adj. 30th MI Infy	CO	10452
Babin, Hosea J.	Med. Director USN	NY	08098
Bache, Alexander Dallas	3rd Class (Supt.US Coast Survey)	PA	00098
Bache, Dallas	Col. Asst Surg. Gen. USA	DC	12176
Bache, George M.	Commander USN	PA	00913
Bachman, Augustus H.	1st Lt. 1st MI L Arty	MI	07283
Bachman, Martin V.	Capt. 107th NY Infy	DC	10332
Bachtell, Samuel	Capt. Sig. Corps BvtLTC USV	OH	07416
Backus, Charles W.	Surg. 203rd PA Infy	MI	05923
Backus, Clarence W.	1st Lt. 97th NY Infy	MO	07382
Backus, Samuel W.	2nd Lt. 2nd CA Cav	CA	01621
Backus, William	Capt. 20th Batt OH L Arty	OH	14270
Bacon, Albert W.	Pay Director USN	DC	00432
Bacon, Francis	1st Lt. 50th NY Eng.	NY	06426
Bacon, Francis H.	Act Ensign USN	CA	03459
Bacon, George M.	Capt. 24th OH Infy	OH	07015 (Dup)
Bacon, George S.	Capt. 29th IA Infy	IA	05484
Bacon, George W.	1st Lt. 91st NY Infy	WI	01550
Bacon, Henry M.	Chap 63rd IN Infy	OH	02974
Bacon, Horace C.	Capt. 11 NH Infy	MA	01456
Bacon, John M.	Col. 8th Cav USA BG USV	DC	02360
Bacon, William P.	LTC 5th NY Cav	NY	13656
Badger, Oscar C.	Commodore USN	DC	10333
Badger, William	Capt. 6th Infy USA BvtMaj	MA	04831

Name	Rank	Commandery	Insignia No.
Badlam, William H.	2nd Asst Eng. USN, PA Eng. USN	MA	01611
Baer, Edward R.	Surg. 1st MD Infy	DC	10773
Baer, George F.	Capt. 133rd Infy	PA	09493
Baer, Louis	1st Lt. 2nd OH H Arty	OH	07125
Baggs, Nicholas	Capt. 2nd PA H Arty	PA	00204
Bagley, Henry A.	2nd Lt. 211th PA Infy	CO	05614
Bailey, Andrew J.	2nd Lt. 5th MA Infy	MA	01609
Bailey, Chesley D.	LTC 9th KY Infy	OH	07129
Bailey, Clarence M.	BG USA	IN	03548
Bailey, Daniel W.	Capt. 78th USCT	NY	15678
Bailey, Edward	Capt. 35th IL Infy	IL	17371
Bailey, George W.	1st Lt. 6th MO Infy	MO	12636
Bailey, James H.	1st Lt. 3rd NY Cav BvtCapt.	NY	08940
Bailey, John M.	1st Lt. Adj 177th NY Infy	NY	07239
Bailey, John R.	Surg. 8th MO Infy BvtLTC	MI	04030
Bailey, Leroy W.	Capt. 128th OH Infy	OH	08538
Bailey, Mahlon	Surg. 1st KS Infy	KS	08366
Bailey, Marcellus	Maj 7th USCT	DC	02490
Bailey, Peter P.	1st Lt. RQM 30th IN Infy	CA	06066
Bailey, Peter S.	Capt. 27th MA Infy	MA	02550
Bailey, Pryce W.	1st Lt. 61st NY Infy	NY	10320
Bailey, Robert	Capt. 6th NY Infy	CO	11015
Bailey, Theodorus	RAdm USN	NY	00727
Bailey, Thomas C.	1st Lt. Adj 14th IN Infy	CA	04758
Bailey, William	Maj Surg. 9th KY Cav	OH	15109
Bailey, William W.	Surg. 1st MO Cav	MO	07383
Bailhache, Preston H.	Surg. 14th IL Cav	DC	07511
Bailhache, William H.	Capt. AQM BvtMaj USV	CA	09835
Bailie, William L.	Passed Asst. Eng. USN	PA	10394
Baily, Elisha I.	BG USA	CA	02719
Baily, Joseph C.	Col. Asst Surg. Gen. USA	CA	02533
Bainbridge, Augustus H.	Col. USA	IL	06389
Bainbridge, Edmund C.	Col. 3rd Arty USA	CA	10361
Baird, Absalom	BG Ins Gen BvtMG USA	DC	01949
Baird, Andrew D.	Maj 79th NY Infy	NY	06746
Baird, Frank J..	2nd Lt. 138th IL Infy	MO	05049
Baird, George W.	BG Paymaster Gen. USA	NY	03500
Baird, George W.	RAdm USN	DC	11387
Baird, William L.	2nd Lt. 4th MA H Arty	MA	14517
Baker, Alpheus W.	2nd Lt. 23rd WI Infy	MA	06991
Baker, Andrew J.	1st Lt. 17th IA Infy	IA	05906
Baker, Benjamin F.	Col. 43rd NY Infy BvtBG	NY	02265
Baker, Charles C.	1st Lt. 6th OH Cav	OH	04390
Baker, Charles E.	Capt. 64th OH Cav	IL	07222
Baker, Charles H.	1st Lt. 20th MA Infy	MA	06180
Baker, Charles H.	Chief Eng. USN	DC	02429
Baker, Charles S.	1st Lt. 27th NY Infy	DC	02276
Baker, Edward D.	Maj QM USA	CA	01379

Name	Rank	Commandery	Insignia No.
Baker, Edward L.	Capt. 3rd MN Infy	WI	04458
Baker, Fisher A.	1st Lt. Adj 18th MA Infy BvtCapt.	NY	12787
Baker, George L.	2nd Lt. 4th USC H Arty	MN	06880
Baker, George W.	LTC CS USV	OH	09018
Baker, Hendrick D.	Capt. 35th KY Infy	KS	05356
Baker, Henry	Act Master USN	MO	08277
Baker, Henry B.	Asst Surg. 20th MI Infy	MI	12577
Baker, Henry R.	Lt. USN	MA	09880
Baker, James H.	Col. 10th MN Infy BvtBG	MN	03694
Baker, Joel C.	1st Lt. 9th VT Infy	VT	09165
Baker, John B.	Capt. 3rd IL Cav	IL	09655
Baker, John P.	LTC USA	MO	04430
Baker, Joseph G.A.	1st Lt. 13th CT Infy	NY	01248
Baker, Livingston L.	3rd Class (Pioneer settler)	CA	04104
Baker, Rienzi H.	2nd Lt. 18th MI Infy	MI	12765
Baker, Robert S.	Capt. 27th MI Infy	MI	10249
Baker, Stephen	Maj 4th Infy USA	CA	03543
Baker, Theodore S.S.	1st Lt. 29th PA Infy	PA	05717
Balch, George B.	RAdm USN	MD	00702
Balding, Thomas E.	Capt. 24th WI Infy BvtMaj	WI	09715
Baldridge, Samuel P.	Capt. 91st OH Infy	OH	09029
Baldwin, Aaron P.	Capt. 6th Batt OH L Arty	OH	03038
Baldwin, Charles P.	LTC 11th ME Infy BvtBG	CO	05778
Baldwin, David C.	1st Lt. 35th OH Infy	OH	13749
Baldwin, Elias B.	LTC 8th MO Cav	KS	16986
Baldwin, Ephriam C.	1st Lt. 1st CA Cav	CA	07720
Baldwin, Frank D.	BG USA	MI	09585
Baldwin, George H.	1st Lt. 40th MA Infy	NY	01111
Baldwin, George W.	Capt. AAG USV	MA	00979
Baldwin, Hugh J.	Capt. 23rd NY Infy	NY	12000
Baldwin, James A.	Capt. 1st MA Cav	IL	09350
Baldwin, James G.	Capt. 137th OH Infy	OH	04192
Baldwin, James M.	Capt. 2nd NJ Cav	NY	06951
Baldwin, John S.	Capt. 51st MA Infy	MA	01268
Baldwin, Norman A.	Capt. 1st OH L Arty	OH	14464
Baldwin, Silas	1st. Lt. RQM 96th OH Infy	IN	13003
Baldwin, Theodore A.	BG USV	OH	16368
Baldwin, Theodore F.	2nd Lt. 14th IA	IA	11901
Baldwin, William H.	LTC 83rd OH Infy BvtBG	OH	03396
Ball Charles J. C.	Capt. 65th NY Infy BvtMaj	NY	03011
Ball, Benjamin A.	Capt. 3rd MA H Arty	MA	03147
Ball, Eustace H.	1st Lt. 53rd OH Infy	OH	04216
Ball, James M.	Capt. 3rd USC H Arty BvtMaj	IL	05916
Ball, Ogilvie D.	1st Lt. RQM 3rd NY L Arty	NY	12553
Ball, Stephen	2nd Lt. 12th CT Infy	MA	09600
Ball, Wallace M.B.	2nd Lt. 2nd MD Infy	PA	05980
Ball, Warren J.	2nd Lt. 2nd MA Cav	MA	08266
Ballard, Henry	2nd Lt. 5th VT Infy	VT	09164

The Roster

Name	Rank	Commandery	Insignia No.
Ballard, Orville W.	Maj Paymaster USV	IL	03866
Ballinger, Richard H.	Col. 53rd USCT	WA	13612
Ballinger, William	2nd Lt. 19th IA Infy	IA	14231
Ballou, Alphonso A.	1st Lt. 52nd MA Infy	MI	06818
Ballou, Barton A.	1st Lt. 16th NH Infy	MA	16438
Ballou, Daniel R.	2nd Lt. 12th RI Infy	MA	08051
Ballwood, Edmond	2nd Lt. Troop "C" 1st Regt US Cav	KS	17521
Balsley, Joseph	Capt. 27th IN Infy	IN	11802
Bampton, Benjamin C.	Passed Asst. Eng. USN	NY	08640
Bancroft, Ambrose	Capt. 32nd MA Infy BvtMaj	MA	13596
Bancroft, Frederick J.	Maj 3rd PA H Arty	CO	05962
Bane, Oscar F.	Capt. 123 IL Infy	IL	03143
Banes, Charles H.	Capt. AAG BvtLTC USV	PA	03222
Bangs, George F.	Capt. 2nd MA Infy	MA	01242
Bangs, Isaac S.	LTC 81st USCT BvtBG	ME	02692
Bankhead, Henry C.	LTC AIG BvtBG USV	NY	08484
Banks, Lyman	Capt. 47th USCT	WA	13613
Banks, Nathaniel P.	MG USV	MA	09472
Bankson, John P.	Capt. 118th PA Infy	PA	01121
Bannister, Dwight	Maj Paymaster USA BvtLTC	IA	11829
Banta, William Jr.	1st Lt. RCS 12th NY Cav	NY	10538
Banzhaf, Charles	Maj 1st MO Cav	PA	00802
Baquet, Camille	2nd Lt. 1st NJ Infy	NY	09948
Barber, Ambrose M.	Capt. 120th NY Infy	NY	08941
Barber, Gershom M.	LTC 197th OH Infy BvtBG	OH	03201
Barber, Merritt	Col. AAG USA BG USV	NY	02614 (Dup)
Barbour, Isaac R.	1st Lt. 35th USCT	MA	08852
Barbour, Joseph H.	1st Lt. 16th USCT	CA	03909
Barclay, Charles J.	RAdm USN	PA	08203
Bard, Cephas L.	Asst Surg. 210th PA Infy	CA	03635
Bard, Sylvester W.	Capt. Bard's Indpt. Co. OH Cav	OH	03485
Bardwell, Abalino C.	Capt. 147th IL Infy	IL	08398
Bargar, Benjamin F.	Maj 33rd OH Infy	OH	08157
Bargar, Fred C.	1st Lt. 49th NY Infy	NY	06019
Barker, Albert S.	RAdm USN	MA	01821
Barker, Eben F.	Capt. 75th USCT	PA	05238
Barker, Edward T.	Actg. Asst Paymaster USN	MA	01731
Barker, Elmer J.	Maj 5th NY Cav	NY	08343
Barker, Frederick	Capt. 26th ME Infy	NY	15210
Barker, James G.	Capt. 36th OH Infy	OH	07207 (Dup)
Barker, John D.	Capt. 1st OH Cav	KS	04094
Barker, Joseph H.	1st Lt. NY H Arty	NY	03608
Barker, Orville A.	1st Lt. Adj. 39th MA Infy	MA	03503
Barker, Thaddeus L.	LTC 39th MA Infy	MA	13047
Barker, Thomas E.	LTC 12th NH Infy	MA	02710
Barker, William W.	Capt. CS BvtMaj USV	PA	07630
Barley, Jonathan W.	Capt. 37th NY Infy	NY	10253
Barlow, Francis C.	MG USV	NY	00333-528

Name	Rank	Commandery	Insignia No.
Barlow, John W.	BG Chief of Eng. USA	DC	03193
Barnard, Albert J.	Capt. 116th NY Infy	NY	16779
Barnard, Benjamin F.	1st Lt. RQM 59th MA Infy	MA	08052
Barnard, Charles A.	1st Lt. 66th USCT	IL	15253
Barnard, Daniel P.	Capt. 139th NY Infy BvtMaj	PA	10523
Barnard, George M.	Capt. 18th MA Infy BvtCol	MA	01004
Barnard, J. Howard	1st Lt. USC H Arty	CA	09046
Barnard, James M.	1st Lt. 24th MA Infy	MA	00856
Barnard, John H.	Capt. 76th NY Infy	DC	14256
Barnard, Levi R.	1st Lt. 2nd NJ Cav	NY	04602
Barnes, Henry E.	Chap 72nd IL Infy	MA	15779
Barnes, Henry L.	Asst Surg. 21st WI Infy	WI	14462
Barnes, John G.	Lt. Commander USN	PA	00139
Barnes, Samuel D.	Capt. 64th USCT	CO	06527
Barnett, James	Col. 1st OH L Arty BvtMG	OH	02889
Barnett, James W.	1st Lt. 10th USCT	PA	16454
Barney, Albert M.	Col. 142nd NY Infy BvtBG	NY	01164
Barney, Benjamin G.	LTC 2nd PA H Arty BvtBG	CA	02332
Barney, Caleb H.	1st Lt. USC H Arty	NY	05417
Barney, Luther L.	Capt. 10th NY Cav	NY	02564
Barney, Martin V.B.	Capt. 3rd MA Cav	KS	06559
Barnhart, Franklin H.	Capt. 50th PA Infy	PA	04807
Barnitz, Albert	Maj BvtCol. USA	OH	06839
Barnum, Frank D.	Capt. 47th NY Infy	DC	12520
Barnum, George G.	1st Lt. RQM 100th NY Infy BvtCapt.	MN	04242
Barnum, William L.	LTC 11th MO Infy	IL	01933
Baroux, Charles L.	1st Lt. 119th PA Infy	PA	01473
Barr, Jacob E.	Capt. 178th PA Infy	PA	02033
Barr, John C.	Act Ensign USN	WA	17536
Barr, Samuel L.	Capt. 5th Infy USA	PA	00652
Barr, Thomas F.	BG Jdge Adv Gen. USA	MA	04039
Barr, William M.	2nd Asst Eng. USN	PA	06986
Barrett, Addison	Capt. Mil. Storekpr. USA BvtMaj	IN	07260
Barrett, Augustus E.	2nd Lt. 8th IL Infy	WA	11067
Barrett, Clarence T.	Capt. ADC BvtMaj USV	NY	01646
Barrett, Daniel E.	Capt. 5th VT Infy	DC	12695
Barrett, David M.	Capt. 89th OH Infy	OH	09383
Barrett, Edward	Commodore USN	NY	01024
Barrett, George V.	1st Lt. 23rd MA Infy	MA	03159
Barrett, Orsmund M.	1st Lt. 38th IA Infy	IA	06200
Barrett, Richard	Capt. 47th MA Infy	MA	04625
Barrett, Samuel E.	Maj 1st IL L Arty	IL	01996
Barrett, Theodore H.	Col. 62nd USCT BvtBG	MN	05340
Barrett, Thomas H.	Act 3rd Asst Eng. USN	NY	04610
Barrett, William H.	Capt. 40th USCT BvtMaj	DC	03583
Barrett. Gregory	LTC 4th MD Infy BvtCol	MD	08311
Barriger, John W.	BG USA	NE	06364
Barron, Florentine W.	1st Lt. 38th IA Infy	IA	11143

Name	Rank	Commandery	Insignia No.
Barrows, Frank	2nd Lt. 30th USCT	KS	06303
Barrows, Walter A.	Capt. 115th USCT	PA	07049
Barrows, William E.	Capt. 19th MA Infy BvtMaj	PA	01864
Barry, Alfred C.	Chap 19th WI Infy	WI	01569
Barry, Garrett R.	Pay Director USN	NY	00231
Barry, George	2nd Lt. 134th IL Infy	IL	13110
Barry, George H.	Capt. 8th NY Cav	IL	09199
Barry, William W.	Pay Inspector USN	MA	12509
Barse, George R.	1st Lt. 5th MI Cav	MO	05885
Barstow, George F.	Maj USA	MA	05336
Barstow, John L.	Maj 8th VT Infy	VT	09173
Barstow, Robert	Act Master USN	MA	05794
Barstow, Wilson	BG USV	NY	00131
Barth, Charles G.	Capt. CS BvtMaj USV	IL	00283
Barth, Charles H.	Capt. 2nd CA Infy	CA	01345
Bartholf, John H.	LTC USA	NY	09304
Bartholomew, Orion A.	BvtBG USV	MN	17897
Bartholomew, Thomas L.	1st Lt. Adj. 9th NY Infy	NY	12399
Bartine, David H.	Surg. 114th PA Infy	PA	01607
Bartleman, Richard M.	Chief Eng. USN	PA	02580
Bartlett, Amos	Capt. 15th MA Infy	MA	09050
Bartlett, Charles E.A.	Capt. 6th MA Infy	MA	05030
Bartlett, Charles G.	Col. 9th Infy USA BvtBG	NY	03695
Bartlett, Edward J.	2nd Lt. 5th MA Cav	MA	02120
Bartlett, Henry A.	Maj USMC	CA	09044
Bartlett, John R.	RAdm USN	DC	03681
Bartlett, Joseph	Capt. 1st OH Light Infy	OH	09019
Bartlett, Lewis C.	1st Lt. 27th & 121st NY Infy BvtMaj	DC	No Number
Bartlett, Prescott	Capt. 7th IL Cav	IL	09873
Bartlett, William C.	LTC 2nd NC Mtd. Infy BvtBG	CA	06051 (Dup)
Bartlett, William F.	BG BvtMG USV	MA	00890
Barto, Alphonso	Capt. 52rd IL Infy	MN	08926
Barton, Frederick	Capt. 10th MA Infy BvtLTC	MA	07450
Barton, Geo. DeForest	Paymaster USN	NY	00543
Barton, Isaac R.	1st Lt. 53rd USCT	NY	18159
Barton, Jonathan Q.	Paymaster USN	DC	04623
Barton, Percival	1st Lt. 7th MN Infy	MN	16343
Barton, Robert	Capt. 86th NY Infy	WA	14616
Barton, Theodore A.	1st Lt. 58th MA Infy	MA	05795
Barton, William H.	Lt. Commander USN	MD	12521
Bascom, Gustavus M.	LTC AAG BvtCol. USV	MA	02690
Basiger, John R.	Capt. 174th OH Infy	KS	15829
Bass, Edgar	QM Sgt. 6th MN Infy Prof. USMA	NY	05293
Bassett, Adams	Capt. 4th Infy USV	CA	11222
Bassford, Abraham	Col. 14th NY Cav	NY	09857
Bast, Ulysses S.	Capt. 48th PA Infy	CA	14902
Batchelder, Greenleaf W.	1st Lt. Adj. 1st MA Cav	MA	13327
Batchelder, Hiram T.	2nd Lt. 26th ME Infy	CA	06140

Name	Rank	Commandery	Insignia No.
Batchelder, John T.	1st Lt. 1st Battn MA H Arty	MA	02067
Batchelder, Moulton	1st Lt. 6th MA Infy	MA	10487
Batchelder, Richard	BG QMG USA	DC	02611
Batcheller, George S.	LTC 115th NY Infy	NY	05412
Batcheller, Oliver A.	Commander USN	ME	04723
Batcheller, Wheelock T.	LTC 28th CT Infy	NY	13448
Bates, Cyrus C.	1st Lt. 13th OH Infy	OH	04405
Bates, Alexander B.	RAdm USN	NY	07601
Bates, Byron W.	1st Lt. 1st NY Mtd. Rifles	NY	17569
Bates, Caleb	Maj ADC USV	OH	02250
Bates, Charles H.	1st Lt. 23rd MA Infy	MA	03050
Bates, Delevan	Col. 30th USCT BvtBG	NE	03921
Bates, Henry C.	1st Lt. 11th NY Cav	MI	07281
Bates, Hervey	Maj 132nd IN Infy	IN	08580
Bates, James A.	Maj BvtLTC USA	DC	00840
Bates, James L.	Col. 12th MA Infy	MA	01068
Bates, John C.	Capt. 11th Infy USA LG USA	MO	05740
Bates, Joshua H.	BG USV	OH	02248
Bates, Marcus W.	1st Lt. 21st MI Infy	MN	08729
Bates, Robert F.	Maj 22nd Iny USA	DC	04814
Bates, William H.	Act Asst Surg. USN	NY	13570
Baugher, Eugene C.	Maj 12th MD Infy	MO	12980
Baum, William T.	1st Lt. 26th PA Infy	PA	11446
Baumbach, Charles Von	Maj 24th WI Infy	WI	07116
Bausman, Edwin W.	2nd Lt. 100th PA Infy	PA	10861
Baxter, Archibald E.	Capt. 141st NY Infy	NY	13755
Baxter, Charles H.	Capt. 47th WI Infy	WI	11847
Baxter, Dewitt C.	BvtBG USV	PA	00512
Baxter, Jedediah H.	BG Surg. Gen. USA	DC	02402
Baxter, Luther L.	LTC 1st MN H Arty	MN	05855
Baxter, Samuel A.	Asst Surg.18th OH Infy	OH	13961
Baxter, William H.	1st Lt. 113th OH Infy	MN	08826
Bayer, Charles T.	2nd Lt. 81st Infy USA	PA	01656
Bayley, William E.	2nd Lt. 9th IL Cav	PA	00284
Baylor, Thomas G.	Col. Ordnance USA	PA	07855
Bayne, Thomas M.	Col. 136th PA Infy	DC	10371
Beach, Albijah I.	Asst Surg. 9th KS Cav	WA	14368
Beach, Alexander	1st Lt. Adj. 11th NJ Infy	NY	09418
Beach, Carmi W.	Capt. 2nd WI Infy	CA	02916
Beach, Dennis	1st Lt. 5th CT Infy	NY	10539
Beach, Edgar A.	2nd Lt. 4th VT Infy	VT	09253
Beach, John N.	Surg. 40th OH Infy	OH	07317
Beach, Myron H.	2nd Lt. 44th IA Infy	IL	05284
Beach, William H.	1st Lt. Adj. 1st NY Cav	WI	04127
Beadle, William H. H.	LTC 1st MI Shpshtrs. BvtBG	WI	04121
Beaham, Thomas G.	Maj ADC USV	MO	11912
Beal, George L.	BG BvtMG USV	ME	00677
Beal, John G.	Capt. 95th OH Infy	CA	16769

The Roster

Name	Rank	Commandery	Insignia No.
Beale, J. Hervey	Chap 1st PA Cav	PA	13284
Beall, Alpheus	1st Lt. Adj. 4th WV Infy	PA	08967
Beals, Thomas P.	Capt. 32nd ME Infy	ME	08588
Beaman, George W.	Pay Director USN	MA	08875
Bean, Irving McC.	Capt. 5th WI Infy	WI	01556
Bean, Theodore W.	Capt. 17th PA Cav BvtLTC	PA	02578
Beane, James W.	1st Lt. 7th Batt MA L Arty	MA	14387
Bearce, Henry M.	1st Lt. 32nd ME Infy	ME	10519A
Beardslee, Lester A.	RAdm USN	DC	05594
Beardsley, George A.	Maj 13th NJ Infy	NY	05116
Beardsley, Grove S.	Med. Director USN	DC	10334
Beardsley, Samuel R.	1st. Lt. 13th NJ Infy	NY	04597
Beardsley, Solomon W.	1st Lt. 154 NY Infy	NE	07171
Beasley, George F.	Act Asst Surg. USN	IN	07154
Beasley, James W.	1st Lt. RQM 40th IN Infy	MA	09803
Beath, Robert B.	Capt. 6th USCT	PA	04938
Beaton, Charles H.	2nd Lt. 13th CT Infy	MA	16991
Beattie, Alexander M.	Capt. 3rd VT Infy	VT	09663
Beatty, James H.	1st Lt. 4th IA Batt Arty	CA	16721
Beatty, John	BG USV	OH	03577
Beatty, William G.	Maj 174th OH Infy	OH	05387
Beaumont, Eugene B.	LTC 3rd Cav USA BvtCol	PA	02737
Beaumont, Horatio N.	Surg. USN	NY	05009
Beaumont, J. C.	Commander USN	NY	00798
Beaver, David R.	Asst Surg. 191st PA Infy	PA	07856
Beaver, James A.	Col. 148th PA Infy BvtBG	PA	04940
Bechel, William F.	1st Lt. 107th OH Infy	NE	03945
Becher, John A.	1st Lt. RQM 34th WI Infy	WI	07196
Bechtel, Henry H.	Capt. 10th PA Infy	PA	09270
Beck, Charles A.	Chap 26th PA Infy	PA	10621
Beck, Henry L.	Bvt Capt. USA	PA	00709
Beck, Moses M.	Capt. 18th Ind Batt IN L Arty	KS	15878
Beck, William H.	BG USV	MN	14331
Beck, Willliam Butler	Capt. 5th Arty BvtLTC USA	NY	02760
Becker, Alexander R.	3rd Class (Act Asst Surg.USA)	MA	00872
Becker, Anton	1st Lt. Adj. 74th PA Infy	DC	06384
Becker, Otto	LTC USA	MO	13954
Beckford, William A.	1st Lt. 8th NH Infy	MA	11740
Beckwith, Warren	Capt. 4th IA Cav	IA	05790
Bedee, Edwin E.	Capt. 12th NH Infy	MA	10045
Bedell, James O.	2nd Lt. 14th NJ Infy	NY	14036
Beebe, Hinckley F.	Maj 34th IA Infy	MO	09629
Beebe, William S.	1st Lt. Ordnance BvtMaj USA	NY	00409
Beem, David E.	Capt. 14th IN Infy	IN	10573
Beers, Alfred B.	Capt. 6th CT Infy	NY	02143
Beers, James R.	Act Vol Lt. USN	NY	06737
Beeson, Byron A.	1st Lt. 2nd IA Cav	IA	07595
Beggs, George W.	Asst Surg. 105th IL	IA	05441

Name	Rank	Commandery	Insignia No.
Behm, Adam O.	Capt. 150th IN Infy	IN	08281
Beidelman, William	2nd Lt. 153rd PA Infy	PA	10622
Belcher, John H.	Maj QM USA	MA	07257
Belcher, Samuel C.	Capt. 16th ME Infy	ME	02879
Belden, Charles O.	Maj 67th NY Infy	NY	00371
Belden, W. Scott	Capt. 2nd IA Cav	DC	14218
Belden, William S.	Capt. 93rd OH Infy	OH	12838
Belfield, Henry H.	1st Lt. Adj. 8th IA Cav	IL	09081
Belknap, Augustus	Capt. 67th NY Infy	NY	01081
Belknap, Charles	Commander USN	DC	04559
Belknap, Charles E.	Capt. 21st MI Infy BvtMaj	DC	07573
Belknap, George E.	RAdm USN	MA	03313
Belknap, William W.	BG BvtMG USV	DC	05647
Bell, Digby V.	1st Lt. RQM 24th MI Infy	MI	04593
Bell, George	Capt. 150th PA Infy	CO	08189
Bell, George	BG USA	DC	10417
Bell, George H.	2nd Lt. 2nd OH H Arty BvtCapt.	OH	13850
Bell, James B.	BvtMaj USV	NY	00534
Bell, James H.	Capt. 6th NY Cav	IL	04144
Bell, James M.	BG USA	DC	05210
Bell, John B.	Maj 15th MI Infy BvtLTC	OH	03066
Bell, John H.	Col. VRC BvtBG	NY	00213
Bell, John N.	Capt. 25th IA Infy	OH	02964
Bell, John T.	2nd Lt. 2nd IA Infy	CA	04310
Bell, Joseph McC.	Capt. AAG BvtLTC USV	WI	01557
Bell, Samuel	Maj Paymaster BvtLTC	PA	01573
Bell, Samuel	Asst Surg. 15th WI Infy	WI	12368
Bell, William B.	LTC 8th IA Infy BvtCol	IA	13588
Bell, William H.	BG Comm. Gen. of Subst. USA	CO	02809
Bellows, Edward	Pay Director USN	CA	10303
Belmer, Herman	BvtCapt. USV	OH	17509
Bemis, William W.	2nd Lt. 16th VT Infy	MA	09051
Bendel, Herman	Surg. 86th NY Infy	NY	02571
Bendel, Herman	Maj 34th MO Infy	CA	01736
Bender, George A.	Capt. 105th IL Infy	IL	09243
Bendire, Charles E.	Capt. 1st Cav BvtMaj USA	DC	03397
Benecke, Louis	Capt. 49th MO Infy	MO	10520
Benedict, David De F.	Surg. 17th OH Infy	OH	07946
Benedict, George G.	2nd Lt. 12th VT Infy	VT	08267
Benét Stephen V.	BG Chief of Ordnance USA	DC	02281-317
Benham, Daniel W.	BG USA	OH	03545
Benham, John H.	1st Lt. 11th Infy USA	CA	12201
Benham, Tower L.	Capt. 7th MI Infy	MA	15780
Benjamin, Charles A.	1st Lt. 21st NY Cav	MA	01594
Benjamin, Park	Ensign USN	NY	16149
Benjamin, Samuel N.	Maj AAG BvtLTC USA	DC	02664
Benkard, James	Capt. ADC USV	NY	02044
Bennet, Thomas	Capt. 37th Infy PA Militia	CA	08880

The Roster

Name	Rank	Commandery	Insignia No.
Bennett, Augustus G.	LTC 21st USCT	CA	07245
Bennett, Daniel A.	1st Lt. 15th USCT	CA	07409
Bennett, Frank T.	LTC 55th PA Infy	PA	00153-1816
Bennett, Harrison	1st Lt. 1st MI Infy	CA	04099
Bennett, Henry	2nd Lt. Stokes Ind Batt IL L Arty	KS	06789
Bennett, Herbert F.	2nd Lt. 11th USC H Arty	MA	14136
Bennett, John W.	LTC 1st VT Cav	IL	15103
Bennett, Jonas L.	Capt. 16th WI Infy	IL	12523
Bennett, Thomas G.	Capt. 29th CT Infy	NY	12626
Benson, Andrew M.	Capt. 1st ME Cav BvtMaj	MA	01501
Benson, Edwin N.	3rd Class	PA	05747
Benson, Frederick S.	1st Lt. Adj. 22 MA Infy BvtCapt.	NY	05114
Benson, Harvey W.	1st Lt. Sig. Corps BvtCapt. USV	PA	02929
Benson, Henry H.	Capt. 8th IA Infy	NE	05911
Benson, Henry M.	Maj USA	CA	03117
Benson, Richard Dale	1st Lt. 114th PA Infy BvtMaj	PA	02123
Benson, Samuel W.	2nd Lt. 7th Batt MA L Arty	MA	13048
Benson, Stephen D.	1st Lt. 31st ME Infy	ME	09099
Bent, Charles	2nd Lt. 147th IL	DC	08613
Bent, Luther S.	Maj 18th MA Infy	MA	01366
Benteen, Frederick W.	Col. 138th USCT BvtBG	OH	11426
Bentley, Charles S.	Capt. 2nd WI Cav	DC	03732
Bentley, Robert H.	LTC 12th OH Cav BvtBG	OH	07017
Bentley, Wilbur G.	Maj 9th NY Cav	DC	02813
Benton, Caleb H.	1st Lt. 5th VT Infy	MN	05770
Benton, Charles H.	1st Lt. RQM 1st WI Infy	WI	03713
Benton, Josiah H.	Act Paymaster USA	NY	06016
Benton, Reuben C.	LTC 1st VT H Arty	MN	05863
Benton, William M.	1st Lt. 9th IL Infy	PA	00360
Bentzoni, Charles	LTC USA	CA	03690
Benyaurd, William H.H.	LTC Corps of Eng. USA	PA	02799
Benzon, John L.	Capt. 191st PA Infy	PA	07327
Berch, Jesse L.	1st Lt. RQM 22nd WI Infy	MI	04365
Berdan, Hiram	Col. 1st US Shpshtrs. BvtBG	DC	08810
Berger, Adolph	1st Lt. RQM 1st LA Cav	DC	05595
Bergland, Eric	Maj Eng. USA	MD	08409
Bering, John A.	Maj 48th OH Infy	OH	17006
Berkey, John M.	LTC 99th IN Infy	CO	05615
Berlin, Carl	1st Lt. 1st NY L Arty BvtMaj	OH	04400
Bernard, George A.	Capt. 65th NY Infy BvtLTC	PA	01715
Bernard, Reuben F.	LTC 9th Cav BvtBG USA	DC	07500
Berry, A. Hun	1st Lt. Adj. 8th MA Infy	MA	01866
Berry, Benjamin N.	1st Lt. 20th MI Infy	CA	10732
Berry, Casper M.	LTC 60th Infy PA Militia	PA	00006
Berry, Ira, Jr.	Capt. 14th NH Infy BvtMaj	ME	11239
Berry, James T.	1st Lt. 26th MO Infy	WA	06907
Berry, John G.	1st Lt. 16th MI Infy	MI	11287
Berry, Mark T.	1st Lt. Hatch's Co. MN Cav	CA	10955

The Roster

Name	Rank	Commandery	Insignia No.
Berry, Thomas H.	1st Lt. 8th MA Infy	MA	14438
Berryman, Wilson	1st Lt. 32nd USCT	NY	15211
Bertelotte, John D.	BvtCol. USV	PA	00553
Bertram, Joseph H.M.	Maj Paymaster USV	MA	01258
Bessie, Adolphe	1st Lt. Adj. 21st USCT	MN	13798
Best, Clermont L.	Col. 4th Arty USA	NY	08793
Bettcher, George A.	Capt. 11th IN Cav	IN	13185
Betts, C. Frederic	Capt. 17th CT Infy	NY	02739
Betts, George F.	LTC 9th NY Infy	NY	09949
Bever, George W.	2nd Lt. 46th IA Infy	IA	05057
Beveridge, John L.	Col. 17th IL Cav BvtBG	CA	02411
Beverly, John	LTC 34th NY Infy	WA	07219
Bevin, Abner A.	1st Lt. 21st CT Infy	PA	04650
Bevins, Silas H.	Act Ensign USA	NY	08942
Bibber, Andrew H.	Capt. AAG USV	CA	06278
Bicker, Henry K.	Capt. 10th USC H Arty BvtMaj	NY	03773
Bickford, Nathan	Capt. CS USV	DC	08003
Bickham, William D.	Maj ADC USV	OH	02773
Bicknell, Francis A.	BvtMaj USV	MA	15515
Bicknell, George W.	1st Lt. Adj. 5th ME Infy	MA	12667
Biddle, Alexander	LTC 121st PA Infy	PA	06248
Biddle, George H.	Col. 95th NY Infy	NY	00638
Biddle, James	BG USA	CA	03534
Biddle, James	Capt. 16th Infy BvtMaj USA	MI	03420
Biddle, James C.	Maj ADC BvtCol. USV	PA	03792
Biddle, William B.	Capt. 87th IN Infy BvtMaj	IN	12860
Biddle, William C.	Capt. 72nd OH Infy	OH	08176
Biddle, William F.	Capt. ADC USV	PA	04939
Bidwell, William B.	1st Lt. 19th KS Infy	WA	14985
Bierce, George N.	1st Lt. Adj. 131st OH Infy	OH	14250
Biese, Charles W.	2nd Lt. 82nd IL Infy	OH	07941
Bigelow, Alexander T.	2nd Lt. 15th VT Infy	MN	04546
Bigelow, Edmund D.	1st Lt. 40th MA Infy	MO	05087
Bigelow, Frank W.	Capt. 4th NY Cav	MA	01798
Bigelow, Henry W.	Capt. 14th OH Infy	OH	02975
Bigelow, John	Capt. 9th Batt MA L Arty BvtMaj	PA	01124
Bigelow, John A.	BvtCapt. USV	MI	06816
Bigger, David P.	Surg. 9th IL Infy	MN	04936
Bigger, Matthew	2nd Lt. 39th OH Infy	PA	08966
Biggs, Herman	Col. QM BvtBG USV	PA	02738
Bigham, John G.	Surg. 68th OH Infy	OH	12602
Billard, Jules F.	Act Asst Surg. USN	DC	15328
Billings, Henry R.	Capt. 20th CT Infy	MA	03847
Billings, John S.	LTC Dept. Surg. Gen. USA	DC	07724
Billings, L. Lorenzo	1st Lt. 35th USCT	MA	11264
Billings, Luther G.	Pay Director USN	DC	08312
Billingsley, Lorenzo W.	Capt. 44th USCT	NE	10059
Billow, George	Capt. 107th OH Infy	OH	03209

Name	Rank	Commandery	Insignia No.
Bingham, Edward B.	Asst Surg. USN	PA	00831
Bingham, Frank	Capt. 75th IL Infy	CO	07670
Bingham, Henry H.	Maj Jdge Adv BvtBG USV	PA	00551
Bingham, John A.	Maj Jdge Adv USV	OH	10282
Bingham, William	3rd Class	OH	03270
Bingmann, Richard	Capt. 7th WV Infy	OH	07714
Binkley, Otho H.	LTC 110th OH Infy BvtCol	OH	07322
Binney, Horace	3rd Class (Atty. supporter of Lincoln)	PA	00096
Biondi, Eugene N.	Acting Master USN	CA	14552
Bird, Charles	BG USA	DC	00290
Bird, Charles M.	Act Ensign USN	PA	13285
Bird, George W.	2nd Lt. 40th WI Infy	WI	10700
Bird, Harlan P.	1st. Lt. 12th WI Infy	WI	13686
Bird, Lewis J.	Capt. 1st Unat. Co. MA Infy	MA	11984
Bird, Samuel W.	1st Lt. 35th IL Infy	CO	15450
Bird, William	Capt. 179th NY Infy	MN	10668
Bird, William H.	1st Lt. 1st DE Cav BvtMaj	CA	04521 (Dup)
Birdseye, John T.	1st Lt. 111th OH Infy	MO	05392
Birge, Manning D.	Maj 6th MI Cav	IL	07438
Birkhimer, William E.	LTC USA Arty Col. USV	CA	08128
Birney, Samuel H.	Surg. 135th IL Infy	CO	06946
Bisbee, George D.	2nd Lt. 16th ME Infy	ME	03531
Bisbee, Horatio	LTC 9th ME Infy	NY	13449
Bisbee, William H.	BG USA	DC	10453
Bishop, Alber W.	LTC 1st AR Cav	PA	00776
Bishop, Edward F.	1st Lt. Adj. 89th IL Infy	CO	04022
Bishop, Francis M.	Capt. 2nd Infy USV	CA	04755
Bishop, John C.	1st Lt. RQM 1st WV Infy	OH	05315
Bishop, John F.	1st Lt. 5th MN Infy	IA	10392
Bishop, John S.	Col. 108th USCT	PA	06294
Bishop, Judson W.	Col. 2nd MN Infy BvtBG	MN	03692
Bishop, Thomas E.	Capt. 25th NY Infy	MN	07951
Bishop, William	1st Lt. RQM 13th CT Infy	NY	09414
Bishop. Herbert M.	Asst Surg. 1st CT Cav	CA	04631
Bissell, Evelyn L.	Surg. 5th CT Infy	NY	01018
Bissell, George P.	Col. 25th CT Infy	NY	01110
Bissell, Josiah W.	Col. 1st MO Eng	MN	06351
Bissell, Julius B.	1st Lt. 15th CT Infy	CO	04776
Bissell, Oliver C.	LTC 44th WI Infy	MN	13515
Bissinger, Philip	Capt. 79th PA Infy	PA	09494
Bixby, Augustus H.	Capt.1st NH Cav BvtMaj	MA	03805
Bixby, James A.	2nd Lt. 5th VT Infy	MN	05855
Bixler, John W.	2nd Lt. 30th IN Infy	DC	15562
Black, George W.Z.	Capt. 107th PA Infy BvtLTC	DC	12952
Black, Henry M.	Col. 23rd Infy USA	MI	06413
Black, James B.	Maj 18th IN Infy	IN	07040
Black, John C.	Col. 37th IL Infy BvtBG	IL	03696
Black, John D.	1st Lt. Adj. 145th PA Infy BvtMaj	MN	10484

Name	Rank	Commandery	Insignia No.
Black, Joseph F.	LTC 111th IL Infy BvtCol	MO	05841
Black, Thomas S.	Capt. 122nd OH Infy	OH	07206
Black, William	2nd Lt. 97th NY Infy	CA	04833
Black, William R.	Capt. 4th MA Infy	MA	13499
Blackburn, David S.	Capt. 21st IL Infy	CA	05460
Blackford, Albert J.	Capt. 107th IL Infy	IL	12661
Blackman, Francis H.	Capt. 11th USCT	MI	06987
Blackman, George N.	1st Lt. 93rd NY Infy	NY	18402
Blackman, Hudson B.	BvtMaj USV	MI	04074
Blackmar, Edwin C.	Capt. 15th IA Infy	IA	11073
Blackmar, Wilmon, W.	Capt. 1st WV Cav	MA	02276
Blackmer, Eli T.	1st Lt. 37th IL Infy	CA	05644
Blackmer, John C.	1st Lt. 135th Infy	VT	13404
Blackstone, Richard	Capt. 32nd OH Infy	OH	09817
Blackwell, Samuel H.	1st Lt. 52nd MA Infy	MN	13614
Blackwell, William B.	1st Lt. 29th NY Infy	WA	06391
Blagden, George	Maj 2nd MA Cav BvtCol	NY	05298
Blair, Andrew A.	Ensign USN	PA	16574
Blair, Austin	3rd Class (Gov. MI)	MI	05177
Blair, Benjamin	Capt. 123rd OH Infy	NY	05299
Blair, Charles W.	Col. 14th KS Cav BvtBG	KS	04088
Blair, Henry W.	LTC 15th NH Infy	DC	08811
Blair, John M.	Capt. 2nd KY Infy	OH	02630
Blaire, George E.	Capt. 17th OH Infy	OH	09641
Blaisdell, Humphrey M.	1st Lt. USC H Arty	MN	03832
Blake, Charles E.	2nd Lt. 40th USCT	CA	09260
Blake, Charles M.	Post Chap USA	CA	03665
Blake, Edward R.	1st Lt. 24th WI Infy	IL	10218
Blake, Fletcher A.	2nd Lt. 11th PA Cav	CO	14811
Blake, George A. H.	Col. 1st Cav BvtBG USA	DC	00827
Blake, Granville	Capt. 29th ME Infy BvtMaj	ME	10049
Blake, Henry J.	Lt. USN	MA	00836
Blake, Henry N.	Capt. 11th MA Infy	CA	04620
Blake, Henry T.	Act Ensign USN	DC	10335
Blake, James H.	1st Lt. 44th MA Infy	MA	00756
Blake, Maurice C.	3rd Class	CA	04105
Blake, Samuel C.	Surg. 39th IL Infy	IL	09824
Blakeman, A. Noel	Act Asst Paymaster USN	NY	02572
Blakeney, Thomas J.	Maj 1st CA Cav	CA	02907
Blakeslee, Bernard F.	2nd Lt. 16th CT Infy	NY	08344
Blakeslee, Erastus	Col. 1st CT Cav BvtBG	MA	01354
Blakesley, Alpheus M.	Capt. 74th IL Infy	IL	11193
Blanchard, Clifton A.	Capt. 35th MA Infy	MA	01393
Blanchard, Henry F.	2nd LT. 1st ME Cav	ME	02691
Blanchard, Horatio	Act Master USN	ME	11621
Blanchard, Ira	Capt. 12th MA Infy	MA	16233
Blanchard, James M.	Capt. 92nd USCT	MA	01734
Blanchet, Auguste D.	Maj 27th NJ Infy	NY	09114

Name	Rank	Commandery	Insignia No.
Bland, Charles C.	Capt. 32nd MO Infy	MO	12389
Bland, Daniel W.	Surg. 96th PA Infy	PA	08204
Blandon, Leander	Col. 95th IL Infy BvtBG	IA	11690
Blasland, Edward B.	Maj 33rd MA Infy BvtLTC	MA	01620
Blazer, Philip	1st Lt. 7th OH Cav	OH	12422
Bleidorn, Charles F.G.	2nd Lt. 20th NY Infy	NY	09858
Blewett, William E.	1st Lt. 2nd NJ Infy	NY	16150
Bliss, Aaron T.	Capt. 10th NY Cav	MI	04718
Bliss, William W.	1st Lt. 49th IL Infy	DC	10809
Bliss, Zenas H.	Capt. 28th USCT	VT	18206
Bliss, Zenas R.	MG. USA	DC	02601
Bliven, Charles E.	Capt. Ast QM. BvtMaj	IL	03067
Bliven, Charles H.	Capt. 13th NJ Infy	NY	01773
Blocklinger, Gottfried	RAdm USN	DC	18220
Blodgett, Aziel Z.	Capt. 96th IL Infy	IL	16603
Blodgett, Edward A.	1st. Lt. Adj. 96th IL Infy BvtCapt.	IL	02423
Blodgett, Gardiner S.	Capt. AQM BvtMaj USA	VT	05026
Blodgett, Pearl D.	Capt. 10th VT Infy	VT	05466
Blodgett, Wells H.	Col. 48th MO Infy	MO	04014
Blood, Henry B.	Lt. Col. QM USV	IA	11379
Bloodgood, Delavan	Med. Director USN	NY	06024
Bloodgood, Edward	Col. 22nd WI Infy	WI	04974
Bloomer, Samuel	2nd Lt. 13th VRC	MN	10215
Bloss, William H.	Capt. 27th IN Infy	KS	06485
Blossom, Edmund W.	1st. Lt. 1st NY Cav	IL	12892
Blue, Richard W.	2nd Lt. 6th WV Cav	KS	11004
Blume, Nils A.	Act Master USN	CA	03460
Blundell, William	Asst Surg. 5th NJ Infy	NY	13657
Blunt, Asa P.	Col. 12th VT Infy BvtBG	MA	01565
Blunt, Charles E.	Col. Eng. USA	DC	05456
Blunt, Edmund	Capt. 5th NY Cav	NY	00795
Blunt, William S.	Asst Paymaster USN	NY	04481
Bluthardt, Theodore J.	Surg. 144th IL Infy	IL	11603
Bly, David	Capt. 131st PA Infy	PA	11326
Blye, Harry C.	Passed Asst. Eng. USN	PA	00023
Blythe, William T.	1st Lt. 149th IL Infy	IL	13415
Blyton, William H.	1st Lt. 2nd USV Infy	WI	05221
Boal, Charles T.	1st Lt. 88th IL Infy	IL	02425
Boals, Albert C.	1st Lt. 108th IL Infy	IA	10552
Boalt, John H.	1st Lt. 11th OH Cav	CA	04442
Boardman, Charles H.	Act Asst Paymaster USN	MA	15000
Boardman, George H.	1st Lt. Coast Guard Battn ME Infy	WA	08618
Boardman, Napoleon	Capt. 2nd MO L Arty	WI	06366
Boas, Edward P.	Capt. 20 IL Infy	PA	00617
Boatman, Isaac	1st Lt. 59th USCT	OH	09757
Bobyshell, Oliver C.	Maj 48th PA Infy	PA	02249
Bockee, Jacob S.	Capt. 114th NY Infy BvtLTC	OH	06323
Bockiuis, Charles J.	1st Lt. RQM 22nd MI Infy	IN	10669

Name	Rank	Commandery	Insignia No.
Boden, Frederick E.	2nd Lt. 117th NY Infy	PA	09268
Bodfish, Sumner H.(Samuel)	2nd Lt. 6th Cav USA	DC	04478
Bodman, Henry A.	1st Lt. 73rd IL Infy	MA	09927
Bogardus, William P.	2nd Lt. 24th USCT	OH	13120
Bogert, Edward S.	Med. Director USN	NY	08099
Boggs, Charles S.	RAdm USN	DC	00701
Boggs, Thomas K.	1st Lt. Adj. 23rd PA Infy	NY	02769
Bogue, Roswell G.	Surg. 19th IL Infy	IL	02800
Bohannan, Daniel	1st Lt. 55th PA Infy	PA	11935
Bohannan, Thomas	1st Lt. 48th PA Infy	PA	07631
Bohm, Edward H.	1st Lt. 7th OH Infy	OH	13619
Bohn, Ahiman V.	1st Lt. RQM 15th IL Infy BvtMaj	CO	05066
Bolan, Albion K.	Col. 14th ME Infy	NY	08100
Boland, Frederick	Capt. 73rd PA Infy	PA	02251
Bolard, Jacob	Capt. 197th PA Infy	CA	16702
Boling, John N.	1st Lt. 16th OH Infy	IA	11223
Bolster, Solomon A.	1st Lt. 23rd ME Infy	MA	04381
Bolton, John T.	BvtCapt. USV	DC	15765
Bolton, William H.	LTC 2nd IL L Arty	IL	03865
Bolton, William J.	Col. 51st PA Infy BvtBG	PA	07632
Boltz, Ferdinand F.	Capt. 88th IN Infy	IN	06579
Bombaugh, Charles C.	Surg. 69th PA Infy	MD	02699
Bomford, George N.	LTC 42nd NY Infy	KS	05604
Bond, Frank S.	Maj ADC USV	NY	04641
Bond, John W.	Surg. 30th IA Infy	OH	07423
Bond, Lewis H.	BvtMaj USV	OH	03007
Bond, Nelson F.	Capt. 31st MA Infy BvtMaj	MA	02804
Bond, Samuel M.	2nd Lt. 2nd WI Infy	NE	15496
Bond, William S.	1st Lt. 45th MA Infy	MA	00986
Bonebrake, George H.	Maj 69th IN Infy	CA	04902
Bonesteel, Jacob P.	Capt. 1st CO Cav	WI	04122
Bonnaffon, Sylvester, Jr.	Capt. 99th PA Infy BvtLTC	PA	02069 (Dup)
Bonnell, Daniel V.	1st Lt. 93rd OH Infy	OH	05375
Bonsal, William H.	2nd Lt. 1st OH H Arty	CA	04857
Book, George M.	RAdm USN	NY	16086
Boone, John L.	1st Lt. Adj. 1st OR Infy	CA	02543
Boone, Thomas C.	Col. 115th OH Infy	OH	09645
Booth, Charles A.	Maj QM USA BvtLTC	CA	03376
Booth, George	2nd Lt. 9th Batt MA L Arty	MA	01141
Booth, Henry	Capt. 11th KS Cav	KS	05452
Booth, William E.	1st Lt. 41st OH Infy	MN	11131
Booz, Albert	2nd Lt. 88th PA Infy	PA	05240
Bope, James A.	LTC 50th OH Infy	OH	08601
Borchardt, Newman	1st Lt. 7th US Vet. Infy	DC	17319
Borcherdt, Julius C.	2nd Lt. 49th NY Infy	IL	04834
Borchers, Lyman T.	Capt. 67th PA Infy	PA	10862
Borck, Edward	Asst Surg. 3rd MD Cav	MO	09148
Borden, George P.	Col. 24th Infy USA	IN	03455

Name	Rank	Commandery	Insignia No.
Boreing, Vincent	1st Lt. 24th KY Infy	DC	13872
Boring, Edwin McC.	1st Lt. 79th PA Infy	PA	07328
Borland, Matthew W.	Capt. 147th IL Infy	CA	06068
Bornarth, Charles	1st Lt. 92nd USCT	DC	12177
Borthwick, John L.D.	Chief Eng. USN	PA	01272
Bosley, Daniel W.	Asst Surg. 3rd USC H Arty	IL	11133
Bostwick, Burr H.	Capt. 7th KS Cav	OH	09901
Bostwick, Henry C.	Surg. 9th KS Cav	WA	04983
Boswell, Charles P.	Capt. 92nd NY Infy	NY	11627
Boswell, Daniel P.	Act Ensign USN	OH	08170
Botimer, William	Capt. 13th USC H Arty	OH	17005
Botsford, Reuben S.	Capt. 39th IL Infy	IL	16604
Botticher, Paul G.	1st Lt. 68th NY Infy	NY	06744
Bottsford, James L.	Capt. AAG BvtMaj USV	OH	03378
Boude, John K.	Asst Surg. 118th IL	DC	10039
Boudinot, William B.S.	Capt. 9th NJ Infy	PA	00476
Boudren, Thomas	Maj 25th USCT	NY	06010
Boughton, Horace	Col. 143rd NY Infy BvtBG	DC	05940
Boughton, John W.	1st Lt. RQM 1st WI Cav	PA	08969
Boughton, William DeL.	1st Lt. 49th NY Infy	NY	02215
Bouldin, Richard E.	Capt. 7th MD Infy	MD	15652
Bourne, Charles W.	Asst Surg. 1st VT H Arty	NY	13756
Bourne, William R.	Maj USA	MN	03496
Bousquet, Henri L.	1st Lt. RQM 4th AR Cav	IA	12656
Boutell, Ira	LTC 6th MO Infy	MO	04280
Boutell, Lewis H.	Maj 45th MO Infy	IL	07003
Boutelle, Charles A.	Capt. USN	DC	02385
Boutelle, Frazier A.	Maj USA	WA	02653
Boutelle, George V.	Maj 21st NY Cav	DC	11011
Boutin, Charles W.	Maj 4th VT Infy	IA	04111
Bouton, Edward	Col. 59th USCT BvtBG	CA	04751
Bouton, Nathaniel S.	1st Lt. RQM 88th IL Infy	IL	12445
Boutwell, Nathan B.	1st Lt. Adj. 13th NH Infy	MA	02393
Bouve', Edward T.	Maj 29th NY Cav	MA	00954
Bouvier, John V.	1st Lt. 80th NY Infy BvtCapt.	NY	14168
Bowditch, Charles P.	Capt. 5th MA Cav	MA	03788
Bowditch, Henry I.	3rd Class (Established Ambulance Sys)	MA	07967
Bowdle, Ancil M.	Capt. 12th USCT	OH	10125
Bowen, Adna H.	BvtCol. USV	OR	16775
Bowen, Amos M.	1st Lt. 3rd RI Infy	MA	08053
Bowen, Edgar C.	Capt. USA	WI	16555
Bowen, Edward R.	LTC 114th PA Infy	PA	05979
Bowen, Edwin A.	LTC 52nd IL Infy	IL	09082
Bowen, George A.	Capt. 12th NJ Infy	PA	11016
Bowen, James	BvtMG USV	NY	01336
Bowen, James A.	Capt. 2nd RI Infy	NY	01336-5905
Bowen, John B.	Surg. 34th NJ Infy	MN	05981
Bowen, William R.	BvtCapt. USV	CA	03948

The Roster

Name	Rank	Commandery	Insignia No.
Bowerman, Richard N.	BvtBG USV	PA	01092
Bowers, Charles E.	1st Lt. 26th NY Cav	MA	01419
Bowers, George	LTC 13th NH Infy	MA	02548
Bowers, John E.	1st Lt. 3rd WV Cav	OH	08037
Bowes, Manning F.	Surg. 51st PA Infy	CA	04869
Bowie, George W.	BvtBG USV	CA	01282
Bowker, Hugh D.	Capt. USA	IL	03867
Bowler, James M.	Maj 113th USCT	MN	10667
Bowles, Albert G.	1st Lt. 2nd MA Cav	MA	01271 (Dup)
Bowley, Freeman S.	1st Lt. 30th USCT	CA	03469
Bowman, Albert L.	1st Lt. 42nd OH Infy	OH	08379
Bowman, Alpheus H.	BG USA	DC	03656
Bowman, Charles W.	1st Lt. Adj. 4th MO Cav	CO	11030
Bowman, Henry	Col. 36th MA Infy	CA	05179
Bowman, Henry	Capt. AQM USV	PA	00289
Bowman, James	Capt. 191st PA Infy	PA	14192
Bowman, Martin T.V.	1st Lt. RCS 1st ME Cav	IA	07303
Bowman, Nathan P.	Maj Paymaster USV	VT	09168
Bown, Alfred	Capt. 146th OH Infy	OH	14658
Bowne, George A.	Capt. 1st NJ Cav	NY	12477
Boyce, Henry H.	Capt. 45th IL Infy	NY	10116
Boyd, Augustus	Capt. AQM Bvt LTC USA	PA	00416
Boyd, Carlile	LTC VRC	PA	00929
Boyd, Charles H.	Maj Volunteer ADC	ME	08193
Boyd, Charles W.	Capt. 34th OH Infy	OH	04350
Boyd, Edward D.	Capt. 2nd CO Cav	DC	04354
Boyd, Francis E.	BvtLTC USV	CO	15655
Boyd, John L.	Chap 135th IN Infy	CO	11031
Boyd, Joseph F.	Col. QM BvtBG USV	PA	06459
Boyd, Robert	LTC 2nd DC Infy	DC	06658
Boyd, Robert	Capt. USN	NY	01010-5301
Boyd, William H.	Capt. 21st PA Cav	PA	08742
Boyer, Samuel Patterson	1st Lt. RQM 3rd PA Cav	PA	12871
Boyer, Samuel Pellman	Act Passed Asst Surg. USN	PA	00547
Boyer, Zaccur P.	LTC 173rd PA Infy	PA	07329
Boyle, James	2nd Lt. 37th NY Infy	MA	07398
Boyle, John	LTC 9th KY Cav	MO	05563
Boyle, John R.	Capt. AQM USV	PA	10522
Boyle, William H.	Col. USA	NY	03328
Boynton, Henry V.	LTC 35th OH Infy BvtBG	DC	02603
Boynton, Nathan S.	Maj 8th MI Cav	MI	08527
Brachman, William E.	Capt. 47th OH Infy	OH	05378
Brackett, Gustavus B.	Capt. 1st MO Eng.	DC	13371
Brackett, L. Curtis	Capt. 57th MA Infy BvtMaj	NY	05405
Bradbury, Albert W.	BvtLTC. USV	ME	No Number
Bradbury, George L.	Capt. 5th MA Cav	IL	07155
Braden, James D.	Maj 9th IN Infy	IN	09007
Braden, William D.	Capt. 7th OH Infy	CA	16910

Name	Rank	Commandery	Insignia No.
Braden, William W.	Capt. 6th MN Infy	MN	03693
Bradfield, George M.	Asst Surg. 111th PA Infy	PA	10256
Bradford, Horace S.	Act Asst Paymaster USN	CA	11092
Bradford, James H.	Col. USA	PA	02577
Bradford, James Henry	Chap 12th CT Infy	DC	06659
Bradford, John	1st Lt. 4th NC Infy	DC	07558
Bradford, John C.	Paymaster USN	NY	00298
Bradford, Joseph M.	Commander USN	PA	00613
Bradford, Royal B.	RAdm USN	ME	16187
Bradish, Albert B.	Capt. 21st WI Infy	IL	04032
Bradley, David C.	1st Lt. Adj. 65th IL Infy	IL	02315
Bradley, John G.	BvtCapt. USV	OR	15962
Bradley, Joseph H.	Chap 10th NY Cav	DC	13148
Bradley, Luther P.	BG USA	WA	01755
Bradley, Thomas W.	Capt. 124th NY Infy BvtMaj	NY	10690 (Dup)
Bradley, William	Chap 40th MO Infy	MA	11288
Bradshaw, Albert M.	Capt. AQM USV	NY	14520
Bradshaw, Centenary B.	Capt. 24th IA	IA	14766
Bradshaw, James M.	Capt. AQM USV	IN	07261
Bradshaw, Robert C.	BvtBG USV	KS	17355
Bradshaw, William H.	2nd Lt. 90th NY Infy	NY	10898
Brady, George K.	LTC 17th Infy USA	IL	03443
Brady, George W.	1st Lt. Adj. 18th CT Infy	MA	01764
Brady, James D.	LTC 63rd NY Infy	DC	05307
Brady, William H.	1st Lt. 119th PA Infy	PA	06460
Bragg, Edward S.	BG USV	DC	02488
Bragg, James	Capt. 40th IN Infy	IN	10793
Braine, Daniel L.	RAdm USN	NY	01338
Brainerd, George	1st Lt. 51st OH Infy	OH	09643
Brainerd, Herbert	1st Lt. RQM 1st VT Cav	VT	03877
Brainerd, Wesley	Co. 15th NY Eng.	CO	02022
Bramhall, Walter M.	Capt. 6th Batt NY L Arty	CA	02471
Branagan, John	1st Lt. 2nd PA Cav	CA	04098
Branch, Charles F.	Capt. 9th VT Infy	VT	09662
Brand, Charles R.	1st Lt. 9th MI Infy	MI	07892
Brand, Thomas T.	Maj USA	OH	03372
Brandon, Calvin K.	Capt. 14th IL Infy	MI	04716
Brandt, John B.	Capt. 114th OH Infy	MO	06856
Brandt, Randolph C.	Chap 2nd KS Infy	CA	09926
Branham, George F.	Capt. 10th IN Cav	IN	06580
Brann, Thomas A.	1st Lt. 2nd ME Cav	MN	15513
Brannan, John M.	BG USV BvtMG USA	CA	05852
Brantingham, Charles H.	Act Master USN	NY	10540
Brasher, Lewis B.	1st Lt. RQM 54th KY Mtd. Infy	CO	02995
Braun, John	Act Ensign USN	DC	09849
Brayton, Charles R.	BvtBG USV	MA	16232
Brayton, George M.	Col. 19th Infy USA	DC	04052
Brayton, William T.	1st Lt. 3rd WI Cav	DC	05596

Name	Rank	Commandery	Insignia No.
Bready, John E.	2nd Lt. 14th PA Cav	IA	12504
Breakey, William F.	Asst Surg. 16th MI Infy	MI	06408
Brearley, Samuel L.	Capt. 4th OH Infy	MN	08542
Brecht, T. C.	Act Asst Eng. USN	PA	00517
Breck, George	Capt. 1st NY L Arty BvtMaj	NY	06247
Breck, Samuel	BG Adj. Gen. USA	DC	03689
Breckinridge, Joseph C.	MG USA	DC	02534
Breed, Henry A.	2nd Lt. 155th PA Infy	PA	06760
Breintnall, Reginald H.	LTC 1st NJ Infy	NY	13391
Breiver, James H.C.	1st Lt. 6 MD Infy	KS	04816
Bremfoerder, Henry	Capt. 47th OH Infy	OH	07526
Bremner, David F.	Capt. 19th IL Infy	IL	07387
Brennan, James	1st Lt. 17th Infy USA	CA	03898
Brent, Columbus P.	Surg. 54th OH Infy	OH	07426
Brett, Benjamin C.	Asst Surg. 21st WI Infy	WI	06368
Brevoort, Henry W.	Maj AAG USV	NY	13946
Brewerton, Henry F.	Maj 5th Arty USA	PA	00934
Brewster, Charles	Capt. CS BvtMaj USV	NE	05052
Brewster, George H.	Capt. 13th NY Cav	NY	12722
Brewster, Henry M.	Capt. 10th VRC BvtMaj	MA	01617
Breyfogle, Charles W.	Capt. 9th OH Cav	CA	04905
Brian, William	Capt. 2nd Batt VRC USV	PA	00069
Briant, Cyrus E.	LTC 88th OH Infy BvtCol	IN	06581
Brice, Calvin S.	Capt. 180th OH Infy	OH	07522
Brice, John J.	Commander, USN	CA	02869
Brice, William H.	Lt. USN	PA	00992
Bricker, John R.	Capt. CS BvtMaj USV	PA	08207
Bricker, Peter D.	Capt. 13th PA Cav BvtMaj	PA	10623
Brickett, George E.	Surg. 21st ME Infy	ME	02881
Bridge, Horatio	Pay Director USN	DC	00169
Bridgeman, Frank	LTC USA	IL	05917
Bridges, Lyman	BvtCol. USV	NY	02205
Briggs, Charles E.	Surg. 54th MA Infy	MO	06178
Briggs, George G.	Col. 7th MI	MI	04004
Briggs, Henry S.	BG USV	MA	01433
Briggs, James F.	1st Lt. RQM 11th NH Infy	MA	03880
Briggs, James J.	Capt. 11 PA Infy	OR	04459
Briggs, James W.	2nd Lt. 44th MA Infy	MA	00871
Briggs, Oliver F.	RQM 19th MA Infy	NE	05109
Briggs, Thomas B.	Capt. 3rd RI H Arty	IL	08718
Brigham, Alfred W.	Capt. 3rd MA H Arty	MA	01505
Bright, George A.	Med. Director USN	DC	11827
Brinker, John M.	Capt. 78th PA Infy	NY	09558
Brinkerhoff, Henry R.	Col. USA	IL	12965
Brinkerhoff, Roeliff	Col. QM BvtBG USV	OH	07015 (Dup)
Brinkle, John R.	Maj USA	PA	08876
Brinton, Bernard	Asst Surg. BvtMaj USA	PA	00406
Brinton, Daniel G.	Surg. BvtLTC USV	PA	04651

Name	Rank	Commandery	Insignia No.
Brinton, John H.	Surg. USV	PA	00349
Brinton, Joseph P.	BvtLTC USV	PA	00276 (Dup)
Brinton, Robert M.	Maj 2nd PA Cav BvtLTC	PA	00195
Brisben, James G.	BvtMG USV	PA	00375
Brisben, John P.	Capt. 98th OH Infy	CO	12475
Briscoe, Benjamin F.	Capt. 23rd MI Infy	MI	06922
Bristol, Eugene S.	1st Lt. 29th CT Infy	NY	12627
Bristol, Henry B.	Capt. 5th Infy BvtLTC USA	DC	06538
Bristol, Jacob	1st Lt. 5th MI Cav BvtCapt.	MI	05580
Britt, James W.	LTC 57th NY Infy	NY	04910
Britton, William B.	Col. 8th WI Infy	WI	06493
Broadhead, Edward H.	3rd Class	WI	05574
Broadhead, James O.	LTC 3rd Cav MO State Militia	MO	07000
Broadhead, William	1st Lt. RQM 14th NY Infy	NY	02371
Broatch, William J.	Capt. 40th Infy USA	NY	03663
Brock, Jesse W.	Surg. 66th OH Infy	KS	04792
Brock, Sidney G.	Capt. 67th OH Infy	MO	07600
Brockett, Andrew J.	Asst Surg. 1st OH Infy	OH	14175
Brockway, Harvey N.	Capt. 32nd IA Infy	IA	07301
Brodie, William	Surg. 1st MI Infy	MI	05926
Brokaw, William B.	Capt. 96th NY Infy	NY	15440
Bromley, Isaac H.	Capt. 18th CT Infy	NY	09420
Bronson, Henry M.	2nd Lt. 145th OH Infy	IN	11515
Bronson, Ira T.	1st Lt. 5th NH Infy	MO	08964
Bronson, John O.	Surg. BvtLTC USV	NY	09950
Brooke, Benjamin	LTC 203rd PA Infy	PA	04652
Brooke, Hunter	1st Lt. 192nd PA Infy	PA	07633
Brooke, John	Maj Surg. USA	PA	08930
Brooke, John R.	MG USA	PA	02434
Brooks, Charles A.	Capt. 9th ME Infy	NY	04601
Brooks, Elisha	2nd Lt. 8th CA Infy	CA	17206
Brooks, Everett W.	Act Asst Paymaster USN	IL	05976
Brooks, James C.	Capt. CS BvtMaj USV	PA	08743
Brooks, Martin L., Jr.	Asst Surg. 93rd OH Infy	OH	03481
Brooks, Newton M.	Capt. 12th NJ Infy	DC	08678
Brooks, Philip	3rd Class (Episcopal Bishop of MA)	MA	06341
Brooks, Thomas B.	Maj ADC BvtCol. USV	NY	09951
Brooks, William B.	Chief Eng. USN	PA	02579
Broome, John L.	LTC USMC	NY	01630
Brother, Ferdinand	Surg. 8th Cav MO St. Militia	MO	07119 (Dup)
Brower, Daniel R.	Asst Surg. BvtCapt. USV	IL	03859
Brown Richard H.	LTC 12th MO Cav	MO	11788
Brown, Aaron M.	Surg. USV	OH	03005
Brown, Allan D.	Commander USN	VT	13770
Brown, Allen G. P.	Capt. 24th NY Cav	NY	06738
Brown, Andrew C.	LTC 13th VT Infy	VT	13865
Brown, Andrew M.	Capt. 13th Infy USA	CA	00435 (Dup)
Brown, Ansel D.	1st Lt. 5th KS Cav	KS	06981

Name	Rank	Commandery	Insignia No.
Brown, Augustus C.	Capt. 4th NY H Arty	NY	08345
Brown, Charles E.	LTC 63rd OH Infy BvtBG	OH	09344
Brown, Charles H.C.	1st Lt. Adj. 7th USCT BvtCapt.	MA	02243
Brown, Charles L.	1st Lt. 114th NY Infy	OH	07524
Brown, Charles S.	1st Lt. Adj. 21st MI Infy	MI	06811
Brown, Clinton C.	Capt. 134th NY Infy	NY	11460
Brown, Cyrus W.	1st Lt. Adj. 3rd USCT	IL	13109
Brown, Edwin F.	Col. 28th NY Infy	OH	04571
Brown, Edwin P.	BvtMaj USV	MA	01370
Brown, Fayette	Maj Paymaster USV	OH	03574
Brown, Francis C.	BvtMaj USV	IL	17586
Brown, Francis S.	Lt. Commander USN	NY	02038
Brown, George	RAdm USN	IN	07847
Brown, George E.	Capt. 5th ME Infy	ME	07111
Brown, George H.	1st Lt. 7th Batt DC Militia	DC	13424
Brown, George J.	1st Lt. 31st ME Infy	ME	15904
Brown, George M.	Maj 1st ME Cav	ME	13397
Brown, George R.	Capt. 9th Batt IN L Arty	IN	06582
Brown, George W.	Act Vol. Lt. USN	NY	03774
Brown, Hiram L.	2nd Lt. 12th MI Infy	MI	16630
Brown, Horatio D.	1st Lt. Adj. 11th MN Infy	MN	12854
Brown, Hugh G.	Maj 12th Infy USA BvtLTC	KS	01316
Brown, James C.	1st Lt. 51st MA Infy	MA	16126
Brown, James F.	LTC 21st CT Infy	MA	15286
Brown, John C.	Capt. 5th PA Cav	PA	07330
Brown, John D.	Capt. 3rd IA Cav	IA	13680
Brown, John M.	Col. 45th KY Mtd. Infy	OH	03480
Brown, John Marshall	LTC 32nd ME Infy BvtBG	ME	00261
Brown, Joseph B.	Col. Surg. BvtBG USA	NY	08346
Brown, Joseph M.	Capt. AQM BvtLTC USV	DC	10855
Brown, Joseph W.	2nd Lt. Sig. Corps	MA	15001
Brown, Joshua K.	Maj 172nd OH Infy	OH	13498
Brown, Justice M.	BG USA	NY	02960
Brown, Marcus L.	2nd Lt. 148th IN Infy	IN	07692
Brown, Orlando	Col. 24th USCT BvtBG	NY	14121
Brown, Philip P., Jr.	BvtBG USV	PA	00162
Brown, Richard A.	LTC 61st NY Infy BvtCol	NY	06626
Brown, Richard B.	Asst Surg. BvtCapt. USA	WI	05019
Brown, Robert B.	Capt. 2nd MA Infy	NY	06023
Brown, Robert M.	2nd Lt. 25th CT Infy	CA	09361
Brown, Robert W.	Act Ensign USN	CO	08190
Brown, Rowland B.	Act Master USN	ME	07729
Brown, Samuel M.	1st Lt. 7th NY Cav	CO	08900
Brown, Seba S.	Capt. 25th ME Infy	MN	10995
Brown, Sewell H.	2nd Lt. 6th US Cav	PA	00278
Brown, Stephen F.	Capt. 17th VT Infy	VT	09178
Brown, T. Frederic	Capt. 1st RI L Arty BvtLTC	MA	01143-2119
Brown, Thomas	Capt. 88 IL Infy	MI	15431

Name	Rank	Commandery	Insignia No.
Brown, Walter J.	1st Lt. 28th NY Infy	CA	06065
Brown, William A.	Surg. 176th OH Infy BvtLTC	DC	09212
Brown, William H.	1st Lt. RQM 11th MA Infy	MA	11201
Brown, William H.	Capt. 5th Cav BvtMaj USA	PA	00449
Brown, William Harvey	LTC 1st Infy USA	PA	02576
Brown, William O.	2nd Lt. 21st NY Infy	NY	15212
Brown, William Rawle	Maj USMC	PA	02076
Brown, William Richardson	Capt. 15th Infy USA	PA	00381-383
Browne, A. Parker	Maj 40th MA Infy	MA	01414
Browne, Daniel R.	Act Master USN	CA	13605
Browne, Edward F.	Capt. 1st USC H Arty BvtLTC	CO	09886
Browne, Edwin H.	1st Lt. 47th NY Infy	NY	No Number
Browne, Frederick W.	2nd Lt. 1st USC Cav	OH	03078
Browne, George	1st Lt. 6th Batt NY L Arty	WA	11414
Browne, J. Edwin	2nd Lt. 48th WI Infy	DC	12206
Browne, John M.	Med. Director USN	DC	02422 (Dup)
Browne, Myron G.	1st Lt. RQM 111th OH Infy	OH	03370
Browne, Oliver L.	Capt. 149th NY Infy BvtMaj	IA	13362
Browne, Robert A.	Chap 100th PA Infy	PA	09762
Browne, Symmes E.	Act Ensign USN	OH	16980
Browne, William H.	Col. 36th NY Infy BvtBG	DC	06026
Brownell, Charles A.	1st Lt. 10th USC H Arty	NY	01230
Brownell, Elias L.	Capt. 9th VT Infy	IA	11310
Brownell, Frank H.	1st Lt. 11th Infy USA	DC	04500
Brownell, John R.	2nd Lt. 22nd OH Infy	OH	10022
Brownell, Seymour	Capt. C.S. BvtLTC USV	MI	05274
Browning, John W.	2nd Lt. 1st NY Eng	CO	10033
Brownlee, J. B.	LTC 9th TN Cav	MA	01171
Brownson, Leonard J.	1st Lt. 5th VT Infy	VT	16302
Brownson, Willard H.	RAdm USN	DC	16050
Bruce, George A.	Capt. 13th NH Infy BvtLTC	MA	01369
Bruce, Gouverneur M.	Capt. 8th IL Infy	CA	08568
Bruce, John	LTC 19th IA Infy BvtBG	OH	08028
Bruce, Sanders D.	Col. 20th KY Infy	NY	12130
Bruckner, Charles	2nd Lt. 5th MI Infy	MI	10276
Brumback, Jefferson	LTC 95th OH Infy BvtBG	KS	04872
Brumm, Charles N.	1st Lt. RQM 76th PA Infy	PA	03312
Brundage, Alfred H.	Surg. 32nd OH Infy	OH	04521 (Dup)
Brunson, Benjamin W.	Maj Paymaster USV	MN	09070
Brunton, William B.	Capt. 2nd IA Cav	CO	14809
Brush, Charles H.	LTC 53rd IL Infy BvtCol	MN	06881
Brush, Daniel H.	LTC 17th Infy USA	IL	03857
Brush, George W.	Capt. 34th USCT	NY	03766
Brush, Samuel T.	1st Lt. Adj. 18th IL Infy	IL	08292
Brutton, Charles H.	Capt. 6th OH Infy	MN	09226
Bryan, Edwin H.	1st Lt. RQM 1st DE Infy BvtCapt.	PA	05239
Bryan, Thomas	3rd Class	IL	05138
Bryan, Thomas J.	Col. 74th IL Infy	WA	09626

Name	Rank	Commandery	Insignia No.
Bryan, William E.	Maj 3rd NJ Infy	PA	05716
Bryant, Benjamin F.	1st Lt. 101st OH Infy	WI	07625
Bryant, Edwin E.	LTC 50th WI Infy	WI	04108
Bryant, Franklin B.	1st Lt. RQM 12th WI Infy	NE	07539
Bryant, Thomas	Capt. 32nd WI Infy	NE	12920
Bryson, Andrew	RAdm USN	DC	08410
Bubb, John W.	BG USA	CA	13631
Bubier, Joseph A.	Asst Surg. USN	MA	01507
Buch, Lemon	1st Lt. 213th PA Infy	PA	09763
Buchan, William J.	1st Lt. 53rd USCT	KS	12750
Buchanan, Alexander S.	1st Lt. 10th MO Infy	PA	08205
Buchanan, Charles J.	1st Lt. 1st US Shpshtrs.	NY	10321
Buchanan, Robert	LTC 7th MO Infy	MO	10597
Bucher, William H.	1st Lt. 176th OH Infy	OH	07845
Buchwalter, Edward L.	Capt. 53rd USCT	OH	04739
Buck, Alfred E.	LTC 51st USCT BvtCol	OH	04564
Buck, Daniel W.	Capt. 8th IL Cav	CA	03932
Buck, Harmon A.	Surg. 150th IL Infy	VT	13405
Buck, James J.	1st Lt. 101st USCT	KS	05110
Buck, Leffert L.	Capt. 60th NY Infy	NY	05523
Buck, Norman	Capt. 7th MN Infy	OR	05713
Buck, Robert H.	Capt. 6th MO Infy	CO	07668
Buck, William T.	Lt. USN	PA	00693
Buckbee, Julian E.	Maj 1st MI Shpshtrs. BvtLTC	IL	14163
Buckingham, George W.	Capt. 23rd MI Infy	MI	10236
Buckland, Ralph P.	BG BvtMG USV	OH	02962
Buckles, Abraham J.	2nd Lt. 20th IN Infy	CA	05848
Buckley, Charles W.	Chap 47th USCT	OH	08911
Buckley, Ralph	Capt. 197th PA Infy	PA	07331
Buckley, Thomas	Capt. 6th CA Infy	CA	02860
Buckley, William J.	Capt. 2nd NJ Infy	NY	10751
Bucklin, George	Capt. 11th USC H Arty	CO	10548
Bucklin, James T.P.	Maj 4th RI Infy BvtCol	MA	10446
Bucklyn, John K.	1st Lt. 1st RI L Arty BvtCapt.	PA	04180
Buckman, Aaron, N.	Capt. 6th USCT BvtMaj	IA	14765
Bucknam, Alvan F.	Asst Surg. 2nd MA Cav	IL	16434
Buckner, Lewis	Capt. 52nd KY Mtd. Infy	OH	09022 (Dup)
Budlong, John C.	Surg. 3rd RI Cav	MA	02307
Buehler, Charles H.	Col. 165th PA Infy	PA	08450
Buehler, Henry B.	Asst Surg. 11th PA Infy	PA	08206
Buehler, William G.	RAdm USN	PA	02124
Buel, Clarence	Col. 169th NY Infy	DC	10370
Buel, Frederick	1st Lt. 80th OH Infy	OH	14028
Buell, James W.	Capt. Asst Surg. USA	MO	11556 (Dup)
Buffan, George R.	2nd Lt. 16th VRC	PA	00088
Bugbee, Samuel H.	1st Lt. 18th MA Infy	MA	08436
Bugh, Alfred	1st Lt. 62nd OH Infy	NE	12532
Buhner, Albert	Act Master USN	WA	13518

The Roster

Name	Rank	Commandery	Insignia No.
Bukey, Van Hartness	Col. 11th WI Infy BvtBG	DC	09747
Bull, Frederick	1st Lt. 80th OH Infy	OH	(see Buel)
Bull, Henry L.	1st Lt. 8th WI Infy	WI	17080
Bullard, Albert F.	Capt. 38th MA Infy	IL	06177
Bullard, Gates B.	Surg. 15th VT Infy	VT	09192
Bullis, George W.	Capt. 20th MI Infy	MI	09583 (Dup)
Bump, Orrin	1st Lt. Adj. 8th MI Infy	MI	05924
Bumpus, Everett C.	1st Lt. 3rd MA H Arty	MA	08054
Bumpus, Lorenzo D.	Lt. Col. 37th PA Infy	DC	06574
Bumstead, Horace	Maj 43rd USCT	MA	10746
Bumstead, N. Willis	Capt. 45th MA Infy	MA	10839
Bunce, Francis M.	RAdm USN	NY	08101
Bundick, Charles P.	2nd Lt. 10th NJ Infy	DC	13027
Bundy, John C.	LTC 1st AR Infy	IL	09351
Bundy, Martin L.	Maj Paymaster, BvtLTC USV	IN	06821
Bunker, David T.	Maj 3rd MA Cav	MA	01677
Bunnell, Mark J.	Capt. 13th NY Infy	DC	12411
Bunting, Thomas E.	Capt. 6th Batt NY L Arty	CA	09536
Burbank, Augustus J.	Capt. 1st ME Cav	IL	10154
Burbank, Horace H.	Capt. 31st ME Infy	ME	09705
Burbank, J. Edward	LTC USA	MA	09601
Burbank, James B.	BG USA	DC	04356
Burch, Sylvester R.	1st Lt. Adj. 12th IA Infy BvtCapt.	DC	06161
Burchard, George W.	Maj 54th USCT	WI	07010
Burchard, Jabez	Asst Eng. USN	PA	15931
Burdett, Samuel S.	Capt. 1st IA Cav	DC	03216
Burdick, Daniel W.	1st Lt. 10th NY H Arty BvtCapt.	NY	13450
Burdon, Levi L.	2nd Lt. 5th RI H Arty	MA	10712
Burdsal, Caleb S.	2nd Lt. Ind Batt CO L Arty	IL	02791
Burger, Joseph	1st Lt. 2nd MI Infy	MI	12497
Burget, Lawrence	2nd Lt. 85th IN Infy	IN	12940
Burhans, Henry N.	Maj 149th NY Infy BvtLTC	NY	10160
Burke, Daniel W.	BG USA	OR	00377
Burke, Francis N.	Surg. BvtLTC USV	OH	10363
Burke, John	1st Lt. 73rd OH Infy	IN	07691
Burke, Joseph W.	Col. 10th OH Infy BvtBG	OH	00144
Burkey, John G.	1st Lt. 11th WV Infy	DC	15563
Burleigh, John L.	Capt. 17th NY Infy BvtCol	NY	01224
Burleson, George W.	Capt. 6th VT Infy	VT	10076
Burlingame, Edwin H.	1st Lt. 11th RI Infy	MA	16069
Burlingame, William L.	1st Lt. 2nd MI Infy	MO	07289
Burnap, George J.	Chief Eng. USN	PA	08388
Burnap, Silas A.	Capt. 7th Batt OH L Arty	CA	12586
Burnell, George W.	Capt. 19th USCT	WI	03712
Burnett, Henry A.	1st Lt. 2nd CA Cav	CA	03242
Burnett, Henry L.	Maj Jdge Adv BvtBG USV	NY	03768
Burnett, Levi F.	Maj USA	CA	09231
Burnett, Robert L.	Capt. 12th Infy BvtMaj USA	NY	01490

Name	Rank	Commandery	Insignia No.
Burnett, Robert W.	3rd Class	OH	03213
Burnham, Arthur H.	Capt. Eng. BvtMaj USA	MA	01597
Burnham, David R.	Maj USA	CA	03976
Burnham, Edwin K.	Capt. 111th NY Infy	NY	15679
Burnham, Franklin J.	1st Lt. 9th NH Infy	MN	07701
Burnham, George H.	2nd Lt. 9th RI Infy	MA	11985
Burnham, George S.	Col. 22nd CT Infy	MA	09234
Burnham, Horace B.	LTC Dept. Jdge Adv Gen. USA	DC	04756
Burnham, John H.	LTC 10th CT Infy	MA	01173 (Dup)
Burnham, John W.	1st Lt. 125th USCT	MN	04543
Burnham, Joseph H.	1st Lt. 30th MA Infy	MA	10713
Burnham, Samuel E.	Capt. 5th VT Infy	VT	07451
Burns, Charles G.	Maj 12th US Infy	NY	16688
Burns, Charles M., Jr.	Act Asst Paymaster USN	PA	00037
Burns, George W.	Maj Paymaster USA	CA	03335
Burns, James M.	Maj USA	OH	03267
Burns, Robert	Maj 4th MI Cav BvtLTC	MI	02816
Burns, Thomas E.	LTC 16th KY Infy	KS	05693
Burns, Walter	1st Lt. 5th CT Infy	MA	09804
Burns, William S.	Capt. 4th MO Cav	NY	04595
Burns, William W.	BG USV	DC	01049
Burnside, Ambrose E.	MG USV	MA	00889
Burnside, James O. P.	LTC 71st IL Infy	DC	02847
Burrage, Henry S.	Capt. 36th MA Infy BvtMaj	ME	03001
Burrell, Isaac S.	Col. 24th MA Infy	MA	02199
Burrell, Thomas	1st Lt. 189th NY Infy	NE	04311
Burrell, Thomas J.	2nd Lt. 82nd NY Infy	DC	12844
Burrill, Treeman N.	BvtMaj USV	DC	07100
Burritt, Ira N.	Capt. 56th PA Infy	DC	02282
Burroughs, George T.	Capt. CS BvtMaj USV	IL	01820
Burrows, Edwin B.	Capt. AQM USV	MA	10961
Burrows, Frank J.	1st Lt. Adj. 49th IL Infy	PA	14052
Burrows, Jerome B.	Capt. 14th Batt OH L Arty	OH	05750
Burrows, Julius C.	Capt. 17th MI Infy	MI	08367
Burrows, Samuel W.	2nd Lt. 1st NY Cav	OH	04537
Burrows, William M.	1st Lt. 127th USCT	NY	09556
Burt, Andrew S.	BG USA	DC	03133
Burt, Charles A.	LTC 159th NY Infy	NY	14283
Burt, Mason W.	BvtCol. USV	OH	04211
Burtis, A. Martin	1st Lt. RQM 83rd NY Infy	NY	05413
Burtis, Arthur	Pay Director USN	NY	00469
Burton, Anthony B.	1st Lt. 5th Batt OH L Arty BvtMaj	OH	03482
Burton, Charles N.	BG USA	CA	16378
Burton, Edward F.	3rd Class (Pioneer settler)	CA	03472
Burton, George W.	LTC CS USV	PA	09269
Burton, John E.	Capt. 11th NY Batt L Arty	NY	16950
Burton, William T.	1st Lt. 7th OH Cav	OH	14359
Buschbeck, Adolph	Col. 27th PA Infy	PA	00163
Bush, Asahel K.	BvtLTC USV	OR	06393

Name	Rank	Commandery	Insignia No.
Bush, Cassius M.	2nd Lt. 42nd WI Infy	IL	06674
Bush, Daniel B.	Col. 2nd IL Cav	OR	06317
Bush, Eurotus H.	Chap 49th OH Infy	OH	08910
Bush, Francis	1st Lt. RQM 44th MA Infy	MA	00813
Bush, Henry H.	Capt. 17th IL Infy	IA	08808
Bush, Thomas J.	Capt. 24th KY Infy	OH	04642
Bush, William D.	1st Lt. 49th MO Infy	MO	16290
Bushnell, Allen R.	Capt. 7th WI Infy	Wi	10892
Bushnell, Ara S.	Capt. 152nd OH Infy	OH	13780
Busse, Gustav A.	Capt. 57th IL Infy	IL	12159
Bussey, Cyrus	BG Bvt MG USV	DC	14439
Bussy, Samuel T.	Col. 76th IL Infy BvtBG	IL	13782
Butler, Benjamin C.	LTC 93rd NY Infy	NY	No Number
Butler, Charles W.	BvtMaj USV	DC	15836
Butler, Edmond	LTC 17th Infy USA	PA	00969
Butler, Edward A.	Act Ensign USN	ME	04895
Butler, George	Maj 11th IN Infy BvtLTC	IN	06583
Butler, George B.	1st Lt. USA	NY	06567
Butler, George H.	Act Passed Asst Surg. USN	NY	08641
Butler, James G.	Maj 3rd MI Cav	MO	02908
Butler, James H.	Capt. 32nd NY Infy BvtMaj	NY	02277
Butler, John G.	BG USA	DC	07501
Butler, John M.	1st Lt. 101st OH Infy	PA	05241
Butler, Lysander S.	1st Lt. 65th USCT	CA	04907
Butler, Richard	Capt. 54th USCT	CO	13683
Butler, Thaddeus J.	Chap 23rd IL Infy	IL	10203
Butler, William P.	2nd Lt. Ordnance USA	CA	02797
Butler, Winthrop	Act Asst Surg. USN	MA	06181
Butt, Richard F.	Capt. 1st NY Eng.	NY	14412
Butterfield, Charles H.	LTC 91st IN Infy	IN	11313
Butterfield, Daniel	MG USV	NY	00123-639
Butterfield, Franklin G.	Capt. 6th VT Infy	VT	02982
Butterfield, Frederick D.	Capt. 8th VT Infy	VT	04470
Butterworth, James	Chief Eng. USN	MA	08853
Buttle, Richard W.	Capt. 133rd NY Infy	NY	09123
Buttrick, Edward K.	Capt. AAG BvtMaj USV	WI	04508
Buttrick, Edwin L.	Col. 39th WI Infy	DC	02338
Butts, Frank A.	Maj 47th NY Infy	DC	02491
Butze, Frank C.	Capt. AQM USV	IL	07915
Buzard, Benjamin F.	Capt. 25th MO Infy	MO	06726
Buzzell, Marcus H.	1st Lt. 16th USCT	IL	13339
Byam, Charles L.	1st Lt. Adj. 24th IA Infy	CA	12856
Byerly, Edgar P.	Capt. 10th MI Cav	MI	08594
Byers, Frederick W.	Asst Surg. 96th IL Infy	IL	02122
Byers, Nelson	Capt. 147th PA Infy	PA	11327
Byers, Samuel H.M.	1st Lt. Adj. 5th IA Infy	IA	07827
Byram, John C.	2nd Lt. 36th IN Infy	CA	06675
Byrne, Charles C.	BG USA	DC	02904
Byrne, Edward	LTC 18th NY Cav	DC	09990

Name	Rank	Commandery	Insignia No.
Byrne, John	LTC 155th NY Infy	NY	09952
Byrnes, Timothy A.	Maj 13th PA Cav	PA	11713
Byron, John W.	Maj 88th NY Infy BvtCol	OH	08382
Byxbee, Theodore	Maj 27th CT Infy	NY	08794
Cable, Charles A.	Capt. 18th OH Infy	OH	03077
Cabot, Edward C.	LTC 44th MA Infy	MA	00852
Cabot, Louis	Maj 4th MA Cav	MA	02483
Cabot, Stephen	Maj 1st Battn MA H Arty	MA	00923
Cadle, Cornelius	LTC AAG BvtCol. USV	OH	02878
Cadle, William L.	Capt. 6th USC H Arty	IL	04153
Cadwalader, Charles E.	Capt. 6th PA Cav BvtLTC	PA	01529
Cadwalader, Charles G.	1st Lt. 100th PA Infy	PA	15662
Cadwalader, George	MG USV	PA	00060
Cadwalader, George B.	Capt. AQM BvtCol. USV	PA	12111
Cadwallader, Albert D.	1st Lt. 85th IL Infy	IL	06397
Cadwell, Luman L.	1st Lt. 2nd NY Cav	IA	11931
Caffee, Amos H.	Surg. 13th KS Infy	MO	07293
Cahill, Edward	Capt. 102nd USCT	MI	12576
Cahill, James	1st Lt. 9th CT Infy	CA	13419
Cain, John H.	Col. 155th PA Infy	PA	08208
Cake, Henry L.	Col. 96th PA Infy	PA	00295
Cake, William M.	Maj Surg. 53rd OH Infy	OR	09137
Caldwell, George B.	1st Lt. Adj. 12th WV Infy BvtLTC	DC	14257
Caldwell, Henry C.	Col. 3rd IA Cav	MO	08134
Caldwell, Henry W.	1st Lt. 10th KY Cav	IL	04701
Caldwell, J. C.	BvtMG	PA	00255
Caldwell, John	2nd Lt. 61st PA Infy	PA	03590
Caldwell, Timothy J.	Asst Surg. 23rd IA Infy	IA	06199
Caldwell, Walter L.	Capt. 9th NY Cav	WI	11972
Caldwell, William C.	Asst Surg. 72nd OH Infy	OH	07309
Caldwell, William M.	Maj Paymaster USV	DC	02824
Calef, Benjamin S.	Capt. ADC USV	MA	01217
Calef, John H.	Col. USA	MO	11909
Calhoun, George A.	Lt. USN	CA	10818
Califf, Joseph M.	LTC Arty USA	CA	10674
Caliger, Thomas M.	2nd Lt. 1st WI Infy	IL	11084
Calkins, Elias A.	LTC 3rd WI Cav	IL	09382
Calkins, William H.	Maj 12th IN Cav	WA	02978
Call, Frank J.	1st Lt. 5th USCT	MN	05338
Callahan, Charles M.	Capt. 4th Cav USA	NY	01780
Callender, Byron M.	Capt. 1st MO L Arty	IL	03854
Callender, Eliot	Act Ensign USN	IL	05130
Callinan, Daniel F.	Maj USA	CA	03330
Calvert, Henry M.	1st Lt. 11th NY Cav	NY	14521
Camac, William	2nd Lt. 1st Trp Phil. City Cav PA Mil	PA	05982
Cameron, William A.	Capt. 16th NY Cav	PA	00488
Cameron, Winfield S.	BvtMaj USV	NY	15213
Camp, George A.	Maj 8th MN Infy	MN	04042

The Roster

Name	Rank	Commandery	Insignia No.
Camp, Jacob A.	Maj Paymaster USV	OH	11278
Camp, Norman N.	BvtMaj USV	DC	02486
Campbell, Andrew 2nd	Capt. 46th MA Infy	MA	07567
Campbell, Benjamin H.	1st Lt. USC H Arty	IL	01946
Campbell, Charles A.	2nd Lt. 40th MA Infy	MA	01367
Campbell, Douglas	Capt. 121st NY Infy	NY	01788
Campbell, Edward	LTC 85th PA Infy	PA	09272
Campbell, Erford A.	1st Lt. Adj. 7th WI Infy	MN	08280
Campbell, Gabriel	Capt. 17th MI Infy	ME	02396
Campbell, Henry	1st Lt. 101st USCT	IN	06584
Campbell, Hugh J.	LTC 18th WI Infy	WI	04379
Campbell, Isaac N.	Capt. 115th OH Infy	OH	11357
Campbell, Jacob M.	Col. 54th PA Infy BvtBG	PA	00348
Campbell, James A.	Capt. AQM USV	MN	13479
Campbell, James D.	Capt. 49th PA Infy	NY	04614
Campbell, James H.	LTC 39th PA Militia	PA	00566
Campbell, John	Capt. 70th OH Infy	OH	04217
Campbell, John	Capt. 82nd OH Infy	OH	09155
Campbell, Lafayette E.	Maj AQM USA	CO	04434
Campbell, Lewis	2nd Lt. 11th ME Infy	MN	07190
Campbell, Nicholas L.	Act Passed Asst Surg. USN	NY	00732
Campbell, Peter	2nd Lt. 18th Infy USA	KS	04809
Campbell, Robert	1st Lt. RQM 4th MI Infy	MI	09582
Campbell, Samuel W.	Capt. 109th USCT	WI	16306
Campbell, William M.	Capt. 19th IN Infy	CA	01417
Campbell, William O.	Capt. 134th PA Infy	PA	15594
Canby, James P.	Col. Asst Paymaster Gen. USA	OR	05591
Canby, Samuel	1st Lt. 4th Arty BvtMaj USA	PA	07050
Candee, Frederick P.	1st Lt. Adjt. 11th IA Infy	CO	10278
Candler, William L.	Capt. ADC BvtCol. USV	MA	00984
Candy, Charles	Col. 66th OH Infy BvtBG	DC	04817
Canfield, Henry R.	1st Lt. 17th USCT	IN	17051
Canfield, Thomas N.	Capt. 114th IL Infy	IA	10805
Canfield, William J.	1st Lt. Adj. 1st NY L Arty	CA	13239
Cannon, Arnout	LTC 97th USCT	NY	08347
Cannon, George B.	1st Lt. Adj. 144th NY Infy	NY	14284
Cannon, LeGrand B.	Col. ADC USV	NY	04609
Cannon, Madison M.	LTC 40th NY Infy	NY	07452
Cantine, William W.	Capt. CS BvtMaj USV	OH	11427
Cantwell, Michael J.	1st Lt. 12th WI Infy	WI	05222
Capehart, Henry	Col. 1st WV Cav BvtMG	DC	10774
Cappell, Peter	Capt. 32nd IN Infy	OH	10284
Capron, Adin B.	1st Lt. Sig. Corps BvtMaj USV	MA	06500
Capron, Horace R.	Col. 14th IL Cav BvtBG	DC	02487
Capron, Thaddeus H.	Maj QM USV	IL	06511
Card, Benjamin C.	BvtBG USA	DC	02349
Card, Joseph P.	1st Lt. 103rd OH Infy	IL	08043
Carey, Asa B.	BG Paymaster Gen. USA	DC	02662

Name	Rank	Commandery	Insignia No.
Carey, Milton T.	Surg. 48th OH Infy	OH	09900
Carey, Samuel S.	1st Lt. RQM 137th OH Infy	CA	17788
Carkener, Stuart	Capt. 33rd MO Infy	MO	06371
Carland, John	Maj 23rd MI Infy	CA	03623
Carleton, Charles A.	LTC AAG BvtBG USV	NY	00211
Carleton, Charles M.	Surg. 18th CT Infy	MA	01351
Carleton, James H.	BG USV BvtMG USA	NY	01157
Carlile, William S.	Capt. 31st OH Infy	OH	11785
Carlin, William P.	BG BvtMG USA	DC	04302
Carlson, Edward	1st Lt. 8th CA Infy	CA	01794 (Dup)
Carlton, Caleb H.	BG USA	DC	02401
Carlton, William J.	Capt. 48th NY Infy	NY	01337
Carman, Ezra A.	Col. 13th NJ Infy BvtBG	DC	03167
Carman, James L.	1st Lt. 13th NJ Infy	NY	11628
Carmody, James D.	2nd Lt. 19th WI Infy	IN	10456
Carmody, John R.	Paymaster USN	DC	07183
Carmody, Patrick J.	Capt. 15th USCT	MO	16393
Carnahan, James R.	Capt. 86th IN Infy	IN	03004
Carnahan, Thomas L.	Paymaster USV	MO	10690 (Dup)
Carnahan, William A.	2nd Lt. 38th OH Infy	KS	16004
Carney, George J.	Capt. AQM USV	MA	01512
Carpenter, Charles C.	RAdm USN	MA	10609
Carpenter, Emlen N.	Capt. 6th PA Cav BvtLTC	PA	03398
Carpenter, George N.	Capt. CS USV	MA	02524
Carpenter, Gilbert S.	BG USV	NY	07258
Carpenter, Hiram H.	1st Lt. RCS 20th NY Cav	DC	09458
Carpenter, J. Edward	Capt. 8th PA Cav BvtMaj	PA	00351
Carpenter, James	Capt. 16th VRC	PA	00084
Carpenter, James B.	1st Lt. 1st TN L Arty	MO	13111
Carpenter, John B.	Chief Eng. USN	NY	02056
Carpenter, John C.	Col. 67th PA Infy	KS	04808
Carpenter, John E.	Capt. 17th OH Infy	DC	03323
Carpenter, John H.	Capt. 9th IL Cav	IL	10155
Carpenter, John Q.	Capt. 150th PA Infy	PA	02070
Carpenter, Lewis E.	Maj 75th NY Infy	NY	04612
Carpenter, Louis H.	BG USA	PA	00433
Carpenter, Thomas H.	Capt. 17th Infy BvtMaj USA	DC	13073
Carpenter, Walter W.	1st Lt. 1st IA Cav	CO	15534
Carpenter, William L.	Capt. 9th Infy USA	NY	10159
Carr, Byron O.	Col. QM USV	WA	03237
Carr, Camillo C.C.	BG USA	KS	03103
Carr, Eugene A.	BG BvtMG USA	MO	02852
Carr, Horace M.	Chap USV	KS	16698
Carr, James G.	Asst Surg. 26th OH Infy	OH	09754
Carr, Joseph B.	BG BvtMG USV	NY	02140
Carr, Joseph H.	LTC 169th OH Infy	OH	08041
Carran, Thomas J.	1st Lt. 124th OH Infy	CA	08571
Carrick, Anthony L.	Surg. 2nd East TN Cav	OH	03573

The Roster

Name	Rank	Commandery	Insignia No.
Carrington, Edward T.	1st Lt. Adj. 45th USCT	MI	08934
Carrington, Henry B.	BG USA	MA	14180
Carrington, Julius M.	2nd Lt. 10th MI Infy	OH	07712
Carroll, Henry	BG USA	CA	12612
Carroll, Samuel S.	MG USA	DC	02980
Carroll, Thomas M.	Capt. 1st WV Cav	KS	06798
Carruth, William W.	Capt. AAG USV	MA	01301
Carruthers, Robert	Capt. 24th MA Infy BvtMaj	MA	11259
Carson, John L.	Capt. CS USV	NE	07541
Carson, John M.	Capt. 27th PA Infy	DC	08313
Carson, John P.	Capt. 1st ME Cav	ME	13398
Carstairs, Thomas	Act Asst Paymaster U.S.N.	PA	00527
Carter, George T.	Capt. 2nd NH Infy	DC	15242
Carter, George W.	Capt. 15th VRC BvtMaj	WI	04114
Carter, James O.	Asst Surg. 136th OH Infy	NE	05645
Carter, John J.	Capt. 1st NY Cav	PA	09972
Carter, John L.	1st Lt. Adj. 118th NY Infy BvtMaj	NY	10962
Carter, Mason	Maj USA	CA	04435
Carter, Richard	Capt. AQM USV	WI	14069
Carter, Robert G.	Capt. USA	MA	01865
Carter, Samuel P.	R.Adm. USN BG USV	DC	00458
Carter, Solon A.	Capt. AAG BvtLTC USV	MA	01727
Carver, Henry L.	Capt. AQM BvtLTC USV	MN	04045
Cary, Eugene	Capt. 1st WI Infy	IL	02192
Cary, George	Capt. 1st ME Cav	ME	10471
Cary, Samuel E.	2nd Lt. 13th MA Infy	NY	09124
Cary, William B.	Capt. 5th NY Cav	NY	09953
Casad, John W.	1st Lt. 5th IA Infy	IA	07593
Case, A. Ludlow	RAdm USN	NY	00637
Case, Alanson B.	1st Lt. Adj. 13th MI Infy	WA	04499
Case, Charles W.	Capt. 19th WI Infy	MN	14332
Case, Halbert B.	Capt. 84th OH Infy	OH	11868
Case, Leverett N.	Capt. 1st MI Shpshtrs. BvtMaj	MI	09920
Case, Theodore S.	Col. QM MO State Militia	MO	04991
Case, William W.	2nd Lt. 10th MN Infy	DC	10775
Casement, John S.	Col. 103rd OH Infy BvtBG	OH	03194
Casey, James	1st Lt. 42nd NY Infy	NY	10322
Casey, Silas	RAdm USN	DC	02604
Casey, Silas	MG USV	NY	00370
Casey, Thomas L.	BG Chief of Engineers USA	ME	00454
Cash, Daniel G.	Maj 27th MI Infy	MN	07750
Cash, John C.	Maj Paymaster USMC	PA	00483
Caskey, Alexander C.	1st Lt. 124th OH Infy	OH	10232
Cassels, John	Maj 11th PA Cav BvtLTC	PA	00770
Casserly, Patrick	1st Lt.15th MI Infy	MI	11695
Cassidy, Ambrose S.	Maj 93rd NY Infy BvtBG	NY	03187
Caster, James	2nd Lt. 95th IL Infy	MN	15618
Castle, Frederick A.	Act Asst Surg. USN	NY	02208

The Roster

Name	Rank	Commandery	Insignia No.
Castle, Henry A.	Capt. 137th IL Infy	MN	03691
Castle, William W.	Act Asst Paymaster USN	MA	13693
Caswell, Cassius C.	1st Lt. 16th NY H Arty	NY	09125
Caswell, Thomas T.	Pay Director USN	DC	10475
Cating, James	Capt. 6th NY Cav BvtMaj	NY	08485
Catlin, George L.	1st Lt. 101st NY Infy	NY	11558
Catlin, Isaac S.	BG USA BvtMG	NY	10084
Catlin, Lyman S.	1st Lt. RQM 5th USC Cav	NY	07777
Catlin, Robert	Capt. 43rd Infy USA	DC	03987
Catterson, Robert F.	BG USV	PA	00773
Caufy, Edward	Capt. 29th MA Infy	WI	06452
Caukin, Gavin E.	Capt. 1st MN Infy	OR	02957
Caulfield, John S.	1st Lt. 114th IL Infy	CA	03946
Cavanaugh, Dennis	Capt. 10th MN Infy	MN	05771
Cavanaugh, Harry G.	LTC USA	PA	13550
Cavett, George W.	1st Lt. Adj. 3rd OH Infy	OH	05810
Cavins, Aden G.	Col. 97th IN Infy	IN	12281
Caziarc, Louis V.	Col. Arty USA	DC	01349
Chacon, Rafael	Maj 1st Mexican Cav	CO	15017
Chadbourne, Alex S.	LTC 88th IL Infy	IA	07444
Chadwick, Charles C.	Capt. 27th OH Infy	MI	06988
Chadwick, French E.	RAdm USN	DC	10856
Chaffee, Adna R.	LTG USA	DC	01074-11698
Challenger, Thomas H.	Capt. 4th DE Infy	PA	07051
Chalmers, James C.	1st Lt. 37th MA Infy	MA	03502
Chalmers, Matthew	Asst Surg. USN	NY	10085
Chamberlain, Charles K.	1st Lt. 38th PA Infy BvtCapt.	PA	09273
Chamberlain, Cyrus N.	Surg. BvtLTC USV	MA	02806
Chamberlain, Daniel H.	1st Lt. 5th MA Cav	PA	04941
Chamberlain, David C.	Surg. 94th NY Infy	MI	09923
Chamberlain, Dwight S.	Surg. 9th NY H Arty	NY	08348
Chamberlain, Frank	LTC 177th NY Infy	NY	07453
Chamberlain, Hiram S.	Capt. AQM USV	OH	04563
Chamberlain, James W.	Maj 178th PA Infy	PA	15595
Chamberlain, Joshua L.	BG BvtMG USV	ME	00062
Chamberlain, Nathaniel A.	Maj 13th IN Infy	IN	17777
Chamberlain, Orville T.	Capt. 74th IN Infy	IN	09008
Chamberlain, Robert H.	Capt. 60th MA Infy	MA	12164
Chamberlain, Robert S.	Capt. 64th OH Infy	IN	09009
Chamberlain, Russell T.	1st Lt. 4th VT Infy	OR	16776
Chamberlain, Samuel E.	Col. 5th MA Cav BvtBG	MA	01615
Chamberlain, Simon E.	Capt. 25th NY Cav	DC	03666
Chamberlain, Val B.	Capt. 7th CT Infy	MA	01180
Chamberlain, William P.	1st Lt. 23rd OH Infy	OH	03293
Chamberlain, William S.	1st Lt. RQM 41st OH Infy	OH	12632
Chamberlin, James R.	Capt. 3rd NY Cav	NY	12786
Chamberlin, John W.	Capt. 123rd OH BvtMaj	OH	04738
Chamberlin, Lewis H.	1st Lt. Adj. 24th MI	MI	05348

Name	Rank	Commandery	Insignia No.
Chamberlin, Lowell A.	Capt. 1st Arty USA	CA	06717
Chamberlin, Thomas	LTC 150th PA Infy	PA	04654
Chamberlin, William H.	Maj 81st OH Infy	OH	03479
Chamberlin, William N.	1st Lt. 17th PA Cav BvtMaj	DC	13721
Chambers, Alex	BG USV	PA	00706
Chambers, David W.	Capt. 36th IN Infy	IN	06897
Chambers, Emmett B.	1st Lt. 33rd IL Infy	DC	11620
Chambers, Thomas P.	2nd Lt. 20th PA Cav	PA	11447
Chambre', A. St. John	Chap 8th NJ Infy	MA	06339
Champion, John C.	Act Master USN	NY	12316
Chance, Jesse C.	BG USA	OH	04539
Chance, Josiah	Capt. 127th USCT	OH	03261
Chandler, Daniel J.	2nd Lt. 14th ME Infy	OH	07029
Chandler, George	1st Lt. 88th IL Infy	IL	02178
Chandler, Harrison T.	1st Lt. RQM 114th IL Infy	OH	13304
Chandler, John G.	BG USA	CA	01371 (Dup)
Chandler, Joseph H.	Capt. 115th USCT	IL	04007 (Dup)
Chandler, Nathan W.	1st Lt. 109th NY Infy	NY	14285
Chandler, Robert	BvtMaj USA	PA	00248
Chandler, Samuel E.	1st Lt. Adj. 7th MO Cav	MA	01730
Chandler, William H.	Capt. 96th OH Infy	OH	13845
Chantland, Peter W.	2nd Lt. 15th WI Infy	IA	11684
Chapin, Edward S.	Capt. 15th Infy USA	IL	11085
Chapin, Howard C.	Capt. 4th VT Infy	CO	10919
Chapin, Lebus C.	Asst Surg. USV	MI	04075
Chapin, Philip E.	1st Lt. 2nd CT H Arty	DC	06971
Chapleau, Samuel E. St.O.	Capt. 16th Infy BvtMaj USA	NY	13948
Chapman, C. Henry	Capt. 41st USCT	MA	06041
Chapman, George D.	Col. 5th CT Infy	MA	05234
Chapman, Justin H.	Capt. 5th CT Infy	IN	03387
Chapman, William	LTC 3rd Infy BvtCol. USA	WI	01856
Chappelear, Henry	1st Lt. 17th IL Cav	CA	13423
Chappell, Sanford A.	2nd Lt. 15th IL Infy	CA	18461
Charles, William S.	2nd Lt. 1st MI L Arty	MI	15547
Charlot, Chapman S.	Maj AAG BvtLTC USV	MO	04267
Charlton, Thomas J.	2nd Lt. 22nd IN Infy	IN	07262
Chase, Constantine	LTC Arty USA	DC	02656
Chase, Dudley H.	Capt. 17th Infy USA	IN	03974
Chase, Edward E.	Capt. 1st RI Cav	NY	05294
Chase, Edward R.	Capt. 23rd VRC	IA	04109
Chase, Franklin A.	Capt. 4th RI Infy	MA	03718
Chase, George H.	1st Lt. 1st CO Cav	WI	04128
Chase, Henry M.	Act Asst Surg. USN	MA	13745
Chase, J. B. Thornton	Capt. 104th USCT	CA	08569
Chase, Martin V.B.	1st Lt. 21st ME Infy	ME	07493
Chase, Milton	1st Lt. 1st MI Infy	MI	16853
Chase, Philip S.	2nd Lt. 1st RI L Arty	MA	11029
Chase, Ransom J.	Capt. 42nd WI Infy	WA	08183

Name	Rank	Commandery	Insignia No.
Chase, Salmon P.	3rd Class (Sec. of the Treasury)	PA	00046
Chase, Winfield S.	2nd Lt. VRC	DC	13028
Chasmar, James H.	Chief Eng. USN	NY	12001
Chatfield, Charles J.	1st Lt. 1st US Vet. Vol. Infy	NY	09421
Chatfield, Isaac W.	2nd Lt. 27th IL Infy	CO	15189
Chatfield, William F.	Act Ensign USN	NY	10493
Chauncey, Charles	Capt. 2nd PA Cav	PA	12770
Cheeseman, Roland C.	Capt. 45th PA lnfy BvtMaj	DC	11871
Chenery, Leonard	Lt. Commander USN	NY	01657
Cheney, Albert G.	Capt. 127th USCT	NY	14413
Cheney, Augustus J.	Capt. 49th WI Infy BvtMaj	WI	03889
Cheney, Benjamin H.	Asst Surg. 41st OH Infy	NY	08102
Cheney, Edward M.	1st Lt. 33rd MA Infy	CO	04347
Cheney, Frank W.	LTC 16th CT Infy	MA	01219
Cheney, Person C.	1st Lt. RQM 13th NH Infy	MA	02329
Chenoweth, William H.	1st Lt. 51st IL Infy	IL	02415
Cherrington, Thomas	Capt. 122nd USCT	OH	09025
Cherry, Elias V.D.	1st Lt. 63rd OH Infy	OH	03297
Cherry, William S.	2nd Asst Eng. USN	CO	09637
Chessrown, James Y.	Capt. 22nd PA Cav	PA	15470
Chester, Colby M.	RAdm USN	DC	07799
Chester, Dean R.	Capt. 88th IL Infy	CA	09636
Chester, Frank S.	Capt. 2nd CT Infy	OH	05816
Chester, Henry W.	Capt. 2nd OH Cav	IL	16355
Chester, James	Maj 3rd Arty USA	DC	03315
Chester, Walter T.	BvtLTC USV	NY	06172
Chetlain, Augustus L.	BG BvtMG USV	IL	01849
Chew, Henry F.	LTC 12th NJ Infy	PA	02252
Child, Benjamin H.	2nd Lt. 1st RI L Arty	MA	09667
Child, Thomas	1st Lt. 36th ME Infy	MA	02598
Childe, Charles B.	Capt. 8th VT Infy	OH	07130
Childs, William A.	1st Lt. Adj. 27th MI Infy	MI	11121
Chipman, E.B.	Lt. USA	MA	01027
Chipman, George A.	2nd Lt. 6th MA Infy	CO	07739
Chipman, Henry L.	Col. BvtBG USA	MI	05170
Chipman, Norton P.	Col. ADC BvtBG USV	CA	03333
Chipman, Richard H.	Act Asst Paymaster USN	NY	07454
Chisman, Homer	1st Lt. 7th IN Infy	OH	05752
Chittenden, Albert A.	2nd Lt. 6th MA lnfy	MA	12372
Chittenden, George P.	Surg. 16th IN Infy	IN	12596
Chope, Charles H.	2nd Lt. 24th MI Infy	MI	06034
Christensen, Charles	Capt. AAG Bvt Maj USV	CA	02470
Christensen, Christian T.	LTC AAG BvtBG USV	NY	01087
Christiancy, Henry C.	Capt. ADC USV	MI	06820
Christie, Harlan P.	1st Lt. 58th OH Infy	OH	17847
Christy, George H.	1st Lt. Adjt. 22nd USCT	PA	09765
Christy, William	Capt. 8th IA Cav	NY	06329
Church, George E.	Col. 11th RI Infy	NY	13947

Name	Rank	Commandery	Insignia No.
Church, John L.	2nd Lt. 1st WI Cav	CO	15319
Church, Nathan	LTC 26th MI Infy	MI	04703
Church, Samuel W.	1st Lt. 24th MI Infy	KS	17726
Church, William C.	Capt. CS BvtLTC USV	NY	00130
Churchill, Charles C.	Maj USA	CA	14319
Churchill, Frederick A.	Capt. Volunteer ADC	MO	08192
Churchill, Gardner A.	Act Ensign USN	MA	01290
Churchill, James O.	Capt. AQM BvtLTC USV	MO	04582
Churchill, Mendal	Col. 27th OH Infy BvtBG	OH	03576
Churchill, Thomas L.	Act 1st Asst Eng. USN	MA	01797
Cilley, John K.	Maj QM USV	NY	03357
Cilley, Jonathan P.	LTC 1st MO Cav Brig. BvtBG	ME	00259-14013
Cist, Henry M.	Maj AAG BvtBG USV	OH	02633
Claflin, Jeremiah G.	2nd Lt. 177th OH Infy	OH	12346
Clagett, Dorsey	1st Lt. 1st MD Cav	DC	11012
Clague, John J.	Col. Asst Com. Gen. USA	MN	13799
Clapp, Albert A.	2nd Lt. 2nd OH Cav	CA	15850
Clapp, John M.	Capt. 121st PA Infy	PA	05242
Clapp, Joseph	Capt. 8th IL Cav	IL	03702
Clapp, William H.	Col. USA	DC	02519
Clare, James P.	Capt. 5th MA Infy	MA	13977
Clark, A. Judson	Capt. 2nd Batt. NJ L Arty BvtMaj	NY	04483
Clark, Allan Jay	Act Asst Paymaster USN	NY	09305
Clark, Ambrose J.	Paymaster USN	NY	00633
Clark, Anson L.	Asst Surg. 127th IL Infy	IL	08913
Clark, Arthur E.	2nd Lt. 1st Batt. CT L Arty	MN	04587
Clark, Augustus M.	Surg. BvtLTC USV	NY	01642
Clark, Charles A.	Capt. AAG BvtLTC USV	IA	05056
Clark, Charles B.	1st Lt. 21st WI Infy	WI	04116
Clark, Charles E.	RAdm USN	VT	09210
Clark, Charles J.	LTC 23rd IA Infy	CO	07809 (Dup)
Clark, Charles P.	ActVolunteer Lt. USN	MA	03678
Clark, Charles T.	Capt. 125th OH Infy	OH	13896
Clark, Davis M.	1st Lt. 83rd IL Infy	OH	07019
Clark, Dillard H.	Maj USA	IA	17850
Clark, Edward J.	1st Lt. 3rd US Resv. Corps	MO	15830
Clark, Edward L.	Chap 12th MA Infy	MA	10488
Clark, Edwin C.	1st Lt. RQM 52nd MA Infy	MA	11402
Clark, Edwin L.	1st Lt. 14th ME Infy	ME	16739
Clark, Egbert B.	2nd Lt. 5th MI Cav	CA	17437
Clark, Embury P.	Col. 2nd MA Infy	MA	14293
Clark, Erastus C.	Capt. 107th NY Infy	IA	05446
Clark, Eugene	Capt. 23rd OH Infy	WA	11500
Clark, Ezra W.	Capt. AAG BvtMaj USV	DC	07185
Clark, Frank A.	1st Lt. 1st ME H Arty	DC	13788
Clark, Frank G.	1st Lt. 26th NY Cav	IA	07302
Clark, Frederick A.	1st Lt. 29th IN Infy	NY	16084
Clark, George A.	Capt. 12th Ind.Batt.NY L Arty	DC	15837

Name	Rank	Commandery	Insignia No.
Clark, George H.	1st Lt. 16th NY Infy	MN	14562
Clark, George J.	Capt. US Sig. Corps	NY	01149
Clark, George Shiras	Capt. 15th PA Cav	PA	07332
Clark, George W.	Col. 34th IA lnfy BvtBG	DC	03166
Clark, George W., Jr.	Capt. 2nd MI Infy	MN	04048
Clark, Gideon	BvtBG USV	PA	00318
Clark, Gideon E.	1st Lt. 108th USCT	IL	08399
Clark, Hiram E.W.	Capt. 5th MA Cav	MA	17312
Clark, Horace S.	1st Lt. 73rd OH Infy	IL	09200
Clark, James A.	1st Lt. Adj. 17th PA Cav	DC	13512
Clark, James S.	Capt. 34th IA Infy	IA	10980
Clark, Jeremiah S.	Capt. 2nd USC L Arty	NY	18050
Clark, John	LTC 32nd PA Infy	PA	00026
Clark, John D.	Capt. Batt. I 3rd NY L Arty	MI	04719
Clark, John G.	Col. 26th IN Infy	IN	06822
Clark, John H.	Med. Director USN	MA	11417
Clark, John R.	1st Lt. 15th OH Infy	NE	04020
Clark, John S.	Maj 8th KY Infy	OH	03071
Clark, John W.	Capt. AQM USV	VT	10074
Clark, Jonathan	Surg. 1st Battn. Mount. CA Infy	CA	03109
Clark, Joseph A.	Capt. 15th ME Infy	ME	08586
Clark, Joseph B.	Capt. 11th NH Infy	MA	04628
Clark, Joseph C.	Maj BvtCol USA	PA	10257
Clark, Joseph H.	Capt. 6th PA Cav BvtLTC	PA	05244
Clark, Joseph H.	Capt. 1st MA H Arty	MA	12489
Clark, Joshua M.	1st Lt. 39th Ohio Infy	DC	13029
Clark, Julius S.	Capt. 80th USCT BvtMaj	MA	09677
Clark, Lewis M.	LTC 4th KY Mounted Infy	OH	15498
Clark, Linus E.	Capt. 61st MA Infy	MA	08055
Clark, Nathan B.	Chief Eng. USN	DC	06027
Clark, Newcomb	LTC 102nd USCT BvtCol.	MI	14074
Clark, Newton	1st Lt. 14th WI lnfy	OR	16548
Clark, Orlando J.	2nd Lt. 38th IA Infy	IA	11309
Clark, Orton S.	Capt. 116th NY Infy	MN	13067
Clark, Randolph M.	1st Lt. 1st MA Cav	MA	01318
Clark, Robert F.	Capt. 24th MA Infy	MA	01391
Clark, Robert M.	Act Ensign USN	MI	06819
Clark, Selden N.	1st Lt. 69th USCT BvtMaj	DC	12100
Clark, Stephen R.	LTC 13th OH Cav BvtCol.	OH	08533
Clark, Terrence	LTC 79th NY IL Infy	IL	15104
Clark, Thomas	Capt. 11th ME Infy	ME	12019
Clark, Warren C.	1st Lt. RCS 2nd IL Cav	OH	03048
Clark, William A.	Capt. 35th IA	NY	04156
Clark, William H.	1st Lt. 1st Battn NV Cav	MA	13470
Clark, William L.	Capt. 13th MA Infy	CA	03337
Clark, William T.	LTC AAG BvtMG USV	CO	06312
Clark, Zerah P.	1st Lt. 1st WI Infy	CA	03470
Clarke, Albert	1st Lt. 13th VT Infy	MA	05950

Name	Rank	Commandery	Insignia No.
Clarke, Alexander S.	Capt. 5th Cav USA	NY	10651
Clarke, Almon	Surg. 1st VT Cav	WI	08086
Clarke, Andrew M.	1st Lt. 9th PA Cav	NY	14829
Clarke, Aug. Pomeroy	Maj 97th USCT	NY	10652
Clarke, Augustus Peck	Surg. 6th NY Cav	MA	06683
Clarke, Charles W.	1st Lt. 63rd USCT	MO	05038
Clarke, Ferdinand L.	Capt. 99th NY Infy	CA	05462
Clarke, Francis	Capt. 22nd Infy BvtMaj USA	MI	07622
Clarke, Frank	Paymaster USN	MA	01468
Clarke, G. J.	Bvt Capt. USV	NY	No Number
Clarke, Haswell C.	Capt. ADC BvtLTC USV	IL	01938
Clarke, Henry F.	Col. Asst Comm. Gen.BvtMG USA	NY	00733
Clarke, John B.	1st Lt. 8th USC H Arty	IL	06706
Clarke, Otis P.G.	Capt. 2nd RI Infy BvtMaj	DC	02493
Clarke, Richard W.	Capt. 120th NY Infy	OH	03389
Clarke, Thomas C.	2nd Lt. 30th MA Infy BvtMaj	IL	02007
Clarke, Thomas William	Capt. 29th MA Infy BvtMaj	MA	04426
Clarke, William E.	Surg. 19th MI Infy	IL	09613
Clarke, William E.	1st Lt. 11th RI Infy	MA	02712
Clarke, William T.	Capt. AAG BvtMaj USV	IA	01867
Clarkson, Floyd	Maj 12th NY Cav BvtLTC	NY	01836
Clarkson, Francis	1st Lt. 125th NY Infy	NY	11848
Clarkson, Thaddeus S.	Maj 3rd AK Cav	NE	03928
Clary, Charles S.	1st Lt. 12th KY Cav	WA	11402
Claxton, William C.	2nd Lt. 1st MO Eng.	MI	12923
Clay, Anthony A.	1st Lt. Adj. 58th PA Infy	PA	00150
Clay, Cecil	Col. 58th PA Infy BvtBG	DC	00149
Clay, Henry DeB.	Capt. 14th Infy USA	DC	01446
Clayton, Powell	BG USV	MO	00772
Clayton, William H.H.	2nd Lt. 124th PA Infy	MO	08805
Clayton, William Z.	Capt. 1st Batt. MN L Arty BvtMaj	ME	02504
Cleary, Joseph P.	BvtLTC USV	CA	04901
Cleaver, Israel	Asst Surg. 1st Reg.MO Marine BG	PA	11535
Cleaves, Henry B.	1st Lt. 30th ME Infy	ME	05871
Cleland, Henry A.	Asst Surg. 2nd MI Infy	MI	11694
Cleland, John E.	Capt. 44th USCT	IN	07263
Clem, John L.	Col. Asst QM Gen BvtMG USA	OR	02740
Clement, Henry S.	Maj 79th OH Infy	NY	10752
Clements, Frank M.	1st Lt. 39th WI Infy	NY	02093
Clements, Isaac	Capt. 9th IL Infy	IL	08719
Clements, John T.	Capt. CS BvtMaj USV	DC	08274
Clemons, Frederick W.	Capt. CS Bvt LTC USV	DC	11261
Clendenin, David E.	Col. 2nd Cav USA BvtBG	IL	03439
Clendenin, Frank	Maj 147th IL	WA	07143
Clendenin, William	1st Lt. 108th USCT	IL	13176
Cleveland, Chester D.	Maj 2nd CT H Arty BvtLTC	WI	05223
Cleveland, Edmund F.	1st Lt. 9th VT Infy	IL	15543
Cline, Cullen E.	2nd Lt. 1st MN H Arty	OR	09713

Name	Rank	Commandery	Insignia No.
Cline, E. Clarke	Chap 11th NJ Infy	NY	12131
Clinton, Charles	Capt. 1st Mo Cav	OH	09021
Clinton, Dewitt	BvtLTC USV	NY	No Number
Clinton, George O.	Capt. 1st WI Cav	WI	04007 (Dup)
Clisson, Henry W.	BG USA	DC	12101
Clitz, Henry B.	Col. 10th Infy BvtBG USA	MI	01082
Cloud, J. Albert	Asst Surg. 1st NJ Infy	PA	01576
Clous, John W.	BG Jdge Adv Gen USA	NY	01107
Clover, Richardson	RAdm USN	DC	16106
Clowery, Robert C.	Capt. AQM BvtLTC USV	NY	06313
Cloyes, Lothrop J.	1st Lt. 12th VT Infy	MA	11741
Clum, Jesse S.	1st Lt. 118th OH Infy	OH	14030
Clymer, George E.	Maj 6th PA Cav	PA	09764
Coan, Alonzo	Capt. 15th ME Infy	CO	13839
Coan, Titus Munson	Act Asst Surg. USN	NY	03122
Coane, Thomas M.	1st Lt. 118th PA Infy	PA	15038
Coates, Benjamin F.	Col. 91st OH Infy BvtBG	OH	04202
Coates, Edwin M.	BG USA	PA	08298
Coates, Joseph R. T.	Capt. 30th PA Infy BvtMaj	PA	14371
Cobb, Amasa	Col. 43rd WI Infy BvtBG	NE	03922
Cobb, John C.	Col. 2nd Regt. Eng. USA	ME	14998
Cobb, Thomas A.	Capt. 10th IN Infy	IN	12535
Cobb, William B.	Act Master USN	CA	04761
Cobb, William S.	Capt. 3rd MA Infy	MA	01104 (Dup)
Coburn, Charles H.	1st Lt. RCS 1st US Cav USA	MA	01515
Coburn, John	Col. 33rd IN Infy BvtBG	IN	13992
Coburn, Lewis L.	Capt. 13th VT Infy	IL	13229
Coburn, William	2nd Lt. 3rd US Vol. Infy	CA	03949
Cochnower, James H.	1st Lt. 74th OH Infy	NY	10753
Cochran, George	Pay Director USN	PA	00542
Cochran, John T.	Capt. 80th IN Infy	NE	08524
Cochran, Melville A.	Col. 6th Infy USA	OH	08161
Cochran, Robert H.	1st Lt. 15th OH Infy	OH	04531
Cochrane, Henry Clay	Col. USMC	PA	00455
Cochrane, John	BG USV	NY	01210
Cochrane, Thomas J.	1st Lt. 77th OH Infy	OH	03972
Cochrane, William H.D.	Maj QM BvtLTC USV	MA	03710
Cockrum, William M.	LTC 42nd IN Infy	IN	11321
Codding, M.O.	1st Lt. US Infy	CA	00805
Coddington, Clifford	Capt. 51st NY Infy	NY	07602
Coddington, Thomas V.	2nd Lt. 52nd USCT	KS	06489
Codman, Charles R.	Col. 45th MA Infy	MA	01352
Coe, Albert L.	Capt. 51st IL Infy BvtMaj	IL	01920
Coe, Eben S.	LTC 196th OH Infy	NY	03266
Coe, George D.	1st Lt. 174th OH Infy	CA	14320
Coe, James N.	Capt. 2nd CT H Arty	NY	11040
Coe, John N.	Col. USA	PA	03399
Coey, James	BvtCol. USV	CA	01578

Name	Rank	Commandery	Insignia No.
Cofer, Thomas J.	Capt. 9th IN Cav	IN	13416
Coffin, Edward W.	Capt. CS BvtMaj USV	PA	01795
Coffin, George W.	Capt. USN	CA	12041
Coffin, Veranus L.	1st Lt. 31st ME Infy	ME	11906
Coffinberry, Henry D.	Act Master USN	OH	10056
Coffman, Daniel M.	LTC 3rd TN Infy	OH	13409
Coffman, Victor H.	Surg. 34th IA Infy BvtLTC	NE	06142
Coggin, Frederick G.	1st Asst Eng. USN	MI	12496
Coghlan, Joseph B.	RAdm USN	NY	02647
Cogswell, Joseph H.	LTC 150th NY Infy	PA	13197
Cogswell, Milton	Col. 2nd NY H Arty	DC	02494
Cogswell, Thomas	Capt. 15th NH Infy	MA	07770
Cogswell, William	Col. 2nd MA Infy BvtBG	MA	00681
Cogswell, William S.	Maj 5th CT Infy BvtLTC	NY	03776 (Dup)
Cohen, Andrew J.	Capt. AAG USV	CO	05616
Cohen, Jacob S.	Act Asst Surg. USA	PA	15663
Cohn, Henry S.	2nd Lt. 106th OH Infy	OH	11187
Coit, Charles M.	Capt. 8th CT Infy BvtLTC	MA	01320
Coit, George M.	Capt. 10th CT Infy	NY	03181
Coit, James B.	Maj 14th CT Infy BvtBG	DC	05231
Colburn, Webster J.	Capt. AQM BvtMaj USV	OH	00354
Colburt, Edward	Capt. 7th KS Cav	KS	10217
Colby, Edward P.	Act Asst Surg. USN	MA	06501
Colby, Harrison G.O.	RAdm USN	DC	16107
Colby, Henry G.	Pay Director USN	CA	06716
Colby, Isaac	Capt. 4th MI Infy	MI	11692
Colby, Leonard W.	BG USV	NE	16293
Cole, Charles C.	Capt. 17th ME Infy	DC	02514
Cole, Daniel W.	2nd Lt. 9th MI Infy	MI	13537
Cole, Henry A.	Col. 1st Regt. MD Cav Potomac Home Brig.	DC	12178
Cole, Horace S.	Capt. 1st ME Cav	MN	06356
Cole, Nathan	Capt. 23rd VCR BvtMaj	WI	04119
Cole, Nelson	Col. 2nd MO Arty BG USV	MO	03700
Cole, Ulysses D.	Capt. 147th OH Infy	IN	12096
Colegrove, James	1st Lt. Adj. 44th IN Infy	IL	08044
Coleman, Asa	Asst Surg. 46th IN Infy	IN	07407
Coleman, Charles Caryl	1st Lt. 100th NY Infy	NY	08310
Coleman, David G.	LTC 8th MO Infy	MO	15154
Coleman, Francis M.	2nd Lt. 3rd MA H Arty	NY	07982
Coleman, Frederick W.	Capt. 15th Infy BvtMaj USA	DC	00788
Coleman, Horace	Surg. 147th OH Infy	OH	05380
Coleman, Nathaniel B.	1st Lt. Asst Surg. 17th ME Infy	CA	16123
Coleman, Silas B.	Act Master USN	MI	05904
Coleman, William B.	Act Asst Paymaster USN	PA	09274
Coler, William N.	Col. 25th IL Infy	NY	09874
Coles, Butler	1st Lt. RQM 2nd NY Cav	NY	05524
Colgate, Christian G.	Col. 15th NY Eng.	NY	01156
Colhoun, Edmund R.	RAdm USN	DC	00894

Name	Rank	Commandery	Insignia No.
Colladay, Samuel R.	Capt. 6th PA Infy	PA	00803
Collamore, George A.	Surg. 100th OH Infy	OH	05374
Collard, James	LTC 155th PA Infy	PA	05717
Collier, Frederick H.	Col. 139th PA Infy BvtBG	PA	07052
Collier, John H.	1st Lt. 12th USCT	IL	08420
Collier, Martin C.	1st Lt. 101st IL Infy	OR	17707
Collier, Thomas W.	Capt. 80th OH Infy	CO	13145
Collins, Albert W.	1st. Lt. 152nd IL Infy	CA	02234
Collins, Charles W. P.	2nd Lt. 103rd PA Infy	KS	06420
Collins, Edward C.	1st Lt. 83rd OH Infy	IA	07594
Collins, George J.	1st Lt. 127th NY Infy	NY	08486
Collins, George K.	1st Lt. 149th NY Infy	NY	10424
Collins, James	Surg. BvtLTC USV	PA	00033
Collins, John T.	Capt. 1st USC H Arty BvtLTC	NY	07559
Collins, Loren W.	1st Lt. 7th MN Infy BvtCapt.	MN	05854
Collins, Walter J.	Capt. 8th US Vet Vols BvtMaj	NY	00214
Collins, William A.	Capt. 10th WI Infy	IL	01561
Collins, William H.	Capt. 1st USC Cav	DC	15483
Collins, Williamson B.	Maj 7th MO Infy	IA	11884
Collis, Charles H.T.	Col. 114th PA Infy BvtMG	NY	08636
Collum, Richard S.	Maj QM USMC	PA	00898
Colman, Edmund C.	1st Lt. 6th MA Militia	MA	16960
Colman, Edward	Col. 49th WI Infy	WI	09042
Colton, William F.	Capt. 15th PA Cav	PA	04653
Colver, George B.	Capt. 12th TN Cav	NY	01645
Colville, John E.	BvtMaj USV	NY	01792
Comba, Richard	BG USA	CA	12692
Combs, George W.	BvtMaj USV	KS	15260
Comey, Henry N.	Capt. 2nd MA Infy	MA	10117
Comfort, A. Ivins	Asst Surg. BvtCapt. USV	WI	07235
Comfort, Samuel	Maj 20th PA Cav	NY	10754
Comly, Clifton	Maj Ordnance USA	NY	03126
Comly, James M.S.	Col. 23rd OH Infy BvtBG	OH	03074
Commerford, John A.	Capt. 3rd MA Cav	DC	05351
Compton, Charles E.	BG USA	DC	03533
Compton, James	Capt. 52nd IL Infy	MN	05263
Compton, John W.	1st Lt. 17th KY Infy	IN	11314
Comstock, Cyrus B.	Col. Eng. USA BvtMG	NY	09559
Comstock, Daniel W.	Capt. 9th IN Cav	IN	04201
Comstock, Edward	1st Lt. Adj. 146th NY Infy BvtMaj	NY	11629
Conant, James S.	2nd Lt. 25th MI Infy	MI	04894
Conant, Sherman	Maj 3rd USCT	NY	01540
Condon, George B.	Maj Paymaster USV	WI	04977
Conely, William H.H.	1st Lt. 6th MI Infy	CO	10188
Congdon, Joseph W.	Act Master USN	NY	08795
Conger, Arthur L.	1st Lt. 115th OH Infy	OH	02967
Conger, Edwin H.	Capt. 103rd IL Infy BvtMaj	IA	04477
Conine, John M.	Capt. 93rd NY Infy	CO	17944

Name	Rank	Commandery	Insignia No.
Conklin, Joseph E.	2nd Lt. 135th IL Infy	KS	06159
Conklin, Norman H.	Act Ensign USN	CA	12591
Conline, John	Maj USA	MI	04926
Conn, Charles G.	Capt. 1st MI Shpshtrs.	DC	06898
Conn, Granville P.	Asst Surg. 12th VT Infy	VT	14302
Conner, Freeman	LTC 44th NY Infy	IL	10848
Conner, Patrick E.	BG BvtMG USV	CA	03108
Conner, Phineas S.	Asst Surg. BvtMaj USA	OH	02952
Conner, Selden	BG USV	ME	02390
Connet, Andrew T.	2nd Lt. 31st NJ Infy	PA	06246
Connolly, James A.	Maj 123rd IL Infy BvtCol.	IL	06398 (Dup)
Conover, John	LTC 8th KS Infy BvtCol.	KS	04799
Conover, Stephen D.	Capt. 125th IL Infy	KS	12909
Conover, William W.	Capt. 14th NJ Infy	NY	15795
Conrad, Casper H.	Maj 8th Infy USA	DC	10442
Conrad, Jacob	2nd Lt. 95th PA Infy	PA	10624
Conrad, Joseph	Col. BvtBG USA	DC	02983
Conrady, Howard C.	Capt. 173rd NY Infy BvtLTC	NY	10161
Conroy, Edward	Act Vol. Lt. Commander USN	PA	00907 (Dup)
Consigny, Eugene A.	1st Lt. Adj. 1st VT Cav	IA	05786
Convis, Charles E.	2nd Lt. 2nd CA Infy	DC	15951
Conway, Edwin J.	Maj USA	PA	09491
Conway, John F.	1st Lt. 15th PA Cav	PA	03794
Conway, William	Capt. USA	NY	10653
Conyngham, Charles M.	Maj 143rd PA Infy	PA	01980
Conyngham, John B.	Col. 52nd PA Infy	PA	00932
Cook, Asa M.	Maj 1st Batt. MA L Arty (Militia)	MA	05149
Cook, Augustus P.	Lt. Commander USN	PA	00138
Cook, David A.	2nd Lt. 12th IL Infy	IL	06399
Cook, Edward L.	Capt. 100th NY Infy	NY	08637
Cook, Francis A.	RAdm USN	DC	06665
Cook, George B.	Maj 1st CT H Arty	CA	05844
Cook, George H.	Capt. AQM BvtLTC USA	NY	05400
Cook, George W.	1st Lt. 179th NY Infy	NE	07538
Cook, Henry C.	BG USA	MA	09370
Cook, John	BG BvtMG USV	MI	14725
Cook, John D.S.	Capt. 80th NY Infy	KS	04798
Cook, John H.	1st Lt. 57th MA Infy BvtMaj	MA	07960
Cook, John L.	2nd Lt. 6th IA Infy	MO	14355
Cook, Stephen G.	Asst Surg. 150th NY Infy	NY	06237
Cook, Thomas J.	1st Lt. 147th IN Infy	IN	12941
Cook, Watson H.	1st Lt. 21st WI Infy	DC	06972
Cook, William C.	Asst Paymaster USN	NY	04655
Cook, William W.	1st Lt. Adj. 9th MI Cav	MI	11010
Cooke, Aaron J.	Capt. 148th NY Infy	MI	08936
Cooke, Albert W.	Capt. 57th MA Infy	MA	09805
Cooke, George H.	Med. Director USN	PA	00172
Cooke, Henry P.	Capt. AAG USV	OH	05670

Name	Rank	Commandery	Insignia No.
Cooke, John S.	Capt. 26th MA Infy BvtLTC	MA	11202
Cooke, Lorenzo W.	LTC 26th Infy USA	WI	12315
Cooke, P. St. George	BG BvtMG USA	MI	03739
Cooke, Sidney G.	2nd Lt. 147th NY Infy	KS	10791
Cooke, Walter H.	Maj 11th Infy PA Militia	PA	07635
Cooke, Warren W.	Capt. 182nd OH Infy	OH	04209
Cooley, Alfred	Capt. 156th NY Infy	NY	06165
Cooley, Earl K.	Act Asst Paymaster USN	CA	10243 (Dup)
Cooley, Francis M.	Capt. 11th Infy BvtLTC USA	CA	02333
Cooley, Gilbert	2nd Lt. 21st IA Infy	IA	14710
Cooley, James C.	Capt. 133rd NY Infy	NY	01250
Cooley, N. Saxton	2nd Lt. 46th MA Infy	MA	12373
Cooley, Sherman P.	Capt. 27th MA Infy	NY	03785
Coolidge, Charles A.	BG USA	CA	08415
Coombs, Eugene C.	1st Lt. 56th USCT	CA	17793
Coon, Datus E.	Col. 2nd IA Cav BvtBG	CA	09404
Coon, John	Maj Paymaster USV	OH	04398
Cooney, Michael	BG USA	DC	12697
Coons, John W.	1st Lt. RQM 11th IN Infy	IN	06585
Cooper, Benjamin G.	Capt. 177th PA Infy	PA	10863
Cooper, Charles B.	Maj 5th OH Cav	IN	12107
Cooper, Charles L.	BG USA	CO	00715
Cooper, Charles S.	Capt. 2nd IL L Arty	CO	16098
Cooper, Daniel E.	4th IA Infy	CO	15944
Cooper, Daniel N.	2nd Lt. 96th OH Infy	OH	14866
Cooper, David B.	2nd Lt. 1st NY H Arty Bvt1stLt	NY	08643
Cooper, Elder	Capt. 42nd IN Infy	IN	10574
Cooper, James J.	Capt. 199th PA Infy	PA	05245
Cooper, John S.	LTC 107th OH Infy	IL	02671
Cooper, John W.	Capt. 43rd IN Infy	IN	07926
Cooper, Joseph J.	BvtMaj USV	MA	16032
Cooper, Philip H.	RAdm USN	NY	00662
Cooper, Poinsett	Capt. 42nd NY Infy	NY	01085
Cooper, Theodore	1st Asst Eng. USN	NY	03611
Cope, Alexis	Capt. 15th OH Infy	OH	03571
Cope, Emmon B.	BvtLTC USV	PA	16672
Copeland, Charles F.	1st Lt. RQM 16th MA Infy	MA	12243
Copeland, Frederick A.	Capt. 3rd WI Cav	WI	04511
Copp, Charles D.	Capt. 9th NH Infy	MA	07684
Copp, Elbridge J.	1st Lt. Adj. 3rd NH Infy	MA	06828
Coppinger, John J.	BG USA MG USV	DC	11226
Copps, Egbert M.	Capt. 98th NY Infy	WI	16901
Corbett, Marshall J.	Capt. 137th NY Infy	NY	11630
Corbin, David T.	Capt. 3rd VT Infy BvtMaj	IL	03961
Corbin, Henry C.	MG USA	DC	02716
Corbin, Job	Surg. USN	NY	06958
Corbus, John C.	Asst Surg. 75th IL Infy	IL	08952
Corby, William	Chap 88th NY Infy	IN	11516

Name	Rank	Commandery	Insignia No.
Corliss, Augustus W.	BG USA	CO	00963
Corliss, Stephen P.	Capt. 4th NY H Arty BvtCol.	NY	02039
Cormack, T.H. Stockton	2nd Lt. 2nd WV Infy	CA	17611
Cornell, Norman B.	Surg. 40th IA Infy	IA	12869
Corning, Clarence M.	LTC 14th NY H Arty	NY	01208 (Dup)
Corning, Edward	Capt. AQM USV	MN	03827
Corning, Standish V.	1st Lt. RQM 80th NY Infy	IL	07697
Cornish, Benjamin L.	1st Lt. 31st WI Infy	WI	16973
Cornwall, John J.	Commander USN	NY	No Number
Cornwell, Robert T.	Capt. 67th PA Infy	PA	09971
Corrie, Frederic H.	BvtCapt. USMC	NY	00791
Corsa, William H.	Capt. 131st NY Infy	NY	08642
Corse, John M.	BG BvtMG USV	MA	01776
Corser, Elwood S.	1st Lt. 93rd NY Infy	MN	05860
Corson, Joseph K.	Maj Surg. USA	PA	01252
Corson, Richard R.	Capt. AQM USV	PA	01197
Corthell, Elmer L.	Capt. 1st RI L Arty	NY	03617
Cortright, Moses W.	1st Lt. 1st NY Mounted Rifles	NY	16584
Corwin, B. Ryder	Maj 35th USCT	NY	00734
Corwin, David B.	LTC 2nd Indian Home Guard KS Infy	OH	10018
Cory, William O.	1st Lt. USA	MN	05153
Cosby, Frank C.	Pay Director USN	DC	09338
Cossitt, Davis	Capt. 122nd NY Infy	NY	08487
Cosslett, Charles	Capt. 116th PA Infy BvtMaj	PA	08209
Cossum, Frederick	1st Lt. 75th NY Infy	NY	11748
Coster, John H.	Capt. 8th Cav USA BvtMaj	NY	03183
Cotlin, Francis X.	1st Lt. 58th IL Infy	CA	17805
Cottle, Pliny D.	1st Lt. 146th OH Infy	OH	07325 (Dup)
Cotton, Charles S.	RAdm USN	CA	08873
Couch, Simon A.	1st Lt. 13th WI Infy	KS	04793
Coudrey, John N.	1st Lt. 2nd MO Cav	MO	06549
Coulson, Washington C.	Act Master USN	DC	08140
Coulter, Richard	Col. 11th PA Infy BvtMG	PA	00604
Coulter, Will A.	Capt. AAG BvtMaj USV	CA	05891
Coulter, William J.	1st Lt. 15th MA Infy	MA	12068
Coursen, Henry A.	Capt. 23rd NJ Infy (Col. 13th PA Infy)	PA	13935
Courtney, Michael L.	LTC 16th USCT	IL	03856
Courtright, George S.	Asst Surg. BvtMaj USV	OH	09022 (Dup)
Coverdale, David S.	Capt. 2nd MN Infy	CA	09407
Coverdale, Robert T.	Capt. AQM USV	OH	03391
Coville, Orson	Capt. 149th NY Infy	NY	08488
Cowan, Andrew	Capt. 1st Batt. NY L Arty BvtLTC	OH	05200
Cowan, George W.	1st Lt. 50th NY Eng.	WA	14333
Cowden, Robert	LTC 59th USCT	OH	09648
Cowdrey, Samuel	Capt. 162nd NY Infy	MA	14518
Cowen, Benjamin R.	Maj Paymaster BvtBG USV	OH	04220
Cowgill, Charles	Capt. 20th MA Infy	PA	13819
Cowie, George	Capt. USN	NY	10899

Name	Rank	Commandery	Insignia No.
Cowin, John C.	Capt. 108th USCT	NE	11513
Cowles, Edward	Capt. Asst Surg. USA	MA	02523
Cowles, John G.W.	Chap 55th OH Infy	OH	08845
Cowles, William S.	RAdm USN	DC	16051
Cox, Charles D.	Maj USV	NY	00391
Cox, Jacob D.	MG USV	OH	04221
Cox, James M.	Capt. 2nd PA Cav	PA	12229
Cox, James N.	1st Lt. 58th MA Infy	MI	03750
Cox, Rowland	Capt. AAG BvtMaj USV	NY	06226
Cox, Theodore	LTC AAG BvtCol. USV	OH	02951
Cox, Whittingham	1st Lt. 4th Infy USA	PA	00564
Coxe, Charles H.	Capt. 24th USCT	PA	01868
Coxe, Frank M.	BG USA	CA	00513
Coy, Lucien W.	1st Lt. 1st MO Eng.	MO	14142
Coye, Charles S.	Act Vol. Lt. USN	NY	08796
Coykendall, Horatio G.	Capt. 71st IL Infy	MN	06151
Coyne, John N.	Capt. 70th NY Infy BvtLTC	NY	07455
Cozier, Benjamin F.W.	Chap 3rd OH Cav	IA	11390
Crabtree, John D.	Capt. 3rd MO Cav BvtMaj	IL	05547
Crader, James W.	2nd Lt. 47th PA Infy	PA	15932
Craft, David	Chap 141st PA Infy	NY	14122
Craft, Elijah R.	1st Lt. 5th Arty BvtMaj USA	NY	09560
Craft, Richard P.	1st Lt. 58th IN Infy	IN	08581
Craft, William S.	Capt. 1st PA Cav	PA	14193
Crafts, Francis H.	2nd Lt. 8th PA Cav	NY	14621
Crafts, Francis M.	1st Lt. Adj. 102nd NY Infy	NY	13268
Crafts, Samuel P.	Act Vol. Lt. USN	NY	09954
Cragin, William S.W.	Act Ensign USN	CA	10731
Craig, George E.	1st Lt. RQM 13th MA Infy	MA	01464
Craig, James	BG USV	MO	04578
Craig, James M.	Capt. 23rd PA Infy	PA	07053
Craig, John	LTC 147th PA Infy	PA	04162
Craig, Robert	LTC USA	DC	16913
Craig, Samuel A.	Capt. 17th VRC	PA	07636
Craig, Thomas H.	LTC 84th PA Infy	CA	11778
Craighill, William P.	BG Chief of Eng. USA	DC	11262
Craigie, David J.	BG USA	DC	03553
Craigue, Nelson F.	LTC 4th WI Cav	MI	04262
Cram, DeWitt C.	Maj 6th IA Cav BvtCol.	IA	11441
Cram, George T.	Capt. 1st NH Cav	MO	02793
Cramer, Michael J.	Post Chap USA	NY	06959
Crampton, Adelbert B.	1st Lt. 48th IN Infy	IN	16966
Crampton, Hiram	BvtCapt. USV	KS	15970
Crandall, Frederick M.	BvtBG USV	CA	12198
Crandall, John B.	Asst Surg. 13th VT Infy	IL	12716
Crandall, John R.	Capt. 1st Regt. Miss.Marine Brigade	MO	04286
Crandon, Thomas F.P.	Capt. AQM BvtMaj USV	IL	05918
Crane, Alexander B.	LTC 85th IN Infy	NY	08797

Name	Rank	Commandery	Insignia No.
Crane, Charles H.	BG USA	PA	00242
Crane, John	1st Lt. Adj. 17th WI Infy	NY	12132
Crane, John P.	Capt. 22nd MA Infy	MA	13129
Crane, Simeon H.	Capt. 67th IN Infy	IL	02014
Crane, William E.	Capt. 4th OH Cav	OH	02632
Cranford, Henry L.	Capt. CS BvtMaj USV	DC	00634
Cranston, Earl	Capt. 60th OH Infy	OR	07432
Cranston, James R.	Capt. 119th USCT	KS	06164
Crary, Charles W.	Surg. 185th NY Infy	IL	09825
Crater, Lewis	1st Lt. Adj. 50th PA Infy	PA	05718
Cravens, Junius E.	Capt. 123rd IN Infy	IN	07264
Crawford, Charles	Maj Paymaster BvtLTC USV	IL	09357
Crawford, Emmet	BvtMaj USV	PA	00716
Crawford, Francis C.	Capt. 85th IN Infy BvtMaj	IN	06586
Crawford, George S.	Capt. 49th OH Infy	OH	06438
Crawford, J. Sidney	Capt. 114th PA Infy	PA	00068
Crawford, James	Capt. 91st OH Infy	OH	06429
Crawford, James H.	1st Lt. 7th MO Cav	CO	15996
Crawford, John A.	Hosp. Chap USV	PA	08993
Crawford, Joseph U.	Capt. 6th NJ Infy	PA	03400
Crawford, LeRoy	Capt. AQM USV	NY	09561
Crawford, Medorem	Capt. AQM USV	OR	03110
Crawford, Phineas W.	Capt. 4th US Veteran Vols.	IA	11374
Crawford, Richard B.	1st Lt. 13th OH Infy	OH	12473
Crawford, Robert	Passed Asst. Eng. USN	PA	10395
Crawford, Robert P.	Capt. AAG BvtLTC USV	PA	07333
Crawford, S. Wylie	BG BvtMG USA	PA	00124
Crawford, Samuel J.	Col. 83rd USCT BvtBG	KS	08365
Crawford, William H.	Capt. 61st PA Infy	PA	07637
Crays, James	1st Lt. 105h OH Infy	MN	06682
Creager, Noble H.	Capt. QM USA (LTC QM USV)	DC	06973
Creasey, George W.	Capt. 35th MA Infy	MA	02624
Cree, Joseph C.	Act 1st Asst Eng. USN	PA	05487
Creecy, Edward W.	Lt. US Revenue Cutter "Denise"	DC	18396
Crehore, Charles F.	Surg. 37th MA Infy	MA	02223
Creigh, A.H.W.	BvtMaj USV	CA	02031
Cremer, Harrison W.	Capt. 7th IA Cav BvtLTC	NE	04780
Cressey, Edward P.	Capt. 3rd Cav BvtLTC USA	CA	09405
Cresson, Charles C.	LTC 73rd PA Infy	CA	03899
Crews, Hanson H.	Capt. 4th Cav USA	CO	08416
Cribben, Henry	Capt. 140th NY Infy	IL	08120
Crilly, Francis J.	Capt. AQM BvtCol. USA	PA	03088
Crispin, Silas	BvtCol. USA	PA	00893
Crittenden, Thomas T.	LTC 7th Cav MO State Militia	MO	14190
Crittenden, Thomas T.	BG USV	CA	05323
Crocker, Frederic W.	Commander USN	OH	10230
Crocker, Frederick	Act Vol. Lt. Commander USN	MA	11586
Crocker, Watson D.	Capt. 9th Batt. WI L Arty	WI	07251

Name	Rank	Commandery	Insignia No.
Crofton, Robert E.A.	Col. 15th Infy USA	DC	02631
Crofts, Wm Elliott	1st Lt. 38th NY Infy BvtCapt.	NY	07456
Crombie, William	1st Lt. 14th USC H Arty	MA	15555
Cromelien, Alfred	1st Lt. 5th PA Cav	PA	00477
Cromwell, Bartlett J.	RAdm USN	Dc	13722
Cronkhite, Henry M.	LTC USA	NY	05773
Crook, George	MG USA	OH	06512
Crooke, George	1st Lt. Adj. 21st IA Infy	WI	08085
Crooke, William D.	Maj 21st OH Infy	IL	07916
Crooker, Lucien B.	Capt. 55th IL Infy	IL	03705
Crooks, William	Col. 6th MN Infy	OR	14568
Crosby, Hiram B.	Col. 21st CT Infy	NY	01215
Crosby, John S.	LTC ADC USA	NY	00800
Crosby, John W.	1st Lt. 5th NH Infy	MA	02596
Crosby, Pierce	RAdm USN	DC	00892
Crosby, Stephen M.	Maj Paymaster BvtLTC USV	MA	00953
Crosby, William	Capt. 7th ME Infy	CA	09833
Crosby, William D.	Capt. 26th MA Infy	OR	16189
Crosby, Wilson	2nd Lt. 14th ME Infy	ME	11095
Crosley, George W.	Capt. 5th US Vet.Vol. BvtCol.	IA	05058
Crosman, George H.	BvtMG USA	PA	00189
Crosman, George H., Jr.	Capt. BvtMaj USA	PA	00192
Cross, Albert T.	2nd Lt. 3rd USC H Arty	PA	16575
Cross, Daniel K.	Capt. ADC BvtLTC USV	CO	01686
Cross, Elisha W.	Surg. 4th MN Infy	MN	04465
Cross, Felix G.	1st Lt. 84th IN Infy	OH	04228
Cross, Harrison C.	Capt. 153rd OH Infy	KS	06305
Cross, Henry M.	Capt. 59th MA Infy	MA	02078
Cross, John	Capt. 4th MO Cav	CA	12928
Cross, Judson N.	Capt. 7th OH Infy	MN	04545
Cross, Samuel	1st Lt. 7th Battn. Infy DC Militia	DC	14157
Cross, Samuel K.	1st Lt. 3rd KS Cav BvtCapt.	KS	06492
Cross, William F.	1st Lt. Hutchins Ind. Batt. Arty	MN	06496
Crossman, Alexander F.	Commander USN	PA	00186
Crossman, Robert 2nd	Capt. 58th MA Infy	MA	01458
Croswell, Micah S.	BvtLTC USV	CA	16766
Crotzer, Henry W.	Capt. 150th PA Infy	PA	11936
Crounse, Lorenzo	Capt. 4th NY L Arty	NE	12976
Crouse, George W.	3rd Class	OH	03310
Crow, Dallas	Capt. 97th PA Infy	PA	10625
Crow, Esrom B.	Capt. 45th OH Infy	OH	11810
Crowe, John T.	Capt. 26th MO Infy	MO	05913
Crowell, John	Capt. AAG USV	OH	02808
Crowell, John T.	Capt. AQM BvtMaj USV	CO	07163
Crowell, Joseph W.	Act Ensign USN	MD	15910
Crowell, Miner B.	Act Vol. Lt. USN	NY	08798
Crowell, William H.H.	Maj 6th Infy USA	OH	03544
Crowninshield, Arent S.	RAdm USN	DC	13149

Name	Rank	Commandery	Insignia No.
Crowninshield, Benjamin W.	Capt. 1st MA Cav BvtCol.	MA	09052
Crowninshield, Caspar	Col. 2nd MA Cav BvtBG	MA	00748
Croxton, John G.	1st Lt.Adj. 51st OH Infy	PA	05243
Crozer, James G.	Capt. 26th IA Infy	IA	15405
Cruger, Stephen V.R.	Capt. 150th NY Infy BvtMaj	NY	02211
Cruice, Robert B.	1st Lt. Asst Surg. USA	PA	02283
Crumbliss, Henry	1st Lt. Adj. 1st TN Infy	OH	08169
Crumit, Charles K.	Capt. 53rd OH Infy	OH	03373
Cryer, John H.	Maj 6th OH Cav	PA	05246
Cryer, Matthew H.	Maj 6th OH Cav	PA	09271
Cudner, Albert M.	1st Lt. Adj. 42nd USCT	NY	03082
Cudworth, Darius A.	Capt. 18th MO Infy	MN	13140
Cudworth, John G.	Maj 20th NY Cav	IA	09402
Culbertson, James C.	Asst Surg. 137th OH Infy	OH	11188
Culbertson, Willilam W.	Capt. 27th OH Infy	OH	08167
Cullen, Edgar M.	Col. 96th NY Infy	NY	07457
Cullen, Robert	Capt. 74th OH Infy	OH	03150
Culp, Edward C.	Maj 25th OH Infy BvtCol.	KS	05536
Culver, Charles G.	Capt. 105th IL Infy	IA	08445
Culver, George B.	1st Lt. 43rd NY Infy	NY	10654
Culver, Jacob H.	Capt. 32nd WI Infy USV	NE	13628
Culver, John O.	Maj Paymaster USA	CA	09693
Cumback, Will	Maj Paymaster BvtLTC USV	IN	06075
Cumings, Henry H.	Capt. 105th OH Infy	PA	05486
Cummings, Finlay O.	Asst Adj. Gen. USV	OH	16788
Cummings, Silas S.	Chap 4th RI Infy	MA	09053
Cummings, Thomas A.	Maj Paymaster USV	MN	13529
Cummings, William G.	LTC 1st VT Cav	IA	05907
Cummins, James H.	Capt. 10th MI Cav BvtMaj	MI	03754
Cumston, James S.	2nd Lt. 44th MA Infy	MA	06182
Cundy, Willam H.	Capt. 40th MA Infy	MA	02547
Cunningham, Charles N.W.	Capt. USA	PA	00486
Cunningham, David	Maj 30th OH Infy BvtCol.	OH	12693
Cunningham, Francis C.	2nd Lt. 147th IN Infy	WI	18312
Cunningham, James A.	LTC 32nd MA Infy BvtBG	MA	01057
Cunningham, James F.	2nd Lt. 96th USCT	CA	08303
Cunningham, John S.	Pay Director USN	NY	01013
Cunningham, John S.	1st Lt. Adj. 13th WV Infy	PA	03284
Cunningham, Thomas D.	1st Lt. 56th PA Infy	PA	06761
Cunningham, Thomas S.	1st Asst Eng. USN	IL	02819
Curie, Charles	Capt. 178th NY Infy	NY	04484
Curran, Richard	Surg. 9th NY Cav	NY	09859
Currie, George E.	LTC 1st Regt. Miss. Marine Brigade	OH	05676
Currier, Alonzo E.	Capt. 106th IL Infy	KS	05602
Currier, Charles A.	Capt. 40th MA Infy	MA	01411
Currier, John C.	2nd Lt. 12th Infy BvtCapt. USA	CA	05069
Curry, Lewis V.B.	2nd Lt. 9th MI Infy	MI	12222
Curry, William L.	Capt. 1st OH Cav	OH	09755

Name	Rank	Commandery	Insignia No.
Curtice, Grovenor A.	Capt. 7th NH Infy	MA	11203
Curtin, Andrew G.	3rd Class (Gov. PA)	PA	00049
Curtis, Caleb A.	Act Master USN	MA	01323
Curtis, Charles A.	Capt. USA	VT	12687
Curtis, David C.F.	1st Lt. RQM 173rd NY Infy	NY	04409
Curtis, David W.	Capt. AQM USV	WI	07011
Curtis, Edward	Asst Surg. BvtMaj USA	NY	09562
Curtis, Edward F.	1st Lt. 3rd RI H Arty	PA	10864
Curtis, Edwin S.	Capt. 2nd Arty USA	NY	09036
Curtis, Elliot M.	Maj 4th US Veteran Vols	PA	05485
Curtis, H. Pelham	LTC Dept. Jdge Adv Gen. USA	NY	02407
Curtis, Hall	Surg. 2nd MA H Arty	MA	00823
Curtis, Harry R.	Asst Surg. 5th PA Cav	PA	01103
Curtis, Henry	Capt. AAG BvtLTC USV	IL	13247
Curtis, James	Maj 10th Cav USA	PA	00760
Curtis, James F.	Col. 4th CA Infy BvtBG	MA	06055
Curtis, John C.	1st Lt. 9th CT Infy	NY	10541
Curtis, N. Martin	BG BvtMG USV	NY	01017
Curtis, Oscar H.	Maj 114th IL Infy	DC	12845
Curtis, Samuel S.	LTC 3rd CO Cav	NE	04767
Curtiss, Amasa S.	1st Lt. 1st Batt. IA L Arty	NY	10994
Curtiss, Charles H.	Capt. 7th MI Infy	MI	03890
Curtiss, James E.	Col. 152nd NY Infy BvtBG	NY	01772
Cushing, Edmund H.	Paymaster USN	NY	00443
Cushing, Harry C.	Maj USA	MA	02148
Cushing, Henry G.	1st Lt. 8th NH Infy	MA	02308
Cushing, Henry K.	Surg. 7th OH Infy	OH	03369
Cushing, Lyman F.W.	2nd Lt. 4th MA H Arty	DC	05896
Cushing, Samuel T.	BG Com. Gen. of Subsistence USA	DC	02778 (Dup)
Cushing, Wainwright	2nd Lt. 1st ME Infy	ME	07227
Cushman, Austin S.	Maj 47th MA Infy	MA	13881
Cushman, Henry T.	1st Lt. RQM 4th VT Infy	VT	09186
Cusick, Cornelius C.	Capt. 22nd Infy USA	ME	06561
Custer, Bethel M.	Capt. 24th Infy USA	PA	00509
Custer, George Armstrong	MG USV	NY	01641
Cutcheon, Byron M.	Col. 27th MI Infy BvtBG	DC	03726
Cuthbert, Mayland	2nd Asst Eng. USN	PA	06762
Cutler, Carroll	1st Lt. 85th OH Infy	OH	03383
Cutter, George F.	Paymaster General USN	DC	01400
Cutter, George H.	1st Lt. 3rd WI Infy	MA	16873
Cutting, Walter	Maj ADC BvtLTC USV	MA	04345
Cutts, Richard D.	Col. ADC BvtBG USV	DC	02352
Dabney, Charles W.	Maj 44th MA Infy	MA	00838
Dabney, Lewis S.	Capt. 2nd MA Cav	MA	11742
Dade, Francis C.	Chief Eng. USN	PA	00592 (Dup)
Daggett, Aaron S.	BG USV	ME	16186
Dahlgren, Charles B.	Act Master USN	PA	09492
Daland, Edward F.	Capt. 45th MA Infy	MA	00860

Name	Rank	Commandery	Insignia No.
Daland, John	Capt. 24th MA Infy	MA	00835
Dale, William J.	3rd Class (Surg. Gen. MA)	MA	01498
Dally, George W.	2nd Lt. 5th NJ Infy	PA	04657
Dalrymple, Aaron P.	Surg. 1st NY Eng. BvtLTC	NY	02565
Dalrymple, Henry M.	Capt. 1st NY Eng. BvtMaj	NY	09115
Dalton, Henry R.	Maj AAG USV	MA	12443
Dalton, Samuel	1st Lt. 1st MA H Arty	MA	01429
Dame, Luther	Capt. 11th MA Infy	MA	11819
Dana, Edmund L.	Col. 143rd PA Infy BvtBG	PA	02742
Dana, George H.	BvtLTC USV	MA	16919
Dana, James J.	BvtBG USA	PA	00446
Dana, Napoleon J.T.	MG USV	DC	10336
Dana, William S.	Lt. Commander USN	NY	No Number
Dance, John	Maj 8th IA Cav	IA	07445
Dandy, George B.	Col. BvtBG USA	CA	03926
Dane, Henry C.	1st Lt. 3rd MA Cav BvtMaj	CA	02861
Danforth, Keyes	1st Lt. 15th IL Infy	PA	00780
Danforth, Willis	Surg. 134th IL Infy	WI	04299
Daniels, Henry H.	Capt. 12th MI Infy	CO	15449
Daniels, Jared W.	Surg. 2nd MN Cav	MN	07105
Daniels, Milton J.	Capt. CS BvtMaj USV	CA	04770 (Dup)
Danison, Michael	Capt. 41st IL Infy	CA	06931
Danks, William N.	Capt. 44th NY Infy	IL	12383
Darling, John A.	LTC USA	ME	06059
Darragh, James C.	1st Lt. Adj. 9th MI Cav	MI	04362
Darragh, Louis H.	1st Lt. 140th PA Infy	Co	08188
Darrow, Edwin	1st Lt. 39th MO Infy	MO	05637
Darte, Alfred	Capt. 4th PA Cav	PA	09766
Dashiell, Alfred H.	Chap, 57th MA Infy	NY	10655
Dauchy, George K.	1st Lt. 12th Batt. NY L Arty	IL	02320
Daugherty, James F.	Capt. 10th MO Infy	IA	11549
Daugherty, Will W.	Maj USA	IN	07816
Davenport, Edward A.	1st Lt. 9th IL Cav	IL	16279
Davenport, Francis O.	Lt. Commander USN	MI	04893
David, Elijah B.	Capt. 30th IL Infy	IL	11979
David, James B.	Maj 7th IA Cav BvtCol.	MA	14181
David, James I.	Col. 9th MI Cav	MI	08823
David, Thomas B.A.	Capt. AQM USV	PA	10865
Davids, Henry S.	Chief Eng. USN	CA	02856
Davidson, Alonzo S.	Capt. 36th MA Infy	CA	14973
Davidson, Andrew J.	Capt. 30th USCT	DC	08314
Davidson, James H.	Col. 122nd USCT	MN	06454
Davidson, John	1st Lt. 6th WI Infy	KS	15093
Davidson, John W.	BvtMG USA	PA	00644
Davidson, Robert B.	1st Lt. 35th OH Infy	OH	07321
Davidson, William R.	Asst Surg. 7th KY Infy	IN	14351
Davies, Edward F.	Capt. 16th ME Infy	ME	09100
Davies, Henry E.	MG USV	NY	00127

Name	Rank	Commandery	Insignia No.
Davies, Samuel W.	Capt. 1st OH Infy	OH	02972
Davies, Thomas M.	LTC 14th NY Infy BvtCol.	NY	01546
Davies, William T.	Capt. 141st PA Infy	PA	05983
Davis, Alexander H.	Maj 16th NY H Arty	NY	01650
Davis, Augustus P.	Capt. 11th ME Infy BvtMaj	PA	01981
Davis, Byron C.	Capt. 71st PA Infy	PA	09973
Davis, Charles	2nd Lt. 39th PA Infy BvtCapt.	PA	11937
Davis, Charles G.	Maj 1st MA Cav	MA	06042
Davis, Charles H.	Capt. CS BvtMaj USV	MA	06102
Davis, Charles H.	RAdm USN	NY	01022
Davis, Charles L.	BG USA	PA	01604
Davis, Charles W.	LTC 51st IL Infy	IL	02012
Davis, Cushman K.	1st Lt. 28th WI Infy	MN	03852
Davis, Donnis A.	2nd Lt. 211th PA Infy	WA	18020
Davis, Edward	BG USA	DC	05895
Davis, Edward J.	1st Lt. 146th NY Infy	MN	14486
Davis, Edwin P.	BvtBG USV	PA	00113
Davis, Ferdinand	1st Lt. 7th NH infy	CA	17807
Davis, Francis F.	Asst Surg. 121st PA Infy	PA	10259
Davis, George B.	BG Jdge Adv Gen. USA	DC	09850
Davis, George E.	Capt. 10th VT Infy	VT	09159
Davis, George R.	Maj 3rd RI Cav	IL	02823
Davis, George T.	Commander USN	MA	07399
Davis, George W.	MG USA	DC	09707
Davis, Guyan I.	1st Lt. RQM 11th IL Infy	PA	08210
Davis, Heber J.	1st Lt. 7th NH Infy	MA	15199
Davis, Henry T.	Capt. 10th Cav BvtMaj USA	PA	00801
Davis, Isaac D.	LTC 188th USCT	MD	17078
Davis, Jefferson C.	BG USV BvtMG USA	NY	01372
Davis, Jefferson D.	1st Lt. 64th NY Infy	DC	13211
Davis, Jerome D.	LTC 52nd IL Infy	CA	14234
Davis, John A.	Act Ensign USN	ME	08330
Davis, John B.	Maj 2nd MN Infy	MN	06150
Davis, John E.	1st Lt. Adj. 43rd WI Infy	OR	14100
Davis, John L.	RAdm USN	DC	04729
Davis, John M.K.	Col. Arty USA	CA	02542
Davis, Joseph	1st Lt. Adj. 30th MA Infy	CO	02254
Davis, Joshua B.	Maj 122nd NY Infy	NE	04027
Davis, Nathaniel R.	Act Ensign USN	CO	11764
Davis, Perry J.	Bvt Capt. USV	MI	11495
Davis, Phineas A.	Maj AAG BvtCol. USV	MA	00821
Davis, Robert	Bvt Capt. USA	PA	00346
Davis, Samuel A.	Surg. 30th MA Infy	MA	12829
Davis, Samuel L.	1st Lt. 7th MN Infy	MN	05688
Davis, Samuel T.	Capt. 77th PA Infy	PA	05744
Davis, Theodore R.	Capt. 15th CT Infy	NY	02266
Davis, Thomas E.	1st Lt. 17th WV Infy	DC	12209
Davis, Walter S.	Capt. 22nd MA Infy BvtCol.	CA	00726

Name	Rank	Commandery	Insignia No.
Davis, William H.	Surg. 195th PA Infy	NY	14123
Davis, William L.	2nd Lt. 59th USCT	IA	09733
Davis, William P.	LTC 23rd IN Infy	DC	04353
Davis, William W.H.	Col. 104th PA Infy BvtBG	PA	00102
Davis, Wilson E.	2nd Lt. 5th PA Cav	CA	15032
Davis, Wirt	BG USA	MD	03447
Davison, James	1st Lt. BvtCapt. USA	OH	12377
Davison, Joseph K.	LTC 29th NJ Infy	PA	02930
Davy, John M.	1st Lt. 108th NY Infy	NY	14334
Dawes, Ephriam C.	Maj 53rd OH Infy BvtLTC	OH	02071
Dawes, Rufus R.	LTC 6th WI Infy BvtBG	OH	06327
Dawes, William J.	Capt. BvtMaj USA	WI	02389
Dawson, Andrew R.Z.	Col. 187th OH Infy BvtBG	OH	08837
Dawson, Byron	Maj USA	IN	06587
Dawson, Lucien L.	Maj USMC	PA	00768
Day, Albion W.	2nd Lt. 20th PA Cav	NY	15380
Day, Augustus P.	1st Lt. 15th CT Infy	NY	06955
Day, Charles M.	1st Lt. 1st US Vet.Vol.Eng.	NY	07458
Day, Hannibal	Col. 6th Infy BvtBG USA	NY	06423
Day, James B.	Maj 6th USC Cav	OH	05376
Day, James G.	Capt. 15th IA Infy	IA	06444
Day, Nicholas W.	Col. 131st NY Infy BvtBG	NY	05291
Day, Samuel H.	2nd Lt. 1st OH L Arty	CA	07410
Day, Selden A.	Col. USA	CA	08566
Day, Warren E.	Asst Surg. 117th NY Infy	CA	13920
Day, William H.	Capt. 10th OH Cav BvtMaj	IA	11308
Dayton, Frederick L.	1st Lt. Adj. 35th IA Infy	IL	13700
Dayton, James H.	RAdm USN	IN	16239
Dayton, Lewis M.	Col. ADC USA	OH	01233
Dayton, Oscar V.	Col. 63rd NY Infy BvtBG	NY	00366
Deacon, Andrew G.	2nd Lt. 5th WI Infy	MO	11913
Deacon, Edward P.	Bvt Maj	MA	01062
Deacon, Howard R.	2nd Lt. 197th PA Infy	PA	04408
Deam, Harrison L.	Capt. 34th IN Infy	DC	13372
Deamude, Daniel C.	1st Lt. 150th IL Infy	OH	13851
Dean, Albert F.	2nd Lt. 1st IA Cav	IL	04296
Dean, Bradley	Capt. 3rd MA Cav	IL	12156
Dean, George W.	Act 2nd Asst Eng. USN	PA	05490
Dean, Henry S.	LTC 22nd MI Infy	MI	04498
Dean, Richard C.	Med. Director USN	DC	03184
Dean, Thomas	Capt. 3rd MI Cav	IL	07756
Dean, William	Capt. 5th IA Infy	IA	05483
Dean, William B.	1st Lt. 127th NY Infy	MO	05636
Deane, Charles T.	Asst Surg. 12th NY H Arty	CA	11781
Deane, Charles W.	Maj 6th MI Cav	WI	12125
Deane, Gardiner A.A.	LTC 60th USCT	MA	11128
Deane, James R.	Act Asst Surg. USN	MA	03145
Deane, John M.	Maj 29th MA Infy	MA	09235

Name	Rank	Commandery	Insignia No.
Dearborn, John G.	Act Asst Surg. USN	MA	10447
Dearborn, Sam G.	Surg. 8th NH Infy	MA	09054
Dearborne, Fred M.	Surg. USN	MA	01430
Deardoff, David P.	1st Lt. 74th IN Infy	IL	11886
DeArmond, James A.	Capt. 15th USCT	OH	12420
Debevoise, George W.	Capt. 17th VRC BvtMaj	NY	12245
DeBus, Henry	Capt. 1st US Cav	OH	02614 (Dup)
Dechert Robert P.	Maj 29th PA Infy BvtLTC	PA	00075
Decker, Westbrook S.	1st Lt. 19th USCT	CO	05617
DeCourcy, Ferdinand E.	Maj USA	CA	08565
Deems, James M.	LTC 1st MD Cav BvtBG	DC	06656
Deering, George A.	Paymaster USN	DC	07725
DeFigh, James J.	Capt. 12th Ohio Cav	OH	08534
DeForest, Cyrus H.	Capt. 2nd CO Cav	OH	11969
DeForest, Newton	Maj 2nd WI Cav	DC	13373
DeGress, Jacob C.	Capt. 9th Cav BvtLTC USA	OH	03069
DeGress, William J.	Capt. 10th MO Cav	CA	04519
DeGroat, Charles H.	Col. 32nd WI Infy BvtBG	WI	09041
DeHart, Richard P.	Col. 128th IN Infy BvtBG	IN	13307
DeHaven, Joseph E.	Lt. Commander USN	IL	01927
Deimling, Francis C.	Col. 10th MO Infy	PA	01239
Deitz, Lewis	Capt. 5th NY H Arty	NY	04600
Deitzler, George W.	BG USV	CA	02901
DeKay, Sidney B.	Capt. 8th CT Infy BvtMaj	NY	01541
DeKrafft, John C.P.	RAdmUSN	DC	03086
DeLaMatyr, Gilbert	Chap, 8th NY H Arty	OH	05624
Delano, Francis H.	RAdm USN	DC	17527
DeLaVergne, George	LTC 8th TN Infy	CA	06944
Delaware, Ambrose S.	2nd Lt. 21st WI Infy	IL	07552
Delevan, J. Savage	Asst Surg. 1st CT H Arty	NY	01778
DeLong, Sidney R.	1st Lt. 1st CA Cav	CA	06139
DeMar, James L.	1st Lt. 83rd OH Infy	OH	07934
Demarest, Abraham G.	Col. 22nd NJ Infy	NY	08644
DeMeritt, John H.	Act Asst Paymaster USN	DC	10810
Demming, Henry C.	1st Lt. 77th PA Infy	PA	04942
Demuth, Albert	Capt. 8th MO Cav	MO	08014
Denby, Charles	Col. 80th IN Infy	IN	10670
Denicke, Earnest A.	Capt. 68th NY Infy BvtMaj	CA	02912
Denig, Edwin C.	Capt. AAG USV	OH	09753
Denison, Andrew W.	Col. 8th MD Infy BvtMG	PA	01193
Denison, D. Stewart	1st Lt. 5th Arty USA	NY	01699
Dennett, John	Act Ensign USN	ME	10470
Dennett, Joseph G.	Act 2nd Asst Eng. USN	MA	06684
Dennis, Charles P.	1st Lt. 47th OH Infy	OH	05472
Dennis, John B.	Maj Paymaster BvtBG USV	NE	03791
Dennis, Roland R.	1st Lt. 111th NY Infy	NY	07603
Dennison, William E.	Act Vol. Lt. USN	ME	07112
Dennison, William Neil	Capt. 2nd Arty BvtLTC USA	CO	13233

The Roster

Name	Rank	Commandery	Insignia No.
Denniston, George C.	2nd Lt. 14th WI Infy	WI	12967
Denniston, Henry M.	Pay Director USN	NY	03401
Denniston, John T.	1st Lt. 155th PA Infy	PA	00618
Denniston, Joseph F.	Capt. CS BvtMaj USV	PA	01718
Denny, Edward W.	1st Lt. 2nd MA H Arty BvtCapt.	NY	04604
Denny, George P.	Capt. 45th MA Infy	MA	01005
Denny, J. Waldo	Capt. 25th MA Infy	MA	00686
Denny, James H.	Asst Surg. 2nd MA H Arty	MA	01769
Dent, Frederick T.	BG USV	CO	08956
Denton, Ansel B.	Capt. 18th Infy USA	MO	10929
DePeyster, Frederic, Jr.	2nd Lt. 8th NY State Militia BvtMaj	NY	01016
DePeyster, John Watts	3rd Class(MG NY Nat. Guard)	NY	00394
DePeyster, Johnston L.	2nd Lt. 13th NY H Arty BvtLTC	NY	00232
DeQueralla, Fernando L.	1st Lt. 82nd PA Infy	NY	01544 (Dup)
Derby, Buel J.	1st Lt. RQM 17th VT Infy	VT	13769
Derby, Isaac W.	2nd Lt. 1st VRC	MA	01732
DeReamer, George C.	Act 2nd Asst Eng. USN	CA	11505
Derickson, Richard	1st Lt. 15th Infy USA	WA	08619
Dering, Charles L.	1st Lt. 3rd WI Infy	WI	17655
Derrom, Andrew	Col. 25th NJ Infy	NY	01447
DeRudio, Charles C.	Maj USA	CA	08150
DeRussy, Isaac D.	BG USA	DC	11381
DesAnges, Robert	Col. 6th Infy USA	NY	01361
Detre, Cyrus S.	1st Lt. Adj. 88th PA Infy	PA	04656
DeTrobriand, Philip R.D.	BG BvtMG USV	IL	11194
DeTurk, Joshua G.	2nd Lt. 82nd IN Infy	CA	05464
Deuel, William A.	Capt. 12th MI Infy	CO	05571
DeValin, Charles E.	Chief Eng. USN	DC	01704
Devendorf, Charles A.	Surg. 48th NY Infy	MI	03760
Devendorf, LaMotte K.	Capt. 1st NC Infy	DC	02285
Devens, Charles	BG BvtMG USV	MA	00863
Devens, Edward F.	Act Vol. Lt. Commander USN	MA	00755
Devereaux, Alfred	2nd Lt. USMC	PA	05489
Devereaux, John	LTC 69th PA Infy	PA	02253
Devereaux, John H.	Col. Vol ADC Supt. Military RR	OH	03580
Devin, Thomas C.	BG BvtMG USC	NY	00846
Devol, Hiram F.	Col. 36th OH Infy BvtBG	MO	04576
Dewees, Jacob H.	LTC 13th PA Cav	PA	00385
Dewees, Thomas B.	Maj 9th Cav USA	NE	04318
Dewey, Dennis A.	Capt. 108th USCT	NY	14451
Dewey, Edward	Capt. AQM USV	VT	06502
Dewey, George	Adm. USN	VT	02397
Dewey, George M.	Capt. 10th NY Infy	NY	11335
Dewey, Israel O.	Maj Paymaster USA	DC	03747
Dewing, Paul F.	Act Asst Paymaster USN	MA	09055
DeWitt, Calvin	BG USA	DC	02668
Dewitt, J. Wilson	Asst Surg. 17th PA Cav	PA	00563
DeWolf, Daniel F.	Maj 55th OH Infy	OH	09153

Name	Rank	Commandery	Insignia No.
DeWolfe, James	2nd Lt. 96th OH Infy	OH	07021
DeWolfe, Thomas S.	Capt. 88th USCT	NY	09563
Dews, Edwin	Capt. 3rd MA H Arty BvtMaj	MA	01317
Dewson, Francis A.	1st Lt. RQM 45th MA Infy	MA	01678
Dexter, Benjamin F.	Capt. 50th NY Eng.	NY	10323
Dexter, James E.	Surg. 40th NY Infy	DC	09526
Dibble, Theodore H.	Capt. 5th CT Infy	PA	11154
DiCesnola, Louis P.	Capt. 4th NY Cav	NY	02141
Dick, George F.	Col. 86th IN Infy BvtBG	IL	13650
Dick, Samuel B.	Col. 56th Infy PA Militia	PA	05984
Dickens, Francis W.	RAdm USN	DC	12028
Dickenson, Charles E.	1st Lt. 134th IL Infy	CO	07162
Dickenson, Chase H.	Capt. AQM USV	MI	06035
Dickenson, Daniel A.	Act Asst Paymaster USN	MN	05769
Dickenson, Joseph	LTC AAG BvtBG USV	DC	04257
Dickenson, Julian G.	1st Lt. Adj. 4th MI Cav BvtCapt.	MI	03751
Dickenson, Leonard A.	Capt. 12th CT Infy	NY	01251
Dickenson, M. Nelson	1st Lt. 118th NY Infy	NY	10324
Dickenson, Martin H.	1st Lt. RQM 1st KS Infy	MO	05886
Dickenson, Samuel M.	Act Paymaster USN	PA	04943
Dickerson, D'Estaing	Surg. 1st NY Cav	MO	04366 (Dup)
Dickerson, Joseph	Capt. 30th OH Infy	WA	14515
Dickey, Charles H.	2nd Lt. 4th IL Cav	CA	14323
Dickey, Joseph M.	2nd Lt. 15th NY H Arty	NY	11631
Dickey, T. Lyle	Col. 4th IL Cav	IL	02004
Dickey, William B.	Capt. AQM USV	DC	12022
Dickman, Theodore	1st Lt. 58th OH Infy	OH	10019
Dickson, Campbell	Capt. 9th NY Cav	MO	10439
Dickson, James N.	Capt. 6th PA Cav	PA	00622
Dickson, John M.	Asst Surg. USA	CA	03452
Dickson, Thomas H.	Act Asst Paymaster USN	MN	12651
Dicus, James A.	1st Lt. 11th MD Infy	OH	17320
Diehl, Edward P.	Capt. 50th MO Infy	KS	04887
Diehl, James B.	1st Lt. 91st PA Infy	PA	00148
Diggs, Dabney W.	Maj 33rd NY Infy	NY	18391
Dill, Albert F.	Act Ensign USN	CA	10200
Dill, Robert G.	Capt. 43rd USCT	CO	10099
Dillenback, John W.	Maj 2nd Arty BvtLTC USA	NY	02854
Diller, William S.	Maj 76th PA Infy	NY	03619
Dillingham, Charles	LTC 8th VT Infy	DC	07715
Dillingham, James S., Jr.	Act Master USN	MA	01415
Dillon, Daniel	Capt. 6th USC H Arty	MO	07379
Dilworth, Caleb J.	Col. 85th IL Infy BvtBG	NE	08523
Dimick, Orlando W.	Capt. 11th NH Infy	MA	04467
Dimmick, Eugene D.	BG USA	DC	13488
Dimon, Charles A.B.	Col. 1st USV BvtBG	MA	01583
Dimon, Theodore	Surg. 3rd NY L Arty	NY	04698
Dimond, William H.	Capt. AAG USV	CA	01768

Name	Rank	Commandery	Insignia No.
Dimpfel, George H.A.	Capt. Mil. Storekeeper USA	CA	06670
Dingwall, George	2nd Lt. 24th MI Infy	MI	04721
Dinsmore, Albert G.	Capt. 49th WI Infy	WI	16663
Dinsmore, John B.	2nd Lt. 9th NY Cav	NE	07170
Dinwiddie, William A.	1st Lt. 2nd Cav USA	IA	06543
DiRozzoli, Octave F.	LTC 96th USCT	MD	16374
DiSay, Isaac	Capt. 27th Infy USA	MO	14023
Diven, Eugene	Capt. AAG USV	PA	00667
Diver, William	Capt. 11th MD Infy	MD	17300
Dix, Henry F.	Capt. 16th VT Infy	PA	00495
Dix, John A.	MG USV	NY	No Number
Dixon, George M.	Capt. 131st OH Infy	CO	12274
Dixon, James W.	1st Lt. 4th Arty BvtCapt. USA	NY	00796
Dixon, William D.	LTC 35th PA Infy BvtBG	PA	10626
Dixon, William H.	1st Lt. 2nd USC L Arty	MN	03831
Doan, Azariah W.	BvtBG USV	OH	09639
Doan, Thomas C.	Act Asst Paymaster USN	MO	05207
Doane, George S.	Capt. 11th IL Infy	OR	08130
Doane, Gustavus C.	Capt. 2nd Cav USA	CA	05325
Dobbins, John R.	1st Lt. 116th NY Infy	NY	11849
Dobbins, Matthias C.	Capt. 26th NJ Infy	NY	13054
Dobie, David F.	Capt. 118th NY Infy	NY	10963
Doborzy, Peter P.	LTC 4th USC H Arty	MO	06857
Dodd, Edward	Asst Surg. USV	NY	04065
Dodd, Levi A.	Col. 112th PA Infy BvtBG	DC	12412
Dodds, Ford S.	Asst Surg. 60th IL Infy	IL	08560
Dodge, Charles E.	BG USV	NY	00393-737
Dodge, Don A.	Capt. 146th NY Infy	MN	07823 (Dup)
Dodge, Francis S.	BG Paymaster Gen. USA	NY	05300
Dodge, Frederick L.	Capt. 23rd Infy USA	MI	06093
Dodge, Grenville M.	MG USV	NY	00484
Dodge, Henry Lee	3rd Class(CA State Senator)	CA	06337
Dodge, James G.C.	Maj 61st MA Infy BvtLTC	MA	01030
Dodge, James H.	Capt. 9th Batt. WI L Arty	DC	06800
Dodge, Richard I.	Col. 11th Infy USA	NY	05836
Dodge, Theodore A.	Maj BvtCol. USA	MA	01691
Dodge, William A.	1st Lt. 9th VT Infy	IL	16825
Dodsley, William R.	Capt. 24th MI Infy	MI	05169
Doherty, Timothy	Capt. 16th IN Infy	MN	08018
Dole, James A.	1st Lt. 1st ME H Arty	ME	10932
Dollard, Robert	Maj 2nd USC Cav	MA	12688
Donagan, Richard	Capt. 118th PA Infy	PA	00205
Donahower, Jeremiah C.	Capt. 2nd MN Infy	MN	08153
Donaldson, Francis Adams	Capt. 118th PA Infy	PA	02072
Donaldson, Jacob C.	Capt. 38th OH Infy	DC	16871
Donaldson, James L.	Col. AQM Gen. BvtMG USA	MA	01398
Donley, Joseph R.	Capt. 83rd IL Infy	PA	10258
Donley, Michael P.	Capt. 3rd NH Infy	MA	10940

Name	Rank	Commandery	Insignia No.
Donn, John W.	Chief Topographer with rank of Capt.	MD	10297
Donnell, John A.	1st Lt. 1st IA Cav	CA	07215
Donnell, William E.	1st Lt. Adj. 20th ME Infy BvtMaj	NY	00672
Donnellan, John W.	LTC 27th USCT	OH	05195
Donnelly, Edward	Surg. 31st PA Infy BvtLTC	CA	06667
Donnelly, James J.	1st Lt. 118th PA Infy	PA	05491
Donnelly, Vincent P.	Capt. 61st PA Infy	PA	00009
Donohoe, Michael T.	Col. 10th NH Infy BvtBG	MA	08056
Doolittle, Charles C.	BG BvtMG USV	OH	06516
Doran, James S.	Act 2nd Asst Eng. USN	PA	08970
D'Orleans, Louis P.A.	Capt. ADC USV (Comte de Paris)	PA	02107
Dornblaser, Benjamin	Col. 46th IL Infy BvtMG	KS	04819
Dornbusch, Henry	Capt. 1st OH Infy	OH	07315
Dorr, Charles P.	1st Lt. 6th ME Infy BvtCapt.	ME	13053
Dorr, Henry G.	1st Lt. 4th MA Cav	MA	01684
Dorr, John	1st Lt. 60th MA Infy	MA	12024
Dorsey, Daniel A.	2nd Lt. 33rd OH Infy	NE	06703
Dorsey, George W.E.	Capt. CS BvtMaj USV	NE	03941
Dorsey, Stephen W.	Capt. 1st OH L Arty BvtLTC	CA	06531
Dorsheimer, William	Maj ADC USV	NY	03352
Dorton, Henry F.	Act Ensign USN	MD	12698
Dorwin, William E.	2nd Lt. 3rd IL Cav	IL	12644
Doten, Frederick B.	Capt. 14th CT Infy	MA	01697
Doty, Charles E.	1st Lt. 17th CT Infy	NY	08103
Doty, Spencer C.	1st Lt. 128th NY Infy	NY	10755
Doubleday, Charles W.	Col. 2nd OH Infy	DC	04561
Doubleday, Ulysses	BvtBG USN	NY	00876
Dougall, Allen H.	Capt. 88th IN Infy	IN	10365
Dougall, William	Capt. 13th USCT	IL	07917
Dougan, Henry M.	1st Lt. Adj. 100th PA Infy	PA	08451
Dougherty, John C.	Capt. 105th PA Infy	DC	14532
Dougherty, William E.	BG USA	CA	02909
Doughty, John E.	Capt. 4th NJ Infy	PA	10132
Doughty, Thomas	Act Chief Eng. USN	MO	07177
Douglas, Archibald	Surg. 10th CT Infy	NY	01906
Douglas, George A.	Capt. 30th MI Infy	OH	13121
Douglas, Henry	Col. 10th Infy USA	KS	06154
Douglas, Orlando B.	2nd Lt. 18th MO Infy	VT	09727
Douglas, William W.	Capt. 5th RI H Arty	MA	01502
Dousman, John P.	1st Lt. 47th WI Infy	WI	07797
Dovener, Blackburn B.	Capt. 15th WV Infy	DC	11415
Dow, Albert F.	2nd Lt. 4th MA Infy	MA	09056
Dowd, Edmund DeW.	Capt. 8th IL Infy	CA	17808
Dowd, John B.	Capt. 13th USCT	DC	10983
Dowden, Francis M.	2nd Lt. 52nd IN Infy	IN	06588
Dowling, Patrick H.	Capt. 111th OH Infy	OH	06648
Downey, George M.	Maj USA	CA	03230
Downing, Columbia	1st Lt. 7th Batt. OH L Arty	OH	12601

The Roster

Name	Rank	Commandery	Insignia No.
Downing, Joseph B.	Capt. 49th PA Infy	PA	12771
Downs, Henry W.	2nd Lt. 8th VT Infy	MA	09881
Downs, Thomas	Capt. AQM USV	IN	13892
Dows, Stephen L.	Capt. 20th IA Infy	IA	06407
Dox, Hamilton B.	LTC 12th IL Cav BvtBG	IL	12394
Doxey, Charles T.	Capt. 16th IN Infy	IN	08392
Doyle, Michael A.	1st Lt. 7th MO Infy	MO	04284
Doyle, Peter C.	Capt. 21st NY Infy	NY	07088
Doyly, Nigel	Act Master USN	CA	06676
Drake, Francis M.	LTC 36th IA Infy BvtBG	IA	05442
Drake, Franklin J.	RAdm USN	DC	18114
Drake, George B.	LTC AAG BvtBG USV	MA	01862
Drake, Henry T.	2nd Lt. 24th WI Infy	WI	03716
Drake, Jay J.	Capt. 7th MO Infy	MI	15822
Drake, John M.	LTC 1st OR Infy	OR	04460
Drake, Ludlum C.	Capt. 114th USCT	MI	12815
Drake, Marquis M.	1st Lt. 120th NY Infy	NY	14830
Drake, Samuel Adams	LTC 17th KS Infy	MA	02364
Dran, Francis A.	Chief Boatswain USN	MA	15781
Draper, Charles S.	1st Lt. VRC	MI	03753
Draper, Daniel M.	LTC 9th MO Cav	CO	08186
Draper, Frank W.	Capt. 39th USCT	MA	02781-2802
Draper, William F.	LTC 36th MA Infy BvtBG	MA	00926
Drennan, James M.	Capt. 25th MA Infy	MA	00754
Dresser, Jasper M.	LTC 86th IN Infy	IN	06823
Drew, Charles H.	Capt. 18th MA Infy	MA	01368
Drew, Charles W.	Col. 76th USCT BvtBG	IL	02409
Drew, Franklin M.	Maj 15th ME Infy BvtCol.	ME	02529
Drew, Harvey L.	1st Lt. 3rd MI Cav	CA	08570
Drew, Jeremiah D.	LTC 4th NH Infy	MA	09668
Dripps, William A.	2nd Asst Eng. USN	PA	02098
Driver, William R.	Maj AAG BvtLTC USV	MA	01508
Drum, John	Capt. 10th Infy USA	CA	10611
Drum, Richard Coulter	BG ADG USA	DC	02361
Drum, William F.	LTC 12th Infy USA	MN	06056
Drumm, Thomas	Hospital Chap USV	NY	07604
Drury, George B.	2nd Lt. 59th USCT	VT	10312
Drury, Lucius H.	Maj 1st WI H Arty	IL	02325
Drury, William P.	Capt. 61st MA Infy	MA	01401
Dryden, Carleton	Capt. 10th IA Infy	IA	16566
DuBarry, Beekman	BG Com. Gen. of Subsistence USA	DC	08315
DuBarry, Hartman	1st Lt. Adj. 88th IN Infy	OH	05813
DuBois, Delafield	Maj 62nd OH Infy	PA	02581
DuBois, Frank L.	Med. Inspector USN	PA	00142
DuBois, Henry A.	Asst Surg. BvtMaj USA	CA	02915
DuBois, John V.D.	Col. 1st MO L Arty	NY	01775
Ducat, Arthur C.	LTC 12th IL Infy BvtBG	IL	01848
Ducey, Patrick A.	2nd Lt. 2nd CO Cav	MI	09924

Name	Rank	Commandery	Insignia No.
Duchesney, Lawrence N.	Capt. 26th NY Cav	MA	04629
Duckhart, Thomas M.	1st Asst Eng. USN	MD	15788
Duckworth, William A.	2nd Lt. 110th USCT	IL	17025
Dudley, Albion M.	1st Lt. 58th MA Infy BvtCapt.	MA	05098
Dudley, Edgar S.	Col. Jdge Advocae USA	NY	02735
Dudley, James S.	BvtMaj USA	CA	03944
Dudley, Nathan A.M.	BG USA	MA	08057
Dudley, William W.	LTC 19th IN Infy BvtBG	DC	02286
Duer, William A.	Act Ensign USN	MO	05039
Duex, Augustus P.	LTC 97th PA Infy	PA	00697
Duff, Levi B.	LTC 105th PA Infy	PA	04407
Duffield, Henry M.	1st Lt. Adj. 9th MI BG USV	MI	01421
Duffield, William W.	Col. 9th MI Infy	DC	03757
Dufloo, Armand	Asst Surg. 25th NY Cav	NY	09955
Dugan, Cornelius	Lt. USN	PA	17993
Dugan, Daniel	2nd Lt. 178th OH	OH	12529
Duggan, Andrew W.	LTC 1st MI Cav	CA	17894
Duggan, Walter T.	Col. 1st Infy USA	OH	10124
Duguid, James	Capt. 65th IL Infy	IL	09794
Dumont, Robert S.	Capt. 5th NY Infy	NY	01209
Dumont, Theodore S.	2nd Lt. 5th NY Infy	PA	02759
Dunbar, Edward L.	2nd Lt. 43rd OH Infy	PA	08452
Duncan, Andrew J.	Capt. 39th USCT	IN	06398 (Dup)
Duncan, Edward A.	Asst Surg. 38th IA Infy	DC	14404
Duncan, Henry T.	Capt. "Companion at Large"	OH	15499
Duncan, John W.	Maj 37th PA Infy	PA	00665
Duncan, Samuel A.	Col. 4th USCT BvtMG	NY	04611
Duncan, Samuel W.	Capt. 50th MA Infy	MA	10911
Duncan, William	Capt. 10th IL Cav	MN	09144
Duncker, Henry	Capt. 2nd MO L Arty	MO	05700
Dunderdale, Cleveland F.	Act Ensign USN	IL	08400
Dundon, Michael	Act 2nd Asst Eng.USN	MA	16592
Dungan, Stephen W.	2nd Lt. 70th IN Infy	IN	15162
Dungan, Warren S.	LTC 34th IA Infy BvtCol.	IA	11136
Dungan, William W.	Chief Eng. USN	PA	08489
Dunham, Abner	1st Lt. 12th IA Infy	IA	13279
Dunham, William	Capt. 3rd MI Cav	MI	13968
Dunham, William G.	1st Lt. 1st VT H Arty	VT	09156
Dunkelberger, Isaac R.	Capt. 1st Cav BvtLTC USA	CA	03539
Dunlap, Horace L.	Capt. 50th IL Infy	KS	11072
Dunlava, Thomas A.	2nd Lt. 24th NY Cav	MN	08544
Dunn, Edwin	1st Lt. 25th NY Cav	MN	05155
Dunn, George W.	Maj 109th NY Infy	NY	15517
Dunn, John Jr.	1st Lt. RQM 184th NY Infy	NY	06735
Dunn, John M.	1st Lt. 1st DE Infy	PA	01664
Dunn, Moncena	Maj 19th MA Infy	MA	10314
Dunn, Rhodomanthen H.	Maj 3rd TN Infy	CA	08022
Dunn, Robert	Capt. 8th USC H Arty	WA	10378

The Roster

Name	Rank	Commandery	Insignia No.
Dunn, Thomas	1st Lt. US Infy	PA	00996
Dunn, Thomas G.	Capt. 7th NJ Infy BvtMaj	OH	11568
Dunn, William M.	Maj 3rd Arty USA	CA	03102
Dunn, Williamson	Act Ensign USN	CA	15417
Dunne, Hugh	Capt. 78th OH Infy	OH	08173
Dunot, Thomas J.	Surg. 1st MD Cav	PA	04163
Dunton, Warren RD.	Capt. VRC BvtMaj	PA	10069
Dunwoody, Henry H.G.	BG USA	DC	16944
DuPlaine, Benoni C.	Act 2nd Asst Eng. USN	PA	08211
Dupont, Charles	Capt. 13th Batt. MI L Arty	MI	06411
Dupont, Henry A.	Capt. 5th Arty BvtLTC USA	DC	10418
Durbin, John W.	1st Lt. 183rd OH Infy	IN	14981
Durbin, Winfield T.	Col. 161st IN Infy	IN	13308
Durfee, George N.	Capt. 7th RI Infy	MA	13927
Durfee, George S.	Capt. 8th IL Infy	IL	13986
Durgin, John C.	1st Lt. Adj. 22nd WI Infy	IL	02795
Durgin, Samuel H.	Asst Surg. 1st MA Cav	MA	14214
Durham, Thomas W.	2nd Lt. 11th IL Infy	KS	06790
Durkee, Joseph H.	Capt. 18th VRC	NY	02560
Durkee, Richard P.H.	Capt. 14th Infy USA	IL	03706
Durland, Coe	LTC 17th PA Cav BvtCol.	PA	05488
Duryea, George	LTC 5th NY Infy BvtCol.	NY	01640
Duryea, Hiram	Col. 5th NY Infy BvtBG	NY	04488
Duryee, Jacob E.	LTC 2nd MD Infy BvtBG	NY	04490
Dusseault, John H.	1st Lt. 39th MA Infy	MA	16591
Dustin, Daniel	Col. 105th IL Infy BvtBG	IL	08421
Dutch, James B.	2nd Lt. 1st IL L Arty	IL	04501
Dutcher, George N.	Capt. 5th MI Cav	IL	03144
Dutton, Charles King	Capt. 146th NY Infy BvtMaj	NY	02761
Dutton, Clarence E.	Maj Ordnance USA	DC	12699
Dutton, Everell F.	LTC 105th IL Infy BvtBG	IL	06214
Dutton, George W.	Maj 9th MA Infy	MA	09330
Dutton, Henry F.	LTC 5th VT Infy	PA	14545
Dutton, Samuel L.	Surg. 4th MA Infy	MA	07772
Dutton, William G.	2nd Lt. 67th PA Infy	PA	00280
Dwight, Charles	2nd Lt. 70th NY Infy	MA	00925
Dwight, G. Lyman	1st Lt. 1st RI L Arty	MA	01090
Dwight, Henry C.	Capt. 27th MA Infy	MA	02597
Dwight, James F.	LTC 11th MO Cav	DC	05942
Dwinel, Lester	Capt. 15th ME Infy BvtMaj	ME	07732
Dwinnell, Benjamin D.	1st Lt. 2nd MA H Arty	MA	16033
Dwyer, Michael T.	1st Lt. 3rd NJ Cav	NY	12723
Dwyer, William M.	Capt. 96th OH Infy	OH	14308
Dye, P. Edwin	Maj Paymaster USV	DC	11388
Dyer, Clarence H.	Maj AAG USV	IL	01923
Dyer, David P.	Col. 49th MO Infy	MO	04270
Dyer, Elisha	Capt. 10th RI Infy	MA	03163
Dyer, George B.	Maj 9th ME Infy BvtCol.	MA	01765

Name	Rank	Commandery	Insignia No.
Dyer, George R.	Capt. AQM USV	IL	06457
Dyer, George W.	Maj Paymaster BvtLTC USV	DC	04472
Dyer, Isaac	Col. 15th ME Infy BvtBG	ME	14012
Dyer, J. Franklin	Surg. 19th MA Infy	MA	01089
Dyer, N. Mayo	RAdm USN	MA	08854
Dyer, Nicholas D.	Capt. 29th MO Infy	KS	16392
Dyer, Reuben F.	Surg.104th IL	IL	08863
Dyke, Robert	2nd Lt. 4th WV Infy	OH	10128
Dysart, Benjamin F.	2nd Lt. 34th IL Infy	IL	08401
Eachus, George W.	1st Lt. RDQM 20th PA Cav PA	PA	10866
Eads, Albert	1st Lt. 51st IL Infy	IL	11086
Eagal, Melzar J.	1st Lt. 64th USCT	IL	04835
Eagan, Charles P.	Capt. CS USA	CA	03326
Eager, Charles H.	Capt. 15th MA Infy	MA	12739
Eager, William B.	Surg. 162nd NY Infy	NY	01115
Eagle, Henry	Commodore USN	NY	01212
Eakin, Chandler P.	Capt. 1st Arty BvtMaj USA	PA	00493
Eakins, William R.	2nd Lt. 2nd NY H Arty	NY	15791
Earle, Charles W.	1st Lt. 96th IL Infy BvtCapt.	IL	03863
Earle, David M.	Capt. 15th MA Infy	MA	02553
Earle, Francis S.	Maj AAG USV	CA	11659
Earnest, Cyrus A.	Capt. 8th Infy BvtLTC USA	CA	02918
Easterbrook, Kimball	1st Lt. RQM 40th MA Infy	MA	13012
Easterbrook, Nathan, Jr.	1st Lt. RQM 34th NY Infy	NY	14414
Eastman, Albert P.	2nd Lt. 1st Me H Arty	DC	13030
Eastman, David W.	1st Lt. Adj. 2nd MO Cav	KS	07954
Eastman, Ermon D.	1st Lt. 7th MN Infy	ME	14014
Eastman, Joseph A.	Asst Surg. 44th USCT	IN	07927
Eastman, Thomas H.	Commander USN	PA	00306
Eastman, William Reed	Capt. 72nd NY Infy	NY	15518
Easton, Fergus A.	2nd Lt. 6th NY Cav	MA	12374
Easton, William T.	Capt. 103rd USCT	PA	10524
Eastwick, Philip G.	2nd Asst Eng. USN	OR	08897
Eaton, Charles W.	Capt. 21st MI Infy	MI	03869
Eaton, George O.	1st Lt. 5th Cav USA	WI	04822
Eaton, Henry Z.	1st Lt. 7th OH Infy	IL	14226
Eaton, John	Col. 63rd USCT BvtBG	DC	04324
Eaton, John B.	Capt. 2nd Cav BvtLTC USA	DC	05125
Eaton, Joseph H.	Maj Paymaster BvtBG USA	OR	04982
Eberhart, Gustavus A.	Col. 32nd IA Infy	IA	13230
Ebersole, Jacob	Surg. 19th IN Infy	OH	10026
Ebi, Monroe	1st Lt. 19th OH Infy	IL	04836
Ebstein, Frederick H.E.	Maj 19th Infy USA	NY	03231 (Dup)
Eckels, William H.	Maj Paymaster USA	MN	03648
Eckerson, Theodore J.	LTC USA	OR	04882
Eckert Thomas T.	BvtBG USV	NY	15796
Eckert, George B.	1st Lt. 3rd Infy USA	PA	02132
Eckley, Ephraim R.	Col. 80th OH Infy BvtBG	OH	10229

Name	Rank	Commandery	Insignia No.
Eddy, Darius F.	2nd Lt. 42nd MA Infy	MA	10315
Eddy, George O.	1st Lt. 3rd RI H Arty	MN	07189
Edes, Benjamin L.	Lt. USN	PA	00972
Edes, Robert T.	Passed Asst Surg. USN	MA	02195
Edgar, James M.	1st Lt. 11th MO Cav	DC	12254
Edgerley, Edward	Capt. 79th PA Infy	PA	05492
Edgerley, J. Homer	Capt. 3rd NH Infy BvtMaj	MA	07400
Edgerton, Alonzo J.	Col. 65th USCT BvtBG	MN	05853
Edgerton, Rollin A.	1st Lt. 72nd OH Infy	OH	04737
Edgett, Isaac H.	1st Lt. 23rd MA Infy	MA	10118
Edgington, Lindsey L.	Capt. 70th OH Infy	OH	10057
Edmands, J. Cushing	Col. 32nd MA Infy BvtBG	MA	00725
Edmands, Thomas F.	LTC 24th MA Infy BvtCol.	MA	00747
Edmonds, Howard	Capt. 3rd PA Cav	DC	12210
Edmunds, Eli D.	Act Master USN	PA	16327
Edsall, Thomas H.	1st Lt. Adj. 176th NY Infy	CO	08021
Edson, Abner B.	1st Lt. 83rd PA Infy	PA	07857
Edson, Benjamin	1st Lt. 10th IL Infy	CA	13253
Edson, P. O'Meara	Surg. 17th VT Infy	MA	03876
Edson, Willis	Capt. 84th IL Infy	KS	14081
Edwards, Alanson W.	1st Lt. Adj. 1st AL Cav BvtMaj	MN	12037
Edwards, Arthur	Chap 1st MI Cav	IL	01948
Edwards, Charles G.	Maj 106th OH Infy BvtLTC	MN	05261
Edwards, David S.	Med. Director USN	NY	01229
Edwards, Eaton A.	LTC USA	DC	09470
Edwards, Eugene E.	1st Lt. 6th IA Infy	CA	06719
Edwards, George B.	2nd Lt. 5th IA Cav	PA	00699
Edwards, Thomas C.	1st Lt. 1st NH Cav	IL	01918
Edwards, William	3rd Class	OH	03273
Edwins, Stanley W.	Asst Surg. 124th IN Infy	IN	09725
Egan, Francis D.	Chap 8th PA Cav	PA	00014
Egan, James J.	1st Lt. 1st MN H Arty	MN	06680
Egan, John	Maj 1st Arty USA	NY	10542
Egbert, Augustus R.	Capt. 2nd Infy USA BvtLTC	CA	03234
Egbert, Harry C.	Col. 22nd Infy USA BvtBG USV	OH	03449
Egbert, Henry	LTC 44th IA Infy	IA	04837
Egbert, Horace	Maj 183rd PA Infy	PA	00771
Egle, William H.	Surg. 116th USCT	PA	04164
Egleston, Melville	1st Lt. Adj. 19th MA Infy	NY	09306
Ehlers, Edward M.L.	Capt. 17th VRC BvtCol.	NY	02574
Eicholtz, George C.M.	Capt. 53rd PA Infy	PA	00407
Eisenbise, Henry A.M.	Caapt. 36th PA Militia	PA	12872
Ekin, James A.	Col. AQMG BvtBG USA	OH	06834
Ekings, Robert M.	LTC 34th NJ Infy	NY	08638
Elcock, George S.	Capt. 84th NY Infy	NY	14335
Elder, Henry G.	Maj 142nd PA Infy BvtLTC	CO	07482
Elder, Robert B.	Act Ensign USN	NY	02272
Elderkin, William A.	Col. Asst Com. Gen. Sub. USA	CA	03325

Name	Rank	Commandery	Insignia No.
Eldredge, Charles H.	Pay Director USN	NY	00941
Eldredge, Daniel	1st Lt. 3rd NH Infy	MA	05233
Eldredge, James E.	Capt. 1st VT H Arty BvtMaj	VT	09172
Eldredge, Joseph C.	Pay Director USN	NY	00731
Eldridge, Cornelius S.	Capt. 29th MI Infy	IL	14227
Eldridge, James W.	1st Lt. 23rd USCT	MA	11614
Eldridge, Stuart	1st Lt. 64th USCT BvtMaj	CA	06138
Elerick, James	Capt. 59th IL Infy	IA	15366
Elfwing, Nere A.	Maj 48th NY Infy BvtLTC	NY	00797
Ellinwood, Charles N.	Surg. 74th IL Infy	CA	01437
Elliot, Joseph P.	Capt. 22nd PA Infy	PA	01982
Elliott, Adjonijah B.	Capt. 1st USC H Arty	IL	14188
Elliott, Alban V.	Maj Paymaster BvtLTC USV	NY	11915
Elliott, Byron K.	Capt. 132nd IN Infy	IN	10794 (Dup)
Elliott, George H.	Col. Eng. USA	CA	02720
Elliott, Henry Hill	LTC 1st LA Infy	NY	00635
Elliott, Isaac H.	Col. 33rd IL Infy BvtBG	IL	02410
Elliott, Jacob T.	Capt. CS BvtMaj USV	PA	01160
Elliott, John	Capt. USA	PA	00451 (Dup)
Elliott, Joseph T.	2nd Lt. 124th IN Infy	IN	16161
Elliott, Samuel M.	Col. 79th NY Infy BvtBG	NY	00369
Elliott, Victor A.	Maj 207th PA Infy	CO	05956
Elliott, Washington L.	BG USV	CA	02027
Elliott, William St. George	Maj 79th NY Infy	DC	08515
Ellis, Clarence	Capt. 2nd MA H Arty	MA	01292
Ellis, Cyrus L.	2nd Lt. 168th OH Infy	CA	17436
Ellis, Erwin	Capt. 8th MI Cav	MO	04290
Ellis, Henry A.	Capt. 15th Infy Bvt LTC USA	NY	01147 (Dup)
Ellis, Henry C.	Capt. 65th NY Infy	NY	01443
Ellis, James	Maj 53rd Infy PA Militia	PA	08453
Ellis, James M.	LTC CS USV	MA	06043
Ellis, Matthew H.	Capt. 175th NY Infy	NY	08349
Ellis, Philip Howard	Col. USA	PA	00675
Ellis, Rudolph	Capt. 6th PA Cav	PA	00920
Ellis, Theodore G.	Col. 14th CT Infy BvtBG	MA	01322
Ellis, W. Irving	Capt. CS BvtMaj USV	MA	01522
Ellison, David	Capt. 3rd US Vol. Infy	MO	05053
Ellison, Henry C.	1st Lt. Adj. 115th OH Infy	OH	03258
Ellsworth, Henry G.	1st Lt. USMC	PA	03402
Ellsworth, Horace D.	Maj 11th NY Cav	NY	17125
Ellsworth, Prosper H.	Surg. 106th IL Infy	IL	08953
Elmer, Horace	Commander USN	PA	06409
Elson, Jerry E.	Capt. 9th IA Infy	IA	11135
Elston, Isaac C.	LTC ADC USV	IN	06589
Elwell, Charles W.	Capt. 34th MA Infy	MA	01170
Elwell, John J.	LTC QM BvtBG USV	OH	02994
Elwood, James G.	Capt. 100th IL Infy	IL	07553
Elwood, Robert D.	Capt. 78th PA Infy	PA	11155

Name	Rank	Commandery	Insignia No.
Ely, Charles U.	1st Lt. 46th MA Infy	NY	05416
Ely, Charles W.	2nd Lt. 27th CT Infy	DC	11963
Ely, John F.	Surg. 24th IA Infy	IA	05443
Ely, William G.	Col. 18th CT Infy BvtBG	MA	02165
Emanuel, Jonathan M.	Passed Asst. Eng. USN	PA	06002
Emanuel, Lyon L.	Capt. 82nd PA Infy	NY	01360
Embick, Frederick E.	Col. 106th NY Infy	PA	01485
Emerson, Edward O.	1st Lt. 19th WI Infy	PA	13286
Emerson, John W.	Maj 47th MO Infy	MO	06090
Emerson, Loring G.	Act Master USN	CA	02755
Emerson, Lowe	1st Lt. RQM 15th NJ Infy	OH	02718
Emerson, William	Capt. 35th USCT	DC	13031
Emerson, William	Col. 151st NY Infy	CA	03924
Emery, Andrew	Capt. USA	IN	16241
Emery, Augustus H.	Capt. 1st MI L Arty	CA	12293
Emery, Charles E.	2nd Asst Eng. USN	NY	04337
Emery, John R.	2nd Lt. 15th NJ Infy	NY	12246
Emilio, Luis F.	Capt. 54th MA Infy	NY	05529
Eminger, Augustus J.	Capt. 93rd OH Infy	OH	07429
Emmerton, Charles S.	1st Lt. 23rd MA Infy	MA	10195
Emmerton, James A.	Surg. 2nd MA H Arty	MA	02305
Emmons, George F.	RAdm USN	PA	00135
Emmons, George W.	Capt. 3rd NH Infy	MA	04333
Emmons, J. Frank	2nd Lt. 45th MA Infy	MA	01859
Emory, Campbell D.	Capt. 9th Infy BvtLTC USA	PA	01471
Emory, William H.	MG USV BG USA	PA	00241
Ende, Charles	1st Lt. 5th IA Cav	IA	16567
Endicott, William C.	3rd Class (Secretary of War)	MA	06342
Eneson, Eugene S.	Capt. 174th NY Infy	NY	00628
Engard, Albert C.	Chief Eng. USN	PA	05330
England, Thomas Y.	Capt. CS USV	PA	03093
Engle, James E.	2nd Lt. VRC	DC	03084
Engle, Jeremiah	1st Lt. 34th OH Infy	OH	14988
Englebert, J. Lee	BvtCol. USV	PA	00438
English, Earl	RAdm USN	DC	02399
English, Thomas C.	LTC 2nd Infy USA	PA	00895
Ennis, Joseph L.	2nd Lt. 6th US Vet. Vols.	PA	00087
Ennis, William	BG USA	DC	10337
Eno, Frank	Maj AAG USV	CA	02037
Enochs, William H.	Col. 1st WV Infy BvtBG	OH	03068
Enos, Herbert M.	LTC BvtCol. USA	WI	01858
Ensign, Edgar T.	Maj 9th IA Cav BvtCol.	CO	09884
Ensinger, Samuel L.	1st Lt. 11th IN Infy	IN	07265
Ensley, Nicholas	2nd Lt. 44th IN Infy	IN	07928
Entwistle, James	RAdm USN	NY	05010
Erb, William S.S.	Capt. 19th OH Infy	DC	15350
Erben, Henry	RAdm USN	NY	00323
Erdelmeyer, Frank	LTC 32nd IN Infy	IN	13309

Name	Rank	Commandery	Insignia No.
Erdman, Adolphus	1st Lt. 15th MO Infy BvtMaj	MN	12653
Erhardt, Joel B.	Capt. 1st VT Cav	NY	01355
Erickson, Christian	1st Lt. 82nd IL Infy BvtCapt.	IL	12204
Ernst, Charles F.	Capt. 12th MO Cav	MO	06725
Ernst, J. Eugene	Act Ensign USN	NY	11850
Ernst, Oswald H.	Col. Eng. USA BvtBG USV	DC	09914
Erwin, Charles K.	Capt. 45th IL Infy	WI	04980
Eskridge, Richard I.	Col. 27th Infy USA	CA	05928
Esmond, Richard	1st Lt. 147th NY Infy BvtMaj	NY	08341
Estabrooks, Henry L.	2nd Lt. 26th MA Infy	MA	12668
Este, William M.	Maj ADC USV	NY	00155-5415
Estes, Stephen A.	Capt. 12th NY Infy	NY	01652
Etting, Charles E.	Capt. 121st PA Infy	PA	01850
Etting, Frank M.	BvtLTC USV	PA	00286
Etting, Henry	Pay Director USN	PA	00310
Etting, Theodore M.	Lt. USN	PA	02099
Euen, Matthias S.	Maj 156th NY Infy BvtCol.	NY	02136
Eustrom, Hans	Capt. 3rd MN Infy	MN	09469
Evans, Amos H.	Capt. 9th NJ Infy	IA	09687
Evans, Charles H.	1st Lt. Baltimore Batt. MD L Arty	DC	10811
Evans, David M.	Col. 20th NY Cav	MN	14561
Evans, Franklin H.	Capt. 8th USCT	PA	03403
Evans, George S.	Col. 2nd Cav BvtBG USA	CA	01283
Evans, George W.	Capt. 21st Infy USA	DC	08925
Evans, Ira H.	Capt. 116th USCT BvtMaj	NY	06954
Evans, Isaac F.	Capt. 2nd CO Cav	CA	04438
Evans, John A.	Capt. 27th OH Infy	OH	07523
Evans, Joseph S.	Chap 124th PA Infy	PA	06249
Evans, Nelson W.	Capt. 173rd OH Infy	OH	05379
Evans, Owen J.	Surg. 40th NY Infy	MN	08731
Evans, Robert D.	1st Lt. 73rd NY Infy	NY	14286
Evans, Robley D.	RAdm USN	DC	01863
Evans, Rowland N.	Maj 20th IL Infy	IL	11976
Evans, Walter	1st Lt. 25th KY Infy	MO	12700
Eveleth, Francis M.	Surg. 1st ME Infy	ME	08832
Everdell, Lyman B.	Capt. 35th WI Infy	MN	14146
Everest, James G.	Capt. 13th IL Infy	IL	06400
Everett, Ambrose S.	Capt. 108th NY Infy	CO	05185
Everett, Edward F.	2nd Lt. 2nd MA H Arty	MA	06912
Everett, James A.	1st Lt. 7th ME Infy	MN	13530
Everett, Walter	1st Lt. 5th MA Infy	MA	01610
Everhard, Henry H.	Capt. 104th OH Infy	OH	10020
Everhart, Isaiah F.	Surg. 8th PA Cav	PA	11156
Everhart, William M.	BvtCapt. USV	PA	10397
Eversfield, Charles	Med. Director USN	NY	00368-529?
Eversz, Moritz E.	2nd Lt. 20th WI Infy	IL	17691
Everts, Orpheus	Surg. 20th IN Infy	OH	03006
Ewen, Clarence	Maj Surg. USA	NY	03557

The Roster

Name	Rank	Commandery	Insignia No.
Ewen, Milton	Capt. 21st WI Infy	WI	07012
Ewen, Warren	Act 1st Asst Eng. USN	IL	06707
Ewers, Ezra P.	BG USA	DC	04382
Ewing, Elmore E.	1st Lt. 91st OH Infy	CA	04200
Ewing, Francis M.	Maj 55th USCT	IN	11315
Ewing, Henry A.	Capt. 58th USCT	KS	17232
Ewing, John	LTC 155th PA Infy BvtCol.	PA	07054
Ewing, Martin B.	LTC 2nd OH H Arty	OH	07131
Ewing, Milton A.	Capt. 135th IL Infy	IL	13337
Ewing, Thomas	BG BvtMG USV	NY	07459
Ewing, William D.	1st Lt. Weaver's Indpt.Co. PA Cav	MA	07744
Eyerly, Josiah B.	1st Lt. 13th IA Infy	IA	07168
Eyre, Edward E.	LTC 1st CA Cav	CA	02859
Eyre, Manuiel, Jr.	Lt. Adj. 3rd DE Infy	PA	00079
Ezekiel, David I.	Capt. 6th Infy USA	CO	05618
Fagan, Louis E.	Capt. USMC	PA	06250
Fagan, Maurice E.	Capt. 19th PA Cav BvtLTC	PA	01983
Fahnestock, Edward G.	LTC 165th PA Infy	MN	13871
Fahrion, Gustave W.	Capt. 5th USCT	OH	08287
Fair, Charles	LTC 54th USCT BvtCol.	DC	04557
Fairbanks, Crawford	1st Lt. 129th IN Infy	IN	06590
Fairbanks, Henry N.	2nd Lt. 30th ME Infy	ME	08082
Fairbanks, John W.	1st Lt. 89th USCT	MA	16468
Fairbanks, William H.	Col. 149th IN Infy	IN	12097
Fairbrass, Frederick J.	1st Lt. 1st MI L Arty BvtMaj	MI	11876
Fairbrother, George W.	2nd Lt. 5th MI Cav	MN	09851
Fairchild, Charles	Asst Paymaster USN	MA	01312
Fairchild, Lucius	BG USV	WI	02387
Fairfax, Donald	RAdm USN	DC	00500
Fairlamb, George A.	LTC 148th PA Infy	PA	00058
Fairman, James	Col. 96th NY Infy	NY	08918
Falck, William	Maj BvtLTC USA	NY	12955
Fales, Samuel B.	3rd Class	PA	00364
Fallows, Samuel	Col. 49th WI Infy BvtBG	IL	03135
Farber, William H.	Capt. 64th OH Infy	OH	09589
Farenholt, Oscar W.	RAdm USN	CA	06503
Farley, Edwin	1st Lt. 3rd USC Cav	IN	10035
Farley, Joseph P.	BG USA	PA	11938
Farley, Porter	Capt. 140th NY Infy	NY	17276
Farmer, Edward	Chief Eng. USN	NY	08645
Farnham, Augustus B.	LTC 16th ME Infy BvtCol.	ME	01726
Farnham, George M.	Capt. 10th MI Cav	IL	02186
Farnham, Roswell	LTC 12th VT Cav	VT	09160
Farnsworth, Ezra, Jr.	Capt. 26th MA Infy	MN	05858
Farnsworth, Henry J.	Maj Inspr. Gen. USA BvtLTC	DC	03649
Farnsworth, John G.	Col. QM USV	NY	02762
Farnum, Edwin J.	Capt. AQM USV	MN	04547
Farquhar, Francis W.	BvtLTC USA	DC	No Number

Name	Rank	Commandery	Insignia No.
Farquhar, Norman H.	RAdm USN	DC	09937
Farragut, David G.	Admiral USN	NY	00221
Farragut, Loyall	2nd Lt. 5th Arty USA	NY	00950
Farrand, Daniel F.	Capt. 36th WI Infy	PA	05720
Farrand, William H.	2nd Lt. 60th OH Infy	OH	08701
Farrar, Bernard G.	Col. 6th USC H Arty BvtBG	MO	06855
Farrar, George D.	Capt. 145th NY Infy	NY	07605
Farrar, Henry W.	Capt. ADC BvtLTC USV	IL	00851
Farrar, Judson S.	Col. 26th MI Infy	MI	03755
Farrell, Lawrence	Capt. 35th NJ Infy	PA	13936
Farrington, George E.	1st Lt. RQM 85th IN Infy	IN	06591
Farrington, Willard	1st Lt. 1st VT Cav	VT	09185
Fassett, Lewis H.	Capt. 64th NY Infy	PA	13820
Fassitt, John B.	Capt. 23rd PA Infy	NY	01362
Faulkner, John K.	Col. 7th KY Cav	OH	02986
Faulkner, L.B.	LTC 136th NY Infy	NY	01108
Faulkner, William D.	1st Lt. 86th IL Infy	MN	05857
Favill, Josiah M.	Capt. 57th NY Infy BvtCol.	NY	10425
Faxon, William	3rd Class (Asst Sec.Navy)	PA	00164
Fay, Edwin G.	2nd Lt. 107th NY Infy BvtCapt.	PA	07638
Fay, Franklin E.	3rd Class (Vice Pres.Sanitary Com)	MA	01497
Fearey, Thomas H.	2nd Lt. Sig. Corps USV	NY	10325
Fearing, George R.	Capt. ADC BvtMaj USV	MA	06044
Febiger, Christian	LTC 5th DE Infy	PA	06251
Febiger, George L.	Col. Asst Paymaster USA	CA	02645
Febiger, John C.	RAdm USN	DC	09038
Fechet', Edmund G.	LTC USA	MI	15179
Fechet', Eugene O.	Maj Sig. Corps USA	CA	04740
Fee, Franklin W.	1st Lt. RQM 1st KY Infy	OH	06885
Fee, Thomas M.	Capt. 36th IA Infy	IA	06947
Feeman, John C.	Capt. 1st NY Cav	WI	12314
Fegan, Joseph D.	Capt. AAG USV	IA	02794
Feldstein, Theodore	Capt. 68th NY Infy	NY	No Number
Felker, Charles W.	Capt. 48th WI Infy	WI	04450
Fell, David N.	2nd Lt. 122nd PA Infy	PA	01240
Fellows, Theodore A.	Capt. 8th WI Infy	WI	12634
Felton, Charles H.	1st Lt. 2nd IL L Arty	IL	12824
Felton, William	Capt. 90th OH Infy BvtMaj	OH	04569
Feltus, Roswell G.	Capt. 75th PA Infy	PA	02932
Fendall, Philip R., Jr.	Maj USMC	PA	00472
Fenn, Augustus H.	Maj 2nd CT H Arty BvtLTC	NY	08943
Fenner, Arnold C.	Capt. 63rd OH Infy	OH	03034
Fenton, Alcenus W.	Capt. 6th OH Cav	OH	08539
Fenton, Charles	Capt. 21st CT Infy	MA	11587
Fenton, Ebenezer B.	2nd Lt. 20th CT Infy (Capt.CS USV)	MI	05925
Fenton, Joseph B.	1st Lt. 8th MI Infy	MI	08092
Ferguson, Benjamin H.	Capt. 114th IL Infy	IL	04502
Ferguson, Edward	2nd Lt. 1st WI Infy	WI	01551

Name	Rank	Commandery	Insignia No.
Ferguson, James F.	Surg. 165th NY Infy	NY	00581
Ferguson, William	1st Lt. 5th NY Infy	NY	07460
Fernald, Albert E.	1st Lt. 20th ME Infy BvtCapt.	ME	07899
Fernald, Cassius M.	1st Lt. 97th USCT	MN	13681
Fernald, Charles H.	Asst Eng. USN	MA	15782
Fernow, Berthold	2nd Lt. 3rd USCT	NY	01153
Ferree, Charles M.	1st Lt. 52nd IN Infy	MO	05037
Ferree, Newton	2nd Lt. 157th OH Infy	DC	12846
Ferrell, Theodore F.	1st Lt. 18th OH Infy	OH	05478
Ferrero, Edward	BG BvtMG USV	NY	04606
Ferril, Thomas J.	Chap 16th KS Cav	MO	09842
Ferris, Alexander M.	Capt. 30th MA Infy	MA	05142
Ferris, Daniel O.	Chap 133rd NY Infy	NY	01158
Ferris, Eddy F.	LTC 14th WI Infy	WI	04378
Ferris, Eugene W.	Capt. 30th MA Infy	IN	10287
Ferris, William G.	Capt. 6th NY H Arty	NY	01211
Ferry, William M.	LTC 14th MI Infy	MI	13392 (Dup)
Fesler, John R.	LTC 27th IN Infy	IN	12861
Fessenden, Anson D.	Capt. 53rd MA Infy	MA	09331
Fessenden, Charles B., Jr.	BvtMaj USV	KS	15416
Fessenden, Francis	MG USV	ME	00253
Fessenden, James D.	BG BvtMG USV	ME	00435 (Dup)
Fessenden, Joshua A.	Maj USA	NY	03609
Fessenden, Samuel	2nd Lt. 1st Batt. ME L Arty	DC	07674
Fetters, Levi	Capt. 175th PA Infy	PA	03223
Fidlar, John B.	1st Lt. 25th IA	IL	04838
Field, Benjamin F.	2nd Lt. 44th MA Infy	MA	01592
Field, Daniel W.	1st Lt. 27th CT Infy	CA	06673
Field, Edward	Col. USA	CA	00930
Field, Francis A.	Capt. 11th Infy USA	DC	09102
Field, Joseph F.	1st Lt. 2nd MA H Arty	MA	09057
Field, Joseph T.	Maj 29th NJ Infy	NY	11749
Field, Lucius	2nd Lt. 36th MA Infy	MA	11418
Field, Maunsell B.	Lt. USN	NY	16151
Field, Putnam	Capt. 10th NY Infy	CA	16836
Field, Richard S.	3rd Class (US Senator NJ)	PA	00910
Field, William M.	1st Lt. 15th PA Cav	PA	08454
Fielder, George B.	2nd Lt. 21st NJ Infy	NY	04485
Fife, George T.	Surg. USN	PA	00413-4830
Filbert, Isaac S.	Capt. 177th PA Infy	DC	11479
Filkins, George E.	1st Lt. 15th USCT	Ca	02919
Fillerbrown, Charles B.	1st Lt. 219th ME Infy BvtCapt.	MA	06045
Fillerbrown, Thomas S.	Commodore USN	DC	00325
Filley, Giles F.	3rd Class (Organized Free Soil Party)	MO	05054
Finch, Cyrus M.	Surg. 9th OH Cav	OH	04218
Finch, Duane D.	2nd Lt. 3rd IA Infy	CO	13146
Finch, George M.	LTC 137th OH Infy	OH	03255
Findley, Robert P.	LTC 74th OH Infy	OH	07846

Name	Rank	Commandery	Insignia No.
Fink, Joseph H.	Act Ensign USN	MO	05041
Finney, Isaac S.	Chief Eng. USN	PA	00915
Fish, Dyer B. N.	Surg. 27th MA Infy	MA	08437
Fish, John B.	Capt. 52nd PA Infy	PA	11448
Fish, John T.	Capt. 13th WI Infy	WI	03192
Fish, Latham A.	Capt. 174th NY Infy	NY	03612
Fish, Laurens B.	Capt. 3rd OH Cav	MO	06372
Fish, Melancthon W.	Surg. 11th MO Infy	CA	01480
Fish, Roswell A.	Capt. 32nd NY Infy	DC	05229
Fisher, Benjamin F.	Col. Chief Signal Off. BvtBG USV	PA	02068
Fisher, Calvin G.	Capt. 1st Regt. Miss. Marine Brig.	MA	09669
Fisher, Chesselden	Surg. 75th IL Infy	OH	09752
Fisher, Clark	Chief Eng. USN	PA	02100
Fisher, Cyrus W.	LTC 54th OH Infy	CO	05963
Fisher, Edward T.	2nd Lt. 139th NY Infy	MA	08547
Fisher, Edwin D.	2nd Lt. 53rd USCT	MO	05972
Fisher, Francis P.	1st Lt. Adj. 55th IL Infy	IL	05543
Fisher, George A.	1st Lt. Sig. Corps BvtCapt.USV	CA	02036
Fisher, Harvey	1st Lt. 150th PA Infy	PA	03404
Fisher, Hiram T.	Capt. 53rd USCT	OH	08031
Fisher, Horace N.	LTC AIG USV	MA	01389
Fisher, John G.	2nd Lt. 14th NJ Infy	NY	12133
Fisher, John K.	Capt. 16th PA Cav	KS	09389
Fisher, Joseph S.	Capt. 84th IN Infy	OH	07316
Fisher, Joseph W.	BG USV	CO	05619
Fisher, Louis G.	1st Lt. 10th MO Cav	NY	07237
Fisher, Newton DeL.	1st Lt. 2nd OH Cav	OH	07527
Fisher, Samuel H.	Capt. McLaughlin's Squadron OH Cav	CO	10101
Fisher, Thomas M.	1st Lt. 190th PA Infy	WA	07809 (Dup)
Fisher, William H.	Capt. 7th MI Cav	MI	08892
Fisher, William J.	2nd Lt. 7ith MA Infy	CA	10241
Fisk, Archie C.	Capt. AAG USV	CO	06941
Fisk, Clinton B.	BG BvtMG USV	NY	07980
Fisk, Daniel W.	Capt. 132 NY Infy	CA	03934
Fisk, Robert E.	Capt. 132nd Ny Infy	CA	03933
Fisk, Smith W.	1st Lt. 9th MI Cav	CA	15724
Fiske, Alexander P.	Capt. AAG BvtLTC USV	NY	13269
Fiske, Asa S.	Chap 4th MN Infy	DC	02917
Fiske, Edward A.	Maj 30th MA Infy	MA	01511
Fiske, Eugene A.	2nd Lt. 8th US Vet. Volunteers	CO	10563
Fiske, Francis S.	LTC 2nd NH Infy BvtBG	MA	13599 (Dup)
Fiske, George A.	Maj Paymaster USV	MA	01175
Fiske, Joseph E.	Capt. 2nd MA H Arty	MA	01435
Fiske, William O.	Col. 1st LA Infy BvtBG	MA	01509
Fitch, Asa B.	Capt. 4th IA Cav	CA	015682
Fitch, Calvin W.	2nd Lt. 76th USCT	MO	17100
Fitch, Edson	Capt. 93rd NY Infy	NY	09307
Fitch, Henry W.	Chief Eng. USN	DC	02685

Name	Rank	Commandery	Insignia No.
Fitch, John A.	Maj 1st IL L Arty	IL	02009
Fitch, Michael H.	LTC 21st WI Infy BvtCol.	CO	06117
Fitch, Thomas W.	Passed Asst. Eng. USN	PA	07055
Fitch, William G.	Capt. USA	PA	05029
Fithian, Edward	RAdm USN	PA	15593
Fithian, Joel A.	Maj 24th NJ Infy	CA	11658
Fitzgerald, Louis	LTC 1st Mississippi Infy	NY	01264
Fitzgerald, Michael J.	Maj USA	PA	09767
Fitzgibbon, Richard	LTC 9th CT Infy	NY	10964
Fitzhugh, Charles L.	Col. 6th NY Cav BvtBG	PA	01182 (Dup)
Fitzhugh, Robert H.	Maj 1st NY L Arty BvtLTC	PA	10627
Fitzpatrick, George W.	Capt. 5th Cav MO State Militia	MO	06858
Fitzsimons, Charles	LTC 21st NY Cav BvtBG	IL	01934
Fitzwilliam, Francis J.	1st Lt. 33rd OH Infy	IL	10801
Flad, Henry	Col. 1st MO Eng.	MO	07599
Flagg, Samuel D.	Asst Surg. USN	MN	10011
Flagler, Benjamin	Capt. 28th NY Infy	NY	10965
Flagler, Daniel	BG Chief of Ordnance USA	DC	05985
Flavin, Edward H.	1st Lt. 84th NY Infy	NY	14336
Fleming, George M.	1st Lt. 11th Infy USA	PA	00899
Fleming, James E.	Capt. 11th PA Cav	NY	03769
Fleming, Robert H.	Capt. 77th OH Infy	OH	03569
Fletcher, George A.	Capt. 56th MA Infy	MA	02196
Fletcher, John W.	Capt. 36th USCT	MA	01413
Fletcher, Joshua S.	LTC 2nd Infy USA	PA	00714
Fletcher, Montgomery	Chief Eng. USA	DC	02871
Fletcher, Robert	Surg. BvtLTC USV	DC	07726
Fletcher, Stephen K.	1st Lt. Adj. 115th IN Infy	IN	06824
Fletcher, Thomas C.	Col. 47th MO Infy BvtBG	MO	04275
Fletcher, Warren H.	1st Lt. 5th NH Infy	KS	16246
Fletcher, William	Maj USA	DC	03514
Flint, Frankllin F.	Col. 47th Infy USA	IL	04839
Flint, James M.	Med. Director USN	DC	02508
Flint, Mortimer R.	Capt. 1st AL Cav	MN	10485
Flint, Samuel	1st Lt. 67th PA Infy	CA	06718
Flood, Philip N.	1st Lt. 2nd Infy USA	CA	17118
Flood, Theodore L.	2nd Lt. 125th PA Infy	PA	07056
Floyd, John G.	Capt. 145th NY Infy	NY	11336
Fockler, Jacob M.	2nd Lt. 198th PA Infy	PA	18436
Foering, John O.	1st Lt. 28th PA Infy BvtCapt.	PA	02073
Fogg, George W.	1st Lt. 1st ME Infy	WA	11799
Fogler, William H.	Capt. 19th ME Infy	ME	03720
Foley, James L.	Maj 10th KY Cav	OH	02339
Foley, James W.	Capt. 181st OH Infy	OH	06891
Folger, William M.	RAdm USN	DC	09852
Follansbee, George S.	Capt. 1st MA H Arty	MA	01706
Follett, Joseph L.	2nd Lt. 1st MO L Arty	NY	01774
Folsom, Norton	Surg. 45th USCT BvtLTC	MA	01493

Name	Rank	Commandery	Insignia No.
Foltz, Jonathan M.	Med. Director USN	PA	00176
Folwell, Mahlon B.	Capt. 50th NY Eng. BvtMaj	NY	10756
Folwell, William W.	BvtLTC USV	MN	15466
Foote, Allen R.	2nd Lt. 21st MI Infy	DC	06437
Foote, Augustus R.S.	Capt. AAG USV	DC	06660
Foote, Charles E.	1st Lt. 22nd MI Infy	CA	06920
Foote, Charles H.	1st Lt. 2nd US Shpshtrs.	VT	15408
Foote, George F.	Maj BvtLTC USA	DC	10691
Foote, John B.	2nd Lt. 12th NY Infy	DC	12413
Foote, Lucien A.	Maj 133rd IN Infy	IN	06592
Foote, Morris C.	BG USA	NY	03659
Foote, Morris J.	Capt. 70th NY Infy	DC	11608
Foraker, Joseph B.	1st Lt. 89th OH Infy BvtCapt.	OH	02179
Forbes, Cornelius H.	1st Lt. Adj. 5th VT Infy	VT	02380
Forbes, John	3rd Class (Fndr. Loyal Publication Soc.)	MA	02498
Forbes, Samuel F.	Surg. 67th OH Infy	OH	03374
Forbes, Stephen A.	Capt. 7th IL Cav	IL	12381
Forbes, Theodore F.	BG USA	DC	04933
Forbes, William H.	LTC 2nd MA Cav	MA	01182 (Dup)
Forbes, William S.	Surg. USV	PA	10260
Force, Jacob F.	Capt. 22nd USCT	MN	06350
Force, Levi	Capt. 179th NY Infy BvtMaj	CA	07211
Force, Manning F.	BG BvtMG USV	OH	02288 (Dup)
Ford, Augustus	Capt. 42nd MA Infy	MA	12807
Ford, Augustus C.	Capt. 31st IN Infy	IN	06593
Ford, Charles H.	Capt. 10th WI Infy	NY	03347
Ford, Charles W.	Capt. AQM USV	ME	07731
Ford, Collin	Maj 100th USCT BvtCol.	OH	06435
Ford, Elias A.	1st Lt. 41st OH Infy	OH	11449
Ford, George E.	Capt. 3rd Cav BvtCol. USA	PA	00408
Ford, George W.	1st Lt. RQM 65th NY Infy	NY	05419
Ford, James M.	2nd Lt. 130th IN Infy	CO	11956
Ford, John D.	RAdm USN	MD	08389
Ford, Silas P.	Capt. 5th CA Infy	CA	02541
Fordyce, Samuel W.	Capt. 1st OH Cav	MO	06089
Forgeus, Solomon F.	1st Lt. 9th USCT	PA	17448
Forney, James	BG USMC	PA	00897
Forrester, Charles W.	Capt. 57th PA Infy	IL	02931
Forse, Albert G.	2nd Lt 1st Cav USA	PA	01043
Forster, Robert H.	Maj 148th PA Infy	PA	08971
Forsyth, James M.	RAdm USN	PA	01128
Forsyth, James W.	MG USA	IL	02170
Forsyth, John	Chap USA	NY	01846
Forsyth, Lewis C.	LTC DQM Gen. USA	DC	02347
Fort, William S.	Passed Asst Surg. USN	PA	01073
Fortescue, Louis R.	1st Lt. 29th PA Infy	PA	05719
Fortescue, William M.	Capt. 2nd WV Cav	KS	04874
Fortner, Sanford	Capt. 101st IN Infy BvtMaj	IN	10366

The Roster

Name	Rank	Commandery	Insignia No.
Forwood, William H.	BG Surg. Gen. USN	DC	03701
Fosdick, Wood	2nd Lt. 3rd OH Cav	NY	17250
Foster, Amos P.	Act Vol. Lt. USN	WI	12969
Foster, Andrew J.	1st Lt. 2nd MI Cav	KS	05216
Foster, Benjamin B.	Maj AAG BvtCol. USV	NY	05519
Foster, Charles W.	Maj QM BvtCol. USA	CA	05084
Foster, David N.	Capt. 83rd NY Infy	IN	07041
Foster, Edward	Pay Inspector USN	NY	00952
Foster, Edward L.	1st Lt. Adj. 1st VT H Arty	NY	10221
Foster, Enoch	1st Lt. 13th ME Infy	ME	03474
Foster, Everett W.	LTC 3rd MN Infy	DC	11130
Foster, H. J.	Capt. USV	NY	No Number
Foster, Henry B.	Capt.	NY	01083
Foster, Henry E.	Capt. 8th VT Infy	VT	09189
Foster, James C.	Maj 59th USCT	OH	08179
Foster, James D.	1st Lt. 14th KY Infy	OH	12839
Foster, John M.	2nd Lt. 8th OH Cav	NY	10494
Foster, John W.	Col. 136th IN Infy	DC	04325
Foster, Joseph	Pay Director USN	MA	13807
Foster, Lafayette S.	3rd Class (US Senator CT)	PA	00048
Foster, Phineas	1st Lt. 1st ME Cav	WA	08620
Foster, Reuben	2nd Lt. 25th NJ Infy	MD	15339
Foster, Robert S.	BG BvtMG USV	IN	02843
Foster, Samuel J.	Capt. 48th NY Infy	MA	14388
Foster, Sidney H.	1st Lt. 1st VT H Arty	VT	09157
Foster, Theodore S.	LTC 21st MA Infy	MA	09332
Foster, William D.	Asst Surg. 7th MO Cav	MO	10286
Foster, William E.	Act Asst Paymaster USN	NY	14415
Foster, William H.	1st Lt. Adj. 14th NJ Infy BvtMaj	NY	13757
Foster, William S.	2nd Lt. 1st PA Cav	PA	06763
Fountain, Samuel W.	BG USA	DC	04207
Fowle, William B.	Capt. 43rd MA Infy	MA	01761
Fowler, DeWitt C.	Asst Surg. 19th NY Cav	MN	11279
Fowler, Edward B.	Col. 84th NY Infy BvtBG	NY	10757
Fowler, Henry P.	2nd Lt. 1st MA H Arty	OH	04198
Fowler, Horace W.	Capt. 16th NY H Arty	NY	01911
Fox, Charles B.	LTC 55th MA Infy Bvt Col.	MA	01394
Fox, Charles J.	Capt. 4th MI Infy	CA	15581
Fox, Charles James	Capt. 107th NY Infy	MI	08712
Fox, George B.	Maj 75th OH Infy	OH	02785
Fox, George H.	1st Lt. Med. Res. Corps. USA	NY	17012
Fox, George W.	1st Lt. VRC	MN	12039
Fox, Gustavus V.	Asst Surg. USN	PA	00157
Fox, Henry	Capt. 59th USCT	IL	10802
Fox, Henry C.	1st Lt. 57th IN Infy	IN	13891
Fox, James A.	Capt. 13th MA Infy	MA	02313
Fox, John A.	1st Lt. Adj. 2nd MA Infy BvtMaj	MA	01386
Fox, Lorenzo S.	Asst Surg. 26th MA Infy	MA	03719

Name	Rank	Commandery	Insignia No.
Fox, Norman	Chap 77th NY Infy	NY	10900
Fox, Perrin V.	LTC 1st MI Eng. BvtCol.	MI	03870
Fox, Philip	Asst Surg. 2nd WI Infy	WI	11119
Fox, Philip L.	Capt. AQM USV	PA	00108
Fox, Simeon M.	1st Lt. Adj. 7th KS Cav	KS	12908
Fox, William F.	LTC 107th NY Infy	NY	09564
Fracker, Charles W.	1st Lt. RQM 16th IA Infy	IA	06542
Frailey, James M.	Commodore USN	PA	00181
Frailey, Leonard A.	Pay Director USN	DC	12886
Frame, Adolphus B.	1st Lt. Adj. 186th OH Infy	OH	09590
Frame, Robert A.	Capt. 76th IL Infy	OR	08545
France, James S.	Capt. 17th NY Infy	CA	03939
Francis, Eben	Chap 127th NY Infy	MA	03784
Francis, James	Maj 2nd MA Infy BvtLTC	MA	03783
Francis, Owen	1st Lt. 57th Ohio Infy	OH	07430
Frank, Adam	Asst Surg. USN	PA	00767
Frank, Emil	1st Lt. 52nd NY Infy	NY	04068
Frank, Mayer	Capt. 82nd IL Infy	IL	10385
Frank, Royal T.	BG USA	DC	01881-2204
Frankle, Jones	Col. 2nd MA H Arty BvtBG	MA	10714
Franklin, Edward C.	Surg. USV	MO	04266
Franklin, George M.	Capt. AAG USV	PA	02101
Franklin, Nelson G.	Maj 45th OH Infy	NE	04312
Franklin, Samuel R.	Commodore USN	PA	00807
Franklin, Walter S.	LTC AIG BvtCol.	DC	06872
Franklin, William B.	MG USV	NY	00789
Franklin, William H.	Capt. 10th NJ Infy	CA	11231
Fraser, Alexander V.	Passed Asst. Eng. USN	NY	08646
Fraser, Dwight	Capt. 128th IN Infy BvtMaj	IN	13994
Fraser, Joshua	2nd Lt. 128th IN Infy	IN	13995
Fraunfelter, Elias	Capt. 120th OH Infy	OH	03196
Frazee, John H.	Chap 3rd NJ Cav	OH	08704
Frazee, John N.	LTC 150th OH Infy	OH	08995
Frazee, John W.	Maj 119th USCT BvtCol.	OH	06649
Frazer, Andrew S.	1st Lt. 34th OH Infy	OH	03483
Frazer, John W.	2nd Lt. 15th NY Cav	CA	06153
Frazer, Persifor	Act Ensign USN	PA	01756
Frazier, Nalbro	Capt. 2nd PA Cav	PA	00070
Frazier, William W.	Capt. 6th PA Cav	PA	05493
Frederick, Calvin H.	LTC 59th IL Infy BvtBG	NE	03925
Frederick, George W.	LTC 209th PA Infy BvtCol.	PA	02582
Freeborn, Thomas	Capt. 7th NY Cav	NY	00793
Freeman, Charles A.	1st Lt. 1st WV Infy	OH	07937
Freeman, Edwin	Surg. USV	OH	13465
Freeman, George P.	1st Lt. 25th NJ Infy	MA	17965
Freeman, George W.	Capt. 11th IL Cav	CO	11276
Freeman, Henry B.	BG USA	KS	03564 (Dup)
Freeman, Henry V.	Capt. 12th USCT	IL	03860

Name	Rank	Commandery	Insignia No.
Freeman, Jason E.	2nd Lt. 10th VT Infy	CO	08901
Freeman, Joseph H.	Capt. 14th ME Infy	IL	12225
Frees, Benjamin M.	Capt. 38th WI Infy	IL	07554
Freeze, John W.	Capt. 1st ME Cav	CA	08881
French, Charles A.	Act Vol. Commander USN	CA	14001
French, Edward L.	1st Lt. 149th IL Infy	CA	17612
French, George F.	Surg. BvtLTC USV	MN	05859
French, George Foster	1st Lt. 8th VT Infy	ME	08589
French, George H.	1st Lt. VRC BvtMaj	DC	12547
French, Horace	Capt. 3rd VT Infy	VT	16906
French, John F.	1st Lt. 21st CT Infy	MN	16734
French, John W.	Col. 22nd Infy USA	CA	04433
French, Lyman P.	1st Lt. USMC	MA	01668
French, Peter	Maj 46th NY Infy BvtCol.	NY	01357
French, Simeon W.	1st Lt. RCS 3rd PA Cav	MO	11069
French, Walton W.	Capt. 115th NY Infy	OH	14212
French, William H.	MG USV	CA	01380
French, William H.	Capt. CS BvtMaj USV	IL	07829
French, Winsor B.	LTC 77th NY Infy BvtBG	NY	04342
Freshour, William	Capt. 8th OH Cav	OH	08603
Freudenberg, Charles G.	LTC BvtCol. USA	DC	02351
Freudenreich, George A.	2nd Lt. Hatch's Ind. Co. MN Cav	MN	10568
Frick, Abraham P.	Surg. 103rd PA Infy	PA	07057
Frick, Alexander J.	Capt. 84th PA Infy	PA	16803
Frick, Charles A.	Capt. 9th IA Cav	IA	11221
Frick, George C.	1st Lt. 7th NY Infy	NY	00794
Frick, John J.	2nd Lt. 130th PA Infy	PA	14633
Friedman, David	Capt. 108th OH Infy	OH	09028
Friesner, William S.	LTC 58th OH Infy	OH	06518
Frink, Charles S.	Surg. BvtLTC USV	IN	06594
Frink, H.A.	BvtBG USA	PA	00072
Frink, Norris J.	Maj 26th MI Infy BvtLTC	MI	05275
Frisbie, Alvah L.	Chap 20th CT Infy	IA	05651
Frisbie, James S.	1st Lt. Adj. 53rd WI Infy	WI	07197
Frisbie, William	Capt. 8th NY Cav	MN	07824
Fritsch, Charles R.	2nd Lt. 3rd Res. Corps MO Infy	MO	05702
Frost, Carlton P.	Surg. 15th VT Infy	MA	11289
Frost, Frank P.	1st Lt. 107th NY Infy	NY	10758
Frothingham, Ward B.	1st Lt. 59th MA Infy	MA	06635
Frothingham, William	Surg. 44th NY Infy	NY	01838
Frow, Thomas J.	Capt. 1st PA Cav	PA	07858
Frowe, Samuel S.	Capt. 18th WI Infy	IL	04155
Fry, Benjamin St. J.	Chap 63rd OH Infy	MO	05889
Fry, James B.	BG USV BvtMG USA	NY	08350
Fry, William H.	Maj 16th PA Cav BvtLTC	PA	00024
Frye, Moses M.	1st Lt. 39th USCT	NY	10759
Fryer, Blencowe E.	Col. USA	MO	04579
Fuger, Frederick	LTC USA	DC	03668

The Roster

Name	Rank	Commandery	Insignia No.
Fuller, Allen C.	3rd Class (Adj. Gen. IL)	IL	06072
Fuller, Andrew J.	BvtCapt. USV	CA	17809
Fuller, Austin W.	2nd Lt. 10th VT Infy BvtCapt.	VT	09166
Fuller, Charles A.	2nd Lt. 11th ME Infy	MA	11204
Fuller, Charles E.	LTC QM USV	MA	01466
Fuller, Charles J.	Capt. 13th CT Infy	MA	10585
Fuller, Edward M.	Maj 39th USCT	IL	15133
Fuller, Eugene C.	2nd Lt. 8th NY H Arty	IL	15846
Fuller, Ezra B.	LTC USA	DC	11553
Fuller, Frederick	2nd Lt. 52nd PA Infy	PA	11714
Fuller, Henry W.	Col. 75th USCT BvtBG	MA	01169
Fuller, James S.	1st Lt. 3rd NY L Arty	NY	13055
Fuller, Jesse B.	Capt. 1st MI L Arty BvtLTC	CA	02651
Fuller, John W.	BG BvtMG USV	OH	02884
Fuller, Sidney L.	Surg. 24th IL Infy	IL	01572
Fuller, Stephen E.	Surg. BvtLTC USV	NY	06232
Fuller, Thomas P.	Capt. 93rd NY Infy	CA	03935
Fuller, Truman K.	Capt. 75th NY Infy	NY	10760
Fuller, William G	Capt. AQM BvtLTC USV	OH	05751
Fullerton, Joseph S.	LTC AAG BvtBG USV	DC	04015
Fullerton, Thomas C.	Capt. 64th IL Infy	IL	06401
Fullwood, Samuel L.	Capt. 102nd PA Infy	PA	08965
Fulmer, David M.	Passed Asst. Eng. USN	PA	08212
Fulton, Christopher C.	1st Lt. 17th USCT	CA	09259
Fulton, James	Pay Director USN	DC	05306
Fundenberg, Walter F.	Surg. 176th PA Infy	PA	09974
Furay, John B.	1st Lt. 11th OH Cav	NE	04305
Furey, John	Paymaster USN	NY	08104
Furey, John V.	BG USA	PA	00451 (Dup)
Furley, Charles C.	Asst Surg. 2nd CA Cav	KS	04876
Furnas, Robert W.	Col. 2nd NE Cav	NE	0557i0
Furness, Frank	Capt. 6th PA Cav	PA	07058
Furness, William Eliot	Maj Jdge Adv USV	IL	02008
Fyffe, Joseph P.	Capt. USN	PA	00905
Fyler, Orsamus R.	1st Lt. 2nd CT H Arty	DC	11872
Gable, William	1st Lt. 101st USCT	PA	04165
Gabriel, Jonas F.	Surg. 11th OH Infy	OH	10025
Gaebel, F.A.	BvtLTC USV	PA	00092
Gafney, Charles B.	1st Lt. 13th NH Infy	MA	07961
Gage, Joseph S.	BvtBG USV	CA	07408
Gageby, James H.	Maj 12th Infy USA	NE	11090
Gager, Edwin V.	Act Master USN	NY	08105
Gahagan, Andrew J.	1st Lt. RQM 1st TN Cav	OH	06123
Gaines, Theopolis	Maj	PA	02287
Gair, Robert	Capt. 79th NY Infy	NY	07606
Galbraith, Alvan S.	1st Lt. 2nd Infy BvtMaj USA	OH	10054
Galbraith, Franklin B.	Surg. 31st MI Infy	MI	04892
Galbraith, Frederick W.	Capt. ADC BvtLTC USV	MA	01669

The Roster

Name	Rank	Commandery	Insignia No.
Galbraith, William J.	1st Lt. Sig. Corps USV	WA	02219
Gale, George A.	Capt. 33rd NY Infy	IL	10528
Gallagher, Joseph P.	Act Ensign USN	CA	10244
Gallaher, Benjamin D.	1st Lt. 152nd NY Infy	NY	01907
Gallaher, William	1st. Lt. 3rd Indian Home Guard KS Infy	KS	07236
Galligher, Michael	1st Lt. 16th PA Infy	OH	04196
Galloupe, Isaac F.	Surg. 17th MA Infy BvtLTC	MA	06685
Galloway, John	Ist Lt. RCS 8th PA Cav	PA	12873
Gallup, James H.	Capt. 55th OH Infy	CO	14810
Galt, Smith P.	Capt. 122nd PA Infy	MO	07380
Galucia, Warren B.	Capt. 56th MA Infy	MA	02644
Galvin, Edward I.	Chap 42nd MA Infy	CA	14204
Galwey, Thomas F.	1st Lt. 8th OH Infy	NY	11041
Gambee, Theodore W.	Capt. 10th TN Cav	OH	14659
Gamble, George H.	Capt. 9th Cav USA	CA	06669
Gandolfo, John B.	LTC 178th NY Infy	MO	02818
Gano, Jacob W.	1st Lt. 75th OH Infy	OH	03567
Gansevoort, Henry S.	Col. 13th NY Cav BvtBG	MA	00759
Gardiner, Asa Bird	LTC USA	NY	00586
Gardiner, Curtis C.	Maj 27th NY Infy BvtCol.	MO	04281
Gardiner, J. Grahame	1st Lt. Adj. 4th USCT	NY	09422
Gardner, Charles Frederic	Act Asst Paymaster USN	NY	06425
Gardner, Edwin F.	Col. USA	CA	03104
Gardner, Harrison	1st Lt. 45th MA Infy	MA	04493
Gardner, Hezekiah	Capt. 44th Infy BvtCol. USA	DC	02246
Gardner, Ira B.	Capt. 14th ME Infy BvtLTC	ME	11474
Gardner, John B., Jr.	1st Lt. RCS 3rd NY Cav	NY	07461
Gardner, John W.	Passed Asst. Eng. USN	NY	08490
Gardner, Peter G.	1st Lt. 15th OH Infy	IL	08293
Gardner, Robert P.	Capt. 1st VRC	NY	01207
Gardner, William H.	LTC Dept. Surg. Gen. USA	DC	02583
Gardner, William H.	Capt. 30th MA Infy	NE	07836
Gardner, William H.	Commodore USN	PA	00499-599
Garland, William J.	Capt. 24th IL Infy	MO	07810
Garman, Charles P.	Capt. 113th OH Infy	OH	10031
Garner, Abram B.	Maj 15th PA Cav	NY	07975
Garnsey, Frank A.	Capt. 2nd ME Infy	ME	10933
Garrard, Jeptha	Col. 1st USC Cav BvtBG	OH	02977 (Dup)
Garretson, Charles	Capt. AQM USV	PA	01200
Garretson, George A.	2nd Lt. 4th Arty USA BG USV	OH	03264
Garrett, George L.	2nd Lt. 4th MO Cav	PA	13663
Garrett, Joseph W.	Capt. 69th PA Infy	PA	08213
Garretty, Frank D.	Maj USA	MN	03446
Garrigus, Milton	Capt. 142nd IN Infy	IN	10367
Garvey, Thomas	Capt. 1st Cav USA	CA	03106
Garvin, Benjamin F.	Chief Eng. USN	PA	00692
Gary, Marco B.	Capt. 1st OH L Arty	OH	08029
Gaskell, Charles B.	Col. 81st USCT	NY	13828

Name	Rank	Commandery	Insignia No.
Gaskell, Henry W.	1st Lt. 12th NJ Infy	PA	03591
Gaston, Alanson D.	Capt. 26th IA Infy	DC	13074
Gaston, William J.	2nd Lt. 47th IA Infy	IA	10310
Gatch, Asbury P.	Capt. 9th OH Cav	OH	16044
Gatch, Conduce H.	LTC 135th OH Infy	IA	06541
Gates, Clarence D.	1st Lt. Adj. 1st VT Cav	VT	11385
Gates, Howard E.	Surg. 189th NY	CO	06008
Gaul, Edward L.	LTC 159th NY Infy	NY	02896
Gaul, Joseph L.	1st Lt. 5th OH Infy	OH	06326
Gause, Harlan	Capt. 4th DE Infy BvtLTC	PA	10867
Gausline, Charles W.	1st Lt. 2nd PA H Arty	CA	03637
Gawthrop, Alfred	Capt. 7th DE Infy	PA	09275
Gaylord, Augustus	3rd Class (Adj. Gen WI)	WI	06618
Geary, Edward C.	LTC 32nd USCT	MN	11905
Geary, John W.	BG BvtMG USV	PA	00198
Geary, William L.	Maj Commissary USA	CA	02103
Geddes, James L.	Col. 8th IA Infy BvtBG	IA	05436
Gein, Louis H.	2nd Lt. 55th NY Infy	NY	12785
Gelray, Joseph W.	Maj 4th MA H Arty BvtLTC USA	MA	01495
Gentry, William F.	LTC 25th Infy USA	MN	03850
Gentsch, Charles	1st Lt. RQM 51st OH Infy	OH	08380
Geoghegan, John D.	1st Lt. 10th Infy USA	WA	05449
George, Milo	LTC 1st Battn. NV Cav	IL	09483
Geraughty, Patrick	Capt. 17th WI Infy	KS	04818
Gere, Thomas P.	1st Lt. Adj. 5th MN Infy	IA	11142
Gerlach, William	LTC USA	MN	08433
Gerrish, David F.	Act 1st Asst Eng. USN	PA	10133
Gerry, Edeon	Maj 12th PA Cav	OR	06390
Gest, Lewis H.	Capt. 26th IN Infy	KS	17596
Getchell, Frank H.	Asst Surg. 3rd ME Infy	PA	05495
Getty, George W.	BG USV BvtMG USA	DC	02602
Getty, James S.	Capt. 44th IN Infy	CA	17810
Gheen, Edward H.	RAdm USN	DC	16108
Gherardi, Bancroft	RAdm USN	PA	00177
Ghiselin, James T.	Maj Surg. BvtCol. USA	CA	06926
Ghost, William C.	2nd Lt. 39th IA Infy	CO	08372
Gibbon, John	MG USV BG USA	OR	06388
Gibbon, William H.	Surg. 15th IA Infy BvtLTC	IA	07140
Gibbons, William C.	1st Lt. 79th USCT	CA	17811
Gibbs, John S.	Capt. 38th USCT BvtMaj	DC	03319
Gibbs, Theodore K.	1st Lt. 1st Arty BvtMaj USA	NY	08944
Gibson, Edwin O.	Capt. 10th Infy USA	NY	07779
Gibson, Fenton W.	2nd Lt. 1st New Orleans Infy	OH	08174
Gibson, Hanson C.	2nd Lt. 165th NY Infy	NY	07780
Gibson, Philip H.	2nd Lt. 13th Infy USA	PA	00968
Gibson, Theodore C.	Maj 53rd IL Infy	IL	14345
Gibson, William	Capt. Purnell Legion MD Infy	DC	03981
Gibson, William C.	Act Asst Eng. USN	PA	00973

The Roster

Name	Rank	Commandery	Insignia No.
Gibson, William H.	Col. 49th OH Infy BvtBG	OH	03566
Gibson, William R.	Col. Asst Paymaster Gen. USA	DC	08316
Giddings, Benjamin F.	Capt. 17th VT Infy	CA	03465
Giddings, Edward L.	Capt. 40th MA Infy	MA	01671
Gifford, Frederick S.	1st Lt. 3rd MA H Arty	MA	01218
Gifford, John H.	Capt. USA	ME	10472
Gift, John W.	Capt. 12th IA Infy	IL	08422
Gihon, Albert L.	Med. Director USN	NY	07462
Gilbert, Calvin	Capt. CS BvtMaj USV	PA	11536
Gilbert, Charles C.	BG USV	PA	02933
Gilbert, Daniel D.	Asst Surg. USN	MA	01751
Gilbert, Foster B.	Act Asst Paymaster USN	NY	05404
Gilbert, Franklin B.	Capt. 91st PA Infy	PA	00004
Gilbert, Franklin T.	LTC 15th IL Infy	OR	05332
Gilbert, Joseph	Capt. 91st PA Infy	PA	05494
Gilbert, William W.	LTC USA	NY	06009
Gilbreath, Erasmus C.	Maj 9th Infy USA	PA	08812
Gilchrist, Alexander	Capt. 148th IN Infy	IN	12334
Gilchrist, George M.	Capt. 3rd IN Cav	IA	07446
Gilder, Wilber F.	1st Lt. 98th USCT	PA	09495
Gildersleeve, Henry A.	BvtLTC USV	NY	No Number
Gile, David H.	Capt. ADC USV	IL	01999
Gile, George W.	Col. USA BvtBG	PA	02743
Gile, William A.	Capt. 117th USCT	MA	02520
Giles, Isaac W.	2nd Lt. 7th MA Infy	MA	10715
Giles, Joseph J.	1st Lt. 39th MA Infy	MA	10119
Gilfillan, James	Col. 11th MN Infy	MN	05427
Gilges, James W.	Capt. 113th USCT	KS	06297
Gill, Adolphus W. H.	Capt. 84th NY Infy BvtMaj	NY	00942
Gill, William H.	Military Storekpr. USA	PA	00765
Gillespie, Charles B.	Capt. 78th PA Infy	PA	15309
Gillespie, George L.	MG USA	DC	04061
Gillespie, George W.	2nd Lt. 102nd PA Infy	CA	17613
Gillespie, John W.	Capt. 57th PA Infy	PA	07859
Gillespie, Robert	Capt. 26th PA Infy	PA	10628
Gillespie, William K.	Capt. 4th PA Cav	PA	11830
Gillett, Charles W.	1st Lt. Adj. 86th NY Infy	NY	11747
Gillett, Edward A.	Capt. 1st CT H Arty	PA	02288 (Dup)
Gillett, Simeon P.	Lt. Commander USN	IN	06436
Gillette, Daniel G.	2nd Lt. 176th NY Infy	NY	12002
Gillette, Fidelio B.	Surg. 9th NJ Infy	NY	06630
Gillette, Theodore W.	1st Lt. RCS 4th WI Cav	WA	13016
Gillingham, Frank C.	1st Lt. 119th PA Infy	PA	08745
Gillis, George H.	2nd Lt. 77th NY Infy BvtCapt.	NY	01789
Gillis, James	Col. AQM Gen. USA	DC	04802
Gillis, James H.	Commodore USN	DC	06570
Gillis, John P.	Commodore USN	PA	00267
Gillman, Coleman	Capt. 173rd OH Infy	OH	08842

Name	Rank	Commandery	Insignia No.
Gillpatrick, James H.	LTC 83rd USCT BvtCol.	KS	04429
Gilman, Augustus H.	Paymaster USN	PA	00591
Gilman, George E.	1st Lt. 1st NH Cav	MI	04891 (Dup)
Gilman, Jeremiah H.	Col. USA	DC	02509
Gilman, John T.	Capt. 22nd ME Infy	ME	11094
Gilman, Lemuel O.	LTC 15th IL Infy	IL	09201
Gilmore, David McK	Capt. 3rd PA Cav	MN	03835
Gilmore, Homer G.	Capt. 10th MA Infy BvtMaj	MA	01682
Gilmore, James R.	Capt. AQM BvtLTC USV	NY	02055
Gilmore, John C.	BG USA	DC	08679
Gilmour, Henry L.	Capt. CS BvtMaj USV	PA	09276
Gilruth, Isaac N.	LTC 27th OH Infy	OH	06646
Gilson, Norman S.	LTC 58th USCT BvtCol.	WI	04120
Ginty, George C.	Col. 47th WI Infy BvtBG	WI	05268
Gist, George W.	Col. 1st US Vet. Vol. Infy	DC	07675
Given, Josiah	Col. 74th OH Infy BvtBG	IA	06540
Givin, Alexander W.	1st Lt. 114th PA Infy BvtCapt.	PA	06765
Gladding, Charles	1st Lt. 72nd IL Infy	CA	05329
Glafcke, Herman	Maj 22nd CT Infy	CO	14047
Glasgow, Samuel L.	BvtBG USV	IA	15346 (Dup)
Glass, Henry	RAdm USN	CA	01117
Glassford, Henry A.	Act Vol. Lt. USN	NY	02216
Glazier, N. Newton	1st Lt. 1st VT H Arty	MA	14182
Gleason, Charles H.	1st Lt. Adj. 7th IN Cav	MO	04369
Gleason, Daniel H.L.	Capt. 1st MA Cav	MA	03510
Gleason, Henry J.	Capt. 72nd IL Infy	IL	04145
Gleason, Levi	Chap 2nd MN Infy	MN	08610
Glen, James	2nd Lt. 2nd MD Infy	MD	14560
Glenn, George E.	Col. Asst Paymaster Gen. USA	NY	11532
Glenn, John F.	Col. 23rd PA Infy	PA	13821
Glenn, William J.	Capt. 61st PA Infy Col. 14th PA Infy	PA	07639
Glidden, Oakman F.	2nd Lt. 2nd ME Cav	ME	17978
Glisson, Oliver S.	RAdm USN	PA	00180
Glover, John J.	Capt. 15th OH Infy	DC	12701
Glover, Samuel C.	Capt. CS BvtMaj USV	IL	14554
Gobin, John P.S.	Col. 47th PA Infy BvtBG:BG USV	PA	03793
Gochenauer, David	Capt. 202nd PA Infy	CA	12199
Goddard, Calvin	LTC AAG USV	NY	02766
Goddard, Charles E.	BvtMaj USA	PA	00964
Goddard, Charles G.	Capt. 17th Infy USA	PA	01183
Goddard, Henry P.	Capt. 14th CT Infy	MD	01521
Goddard, Henry S.	Maj Paymaster USV	PA	00032
Goddard, Joseph A.	Capt. 4th OH Cav	IN	11896
Goddard, Kingston, Jr.	Act Asst Surg. USN	PA	01407
Goddard, Paul L.	Capt. 8th PA Cav	PA	00294
Goddard, Robert H.I.	Capt. ADC BvtLTC USV	MA	01142
Goddard, William	Maj 1st RI Infy BvtCol.	MA	01900
Godfrey, Edward S.	Col. 9th Cav USA	KS	03966

Name	Rank	Commandery	Insignia No.
Godfrey, George L.	LTC 1st AL Cav	IA	05435
Godfrey, Henry T.	Asst Surg. 156th IL Infy	IL	14730
Godman, John M.	Capt. 96th OH Infy	OH	12972
Godon, Sylvanus W.	RAdm USN	PA	00538
Godwin, Edward A.	Col. 14th Cav USA	DC	04212
Goebel, August	Capt. 2nd MI Infy	MI	03873
Goff, Nathan, Jr.	Col. 37th USCT BvtBG	MA	03148
Gold, Cornelius B.	Act Asst Paymaster USN	NY	12247
Golden, Henry C.	1st Lt. 11th NY Infy	IA	07596
Golden, Michael A.	1st Lt. 6th PA Cav	PA	08746
Goldie, William	Capt. AQM BvtLTC USV	IL	08423
Goldsborough, John R.	Commodore USN	PA	00891
Goldsborough, Worthington	Pay Inspector USN	PA	05721
Goldsmith, Edwin	1st Lt. Adj. 100th IN Infy	OH	14466
Goldsmith, Joseph	1st Lt. RQM 15th OH Infy	OH	07765
Goldsmith, Sanford K.	Capt. 59th MA Infy	MA	03676
Gondon, Louis N.	1st Lt. 2nd Regt. Potomac Home Brig. MD	NE	08087
Gonings, H.H.	Lt. Commander USN	NY	00537
Good, Joseph	LTC 108th OH Infy	OH	07433
Goodale, Greenleaf A.	BG USA	MA	03662
Goodale, Warren	1st Lt. 114th USCT BvtCapt	CA	04522
Goodall, Wallace B.	1st Lt. 9th IA Cav	NE	09369
Goodbrake, Christopher	Surg. 20th IL Infy	IL	05131
Goodell, Arthur A.	BvtBG	MA	00837
Goodell, Henry H.	1st Lt. 25th CT Infy	MA	09473
Goodell, John B.	Capt. 51st MA Infy	MA	11361
Goodhue, Justin A.	2nd Lt. 26th OH Infy	CA	04622
Goodhue, Stephen W.	Capt. 68th USCT	IL	11602
Gooding, Henry C.	1st Lt. 122nd IL Infy	CA	16297
Goodloe, Green Clay	Col. Paymaster USMC	DC	02166
Goodloe, William C.	Capt. AAG USV	OH	02885
Goodman, Andrew T.	Maj 215th PA Infy	PA	00104
Goodman, H. Earnest	Col. Med. Director USV	PA	00201
Goodman, James B.	1st Lt. 35th PA Infy BvtCapt	IL	06936
Goodman, Joseph E.	2nd Lt. VRC	PA	01039
Goodman, Richard F.	Act Asst Paymaster USN	NY	13392 (Dup)
Goodman, Samuel	1st Lt. Adj. 28th PA Infy BvtCol.	PA	01037
Goodman, Theodore	Capt. 2nd CA Cav	CA	01038
Goodnow, Edgar W.	1st Lt. 4th MA Cav	OH	07027
Goodnow, James	LTC 12th IN Infy	MN	08563
Goodrell, Mancil C.	Col. USMC	DC	02357
Goodrell, William H.	Capt. 15th IA Infy BvtMaj	IA	07167
Goodrich, Benjamin F.	Asst Surg. 35th NY Infy	OH	03298
Goodrich, Caspar F.	RAdm USN	DC	12179
Goodrich, Elam T.	Capt. 8th CT Infy	NY	06015
Goodrich, George E.	Capt. 34th MA Infy	MA	01500
Goodrich, Ira B.	1st Lt. 21st MA Infy	MA	10510
Goodrich, John E.	Chap 1st VT Cav	VT	09163

THE ROSTER

Name	Rank	Commandery	Insignia No.
Goodrich, William	1st Lt. 15th CT Infy	PA	06764
Goodrich, Willis L.	Capt. 107th USCT BvtMaj	NY	14622
Goodspeed, Joseph M.	1st Lt. 75th OH Infy	OH	02971
Goodspeed, Wilbur F.	Maj 1st L Arty	OH	03039
Goodwillie, Thomas	1st Lt. Adj. 150th OH Infy	MD	03965
Goodwin William W.	Act Asst Paymaster USN	PA	01162
Goodwin, Almon	2nd Lt. 19th ME Infy	NY	07463
Goodwin, David M.	Surg. 3rd VT Infy	MN	08927
Goodwin, Edward M.	Act Asst Surg. USN	OH	03955
Goodwin, Francis E.	Capt. 25th MA Infy	MA	13928
Goodyear, Charles P.	1st Lt. 9th USCT	DC	08813
Gordon, Albert C.	Med. Director USN	PA	00546
Gordon, Charles G.	Capt. 6th Cav USA	DC	08696
Gordon, David S.	BG USA	DC	03440
Gordon, George H.	BG BvtMG USV	MA	01139
Gordon, John A.	Capt. 4th MI Infy	CA	02151
Gordon, John A.	Capt. 15th WI Infy	NE	05759
Gordon, Leonard J.	1st Lt. Adj. 6th NJ Infy	NY	11914
Gordon, Mount A.	1st Lt. 19th KS Cav	CA	16615
Gordon, Roy T.	1st Lt. USA	NY	07090
Gordon, Seth C.	Surg. 1st LA Infy	ME	02383
Gorham, Selden H.	LTC 2nd MI Cav	MI	05172
Gorley, Hugh A.	Capt. 1st CA Infy	CA	09360
Gorman, Richard L.	Capt. 34th NY Infy	MN	04238
Gorsuch, Joseph T.	Capt. 97th OH Infy	OH	07947
Goss, Henry	Capt. 14th NY Infy	MO	05051
Gott, Benjamin F.	Col. 174th NY Infy	NY	02900
Gottschalk, Frederick	Capt. 1st IA Infy	MO	10644
Gottschall, Oscar M.	1st Lt. 93rd OH Infy	OH	02950
Gould, Charles G.	Capt. 5th VT Infy BvtMaj	DC	08814
Gould, Ezra P.	Maj 59th MA Infy	PA	01679
Gould, Francis	1st Lt. 40th NY Infy	MA	01518
Gould, George S.	2nd Lt. 68th IN Infy	CA	14322
Gould, J. Henry	Capt. 3rd RI H Arty	MA	05800
Gould, John M.	Maj 29 ME Infy	ME	02505
Gould, John T.	2nd Lt. 6th MI Cav	MI	13969
Gould, Ozro B.	Capt. 55th OH Infy	MN	06074
Gould, William O.	Maj 14th KS Cav	CA	02079
Gould, William P.	Maj Paymaster USA BvtLTC	IN	07156
Goulding, Joseph H.	1st Lt. 6th USCT	VT	08734
Gourard, George E.	BvtLTC USV	NY	10426
Gove, E. Aaron	1st Lt. Adj. 33rd IL Infy BvtMaj	CO	05957
Gove, Frank M.	Lt. USN	WI	01566
Gove, Richard L.	1st Lt. Adj. 1st WI Cav	WI	06565
Gove, Wesley A.	Capt. 3rd MA Cav	MA	02242
Gowdy, William F.	Capt. 47th IL Infy	CA	15536
Grace, John	Capt. 34th OH Infy	OH	07842
Grace, Peter	Capt. 83rd PA Infy	PA	10261

The Roster

Name	Rank	Commandery	Insignia No.
Graeffe, Richard A.	Capt. 47th PA Infy	MI	07821
Grafly, Daniel W.	1st Asst Eng. USN	PA	01952
Gragg, Isaac P.	1st Lt. 61st MA Infy BvtCapt	MA	03160
Graham, Andrew S.	Capt. 9th NY Infy	OH	10786
Graham, Charles C.	1st Lt. 29th ME Infy BvtCapt	ME	11240
Graham, Charles K.	BG BvtMG USV	NY	00578
Graham, George	1st Lt. 37th WI Infy	WI	04298
Graham, George R.	Maj USMC	DC	02659
Graham, George R.	1st Lt. 5th MD Infy	MD	08584
Graham, Harvey	BvtBG USV	IL	15182
Graham, James D.	Commander USN	CA	06925
Graham, James S.	Capt. 21st NY Cav	NY	08647
Graham, John H.	Capt. 5th NY H Arty BvtLTC	NY	06238
Graham, John W.	Capt. 211th PA Infy	CO	09740
Graham, Joseph H.	Capt. 13th IL Cav	MI	12082
Graham, Matthew J.	1st Lt. 9th NY Infy	NY	12554
Graham, Niel F.	Surg. 12th OH Infy	DC	02828
Graham, Thomas	Maj 8th IN Cav	IN	12680
Graham, Thomas	Capt. 71st NY Infy	PA	00011
Graham, William G.	Capt. 143rd PA Infy	PA	06252
Graham, William Montrose	BG USA MG USV	CA	09531
Graham, William R.	2nd Lt. 3rd WI Cav MajPaymstr USV	IA	13802
Graham, Ziba B.	1st Lt. 16th MI Infy	MI	05270
Gramlich, Christian F.	1st Lt. 2nd PA H Arty	PA	06461
Granger, Gordon	MG USV	NY	00642
Granger, James N.	1st Lt. 2nd RI Infy	MA	10716
Granger, Moses M.	LTC 122nd OH Infy BvtCol.	OH	05377
Granger, Warren	LTC 100th NY Infy	MN	06497
Granger, William W.	Asst Surg. 3rd MO Cav	DC	03584
Grant, Charles E.	Capt. 55th MA Infy BvtMaj	MA	10912
Grant, Claudius B.	LTC 20th MI Infy	MI	05171
Grant, Cyrus	LTC 31st OH Infy	OH	08605
Grant, Gabriel	Surg. USV	NY	00842
Grant, George W.	1st Lt. 88th PA Infy	MN	10996
Grant, Heman W.	1st Lt. 4th MI Cav	OH	14029
Grant, Henry C.	1st Lt. 1st OH L Arty	OH	12837
Grant, Hiram L.	Maj 6th CT Infy	DC	13723
Grant, James	1st Lt. 36th NY Infy	NY	06169
Grant, John	2nd Lt. 38th NJ Infy	NE	07542
Grant, Lewis A.	BG BvtMG US	MN	04584
Grant, Oscar B.	1st Lt. USMC	PA	14372
Grant, Robert E.	1st Lt. 157th NY Infy	DC	12493
Grant, Ulysses S.	General USA	NY	02006
Grant, William	1st Lt. Adj. 91st IL Infy	OH	08035
Grantman, William	LTC 13th NH Infy	MA	05157
Graves, Charles H.	Maj AAG USV BvtLTC USA	MN	04041
Graves, Cyrus E.	Capt. 33rd MA Infy BvtMaj	MA	03845
Graves, Edward P.	Capt. AQM BvtMaj USV	NY	09565

Name	Rank	Commandery	Insignia No.
Graves, George E.	Capt. CS USV	DC	09037
Graves, William P.	Capt. 2nd Arty BvtMaj USA	DC	03730
Gray, A. Judson	Asst Surg. 5th USCT	CA	09840
Gray, Albert Z.	Chap 4th MA Cav	IL	05919
Gray, Allen W.	1st Lt. 51st IL Infy	IL	18013
Gray, Augustus	1st Lt. 12th CT Infy	NY	15868
Gray, Charles C.	2nd Lt. 1st RI L Arty	MA	09602
Gray, Clark	Capt. 93rd IL Infy	CO	05581
Gray, Edmund B.	Col. 28th WI Infy	WI	11397
Gray, F. Edward	Capt. 37th MA Infy	CA	01743
Gray, George N.	2nd Lt. 53rd OH Infy	OH	09592
Gray, James R.	1st Lt. 7th MO Cav	MO	15400
Gray, John B.	Col. 1st Infy MO State Militia	NY	10495
Gray, John C.	Maj Jdge Adv USV	MA	10717
Gray, John D.	Capt. CS BvtMaj USV	CA	09406
Gray, John F.S.	Capt. AAG USV	CA	05187
Gray, O.B.	1st Lt. 16th VRC	PA	00089
Gray, Philander R.	1st Lt. RQM 121st PA Infy	NY	06631
Gray, Samuel F.	LTC 49th OH Infy	IN	10795
Gray, Theodore	Capt. 17th CT Infy	NY	07607
Graybill, George	2nd Lt. 3rd USCT	PA	13664
Greeley, Carlos S.	3rd Class (Treas. West. Sanitary Com)	MO	05055
Greeley, Edwin S.	Col. 10th CT Infy BvtBG	NY	02200
Greeley, Moses R.	Asst Surg. 3rd MN Infy	MA	08058
Greely, Adolphus W.	MG USA	DC	04556
Green, Alfred L.	Surg. 36th PA Infy	PA	00616
Green, Charles L.	Passed Asst Surg. USN	MA	03504
Green, David B.	LTC 37th Infy PA Militia	PA	08216
Green, Edward H.	Capt. 107th PA Infy BvtMaj	MI	12526
Green, Edward N.	1st Lt. 9th NJ Infy	PA	15471
Green, George	Maj 78th IL Infy	IL	03861
Green, George B.	1st Lt. 23rd MI Infy	MI	05579
Green, Harry H.	Capt. 2nd IA Infy	IA	12657
Green, James G.	RAdm USN	NY	09423
Green, John P.	Capt. AAG USV	PA	03224
Green, Milbrey	1st Lt. 10th Batt MA L Arty BvtMaj	MA	01618
Green, Samuel A.	BvtLTC USV	MA	17220
Green, Samuel K.	Capt. 8th NY H Arty	NY	16152
Green, William	1st Lt. 37th WI Infy	KS	11035
Green, William H.	Capt. 17th ME Infy BvtMaj	ME	08336
Greenawalt, John C.	2nd Lt. 73rd IN Infy	DC	07800
Greene, Albert S.	Chief Eng. USN	PA	02102
Greene, Arthur M.	Maj 127th USCT	PA	16328
Greene, Charles H.	Capt. 17th Infy USA	CA	04092
Greene, Charles M.	1st Lt. 3rd AR Cav	MO	11129
Greene, Charles S.	LTC 61st PA Infy	PA	00041-1660
Greene, Charles T.	Maj USA	NY	12003
Greene, David M.	1st Asst Eng. USN	NY	02144

Name	Rank	Commandery	Insignia No.
Greene, George S.	BG BvtMG USV	NY	05520
Greene, Jacob L.	Maj AAG BvtLTC USV	NY	09126
Greene, Joseph S.	Asst Eng. USN	NY	11632
Greene, Levi R.	1st Asst Eng. USN	MA	01728
Greene, Oliver D.	Col. AAG BvtBG USA	CA	02955
Greene, Roger S.	Capt. 51st USCT	WA	16063
Greene, Thomas S.	Capt. 47th USCT	MO	05655
Greenhut, Joseph B.	Capt. 82nd IL Infy	IL	12748
Greenleaf, Charles D.	BG USA	CA	03073
Greenleaf, Edward E.	1st Lt. 1st Batt VT L Arty	VT	09467
Greenleaf, Robert G.	Capt. Batt A Ore. L Arty	OR	13434
Greenleaf, William L.	1st Lt. 1st VT Cav	VT	09158
Greenlee, David R.	Asst Surg. 5th PA H Arty	MI	10726
Greenman, John W.	1st Lt. 8th WI Cav	CA	04757
Greeno, Charles L.	Maj 7th PA Infy BvtLTC	OH	06884
Greenough, George G.	Col. Arty USA	MA	03806
Greenough, William S.	Capt. 18th NH Infy BvtMaj	MA	01450
Greer, James A.	Capt. USN	PA	00160
Gregg, Aaron T.	Capt. 140th PA Infy	PA	07048
Gregg, David McMurtrie	BG BvtMG USV	PA	00342
Gregg, J. Irvin	Col. 8th Cav USA BvtMG	PA	00378
Gregg, Thomas J.	Capt. 2nd Cav BvtMaj USA	PA	00935
Gregg, William L.	1st Lt. 3rd PA Cav	PA	02167
Gregory, Augustus C.	2nd Lt. 32nd WI Infy	IN	12758
Gregory, Henry P.	2nd Asst Eng. USN	CA	02857
Gregory, Henry S.	Act Asst Paymaster USN	MI	08894
Gregory, Hugh M.	Act Vol. Lt. USN	CA	04189
Gresham, Walter Q.	BG BvtMG USV	IL	02833
Greusel, Nicholas	Col. 36th IL Infy	IL	04826
Grier, David P.	Col. 77th IL lnfy BvtBG	MO	04294
Grier, John A.	Chief Eng. USN	IL	05722
Grier, Matthew C.	1st Lt. 4th Arty USA	MA	11290
Grier, William	Med. Director USN	DC	00790
Grier, William N.	Col. 3rd Cav BvtBG USA	NY	02046
Grierson, Benjamin H.	MG USV	MO	05364
Griest, Thomas	1st Lt. Ind.Co. PA Eng.	PA	07640
Griffin, George W.	Act Asst Paymaster	PA	00042
Griffin, Levi T.	Capt. 4th Mi Cav BvtMaj	MI	03422
Griffin, Michael	2nd Lt. 12th WI Infy	WI	06211
Griffin, Simon G.	BG BvtMG USV	MA	01289
Griffin, William F.	Capt. 49th USCT	MA	05931 (Dup)
Griffin, William H.	Capt. 102nd NY Infy	NY	08945
Griffing, George H.	Pay Inspector USN	PA	00341
Griffith, Lewis Edmund	2nd Lt. 192nd NY Infy	NY	15574
Griffith, William E.	Capt. 22nd PA Cav	DC	03171
Griffiths, Joseph M.	Col. 39th IA Infy	IA	14767
Griggs, Chauncey W.	Col. 3rd MN Infy	WA	11413
Grill, Frederick	1st Lt. 3rd PA H Arty	PA	08214

THE ROSTER

Name	Rank	Commandery	Insignia No.
Grimes, George S.	Co. Arty USA	CA	00717
Grimes, James F.	Capt. 17th Infy BvtLTC USA	MA	06992
Grimes, James McF.	Lt. Commander USN	IL	17103
Grimes, John	LTC 13th NJ Infy	NY	15575
Grimes, Silas	Maj 31st IN Infy	IN	12335
Grimm, John H.	2nd Lt. 32nd Batt NY L Arty	OH	11070
Grinager, Mons	Capt. 5th WI Infy	MN	06280
Grindlay, James G.	Col. 140th NY Infy BvtBG	NY	02212
Grinnell, H. Walton	Act Vol. Lt. USN	MA	05099
Griswold, Charles	Capt. 29th CT Infy	NY	10162
Griswold, Charles A.	Surg. 93rd IL lnfy	IL	13630
Griswold, Edward F.	Capt. 1st VT H Arty	PA	04944
Griswold, Elisha	Surg. BvtCol. USV	PA	06253
Griswold, Joseph B.	Ass. Surg. 4th MI Infy	MI	04011
Griswold, Norman W.	1st Lt. 75th USCT	CA	04864
Groenendyke, Edward	1st Lt. 97th IN Infy	CA	14972
Groesbeck, Stephen W.	BG USA	CA	03624
Grosh, Jeremiah M.	1st Lt. Adj. 89th IL Infy	PA	12981
Gross, Frank P.	1st Lt. 9th Cav USA	DC	03028
Grosse, Guy E.	Capt. 63rd PA Infy	CA	03112
Grosvenor, Charles H.	Col. 18th OH Infy BvtBG	OH	02771
Grosvenor, Samuel L.	1st. Lt. 36th OH Infy	OH	09750
Grout, Josiah	Maj 26th NY Cav	VT	09170
Grout, William W.	LTC 15th VT Infy	DC	02695
Grove, Abraham C.	Capt. 140th PA Infy	PA	12982
Grove, John H.	Surg. BvtLTC USV	PA	08215
Grubb, E. Burd	Col. 37th NJ Infy BvtBG	PA	01127
Grugan, Florence W.	1st Lt. Adj. 2nd PA H Arty	PA	02074
Grumley, Edward I.	Capt. USA	DC	07253
Grunwell, Alfred B.	1st Lt. 14th NY Infy BvtCapt	DC	13489
Guenther, Francis L.	BG USA	OH	02736
Guernsey, David W.	Act Asst Paymaster USN	MO	10521
Guernsey, Frank W.	Capt. 32nd WI Infy	WI	09320
Guest, John	Commodore USN	PA	00183
Guffin, Ross	Capt. 52nd IN Infy	MO	07748
Guild, Charles F.	Paymaster USN	PA	01098
Guiney, Patrick B.	Col. 9th MA Infy BvtBG	MA	01754
Guion, George M.	Col. 148th NY Infy	IL	09484
Gunn, Otis B.	Maj 4th KS Infy	MO	05218
Gunnell, Robert H.	Passed Asst. Eng. USN	DC	07676
Gunther, Arthur	Capt. 2nd KS Cav	WI	05020
Gurler, Henry B.	2nd Lt. 132nd IL Infy	IL	16421
Gurlitz, Augustus T.	1st Lt. 2nd KY Cav	NY	11042
Gurm, John T.	1st Lt. 21st KY Infy	OH	18130
Gushee, Edward M.	Chap 9th NH Infy	MA	11205
Guthrie, Alexander M.	2nd Lt. 4th Battn. OH Cav	PA	07860
Guthrie, James V.	Maj 19th IL Infy	OH	02774
Guthrie, John B.	Maj 15th Infy USA	DC	12702

Name	Rank	Commandery	Insignia No.
Guthrie, Thomas S.	Chap 152nd OH Infy	IN	08139
Guyer, Henry	Capt. 13th NJ Infy	NY	11559
Gwyn, James	Col. 118th PA Infy BvtMG	PA	00034
Gwynne, Thomas	Capt. 50th OH Infy	WI	02088
Haanel, Eugene E.F.R.	1st Lt. 2nd MD Vet. Vols.	MD	18395
Haas, Maximilian A.F.	1st Lt. Adj. 3rd MO Infy BvtCapt	IL	04133
Habighurst, Conrad J.	Chief Eng. USN	PA	06766
Hackett, Charles W.	Cap. 10th MN Infy	MN	03688
Hackett, Frank W.	Act Asst Paymaster USN	DC	10040
Hackett, Horatio B.	1st Lt. 81st PA Infy	PA	08455
Hackley, Charles E.	Surg. 2nd NY Cav	NY	06747
Hackney, William P.	Capt. 7th IL Infy	KS	04918
Haddock, Charles	Surg. 8th MA Infy	MA	01524
Hadley, Elridge D.	1st Lt. 14th NH Infy BvtCapt IA	IA	11801
Hadley, John V.	1st Lt. 7th IN Infy	IN	11517
Hady, Alpheus H.	1st Lt. 45th MA Infy	MA	01055
Haeseler, Charles H.	Asst Surg. 20th PA Cav	PA	11939
Hagans, Edwin B.	2nd Lt. 1st NV Cav	CA	09694
Hagar, George I.	2nd Lt. 1st VT Infy	VT	10077
Hageman, George C.	1st Lt. 41st NY Infy	Ca	11504
Hagen, Joseph J.	Capt. 2nd NY Infy	NY	07981
Hagenhorst, William N.	1st Lt. 79th IN Infy	IN	17423
Hagenman, John W.	Lt. Commander USN	PA	16330
Hager, Jonathan B.	Capt. 14th Infy USA	OH	No Number
Haggerty, Robert A.	Maj Paymaster USV	NY	01492
Hagner, Peter V.	Co. Ordnance BvtBG USA	DC	06377
Hahn, William J.	1st Lt. 25th MO Infy	NE	15789
Haight, Charles C.	Capt. 39th NY Infy	NY	11043
Haight, Edward	Capt. 16th Infy BvtLTC USA	NY	01375
Haight, Edward R.	1st Lt. 107th NY Infy	NY	08106
Haight, Theron W.	1st Lt. 24th NY Infy	WI	05082
Haine, Arthur	2nd Lt. 2nd CA Infy	OR	03912
Haines, Abner, Jr.	Capt. 2nd Infy USA	OH	07716
Haines, Thomas J.	Maj CS BvtBG USA	MA	01819
Hains, Peter C.	BG USA	DC	00344
Hair, Richard M.	1st Lt. 78th USCT	MO	11808
Haldeman, Horace L.	Capt. 20th PA Cav	PA	03795
Halderman, John A.	Maj 1st KS Infy	KS	05078
Hale, Charles H.	Capt. 19th Infy USA	PA	00904
Hale, Charles R.	Chap USN	IL	09077
Hale, Clayton	LTC 59th IL Infy	IA	04396
Hale, Edward Everett	3rd Class (Unitarian Minister, author)	MA	06343
Hale, George W.	2nd Lt. 29th WI Infy	IL	02675 (Dup)
Hale, Henry A.	Capt. AAG BvtLTC USV	MA	02688
Hale, Hiram F.	Maj Paymaster USV	MI	12084
Hale, John H.	Capt. 13th MI Infy	IA	10553
Hale, Joseph	Capt. 3rd Infy USA	MN	05903
Hale, William D.	Maj 4th USC H Arty	MN	05869

Name	Rank	Commandery	Insignia No.
Hall, Augustus O.	1st. Lt. Battn QM 3rd WI Cav	IL	10579
Hall, Austin H.	1st Lt. Adj. 3rd VT Infy	VT	09176
Hall, Benjamin L.	Capt. 5th RI H Arty	MA	15832
Hall, Charles B.	Col. 8th Infy USA	NY	08217
Hall, Daniel	Capt. ADC USV	MA	09603
Hall, David A.	Act Ensign USN	DC	03628
Hall, DeLos E.	Maj 97th NY Infy	OR	04309
Hall, Edward H.	Chap 44th MA Infy	MA	01803
Hall, Frank H.	1st Lt. 54th IN Infy	CA	15976
Hall, George W.	2nd Asst Eng. USN	NY	02557
Hall, H. Seymour	BvtBG USV	KS	07218
Hall, Hamilton W.	Capt. 59th IL Infy	MN	09604
Hall, Henry B.	Capt. 6th NY H Arty	NY	09956
Hall, Henry H.	Maj USA	CA	16296
Hall, Henry T.	1st Lt. 34th MA Infy	MA	04331
Hall, Hillman A.	Capt. 6th NY Infy	DC	10936
Hall, Hiram H.	1st Lt. 124th NY Infy	CA	17782
Hall, James A.	Col. 2nd US Vet.Vols. BvtBG	ME	02395
Hall, James F.	Col. 1st NY Eng. BvtBG	NY	01295
Hall, James L.	1st Lt. 1st MA H Arty	MA	06636
Hall, Jarvis W.	BG USV	NY	02047
Hall, Joseph E.	1st Lt. 183rd PA Infy	OR	16190
Hall, Josiah C.	Capt. 55th MA Infy BvtMaj	OH	03973
Hall, Matthew	Capt. 91st PA Infy	PA	06767
Hall, Nathaniel B.	Maj 14th VT Infy	MI	06982
Hall, Peter P.G.	Maj Paymaster USV	PA	01120
Hall, Robert A.	1st Lt. 141st Ny Infy	NY	15214
Hall, Robert H.	BG USA	DC	04025
Hall, Samuel K.	1st Lt. RQM 7th Cav MO St.Militia	DC	14112
Hall, Theron E.	LTC QM BvtCol. USV	MA	01144
Hall, Thomas S.	Maj 92nd NY Infy	CA	05457
Hall, William D.	Capt. 3rd V.H.C. BvtMaj	CA	07256
Hall, William H.	Asst Surg. 36th NY Infy	NY	No Number
Hall, William K.	Chap 17th CT lnfy	NY	13451
Halladay, Charles S.	Act Asst Paymaster USN	MA	01582
Halleck, Walter F.	Capt. USA	DC	14405
Haller, Granville O.	Col. 23rd Infy USA	WA	03097
Hallet, Daniel B.	Act Ensign USN	MA	10586
Hallett, Charles O.	Capt. 103rd USCT	CA	02913
Halliday, Francis A.	1st Lt. USA	DC	15803
Halliday, Frank S.	1st Lt. 2nd RI Infy BvtCapt	NY	03604
Halloran, James	Capt. 12th Infy USA	CA	03554
Hallowell, Edwkard N.	Col. 54th MA Infy BvtBG	MA	00958
Hallowell, James R.	LTC 31st IN Infy BvtCol.	KS	04797
Hallowell, John R.	2nd Lt. 4th IA Cav	PA	07325 (Dup)
Hallowell, Norwood P.	Col. 55th MA Infy	MA	03054
Hallowell, William P.	1st Lt. Adj. 55th MA Infy	PA	04412
Halpine, Charles G.	LTC AAG BvtBG USV	NY	00111

The Roster

Name	Rank	Commandery	Insignia No.
Halsey, Edmund D.	1st Lt. Adj. 15th NJ Infy	NY	10163
Halsey, Milton W.	Capt. 18th OH Infy	MO	15490
Halsey, Thomas H.	Maj Paymaster BvtLTC USA	NY	00303
Halstead, Eminel P.	Capt. AAG BvtMaj USV	DC	00721
Halstead, Willard G.	2nd Lt. 26th NY Infy	CA	08573
Hambleton, Charles E.	Maj 2nd WV Cav	IL	07830
Hamblin, Joseph E.	BG BvtMG USV	NY	00636
Hambright, Henry A.	Col. 79th PA Infy BvtBG USV	PA	04946
Hamersly, George W.	1st Lt. RQM 186th PA Infy BvtMaj	PA	00319
Hamersly, Lewis R.	2nd Lt. USMC	PA	04182
Hamil, Hugh	Capt. 3rd RI H Arty	PA	11162
Hamilin Cyrus	BG BvtMG USV	PA	00521
Hamill, David B.	1st Lt. 45th IA Infy	IA	09688
Hamilton, Alfred	Capt. 119th NY Infy	DC	06653 (Dup)
Hamilton, Benjamin A.	1st Lt. 71st OH Infy	OH	15019
Hamilton, Benjamin B.	Chap 61st IL Infy	IL	06521
Hamilton, C.A.	LTC 7th WI Infy	WI	02083
Hamilton, Charles B.	1st Lt. 23rd IL Infy	KS	06865
Hamilton, Charles S.	MG USV	WI	01552
Hamilton, David B.	Capt. 5th CT Infy	NY	01905
Hamilton, Elisha B.	1st Lt. 118th IL Infy	IL	04138
Hamilton, Frank B.	Maj 3rd Arty USA	DC	03586
Hamilton, James K.	Capt. 113th OH Infy	OH	03206
Hamilton, John	Col. 5th Arty USA	NY	04487
Hamilton, John F.	Surg. 1st CO Cav	CA	03905
Hamilton, Samuel T.	Maj USA	MD	03089
Hamilton, Schuyler	MG USV	NY	01216
Hamilton, Thomas J.	Capt. 28th PA Infy	PA	09497
Hamilton, William	Act Vol. Lt. Commander USN	NY	01015
Hamilton, William D.	Col. 9th OH Cav BvtBG	OH	04640
Hamlih, Norman S.	Surg. 15th MO Infy	CA	05459
Hamlin, Augustus C.	LTC Med. Inspector USV	ME	02381
Hamlin, Charles	Maj AAG BvtBG USV	ME	00258-9374
Hamlin, Hannibal	3rd Class (VP US)	ME	00047
Hammann, Edward	2nd Lt. Batt E. PA L Arty	PA	09277
Hammatt, Charles H.	Act Asst Paymaster USN	NY	02621
Hammer, Charles D.	1st Lt. 124th OH Infy	MA	05550
Hammer, John S.	LTC 16th KY Infy	KS	06787
Hammer, Seth R.	1st Lt. RCS 1st OR Cav	OR	12196
Hammond, Daniel W.	Capt. 23rd MA Infy	MA	13130
Hammond, David	1st Lt. 1st KY Infy	OH	09027
Hammond, Edwin P.	LTC 87th IN Infy BvtCol.	IN	12336
Hammond, John	Col. 5th NY Cav BvtBG	NY	06639
Hammond, Joseph B.	Capt. 32nd ME Infy	ME	13399
Hammond, Josiah T.	1st Lt. 20th MI Infy	MI	10234
Hammond, Lafayette	Maj 2nd OH H Arty	PA	01236
Hammond, William A.	BG Surg. General USA	DC	06969
Hamner, William H.	LTC USA	CA	04786

Name	Rank	Commandery	Insignia No.
Hampson, Jesse A. P.	LTC 12th Infy USA	MI	03871
Hampton, Charles G.	Capt. 15th NY Cav	MI	11124
Hamrick, James W.	Capt. 1st IN H Arty	IN	13310
Hanback, Louis	Capt. 27th IL Infy	DC	03520
Hancock, Elisha A.	Maj 9th PA Cav	PA	01486
Hancock, John	Maj AAG Bvt LTC USV	DC	12029
Hancock, Winfield Scott	MG USA	PA	00161
Hand, Albert E.	1st Lt. 38th NJ Infy	PA	05987
Hand, Charles H.	Capt. 118th PA Infy	PA	00035
Hand, Daniel W.	Surg. BvtLTC USV	MN	04051
Hand, Peter	Capt. 24th IL Infy	IL	09875
Handren, John W.	Act 3rd Asst Eng. USN	NY	01653
Handy, George W.	1st Lt. 22nd IA Infy	CA	06137
Handy, William J.	BvtLTC USV	MI	07285
Hanford, Franklin	RAdm USN	NY	16262
Hanington, Henry	2nd Lt. 27th NY Infy	CO	05779
Hankey, Christopher F.	2nd Lt. 10th IL Infy	MI	16661
Hanks, Horace T.	Asst Surg. 30th NY Infy	NY	11242
Hanley, Patrick T.	LTC 9th MA Infy BvtCol.	MA	08438
Hanna, Howard M.	Paymaster USN	OH	04394
Hanna, Marcus A.	2nd Lt. 150th OH Infy	OH	13750
Hanna, Robert B.	Capt. 72nd IN Infy	IL	08424
Hannaford, George A.	LTC 124th USCT	IA	04634
Hannahs, Harrison	Maj 50th MO Infy	CO	11489
Hannay, John W.	LTC 12th Infy USA	PA	00524
Hannifen, Dennis	2nd Lt. 75th IL Infy	MN	11552
Hanscom, Irving D.	1st Lt. 22nd MI Infy	MI	08025
Hanscom, John F.	Naval Constructor USN	PA	10868
Hanscom, Sanford	1st Lt. Adj. 11th ME Infy	MA	09806
Hansel, Jacob C.	1st Lt. 2nd IL L Arty	IL	06653 (Dup)
Hansen, Ferdinand A.H.	Capt. 5th MO Cav	IA	No Number
Hanson, E. Hunn	Capt. ADC USV	CA	06462
Hanson, James W.	Act Asst Paymaster USN	CA	11233
Hanson, Zenas P.	Surg. 42nd IL Infy	IL	09614
Hapeman, Douglas	LTC 104th IL BvtCol.	IL	03488
Hapgood, Charles E.	Col. 5th NH Infy	MA	01703
Happer, Andrew G.	Capt. 11th PA Infy BvtMaj	PA	08219
Harbach, Abram A.	BG USA	PA	04659
Harbaugh, Thomas J.	1st Lt. 81st OH Infy	OH	14273
Harcourt, Thomas J.	2nd Lt. 89th USCT	OH	12218
Hard, George M.	Capt. 13th NJ Infy	NY	02220
Hardacre, George W.	Capt. 23 IL Infy	MN	06554
Hardenbergh, James R.	1st Lt. 9th Infy USA	CA	01416
Hardie, James A.	BG USV BvtMG USA	PA	01709
Hardin, Martin D.	BG USA	IL	02419
Harding, Amos J.	1st Lt. 6th MO Cav BvtCapt	IL	01928
Harding, Charles H.	2nd Lt.195th PA Infy	PA	14539
Harding, William J.	Capt. 38th USCT	NY	03775

Name	Rank	Commandery	Insignia No.
Hardy, Alexander	Capt. 24th Batt IN L Arty	IN	08282
Hardy, Anthony C.	Chap 18th NH Infy	MA	09188
Hardy, Frank A.	Capt. 94th OH Infy	OH	11812
Hardy, Frederick P.	Capt. 6th NH Infy	WA	18019
Hardy, James G.W.	2nd Lt. 11th IN Cav	IN	07266
Hardy, John C.	Capt. 2nd MI Infy	MI	09723
Hardy, Thomas M.	2nd Lt. 16th IN Infy	IN	15098
Haring, Abram P.	1st Lt. 132nd NY Infy	NY	08351
Haring, Charles B.	2nd Lt. 2nd NJ Infy	DC	13032
Harkins, Charles	Maj USA	CA	02730
Harkins, Daniel	Maj 1st NY Cav	CA	04017
Harkisheimer, William J.	Capt. 88th PA Infy Bvt Maj	PA	09278
Harkness, Daniel M.	1st Lt. RQM 72nd OH Infy Bvt Capt	OH	07308
Harkness, Edson J.	Capt. 6th USCT Bvt Maj	PA	03137
Harlan, George C.	Surg. 11th PA Cav	PA	02168
Harlan, James	3rd Class (U.S. Senator from Iowa)	IA	06545
Harlan, John M.	Col. 10th KY Infy	DC	03519
Harlow, John B.	2nd Lt. 47th IL Infy Bvt Capt	MO	04272
Harlow, William T.	Capt. 21st MA Infy	MA	11265
Harman, Joseph L.	1st Lt. 175th OH Infy	MO	12457
Harmon, George M.	Capt. 1st CT H Arty	NY	08491
Harmon, George W.	1st Lt. 17th MI Infy	MI	05175
Harmon, Joseph W.	Asst Surg. 42nd OH Infy	IL	07388
Harmony, David B.	Capt. USN	NY	00322
Harmount, William R.	1st Lt. RQM 97th USCT	MI	08895
Harnden, Henry	LTC 1st WI Cav Bvt BG	WI	10479
Harover, Francis M.	Capt. 175th OH Infy	OH	15140
Harper, Brainerd D.	Capt. 45th IA Infy	CO	07791
Harries, William H.	Capt. 3rd US Vet. Vol	MN	10725
Harriman, David S.	1st Lt. 12th ME Infy	MA	02245
Harriman, Horace M.	Act Asst Paymaster USN	PA	10629
Harrington, Henry S.	1st Lt. 11th MA Infy	ME	16774
Harrington, Purnell F.	RAdm USN	NY	16399
Harrington, Samuel	Capt. 25th MA Infy	MA	03674
Harrington, Stephen R.	Maj 5th KS Cav	OR	06193
Harris, Andrew L.	Col. 75th OH Infy Bvt BG	OH	09347
Harris, Benjamin F.	LTC 6th Me Infy Bvt BG	ME	02528
Harris, Benjamin F.	Capt. 25th NY Infy	IL	11392
Harris, Charles B.	1st Lt. 19th Ind.Batt OH L Arty	NY	15274
Harris, Charles L.	Col. 11th WI Infy Bvt BG	NE	13982
Harris, Charles W.	Capt. 7th MI Infy	MA	10342
Harris, Franklin M.	1st Lt. 95th PA Infy	Paa	12230
Harris, Frederick H.	LTC 13th NJ Infy BvtCol.	NY	11916
Harris, George F.	Asst Surg. 7th PA Cav	PA	07059
Harris, George L.	Act 1st Asst Eng. USN	CA	02479
Harris, Henry T.B.	Pay Director USN	DC	03125
Harris, Ira	Lt. Commander USN	IL	03199
Harris, J. Louis	Act Ensign USN	MA	05874

Name	Rank	Commandery	Insignia No.
Harris, James	Capt. CS BvtMaj USV	PA	13287
Harris, James W.	1st Lt. 2nd IN Cav	IN	07819
Harris, John H.	Act Master USN	NY	02562
Harris, Joseph N.	1st Lt. 179th OH Infy	NY	13393
Harris, Leonard A.	Col. 2nd OH Infy	OH	04222
Harris, Loyd G.	1st Lt. 6th WI Infy	MO	04273
Harris, Moses	Maj 8th Cav USA	NY	02649
Harris, Samuel	1st Lt. 5th MI Cav	PA	08121
Harris, Thomas A.	Act Vol. Lt. Commander USN	MA	07568
Harris, Thomas H.	LTC AAG USV	MO	09326
Harris, William A.	Capt. 34th OH Infy	OH	08699
Harris, William H.	Chief Eng. USN	MA	09236
Harris, William Hamilton	Capt. Ordnance BvtLTC USA	NY	02810 (Dup)
Harris, Wyatt	Capt. 24th MO Infy	OR	11501
Harrison, Benjamin	Col. 70th IN Infy BvtBG (Pres. USA)	IN	02454
Harrison, James B.	Maj 12th KY Cav	MO	08393
Harrison, Robert W.	Capt. 116th IN Infy	MO	11405
Harrison, Samuel A.	LTC 58th USCT	WI	09096
Harrison, Thomas S.	Act Paymaster USN	PA	01535
Harrison, W.H.	1st Asst Eng. USN	MA	02780-2801
Harrison, William H.	LTC 214th PA Infy BvtCol.	PA	04167
Harrower, Benjamin S.	Capt. 1st IN H Arty	MI	13354
Harshaw, Henry B.	2nd Lt. 2nd WI Infy	WI	02061
Hart, Abraham	Capt. 73rd PA Infy	DC	12430
Hart, Albert G.	Surg. 41st OH Infy	OH	09649
Hart, Charles E.	Capt. 109th USCT	NY	08492
Hart, Francis B.	Capt. 144th NY Infy	MN	06096
Hart, Frederick J.	2nd Lt. 100th USCT	DC	08493
Hart, George P.	1st Lt. 1st NY L Arty	NY	08097
Hart, Lane S.	Maj 51st PA Infy	PA	04168
Hart, Samuel C.	LTC 4th MA H Arty	MA	07533
Hart, William B.	Capt. AAG USV	PA	04945
Hart, William W.	Capt. 14th CT Infy	PA	08747
Harter, George D.	1st Lt. 115th OH Infy	OH	03257
Harter, Lafayette	Act Asst Paymaster USN	MI	08935
Hartley, Edward	Capt. 8th MN Infy	NY	09566
Hartley, James	1st Lt. RQM 114th PA Infy BvtCapt	PA	07641
Hartley, John	Capt. 22nd US Infy	PA	00965
Hartranft, John F.	BG BvtMG USV	PA	00199
Harts, Peter W.	Capt. 106th IL Infy	IL	15635
Hartshorn, Dana W.	Surg. USV	OH	07420
Hartshorn, Edwin A.	Capt. 125th NY Infy	NY	12004
Hartshorn, Eldin J.	Capt. 17th VT Infy	IA	11077
Hartstuff, Albert	BG USA	MI	07543
Hartsuff, William	BvtBG USV	MI	09722
Hartwell, Alfred S.	Col. 55th MA Infy BvtBG	MA	01056
Hartwell, Cephas L.	1st Lt. 7th Batt MA L Arty	MA	03675
Hartz, Wilson T.	LTC 22nd Infy USA	IL	00466

Name	Rank	Commandery	Insignia No.
Hartzell, John C.	Capt. 105th OH Infy	OH	09453
Harvey, George T.	Capt. 104th PA	PA	02289
Harvey, Leonard S.	Capt. 11th ME Infy	CA	13019
Harvey, Samuel W.	1st Lt. 36th OH Infy	OH	09893
Harvey, William J.	1st Lt. Adj. 36th PA Infy	PA	02744 (Dup)
Harwood, Andrew A.	RAdm USN	PA	00265
Harwood, George W.	1st Lt. 31st MA Infy	IL	15701
Harwood, Nathan S.	1st Lt. 46th IA Infy	NE	04315
Harwood, Paul	Col. 57th USCT	PA	05723
Hasbrouck, Henry C.	BG USA	NY	01806
Hascall, Milo S.	BG USV	IL	06132
Haseltine, Charles P.	1st Lt. USCT	MN	05689
Haseltine, John W.	Capt. 2nd PA Cav	PA	01722
Hasie, Montague S.	Maj 1st MO Eng.	MO	13841
Haskell, Harry L.	BG USA	CA	03626 (Dup)
Haskell, Horace C.	Maj 30th ME Infy	ME	15673
Haskell, Joseph T.	LTC 17th Infy USA BvtBG USV	KS	06146
Haskell, Otis L.	Act Ensign USN	CO	11275
Haskell, Phineas B.	Capt. 75th OH Infy	OH	08160
Haskin, William L.	BG USA	CA	03101
Haskins, Charles R.	Act Ensign USN	OH	15452
Haskins, Kittredge	1st Lt. 16th VT Infy	VT	13263
Hassan, William H.	1st Lt. 37th WI Infy	CO	10647
Hassinger, David S.	1st Lt. 119th PA Infy BvtCapt	PA	01742
Hassler, Charles W.	Paymaster USN	NY	01047
Hasson, Benjamin F.	2nd Lt. 22nd PA Cav	DC	14406
Hastings, Charles W.	Capt. 12th MA Infy	MA	08059
Hastings, David R.	Maj 12th ME Infy	ME	02779
Hastings, George G.	Maj 1st US Shrpshtrs. BvtCol.	NY	00222
Hastings, Russell	LTC 23rd OH Infy BvtBG	OH	06835
Hastings, Smith H.	Col. 5th MI Cav	CO	05966
Haswell, Governur K.	Commander USN	CA	16520
Hatch, Charles P.	1st Lt. Adj. 53rd PA Infy	PA	08456
Hatch, Edward	BG USV BvtMG USA	DC	02700
Hatch, Hiram F.	1st Lt. N.O. Infy	MI	07893
Hatch, Hobart H.	Capt. 7th IL Infy	OH	08164
Hatch, John P.	BG USV	CA	03639
Hatch, Ossian L.	1st Lt. 7th CT Infy	MA	00957
Hatch, Zethro A.	Maj Surg. 36th IL Infy	IN	15160
Hatfield, Samuel P.	Maj 1st CT H Arty	NY	04613
Hathaway, Forrest H.	BG USA	OR	05701
Hathaway, John L.	Capt. CS BvtLTC USV	WI	01562
Hatten, Jasper	2nd Lt. 45th KY Mounted Infy	KS	17595
Hatton, Frank	2nd Lt.l 184th OH Infy	DC	02977 (Dup)
Haugh, Joseph R.	Maj 5th IN Cav	CA	07510
Haughey, James A.	Capt. 21st Infy USA	CA	03329
Hausdorf, Charles F.	LTC 1st Battn. MN Infy	MN	05856
Hausmann, Charles A.	1st Lt. 30th Batt NY L Arty	NY	12317

Name	Rank	Commandery	Insignia No.
Haven, Franklin	LTC 2nd CA Cav	MA	01260
Haven, Samuel R.	Surg. USV	IL	07831
Havens, Benjamin F.	1st Lt. 89th IN Infy	IN	09010
Haverstick, John W.	1st Lt. 36th PA Infy	PA	00518
Haviland, Thomas P.	Maj Paymaster USV	PA	02255
Haviland, William K.	Capt. 142nd PA Infy	MI	13017
Haw, George	1st Lt. 35th WI Infy	IA	15404
Hawes, Alexander G.	LTC 149th IL Infy	CA	01629
Hawes, Gardiner S.	BvtMaj USV	NY	01790
Hawes, Granville P.	Capt. CS USV	NY	04425
Hawes, John A.	Capt. 3rd MA Infy	MA	01288
Hawk, Elbridge L.	Capt. 114th OH Infy	CA	03113
Hawk, Robert M. A.	Capt. 93rd IL Infy BvtMaj	DC	02431
Hawke, James A.	Med. Director USN	MA	07962
Hawkes, Benjamin F.	LTC 78th OH Infy	DC	13150
Hawkins, Gardiner C.	1str Lt. 3rd VT Infy	MA	03251
Hawkins, Hamilton S.	BG USA MG USV	DC	04886
Hawkins, John P.	BvtMG USV	NE	04304
Hawkins, John T.	1st Asst Eng. USN	MA	06504
Hawkins, March P.	2nd Lt. 3rd NH Infy	MN	05866
Hawkins, Morton L.	1st Lt. 36th OH Infy	OH	03075
Hawley, John M.	RAdm USN	DC	16109
Hawley, Joseph B.	BG BvtMG USV	DC	01064
Hawley, Joseph W.	Col. 124th PA Infy	PA	05986
Hawley, Thomas S.	Surg. 11th MO Infy	MO	08011
Hawley, William	LTC USA	CA	03100
Haws, John J.	2nd Lt. 1st US Arty	NY	00442
Hawthorn, Joseph W.	Act Ensign USN	ME	09703
Hawthorne, Leroy R.	Capt. CS BvtMaj USV	OH	03394
Hay, Charles	Capt. CS USA	CO	07306
Hay, Charles E.	1st Lt. 3rd Cav BvtCapt USA	IL	03307
Hay, John	Maj AAG BvtCol. USV	DC	02891
Hay, Leonard	Maj USA	CA	03549
Haycock, George B.	Capt. USMC	DC	06381
Hayden, Edward D.	Act Asst Paymaster USN	MA	01585
Hayden, James R.	Capt. 19th IL Infy	WA	02237
Hayden, Obadiah B.	Capt. 9th IN Cav	WA	07192
Hayes, Albert W.	Capt. 6th NH Infy	MA	10587
Hayes, Calvin L.	1st Lt. Adj. 32nd ME Infy	ME	09847
Hayes, Charles C.	Surg. 43rd WI Infy	MN	04259
Hayes, Edward	LTC 29th OH Infy	DC	07025
Hayes, Edward M.	BG USA	DC	05603
Hayes, Hiram	LTC QM USV	WI	10699
Hayes, Job J.	Capt. CS BvtMaj USV	IN	07503
Hayes, John	2nd Lt. 16th IA Infy	IA	10807
Hayes, Joshua B.	Surg. 72nd PA Infy	DC	12378
Hayes, Philip C.	LTC 103rd OH Infy BvtBG	IL	06215
Hayes, Rutherford B.	BG BvtMG USV (Pres. USA)	OH	02175

Name	Rank	Commandery	Insignia No.
Haynes, Charles H.	Capt. 14th KS Cav	KS	05774
Haynes, Edwin M.	Chap 10th VT Infy	VT	10073
Haynes, Moses H.	Surg. 167th OH Infy	IN	11895
Haynes, William E.	LTC 10th OH Cav	OH	03198
Hays, Henry B.	Capt. 6th Cav USA	PA	00902
Hays, John	1st Lt. Adj. 130th PA Infy	PA	01041
Hays, John B.	Capt. 19th Infy BvtMaj USA	NY	07990
Hays, Peter B.	2nd Lt. 1st OH H Arty	OH	09820
Hays, William W.	Surg. 6th CA Infy	CA	05181
Hayward, Eugene B.	Capt. 5th NY Cav	IL	04840
Hayward, John K.	1st Lt. 39th MO Infy	MO	04529
Hayward, William E.	Capt. 2nd US Vol.Infy	IN	12942
Hayward, William H.	Col. 150th OH Infy	OH	12149
Hazard, Jeffery	Capt. 1st RI L Arty	MA	01698
Hazard, John G.	Col. 1st RI L Arty BvtBG	MA	01054
Hazard, William P.	2nd Lt. 97th IL Infy	MO	07385
Hazeltine, Francis S.	LTC 13th ME Infy	MA	00975
Hazelton, Isaac H.	Asst Surg. USN	MA	01387
Hazen, William B.	MG USV	DC	03155
Hazlelton, Dwight W.	2nd Lt. 22nd NY Cav	PA	12541
Hazlett, Andrew H.	1st Lt. 14th IA Infy	IA	11140
Hazlett, Isaac	Commander USN	DC	16194
Hazzard, Chillion C.W.	Capt. 41st PA Infy BvtMaj	PA	13557
Head, Albert	Capt. 10th IA Infy	IA	05445
Head, George E.	LTC 11th Infy USA	OH	07202
Head, John F.	BG USA	DC	14713
Headington, John W.	LTC 100th IN Infy	IN	11803
Heafford, George H.	1st Lt. Adj. 72nd IL Infy	IL	02776
Healy, John G.	LTC 9th CT Infy	NY	02372
Healy, Robert W.	Col. 58th IL Infy BvtBG	OH	01445
Healy, William J.	Passed Asst Paymaster USN	NY	00948
Hean, Benjamin F.	BvtMaj USV	PA	04411
Heap, David P.	BG USA	CA	04724
Heard, J. Theodore	LTC Med. Director USV	MA	00826
Heard, William A.	1st Lt. RQM 14th NH Infy	MA	10120
Hearn, James A.	Capt. 16th Infy BvtMaj USA	OH	05312
Heath, Francis E.	Col. 19th ME Infy BvtBG	ME	02506
Heath, Lewis W.	Capt. 11th MI Infy	MI	03759
Heath, Thomas T.	Col. 5th OH Cav BvtBG	OH	03570
Heberton, George A.	1st Lt. 110th PA Infy	PA	04658
Hecker, Frank J.	Co. QM USV	MI	13355
Heckscher, John G.	1st Lt. 12th Infy USA	NY	08107
Hedberg, Alfred	Capt. 15th Infy USA	PA	00558
Hedden, Warren R.	1st Lt. 65th NY Infy	NY	01847
Hedge, Thomas	2nd Lt. 106th NY Infy	IA	11141
Hedge, William	1st Lt. 44th MA Infy	MA	00921
Hedges, Samuel P.	1st Lt. Adj. 112th NY Infy	IL	04635
Hedley, Fenwick Y.	1st Lt. Adj. 32nd IL Infy BvtCapt	MO	06419

Name	Rank	Commandery	Insignia No.
Heermance, William L.	Capt. 6th NY Cav	NY	03770
Heffelfinger, Christopher B.	Maj 1st MN H Arty	MN	04246
Heffelfinger, Jacob	1st Lt. 36th PA Infy BvtCapt	PA	03405
Heffron, Henry G.	LTC 79th NY Infy	CO	08556
Heger, Anthony	BG USA	DC	03647
Hegler, Allen	Capt. 114th OH Infy	OH	08172
Heilman, William H.	Capt. 15th Infy USA	PA	06000
Heine, William	Col. 103rd NY Infy BvtBG	NY	01166
Heinmiller, Henry	1st Lt. 108th Infy	OH	10209
Heintzelman, Samuel P.	MG USA	NY	00582
Heisey, Augustus H.	Capt. 155th PA Infy	OH	16896
Heishley, John F.	Capt. 2nd DE Infy	DC	09527
Heitshu, Daniel H.	1st Lt. 122nd PA Infy	PA	08748
Helmer, Albert M.	Surg. 28th NY Infy	WI	05534
Helveti, Francois M.	LTC 1st KY Infy	OH	07305
Hemingway, Anson T.	1st Lt. i70th USCT	IL	11435
Hemphill, Joseph N.	RAdm USN	DC	16052
Hemstreet, William	Capt. 18th MO Infy BvtLTC	NY	11461
Hemstreet, William J.	1st Lt. 179th NY Infy	IL	03140
Hendee, George E.	Pay Director USN	CA	10728
Henderson, Alexander	Chief Eng. USN	NY	02831
Henderson, David B.	Col. 46th IA Infy	IA	03179
Henderson, John B.	3rd Class (US Senator MO)	DC	06053
Henderson, Paris P.	Col. 10th IA Infy	IA	14048
Henderson, Reese R.	Maj 121st OH Infy BvtCol.	MN	04247
Henderson, Richard P.	1st Lt. 36th PA Infy BvtMaj	PA	02290
Henderson, Robert B.	1st Lt. 13th MA Infy	MA	11291
Henderson, Robert M.	LTC 36th PA Infy BvtBG	PA	00154
Henderson, Thomas J.	Col. 112th IL Infy BvtBG	IL	02512
Henderson, William	1st Lt. Adj. 145th NY Infy	KS	11006
Henderson, William F.	Capt. 63rd IN Infy	KS	17275
Henderson, William L.	Capt. 12th IA Infy	IA	11146
Henderson, William P.	Capt. 2nd AK Infy	IA	05787
Hendrick, Albert C.	Capt. 12th CT Infy	NY	01247
Hendrickson, Eliphalet	1st Lt. Adj. 40th NY Infy	NY	05528
Hendrickson, John	Col. 83rd NY Infy BvtBG	NY	12788
Hendrickson, William M.	Asst Surg. 4th NY H Arty	WA	12623
Henley, William M.	Capt. 47th IN Infy	IN	11644
Henning, Benjamin S.	Maj 3rd WI Cav	NY	05704
Hennisee, Argalus G.	BG USA	CA	14003
Henry, Archibald R.	2nd Lt. 34th IA Infy	MI	15548
Henry, Charles E.	1st Lt. Adj. 42nd OH Infy	OH	12194
Henry, George E.	Capt. 1st MA Infy BvtMaj	MA	08060
Henry, Guy V.	BG USA BvtMG USV	DC	00125
Henry, Hugh	2nd Lt. 16th VT Infy	VT	09167
Henry, James R.	2nd Lt. 21st IN Infy	IN	10796
Henry, Robert H.	1st Lt. 42nd WI Infy	NE	09366
Henry, Wilbur F.	Capt. 108th IL Infy	MO	15435

Name	Rank	Commandery	Insignia No.
Henry, William	1st Lt. 79th IN Infy	IN	17420
Henry, William W.	Col. 10th VT Infy BvtBG	VT	05875
Hensey, Thomas G.	1st Lt. RCS 7th NY Cav	DC	13374
Henton, James	LTC 23rd Infy USA	CA	10610
Hepburn, William P.	LTC 2nd IA Cav	IA	04476
Herbert, George R.	2nd Lt. 159th NY Infy	NY	05121
Herbert, William P.	Capt. 139th PA Infy	PA	07642
Herbst, John E.	Surg. BvtLTC USV	MO	08133
Herenden, George B.	1st Lt. Adj. 44th NY Infy	IL	04997
Heritage, Lemuel T.	Capt. 11th KS Cav	KS	05358
Herkner, Joseph C.	Capt. 1st MI Eng.	MI	08197
Herr, Samuel K.	Capt. 191st PA Infy BvtLTC	DC	13178
Herren, Edwin R.	Capt. 4th WI Infy BvtMaj	WI	08809
Herrick, George H.W.	Surg. 1st US Vols.	MA	01426
Herrick, Henry J.	Surg. 17th OH Infy	OH	03254
Herrick, John F.	LTC 12th OH Cav	OH	02970
Herrick, Merton	1st Lt. 48th WI Infy	WI	04452
Herrick, Osgood E.	Maj Chap USA	DC	08680
Herring, Charles P.	LTC 118th PA Infy BvtBG	PA	01483
Herriott, George F.	Maj 10th IN Cav	MO	06595
Herron, Francis J.	MG USV	NY	01835
Herron, William C.	Act Ensign USN	OH	06128
Herron, William P.	Capt. 72nd IN Infy	IN	06596
Hersey, Philo	LTC 26th ME Infy	CA	08872
Hersey, Roscoe F.	Capt. 1st ME H Arty BvtCol.	MN	06455
Hershey, Andrew H.	1st Lt. Adj. 15th IL Infy	IL	12894
Hess, Alexander	Capt. 2nd IN Cav	IN	11406
Hess, Frank W.	LTC USA	PA	04322
Hess, Julius	1st Lt. 1st NY Eng.	MI	06983
Hester, William W.	LTC 48th KY Infy	IL	07580
Hetrich, Frank D.	2nd Lt. 9th PA Infy	CA	13347
Heubel, John L.	1st Lt. 46th PA Infy	DC	03524
Heuberer, Charles E.	Capt. 6th NY Infy	NY	08352
Heuer, William H.	Col. USA	CA	16379
Heusted, Wellington V.	Capt. 22nd USCT	KS	16245
Hewett, James H.H.	Capt. 8th ME Infy BvtMaj	ME	08833
Hewitt, Charles N.	Surg. 50th NY Eng.	MN	05265
Hewitt, Edward L.	2nd Asst Eng. USN	PA	12231
Heyerman, Oscar F.	Commander USN	MI	06536
Heyl, Edward M.	Col. Inspector Gen. USA	PA	00452
Heysinger, Isaac W.	Capt. 48th USCT	PA	11157
Heywood, Charles	MG Commandant USMC	DC	06571
Heywood, John R.	Capt. 6th USC Cav	MA	16034
Hibbard, Curtis A.	2nd Lt. 9th VT Infy	VT	10080
Hibbard, Elisha C.	LTC 24th WI Infy	WI	01567
Hibbard, George B.	BvtMaj USV	NY	09116
Hibbard, Harmon R.	Capt. 119th IL Infy	KS	06298
Hibbs, David R.P.	1st Lt. 104th PA Infy	MN	08152

Name	Rank	Commandery	Insignia No.
Hick, William H.	Maj 1st NJ Cav	PA	01075
Hickenlooper, Andrew	LTC AIG BvtBG USV	OH	02299
Hickey, James B.	LTC 1st Cav USA	NY	03943
Hickman, Job T.	1st Lt. 23rd PA Infy	PA	09496
Hickman, William H.	2nd Lt. 2nd MD Infy	DC	12102
Hickox, Charles R.	1st. Lt. 5th Arty USA	NY	06953
Hicks, Alfred	Capt. 76th PA Infy	PA	06463
Hicks, Borden M.	Capt. 11th MI Infy	MN	10458
Hicks, George A.	Capt. AAG BvtMaj USV	NY	03765
Hicks, Henry G.	1st Lt. Adj. 93rd IL Infy BvtMaj	MN	04034
Hicks, Ira E.	1st Lt. 7th CT Infy	NY	17642
Hicks, Lewis E.	LTC 69th OH Infy	CA	11227
Hicks, Philemon N.	1st Lt. RQM 76th PA Infy	KS	13093
Hicks, Sidney S.	1st Lt. 6th CT Infy	MA	14086
Hieronymus, Benjamin R.	1st Lt. 117th IL Infy	IL	13248 (Dup)
Hiestand, Joseph M.	Capt. 175th OH Infy	OH	11892
Higbee, Chester G.	Capt. 12th WI Infy	MN	03834
Higbee, George H.	Capt. 11th Infy BvtLTC USA	IA	09968
Higbee, John H.	LTC USMC	MA	01280
Higbee, William H.	Act Asst Paymaster USN	NY	12005
Higgins, Thomas	Act Asst Paymaster USN	NY	14124
Higginson, Francis J.	RAdm USN	DC	02495
Higginson, Francis L.	Capt. 5th MA Cav	MA	01071
Higginson, Henry L.	Maj 1st MA Cav BvtLTC	MA	06144
Higginson, James J.	Capt. 1st MA Cav BvtMaj	NY	05295
Higginson, Samuel S.	Chap 9th USCT	IL	10248
Higginson, Thomas W.	Col. 33rd USCT	MA	06913
Higgs, Augustus F.	1st Lt. 127th IL Infy	PA	04410
High, James L.	1st Lt. Adj. 49th WI Infy	IL	04148
Hight, Henry O.	Capt. 82nd USCT BvtMaj	MA	13168
Higley, Mortimer A.	Capt. CS USV	IA	04841
Hildreth, Charles F.	Surg. 40th MA Infy	MA	02117
Hildreth, James M.	LTC 16th IN Infy	IN	06889 (Dup)
Hildt, George H.	LTC 30th OH Infy	OH	09742
Hildt, John McL.	BvtLTC USV	NY	No Number
Hill, Benjamin J.	Capt. 9th ME Infy	ME	09101
Hill, Charles A.	Capt. 1st USCT	IL	06522
Hill, Edgar P.	LTC 23rd WI Infy	NY	02925
Hill, Edward	LTC 16th MI Infy	CA	11091
Hill, F. Stanhope	Act Vol. Lt. USN	MA	08548
Hill, George D.	Capt. 42nd Infy USA	OR	02236
Hill, George H.	Maj USV	PA	00467
Hill, George W.	Capt. 13th Infy USA	MA	09058
Hill, Harry C.	Maj Volunteer ADC	CA	11598
Hill, Hollis B.	2nd Lt. 60th ME Infy	ME	05344
Hill, J. Augustus	Col. 11th ME Infy BvtBG	NY	04482
Hill, James G.	Capt. 97th USCT	MA	00922
Hill, Jerry N.	Maj 66th IL Infy	CO	05958

Name	Rank	Commandery	Insignia No.
Hill, John E.	Capt. 11th OH Infy	NE	07209
Hill, John E.	Capt. 2nd CA Infy	CA	11863
Hill, Joseph C.	LTC 6th MD Infy	DC	06379
Hill, Joseph C.	Capt. 5th KY Cav	DC	05586
Hill, Lester S.	2nd Lt. 11th USC H Arty	MA	10718
Hill, Lysander	Capt. 20th ME Infy	IL	04503
Hill, Norman N.	1st Lt. 3rd MO Cav	DC	13375
Hill, Robert	Capt. 1st WI Infy	WI	01571
Hill, Robert F.	1st Lt. 1st MI Shrpshtrs.	DC	06974
Hill, Robert J.	Asst Surg. 45th OH Infy	MO	04370
Hill, Wareham C.	Maj 4th USCT BvtCol.	DC	14219
Hill, William A.	Capt. 19th MA Infy	MA	10046
Hiller, Allen M.	1st Lt. 199th PA Infy	PA	18407
Hilles, Samuel	1st Lt. 15th OH Infy	OH	09744
Hillman, Beriah T.	2nd Lt. 60th MA Infy	MA	13859
Hillman, William C.	1st Lt. RQM 142nd PA Infy	OH	14491
Hills, Charles F.	1st Lt. 51st IL Infy	IL	02672
Hills, Charles S.	LTC 10th KS Infy BvtCol.	MO	04580
Hills, Leander B.	1st Lt. 10th WI Infy	WI	04454
Hillyer, William R.	Capt. 7th NJ Infy	DC	12057
Hilt, Joseph L.	Capt. 12th OH Infy	OH	07121
Hilton, Charles L.	BvtCapt. USV	KS	05535
Himes, Isaac N.	Surg. 73rd OH Infy	OH	03371
Himoe, Stephen O.	Surg. 15th WI Infy	MO	09843
Hinckley, Henry L.	Capt. 96th USCT	NY	07608
Hinckley, S. Alexander	Act Ensign USN	MA	11292
Hincks, Edward W.	BG BvtMG USV	MA	01205
Hincks, William B.	1st Lt. Adj. 14th CT Infy	NY	06011
Hindes, George W.	LTC 96th NY Infy	CA	14062
Hindman, Samuel	1st Lt. 19th IN Infy	KS	06797
Hinds, Charles C.	1st Lt. 24th ME Infy	WA	15013
Hinds, Henry H.	Capt. 57th PA Infy	MI	05271
Hinds, William H.W.	Surg. 12th MA Infy	MA	02805
Hine, Elmore C.	Asst Surg. 7th CT Infy	PA	07336
Hine, Lemon G.	1st Lt. 44th IL Infy	DC	10692
Hinkley, Julian W.	Capt. 3rd WI Infy	MN	05851
Hinkley, Lucius D.	1st Lt. 10th WI Infy	WI	04506
Hinman, Frank H.	Paymaster USN	NY	04489
Hinman, Hugh C.	1st Lt. 72nd NY Infy	CA	03244
Hinman, Stephen N.	2nd Lt. 1st CT Cav	IA	11312
Hinsdill, Chester B.	Capt. CS BvtLTC USV	MI	12221
Hinson, Daniel K.	Capt. 35th NJ Infy	ME	15819
Hinson, Joseph	Col. 33rd OH Infy	WA	07195
Hipp, Charles	Maj 37th OH Infy	OH	06514
Hirst, Thomas C.	1st Lt. 180th OH Infy	OH	08290
Hitchcock, Alfred O.	Capt. 57th MA Infy BvtMaj	MA	09333
Hitchcock, Elizur	Asst Surg. 7th OH Infy	OH	08705
Hitchcock, Frank	Capt. 86th IL Infy	IL	08720

Name	Rank	Commandery	Insignia No.
Hitchcock, Frederick L.	Col. 25th USCT	PA	15596
Hitchcock, Henry	Maj AAG BvtLTC USV	MO	04274
Hitchcock, Peter M.	1st Lt. RQM 20th OH Infy	OH	03057
Hitchcock, Roswell D.	Commander USN	CA	08574
Hitt, Wilbur F.	1st Lt. Adj. 123rd IN Infy BvtMaj	IN	06597
Hizar, Thomas B.	Capt. 1st DE Infy	MN	08435
Hoag, Edward H.	1st Lt. 18th MI Infy	KS	07173
Hoag, John M.	Maj BvtLTC USA	IL	05544
Hoagland, Cornelius N.	Surg. 71st OH Infy	NY	06956
Hobart, Andrew J.	Surg. 1st MI Infy	IL	02670
Hobart, Charles	LTC 8th Infy USA	IL	04515
Hobart, Edwin L.	1st Lt. 58th USCT	CO	15321
Hobart, Harrison C.	Col. 21st WI Infy BvtBG	WI	01601
Hobbs, Charles W.	BG USA	CA	05893
Hobbs, George W.	Capt. 91st NY Infy	NY	12724
Hobbs, Horace	Capt. 61st MA Infy	MA	08855
Hobson, Edward H.	BG USV	OH	07122
Hodgdon, Caleb W.	Capt. 14th NH Infy	MA	07963
Hodgdon, Charles O.	Act Asst Paymaster USN	MO	10213
Hodge, Ambrose	Capt. 4th IA Cav BvtMaj	OH	08288
Hodge, Newton D.	1st Lt. 10th MI Infy	CA	05643
Hodge, Noah	1st Lt. Adj. 52nd USCT	OH	03211
Hodge, Patrick F.	Capt. 55th PA Infy	PA	07337
Hodge, William E.	2nd Lt. 5th MD Infy	DC	07677
Hodges, Almon D.	2nd Lt. 42nd MA Infy	MA	07401
Hodges, Charles L.	LTC 23rd Infy USA	MN	04043
Hodges, Henry C.	BG USA	CA	03643
Hodges, James L.	Capt. 3rd MN Infy	CO	10646
Hodges, Thorndike D.	BvtMaj USV	NY	03351
Hodges, William R.	Capt. 32nd WI Infy	MO	09285 (Dup)
Hodgkins, William H.	Capt. 36th MA Infy BvtMaj	MA	06103
Hodskin, Charles H.	Capt. 2nd MI Infy	MI	05345
Hoehling, Adolph A.	Med. Director USN	DC	06657
Hoeltge, Augustus	Asst Surg. 47th OH Infy	OH	06190
Hoff, Henry K.	RAdm USN	PA	00175
Hoff, William Bainbridge	Capt. USN	DC	09103
Hoffman, Edward G.	Capt. 165th NY Infy	DC	02613
Hoffman, John W.	Col. 56th PA Infy BvtBG	PA	00151
Hoffman, Louis	Capt. 4th Batt OH L Arty	OH	05749
Hoffman, Southard	LTC AAG USV	CA	02028
Hoffman, William	Maj USA	DC	08815
Hogarty, Michael J.	Capt. USA	CO	05620
Hogarty, William P.	2nd Lt. 45th Infy BvtCapt USA	KS	05104
Hoge, Holmes	Capt. AQM USV	IL	05806
Hoge, Solomon L.	Capt. 82nd OH BvtMaj	OH	01661
Hogeboom, George W.	Surg. BvtLTC USV	KS	06484
Hogin, George B.	Maj Paymaster USV	IA	03139
Hogle, Austin W.	2nd Lt. 76th IL Infy	CO	05621

Name	Rank	Commandery	Insignia No.
Hoit, James B.	LTC 3rd MN Infy	MN	11492
Hoitt, Augustus J.	Capt. 5th NH Infy	MA	12375
Holabird, G.B.	BvtBG USA	DC	02405
Holbrook, Andrew J.	2nd Lt. Sig. Corps USV	MA	11362
Holbrook, Arthur	1st Lt. ADJ 39th WI Infy	WI	04125
Holbrook, William C.	Col. 7th VT Infy	NY	01781
Holcomb, Irving	Capt. 121st NY Infy	NY	16320
Holcomb, William N.	Capt. 36th USCT	NE	08026
Holden, Delos L.	2nd Lt. 50th NY Eng	CO	06115
Holden, Edgar	Asst Surg. USN	NY	04914
Holdridge, Hiram A.	1st Lt. 192nd OH Infy	OH	07766
Holiday, Joshua W.	Capt. 8th IA Cav	IA	11076
Holihan, James W.	Passed Asst. Eng. USN	CA	08307
Holl, Mathias	1st Lt. 6th MN Infy	MN	07624
Holliday, Samuel V.	Major, Paymaster BvtLTC USV	DC	08411
Holliday, Vinton G.	1st Lt. 2nd IN Cav	CA	15320
Hollister, Albert H.	1st Lt. 30th USCT	WI	04510
Hollister, Benjamin F.	1st Lt. RQM 111th OH Infy	OH	11100
Hollister, Edward P.	LTC 57th MA Infy	NY	08494
Hollister, Uriah S.	Capt. 13th WI Infy	CO	12052
Holloway, George A.	Capt. AAG USV	IL	04147
Holman, Samuel	Act Asst Surg. USN	PA	10869
Holmes, Adoniram J.	1st Lt. 37th WI Infy	IA	03813
Holmes, Anthony F.	Act Master USN	PA	00526
Holmes, Charles A.	Capt. 29th WI Infy	NE	04984 (Dup)
Holmes, Edwin F.	Capt. 10th MI Infy	MI	06813
Holmes, George W.	Capt. 6th IA Infy	MA	07297
Holmes, Henry T.	1st Lt. 50th MA Infy	MA	01455
Holmes, Hiram C.	Capt. 1st USCT	WA	08628
Holmes, Joseph W.	1st Lt. Adj. 27th MA Infy	MA	00859
Holmes, Levi E.	2nd Lt. 96th USCT	CA	04700 (Dup)
Holmes, Oliver Wendell	Capt. 20th MA Infy BvtCol.	DC	14158
Holmes, Roswell H.	1st Lt. 7th MI Cav	MI	11693
Holmes, Sebastian D.	Capt. 111th NY Infy	NY	09567
Holmes, Walter H.	Capt. 170th NY Infy	CA	02080
Holsinger, Frank	Capt. 19th USCT BvtMaj	KS	05353
Holstein, Charles	Maj 52nd USCT	OH	17987
Holstein, Charles L.	Capt. AAG BvtMaj USV	IN	12454
Holt, Alexander H.	LTC 138th IL Infy	DC	02515
Holt, Alfred F.	LTC 1st TX Cav	MA	03146
Holt, Frederick V.	Act 2nd Asst Eng. USN	PA	04413
Holt, George R.	2nd Asst Eng. USN	PA	08218
Holter, Marcellus J.W.	LTC 195th OH Infy BvtBG	OH	03384
Holton, Charles M.	1st Lt. 7th MI Infy	WA	07191
Holton, Edward K.	1st Lt. 24th WI Infy	MO	04785
Holton, W.A.N.	1st Lt. 16th VRC	PA	00091
Holton, William H.H.	1st Lt. VRC BvtMaj	NY	07464
Holtzman, Samuel E.	Surg. 58th IN Infy	IL	12643

Name	Rank	Commandery	Insignia No.
Holway, Daniel N.	Capt. 17th MI Infy BvtMaj	IL	02417
Holzhauer, Frederick	2nd Lt. 1st MI L Arty	MI	11604
Homan, Joseph B.	Capt. 99th IN Infy	IN	11519
Homans, George H.	Capt. 45th ME Infy	MA	01465
Homans, John	Asst Surg. USA	MA	08549
Homans, William H.	Capt. 54th MA Infy	CO	07907
Homer, Arthur B.	Act Ensign USN	PA	03090
Homiston, Joseph M.	Surg. 19th NY Cav Bvt LTC	NY	00880
Honey, Samuel R.	Capt. 33rd Infy USA	MA	14240
Hood, Calvin	Capt. 11th MI Infy	KS	06302
Hood, Charles C.	BG USA	PA	09768
Hood, John	Capt. 80th IL Infy	KS	05792
Hood, Robert N.	Capt. 2nd TN Cav	OH	05477
Hood, Thomas B.	Surg. BvtLTC USV	DC	02608
Hoodless, William J.	Act Asst Paymaster USN	NY	03016
Hooker, Edward	Commander USN	NY	02569
Hooker, George W.	Capt. AAG BvtLTC USV	VT	10666
Hooker, Horace B.	1st Lt. 1st MO Eng.	NY	16891
Hooker, Samuel J.	1st Lt. 31st WI Infy	WI	07627
Hooper, Charles E.	2nd Lt. 1st CO Infy	CO	10106
Hooper, Charles H.	LTC 24th MA Infy	MA	01600
Hooper, Henry N.	LTC 54th MA Infy	CA	11104
Hooper, I. Harris	Maj 15th MA Infy	MA	00816
Hooper, Shadrach K.	1st Lt. 23rd IN Infy BvtMaj	CO	06121
Hooper, William B.	Capt. CS BvtMaj USV	CA	02030
Hooton, Francis C.	LTC 175th PA Infy	PA	00664
Hooton, Mott	BG USA	PA	01009
Hoover, James A.	2nd Lt. 2nd WVA Cav	IL	07439
Hoover, John S.	Maj ADC BvtCol. USV	NE	07047
Hopkins, Alfred	Lt. Commander USN	CA	01329
Hopkins, Amos L.	Maj 1st MA Cav	NY	06166
Hopkins, Archibald	Capt. 37th MA Infy BvtLTC	DC	03322
Hopkins, Charles A.	Capt. 13th NJ Infy BvtMaj	MA	06104
Hopkins, Dewitt C.	Capt. 1st Arkansas Cav	MO	08016
Hopkins, Elisha	Asst Surg. 14th ME Infy	ME	14608
Hopkins, Franklin	Act Master USN	MA	01675
Hopkins, George G.	Capt. 5th RI H Arty BvtMaj	NY	06014
Hopkins, George H.	Maj AAG USV	MI	13356
Hopkins, Henry	Chap. 120th NY Infy	MA	05048
Hopkins, Henry F.	2nd Lt. 3rd NH Infy	MA	03843
Hopkins, Marcus S.	1st Lt. 7th OH Infy BvtMaj	DC	05400
Hopkins, Robert E.	Capt. 149th NY Infy	NY	09860
Hopkins, Stephen G.	1st Lt. 160th NY Infy	NY	16090
Hopkins, William E.	Commodore USN	CA	08870
Hopkins, Woolsey R.	LTC QM USV	NY	07984
Hopper, George C.	Maj 1st MI Infy	MI	06814
Hopper, George F.	LTC 10th NY Infy	NY	06428
Hoppin, William W.	3rd Class	MA	06344

Name	Rank	Commandery	Insignia No.
Hord, William T.	Med. Director USN	DC	02696
Horn, John W.	Col. 6th MD Infy BvtBG	DC	06378
Hornbrook, Saunders R.	Capt. 65th IN Infy	IN	11316
Horne, Othniel	1st Lt. Adj. 100th IL Infy	NE	06695
Horne, Samuel B.	Capt. 11th CT Infy	PA	08221
Horner, Caleb W.	Surg. BvtLTC USV	PA	06254
Horner, Gustavus R. B.	Surg. & Med. Director USN	PA	00401
Horner, James B.	Capt. 17th NY Infy	NY	04054
Horner, Richard C.	Capt. 2nd PA H Arty	MA	11986
Horr, John F.	1st Lt. 2nd OH Infy	OH	06893
Horsack, William H.	Capt. CS BvtCol. USV	OR	07148
Horton, Charles C.	LTC 2nd IA Cav	IA	09076
Horton, Charles P.	Capt. ADC BvtLTC USV	MA	00999
Horton, Everett S.	Maj 58th MA Infy	MA	06183
Horton, Joseph H.	LTC 141st PA Infy	NY	06523
Horton, Nathan W.	Capt. 9th PA Cav	NY	04069
Horton, Samuel M.	Col. USA	CA	11815
Horton, William E.	1st Lt. 11th CT Infy BvtMaj	DC	08412
Horton, William L.	1st Lt. 24th MA Infy	MA	00862
Horton, William T.	2nd Lt. 141st PA Infy	PA	13665
Horwitz, Phineas J.	Med. Director USN	PA	00168
Hoschett, John	Capt. 35th IN Infy	KS	04878
Hosea, Lewis M.	Capt. 16th Infy BvtMaj USA	OH	02786
Hosford, Albert W.	Capt. 1st IA Cav	IA	08867
Hoskins, John D.C.	LTC Arty USA	DC	14407
Hoskinson, Thomas J.	Capt. CS BvtMaj USV	OH	10231
Hosmer, Addison A.	Maj Jdge Adv BvtLTC USV	DC	05003
Hotchkiss, Chardles T.	Col. 89th IL BvtBG	IL	03858
Hotchkiss, Frederick E.	1st Lt. 1st NY Cav	CA	13919
Hottel, Martin V.	Capt. 59th IN Infy	DC	13580
Hough, A. Barton	1st Lt. 50th NY Eng.	CO	07490
Hough, Alfred L.	BG USA	PA	00067
Houghton, Albert C.	Capt. 2nd OH Cav BvtMaj	OH	09745
Houghton, Charles W.	Surg. 214th PA Infy	PA	02435
Houghton, Edwin B.	Capt. 17th ME Infy	ME	00670
Houghton, Francis H.	2nd Lt. 17th Batt OH L Arty	OH	06347
Houghton, George C.	Capt. 1st. NH H Arty	MA	11206
Houghton, Thomas F.	Act Asst Paymaster USN	NY	09424
Hoult, Cornelius M.	1st Lt. 14th WVA Infy	MD	15341
House, Charles J.	1st Lt. 1st ME H Arty	ME	09097
House, Leroy Delos	Capt. 108th USCT	OH	06837
Houston, A. Ross	1st Lt. 78th USCT	WI	02025
Houston, David C.	Col. Eng. USA	NY	02092
Houston, George P.	BvtLTC USMC	PA	00188
Houston, James B.	1st Asst Eng. USN	NY	05706
Hovey, Charles H.	LTC 13th MA Infy	MA	08546
Hovey, John G.	Capt. 13th MA Infy	PA	03406
Hovey, Samuel D.	Capt. 31st MA Infy	CA	04520

Name	Rank	Commandery	Insignia No.
Hovey, Solomon, Jr.	Capt. 21st MA Infy	MA	02427
How, James F.	LTC 27th MO Infy	MO	04016
Howard, Charles	1st Lt. 1st MA H Arty	MA	08338
Howard, Charles H.	Col. 128th USCT BvtBG	IL	09244
Howard, Charles R.	Act Asst Paymaster USN	MA	01591
Howard, Edward B.	1st Lt. 14th NH Infy	CA	13238
Howard, Frank A.	1st Lt. 1st MO L Arty	PA	08749
Howard, George F.	Capt. 40th MA Infy	MA	05235
Howard, George N.	1st Lt. 16th MA Infy	MA	15625
Howard, Hartley	Capt. 38th PA Infy BvtMaj	PA	07060
Howard, Horace Z.	Act Ensign USN	CA	04446
Howard, John E.	Capt. CS BvtMaj USV	IL	09656
Howard, John R.	2nd Lt. 2nd MN Cav	MN	09396
Howard, John R.	Capt. ADC USV	NY	12318
Howard, Nelson	1st Lt. 30th ME Infy	ME	07730
Howard, Oliver Otis	MG USA	VT	03808
Howard, Richard L.	Chap 124th IL Infy	ME	09845
Howard, S. Edward	Capt. 8th VT Infy	MA	07534
Howard, W. C.	2nd Lt. 17th Batt OH L Arty	OH	02835
Howard, Willard	Capt. 54th MA Infy	MO	03176
Howe, Albion P.	BG USV BvtMG USA	MA	10489
Howe, Church	Capt. 15th MA Infy BvtMaj	NE	04079
Howe, Elwin A.	Capt. 108th USCT	VT	14303
Howe, George W.	1st Lt. 1st OH L Arty	OH	02984
Howe, H. Warren	2nd Lt. 30th MA Infy	MA	04632
Howe, Henry S.	Maj USA	DC	02935
Howe, James H.	Col. 32nd WI Infy	WI	01563
Howe, Timothy O.	3rd Class (US Senator from WI)	WI	No Number
Howe, Walter	BG USA	DC	16829
Howe, Wesley C.	1st Lt. 2nd MA Cav	MO	13916
Howe, William A.	Capt. 7th OH Infy	OH	09898
Howe, William G.	Capt. 30th MA Infy	MA	01901
Howe, William R.	Capt. AAG USV	PA	08972
Howell, Benjamin R.	Capt. 81st OH Infy	OH	08602
Howell, Franklin D.	1st Lt. 17th Infy USA	PA	00352
Howell, Horatio S.	Capt. 4th NJ Infy	PA	04166
Howell, John C.	RAdm USN	PA	00374
Howell, Richard S.	Capt. AAG USV	PA	00474
Howell, Seymour	LTC USA	MI	09922
Howes, Willis	Act Master USN	MA	10121
Howison, George	1st Lt. 79th NY Infy	IL	18380
Howison, Henry L.	RAdm USN	NY	02353
Howland, Charles C.	Capt. 38th MA Infy	MA	06993
Howland, Levi	Maj 1st WI Cav	WI	03715
Howlett, James P.	1st Lt. 3rd MN Infy	OR	08405
Hoxie, Richard L.	LTC Eng. USA	DC	02511
Hoyt, Alfred	Act Asst Eng. USN	MD	15847
Hoyt, Charles H.	Col. QM BvtBG USV	DC	03982

The Roster

Name	Rank	Commandery	Insignia No.
Hoyt, Charles S.	Surg. 39th NY Infy	NY	07086
Hoyt, Eben, Jr.	Chief Eng. USN	PA	00307
Hoyt, George S.	Maj 7th WI Infy	MO	04789
Hoyt, Henry A.F.	Chap 6th PA Infy	PA	16329
Hoyt, Henry M.	Col. 52nd PA Infy BvtBG	PA	01984
Hoyt, Henry W.B.	Capt. 113th IL Infy	IL	02424
Hoyt, Isaiah F.	1st Lt. 32nd MA Infy	MA	10511
Hoyt, James J.	Capt. 156th NY Infy BvtLTC	IL	01265
Hoyt, John M.	Capt. 7th WI Infy	MO	15707
Hoyt, William	2nd Lt. 112th NY Infy	OH	11891
Hubbard, Charles T.	Asst Surg. USN	MA	06994
Hubbard, Cyrus H.	1st Lt. 23rd OH Infy	CA	03468
Hubbard, Gurdon S., Jr.	BvtMaj USV	IL	02180
Hubbard, James F.	Capt. 30th NJ Infy	NY	08648
Hubbard, John U.	Capt. 21st ME Infy	ME	03346
Hubbard, Lucius F.	Col. 5th MN Infy BvtBG	MN	03714
Hubbard, Nathaniel M.	Capt. 20th IA Infy	IA	09732
Hubbard, Thomas H.	Col. 30th ME Infy BvtBG	NY	02392
Hubbard, William F.	Maj Chap USA	CA	08649
Hubbell, Augustus B.	1st Lt. 42nd OH Infy	OH	16236
Hubbell, Henry W.	BG USA	NY	00233
Hubbell, John McC.	1st Lt. 5th OH Cav	OH	08177
Hubbell, Johnson	1st Lt. 203rd PA Infy	PA	07861
Hubbell, Silas H.	1st Lt. Adj. 107th IL Infy	MO	16569
Hubbell, William L.	Capt. 17th CT Infy	NY	07609
Hubbell, William S.	Capt. 21st CT Infy BvtMaj	NY	06962
Huber, Levi	Maj 96th PA Infy	PA	07643
Hudson, Abijah T.	Surg. 26th IA Infy	CA	07247
Hudson, Adrian	Med. Director USN	CA	05126
Hudson, Frank	2nd Lt. 3rd US Vol. Infy	MO	11401
Hudson, Haynes E.	Capt. 1st MO Eng.	TN	00355
Hudson, James S.	1st Lt. 11th RI Infy	MA	03515
Hudson, John W.	LTC 35th MA Infy	MA	01300
Hudson, Joseph K.	Maj 62nd USCT BG USV	KS	06792
Huested, Alfred B.	Surg. 21st NY Cav	NY	14416
Huey, Pennock	Col. 8th PA Cav BvtBG	PA	06255
Huey, Robert	1st Lt. 2nd TN Infy	PA	06256
Huey, Samuel B.	Act Asst Paymaster USN	PA	01721
Huffman, Albert G.	Asst Surg. 1st KY Cav	KS	05450
Hufty, Samuel	LTC 9th NJ Infy	PA	13937
Hugg, Joseph	Surg. USN	NY	03603
Huggins, Eli L.	BG USA	IL	02125
Hughes, Aaron K.	RAdm USN	DC	09104
Hughes, Charles H.	Surg. 1st Infy MO S.M.	MO	05396
Hughes, James E.	1st. Lt. 2nd CA Infy	CA	02478
Hughes, Robert P.	MG USA	NY	03995
Hughes, Rossel B.	Capt. 2nd MO Cav	MI	08091
Hughes, Thomas	1st Lt. 5th US Vol. Infy	KS	08080

Name	Rank	Commandery	Insignia No.
Hughes, Thomas W.B.	2nd Lt. 90th NY Infy	NY	01636
Hughson, Egbert E.	1st Lt. 8th MN Infy	MN	06556
Huidekoper, Arthur C.	Capt. 211th PA Infy	PA	06257
Huidekoper, Henry S.	LTC 150th PA Infy	PA	02934
Huiskamp, Herman J.	Capt. 6th MO Cav (1st Lt. 50th IA Infy)	IA	11550
Huiskamp, Luke	1st Lt. 6th MO Cav	IA	11378
Hulaniski, Edmund T.	Capt. 12th USC H Arty	IL	17690
Hull, Andress B.	Capt. 20th USCT	IL	09826
Hull, Charles B.	Capt. 67th IL Infy	MI	03733
Hull, George C.	Capt. 97th OH Infy	MO	15155
Hull, Gustavus A.	Capt. Military Storekpr. USA	CA	02725
Hull, Harmon D.	LTC 5th NY Infy	NY	02214
Hull, John A.T.	Capt. 23rd OH Infy	IA	05438
Hull, William	1st Lt. 6th MI Cav	MI	04711
Hull, William E.	Capt. 2nd CA Infy	MN	06882
Hulse, Charles F.	Capt. 121st PA Infy	PA	00025
Humphrey, Charles B.	Capt. 5th Batt WI L Arty	CA	07514
Humphrey, Charles F.	BG QMG USA	DC	02536
Humphrey, George M.	Capt. 42nd WI Infy	NE	03940
Humphrey, Hervey A.	Capt. 8th IL Cav	MN	17933
Humphrey, Lyman U.	1st Lt. 76th OH Infy	KS	06796
Humphrey, P.H.	Surg. 48th & 58th NY Infy	CA	01626
Humphrey, William H.	1st Lt. 2nd US Shrpshtrs.	VT	09252
Humphreys, Charles	LTC Arty USA	CA	12585
Humphreys, Charles A.	Chap 2nd MA Cav	MA	10047
Humphreys, George H.	Surg. 9th NY Infy	NY	03363
Hunt, Andrew L.	1st Lt. 134th IL Infy	IL	11600
Hunt, Charles	Capt. 44th MA Infy	MA	00819
Hunt, Charles B.	LTC 2nd MO Cav (Col. 1st OH Infy)	OH	02713
Hunt, Charles C.	Capt. 4th MN Infy	CA	05461
Hunt, Charles C.	Asst Surg. 107th OH Infy	IL	11978
Hunt, David R.	Capt. 25th OH Infy	OH	12267
Hunt, Edward H.	1st Lt. 8th NY Cav	MI	08199
Hunt, George	Capt. 12th IL Infy	IL	04149
Hunt, Henry J.	BG USV BvtMG USA	DC	04327
Hunt, James H.	2nd Lt. 14th NH Infy	MA	16915
Hunt, John W.	Maj Surg. USV	CA	15265
Hunt, Leavitt	BvtLTC	NY	01221
Hunt, Lewis C.	Col. 14th Infy BvtBG USA	OR	03638
Hunt, Philemon B.	LTC 4th KY Infy	IN	15883
Hunt, Robert H.	Maj 15th KS Cav BvtLTC	KS	04921
Hunter, David	BvtMG	NY	00579
Hunter, George B.	2nd Lt. 13th IA Infy	IA	11760
Hunter, James B.	Surg. 60th IN Infy	NY	06021
Hunter, Morton C.	Col. 82nd IN Infy BvtBG	IN	11179
Hunter, Robert	Capt. 74th OH Infy	OH	03564 (Dup)
Hunter, Samuel B.	Surg. 7th ME Infy	ME	08587
Hunter, Thomas	Capt. 110th NY Infy	NY	07610

The Roster

Name	Rank	Commandery	Insignia No.
Hunter, William	LTC 32nd IL Infy	PA	00353
Hunting, George F.	1st Lt. 3rd Arty USA	MI	04076
Huntington, Charles L.	Commander USN	PA	01011
Huntington, Charles P.	Maj 1st US Vet. Vols. Eng.	WI	06451
Huntington, David L.	LTC Dept. Surg. Gen. USA	DC	11389
Huntington, Edward S.	Capt. 29th Infy USA	MA	09670
Huntington, Henry A.	1st Lt. 4th Arty BvtMaj USA	IL	01941
Huntington, Robert W.	Col. USMC	PA	08457
Huntley, Silas S.	1st Lt. 37th NY Infy	KS	08079
Huntoon, Andrew J.	Capt. 12th NH Infy	DC	03728
Huntt, George G.	Col. 2nd Cav USA	PA	08458
Hurd, Charles H.	Capt. AAG BvtMaj USV	MA	01424
Hurd, Ethan O.	Capt. 39th OH Infy	OH	02851
Hurd, Orin D.	LTC 30th IN Infy	IN	09461
Hurd, Theodore C.	2nd Lt. 45th MA Infy	MA	01409
Hurd, William H.	2nd Lt. 50th MA Infy	MA	06914
Hurlburt, Herbert W.	2nd Lt. 2nd WI Infy	MO	16117
Hurlburt, James S.	Act Ensign USN	MO	12803
Hurlburt, Samuel D.	Passed Asst Paymaster USN	NY	01441
Hurlburt, Ward B.	Capt. 2nd VT Infy	VT	13645
Hurst, John L.	Maj 3rd WVA Cav BvtLTc	OH	13467
Hurst, Joseph H.	Capt. 12th Infy USA	PA	03555
Husk, Lewis W.	Col. 111th NY Infy	WI	09944
Hussey, Cyrus	LTC 192nd OH Infy	OH	07942
Hustead, James M.	1st Lt. 14th PA Cav	PA	08973
Husted, Albert N.	Capt. 44th NY Infy	NY	15792
Husted, Gilbert M.	Capt. AQM USV	DC	11296
Hutchings, Jasper	LTC 78th USCT	ME	10935
Hutchings, William V.	LTC QM USV	MA	00632
Hutchins, Benjamin F.	BvtMaj US Cav	PA	00713
Hutchins, Charles J.	Chap 39th WI Infy	CA	02866
Hutchins, Charles T.	RAdm USN	DC	17700
Hutchins, Chauncey B.	Surg. 116th NY Infy	CA	02303
Hutchins, Horace A.	BvtLTC USV	OH	04643
Hutchins, John	3rd Class (Representative OH)	OH	05353
Hutchins, John C.	1st Lt. 2nd OH Cav	OH	03195
Hutchins, Morris C.	Capt. 10th KY Infy	OH	07940
Hutchinson, Buel E.	Capt. CS USV	WI	06852
Hutchinson, Calvin G.	Act Asst Paymaster USN	MA	15516
Hutchinson, Eben	LTC 24th ME Infy	MA	01759
Hutchinson, Edwin	Surg. 137th NY Infy	NY	01637
Hutchinson, James W.	2nd Asst Eng. USN	IL	07581
Hutchinson, John H.	Surg. 15th MI Infy	MO	00779-11351
Hutchinson, John J.	1st Lt. 7th CT Infy	MA	08061
Hutchinson, John W.	1st Lt. 13th NY Cav	NY	15576
Hutchinson, Joseph G.	Capt. 28th PA Infy	IA	06203
Hutchinson, William F.	Surg. 22nd NY Infy	PA	01533
Hutsinpiller, John C.	2nd Lt. 1st OH H Arty	OH	07841

Name	Rank	Commandery	Insignia No.
Hutt, George W.	1st Lt. 1st KS Infy	CA	18204
Huttman, Berend H.	Capt. 72nd NY Infy	NY	04486
Hutton, Charles G.	Capt. ADC BvtMaj USV	NY	06961
Huxford, William P.	Maj USA	DC	04355
Huxley, Edward C.	1st Lt. RQM 2nd CT H Arty	MA	09807
Hyatt, Charles E.	1st Lt. 20th NY Cav	NY	10164
Hyatt, Chauncey W.	1st Lt. 38th WI Infy	CA	06365
Hyatt, Henry H.	1st Lt. 24th IN Infy	IN	07267
Hyde, George H.	Capt. 37th MA Infy	KS	07733
Hyde, James N.	Passed Asst Surg. USN	IL	02017
Hyde, Joel W.	Asst Surg. 29th CT Infy	NY	09425
Hyde, John McE.	BG USA	CA	03186
Hyde, Joseph	LTC 125th NY Infy	CA	07244
Hyde, Marcus D.	Master USN	CA	02875 (Dup)
Hyde, Simeon T.	1st Lt. 15th CT Infy	NY	01339
Hyde, Thomas W.	Col. 1st ME Infy BvtBG	ME	00260
Hyde, William L.	Chap 112th NY Infy	NY	10496
Hyland, George	Maj 13th NY Infy	NY	11044
Hyndman, William	Capt. 4th PA Cav	NY	04904
Hynes, Dennis J.	LTC 17th IL Cav BvtCol.	IL	13546
Hysell, James H.	Surg. 1st WVA Infy	OH	09452
Ide, Horace K.	Capt. 1st VT Cav BvtMaj	VT	11641
Igel, Richard L.	2nd Lt. 32nd IN Infy	KS	07623
Ijams, William H.	Capt. 30th OH Infy	NE	04080
Iler, Jacob W.	Capt. 49th OH Infy	NE	05758
Ilsley, Charles S.	LTC 6th Cav USA	MA	04243 (Dup)
Ilsley, Edwin	LTC 12th ME Infy	ME	11584
Inch, Philip	Chief Eng. USN	DC	04474
Inch, Richard	RAdm USN	PA	08974 (Dup)
Inches, Charles E.	Asst Surg. 37th MA Infy	MA	01069
Ingalls, James M.	Col. USA	VT	12686
Ingalls, John J.	3rd Class (US Senator KS)	KS	07174
Ingalls, Joseph A.	1st Lt. AQM 8th MA Infy	MA	01388
Ingalls, Rufus	BG QMG BvtMG USA	OR	00588
Ingalls, William	Surg. 59th MA Infy	MA	01186
Ingersoll, Joseph	Capt. 76th IL Infy	OH	05669
Ingersoll, Royal R.	RAdm USN	DC	16166
Ingham, George T.	1st Lt. 11th Infy BvtMaj USA	PA	04414
Ingle, John	1st Lt. 10th IN Cav	IN	08142
Ingledew, Lumley	Capt. CS BvtMaj USV	IL	08402
Inglis, James, Jr.	Capt. 25th NJ Infy	NY	07241
Ingraham, Timothy	1st Lt. 38th MA Infy	OH	07767
Inman, Henry	BvtMaj USA	PA	00555
Inman, James	2nd Lt. 17th MA Infy	MO	07811
Innes, John C.	Capt. 2nd CA Infy	CA	03336
Innes, Robert S.	1st Lt. RQM 1st MI Eng.	PA	06838
Innes, William	Col. 15th USCT	KS	04804
Insley, Merritt H.	Capt. AQM USA	KS	04436

Name	Rank	Commandery	Insignia No.
Ireland, John	Chap 5th MN Infy	MN	05686
Ireland, Oscar B.	2nd Lt. Sig. Corps BvtCapt USV	MA	10382
Irish, Dallas C.	Capt. 13th Infy BvtLTC USA	PA	11158
Irish, Francis	Capt. 45th NY Infy	NY	07988
Irvin, Edward A.	Capt. 42nd PA Infy	PA	05988
Irving, Alexander D.	1st Lt. 176th NY Infy	NY	06749
Irwin, Bernard J.D.	BG USA	CA	00640
Irwin, David A.	Capt. 4th Cav USA	DC	06799
Irwin, George McL.	Maj 5th PA H Arty	PA	07644
Irwin, John	RAdm USN	CA	02905
Irwin, Lambdin E.	1st Lt. Adj. 14th MO Cav	MO	07292
Irwin, Richard B.	LTC AAG USV	NY	01343
Isham, Asa B.	1st Lt. 7th MI Cav	OH	03377
Isom, John F.	Capt. 25th IL Cav	OH	03259
Itsell, Andrew J.	Capt. 10th MI Cav	CA	14010
Ives, Brayton	Col. 1st CT Cav BvtBG	NY	10497
Ives, William	Capt. 33rd Infy PA Militia	PA	11831
Jacklin, Rufus W.	Maj 10th MI Infy BvtLTC MI	MI	10388
Jackman, Lyman	Capt. 6th NH Infy	MA	16623
Jackson, Albert	2nd Asst Eng. USN	MA	15867
Jackson, Albert J.	2nd Lt. 2nd IL Cav	IL	11280
Jackson, Allan H.	LTC 134th NY Infy	CA	12216
Jackson, Amos M.	Maj 10th USC H Arty BvtLTC	MA	09237
Jackson, Andrew	2nd Lt. 42nd WI Infy	WI	05371
Jackson, Calvin C.	Pay Director USN	PA	00372
Jackson, Charles H.	Col. 18th WI Infy	IA	12507
Jackson, Edward C.	Capt. 125th NY Infy	NE	05454
Jackson, Elias G.	1st Lt. 41st WI Infy	WI	16900
Jackson, Heman B.	2nd Lt. 2nd WI Infy	IL	02082
Jackson, Henry	BG USA	KS	00645
Jackson, Huntington W.	1st Lt. 4th NJ Infy BvtLTC	IL	01924
Jackson, James	Col. USA	OR	03537
Jackson, John P.	LTC 23 KY Infy	CA	12305
Jackson, John W.	Surg. 48th MO Infy	MO	07175
Jackson, Joseph R.	Capt. 69th IN Infy	IN	04542
Jackson, Mason	Maj USA	CA	05533
Jackson, Patrick T.	1st Lt. 5th MA Cav	MA	01003
Jackson, Richard H.	BG BvtMG USV	NY	00223
Jackson, Riel E.	Capt. 11th WI Infy	WI	04978
Jackson, Robert F.	1st Lt. Adj. 32nd OH Infy	CA	17615
Jackson, Robert W.	1st Lt. 21st WI Infy	WI	05468
Jackson, Samuel	Med. Director USN	DC	05468
Jackson, Samuel McC	Col. 40th PA Infy BvtBG	PA	04169
Jackson, Thomas M.	Capt. 3rd NH Infy	MA	16112
Jacobi, Otto F.	Capt. 10th TN Infy	IN	10036
Jacobs, Ferris	LTC 26th NY Cav BvtBG	DC	02433
Jacobs, Gustavus	2nd Lt. 21st WI Infy	OH	13122
Jacobs, Horace G.	2nd Lt. 6th ME Infy Bvt1stLt	DC	11609

Name	Rank	Commandery	Insignia No.
Jacobs, Jesse E.	Capt. AAG BvtCol. USV	DC	02065
Jacobs, Joseph T.	1st Lt. Adj. 178th OH Infy	MI	05273
Jacobs, William C.	Surg. 81st OH Infy	OH	03204
Jacobs, William H.	Capt. 20th OH Infy	MO	11273
Jacoby, Lawrence	Capt. 1st Batt IN L Arty	KS	08592
James, Edward C.	Col. 106th NY Infy	NY	11917
James, Frank B.	Capt. 52nd OH Infy BvtMaj	OH	02883
James, Garth W.	Capt. 54th MA Infy	WI	00864
James, Martin S.	Capt. 3rd RI H Arty	MA	15866
James, Robertson	Capt. 55th MA Infy	WI	02060
James, William	Capt. 33rd USCT	OH	15613
James, William A.	Capt. 3rd RI Cav BvtMaj	IL	06937
James, William G.	1st Lt. 2nd LA Cav	CA	12307
James, William L.	Capt. AQM BvtBG USV	PA	01659
Jameson, Albion B.	1st Lt. 35th PA Infy BvtCapt	DC	06876
Jameson, Robert E.	1st Lt. 29th MA Infy	MA	11824
Janes, Henry	Surg. 3rd VT Infy Bvt LTC	VT	09169
Janes, Henry W.	Maj QM BvtLTC USA	PA	00288
Janeway, Jacob J.	LTC 14th NJ Infy BvtCol.	PA	07862
Janeway, John H.	Col. USA	NY	06134
Janeway, John L	Chap 30th NJ Infy	PA	06464
Janney, Bernard T.	Capt. 197th PA Infy	DC	10937
Janney, George	2nd Lt. 198th PA Infy	PA	00209
Janney, Joseph J.	2nd Lt. Purnell Legion MD Cav	MD	09105
Janney, Spencer M.	1st Lt. RQM 197th PA Infy	PA	01851
Janney, Thomas J.	1st Lt. 25th OH Infy	MN	04248
Janney, William S.	Surg. 22nd NJ Infy	PA	08750
Janvrin, Joseph E.	Asst Surg. 15th NH Infy	NY	11243
Jaques, William H.	Lt. USN	MA	16360
Jaques, William H.C.	Capt. 56th USCT	IA	11079
Jardine, Edward	LTC 17th NY Infy BvtBG	NY	01191
Jarves, Deming	2nd Lt. 24th MA Infy	CA	02418
Jarvis, Dwight	Col. 13th OH Infy BvtBG	OH	13591
Jarvis, George C.	Surg. 7th CT Infy	MA	01201
Jarvis, Horatio D.	LTC 24th MA Infy	MA	00824
Jasnowski, Saturnin	1st Lt. 27th MI Infy	MI	10593
Jastram, Pardon S.	1st Lt. 1st RI L Arty	MA	05158
Jay, William	Capt. ADC BvtLTC USV	NY	05406
Jeancon, John A.	Maj 32nd IN Infy	OH	11622
Jeffrey, John H.	Capt. 56th MA Infy	CA	16282
Jeffrey, Thomas	Capt. 14th Batt OH L Arty	OH	15611
Jeffries, Enos P.	2nd Lt. 17th PA Cav	PA	08974 (Dup)
Jeffries, Noah L.	Col. Vet. Res. Corps BvtBG	DC	04773
Jenings, Jefferson H.	1st Lt. 17th KY Infy	DC	02832
Jenkins, Cardoc C.	1st Lt. 115th USCT	OH	06890
Jenkins, David P.	LTC 14th IL Cav	OR	05589
Jenkins, Horatio, Jr.	BvtBG USV	MA	01449
Jenkins, James H.	1st Lt. Adj. 21st WI Infy	WI	02193

Name	Rank	Commandery	Insignia No.
Jenkins, Richard W.	Capt. 2nd CO Cav	KS	06295
Jenkins, Thornton A.	RAdm USN	DC	00158
Jenkins, Wilton A.	LTC 5th KS Cav	IL	02678
Jenks, Albert	LTC 36th IL Infy	CA	03461
Jenks, George W.	1st Lt. 10th MI Infy	MI	05347
Jenks, James D.	BvtLTC USV	CA	04090
Jenness, Joseph K.	2nd Lt. 11th NY Cav	MA	01748
Jenness, Lyndon Y.	2nd Lt. 32nd MA Infy	MA	07133
Jenney, William Le B.	Capt. ADC BvtMaj USV	IL	02188
Jennings, Benjamin F.	1st Lt. 155th PA Infy	PA	05248
Jennings, John H.	2nd Lt. 3rd IL Cav	IL	12645
Jennings, Wallace H.	Capt. 1st WI H Arty	WA	08902
Jennings, William	Act Master USN	MN	12090
Jennings, William W.	Col. 127th PA Infy	PA	04927
Jennison, Samuel P.	LTC 10th MN Infy BvtBG	MN	03494
Jensen, John	2nd Lt. 12th USC H Arty	NE	07169
Jerome, David H.	3rd Class	MI	06990
Jerome, Edward B.	2nd Lt. 71st PA Infy	CA	02709
Jessup, Jonathan	2nd Lt. 187th PA Infy	PA	16934
Jessup, Robert B.	Surg. 24th IN Infy	IN	07268
Jewell, Charles A.	1st Lt. Adj. 22nd CT Infy	NY	06736
Jewell, James A.	LTC 59th NY Infy	DC	06875
Jewell, Orville D.	Capt. 156th NY Infy BvtLTC	NY	01299
Jewell, Theodore F.	RAdm USN	DC	11370
Jewell, William H.	Capt. 38th MA Infy	NY	01638
Jewett, Erastus W.	1st Lt. 9th VT Infy	VT	05876
Jewett, George	Surg. 51st MA Infy	MA	09238
Jewett, George D.	1st Lt. 13th Batt MI L Arty	MI	08024
Jewett, Horace	Col. 21st Infy USA	MN	00434
Jewett, John E.	LTC 193rd OH Infy	KS	10097
Jewett, John H.	2nd Lt. Vet. Res. Corps.	NY	16585
Jewett, Leonidas M.	Capt. 61st OH Infy BvtMaj	OH	06840
Jewett, Pliny A.	Surg. BvtCol. USV	NY	00875
Jewett, Richard H.L.	Capt. 54th MA Infy	MN	05687
Jocelyn, Stephen P.	Capt. 3rd CA Infy	KS	03327
Jocelyn, Stephen P.	Col. 14th Infy USA	VT	03327
Johnson, Albert H.	1st Lt. 10th ME Infy	CA	08883
Johnson, Andrew W.	Capt. USN	PA	00327
Johnson, Charles A.	Col. 25th NY Infy BvtBG	NY	01263
Johnson, Charles A.	Capt. 14th Infy USA	OR	05463
Johnson, Daniel	Act 2nd Asst Eng. USN	DC	15225
Johnson, Daniel H.	Capt. 40th MA Infy	NY	05832
Johnson, Edward C.	1st Lt. Adj. 44th MA Infy	MA	01131
Johnson, Edward P.	2nd Lt. 68th IN Infy	CA	05465
Johnson, Edward S.	Maj 7th IL Infy BvtLTC	IL	14729
Johnson, Elias H.	Act Asst Paymaster USN	PA	07863
Johnson, Elizur G.	Capt. 8th OH Infy	OH	14660
Johnson, George K.	LTC Med. Inspector BvtCol. USV	MI	03743

Name	Rank	Commandery	Insignia No.
Johnson, George R.	Chief Eng. USN	DC	07396
Johnson, George W.	1st Lt. RQM 8th MD Infy	DC	10554
Johnson, George W.	Capt. 3rd IA Cav BvtMaj	CA	03238
Johnson, Hannibal A.	1st Lt. 1st Battn. ME Infy	MA	07964
Johnson, Henry	Capt. Med. Storekpr. USA	CA	03664
Johnson, Henry J.	1st Lt. Adj. 2nd WVA Infy	DC	03027
Johnson, Henry W.	Capt. AQM BvtMaj USV	IL	07582
Johnson, Hosmer	3rd Class	IL	05139
Johnson, Hugh M.	1st Lt. 5th Infy USA	PA	00933
Johnson, Isaac	Capt. 114th USCT	PA	11832
Johnson, James B.	1st Lt. RCS 3rd MI Cav	DC	09915
Johnson, James W.	Capt. 3rd USCT	NY	01548
Johnson, Jerome B.	1st Lt. 6th WI Infy	WI	04123
Johnson, John	Chief Eng. USN	PA	00404
Johnson, John B.	2nd Lt. 5th Batt NY L Arty	NY	13758
Johnson, John Blosser	Capt. 137th IL Infy	KS	04820
Johnson, John Bucher	Capt. 6th Cav BvtLTC USA	PA	00461
Johnson, John Burgess	Capt. 3rd Cav USA	MO	03092
Johnson, John C.	Maj 110th PA Infy	PA	09769
Johnson, John D.	1st Lt. RQM 38th MO Infy	MO	13903
Johnson, John O.	Act Master USN	ME	11478
Johnson, John R.	1st Lt. 23rd PA Infy	NY	02561
Johnson, Joseph E.	Capt. 58th PA Infy BvtMaj	PA	00320
Johnson, Joseph W.	3rd Class	PA	00119
Johnson, Laurence	1st Lt. 8th USC H Arty	NY	05833
Johnson, Lewis	Col. 44th USCT BvtBG	IN	04811
Johnson, Mortimer L.	RAdm USN	MA	12427
Johnson, Parish B.	Capt. AQM USV	WA	03111
Johnson, Philip C.	RAdm USN	DC	00140
Johnson, Richard W.	MG USA	IL	00099
Johnson, Robert S.	Capt. 1st CA Cav	CA	03907
Johnson, Robert Z.	2nd Lt. 7th NY Cav	CA	07216
Johnson, Ruel M.	Col. 100th IN Infy	IN	05192
Johnson, Sherman A.	2nd Lt. 123rd OH Infy	DC	10089
Johnson, Thomas H.	2nd Lt. 2nd Corps Cadets MA Infy	MA	05027
Johnson, Thomas S.	Capt. 176th NY Infy	NY	07465
Johnson, William C.	2nd Lt. 42nd USCT	OH	06887
Johnson, William E.	Maj Surg. 109th NY Infy	NY	15790
Johnson, William J.	Surg. USN	PA	00428
Johnson, William P.	Surg. 18th OH Infy	IN	06598
Johnston, James	Asst Surg. 141st OH Infy	OH	07421
Johnston, James B.	2nd Lt. 12th IL Infy	IL	17116
Johnston, James W.	Capt. 121st NY Infy BvtMaj	NY	14452
Johnston, John L.	Maj USA	NY	16319
Johnston, John V.	Act Vol. Lt. USN	MO	11127
Johnston, John W.	Capt. 12th NH Infy	MA	11266
Johnston, Joseph R.	2nd Lt. 25th Batt OH L Arty	OH	05001
Johnston, Thomas B.	Capt. 30th MA Infy BvtMaj	MA	08735

The Roster 269

Name	Rank	Commandery	Insignia No.
Johnston, Walter S.	Capt. 184th PA Infy	NY	02820
Johnston, William H.	Maj Paymaster BvtLTC USA	PA	00993
Johnston, William N.	Capt. 102nd NY Infy	NY	06732
Johnstone, Louis M.	1st Lt. Batt I, PA L Arty	NY	12400
Jolly, John H.	BvtLTC USV	DC	15226
Jonas, Edward	Capt. ADC BvtLTC USV	OH	07422
Jones, Abram	Capt. 1st NY Cav	CA	17616
Jones, Albert K.	Act Master USN	MA	07971
Jones, Albert W.	1st Lt. 17th IL Infy	CO	06311
Jones, Charles H.	1st Lt. 97th OH Infy	OH	09896
Jones, Charles H.	Chief Sailmaker USN	PA	14473
Jones, David	1st Lt. RQM 97th PA Infy	PA	00439
Jones, David J.	Capt. 1st KY Infy	OH	10559
Jones, David Lloyd	1st Lt. Adj. 16th WI Infy	WI	01332 (Dup)
Jones, David Paul	Capt. 85th PA Infy	CA	02094
Jones, David Phillips	Chief Eng. USN	IL	06299
Jones, Delancy Floyd	Col. 3rd Infy USA	NY	02267
Jones, Edward F.	Col. 26th MA Infy BvtBG	NY	04688
Jones, Edward J.	Capt. 11th Batt MA L Arty BvtMaj	MA	01452
Jones, Edward W.	Maj 2nd CT H Arty BvtLTC	CA	04900
Jones, Francis B.	LTC USA	NY	00103
Jones, Frank J.	Capt. AAG BvtMaj USV	OH	02717 (Dup)
Jones, Frank J.	1st Lt. 1st CT H Arty	NY	11851
Jones, George E.	Act Asst Surg. USN	OH	03043
Jones, Henry B.	1st Lt. 3rd MA H Arty	MA	01812
Jones, Henry E.	Capt. 146th NY Infy BvtMaj	OR	03634
Jones, Henry R.	Capt. USA	PA	05247
Jones, Horatio M.	2nd Lt. 4th US Arty & 58th PA Infy	PA	01527
Jones, James H.	Col. USMC	PA	00471
Jones, James K.	2nd Lt. 24th OH Infy	OH	02784
Jones, John A.	1st Lt. 21st IL Infy	OH	16365
Jones, John G.	Capt. 24th MA Infy	MA	01384
Jones, John P.H.	1st Lt. 2nd PA Cav	PA	00603
Jones, John S.	Col. 174th OH Infy BvtBG	OH	09450
Jones, Julius M.	Maj Paymaster USV	IA	10982
Jones, Leon E.	1st Lt. 12th PA Cav	CA	09542
Jones, Marcellus E.	Capt. 8th IL Cav	IL	12161
Jones, Martin	Cap. 134th NY Infy	CA	11525
Jones, Merriweather P.	Lt. Commander USN	PA	00185
Jones, Owen	1st Asst Eng. USN	PA	10398
Jones, Paul T., Jr.	Capt. 2nd PA H Arty	PA	01608
Jones, Richard H.	Capt. 128th PA Infy	PA	07645
Jones, Samuel B.	2nd Lt. 11th VT Infy	NE	04308
Jones, Theodore	Col. 30th OH Infy BvtBG	OH	14026
Jones, Thomas	1st Lt. 22nd IN Infy	IN	12282
Jones, Thomas H.	1st Lt. Adj. 50th IN Infy	MO	14699
Jones, Thomas R.	Capt. 131st PA Infy	DC	11666
Jones, Toland	LTC 113th OH Infy	OH	07199

Name	Rank	Commandery	Insignia No.
Jones, Wells S.	Col. 53rd OH Infy BvtBG	OH	06517
Jones, William A.	LTC 142nd NY Infy BvtCol.	NY	12628
Jones, William A.	Col. Eng. USA	DC	02903
Jones, William C.	Capt. 10th KS Infy & LTC 19th KS Cav	KS	04873
Jones, William H.	1st Lt. 126th IL Infy	CA	12275
Jones, William Hatch	1st Lt. 29th NY Cav	MA	01528 (Dup)
Jones, William N.	Capt. 106th PA Infy	PA	06258
Jones, William R.	Capt. 97th PA Infy	PA	05989
Jones, William W.	Capt. 2nd WI Infy	DC	08690
Jordan, Francis	Maj Paymaster USV	PA	08459
Jordan, Franklin	Act Ensign USN	CA	04524
Jordan, John W.	Maj 57th IN Infy BvtLTC	IN	10671
Jordan, Thomas A.	2nd Lt. 13th NY Infy	OR	04186
Jordan, Thomas J.	Col. 9th PA Cav BvtBG	PA	01346
Jordan, William H.	Col. 19th Infy USA	OR	10460
Jose', Horatio N.	1st Lt. 12th ME Infy	PA	00678
Joslin, George C.	LTC 15th MA Infy	MA	01558
Josselyn, Simeon T.	1st Lt. 13th IL Infy	NE	04085
Jouett, James E.	RAdm USN	DC	00583-386
Joy, Charles F.	Capt. 54th MA	MA	02311
Joy, Edmund L.	Maj Jdge Adv USV	NY	05120
Joyce, John A.	1st Lt. 24th KY Infy	DC	15838
Juarez, Benito	3rd Class (President of Mexico)	PA	00156
Judd, Edward D.	Capt. 1st MI Infy	CA	02727
Judd, Edwin D.	LTC USA	NY	02924
Judd, George E.	Maj USA	MI	07280
Judson, J.A.	Capt. AAG USV	MA	02194
Judson, Oliver A.	Surg. BvtCol. USV	PA	05496
Julian, George N.	Capt. 13th NH Infy	MA	05103
Jussen, Carl	1st Lt. Adj. 23rd WI Infy	NY	02367
Justice, Jefferson	1st Lt. RQM 100th PA Infy	PA	11717
Kafer, John C.	Passed Asst. Eng. USN	NY	05725
Kahlo, Chales	1st Lt. 163d OH Infy	IN	06599
Kaiser, Julius A.	Passed Asst Eng. USN	PA	03091
Kallman, Herman F.	Col. 2nd US Reserves MO Infy	MI	11411
Kammerling, Gustav	Col. 9th OH Infy	IN	11897
Kane, Aloysius Jose'	Ensign USN	WA	09717
Kane, James J.	Chap USN	WA	10688
Kane, Theodore F.	Capt. USN	NY	00305
Kappner, Ignatz	Col. 3rd USC H Arty	MO	05281
Kaps, John	Capt. 91st OH Infy	OH	15708
Kaps, Peter	1st Lt. 15th KY Infy	OH	16377 (Dup)
Kapus, William	1st Lt. 1st WA Infy	OR	00620
Karge, Joseph	Col. 2nd NJ Cav BvtBG	PA	02436
Kattenstroth, John H.	1st Lt. 9th CT Infy	NY	06745
Kauffman, Albert B.	LTC USA	MO	05201
Kauffman, Joseph A.	1st Lt. 154th PA Infy	PA	04415
Kautz, August V.	BG USV BvtMG USA	DC	03095

Name	Rank	Commandery	Insignia No.
Kay, Samuel W.	Act Asst Paymaster USN	PA	01757
Kaye, John W.	2nd Lt. 3rd PA H Arty	PA	02634
Keam, Thomas V.	2nd Lt. 1st NM Cav	PA	08232
Kearney, James A.	Act Ensign USN	CA	17812
Keatley, John H.	1st Lt. 104th PA Infy	DC	17812
Kedzie, Robert C.	Surg. 12th MI Infy	MI	12266
Keeffe, Joseph	Capt. 4th Infy USA	NE	04827
Keeler, Charles F.	1st Lt. 1st CT Cav	IL	02675 (Dup)
Keeler, William B.	LTC 35th IA Infy BvtCol.	IL	02422 (Dup)
Keen, William W.	Asst Surg. 1st Lt. 5th Infy USA	PA	16218
Keene, Henry C.	Lt. USN	MA	09059
Keene, Henry E.	3rd Class	PA	00118
Keene, William H.	2nd Lt. 8th MA Infy	MA	15262
Keese, Francis S.	LTC 128th NY Infy BvtCol.	PA	04660
Keifer, J. Warren	Col. 110th OH Infy BvtBG BvtMG USV	OH	02484
Keith, Alfred H.	Capt. 6th VT Infy BvtLTC	PA	07338
Keith, Edwin H.	Act 2nd Asst Eng. USN	MA	03164
Keith, Fordyce M.	Capt. 1st USC H Arty	CO	09229
Keith, Theodore S.	Act Passed Asst Surg. USN	MA	04243 (Dup)
Keith, Walter D.	Capt. 26th Unattached Co. MA Infy	NY	06218
Keith, William	1st Lt. 5th MI Cav	MI	06919
Kell, William H.	Maj USA	DC	03956
Kellam, Alphonso G.	Capt. 22nd WI Infy	WI	07796
Keller, Augustus R.	Capt. AQM USV	OH	08156
Keller, Jacob W.	Maj USA	NY	09113
Keller, Louis	Capt. 58th OH Infy	OH	07313
Keller, Theodoric G.	Capt. 66th OH Infy	OH	07022
Kelley, Benjamin F.	BG BvtMG USV	DC	05938
Kelley, Duren F.	1st Lt. 65th USCT	MN	16795
Kelley, Frank M.	2nd Lt. 44th NY Infy BvtCapt	NY	03779
Kelley, George W.	Capt. 103rd PA Infy	CA	07248
Kelley, Harrison	1st Lt. Adj. 44th NY Infy	IL	09202
Kelley, Hiram L.	1st Lt. 2nd MO L Arty	MO	06051 (Dup)
Kelley, John G.	Capt. 1st NV Infy	CO	10186
Kelley, John G.	LTC 7th WVA Infy	PA	11949
Kelley, Joseph M	Maj 10th Cav USA	PA	01256
Kelley, Leverett M.	Capt. 36th IL Infy	DC	07897
Kelley, Samuel H.	Capt. 9th VT Infy	VT	09191
Kelley, William H.H.	Capt. 5th KS Cav	KS	06976
Kelliher, John	Maj 20th MA Infy	MN	03833
Kellogg, Augustus G.	Commander USN	DC	02358
Kellogg, Charles W.	Capt. 29th OH Infy	MA	03381
Kellogg, Edgar R.	BG USA	KS	05352
Kellogg, John A.	Col. 6th WI Infy BvtBG	WI	02097
Kellogg, Justin P.	1st Lt. 52nd MA Infy	MA	13191
Kellogg, Racine D.	Maj 34th IA Infy	IA	10293
Kellogg, Rowland C.	Capt. CS BvtMaj USV	NY	05411
Kellogg, Sanford C.	Maj 4th Cav BvtLTC USA	DC	03816

Name	Rank	Commandery	Insignia No.
Kellogg, Theodore H.	1st Lt. 7th Squadron RI Cav	NY	16780
Kellogg, William L.	Col. 5th Infy USA	CA	03646
Kellogg, William P.	Col. 7th IL Cav	DC	10372
Kelly, Bernard	Maj Chap USA	KS	06155
Kelly, Henry K.	Capt. 118th PA Infy	PA	02126
Kelly, John	Capt. 16th WI Infy	WI	14487
Kelly, Joseph J.	Col. 107th IL Infy	NE	05760
Kelly, Robert M.	Col. 4th KY Infy	OH	03072
Kelly, Samuel B.	2nd Lt. 10th KY Cav	OH	07204
Kelly, William	1st Lt. 8th USCT	KS	08929
Kelsey, Percival G.	Capt. 26th IN Infy	IN	09011
Kelsey, William A.	Capt. 152nd IN Infy	IN	18138
Kelton, John C.	BG USA	DC	05335
Kemble, Arthur	Act Asst Eng. USN	MA	01138
Kemble, Edward C.	Maj Paymaster BvtLTC USV	NY	02895
Kemp, Joseph R.	Maj 6th PA H Arty	MD	14236
Kemper, Adam	Capt. 6th USC H Arty	KS	06300
Kemper, Andrew C.	Capt. AAG USV	OH	02585
Kemper, General W.H.	Asst Surg. 17th IN Infy	IN	04648
Kempff, Louis	RAdm USN	CA	03236
Kempster, Walter	1st Lt. 10th NY Cav	WI	01588
Kempton, Frank H.	Capt. 58th MA Infy	MA	14389
Kenaga, William, Jr.	2nd Lt. 76th IL Infy	IL	16487
Kendall, Alva F.	Capt. 91st OH Infy	OH	09345
Kendall, Charles B.	Capt. 25th MA Infy	CA	07848
Kendall, Frederic A.	Maj USA	OH	00736
Kendall, Henry M.	Maj USA	DC	08299
Kendall, Joseph R.	Capt. 44th MA Infy	MA	10747
Kendall, Joseph V.	1st Lt. 50th PA Infy	MO	09390
Kendall, Robert B.	1st Lt. Adj. 12th ME Infy	MA	04972
Kenderdine, Harry M.	1st Lt. 17th IA Infy	KS	15492
Kendig, Daniel	Maj Chap USA	CA	01026 (Dup)
Kendrick, Frederick H.M.	Maj 7th Infy USA	MN	03999
Kendricken, Paul H.	Act 2nd Asst Eng. USN	MA	06995
Kenfield, Frank	Capt. 17th VT Infy	VT	09179
Kenly, William L.	Capt. CS BvtMaj USV	DC	06873
Kennan, Thomas L.	1st Lt. 10th WI Infy	WI	04380
Kennedy, Charles W.	Capt. 156th NY Infy	NY	03781
Kennedy, Crammond	Chap 79th NY Infy	DC	11667
Kennedy, George B.	Capt. 196th OH Infy	CA	03632
Kennedy, John C.	Capt. 13th IL Cav	CA	08557
Kennedy, Josiah F.	Asst Surg. USA	IA	13436
Kennedy, Robert P.	BvtBG USV	OH	05818
Kennedy, William B.	Maj 4th Cav USA	OH	04091
Kennett, John	Col. 4th OH Cav	OH	07936
Kenney, Charles A.	1st Lt. 104th NY Infy	CA	02708
Kenney, Clesson	2nd Lt. 53rd MA Infy	MA	07956
Kenniston, George B.	1st Lt. 5th ME Infy	ME	05681

Name	Rank	Commandery	Insignia No.
Kenny, Albert S.	Paymaster Gen. USN	DC	08650
Kent, Alba M.	1st Lt. 29th WI Infy	NY	07989
Kent, Frederick R.	1st Lt. 3rd PA H Arty	PA	05497
Kent, J. Ford	BG USA	NY	00215
Kent, John	Capt. 5th MA Infy	MA	01593
Kent, Lewis A.	Capt. 6th WI Infy	CA	07792
Kent, Lindley C.	Maj 109th USCT	PA	15472
Kent, Stephen M.	1st Lt. 16th MI Infy	MI	12843
Kent, William L.	Capt. 23rd MA Infy	NY	12401
Kenyon, John S.	2nd Lt. 3rd NY Cav	NY	08651
Kenyon, Nathaniel C.	LTC 11th IL Infy	DC	18352
Kenyon, Norman S.	1st Lt. 16th NY H Arty	NY	15519
Kepler, Charles W.	Capt. 13th IA Infy BvtMaj	IA	06201
Kepner, Daniel K.	1st Lt. RQM 179th PA Infy	PA	11715
Kerens, Richard C.	3rd Class (Amb.to Austria-Hungary)	MO	06054
Kerin, Joseph	BvtCapt USA	PA	00508
Kern, Louis	1st Lt. 6th Batt IN L Arty	IN	10797
Kerr, Charles D.	Col. 16th IL Infy	MN	03838
Kerr, Daniel	1st Lt. 117th IL Infy	IA	06194
Kerr, Henry C.	Capt. 16th Vol.Res.Corps	PA	00081
Kerr, Robert W.	1st Lt. 121st OH Infy	DC	13955
Kerr, Thomas R.	Capt. 14th PA Cav	PA	07646
Kershner, Edward	Med. Inspector USN	NY	03364
Kessler, Henry C.	1st Lt. 104th PA Infy Col. 1st MT Infy	CA	04097
Kester, John W.	Col. 1st NJ Cav	PA	00105
Ketcham, John L.	1st Lt. 70th IN Infy	IN	12943
Ketcham, William A.	Capt. 13th IN Infy	IN	11645
Ketchum, Alexander P.	Capt. 128th USCT BvtCol.	NY	09426
Ketchum, Edgar	2nd Lt. Sig. Corps BvtCapt USV	NY	00787
Ketchum, Edwin N.	Capt. 176th NY Infy	NY	12725
Ketchum, Hiram H.	Maj 22nd Infy USA	NY	00710
Ketchum, Thomas E.	Capt. 3rd CA Infy	CA	02652
Keteltas, Henry	Capt. 15th Infy BvtLTC USA	NY	01021
Keyes, Addison A.	Capt. 127 IL Infy	NY	02563
Keyes, Alexander S.B.	LTC USA	MO	01348
Keyes, Charles M.	1st Lt. 123rd OH Infy	OH	13314
Keyes, Charles W.	1st Lt. 32nd ME Infy BvtCapt	ME	10745
Keyes, Dwight W.	1st Lt. RQM 1st WI Infy	WI	06287
Keyes, Edward L.	Capt. ADC USV	NY	14625
Keyes, Erasmus D.	BG BvtMG USV	CA	02466
Keyser, Peter D.	Capt. 91st PA Infy	PA	00003
Kidd, James H.	Col. 6th MI Cav BvtBG	MI	03749
Kidd, William	1st Lt. 44th NY Infy	NY	09308
Kidder, Henry M.	LTC 5th USC Cav BvtCol.	IL	04152
Kidder, Henry P.	3rd Class (Financier, supported Union)	MA	02462
Kidder, Jerome H.	Surg. USN	NY	00411
Kiddoo, Joseph B.	BG USA BvtMG	NY	00053
Kiefaber, John C.	1st Lt. 11th OH Infy	OH	10701

Name	Rank	Commandery	Insignia No.
Kiefer, Andrew R.	Capt. 2nd MN Infy	MN	06354
Kieffer, Lorenzo M.	Capt. 48th USCT	PA	09498
Kies, Lewis G.	1st Lt. RQM 24th OH Infy	OH	11358
Kilbourn, Byron H.	2nd Lt. 3rd WI Cav	WI	02024
Kilbourne, James	Capt. 95th OH Infy BvtCol.	OH	02840
Kilbreth, John W.	Capt. 79th OH Infy	NY	06221
Kilburn, Charles S.	BG USA	PA	00190
Kile, John W.	Capt. 113th OH Infy	OH	10053
Kilgore, William Foss	Act Ensign USN	WA	14891
Kilgore, William H.	1st Lt. 1st PA L Arty	NE	06700
Killian, John E.	1st Lt. 28th MA Infy	MA	01904
Kilpatrick, Judson	BvtMG USA	PA	00063
Kilpatrick, Robert L.	Col. USA	OH	02584
Kilty, Augustus H.	RAdm USN	PA	00991
Kimball, Abner S.	BG USA	DC	06057
Kimball, Charles H.	1st Lt. 103rd USCT	KS	08694
Kimball, George H.	1st Lt. 76th USCT	CA	02473
Kimball, James Peleg	LTC Dept. Surg. Gen. USA	Ny	03127
Kimball, James Putnam	Capt. AAG BvtMaj USV	NY	01294
Kimball, John W.	Col. 53rd MA Infy BvtBG	MA	09334
Kimball, Lewis	2nd Lt. 4th USCT	CA	15582
Kimball, Nathan	BG BvtMG USV	NE	07045
Kimball, Spencer S.	2nd Lt. 1st IL L Arty	IL	09245
Kimball, Thomas D.	Capt. 2nd MA H Arty	MO	06175
Kimball, William A.	Capt. 2nd NY Cav	MA	01514
Kimball, William C.	Capt. CS USV	OH	04645
Kimberly, Benjamin E.	Capt. 44th NY Infy	CO	10920
Kimberly, Lewis A.	RAdm USN	DC	03033
Kimes, Jesse B.	Capt. 100th USCT	PA	07647
Kindrick, James P.	Capt. 8th TN Cav	OH	08038
King, Adam E.	LTC AAG BvtBG USV	DC	04359
King, Alonzo L.	Capt. 146th NY Infy	NY	12956
King, Charles F.	Capt. Coast Guard Battn. ME Infy	MA	07972
King, Cornelius L.	Capt. 12th Infy USA	VT	03175
King, Dana W.	Capt. 8th NH Infy	MA	06829
King, David	LTC 94th OH Infy	OH	07324
King, Henry	1st Lt. RQM 50th IL Infy	MO	11790
King, Henry H.	Capt. AAG USV	PA	05274
King, Horatio C.	Maj QM BvtCol. USV	NY	00132
King, James	Surg. USV	PA	00919
King, James W.	Chief Eng. USN	PA	10134
King, James W.	2nd Lt. 32nd MA Infy	MA	11846
King, John H.	BG USV BvtMG USA	MI	04029
King, John R.	1st Lt. 6th MD Infy	DC	09213
King, John S.	1st Lt. 124th NY Infy	NY	04691
King, Joseph DeW	1st Lt.1st OH L Arty	CA	16177
King, Josias R.	LTC 2nd US Vol. Infy	MN	04528 (Dup)
King, Robert B.	Ist. Lt. 2nd MA H Arty	MO	07502

Name	Rank	Commandery	Insignia No.
King, Rufus	Capt. 4th Arty BvtMaj USA	NY	03180
King, William H.	Chief Eng. USN	PA	00595
King, William M.	Med. Inspector USN	PA	00691
King, William S.	Col. Surg. USA	PA	06259
Kingman, Martin	2nd Lt. 86th IL Infy	IL	07004
Kingsbury, David L.	2nd Lt. 8th MN Infy	MN	09356
Kingsbury, Isaac F.	1st Lt. Adj. 32nd MA Infy	MA	01519
Kingsland, Phineas C.	1st Lt. 102nd NY Infy	NY	13571
Kingsley, Henry W.	Capt. CS BvtMaj USV	VT	09250
Kingsley, Levi G.	Maj 12th VT Infy	VT	09177
Kinipe, Thomas J.	Act Master USN	CA	09408
Kinne, C. Mason	Capt. AAG USV	CA	01581
Kinnear, George	Capt. 47th IL Infy	WA	14516
Kinney, Coates	Maj Paymaster BvtLTC USV	OH	08700
Kinney, John C.	1st Lt. 13th CT Infy	PA	03796
Kinney, William C.	1st Lt. 93rd IL Infy	IL	05551
Kinsey, William B.	LTC 161st NY Infy BvtBG	PA	06004
Kinsler, James T.	Asst Surg. 164th NY Infy	NE	05455
Kinsley, Alfred H.	1st Lt. 2nd MA H Arty	MA	09371
Kinsley, Edward W.	3rd Class	MA	00980
Kinsman, Charles C.	1st Lt. 4th VT Infy	VT	09468
Kinsman, Josiah B.	LTC ADC BvtMG USV	DC	05939
Kinsman, Oliver D.	Capt. AAG BvtLTC USV	DC	14237
Kinzie, David H.	BG USA	CA	12780
Kipp, Charles J.	Surg. BvtLTC USV	NY	01827
Kirby, Absalom	Chief Eng. USN	DC	08681
Kirby, Thomas H.	1st Lt. 36th IN Infy	IN	05936
Kirby, William M.	LTC 3rd NY Infy	NY	08946
Kirchner, William F.	2nd Lt. 15th NY H Arty	NY	09861
Kireker, Charles	LTC 116th USCT	NY	07781
Kirk, Charles H.	1st Lt. 15th PA Cav	PA	07339
Kirk, Ezra B.	Maj QM BvtLTC USA	OH	04214
Kirk, Marcus D.	Capt. 30th IN Infy	OH	10480
Kirk, Newton T.	Capt. 118th USCT	CA	15640
Kirkman, Joel T.	Col. USA	DC	13376
Kirkup, Robert	LTC 5th OH Infy	OH	07018
Kirkwood, Samuel J.	3rd Class (Gov. IA)	IA	03169
Kirwan, John S.	LTC 12th TN Cav	MO	08013
Kisselburgh, William E.	1st Lt. Adj. 169th NY Infy	NY	03129
Kitchel, Simon B.	1st Lt. 43rd USCT	MI	10389
Kitchen, Marcus L.W.	LTC 2nd NJ Cav	NY	01046
Kitchen, Samuel	Asst Surg. BvtCapt USV	MI	12639
Kitchen, Theodore	Act Asst Eng. USN	PA	01534
Kitchin, Elias C.	Surg. 155th PA Infy	PA	12466
Kittle, Johathan G.	3rd Class	CA	03248
Kittleson, Charles	Capt. 10th MN Infy	MN	03826
Kittoe, Edward D.	LTC Med. Inspector BvtCol. USV	IL	04636
Kittredge, William T.	BvtMaj USV	CA	05845

The Roster

Name	Rank	Commandery	Insignia No.
Kitzmiller, John E.	2nd Lt. 26th OH Batt L Arty	CA	17813
Kleinfeld, Joseph	BvtCapt USV	KS	06870
Kleutsch, John D.	1st Lt. 82nd IL Infy	NE	10183
Kline, Jacob	BG USA	KS	05360
Klokke, Ernest F.C.	1st Lt. 24th IL Infy BvtMaj	CA	06458
Knaggs, Robert C.	BvtMaj USV	IL	17301
Knap, Charles	3rd Class	DC	03031
Knap, James G.	1st Lt. 1st Batt PA L Arty	PA	17514
Knap, Joseph M.	Maj Independent Battn. PA L Arty	NY	00903
Knapp, Alexander A.	Capt. 40th OH Infy	IN	03064
Knapp, Jacob	Capt. 149th NY Infy	NY	10543
Knapp, John	2nd Lt. 97th PA Infy	CA	12977
Knapp, Lyman E.	LTC 17th VT Infy	WA	13715
Knapp, Obadiah M.	Maj 125th USCT	NY	09427
Knapp, William	Act Master USN	Ca	02754
Knapp, William A.	Capt. 19th OH Infy	DC	06801
Knappen, Prosper L.	1st Lt. RCS 2nd WI Cav	NE	11421
Knee, Samuel G.	LTC 12th IA Infy	IA	07597
Kneeland, Samuel	Surg. BvtLTC USV	MA	01725
Knefler, Fred	Col. 70th IN Infy BvtBG	IN	02846
Knickerbocker, Henry M.	Capt. 7th NY H Arty	IL	02318
Kniffin, Charles W.	1st Lt. 49th MA Infy	MA	06046
Kniffin, Gilbert C.	LTC CS USV	DC	02684
Kniffin, Sylvester W.	1st Lt. Adj. 44th USCT	MO	07176
Knight, Alva A.	Capt. 34th USCT	WA	08621
Knight, Charles C.	LTC 44th Infy PA Militia	PA	01719
Knight, Edwin L.	BvtMaj USV	MA	15505
Knight, George A.	Capt. 188th OH Infy	PA	08751
Knight, John H.	Capt. 18th Infy BvtLTC USA	PA	00523
Knight, John H.	1st Lt. 25th ME Infy	ME	03530
Knipe, Joseph F.	BG USV	PA	01035
Knott, John M.C.	1st Lt. 186th OH Infy	IA	16568
Knowles, Alfred H.	1st Lt. 54th MA Infy	MA	15929
Knowles, Charles R.	Capt. 92nd NY Infy	NY	02218
Knowlson, John	Surg. 169th NY Infy	VT	13971
Knowlton, Julius W.	2nd Lt. 14th CT Infy	NY	01648 (Dup)
Knox, Edward B.	Maj 44th NY Infy BvtLTC	IL	01944
Knox, Edward M.	2nd Lt. 15th Batt NY L Arty	NY	09309
Knox, George G.	Capt. ADC USV	IL	16996
Knox, James C.	Capt. 4th IN Cav	IN	08143
Knox, Kilburn	Capt. 13th Infy BvtLTC USA	WI	00065
Kobbe', William A.	MG USA	CA	12291
Koch, Charles R.E.	Capt. 49th USCT	IL	02324
Koerner, Max	2nd Lt. 3rd US Reserve Corps MO Infy	CA	11780
Koerper, Egon A.	Col. USA	DC	03930
Kohler, Charles	3rd Class (Vintner and Civic Leader)	CA	04103
Kollock, John M.	BvtLTC USV	PA	00010
Kopper, Henry J.	Capt. 4th NY H Arty	NY	16586

Name	Rank	Commandery	Insignia No.
Korn, Gustave	Maj 45th NY Infy	NY	12478
Korns, Daniel	Capt. 80th OH Infy	OH	10787
Korty, Louis H.	3rd Class	NE	07591
Kothe, Gustav C.	Capt. 58th IL Infy	KS	13890
Krafft, James F.	1st Lt. 177th IL Infy	MN	16619
Kramer, Adam	Maj 6th Cav USA	KS	04289
Krause, Charles A.	Capt. 2nd DC Infy	DC	06661
Krause, David	Maj 11th Infy USA	PA	01198
Krause, William	1st Lt. 37th US Infy	PA	01199
Krebs, Adolf	1st Lt. 4th MO Cav	MA	14161
Krebs, Henry	1st Lt. 35th USCT	CA	09540
Kreps, John W.	Capt. 77th PA Infy	PA	09975
Kress, John A.	BG USA	MO	12915
Kress, John F.	1st Lt. 215th PA Infy	PA	14195
Kreutzer, William	LTC 98th NY Infy	NY	09568
Kridler, John C.	1st Lt. 1st TN L Arty	WA	15207
Kroesen, William B.	2nd Lt. 103rd PA Infy	PA	07340
Kruger, Anthony O.	Act Ensign USN	MI	11123
Krughoff, Louis	Capt. 49th IL Infy BvtMaj	IL	12053
Kuhn, Henry H.	Capt. USA	PA	07864
Kuhn, William E.	Capt. AAG USV	OH	02877
Kummer, Arnold	Maj 68th NY Infy	MD	15340
Kurtz, Christian H.	1st Lt. 24th IA Infy	IA	06204
Kurtz, Samuel L.	Surg. 85th PA Infy	PA	09506
Kutz, George F.	Chief Eng. USN	CA	03671
Lacey, Anderson P.	Capt. 98th OH Infy	DC	05892
Lacey, Francis E.	Col. USA	KS	04812
Lacey, Mayberry M.	Capt. 8th IN Infy	IN	14880
Laciar, Jacob D.	Capt. 202nd PA Infy	PA	13938
Lackner, Francis	Maj 20th WI Infy BvtLTC	DC	05285
Ladd, Charles H.	2nd Lt. 5th MA H Arty	MA	16439
Ladd, James O.	Capt. 35th USCT	OH	17032
Ladd, Nathaniel E.	Capt. 55th MA Infy BvtMaj	MA	11207
Ladd, William J.	1st Lt. 13th NH Infy BvtCapt	MA	02460
Lademann, Otto C.B.	Capt. 3rd MO Infy	WI	11973
Ladner, Louis J.	1st Lt. 98th PA Infy	PA	01531
Ladue, William N.	1st Lt. Adj. 5th MI Infy	MN	07152
Lafferty, John	Capt. 8th Cav USA	CA	02469
Lafferty, Nelson B.	Asst Surg. 1st OH H Arty	OH	04647
LaForce, Daniel A.	Surg. 56th USCT	DC	11902 (Dup)
LaGrange, Oscar H.	Col. 1st WI Cav BvtBG	CA	01334
Lahee, Horace R.	Capt. 14th NY Infy	WI	08185
Laine, Richard W.	Ensign USN	CA	02920
Laird, George F.	Capt. 4th OH Infy	OH	03207
Laird, Seth M.	Capt. 14th Batt OH L Arty	OH	09023
Lake, Henry F.	2nd Lt. 22nd MI Infy	CO	07671
Lakin, Albert G.	Capt. 74th IL Infy BvtLTC	KS	12261
Lamb, Charles D.	Capt. 56th MA Infy	MA	01259

Name	Rank	Commandery	Insignia No.
Lamb, David A.	Capt. 73rd OH Infy	OH	09640
Lamb, Robert N.	Capt. AQM USV	IN	07929
Lamb, Samuel T.	Capt. AQM USV	OR	04461
Lamb, William P.	2nd Lt. 39th USCT	NY	No Number
Lambert, George H.	Capt. 116th USCT BvtMaj	NY	11750
Lambert, Henry S.	Act Master USN	NY	06742
Lambert, John J.	Capt. 9th IA Cav	CO	07483
Lambert, Louis E.	Capt. 37th OH Infy	OH	09821
Lambert, William H.	Capt. 33rd NJ Infy BvtMaj	PA	01985
Lamberton, Benjamin P.	RAdm USN	DC	12180
Lamborn, Charles B.	LTC 15th PA Cav	NY	05017-5151
LaMotte, Charles E.	Col. 6th US Vet. Vols. BvtBG	PA	00020
LaMotte, Robert S.	Col. 13th Infy USA	PA	00193
LaMotte, William A.	Capt. AAG BvtLTC USV	PA	00249
Lampson, Mortimer	Asst Surg. 36th USCT	NY	10966
Lamson, Daniel S.	LTC 16th MA Infy	MA	00629
Lamson, Roswell H.	Lt. USN	OR	07912 (Dup)
Lancaster, James M.	LTC 3rd Arty USA	DC	05227
Lancaster, Littleton R.	1st Lt. 2nd Battn. 1st MO Eng.	Ca	12588
Lancey, John A.	1st Lt. 1st ME H Arty	MA	05796
Lancey, Samuel N.	1st Lt. Chap 2nd CT Infy	ME	15118
Land, Joseph F.	Capt. 20th ME Infy BvtMaj	NY	08495
Landell, Edwin A.	Maj 119th PA Infy BvtLTC	PA	00076
Landers, Thomas	BvtCapt. USV	DC	03030
Landis, Abraham H.	Asst Surg. 35th OH Infy	IN	06825
Landis, Isaac D.	1st Lt. Adj. 9th PA Cav	PA	09500
Landis, John B.	Capt. 209th PA Infy	PA	07061
Landon, Henry B.	Asst Surg. 7th MI Infy	MI	08827
Landon, Walter C.	Capt. 12th VT Infy	VT	14105
Landram, John J.	LTC 18th KY Infy	OH	07124
Landram, William J.	Col. 10th KY Infy BvtBG	OH	07231
Lane, Barent H.	2nd Lt. 1st NY Marine Arty	NY	07466
Lane, Everett	Maj 43rd MA Infy	MA	01692
Lane, John S.	1st Lt. 8th CT Infy	NY	11105
Lane, Philander P.	Col. 11th OH Infy	OH	02256
Lane, Samuel W.	Capt. 25th USCT	ME	02619
Lane, Wilbur F.	Capt. 8th ME Infy	MA	13598
Lane, William B.	Maj 3rd Cav BvtLTC USA	DC	04616
Langan, Daniel	1st Lt. 1st DE Infy	IA	12655
Langdon, Charles S.	Capt. CS BvtMaj USV	NY	02048
Langdon, Loomis L.	BG USA	DC	00224
Langley, James W.	Col. 125th IL Infy	WA	13717
Langworthy, Daniel A.	Capt. 85th NY Infy	MN	16027
Laning, Sylvester	Surg. 48th IN Infy	KS	10274
Lanius, William H.	Capt. 87th PA Infy	PA	06260
Lansing, Edwin G.	Capt. 13th NY Cav BvtMaj	OR	13647
Lansing, Henry S.	Col. 17th NY Infy BvtBG	PA	01238
Lanstrum, Christian E.	Capt. 15th IA Infy	IL	07389

Name	Rank	Commandery	Insignia No.
Lapham, Oscar	Capt. 12th RI Infy	MA	07685
Lapham, William B.	Capt. AQM BvtMaj USV	ME	02622
Larabee, George H.	Asst Surg. 1st MA H Arty	MA	04551
Lardner, James L.	RAdm USN	PA	00425
Lardner, Lynford	Act Asst Paymaster USN	PA	04948
Larkin, Courtland P.	Maj 38th WI Infy	WI	10478
Larkin, James E.	Maj 5th NH Infy	MA	04552
Larkin, Lawrence F.	Capt. 10th NH Infy	CO	15609
Larned, Daniel R.	LTC USA	DC	01499
Larrabee, Charles F.	1st Lt. Adj. 30th ME Infy BvtMaj	DC	10938
Larrabee, Charles S.	Capt. 19th ME Infy	ME	09550
Lashells, Theodore B.	Surg. 171st PA Infy	PA	07341
Lasher, George W.	Chap 5th CT Infy	OH	14358
Lasley, Jonathan H.	2nd Lt. 53rd OH Infy	KS	14427
Lathrop, John	Capt.35th MA Infy	MA	01058
Lathrop, Joseph H.	1st Lt. Adj. 4th MA Cav	MA	01059
Lathrop, Solon H.	Capt. 35th Infy USA	NY	No Number
Latta, James W.	Capt. AAG BvtLTC USV	PA	01606
Laubach, Amandus J.	Capt. 202nd PA Infy	IN	07930
Laughlin, George McC.	Capt. 155th PA Infy BvtMaj	PA	02936
Lauriat, George W.	Capt. 32nd MA Infy BvtMaj	MA	02224
Law, David H.	Asst Surg. 10th MO Cav	IL	11436
Law, Galelma	Capt. 6rth WVA Cav	CO	05967
Law, Samuel A.L.	1st Lt. RQM 47th IL Infy	IL	13167
Lawder, Rynd E.	Maj 2nd OH Cav	MO	07288
Lawrence, Abram B.	LTC QM USV	NY	05288
Lawrence, A. Gallatin	Capt. 2nd USC Cav BvtBG	NY	00624
Lawrence, Adley B.	1st Lt. Batt D, PA L Arty	CO	14235
Lawrence, Centre H.	Capt. AAG BvtMaj USV	DC	06244
Lawrence, Charles	Act Master USN	PA	04661
Lawrence, Elijah C.	2nd Lt. 55th IL Infy	MA	09928
Lawrence, Frank B.	2nd Lt. 99th NY Infy	NE	04154
Lawrence, Frederick H.	Capt. 16th NY H Arty	NY	06236
Lawrence, Henry C.	1st Lt. 126th NY Infy	CO	09883
Lawrence, James V.	Capt. CS BvtMaj USV	NY	07240
Lawrence, John J.	Col. 46th Infy PA Militia	PA	07062
Lawrence, Joseph H.	2nd Lt. 2nd DC Infy	DC	08682
Lawrence, Samuel B.	LTC AAG USV	NY	01262
Lawrence, Samuel C.	Col. 5th MA Infy	MA	14390
Lawrence, Samuel W.H.	BvtBG USV	NY	01187
Lawrie, Alexander	Capt. 121st PA Infy	IN	00293
Lawson, Gaines	Maj BvtLTC USA	CA	04241
Lawton, George W.	Capt. 4th MI Cav BvtMaj	IL	03490
Lawton, Henry W.	Col. Insp. Gen USA MG USV	DC	09528
Lawyer, J.C.	Maj 6th US Vet. Vols.	PA	00080
Lawyer, Joseph A.	Maj Paymaster BvtLTC USV	NY	08108
Lay, Richard G.	Capt. 3rd Infy BvtCol. USA	NY	04690
Laycock, Henry A.	LTC 56th PA Infy BvtCol.	PA	09771

Name	Rank	Commandery	Insignia No.
Laycock, Thomas F.	Act Master USN	CA	04865
Layman, James T.	Capt. 55th IN Infy	IN	06600
Lazarus, Aaron	1st Lt. 28th PA Vols.	PA	01986
Lazelle, Henry M.	BG USA	MA	13981
Lea, Joseph T.	1st Lt. Adj. 114th PA Infy	PA	03593
Lea, William, Jr.	2nd Lt. Independent Batt DE L Arty	PA	09499
Leach, Andrew J.	Capt. 19th NY Cav BvtMaj	MN	12834
Leach, Joseph A.	Chap 19th Infy USA	ME	02705
Leach, William B.	Capt. AAG USV	MN	04842
Leake, Joseph B.	LTC 20th IA Infy BvtBG	IL	02010
Leale, Charles A.	Asst Surg. USV	NY	03622
Leaming, Mack J.	Maj 6th TN Cav	CA	05458
Leamy, George W.	2nd Lt. 9th PA Cav	PA	15301
Learnard, Oscar E.	LTC 1st KS Infy	KS	10207
Learned, Bela P.	Capt. 1st CT H Arty BvtMaj	NY	01179
Leary, Michael	Maj USA	KS	06036
Leary, Peter, Jr.	BG USA	MD	09706
Leary, Richard P.	Capt. USN	CA	07217
Leasure, Daniel	Col. 106th PA Infy	MN	03824
Leatz, Axel	Capt. 5th NY Infy BvtMaj	PA	01717
Leavens, Leander C.	1st Lt. 32nd USCT	VT	13586
Leavenworth, Abel E.	Capt. 9th VT Infy	VT	09183
Leavitt, Guilford A.	2nd Lt. 29th MI Infy	DC	11995
Leavitt, Samuel D.	1st Lt. 15th ME Infy	ME	08331
Leavitt, Sheldon	1st Lt. 4th MA Cav BvtCapt.	NY	01358
Leavitt, William W.	Asst Surg. USN	MA	09138
LeBarron, Robert	Asst Surg. 4th MI Infy	MI	13933
Lebo, Thomas C.	BG USA	DC	13724
Ledlie, Gilbert W.	1st Lt. RQM 16th NY H Arty	NY	01839
Ledlie, James H.	BG USV	NY	01439
LeDuc, William G.	BvtBG USV	MN	17363
Lee, Albert L.	BG USV	NY	07782
Lee, Benjamin F.	2nd Lt. 8th IL Cav	IL	07555
Lee, Benjamin F.	1st Lt. 12th NJ Infy	PA	07063
Lee, Daniel W.	Capt. 29th MA Infy	MA	01395
Lee, David B.	Capt. CS BvtMaj USV	MO	04278
Lee, Ethan A.	Surg. 54th IL Infy	CO	12476
Lee, Francis L.	Col. 44th MA Infy	MA	01065
Lee, Harrison A.	1st Lt. 171st OH Infy	KS	15969
Lee, Henry	3rd Class (LTC staff Gov. of MA)	MA	00928
Lee, Henry T.	Maj 4th NY H Arty	CA	05639
Lee, Horace C.	Col. 27th MA Infy BvtBG	MA	00814
Lee, James G.C.	BG USA	Ca	01688
Lee, James H.	2nd Lt. 4th MA H Arty	MA	13599 (Dup)
Lee, Jesse M.	BG USA	IN	11407
Lee, John	Capt. 4th Cav USA	CA	07513
Lee, John	2nd Lt. 203rd PA Infy	PA	10870
Lee, Samuel P.	Maj BvtCol. USV	MA	01392

The Roster 281

Name	Rank	Commandery	Insignia No.
Lee, Simeon L.	2nd Lt. 8th IL Infy	CA	09594
Lee, William Raymond	Col. 20th MA Infy BvtBG	MA	00990
Leech, William A.	LTC 90th PA Infy BvtBG	PA	00039
Leefe, John G.	LTC 30th Infy USA	NY	04439
Lees, George W.	2nd Lt. 28th PA Infy	PA	13939
Leeson, Richard L.	Capt. 68th IN Infy BvtLTC	IN	07504
LeFavor, George W.	Capt. 24th MA Infy	MA	06105
Leffingwell, Douglass	Capt. 3rd IA Infy	PA	10630
Leggett, Francis W.	Capt. 9th MI Cav	NY	09728
Leggett, Henri F.	Capt. 9th KY Infy	PA	00806
Leggett, Mortimer D.	MG USV	OH	02177
Leggett, Wells W.	Capt. ADC USV	MI	04715
Lehe, Eugene	2nd Lt. 2nd CA Infy	CA	06935
Lehman, Albert E.	1st Lt. RQM 67th PA Infy	PA	00008
Leib, Frank R.	Capt. 116th PA Infy BvtMaj	PA	10525
Leibhardt, David P.	1st Lt. RQM 57th IN Infy	DC	14159
Leidy, Philip	Surg. 119th PA Infy	PA	03407
Leighton, George E.	Maj 5th Cav MO St. Militia	MO	04292
Leighton, Walter H.	Asst Surg. 188th PA Infy	MA	03711
Leighton, William E.	Capt. 1st Battn. ME Infy	ME	15990
Leighty, Jacob D.	1st Lt. 11th IN Infy	IN	06900
Leiper, Charles L.	Col. 6th PA Cav BvtBG	PA	08752
Leisen, Jacob	Capt. 45th WI Infy	MI	09798
Leisenring, Thomas D.	Capt. 47th PA Infy	PA	12340
Leland, Cyrus, Jr.	1st Lt. 10th KS Infy	KS	07795
Leland, Francis L.	LTC 1st NY Infy	NY	01782
Lelong, Alexander	Asst Surg. BvtCapt. USV	NY	08947
LeMaistre, George A.	2nd Lt. 97th PA Infy	PA	00601
Lemert, Wilson C.	Col. 86rth OH Infy	OH	14422
Lemmon, John M.	Capt. 73rd OH Infy	OH	07307
Lennig, Thompson	1st Lt. 6th PA Cav	PA	01040
Lennon, John A.	Maj 3rd MO Cav	CO	05622
Lennon, Peter	2nd Lt. 5th MI Infy	MI	08529
Lentz, David H.	Capt. AQM USV	CA	06135
Leonard, Hiram	LTC Dept. Paymaster Gen. BvtBG USA	CA	01275
Leonard, Isaac N.	1st Lt. 9th IN Infy	DC	17471
Leonard, Orville W.	Capt. 42nd MA Infy	NY	02556
Leonard, Robert W.	Maj 162nd NY Infy Col. 12th NY Infy	NY	01106
Leonard, William H.	Surg. 5th MN Infy	MN	05444
Leoser, Charles McK.	Col. 11th NY Infy	NY	03014
Leoser, Christopher	Capt. 11th NY Infy	PA	04662
Leser, Frederick	1st Lt. Adj. 17th MO Infy	PA	07865
Leslie, John A.	1st Lt. Adj. 203rd PA Infy	NY	06220
Lessig, William H.	Capt. 96th PA Infy	PA	00489
Lester, Elias	Surg. 97th USCT	NY	10423
LeTourneau, William	1st Lt. 91st PA Infy	PA	11020
Letterman, Jonathan	Maj Surg. USA	CA	01281
Letton, Theodore W.	1st Lt. Adj. 50th IL Infy	IL	02190

Name	Rank	Commandery	Insignia No.
Leutze, Eugene H.C.	Capt. USN	DC	12855
Levensaler, Henry C.	Surg. 8th ME Infy BvtLTC	ME	08834
Levering, John	Maj AAG BvtCol. USV	IN	06654
Levis, Paul L.	2nd Lt. 1st Battn. PA Infy	PA	12772
Levy, Benjamin J.	Capt. CS BvtMaj USV	NY	02568
Lewis, Alfred E.	Maj 1st PA L Arty	NY	00456
Lewis, Charles F.	Capt. 119th NY Infy	DC	04560
Lewis, Charles H.	1st Lt. Adj. 27th IA Infy	IA	11137
Lewis, David W.	Capt. 9th VT Infy	MA	05095
Lewis, Edwin E.	Capt. Batt G. 1st MI L Arty	MI	17246
Lewis, Edwin R.	Capt. 21st MA Infy	DC	06513
Lewis, Elnathan	Act Master USN	CA	08002
Lewis, Frederick B.A.	Lt. Asst Surg. USN	CA	17620
Lewis, Frederick W.	LTC 1st MO Cav	MO	05036
Lewis, George C.	1st Lt. 1st VT Cav	DC	16110
Lewis, George R.	Surg. 61st PA Infy	MN	12905
Lewis, George W.	2nd Lt. 111th OH Infy	OH	06082
Lewis, Grenville	Act 2nd Ass. Eng. USN	DC	13789
Lewis, J. Van H.	Capt USV	PA	02440
Lewis, James	Col. 144th NY Infy	IL	11800
Lewis, James	1st Lt. 1st DE Infy	PA	08223
Lewis, James	Maj USMC	PA	00380
Lewis, James M.	Col. 29th WI Infy	KS	00774-6293
Lewis, John B.	Surg. BvtLTC USV	MA	03507
Lewis, John C.	Capt. 167th OH Infy	IL	07757
Lewis, John P.	Capt. 5th IA Cav	MO	04583
Lewis, John R.	Col. USA BvtBG	DC	04351
Lewis, John W.	Capt. 4th KY Cav	DC	14113
Lewis, Juan W.	Capt. 102nd NY Infy	DC	13377
Lewis, Morgan D.	1st Lt. Adj. 6th NY Infy	DC	10984
Lewis, Robert H.	1st Lt. 1st Indpt. Batt DE H Arty	IL	04389
Lewis, Samuel N.	1st Lt. 118th PA Infy	PA	00114
Lewis, William D., Jr.	Col. 110th PA Infy BvtBG	PA	00621
Lewis, William H.	LTC 19th Infy USA	NY	01150
Lewis, William M.	Capt. ADC USV	IN	13186
Leyden, Maurice	Capt. 3rd NY Cav BvtMaj	NY	11337
Libbe, Elias D.	Lt. 6th ME Mt. Arty	MN	04734
Libby, Horatio S.	1st Lt. 1st ME Cav	MA	01689
Lichty, Jacob	1st Lt. 107th OH Infy	IA	13025
Liddell, Oliver B.	1st Lt. 68th IN Infy	CO	06942
Liebenau, Joseph H.	Capt. AAG USV	NY	00630
Lieber, G. Norman	BG Jdge Adv Gen. USA	DC	05226
Light, Harvey E.	Maj 10th MI Cav	MI	14307
Lightburn, Calvin L.	1st Lt. 2nd WVA Infy	CO	14531
Lillibridge, George H.	1st Lt. 14th CT Infy	DC	13956
Lillie, Abraham B.H.	RAdm USN	NY	01444
Lilly, Eli	LTC 9th IN Cav	IN	02844
Lilly, James E.	1st Lt. 43rd IN Infy	IN	07505

Name	Rank	Commandery	Insignia No.
Limbocker, Jerry M.	Capt. 5th IA Cav	KS	05538
Lincoln, Abraham	Pres. US. (Posthumous Enrollment)	PA	No Number
Lincoln, Albert R.	Asst Surg. 1st ME H Arty	ME	08831
Lincoln, Charles P.	Capt. 19th MI Infy	DC	02667
Lincoln, Frederick W.	3rd Class (Mayor of Boston MA)	MA	07138
Lincoln, Levi	1st Lt. 34th MA Infy	MA	11482
Lincoln, Robert Todd	Capt. AAG USV	IL	02408
Lincoln, Rufus P.	LTC 37th MA Infy BvtCol.	NY	06640
Lincoln, Sumner H.	BG USA	DC	09106
Lindenberg, Charles H.	1st Lt. 13th OH Infy	OH	10055
Linderman, Charles	2nd Lt. 8th IA Cav	IA	09481
Lindley, John H.	Capt. 11th IN Cav	IN	06601
Lindsay, C. Seton	1st Lt. 36th NY Infy	NY	06672
Lindsay, Cary D.	1st Lt. 67th OH Infy	OH	04199
Lindsay, James P.	Act Master USN	PA	05990
Lindsey, Barnett W.	Capt. 98th OH Infy	OH	06888
Lindsey, Robert F.	Capt. 6th WVA Cav	CA	17814
Linen, James A.	1st Lt. 26th NJ Infy	PA	11941
Lineweaver, Washington K.	Capt. 4th PA Cav	PA	02437
Link, Harry H.	1st Lt. 36th Infy USA	PA	00649
Linn, Henry C.	Asst Surg. 12th MO Cav	KS	06795
Linquist, Gusavus F.	1st Lt. 165th NY Infy	WA	08622
Linscott, Benjamin H.	Capt. 40th MA Infy	IL	16867
Linsley, Nelson E.	1st Lt. 120th NY Infy	WA	12624
Lintner, William H.H.	1st Lt. 177th NY Infy	NY	02897
Linton, Samuel S.	Maj 139th IL Infy	MN	08611
Lipman, Louis	1st Lt. 8th MO Infy	MO	09581
Lipp, Leodegar M.	Capt. 56th MA Infy	NY	No Number
Lippincott, Thomas W.	Capt. 6th IL Infy	CA	17785
Liscum, Emerson H.	Col. 9th Infy USA BG USV	VT	08736
Lisle, Robert P.	Pay Director USN	PA	12874
Litchfield, James A.	1st Lt. 40th MA Infy	MA	09808
Little, Arthur	Chap 1st VT H Arty	MA	06402
Little, David	Surg. 13th NY Infy	NY	10326
Little, Edward H.	LTC 127th NY Infy	NY	05527
Little, George W.	1st Lt. 60th OH Infy	OH	06126
Little, Horace C.	Capt. 23rd ME Infy	ME	11050
Little, James L.	3rd Class (Cared for soldier's families)	MA	02463
Little, John	Capt. 15th Infy USA	NY	01543
Little, Thomas J.	Capt. 1st MA H Arty	ME	02501
Littlefield, Aaron D.	Act Master USN	MA	13860
Littlefield, Charles R.	Maj Paymaster BvtLTC USV	ME	08830
Littlefield, Henry W.	1st Lt. 54th MA Infy	PA	05498
Littlefield, John	1st Lt. 23rd MA Infy	PA	08976
Littlefield, Roger S.	Capt. 1st MA H Arty	OR	04496
Littlejohn, Harry	Capt. 3rd MD Infy	NY	06625
Littlewort, Richard J.	1st Lt. 11th NY Cav	KS	07113
Livermolre, Thomas L.	Col. 18th NH Infy	MA	01135

Name	Rank	Commandery	Insignia No.
Livermore, Oliver C.	Capt. 13th MA Infy	MA	05148
Livingston, George B.	Master USN	NY	01080
Livingston, Josiah O.	Capt. 9th VT Infy	VT	09180
Livingston, LaRhett L.	Col. 3rd Arty USA	DC	00815
Livingston, Mortimer	2nd Lt. 14th NY H Arty	NY	07611
Livingston, Robert R.	Col. 1st NE Cav BvtBG	NE	04024
Lloyd, Harlan P.	Capt. 22nd NY Cav BvtMaj	OH	03256
Lloyd, Isaac	1st Lt. 9th PA Cav	PA	03408
Lloyd, James H.	Capt.15th PA Cav	MO	12665
Lloyd, William P.	1st Lt. Adj. 1st PA Cav	PA	06262
Lochren, William	1st Lt. 1st MN Infy	MN	05557
Lochte, Henry	1st Lt. 1st TX Cav	CA	12589
Locke, Charles E.	Surg. 1st CO Infy	CO	13414
Locke, Frederick T.	LTC AAG BvtBG USV	NY	01643
Locke, Joseph L.	1st Lt. 33rd MA Infy	IL	11134
Locke, Joseph M.	Capt. 14th Infy BvtLTC USA	OH	06077
Lockhart, John	Capt. 73rd PA Infy	PA	05241
Lockman, John T.	Col. 119th NY Infy BvtBG	NY	05829
Lockwood, Benjamin C.	Col. 29th Infy USA	MI	07497
Lockwood, Benoni	Capt. 6th PA Cav	NY	05410
Lockwood, Henry C.	Capt. ADC BvtMaj USV	NY	00212
Lockwood, John B.	Maj Paymaster USV	NY	01823
Lodge, John W.	Asst Surg. 31st PA Infy	PA	02438
Lodor, Richard	BG USA	CA	06129
Loeffler, Charles D.A.	Maj USA	OH	14386
Lofland, Gordon C.	BvtLTC USV	KS	06791
Logan, John A.	MG USA	OH	01947
Logo, Franklin	Capt. 119th PA Infy	PA	15473
Lombard, George B.	Capt. 44th MA Infy	MA	01028
Lombard, Jacob H.	Capt. 44th MA Infy	MA	00888
Lombard, John E.	Lt. USN	OR	04187
Lombard, Richard T.	Maj 11th MA Infy	MA	16816
Long, Charles L. H.	LTC 35th OH Infy	PA	01254
Long, Henry C.	1st Lt. RQM 128th IN Infy	IN	09631
Long, Hiram	Surg. 205th PA Infy	PA	07064
Long, James T.	2nd Lt. 2nd PA Cav	PA	16130
Long, John H.	Chief Eng. USN	NY	00627
Long, Owen M.	Surg. 11th IL Infy	NY	01165
Long, William H.	Maj AAG BvtCol. USV	MA	01745
Longacre, Orleans	1st Asst Eng. USN	NY	00314
Longenecker, Jacob H.	1st Lt. Adj. 101st PA Infy	PA	06261
Longfellow, Charles Appleton	1st Lt. 1st MA Cav	MA	01476
Longnecker, Henry C.	Col. 9th PA Infy	PA	00350
Longshore, William R.	Surg. 147th PA Infy	PA	04949
Longstreth, Thaddeus	Capt. 183rd OH Infy	OH	07126
Longwell, William H.	Capt. 114th NY Infy	PA	07342
Looker, Thomas H.	Pay Director USN	DC	12255
Loomis, Henry	Capt. 146th NY Infy	CA	11230 (Dup)

The Roster

Name	Rank	Commandery	Insignia No.
Loomis, Henry C.	LTC 154th NY Infy	KS	05605
Loomis, Joel P.	Pay Inspector USN	CA	09534
Loomis, John Mason	Col. 29th IL Infy	IL	01739
Loomis, William S.	2nd Lt. 46th MA Infy	MA	09993
Loop, Charles B.	Maj 95th IL Infy	IL	12158
Lopes DeQueralta, Ferdinand	1st Lt. 82nd PA Infy	NY	01544 (Dup)
Lord, Charles V.	1st Lt. RQM 2nd ME Infy	ME	09552
Lord, Frederick C.	Capt. 3rd NY Cav BvtMaj	CA	05186
Lord, George W.	Act Ensign USN	ME	14808
Lord, Henry E.	Capt. CS BvtLTC USV	NY	02134
Lord, James	Capt. Purnell Legion MD Cav	PA	13288
Lord, James H.	Maj QM USA	CA	01381
Lord, T. Ellery	Maj 3rd NY Infy BvtBG	NY	01831
Lord, Thomas W.	Capt. USA	DC	02937
Lord, William A.	BvtMaj USV	WA	14986
Lorimer, William A.	Capt. 17th IL Infy	IL	10604
Loring, Charles G.	LTC AIG BvtMG USV	MA	01408
Loring, Charles H.	Chief Eng. USN	DC	01693
Loring, Francis H.	Capt. 92nd OH Infy BvtMaj	IA	07826
Loring, Francis W.	1st Lt. ADJ 38th MA Infy BvtMaj	MA	01245
Loring, Henry W.	Act Ensign USN	MA	02309
Loring, Selden H.	2nd Lt. 30th MA Infy	MA	08439
Lostutter, David, Jr.	Capt. 7th IN Infy	IN	03149
Lothrop, Charles H.	Surg. 1st IA Cav	IA	05481
Lothrop, John S.	Capt. 26th IL Infy	IA	11902 (Dup)
Lott, George G.	Maj USA	OH	03721
Lotz, George	Surg. 28th Infy PA Militia	MA	01539
Loud, Edward DwC.	1st Lt. 2nd PA Arty	PA	01720
Loud, John S.	LTC USA	DC	01235
Loudon, DeWitt C.	LTC 70th OH Infy	OH	07417
Loughran, Robert	Surg. 80th NY Infy BvtLTC	NY	05401
Lounsberry, Clement A.	LTC 20th MI Infy	MN	12365
Lounsberry, Thomas R.	1st Lt. 126th NY Infy	NY	15794
Love, James E.	Capt. 8th KS Infy	MO	06310
Love, John J.H.	Surg. 13th NJ Infy	NY	05824
Love, Robert	1st Lt. 10th NJ Infy	PA	11328
Lovelace, Chauncey F.	Capt. CS BvtMaj USV	IA	13603
Loveland, Frank C.	LTC 6th OH Cav	NY	06952
Lovell, Don G.	Maj 6th MI Cav	WA	08623
Lovell, Edward C.	Capt. 153rd IL Infy	IL	08914
Lovell, Robert A.	1st Lt. 14th US Infy	CA	05072
Lovering, J.F.	Chap 17th ME Infy	MA	02458
Loving, Starling	Surg. 6th OH Infy	OH	04205
Low, David W.	Maj 8th MA Infy	MA	01091
Low, Frederick C.	Cap. 1st ME H Arty BvtMaj	MA	11363
Low, Frederick F.	3rd Class (Gov.of CA)	CA	02481
Low, James	Maj 8th NY H Arty	NY	11338
Low, Philip B.	Act Ensign USN	NY	05013

The Roster

Name	Rank	Commandery	Insignia No.
Lowber, William	Med. Inspector USN	PA	00808
Lowe, A.S.	BvtCapt. USV	PA	00668
Lowe, John	RAdm USN	DC	06333
Lowe, William R.	Capt. 19th Infy BvtMaj USA	OH	02836
Lowe, William W.	Col. 5th IA Cav BvtBG	NE	01603
Lowell, Abner I.	Act Ensign USN	CA	10050
Lowell, Charles	2nd Lt. 7th ME Infy	DC	06031
Lowell, Frederick E.	1st Lt. 40th MA Infy	MA	13746
Lowell, James Russell	3rd Class (Poet,Amb. to Spain, GBrit)	MA	07968
Lowery, Joseph S.	Capt. 146th NY Infy BvtMaj	NY	01783
Lowes, John H.S.	1st Lt. 7th IN Cav	IN	10005
Lowman, Webster B.	Capt. 5th PA H Arty	PA	09976
Lowrie, James A.	Maj AAG USV	CO	04618
Lowry, Alexander M.	1st Lt. 112th NY Infy	NY	12007
Lowry, Horatio B.	Maj QM USMC	DC	02439
Lowry, Reigart B.	Commander USN	NY	00440
Loxley, Benjamin O.	1st Lt. 58th PA Infy	PA	02291
Loyd, Hinton S.	Chap 16th NY Cav	NY	13452
Loyd, John	Act 1st Asst Eng. USN	NY	12789
Loyd, William H.	Capt. 11th NJ Infy	PA	02257
Lucas, Albert G.	1st Lt. 111th PA Infy	CO	15654
Lucas, Daniel R.	Chap 90th IN Infy	IN	07506
Lucas, William D.	Capt.5th NY Cav	IA	04843
Luce, Enos T.	LTC 23rd ME Infy	MA	13328
Luce, Stephen B.	RAdm USN	NY	13113
Lucia, Joel H.	1st Lt. 17th VT Infy	VT	14103
Luckenbach, Andrew A.	Capt. 129th PA Infy	PA	09770
Luckenbach, John L.	Capt. 196th PA Infy	PA	14264
Luckenbach, W. D.	1st Lt. 202nd PA Infy	PA	00554
Luckey, James B.	Capt. 3rd OH Cav	OH	05933
Ludden, Samuel D.	Maj 8th NY H Arty	IL	08045
Ludington, Horace	Surg. 100th PA Infy	NE	03929
Ludington, Marshall I.	MG USA	DC	00251
Ludlow, Albert S.	Act Ensign USN	WI	04979
Ludlow, Jacob R.	Surg. BvtCol. USV	PA	09977
Ludlow, Nicoll	RAdm USN	CA	06664
Ludlow, William	BG USA MG USV	NY	03592
Ludwig, John	2nd Lt. 9th WI Infy	MN	10193
Ludwig, Oscar	Capt. 20th IL Infy	IL	11599
Ludwig, Walter K.	1st Lt. 119th PA Infy	PA	08460
Luff, William M.	Capt. 12th IL Cav BvtMaj	IL	02811
Lugenbeel, Pinkney	Col. 5th Infy USA	NY	02217
Luhn, Gerhard L.	Maj USA	WA	15987
Lukens, E.J.	1st Lt. 2nd OH Infy	PA	02635
Lull, Edward P.	Capt. USN	PA	00178
Lum, Charles M.	Col. 10th MI Infy	MI	05174
Lund, George	1st Lt. 1st WI Infy	WI	06286
Lunt, Henry	Act Asst Paymaster USN	MA	01410

Name	Rank	Commandery	Insignia No.
Lusk, James Q.	1st Lt. 12th WI Infy	MN	06283
Lusk, William D.	2nd Lt. 151st PA Infy	PA	11159
Lusk, William T.	Capt. AAG USV	NY	04913
Luther, C. Frank	2nd Lt. 82nd USCT	MA	09063
Lutje, William F.	1st Lt. Batt B PA L Arty	PA	10871
Luxton, Edward D.	Maj 2nd WI Cav	NY	02206
Lybarger, Edwin L.	1st Lt. 43rd OH Infy	OH	07435
Lybrand, Archbald	Capt. 73rd OH Infy	OH	02839
Lybrand, Robert G.	Capt. 192nd OH Infy	OH	05474
Lydecker, Garrett J.	Col. Engineers USA	NY	00392
Lyford, Stephen C.	Maj Ordnance BvtLTC USA	NY	00532
Lyke, Hiram F.	1st Lt. 28th WI Infy	WI	11274
Lyle, Jabez M.	1st Lt. 3rd MA Infy	NY	08496
Lyle, Peter	Col. 90th PA Infy BvtBG	PA	00071
Lyman, Charles	2nd Lt. 14th CT Infy	DC	05309
Lyman, Cornelius M.	2nd Lt. 78th USCT	CA	17256
Lyman, Frank E.	2nd Lt. 12th NY Cav	IA	12654
Lyman, George H.	LTC Med. Inspector USV	MA	02163
Lyman, Henry H.	1st Lt. Adj. 147th NY Infy	NY	11462
Lyman, Joel B.	1st Lt. 7th Infy USA	NY	10427
Lyman, Joseph	Maj 29th IA Infy	IA	04684
Lyman, Luke	LTC 27th MA Infy BvtBG	MA	00868
Lyman, Theodore	LTC Volunteer ADC	MA	01822
Lyman, Wyllys	Maj BvtLTC USA	DC	02849
Lynch, Augustine T.	LTC 183rd PA Infy	PA	00059
Lynch, Bennet B.	1st Lt. 183rd PA Infy	PA	13194
Lynch, Edward	Capt. USA	DC	07046
Lynch, Frank	LTC 27th OH Infy	OH	04747
Lynch, James M.	1st Lt. 2nd PA Cav	PA	15859
Lynch, John	Maj 114th OH Infy	CA	02872
Lynch, John	Col. 6th IL Cav	IL	09485
Lynch, John C.	1st Lt. 3rd WI Cav	KS	05698
Lynch, John W.	Capt. 106th PA Infy	PA	05726
Lynch, Joseph E.	Surg. 1st MO Cav	PA	No Number
Lynde, Edward	Col. 9th KS Cav	KS	06793
Lyon, Augustus W.	1st Lt. 3rd VT Infy	VT	16695
Lyon, Charles D.	Capt. 3rd MI Infy	MI	04705
Lyon, David M.	Capt. 138th IL Infy	IL	10706
Lyon, Farnham	Capt. AQM BvtMaj USV	MI	04031
Lyon, George A.	Pay Director USN	PA	08306
Lyon, George W.	1st Lt. Adj. 1st LA Cav BvtCapt.	NY	06424
Lyon, Henry W.	RAdm. USN	MA	16115
Lyon, James	1st Lt. 4th NY Cav	NY	06012
Lyon, Oliver T.	1st Lt. 2nd Eastern Shore MD Infy	MO	06373
Lyon, Phoebus W.	1st Lt. 176th NY Infy	NY	12479
Lyon, William P.	Cjol. 13th WI Infy BvtBG	WI	03683
Lyster, Henry F.	Surg. 5th MI Infy	MI	03736
Lyster, William J.	Col. 19th Infy USA	IL	06403

Name	Rank	Commandery	Insignia No.
Lyte, Eliphalet O.	2nd Lt. Batt I PA L Arty	PA	05499
Maars, Robert W.	Act 2nd Asst Eng. USN	MN	15433
MacAdams, James G.	Capt. 2nd Cav USA	CA	03540
MacAllister, Samuel A.	1st Lt. 1st DE Infy	PA	02104
MacArthur, Arthur	Col. 24th WI Infy LtG USA	WI	00648
Macauley, Daniel	Col. 11th IN Infy BvtBG	DC	04406
Macauley, Daniel T.	Capt. 7th US Vet. Vols	IN	15763
MacBride, James G.	Capt. 9th MI Cav	MI	03875
MacBride, Thomas H.	Capt. 39th USCT	OH	07427
MacCauley, Clay	2nd Lt. 126th PA Infy	MA	01453
MacConnell, Charles C.	Maj USA	NY	04375
MacConnell, John G.	1st Lt. Batt G Indpt. PA L Arty	PA	09778
MacCoun, Robert T.	Med. Director USN	PA	00338
Macdonough, Joseph	Capt. 63rd NY Infy	CA	02707
MacDougall, Clinton D.	Col. 111th NY Infy BvtBG	NY	08353
Macfarlane, Carrington	Surg. 115th IL Infy	NY	08652
Macfarlane, Victor W.	1st Lt. Adj. 165th NY Infy	ME	13642
Macfarren, Samuel J.	1st Lt. Adj. 6th PA H Arty	PA	12232
MacGowan, Alexander	Capt. 12th Infy BvtMaj USA	CA	08877
Machette, Henry C.	Paymaster USN	PA	02298
MacIntyre, James	1st Lt. 115th PA Infy	PA	00110
Mack, Uziah	1st Lt. 100th IL Infy	IL	10004
Mackay, George	Civil Eng. USN	DC	09916
Mackenzie, Alexander	BG Chief of Engineers USA	DC	05286
Mackenzie, Charles	1st Lt. Adj. 9th IA Infy	IA	09322
Mackey, Charles W.	1st Lt. 39th PA Infy	NY	07986
Mackey, Silas G.	Capt. 95th NY Infy	NY	10544
Mackey, William J.	Capt. 147th PA Infy	PA	00562
Mackie, John H.	Act Asst Surg. USN	MA	05094
Macklin, James E.	LTC 3rd Infy USA	KS	04889
Macklind, Thomas H.	Capt. 3rd Cav MO State Militia	MO	10663
MacKnight, Owen B.	Capt. 9th PA Cav	PA	07343
Maclean, Duncan	Capt. 12th IL Infy	PA	00359
Macmillan, Andrew T.	2nd Lt. 1st RI L Arty	MA	01614
MacMurray, Junius W.	Maj 1st Arty BvtLTC USA	OR	02910
MacNamara, Daniel G.	1st Lt. RQM 9th MA Infy	MA	09064
MacNulty, Francis B.	LTC QM USV	NY	No Number
Macomb, David B.	Chief Eng. USN	MA	07686
Macomb, William H.	Commodore USN	PA	00373
Macomber, John H.	Maj Chap USA	CA	03558
Macpherson, William	Asst Surg. 101st PA Infy	PA	04952
Macy, George N.	Col. 20th MA Infy Bvt MG	MA	01067
Macy, William W.	Capt. 20th IN Infy	DC	02657
Madden, Daniel	Maj 7th Cav USA	DC	10985
Madden, Frank	1st Lt. USA	NY	09127
Madden, Thomas	Capt. 9th IN Infy	IN	14207
Maddigan, Matthew F.	1st Lt. 27th OH Infy	OH	06124
Maddox, William A.T.	Capt. AQM USMC	PA	00460

Name	Rank	Commandery	Insignia No.
Madeira, John D.	Capt. 73rd OH Infy	OH	04397
Magdeburg, Fred H.	Capt. 14th WI Infy	WI	07119 (Dup)
Magee, Edward A.	Chief Eng. USN	NY	08109
Magee, Frank J.	Capt. 76th PA Infy	NY	05732
Magee, George W.	Chief Eng. USN	NY	02368
Magill, Arthur E.	Capt. 14th MI Infy	CA	02069 (Dup)
Maginnis, Martin	Maj 11th MN Infy	DC	02403
Magnitzky, Gustave	Capt. 20th MA Infy	MA	08062
Magruder, David L.	BG USA	PA	03594
Mahan, Isaac L.	Capt. 133rd IN Infy	MN	12364
Mahnken, John H.	Capt. 8th Cav BvtMaj USA	NY	00944
Mahon, Samuel	Maj 7th IA Infy	IA	05789
Main, Edwin M.	Maj 3rd USC Cav	IN	13623
Mainzer, Jacob	1st Lt. 2nd MN Infy	MN	08151
Maish, Levi	Col. 130th PA Infy	DC	08981
Maize, William R.	Maj USA	CA	05847
Majors, Thomas J.	Capt. 14th CT Infy	NE	08408
Maker, John C.	Capt. 24th MA Infy	MA	09372
Male, William H.	Capt. ADC BvtMaj USA	NY	03780
Mali, Henry W.T.	Capt. 20th MA Infy	MA	01269
Mallam, Charles E.	Capt. AAG BvtMaj USV	DC	10373
Mallett, Edmund B.	Act Master USN	ME	08333
Mallory, William H.	Maj 2nd NY Cav	NY	01174
Malloy, Adam G.	Col. 17th WI Infy BvtBG	CA	04870
Malone, Francis M.	LTC 17th KS Cav	MN	12227
Malpas, Alfred	1st Lt. 40th NY Infy	CA	02477
Maltrie, Seth W.	Capt. 4th USCT	IA	10295
Maltz, George L.	1st Lt. Adj. 4th MI Infy	MI	04708
Man, Frederick H.	Capt. 84th USCT BvtMaj	NY	04596
Manchester, Charles N.	Maj 2nd RI Cav	NY	08110
Manchester, John R.	Capt. 97th NY Infy	NE	03936
Manchester, Thomas W.	Capt. 97th USCT	PA	03409
Manderbach, Benjamin F.	1st Lt. 29th OH Infy	OH	08289
Manderson, Charles F.	Col. 19th OH Infy BvtBG	NE	02825
Manges, Henry F.	Capt. 53rd PA Infy	PA	05991
Manker, John J.	Capt. 50th OH Infy	OH	14662
Manley, Henry D.H.	Commander USN	DC	00498-3219
Mann, Asahel	1st Lt. 4th IA Cav	IA	15365
Mann, Cyrus S.	Asst Surg. 31st MA Infy	MA	14391
Mann, Horace E.	1st Lt. Adj. 1st. MS Mounted Rifles	WI	06288
Mann, William d'A.	Col. 7th MI Cav	NY	05516
Manning, Charles H.	Passed Asst. Eng USN	MA	09139
Manning, Edward	Act Ensign USN	NY	09117
Manning, Edwin C.	1st Lt. 1st Indian Home Guard KS Infy	KS	12077
Manning, Frederick L.	LTC 148th NY Infy BvtCol.	NY	06427
Manning, Henry S.	1st Lt. 82nd USCT BvtCapt.	NY	01649
Manning, Stephen H.	Col. QM BvtBG USV	ME	02605
Manning, Thomas H.	2nd Lt. 4th MA L Arty	CA	17984

Name	Rank	Commandery	Insignia No.
Manning, William C.	Maj USA	ME	10583
Mannix, D. Pratt	Capt. USMC	DC	00506
Mannng, William R.	1st Lt. 10th IA Infy	IA	05650
Mansfield, Henry T.	Act Asst Paymaster USN	MA	10840
Mansfield, Ira F.	1st Lt. 105th OH Infy	OH	03957
Mansfield, Samuel M.	BG USA	MA	12926
Manson, Mahlon D.	Bg USV	IN	07815
Mansur, Alvah	1st Lt. 19th IL Infy	MO	05090
Manton, Benjamin D.	Act Vol. Lt. USN	PA	11942
Mapes, Smith H.	Surg. 60th NY Infy	IN	09207
Mapes, William H.	Maj 2nd NY Mounted Rifles	KS	16984
Marble, Frank E.	Capt. 1st US Shpshtrs.	MA	02694
Marble, John M.C.	Col. 151st OH Infy	CA	09691
Marchand, John B.	Commodore USN	PA	00266
Marcotte, Henry	Capt. USA	NY	11809
Marcus, Leopold	1st Lt. 72nd NY Infy	NY	09128
Marcy, Henry O.	Surg. 35th USCT	MA	02222
Marcy, William G.	Paymaster USN	NY	00387
Marden, George A.	1st Lt. RQM 1st US Shpshtrs.	MA	01815
Margedant, William O.	Capt. 10th OH Infy	OH	08536
Markbreit, Leopold	Capt. 28th OH Infy	OH	06432
Markham, Edwin C.	1st Lt. 2nd USC Cav	IL	03698
Markham, Henry H.	2nd Lt. 32nd WI Infy	CA	07516
Markle, John E.	1st Lt. 34th IN Infy	IN	13812
Markley, Alfred C.	Col. 13th Infy USA	PA	05500
Markley, Arthur D.	Act Asst Surg. USN	PA	05730
Markley, William H.R.	1st Lt. 16th KY Infy	OH	07939
Markoe, John	LTC 71st PA Infy BvtBG	PA	04663
Marks, Arthur	Capt. 22nd USCT	MI	06921
Marks, Jacob F.	Captl 40th IN Infy	IN	12455
Marks, Morton L.	Capt. 122nd NY Infy	IL	04844
Marks, Solon	Surg. 10th WI Infy	WI	01570
Marland, William	Capt. 2nd Batt MA L Arty BvtMaj	MA	07957
Marple, Alfred	Capt. 104th PA Infy	PA	08980
Marple, William W.	BvtBG USV	WA	17270
Marquart, Louis	Capt. 46th OH Infy	PA	16673
Marriott, Cary M.	Capt. 76th OH Infy BvtMaj	OH	12840
Marsh, Albert O.	Capt. 59th USCT	IN	11317
Marsh, Carmi L.	2nd Lt. 13th VT Infy	VT	06106
Marsh, Charles M.	1st Lt. 25th NJ Infy	NY	08948
Marsh, Daniel E.	2nd Lt. 2nd CT H Arty	NY	11045
Marsh, Daniel J.	2nd Lt. 46th MA Infy	MA	01667
Marsh, Edward L.	Capt. 2nd IA Infy	IA	05649
Marsh, Edward T. T.	Act Asst Surg. USN	NY	03777
Marsh, Edward W.	Capt. 2nd CT H Arty	NY	09118
Marsh, Elias J.	Asst Surg. BvtMaj USA	NY	07612
Marsh, Fletcher E.	Capt. 17th USCT BvtMaj	IN	06602
Marsh, Frederick H.	Capt. 46th IL Infy	IL	06334

The Roster

Name	Rank	Commandery	Insignia No.
Marsh, John F.	LTC 12th NH Infy BvtCol.	MA	02306
Marsh, Lucius B.	Col. 47th MA Infy	MA	09373
Marsh, Vincent R.	Capt. 14th NJ Infy	CA	16963
Marsh, Benjamin F.	LTC 2nd IL Cav	DC	12211
Marshall, Alexander	Capt. 1st OH L Arty	IL	07918
Marshall, Casper E.	1st Lt. 8th ME Infy	ME	11907
Marshall, Edward	1st Lt. 15th PA Cav	PA	08977
Marshall, Elisha G.	Col. BvtMG USA	NY	02273
Marshall, George C.	Capt. 130th PA Infy	PA	16974
Marshall, Isaac N.	2nd Lt. 6th MA Infy	MA	07958
Marshall, James	Chap USA	IA	09731
Marshall, John E.	Capt. AAG BvtLTC USV	NY	08653
Marshall, John G.	Capt. Dental Surg. USV	CA	16552
Marshall, Jonathan T.	1st Lt. RQM 11th PA Infy	PA	00515
Marshall, Samuel D.	Asst Surg. 1st DE Infy	PA	08753
Marshall, Thomas P.	Maj 13th IA Infy	OH	10675
Marshall, Thomas R.	Lt. US Revenue Service	DC	18268
Marshall, William L.	LTC Eng. USA	WI	03418
Marshall, William S.	Maj 5th IA Infy	OH	05672 (Dup)
Marshall, Woodson S.	Capt. 46th IN Infy	IN	15411
Marston, Hiram P.	Capt. 33rd MA Infy	DC	13212
Marten, Benjamin T.	1st Lt. 47th NY Infy BvtMaj	NY	08354
Marthon, Joseph	Lt. Commander USN	NY	01377
Martin, Archer N.	Capt. 16th PA Cav BvtLTC	NY	00078
Martin, Augustus P.	Capt. 3rd Batt MA L Arty BvtCol.	MA	01257
Martin, Charles	Med. Director USN	NY	00225
Martin, Edward	1st Lt. 57th IL Infy	OR	07151
Martin, Edward A.	Capt. 108th USCT	NY	12726
Martin, George H.	2nd Lt. 14th Batt MI L Arty	IL	13783
Martin, George W.	Surg. 2nd ME Cav	ME	05343
Martin, George W.	1st Lt. 25th OH Infy	MO	07118
Martin, Henry V.	Capt. 42nd USCT	CA	06330
Martin, James N.	BvtMaj USV	IA	16614
Martin, James P.	LTC AAG USA	IL	00246
Martin, James W.	Capt. 24th IA Infy	IA	11311
Martin, John A.	Col. 8th KS Infy BvtBG	KS	05451
Martin, John C.	1st Lt. 157th PA Infy	PA	11560
Martin, John P.	Capt. 88th PA Infy	PA	03226
Martin, Oramel	Surg. USV	MA	01267
Martin, Samuel W.	1st Lt. 70th IN Infy	CA	09572
Martin, Sylvester H.	Capt. 88th PA Infy	PA	11537
Martin, Thomas H.	Capt. 123rd IN Infy	IN	07507
Martin, William A.	Capt. 3rd MI Cav	IL	04504
Martin, William P.	Capt. Mil. Storekpr. BvtCol. USA	CA	01623
Martin, William W.	1st Lt. 154th IN Infy	KS	04813
Martindale, Edward	Col. 81st USCT	CA	05482
Martine, Charles A.	2nd Asst Eng. USN	CO	08958
Marvin, Azor S.	Capt. AAG BvtLTC USV	NY	07468

Name	Rank	Commandery	Insignia No.
Marvin, Edwin E.	Capt. 5th CT Infy	MA	13013
Marvin, Selden E.	Maj Paymaster USV	NY	00575
Marvin, Ulysses L.	Capt. 5th USCT BvtMaj	OH	04206
Marvine, George H.	Asst Surg.USN	NY	00234
Mason, A. Judson	Capt. 35th MA Infy BvtMaj	CA	08629
Mason, Addison G.	Capt. ADC BvtLTC USV	PA	06264
Mason, Charles F.	1st Lt. 1st RI L Arty	MA	02457
Mason, Darius	Surg. 31st WI Infy	WI	04118
Mason, E. Porter	1st Lt. 1st CT H Arty BvtCapt.	PA	01140
Mason, Edwin C.	Col. 3rd Infy BvtBG USA	MN	04235
Mason, Frank H.	Capt. 12th OH Cav	OH	06647
Mason, George	1st Lt. Adj. 12th IL Infy BvtMaj	IL	01935
Mason, Henry W.	Capt. 9th NY Cav	MA	16206
Mason, Herbert C.	Capt. 20th MA Infy BvtMaj	MA	01674
Mason, John E.	1st Lt. 9th NH Infy	DC	05977
Mason, John S.	BG USV	DC	10857
Mason, Lorenzo D.	1st Lt. 1st MI Eng.	CA	04523
Mason, Oliver P.	3rd Class	NE	04829
Mason, Reuben S.	1st Lt. 55th USCT	OH	09894
Mason, Roswell H.	Capt. 72nd IL Infy	IL	01916
Mason, Theodore B.M.	Lt. Commander USN	DC	01844
Mason, Thomas	Act Ensign USN	NY	14125
Mason, William B.	Capt. 8th NJ Infy	NY	11244
Mason, William E.	Capt. 58th MA Infy	MA	11743
Massay, George V.	LTC AAG USV	PA	17035
Massey, Frederick I.	1st Lt. 9th NY Infy BvtCapt.	IL	04134
Massey, John	1st Lt. 37th NY Infy	CA	09541
Masten, Cornelius S.	Capt. 4th NY Cav BvtMaj	CA	06927
Masten, George G.	1st Lt. 80th NY Infy	NE	07210
Masters, Hibbert B.	Capt. CS BvtMaj USV	NY	08654
Masury, Charles H.	2nd Lt. 1st MA H Arty	MA	12064
Matchette, Joseph	Capt. 46th PA Infy	PA	15119
Mather, Andrew E.	LTC 20th USCT	NY	01833
Mather, Fred	1st Lt. 7th NY H Arty	WI	08355
Mather, Mason W.	2nd Asst Eng. USN	CA	08899
Mathews, Joseph H.	Act 2nd Asst Eng. USN	CA	11910
Mathews, Joseph S.	Maj 112th NY Infy	NY	00584
Mathews, Sallmon S.	LTC 5th MI Infy BvtBG	MI	03748
Mathewson, Arthur	Surg. USN	NY	10761
Mathewson, Joseph H.	Capt. 1st NV Cav	CA	03908
Mathey, Edward G.	Maj USA	CO	11861
Mathot, Louis	1st Lt. 40th MA Infy BvtCapt.	NY	11556 (Dup)
Matile, Leon A.	BG USA	DC	08816
Matlack, Lewis T.	1st Lt. 91st PA Infy	PA	07648
Matrau, Henry C.	Capt. 6th WI Infy	NE	13844
Matson, Daniel	Capt. 4th USC H Arty	IA	11078
Matteson, Charles F.	Capt. 103rd IL Infy	IL	02322
Matthews, Ambrose M.	Capt. 13th NJ Infy	NY	05826

The Roster 293

Name	Rank	Commandery	Insignia No.
Matthews, Asa C.	BvtCol. USV	DC	07801
Matthews, Charles W.	1st Lt. 53rd PA Infy	PA	01532
Matthews, Edmund O.	RAdm USN	DC	10555
Matthews, Ezra W.	Maj 1st PA L Arty	PA	01574
Matthews, Stanley	Col. 51st OH Infy	DC	02258
Matthews, Thomas L.	1st Lt. 2nd MD Infy	MD	14559
Matthews, William S.	1st Lt. 60th OH Infy BvtCapt.	OH	03572
Mattison, William R.	Maj 2nd NY Cav	NY	07976
Mattocks, Brewer	1st Lt. Asst Surg. 7th MN Infy	MN	16870
Mattocks, Charles P.	Col. 17th ME Infy BvtBG	ME	02382
Mattox, Absalom H.	1st Lt. 17th Batt OH L Arty	OH	02341
Mattson, Hans	Col. 3rd MN Infy	MN	04736
Maulsby, George	Surg. Med. Director USN	PA	00179
Mauran, Edward C.	3rd Class (Adj. Gen. RI)	MA	02497
Maurice, Charles S.	2nd Asst Eng. USN	PA	15121
Mauzy, James H.	Capt. 68th IN Infy	IN	07157
Maxim, Alfonzo A.	1st Lt. RQM 10th MI Cav	DC	13725
Maxon, Mason M.	Capt. 10th Cav USA	OH	16490
Maxwell, Charles A.	2nd Lt. 3rd OH Infy	DC	09339
Maxwell, Edward L.	Capt. 15th KY Cav	KS	16697
Maxwell, Harlan P.	1st Lt. 59th USCT	DC	09853
Maxwell, John A.	1st Lt. 1st AK Cav	IN	12337
Maxwell, Norman J.	Col. 100th PA Infy BvtBG	PA	13289
Maxwell, Obadiah C.	LTC 194th OH Infy BvtBG	PA	01253
Maxwell, Thomas J.	Surg. 138th USCT	IA	11377
May, Charles W.	Capt. 101st PA Infy	PA	08754
May, Darwin R.	Capt. 22nd WI Infy	WI	01553
May, Edward	Pay Director USN	MA	08317
May, Elisha	1st Lt. 26th NY Cav	VT	16181
May, James	1st Lt. 48th PA Infy	PA	05729
May, James R.	Act Asst Surg. USN	MA	17179
Mayer, Brantz	Maj Paymaster BvtLTC USV	PA	00316
Mayer, Daniel	Asst Surg. 5th WV Infy	PA	03787
Mayer, Leopold	Capt. 12th PA Cav	IL	15233
Mayers, Charles G.	1st Lt. RQM 11th WI Infy BvtMaj	WI	05224
Mayhew, Hebron	Capt. 10th ME Infy	ME	08835
Maynadier, William M.	Maj Paymaster USA	CA	09532
Maynard, Charles W.	1st Lt. 20th MI Infy	MI	17945
Maynard, George H.	BvtMaj USV	MA	15258
Maynard, Henry H.	Surg. 2nd AK Cav	CA	06058
Maynard, Horatio B.	LTC 44th OH Infy	OH	08908
Maynard, Washburn	RAdm USN	DC	16167
Mayo, Lewis	Capt. 87th IL Infy	KS	13224
Mayo, William E.	Commodore USN	NY	03355
McAdams, James M.	BvtCapt. USV	KS	16799
McAllister, Arthur	Capt. 10th USCT BvtLTC	OH	03269
McAllister, Edward	Capt. 1st IL L Arty	IL	11281
McAllister, Henry	Maj 15th PA Cav	CO	12675

Name	Rank	Commandery	Insignia No.
McAlpine, Thomas D.	2nd Lt. VRC	DC	06184
McAlpine, William T.	1st Lt. 2nd MA Infy	MA	06505
McArthur, Henry C.	BvtMaj USV	IA	15437
McArthur, James N.	Col. 4th USC H Arty	NY	14453
McArthur, John	BG BvtMG USV	IL	08721
McAuley, John T.	Capt. 55th IL Infy	IL	01931
McAuliffe, Frank	1st Lt. 22nd CT Infy	NY	09310
McBride, Joseph C.	BvtCapt. USV	IL	02788
McBride, Patrick H.	1st Lt. RQM 2nd OH Cav	MI	13712
McCafferty, Matthew J.	Maj 25th Ma Infy	MA	00722
McCagg, Ezra B.	3rd Class (Pres. NW Sanitary Com)	IL	02316
McCain, Thomas H.B.	1st Lt. 88th IN Infy	IN	06603
McCall, Charles A.	Asst Surg. BvtMaj USA	PA	05502
McCall, Ebenezer H.	1st Lt. Adj. 80th OH Infy	OH	13617
McCall, Joseph W.	Asst Surg. 7th TN Cav	OH	11394
McCall, Matthew H.	1st Lt. RQM 187th PA Infy	PA	09773
McCalla, Bowman H.	RAdm USN	IL	12444
McCalla, Theodore H.	Maj 95th PA Infy BvtLTC	PA	07344
McCallay, Edmund L.	1st Lt. Adj. 27th USCT	OH	06892
McCallum, Alexander	Capt. 8th PA Cav	PA	01008
McCalmont, John S.	Col. 39th PA Infy	DC	10176
McCamant, Thomas	2nd Lt. 125th PA Infy	PA	04416
McCammon, William W.	Maj 6th Infy USA	OR	08127
McCandless, James N.	Surg. 77th PA Infy	CA	13998
McCandless, William	Col. 31st PA Infy	PA	00769
McCandless, William G.	Maj 5th PA Cav	PA	04664
McCarter, John G.	1st Lt. 25th MA Infy	MA	09809
McCarthy, Thomas	Capt. 101st NY Infy	NY	01448
McCartney, Daniel P.	Chief Eng. USN	DC	10693
McCartney, James	Cap. 112th IL Infy	IL	03138
McCartney, William H.	Capt. 1st Batt MA L Arty	PA	02741
McCaskey, William S.	BG USA	KS	00712
McCauley, Edward Y.	RAdm USN	PA	00184-3227
McCauley, John R.	1st Lt. 15th NJ Infy BvtCapt.	PA	12773
McCauley, Levi G.	Capt. 36th PA Infy	PA	02106
McCawley, Charles G.	Col. Commandant USMC	PA	08224
McChesney, Robert W.	1st Lt. 113th USCT	CA	11662
McClaskey, Ebenezer P.	Capt. 120th IN Infy	IN	08726
McClaughry, Robert W.	Maj Paymaster USV	KS	02680
McClay, John H.	2nd Lt. 47th IL Infy	NE	04317
McCleary, John	LTC 28th Infy PA Militia	PA	10396
McCLeave, William	Maj 1st CA Cav BvtLTC	CA	04752
McClellan, George B.	MG USA	NY	01373
McClelland, George P.	Capt. 155th PA Infy BvtMaj	IL	04845
McClelland, Joseph S.	1st Lt. 5th USCT	CO	12676
McClelland, William	Capt. 1st PA L Arty	PA	04954
McClintock, Joel M.	Capat. 57th USCT	MO	15880
McCloskey, Francis E.	2nd Lt. Sig. Corps USV	PA	02230

Name	Rank	Commandery	Insignia No.
McClung, Charles L.	Ensign USN	KS	16243
McClung, David W.	Capt. AGM USV	OH	03047
McClure, Charles	LTC Dept. Paymaster Gen. BvtCol. USA	DC	03516
McClure, James R.	Capt. 2nd KS Infy	KS	04443
McClure, John	Maj 57th OH Infy	MO	06370
McClure, John D.	Col. 47th IL Infy	IL	09486
McClurg, Alexander C.	LTC AAG BvtBG USV	IL	01922
McClurg, John R.	Surg. BvtLTC USV	PA	09279
McClymonds, J. Walter	1st Lt. 104th OH Infy	OH	03303
McCoid, Moses A.	2nd Lt. 2nd IA Infy	IA	03032
McComas, Joseph E.	1st Lt. 5th KS Cav	CA	06720
McComas, William R.	Capt. 83rd OH Infy BvtMaj	OH	03210
McConihe, Samuel	Maj 93rd NY Infy BvtBG	KS	07259
McConnell, Benton	Maj Act Paymaster USV	NY	15520
McConnell, Charles C.	BvtMaj USA	PA	00655
McConnell, Daniel	Col. 3rd MI Infy	MI	11386
McConnell, Ezra	1st Lt. 30th OH Infy	OH	06515
McConnell, George E.	Act Master USN	DC	15650
McConnell, Henry A.	2nd Lt. 10th MN Infy	MN	11368
McConnell, Thomas	Capt. 66th OH Infy BvtMaj	OH	06841
McConville, Michael S.	Capt. 3rd Battn. MA Rifles (Infy)	MA	01063
McConway, William	2nd Lt. 102nd PA Infy	PA	03410
McCook, Alexander McD.	MG USA	KS	04992
McCook, Anson G.	Col. 194th OH Infy BvtBG	NY	00197
McCook, Edward M.	BvtMG USA	PA	00196
McCook, Henry C.	Chap 41st IL Infy	PA	06469
McCook, John J.	Capt. ADC USV	NY	01079
McCook, John James	2nd Lt. 1st WVA Infy	NY	07987
McCord, William B.	LTC 55th USCT	MN	05867
McCormick, Andrew W.	Capt. 77th OH Infy BvtLTC	OH	03380
McCormick, Charles	Col. Asst Surg. Gen. USA	CA	01378
McCormick, Isaiah H.	Capt. 148th OH Infy	OH	06080
McCormick, Samuel C.	Surg. 202nd PA Infy	MN	04239
McCormick, William H.	Act Ensign USN	PA	11833
McCourt, John	Act 1st Asst Eng. USN	PA	01994
McCown, Albert F.	Maj 13th WVA Infy	OH	04532
McCown, Ferdinand O.	Capt. 1st OR Infy	OR	07149
McCoy, Andrew J.	Capt. CS BvtCol. USV	MO	05040
McCoy, James B.	1st Lt. 25th WI Infy	WI	06566
McCoy, Milton	Capt. 2nd OH Infy	OH	06889 (Dup)
McCoy, Robert A.	LTC 40th PA Infy BvtBG	PA	00274
McCracken, Aaron H.	1st Lt. Adj. 38th WI Infy	IL	14403
McCracken, William V.	Capt. 123rd OH Infy	NY	05111
McCrackin, Alexander	Capt. USN	IA	10803
McCrary, George W.	3rd Class (Sec. of War)	MO	05093
McCrea, Tully	BG USA	DC	14533
McCreary, B. Daniel	Ltc 145th PA Infy BvtBG	PA	08982
McCreery, Charles H.	BvtMaj USV	MN	15658

Name	Rank	Commandery	Insignia No.
McCreery, William B.	Col. 21st MI Infy	MI	03741
McCrory, William	1st Lt. 7th Co. OH Sharpshtrs.BvtCapt.	MN	04237
McCue, Wilbur F.	1st Lt. 71st OH Infy	CO	11606
McCullough, Samuel M.	1st Lt. 5th WVA Infy	OH	05931 (Dup)
McCurdy, John	Surg. 11th OH Infy	OH	06122
McCurley, Felix	Commander USN	PA	10262
McCutchan, Andrew J.	Capt. 42nd IN Infy	IN	11318
McDaniel, Charles A.	Paymaster USN	PA	00544
McDavitt, Virgil	1st Lt. 1st AL Cav	IL	09246
McDermid, J.J.	BvtLTC USV	IL	02182
McDermott, James	1st Lt. 4th KY Mounted Infy	KS	06162
McDermott, Thomas	Capt., 9th TN Cav	OH	10991
McDonald, Benjamin	3rd Class	KS	04879
McDonald, Christopher R.	Col. 47th NY Infy	NY	00134
McDonald, Henry J.	LTC 11th CT Infy	IA	11687
McDonald, Isaiah H.	2nd Lt. 9th Cav USA	OH	05373
McDonald, James H.	Maj 50th NY Eng. BvtLTC	NY	11106
McDonald, John	Maj USA	DC	12030
McDonald, Stuart A.	Capt. 123rd NY Infy	OH	08381
McDonald, William O.	Surg. BvtLTC USV	NY	11107
McDougall, Charles J.	Commander USN	CA	01278
McDougall, John E.	1st Lt. 9th NY Infy	NY	15441
McDougall, S.P.	2nd Lt. 16th VRC	PA	00090
McDowell, Henry C.	Capt. AAG USV	OH	03061
McDowell, Robert M.	Maj 141st NY Infy	MO	04283
McDowell, William H.H.	2nd Lt. 129th IL Infy	IL	09657
McElderry, Henry	Maj Surg. USA	KS	11699
McElhaney, William	Capt. 4th NJ Infy BvtLTC	PA	08984
McElmell, Edward F.	Asst Eng. USN	PA	13551
McElmell, Jackson	Chief Eng. USN	PA	00287
McElmell, Thomas A.	Act Asst Eng. USN	PA	06768
McElroy, Joseph C.	Capt. 18th OH Infy	OH	14309
McEntee, Charles S.	Capt. AQM BvtLTC USV	IL	05784
McEntee, John	LTC 80th NY Infy BvtCol.	NY	07977
McEwan, Henry D.	Chief Eng. USN	PA	05728
McEwan, John S.	Capt. 7th NY H Arty BvtMaj	NY	20581
McEwan, M.G.	BvtLTC USV	NY	02136
McFarland, Edwin C.	Capt. 41st USCT	MA	11674
McFarland, Walter	LTC Eng. USA	NY	05399
McFeely, Aaron	Capat. 16th IN Infy	IN	10368
McFeeters, James L.	Capt. 100th PA Infy	PA	08983
McGannon, Pleasant C.	Capt. 6th IN Infy	IN	07269
McGaughey, James H.	2nd Lt. 1st AL Cav	MN	08609
McGill, George M.	Capt. Asst Surg. BvtCol. USA	PA	00347
McGilvray, John	Capt. 2nd Arty USA	CO	03517
McGinness, John R.	BG USA	MO	00507
McGinnis, George F.	BG USV	IN	02845
McGinnis, William A.	1st Lt. 19th MA Infy	MA	06915

Name	Rank	Commandery	Insignia No.
McGinniss, James T.	Capt. 13th Infy BvtMaj USA	OH	04574
McGonigal, James B.	2nd Lt. 99th IN Infy	KS	06359
McGonigle, James A.	1st Lt. 1st KS Infy	PA	04917
McGorrisk, Edward J.	Surg. 9th IA Infy	IA	06689
McGowan, Francis	1st Lt. 29th IN Infy	OR	15963
McGowan, George	Maj BvtLTC USA	NY	07783
McGowan, John	RAdm USN	DC	00598
McGowan, Jonas H.	Capt. 9th MI Cav	DC	03526
McGrath, John M.	Surg. 78th PA Infy	PA	01575
McGrath, Maurice J.	Capt. 52nd IL Infy	IL	07919
McGraw, Theodore A.	Asst Surg. BvtCapt. USV	MI	10817
McGreevey, Cornelius	Maj 74th OH Infy	IN	15324
McGregor, Charles	Commander USN	OH	01680
McGregor, Duncan	1st Lt. RQM 2nd IA Cav	NY	02369
McGregor, Duncan	Capt. 42nd WI Infy	WI	15023
McGregor, James	Maj 139th PA Infy	PA	08225
McGregor, John G.	Capt. 8th MN Infy	MN	03317
McGregor, Thomas	BG USA	CA	03442
McGrew, John S.	Surg. BvtLTC USV	Ca	02923
McGuire, John F.	Capt. 153rd NY Infy	IL	04139
McGuire, Michael A.	Capt. 108th OH Infy	OH	07839
McIlvaine, Charles	Maj 97th PA Infy	PA	00492
McIlvaine, Henry C.	1st Asst Eng. USN	PA	00525
McIlwaine, David B.	Capt. 14th WVA Infy	OH	04225
McIntosh, Alexander	Capt. 188th OH Infy	OH	17487
McIntosh, Isaac R.	Capt. 2nd MA Cav	CA	03467
McIntosh, John B.	BvtMG USV	PA	00272
McIntyre, Martin V.B.	1st Lt. 7th Batt NY L Arty	PA	07065
McIntyre, Richard H.	Capt. 72nd IN Infy	IN	14300
McIntyre, William J.	2nd Lt. 11th IL Infy	CA	14321
McJohnston, Robert P.	1st Lt. 65th IN Infy	CA	15977
McKaig, Robert N.	2nd Lt. 6th IN Cav	MN	04763
McKay, Charles E.	Lt. Commander USN	NY	06642
McKay, George A.	Capt. 7th OH Infy	OH	10992
McKay, George F.	BvtMaj USV	MA	00978
McKay, Horace	Capt. 15th USCT	IN	06604
McKay, James	2nd Lt. 2nd RI Infy	MA	04627
McKay, John E.	Act 1st Asst Eng. USN	NY	09428
McKay, Robert G.	1st Lt. 1st MI Cav	WA	13716
McKay, William	Maj 27th MA Infy	CA	04514
McKean, Frederick G.	Chief Eng. USN	DC	11371
McKean, Henry B.	Col. 35th Infy PA Militia	DC	03177
McKee, Edward R.	1st Lt. 149th OH Infy	OH	16011 (Dup)
McKee, George W.	Maj Ordnance USA	NY	01277
McKee, James C.	LTC Surg. USA	PA	01694
McKee, Thomas H.	1st Lt. 1st WVA Infy	DC	02876
McKeen, William	3rd Class	IN	06906
McKeever, Chauncey	Col. AAG BvtBG USA	DC	01223

Name	Rank	Commandery	Insignia No.
McKeever, Samuel	Capt. 2nd Infy BvtLTC USA	MA	04077
McKell, James C.	Capt. 73rd OH Infy	NE	08027
McKellip, William A.	LTC 6th MD Infy	DC	10338
McKenney, Wilbur W.	2nd Lt. 40th USCT	ME	15067
McKercher, Duncan	Maj 10th WI Infy	KS	05776
McKevitte, Charles A.	1st Lt. 3rd NY Infy	Dc	08318
McKibbin, Chambers	BG USA	DC	00658
McKibbin, David B.	Col. 214th PA Infy BvtBG	DC	00653
McKibbin, Gilbert H.	Capt. AAG BvtBG USV	NY	01829
McKibbin, Joseph C.	Col. AADC USV	DC	03024
McKibbin, Robert P.	Capt. 4th Infy BvtLTC USA	PA	00599
McKiernan, Samuel G.	1st Lt. 25th NJ Infy	NY	07242
McKim, James	Capt. 39th Infy USA	WA	10729
McKim, John W.	Capt. AQM BvtMaj USV	MA	07402
McKim, Robert V.	Surg. 57th NY Infy	NY	03366
McKim, William W.	Col. QM BvtCol. USA	MA	00414
McKinley, William	Capt. 23rd OH Infy BvtMaj (Pres. US)	OH	03029
McKinney, Albert	Maj Paymaster BvtLTC USV	MO	07290
McKinney, Edward P.	BvtMaj USV	NY	15869
McKinsey, William P.	1st Lt. RQM 40th IN Infy	IN	14431
McKinstry, James P.	Commodore USN	PA	00308
McKnight, Harvey W.	Capt. 210th PA Infy	PA	06468
McKnight, Joseph H.	1st Lt. 128th PA Infy	PA	09502
McKown, Hillis	1st Lt. Adj. 105th PA Infy	PA	07345
McLanahan, Samuel C.	2nd Asst Eng. USN	PA	17085
McLaren, Donald	RAdm USN	CA	15638
McLaren, John	1st Lt. Adj. 1st MO Eng.	IL	01919
McLaren, Robert N.	Col. 2nd MN Cav BvtBG	MN	03839
McLean, Cornelius	2nd Lt. 42nd NY Infy	NY	15057
McLean, Hugh D.	Asst Surg. 106th PA Infy	PA	13552
McLean, John	2nd Lt. 40th IL Infy	IL	05920
McLean, LeRoy	Surg. 2nd NY Infy	NY	05823
McLean, William A.	Capt. CS BvtMaj USV	IL	02021
McLean, William E.	Col. 43rd IN Infy	IN	04328
McLellan, Charles R.	Act Ensign USN	DC	06147
McLellan, Curwen B.	LTC 1st Cav USA	MO	10051
McLeod, Harvey S.	1st Lt. 148th NY Infy	NY	15442
McLyman, William H.	BvtMaj USV	OH	07713
McMahan, William R.	1st Lt. 58th IN Infy	IN	10798
McMahon, Abraham	Surg. BvtLTC USV	CA	03904
McMahon, Daniel	Capt. 80th NY Infy	DC	03318
McMahon, James	Capt. 41st OH Infy	OH	10211
McMahon, Lawrence C.	1st Lt. 38th NJ Infy	CA	17784
McMahon, Martin T.	LTC AAG BvtMG USV	NY	00128
McManus, Parker W.	1st Lt. Adj. 27th MA Infy	DC	04846
McManus, Thomas	Maj 22nd CT Infy	PA	04955
McManus, William S.	Capt. 15th Infy BvtMaj USA	PA	00505
McMichael, Clayton	Capt. 9th Infy BvtMaj USA	PA	03025

Name	Rank	Commandery	Insignia No.
McMicken, James A.	Capt. 43rd NY Infy	NY	05115
McMicken, William	Capt. 10th MN Infy	WA	06392
McMillan, Alexander F.	Capt. 1st USC H Arty	DC	06382
McMillan, Charles	Surg. 71st Infy NY St. Militia BvtLTC	DC	01076
McMillan, James W.	BG BvtMG USV	DC	03521
McMillan, Putnam D.	1st Lt. RQM 15th VT Infy	MN	05559
McMillan, Thomas	1st Lt. 27th WI Infy	MN	07704
McMillen, William L.	Col. 95th OH Infy BvtMG	OH	03302
McMillin, Emerson	2nd Lt. 2nd WVA Cav	NY	05385
McMillin, William A.	2nd Lt. 140th PA Infy	MO	09630
McMinn, William H.	Capt. 213th PA Infy	CA	03225 (Dup)
McMullen, John W.T.	Col. 57th IN Infy	IN	13311
McMurtrie, Daniel	Med. Director USN	DC	00908
McMurtrie, Horace	1st Asst Eng. USN	MA	01425
McMurty, Alexander C.	Capt. 88th IL Infy	IL	14874
McMynn, John G.	Col. 10th WI Infy	WI	04507
McNair, Anton DeR.	Lt. Commander USN	PA	00268-269
McNair, Frederick V.	RAdm USN	DC	03411
McNally, Michael	Capt. 201st PA Infy	DC	14992
McNary, Oliver R.	1st Lt. RQM 103rd PA Infy	KS	06038
McNary, William P.	1st Lt. Adj. 123rd PA Infy	MO	11567
McNaught, John S.	Maj USA	OH	00656-3962
McNeil, Henry C.	2nd Lt. 2nd IA Infy	IA	05440
McNeil, John	BG BvtMG USV	MO	04686
McNeil, Rollin	Surg. 9th CT Infy	NY	12884
McNulta, John	Col. 94th IL Infy BvtBG	IL	05287
McNulty, James M.	Surg. BvtCol. USV	CA	01284
McNulty, John	Surg. BvtLTC USV	IA	11689
McNulty, Patrick H.	Col. Surg. 6th PA Cav	DC	14998
McNutt, William F.	Act Asst Eng. USN	CA	03629
McParlin, Thomas A.	Col. Surg. BvtBG USA	DC	05106
McPherson, John	1st Lt. RCS 1st WI Cav	KS	14187
McPherson, Theodore H.N.	1st Lt. 107th PA Infy	DC	12703
McQuade, James	Col. 14th NY Infy BvtMG	NY	00879
McQuiston, Henry	2nd Lt. 6th Cav BvtCapt. USA	OH	10702
McReynolds, Benjamin F.	1st. Lt. RQM 1st NY Cav	MI	08196
McVean, Donald C.	Capt. VRC BvtLTC	MO	04113
McVey, Archibald	Act Asst Paymaster USN	MO	14566
McVickar, James R.	3rd Class	IL	05140
McWhorter, Henry C.	Capt. 9th WVA Infy	OH	09756
McWhorter, Paul W.	2nd Lt. 54th USCT	WI	14342
McWilliams, John	1st Lt. RQM 129th IL Infy	IL	06069
McWilliams, John G.	Capt. 51st IL Infy	IL	02019
McWilliams, Lafayette	Capt. 157th NY Infy	IL	02812
Meacham, Florus U.	2nd Lt. Chicago Merch.Batt IL L Arty	IL	11887
Meacham, Franklin	Surg. BvtLTC USA	CA	03536
Meacham, Justin W.	Act Asst Paymaster USN	WI	14461
Mead, David W.	1st Lt. 17th CT Infy	WA	13718

Name	Rank	Commandery	Insignia No.
Mead, Francis W.	Surg. 2nd DC Infy	DC	08722
Mead, George L.	Paymaster USN	NY	00587
Mead, Richard T.	Asst Surg. 79th NY Infy	MI	08713
Mead, Warren H.	1st Lt. 6th KY Cav	MN	06755
Mead, William G.	1st Lt. 72nd IL Infy	IL	03704
Meade, Alfred N.	Capt. 128th OH Infy	OH	03382
Meade, George	Capt. 1st Arty BvtLTC USA	PA	02105
Meade, Richard W.	RAdm USN	PA	00187
Meade, Robert L.	Col. BvtBG USMC	PA	00271
Means, Archibald	Capt. 14th KY Infy	IL	09392
Mears, Charles E.	Maj 1st NY Marine Arty	NY	02927
Mears, Frederick	LTC 4th Infy USA	CA	03324
MeCutchen, John F.	Act Chief Eng. USN	PA	05727
Medart, Philip	Capt. 3rd MO Infy	MO	10178
Meday, Chrstian H.	1st Lt. NY State Nat. Guard	CA	15115
Meding, John J. A.	2nd Lt. 178th NY Infy	DC	17415
Meeker, Carnot R.	1st Lt. 2nd NJ Cav	NY	09129
Meeker, Edward P.	Capt. USMC	NY	08497
Meeks, Albert V.	Capt. 62nd NY Infy	NY	04071
Meeks, Joseph W.	1st Lt. RQM 38th NY Infy	NY	07467
Meginn, James A.	1st Lt. RQM 5th US Vol. Infy	MN	14143
Megler, Joseph G.	Act Ensign USN	OR	04462
Megrew, John P.	Capt. 11th IN Infy	DC	11575
Meier, Edward D.	1st Lt. 1st LA Cav	NY	08912
Meigs, John F.	Lt. USN	DC	16482
Meigs, John J.	Surg. 3rd VT Infy	Ca	03631
Meigs, Montgomery C.	BG BvtMG USA	DC	00315
Meigs, Samuel E.	Capt. AQM USV	PA	00719
Meiser, Herman	1st Lt. 27th PA Infy	MI	09584
Melcher, Holman S.	Capt. 20th ME Infy BvtMaj	ME	03807
Melcher, Samuel H.	LTC 6th Cav MO St. Militia	IL	14162
Meldrum, Norman H.	1st Lt. 21st NY Cav	CA	11114
Mellor, James W.	Act 2nd Asst Eng. USN	NY	08356
Meloy, William T.	2nd Lt. 122nd OH Infy	IL	13987
Melville, George W.	RAdm USN	PA	04682
Melvin, Thayer	Capt. AAG BvtLTC USV	DC	14258
Mendell, George H.	Col. Eng USA	CA	02902
Mendenhall, John	Col. 2nd Arty USA	MA	02201
Mendenhall, Wash. B.	Maj Paymaster BvtLTC USV	PA	00437
Menken, J. Stanwood	Capt. 27th OH Infy	NY	01363
Menken, Nathan D.	Capt. 1st OH Cav	PA	00608
Menninger, Henry J.	Surg. 2nd NC Infy	NY	03356
Menzies, Gustavus V.	Lt. Commander USN	IN	10672
Mercer, Frederick W.	Surg. 20th MA Infy	MA	05613
Mercer, John J.	Capt. 78th IL Infy	NE	13521
Mercer, Samuel D.	Asst Surg. 140th IL Infy	NE	04307
Merchant, Clarke	Lt. Commander USN	PA	00550
Merchant, Thomas E.	1st Lt. Adj. 57th PA Infy BvtCapt.	PA	02745

THE ROSTER

Name	Rank	Commandery	Insignia No.
Meredith, Madison M.	Capt. 103rd PA Infy	PA	04725
Meredith, William M.	Capt. 70th IN Infy	DC	07560
Meredith, William M.	3rd Class (Atty Gen PA)	PA	00097
Meredith, William T.	Paymaster USN	NY	07985
Merrell, Albert	1st Lt. 1st OH L Arty	MO	05366
Merrell, Nathaniel A.	Capt. 29th IA Infy	IA	11139
Merriam, Henry C.	MG USA	ME	03345
Merriam, Lewis	Capt. USA	DC	04083
Merriam, Thomas	Capt. 149th NY Infy	NY	10762
Merrick, Franklin A.	2nd Lt. Batt F PA L Arty	PA	16501
Merrick, George W.	Maj 187th PA Infy	PA	13290
Merrifield, Charles E.	Act Asst Paymaster USN	IN	11183
Merrill, Charles B.	LTC 17th ME Infy	ME	00262
Merrill, Edward I.	Capt. 17th ME Infy BvtMaj	ME	03709
Merrill, Edward R.	1st Lt. 1st MA Cav	NY	06949
Merrill, Elias	Paymaster USV	ME	00673
Merrill, George S.	Capt. 4th MA Infy	MA	01496
Merrill, George W.	Capt. 60th IN Infy	CA	05184
Merrill, Henry P.	Capt. 4th KY Mounted Infy	MI	05927
Merrill, James F.	1st Lt. 7th RI Infy	MA	16414
Merrill, James W.	1st Lt. RQM 28th ME Infy	IA	11933
Merrill, Jesse	Capt. Sig. Corps BvtMaj USV	PA	10136
Merrill, John P.	RAdm USN	CA	16251
Merrill, Lewis	Col. 2nd MO Cav BvtBG	PA	00100
Merrill, Philo G.C.	1st Lt. 3rd IA Infy	IA	09395
Merrill, Samuel	LTC 70th IN Infy	CA	14064
Merrill, Simeon H.	Capt. 11th ME Infy	DC	08514
Merrill, William E.	LTC Eng. BvtCol. USA	OH	02990
Merrill, William F.	1st Lt. 3rd MA H Arty	NY	09203
Merrill, William G.	Capt. 2nd WVA Cav	OH	15612
Merriman, Charles H.	1st Lt. Adj. 1st RI Infy	MA	05877
Merriman, Daniel	1st Lt. Adj. 132nd IL Infy	MA	10989
Merriman, Edgar C.	Capt. USN	PA	03225 (Dup)
Merriman, Elijah R.	Capt. 5th WVA Infy	CA	03114
Merriman, Orlando C.	Capt. 6th MN Infy	MN	08728
Merritt, Abram	2nd Lt. 80th NY Infy	NY	05289
Merritt, Adoniram J.	Capt. Regt. W MO Eng.	MN	06281
Merritt, Edwin A.	Capt. CS USV	NY	02218
Merritt, Wesley	MG USA	IL	00243-8009
Merry, Benjamin G.	Maj 21st ME Infy	MN	05560
Merry, John F.	1st Lt. 46th IA Infy	IA	08686
Merry, John F.	RAdm USN	MA	02404
Merry, Lemuel E.	Capt. 34th OH Infy	OH	11395
Merryman, John D.	1st Lt. 25th OH Infy	OR	08404
Meserole, Nicholas W.	Capt. 133rd NY Infy	NY	03610
Meserve, William N.	Maj 4th MA H Arty	CA	11228
Meservey, Benjamin F.	Capt. 18th MA Infy BvtMaj	MA	02198
Messer, Ervin B.	LTC 156th IL Infy	IA	08684

Name	Rank	Commandery	Insignia No.
Messer, Nathaniel T.	1st Lt. 20th MA Infy Capt. CS USV	CA	01482
Messersmith, John S.	Med. Director USN	PA	04170
Messick, Jacob W.	Capt. 42nd IN Infy	IN	11322
Messimer, Hilary	2nd Asst Eng. USN	MI	10816
Messinger, William	2nd Lt. 55th MA Infy	IL	18120
Messinger, William H.	1st Asst Eng. USN	MA	13014
Metcalf, Frederick A.	1st Lt. 2nd ME Cav	CO	05623
Metcalf, Henry H.	1st Lt. 3rd RI H Arty	CO	05780
Metcalf, Joseph H.	Capt. AAG USV	NY	03353
Metcalfe, Lyne S.	Capt. AQM BvtLTC USV	MO	07381
Methudy, Leopold	Capt. 3rd USC H Arty	MO	05657
Metschan, Franz F.	1st Lt. 12th MO Infy	KS	06296
Metzger, James	LTC 55th PA Infy	PA	08978
Metzner, Adolph	Capt. 32nd IN Infy	OH	08378
Meyer, Charles F.	Capt. 2nd MN Infy	MN	10010
Meyer, Edward S.	Maj 5th US Vet.Vols.BvtBG	OH	06125
Meyer, George W.	2nd Lt. 37th IN Infy	OH	12148
Meyer, Henry C.	Capt. 24th NY Cav	NY	02054
Meyers, Charles W.	Surg. 82nd OH Infy	IL	02416
Meylert, Asa P.	Surg. USV	NY	05828
Meysenburg, Theodore A.	LTC AAG USV	MO	06546
Michael, William H.	Act Ensign USN	DC	04087
Michaelis, Otho E.	Maj Ordnance USA	ME	00882
Michaels, Lewis	BvtLTC USV	OH	07763
Michie, James C.	Capt. 1st US Vet. Vols.	OH	02993
Michie, Peter S.	LTC AIG BvtBG USV	NY	04697
Mickley, Joseph P.	Commander USN	PA	06466
Middleton, George A.	1st Lt. Adj. 137th OH Infy	OH	13848
Middleton, George M.	2nd Lt. 97th PA Infy	PA	07066
Middleton, Johnson V.D.	Col. USA	DC	04800
Middleton, Orlando F.	BvtLTC USV	NY	10165
Middleton, Passmore	Maj Surg. USA	KS	04790
Middleton, Richard	Capt. 50th NY Eng. BvtMaj	DC	03815
Mifflin, Benjamin C.	1st Lt. Adj. 49th MA Infy	MA	01123
Mihills, Merrick A.	2nd Lt. 178th OH Infy	IL	16354
Milburn, Henry	Capt. 48th IN Infy	KS	05601
Milchrist, Thomas E.	Capt. 65th IL Infy	IL	07758
Miles, Evan	BG USA	CA	00657
Miles, Nelson Appleton	LG USA	DC	01818
Milhau, John J.	Surg. BvtBG USA	NY	00301
Millar, Robert	Asst Surg. 4th RI Infy BvtMaj	MA	02600
Millard, Charles S.	1st Lt. Adj. 117th NY Infy	IN	02421
Millard, Edward E.	2nd Lt. 11th NY Infy	NY	17570
Millard, Harrison	1st Lt. 19th Infy USA	CA	02558
Miller, Allen T.	2nd Lt. 36th OH Infy	OH	14465
Miller, Charles H.	LTC 106th IL Infy	OH	16397
Miller, Crosby P.	LTC DepQMG USA	DC	07005
Miller, Daniel B.	Capt. CS BvtMaj USV	PA	05733

The Roster

Name	Rank	Commandery	Insignia No.
Miller, Daniel McL.	Asst Surg. 28th WI Infy	WI	03687
Miller, David	Capt. 65th NY Infy	NY	09429
Miller, David H.	Maj 23rd CT Infy	NY	15215
Miller, E. Rittenhouse	2nd Lt. USMC	PA	00473
Miller, Edgar T.	Capt. 15th IA Infy BvtMaj	PA	06001
Miller, Edward G.	Capt. 20th WI Infy	IA	12936
Miller, Edward H.	2nd Lt. 73rd OH Infy	OH	10676
Miller, Franklin E.	Maj 66th USCT	NY	07784
Miller, Frederick A.	Lt. Commander USN	DC	11267
Miller, Frederick C.	2nd Lt. 1st OH L Arty	OH	05196
Miller, George A.	LTC 3rd TN Cav	OR	04190
Miller, Harmon L.	Capt. 1st IN Cav	DC	13425
Miller, Harvey H.	2nd Lt. 20th IN Infy	IN	07270
Miller, Henry H.	BvtMaj USV	CA	16292
Miller, Henry W.	Lt. Commander USN	NY	09430
Miller, James	BG USA	MA	14294
Miller, Jesse S.	Maj 11th WI Infy	NE	07540
Miller, John	Act 2nd Asst Eng. USN	NY	08498
Miller, John F.	BG BvtMG USV	DC	01330
Miller, John W.	2nd Lt. 1st CT H Arty	CA	08302
Miller, Joseph N.	RAdm USN	NY	09431
Miller, Joseph W.	Capt. 2nd KY Infy	OH	08782
Miller, Madison	Col. 18th MO Infy BvtBG	MO	11068
Miller, Marcus P.	BG USA	DC	11908
Miller, Matthew M.	Capt. 5th USC L Arty	KS	16912
Miller, Milton B.	Capt. 74th NY Infy	IL	05132
Miller, Robert	1st Lt. 89th IL Infy	MI	06986
Miller, Roswell	1st Lt. 3rd NY L Arty	WI	06285
Miller, Samuel J.F.	Asst Surg. 5th KY Infy	OH	03153
Miller, Samuel L.	2nd Lt. 20th ME Infy	ME	07900
Miller, Samuel R.	Capt. 14th MN Infy	MN	14206
Miller, Thomas P.	1st Lt. 68th PA Infy	DC	13726
Miller, Wells W.	Capt. 8th OH Infy	OH	14575
Miller, William A.	Maj USA	DC	03450
Miller, William B.E.	1st Lt. 143rd IL Infy	PA	06266
Miller, William DeW.	Capt. ADC BvtMaj USV	NY	02778 (Dup)
Miller, William E.	Capt. 3rd PA Cav	PA	02229
Miller, William H.	1st Lt. 12th MI Infy	MI	16856
Miller, William H.	Capt. 35th MO Infy	MO	05042
Miller, William H.	Capt. USA	MO	12570
Miller, William H.	1st Lt. 95th PA Infy	PA	08226
Miller, William H.H.	2nd Lt. 84th OH Infy	IN	10575
Miller, Wilson S.	Capt. 41st OH Infy	OH	11784
Millett, Henry R.	LTC 5th ME Infy	ME	10615
Milligan, Francis H.	Asst Surg. 3rd & 10th MO Infy	MN	04585
Milligan, James G.	Capt. 22nd KY Infy	WA	10239
Milligan, William	1st Lt. 62nd NY Infy	MN	16028
Milliken, Elias	LTC 14th ME Infy	ME	02880

Name	Rank	Commandery	Insignia No.
Milliken, Robert B.	1st Lt. 93rd OH Infy	OH	10227
Milliken, William	1st Lt. 27th ME Infy	CO	11013
Mills, Abraham G.	2nd Lt. 105th NY Infy	NY	07469
Mills, Anson	BG USA	DC	04513
Mills, Anson B.	1st Lt. 65th USCT	KS	05949
Mills, Daniel W.	Capt. 180th OH Infy	IL	07144
Mills, Hiram R.	Asst Surg. 8th MI Cav	MI	14383
Mills, James H.	Capt. 40th PA Infy BvtLTC	CA	03931
Mills, Mason P.	1st Lt. RQM 12th IL Cav	IA	05785
Mills, William	Capt. 2nd Infy USA	NE	05061
Miln, David I.	LTC 65th NY Infy	NY	01298
Milner, Duncan C.	1st Lt. Adj. 98th OH Infy	IL	13132
Milnor, Francis W.	Col. 23rd NJ Infy	PA	06465
Milroy, Robert H.	MG USV	OR	07752
Milton, Richard S.	Capt. 9th Batt MA L Arty	MA	00723
Milward, Hubbard K.	LTC 18th KY Infy BvtCol.	OH	03009
Milward, William R.	LTC 21st KY Infy BvtCol.	OH	07314
Mimmack, Bernard P.	Capt. 30th Infy BvtMaj USA	DC	06802
Mindil, George W.	Col. 33rd NJ Infy BvtMG	NY	00696
Miner, Charles W.	BG USA	OH	10990
Miner, Charles W.	2nd Lt. Infy USA	PA	00966-10990
Minnis, John B.	LTC 3rd TN Cav	OH	11926
Minor, Edward S.	1st Lt. 2nd WI Cav	WI	04494
Minor, Thomas T.	Asst Surg. 33rd USCT	CA	02238
Mintie, Alexander E.	1st Lt. 20th CT Infy	CA	06934
Minty, Robert H. G.	BvtMG USV	CA	04023
Mintzer, Frederick W.	Act Ensign USN	PA	00549
Mintzer, William M.	Col. 53rd PA Infy BvtBG	PA	08461
Mitchel, Frederick A.	Capt. ADC USV	NY	13435
Mitchel, John B.	1st Lt. 83rd OH Infy	OH	04994
Mitchell, Alfred	Asst Surg. 9th ME Infy	ME	07228
Mitchell, Benjamin B.	Capt. 11th PA Cav	PA	10526
Mitchell, Charles D.	1st Lt. Adj. 7th OH Cav	OH	11702
Mitchell, Eugene O.	1st Lt. 128th OH Infy	OH	11051
Mitchell, Frederick W.	Capt. 12th IL Infy	DC	03170
Mitchell, George	Asst Surg. 102nd OH Infy	OH	10299
Mitchell, Harrison	Capt. 14th MO Infy	MO	05393
Mitchell, James H.	Capt. 81st PA Infy BvtMaj	IN	12193
Mitchell, James S.	1st Lt. 57th PA Infy	CA	08001
Mitchell, John	1st Lt. 32nd OH Infy	OH	03268
Mitchell, John F.B.	Capt. 2nd NY Cav	NY	11108
Mitchell, John G.	BG BvtMG USV	OH	02772
Mitchell, John L.	1st Lt. 24th WI Infy	WI	01568
Mitchell, John T.	LTC 66th OH Infy	OH	03212
Mitchell, John W.	Capt. 12th NJ Infy	IN	16796
Mitchell, Lewis B.	Capt. ADC BvtMaj USV	IL	02020
Mitchell, Louis Y.	Capt. 5th USC H Arty	Dc	07561
Mitchell, N. Chapman	LTC 4th USC Cav	PA	00415

Name	Rank	Commandery	Insignia No.
Mitchell, Oreb F.	Capt. 40th MA Infy	MA	02522
Mitchell, Pierson R.	1st Lt. 137th OH Infy	OH	13618
Mitchell, Samuel B. W.	Surg. 8th PA Cav BvtLTC	PA	00001
Mitchell, Samuel M.	1st Lt. 194th PA Infy	PA	12355
Mitchell, Thomas	Capt. 198th PA Infy	CO	00016
Mitchell, William	Capt. 3rd Infy USA	NY	05711
Mitchener, Charles E.	Maj 129th OH Infy	OH	10788
Mizner, Henry R.	BG USA	MI	02379
Mizner, John K.	BG USA	DC	04784
Moale, Edward	BG USA	CA	06714
Moderwell, Erastus C.	Maj 12th OH Cav	IL	08046
Moffat, David H.	Capt. 3rd CA Cav	CA	15114
Moffat, Edward S.	2nd Lt. Sig. Corps BvtCapt. USV	PA	10135
Moffitt, John	1st Lt. 3rd Indian Home Guard. KS Infy	CA	03947
Moffitt, Stephen	Col. 96th NY Infy BvtBG	VT	08655
Mohler, Jeremiah G.	Capt. 115th OH Infy	KS	05361
Mohr, Oscar	Capt. 29th WI Infy	WI	02085
Mohr, Richard J.	Surg. 10th IA Infy	CA	12292
Molineux, Edward L.	Col. 159th NY Infy BvtMG	NY	00216
Molyneaux, Joseph B.	Capt. 7th OH Infy	OH	04403
Monahan, Deane	Maj USA	CO	06116
Monfort, Elias B.	Capt. 75th OH Infy	OH	02758
Monroe, Frank A.	Capt. 5th NY Cav	NY	07470
Monroe, Joseph W.	Act Ensign USN	CA	10065
Monroe, L. Dow	1st Lt. 58th MA Infy	MA	08063
Monroe, William N.	1st Lt. 7th IA Cav	CA	08979
Montague, Harrison	1st Lt. 10th NY H Arty	CO	14046
Montague, Theodore G.	1st Lt. Adj. 140th OH Infy	OH	14574
Montague, Wilfred W.	3rd Class	CA	03247
Monteith, George	Capt. AAG BvtMaj USV	OH	07020
Monteith, Robert	Capt. 7th WI Infy	WI	04129
Montgomery, A. Schuyler	Capt. 1st New Orleans Infy BvtMaj	MI	06985
Montgomery, Alexander	LTC USA	MA	01469
Montgomery, James E.	Maj AAG USV	NY	00055
Montgomery, Milton	Col. 25th WI Infy BvtBG	NE	04313
Montgomery, Robert H.	Maj 10th Cav USA	DC	05654
Montgomery, Thomas	Capt. 65th USCT BvtMaj	MN	11502
Montgomery, William A.	Capt. 15th WI Infy	IL	02018
Montooth, Edward A.	1st Lt. Adj. 155th PA Infy BvtMaj	PA	09280
Moody, Joel	Capt. 2nd Indian Home Guard KS Infy	KS	06867
Moody, William H.	2nd Lt. 2nd ME Cav	ME	13879
Moonlight, Thomas	Col. 11th KS Cav BvtBG	KS	04428
Moore, Adolph E.L.	Capt. 2nd MI Infy	MI	04497
Moore, Clement C.	Capt. 20th MA Infy	NY	05113
Moore, David H.	LTC 125th OH Infy	OH	07318
Moore, Edward	Capt. 17th ME Infy BvtLTC	ME	02546
Moore, Edward B.	Capt. CS BvtMaj USV	PA	06265
Moore, Edwin K.	RAdm USN	DC	18340

Name	Rank	Commandery	Insignia No.
Moore, Francis	BG USA	KS	00487
Moore, Frederick W.	Col. 83rd OH Infy BvtBG	OH	02838
Moore, George W.	1st Lt. 111th OH Infy	OH	07943
Moore, Gurdon G.	1st Lt. 93rd NY Infy	IL	02326
Moore, Henry H.	2nd Lt. 19th Batt NY L Arty	NY	12727
Moore, Henry M.	Capt. CS USV	KS	05349
Moore, Herman N.	Capt. 7th MI Cav BvtLTC	MI	03892
Moore, J. Ridgway	1st Lt. 116th PA Infy	NY	06643
Moore, James D.	Capt. 57th PA Infy	CO	09738
Moore, James D.	Act Ensign USN	PA	00916
Moore, James H.	1st Lt. RQM 71st IL Infy	IL	08864
Moore, James M.	BG USA	DC	04037
Moore, James P.	Capt. 145th IL Infy	CA	04771
Moore, Jeremiah B.	LTC 3rd CA Infy	CA	02468
Moore, John	BvtLTC USA	DC	03098
Moore, John M.	1st Lt. 84th IN Infy	IN	15161
Moore, John P.	Capt. 3rd WI Cav	WI	08088
Moore, John W.	Chief Engineer USN	CA	00340
Moore, John W.	Maj 27th MA Infy	MO	14821
Moore, Jonathan O.	Capt. 3rd NY Infy	NY	15443
Moore, Joseph	Maj Paymaster USV	PA	07346
Moore, Joseph A.	Caapt. 17th MA Infy	MA	13808
Moore, Joseph A.	Capt. 28th PA Infy	PA	05250
Moore, Joseph F.	1st Lt. 1st PA Cav	NY	02892
Moore, Joseph L.	Capt. CS BvtMaj USV	MO	06724
Moore, Malcolm M.	BvtMaj USV	MI	04704
Moore, Milton N.	1st Lt. 16th IN Infy	IN	14042
Moore, Risdon M.	Col. 117rth IL Infy	MO	08431
Moore, Russell L.	1st Lt. 7th WI Infy	MN	05262
Moore, Thomas W.	Col. 148th OH Infy	OH	07428
Moore, Timothy C.	BvtBG USV	WI	07115
Moore, Webster P.	Col. 4th WI Cav	WI	15250
Moore, William	1st Lt. 62nd NY Infy	NY	02280
Moore, William G.	Capt. 55th PA Infy	PA	06467
Moore, William G.	Maj Paymaster BvtLTC USA	DC	11191
Moore, Winthrop A.	Capt. 7th RI Infy	OH	05197
Moores, Adolph E.L.	Capt. 2nd MI Infy	MI	04497
Moores, Frank E.	Capt. 8th OH Cav	NE	03938
Moorhead, Maxwell K.	1st Lt. RQM 13th PA Infy	PA	10874
Moorhead, William J.	Capt. 17th Infy BvtMaj USA	PA	04953
Moorhead, William S.	Maj 76th PA Infy	PA	06263
Mordecai, Alfred	BG USA	DC	13345
More, Enoch A.	BG MO State Militia	MO	09719
More, John R.	Maj Commissary MO State Militia	OH	11703
Morehouse, Roderick D.	Capt. 142nd NY Infy BvtMaj	MA	09810
Moreland, Henry	Capt. 8th IA Cav	IA	10948
Morey, Arthur P.	Capt. 22nd USCT BvtMaj	MA	06414
Morey, Henry L.	Capt. 75th OH Infy	OH	02834

Name	Rank	Commandery	Insignia No.
Morey, Joseph W.	1st Lt. 17th NY Infy	CA	03115
Morey, Lorenzo B.	Capt. 37th IL Infy	IL	13649
Morford, William E.	LTC QM USV	CA	04899
Morgan, Algernon S. M.	Col. 63rd PA Infy	PA	07067
Morgan, Bankson T.	LTC 54th NY Infy	NY	10428
Morgan, Benjamin H.	1st Lt. 3rd NV Cav	MN	12038
Morgan, Charles	Capt. 21st WI Infy	OH	03178
Morgan, Francis	Capt. 1st IL L Arty	IL	01925
Morgan, Frank	1st Lt. 1st WI Infy	MN	04495
Morgan, George W.	BG USV	OH	09741
Morgan, H.C.	BvtLTC Surg. USV	NY	00728
Morgan, J. Frank	Capt. 14th CT Infy	NE	08406
Morgan, James B.	1st Lt. 12th IA Infy	IL	04847
Morgan, James N.	LTC 144th IL Infy	MO	04796
Morgan, John C.	Capt. 1st OH H Arty	DC	13729
Morgan, John T.	Capt. 83rd IL Infy	CA	08567
Morgan, John T.	Capt. 66th OH Infy	OH	07319
Morgan, Joseph, Jr.	2nd Asst Eng. USN	PA	09501
Morgan, Michael R.	BG, Com. Gen. of Subsistence USA	MN	02853
Morgan, Otho H.	Capt. 7th Batt IN L Arty	IL	02821
Morgan, Robert C.	Capt. 10th Infy BvtLTC USA	NY	00335
Morgan, Thomas J.	Col. 14th USCT BvtBG	NY	10429
Morgan, William A.	1st Lt. 23rd KY Infy	KS	11005
Morgan, William A.	Commander USN	CA	06107
Morgan, William H.	1st Lt. 157th NY Infy	NY	16005
Morgan, William J.	Capt. 116th NY Infy	NY	10327
Morgan, William J.	Capt. 41st OH Infy	OH	04404
Morisey, George H.	1st Lt. 12th IA Infy	DC	13581
Morissey, John	Maj 3rd MA Infy	MA	01432
Morong, John C.	Capt. USN	CA	15739
Morrill, Edmund N.	Capt. CS BvtMaj USV	KS	04875
Morrill, Edward P.	1st Lt. 11th Batt MA L Arty	MA	08737
Morrill, Ezekiel	Surg. 1st NH H Arty	MA	13329
Morrill, F. Gordon	Act Ensign USN	MA	03511
Morrill, Henry L.	1st Lt. Adj. 1st IA Cav BvtMaj	MO	05083
Morrill, Joseph C.	Capt. 3rd CA Infy	CA	04861
Morrill, Wells C.	1st Lt. 37th IL Infy	KS	06156
Morris, Arthur	Capt. 4th Arty Bvt Maj USA	NY	03509
Morris, Caspar W.	1st Lt. Adj. 14th PA Cav	PA	05731
Morris, Fordham	1st Lt. 6th NY H Arty	NY	01231
Morris, James H.	2nd Lt. 10th NY H Arty	MN	09397
Morris, John A.	BvtMaj USV	CA	17617
Morris, John R.	Capt. 31st USCT	PA	05992
Morris, Louis T.	LTC 4th Cav USA	CA	04924
Morris, Richard H.	Capt. 9th NY Infy	PA	03595
Morris, Thomas A.	BG IN Volunteers	IN	07271
Morris, William H.	Capt. 15th KS Cav	KS	12078
Morris, William H.	BG BvtMG USV	NY	00336

Name	Rank	Commandery	Insignia No.
Morris, William G.	Capt. AQM BvtMaj USV	CA	01285
Morrison, Albert R.	1st Lt. 173rd OH Infy	OH	08843
Morrison, David	Col. 79th NY Infy BvtBG	NY	01837
Morrison, John W.	2nd Lt. 100th PA Infy	PA	09779
Morrison, Joseph B.	Capt. 7th IA Infy BvtLTC	IA	11059
Morrison, Joseph B.	Surg. BvtLTC USV	MO	00297
Morrison, Mortier L.	1st Lt. RQM 13th NH Infy	MA	05100
Morrison, Samuel H.	1st Lt. 2nd WI Infy	NE	06206
Morrison, Walter	Capt. 9th OH Cav	OH	02887
Morrow, Albert P.	Col. 3rd Cav USA	CO	09634
Morrow, Henry A.	Col. 21st Infy BvtMG USA	NE	00646
Morse, Allen B.	1st Lt. Adj. 21st MI Infy	MI	05272
Morse, Charles F.	Col. 2nd MA Infy	MO	05045
Morse, Charles H.	LTC 117th USCT BvtCol.	MI	11497
Morse, Edmund A.	Capt. AQM USV	NY	07089
Morse, George W.	1st Lt. 1st MA Infy	MA	01752
Morse, Joseph E.	1st Lt. RCS 1st NY Mtd. Rifles	PA	05501
Morse, Lemuel	1st Lt. 129 IL Infy	MO	17187
Morse, William F.	Capt. 3rd MN Infy BvtMaj	NY	05308
Morse, William R.	Capt. VRC BvtMaj	MI	11555
Morse, Worcester H.	1st Lt. 22nd WI Infy	MO	11034
Morsman, Westel W.	Capt. 22nd IA Infy	NE	08407
Morton, Alfred	Maj USA	CA	03232
Morton, Charles	Col. 7th Cav USA	WI	09716
Morton, Charles A.	LTC CS USV	IL	05552
Morton, Francis R.	1st Lt. 19th WI Infy	CA	03241
Morton, William A.	1st Lt. 1st MO Eng.	MO	16016
Morton, Willis W.	1st Lt. 4th VT Infy	VT	10845
Moseley, John L.	Capt. 7th VT Infy	VT	13646
Moses, Isaac	Maj AAG BvtLTC USV	NY	06740
Moses, Robert H.	1st Lt. Adj. 122nd NY Infy BvtCapt.	NY	06422
Moses, William P.	1st Lt. RQM 9th NH Infy	MA	09474
Mosher, Frederic S.	Capt. 115th NY Infy	IL	13063
Mosler, Henry	Lt. Vol. ADC	NY	11581
Mosler, Max	2nd Lt. 108th OH Infy	OH	03565
Mosman, Chesley A.	1st Lt. 59th IL Infy	MO	11352
Mosscrop, Thomas D.	Capt. 10th NY Infy	NY	12790
Mothersell, Philip	Capt. 5th MI Cav BvtMaj	MI	03734
Motley, Thomas L.	Maj AAG BvtCol. USV	MA	10719
Mott, Alexander	Capt. 5th OH Infy	OH	10942
Mott, Alexander B.	Surg. BvtLTC USV	NY	00326
Mott, Amos B.	Capt. CS USV	CO	10102
Mott, Edgar J.	1st Lt. Adj. 5th NY H Arty	NY	07613
Mott, Gershom	MG USV	PA	00810
Mott, Henry H.	Capt. 57th NY Infy	NY	11245
Mott, John O.	Maj Paymaster USV	NY	06222
Mott, John S.	1st Lt. 8th TN Cav	MO	07291
Mott, Smith B.	1st Lt. 52nd PA Infy	PA	16133

Name	Rank	Commandery	Insignia No.
Moulton, Daniel S.	1st Lt. 4th IN Cav	CA	13635
Moulton, George H.	1st Lt. 1st MI L Arty	CO	08960
Moulton, John	BvtLTC US	PA	02293
Moulton, Orson	LTC 25th MA Infy	MA	00685
Mountford, Hollis R.	2nd Lt. 25th ME Infy	ME	17230
Mower, Samuel C.	Capt. 4th WI Cav	WI	03684
Mowry, James R.	2nd Lt. 20th MI Infy	MI	12816
Mowry, William A.	Capt. 11th RI Infy	MA	14392
Moyer, Joseph	Act Ensign USN	OH	09020
Moylan, Myles	Maj 10th Cav USA	CA	08697
Moynahan, James	Capt. 27th MI Infy	CO	10103
Moynihan, Daniel C.	Capt. 164th NY Infy	NY	08656
Mudge, Melvin	LTC 11th MI Infy	CA	14317
Muehlburg, Hermann	Capt. 5th MN Infy	MN	10013
Mueller, Rudolph	Capt. 8th IL Infy BvtMaj	MN	10307
Muffly, Joseph W.	1st Lt. Adj. 148th PA Infy	IA	06544
Muhlenberg, Frank P.	Capt. 13th Infy BvtMaj USA	MI	04003
Muirheid, Henry P.	Capt. 6th PA Cav	PA	00718
Mulcahy, Thomas	LTC 39th NY Infy BvtBG	NE	05279
Mulhall, Stephen J.	Capt. USA	DC	03458
Mulholland, St. Clair A.	Col. 116th PA Infy BvtMG	PA	04950
Mullally, John E.	Capt. 17th MA Infy	IL	15181
Mullen, John H.	Capt. 12th CT Infy	MN	04549
Muller, Charles F.	2nd Lt. 29th PA Infy	OH	09897
Mulligan, James E.	Capt. 4th MA Cav	OR	07221
Mullikin, James R.	Capt. USA	NY	05530
Mullins, Mathew	LTC 40th KY Infy	OH	09151
Mulloy, John B.	Capt. 37th MA Infy	MA	07973
Mumford, Thomas N.	1st Lt. 112th PA Infy	PA	01987
Munday, John W.	2nd Lt. 73rd IN Infy	IL	07832
Mundy, William H.	1st Lt. Adj. 23rd KY Infy	OH	03476
Munger, Orett L.	Capt. 44th Ny Infy	IL	13108
Munhall, Leander W.	1st Lt. Adj. 79th IN Infy	PA	10873
Munn, Curtis E.	Surg. USA	CA	06671
Munns, Harry C.	1st Lt. 114th PA Infy	PA	11163
Munroe, Benjamin F.	Act Asst Paymaster USN	NY	08657
Munroe, James A.	1st Lt. 37th USCT	MA	13500
Munroe, Martin A.	2nd Lt. 4th MA H Arty	MA	02521
Munroe, Thomas	1st Lt. 28th PA Infy	PA	08227
Munroe, William C.	2nd Asst Eng. USN	NY	09946
Munson, Charles N.	1st Lt. 106th NY Infy	CA	17792
Munson, Franklin A.	Capt. 10th IL Infy	CA	16521
Munson, Gilbert D.	LTC 78th OH Infy BvtCol.	OH	02969
Munson, Jacob F.	Maj USA	IL	03654
Murdoch, James B.	Surg. 24th NY Infy	PA	07068
Murdoch, James E.	3rd Class (Entertainer in soldier's camp)	OH	03162
Murdoch, James E., Jr.	Capt. 2nd OH Infy	OH	10527
Murdoch, Joseph	Capt. 45th MA Infy	MA	01672

Name	Rank	Commandery	Insignia No.
Murdock, Daniel H.	Capt. 6th Infy USA	CA	03653
Murdock, George W.	Asst Surg. 15th MI Infy	NY	08949
Murdock, Henry C.	1st Lt. Adj. 35th MO Infy	MO	06049
Murdock, James H.	2nd Lt. 3rd OH Infy	PA	04951
Murdock, Marcus W.	Capt. 111th NY Infy	NY	13219
Murphy, Benjamin	Capt. 8th NJ Infy	NY	09119
Murphy, Charles J.	1st Lt. 38th NY Infy	CA	15418
Murphy, Daniel	2nd Lt. 27th USCT	OH	07128
Murphy, Elisha B.	2nd Lt. 3rd ME L Arty	CA	17052
Murphy, Frankin	1st Lt. 13th NJ Infy	NY	05525
Murphy, John	LTC USA	OR	06113
Murphy, John	LTC 168th PA Infy	PA	10872
Murphy, John H.	Surg. 8th MN Infy	MN	03836
Murphy, Michael	Capt. 163rd NY Infy	CA	07999
Murphy, Patrick E.	1st Lt. 9th MA Infy	MA	05952
Murphy, William H.	Capt. 2nd OH H Arty	MN	11305
Murphy, William J.	2nd Lt. 1st IL L Arty	IL	06331
Murphy, Wyman	1st Lt. 21st WI Iny	CA	02476
Murray, Alexander	RAdm USN	PA	00569
Murray, Benjamin B.	LTC 15th ME Infy BvtBG	ME	02500
Murray, Eli H.	Col. 3rd KY Cav BvtBG	CA	03900
Murray, James D.	Pay Director USN	PA	00312
Murray, Samuel P.	Capt. 69th OH Infy	IL	17877
Murray, William W.	1st Lt. 7th TN Cav	OH	09451
Murrin, Luke	Col. 14th OH Infy	PA	00650
Musselman, DeLafayette	2nd Lt. 86h IL Infy	IL	15871
Mussey, Reuben D.	Col. 100th USCT BvtBG	DC	02292
Muzzay, David P.	Maj 3rd MA Cav	MA	15200
Muzzey, Loring W.	Capt. CS BvtMaj USV	MA	01303
Myers, Andrew G.	Act Asst Paymaster USN	CA	02593
Myers, Francis	Capt. 12th NY Cav	NY	15521
Myers, Frederick A.	Capt. 72nd PA Infy	OH	08083 (Dup)
Myers, George R.	Col. 18th NY Infy BvtBG	OH	08844
Myers, John A.	Capt. 176th OH Infy	OH	13316
Myers, John W.	Capt. 82nd PA Infy	OH	10210
Myers, Joseph M.	Capt. 34th IL Infy	IL	14135
Myers, Lorenzo D.	Capt. AQM USV	OH	06188
Myers, Murray	Capt. 44th IL Infy	KS	06158
Myers, Reuben J.	Capt. 111th NY Infy	NY	10545
Myers, William	LTC DQMGen BvtBG USA	NY	01939
Myers, William H.	Capt. 198th OH Infy	DC	13033
Myers, William H.	2nd Lt. 38th Infy USA	KS	17594
Myers, William R.	Capt. 47th IN Infy	IN	10799
Myers, William W.	Act Asst Surg. USN	PA	09772
Myers, Winslow S.	2nd Lt. 49th USCT	OR	06909
Myler, Alfred	Capt. 42nd IN Infy	IN	11323
Myrick, John R.	Col. Arty USA	NY	12134
Naegeley, Henry	Capt. 6th WI Infy	MI	16513

Name	Rank	Commandery	Insignia No.
Nagle, Charles F.	Lt. Commander USN	NY	16400
Nagle, Hiester M.	Surg. 11th PA Cav	PA	09403
Naglee, Henry M.	BG USV	CA	04427
Naile, Frederick I.	Lt. Commander USN	PA	11017
Nanscawen, Lloyd V.	2nd Lt. 42nd WI Infy	CA	10819
Nash, Charles E.	Capt. 19th ME Infy	ME	02704
Nash, Alfred	Surg. 9th MI Cav	IL	11980
Nash, James M.	LTC 19th OH Infy	OH	09892
Nash, Sumner	1st Lt. 115th OH Infy	OH	05662
Nash, William H.	BG Com. Gen. of Subsistence USA	OR	08896
Nave, Orville J.	Maj Chap USA	OH	13897
Nazro, Charles A.	1st Lt. 26th IL Infy	CA	05625
Neal, William A.	Asst Surg. 1st MO Eng.	IN	07693
Neely, John C.	Capt. 1st IL L Arty	Il	01932
Neely, Shaw F.	Asst Surg. 165th PA Infy	KS	04444
Neff, Cyreneus D.	Capt. 9th IA Infy	CO	10562
Neff, Edmund W.S.	2nd Lt. 1st OH H Arty	OH	03964
Neff, George W.	Col. 88th OH Infy BvtBG	OH	02985
Neff, Harmanus	Col. 196th PA Infy	PA	00038
Neff, James I.	1st Lt. Adj. 101st OH Infy	IL	03853
Neide, Horace	LTC VRC BvtBG	PA	12774
Neil, Henry M.	Capt. 22nd Batt OH L Arty	OH	02954
Neil, Moses H.	Maj 1st OH Cav	OH	04565
Neill, Edward D.	Chap 1st MN Infy	MN	03499
Neill, Edward M.	Maj AAG BvtCol. USV	NY	08800
Neill, John	BvtLTC USV	PA	00828
Neill, John B.	Maj 46th OH Infy	OH	03060
Neill, Richard R.	1st Lt. USMC	PA	01237
Neill, Thomas H.	BvtBG USV	PA	00343
Neill, Thomas W.	1st Lt. 6th PA Cav	DC	00043
Neilson, Robert	Capt. 114th PA Infy	PA	03412
Nelson, Adolph	1st Lt. 66th NY Infy	NY	05708
Nelson, Frank M.	Capt. 3rd PA Vet. Res. Corps	MD	16309
Nelson, George F.	1st Lt. 13th USCT	NY	16082
Nelson, Henry C.	Med. Inspector USN	DC	02669
Nelson, James H.	BvtLTC USA	CA	01328
Nelson, John C.	Capt. 70th OH Infy	IN	10576
Nelson, Nels	1st Lt. 43rd IL Infy	IL	08425
Nelson, Thomas	Commander USN	DC	03523
Nelson, Thomas	1st Lt. 45th WI Infy	WI	04377
Nelson, William	Maj USA	IN	11180
Nelson, William H.	Capt. USA	OH	16669
Nesbitt, William B.	LTC 176th OH Infy	OH	03478
Nesmith, Clarence E.	Capt. 6th Cav BvtMaj USA	NY	00577
Netterville, William C.	Capt. USA	PA	01271 (Dup)
Nettleton, A. Bayard	Col. 2nd OH Cav BvtBG	DC	04251
Nettleton, Edward	2nd Lt. 18th NH Infy	CA	11232
Nettleton, Edward P.	LTC 31st MA Infy BvtCol.	MA	01052

Name	Rank	Commandery	Insignia No.
Neubert, Henry C.	Capt. 14th OH Infy	OH	03385
Neuman, Louis E.	Capt. 175th NY Infy	NY	09130
Neville, Edward M.	Capt. 1st CT Cav	NY	01214
Nevin, David R.B.	Capt. 109th PA Infy	PA	04956
Nevin, Edwin H., Jr.	Capt. USV	PA	01796
Nevin, Robert J.	Capt. Batt "I" PA L Arty BvtMaj	NY	01716
Nevin, William W.	Capt. AAG USV	NY	01663
Nevius, Henry M.	2nd Lt. 7th MI Cav	NY	10328
Nevius, John D.	2nd Lt. 48th OH Infy	PA	17765
Newall, George E.	Capt. 8th MI Cav	MI	11009
Newall, James M.	1st Lt. 115th OH Infy	CA	16962
Newberry, Walter C.	Col. 24th NY Cav BvtBG	IL	05545
Newbold, Charles	LTC USA	DC	03081
Newbury, William S.	1st Lt. 8th KS Infy	OR	07153
Newcomb, Carman A.	Capt. 3rd IA Infy	MO	06548
Newcombe, George K.	Maj 7th MI Infy	MI	03818
Newell, Cicero	Maj 10th MI Cav	WA	11099
Newell, Henry S.	2nd Lt. 27th MA Infy	MA	09065
Newell, John S.	Commander USN	PA	11160
Newell, John W.	Maj Paymaster BvtLTC USV	PA	07347
Newland, John T.	Capt. 79th IN Infy	OR	06908
Newlin, Alfred S.	Capt. 114th PA Infy BvtMaj	PA	00207
Newlin, George E.	1st Lt. 18th PA Cav	IL	07583
Newman, George S.	1st Lt. 17th MI Infy	CO	10147
Newman, John L.	Maj 43rd NY Infy	NY	02145
Newman, Stephen L.	1st Lt. 81st USCT BvtCapt.	MA	11293
Newman, William H.	Capt. 39th OH Infy	CA	07187
Newport, Reece M.	Col. QM BvtBG USV	MN	04036
Newsham, Thomas J.	Maj 117th IL Infy	MO	05652
Newton, Charles H.	1st Lt. 2nd OH H Arty	OH	07127
Newton, Charles W.	1st Lt. 20th CT Infy	MD	02848
Newton, Don Carlos	Capt. 52nd IL Infy	IL	06708
Newton, George B.	BvtMaj USV	PA	00275
Newton, John	MG USV	NY	05118
Newton, John W.	Capt. 1st VT Cav	MA	05422
Newton, Joseph B.	Capt. 14th OH Infy	OH	09819
Newton, Matthew T.	Surg. 10th CT Infy	MA	01308
Nicar, Edwin	Capt. 15th IN Infy	IN	11181
Niccolls, Samuel J.	Chap 126th PA Infy	MO	06553
Nichelson, Marmaduke	1st Lt. Adj. 56th IL Infy	IL	08394
Nicholas, William	Capt. 51st OH Infy	OH	12347
Nichols, Alphonso N.	Maj Paymaster USV	IA	06441
Nichols, Andrew J.	1st Lt. 2nd ME Cav	MA	01702
Nichols, Daniel F.	Capt. 5th USC H Arty	PA	10263
Nichols, Edward T.	RAdm USN	DC	01690
Nichols, Erastus A.	Capt. 2nd IL L Arty	CA	04093
Nichols, George Ward	Capt. ADC BvtLTC USV	OH	02890
Nichols, Henry E.	Lt. Commander USN	CA	06666

Name	Rank	Commandery	Insignia No.
Nichols, Henry B.	Capt. 19th WI Infy	DC	07562
Nichols, James B.	Capt. 24th MA Infy	MA	01178
Nichols, Marshall C.	Capt. 42nd WI Infy	WI	05372
Nichols, Smith W.	Commander USN	MA	12669
Nichols, William A.	Col. AAG BvtMG USA	PA	00522
Nicholson, Augustus S.	Maj USMC	PA	00170
Nicholson, Edward W.	Capt. 22nd Batt IN L Arty	DC	08004
Nicholson, James W.A.	RAdm USN	NY	03607
Nicholson, John Page	1st Lt. RQM 28th PA Infy BvtLTC	PA	01870
Nicholson, William A.	1st Lt. 13th NJ Infy	MO	05394
Nickerson, Albert A.	BvtMaj USV	ME	15992
Nickerson, Alfred E.	1st Lt. 9th ME Infy	ME	11476
Nickerson, Azor R.	Maj AAG USA	CA	01418
Nickerson, Linus M.	Chap 122nd NY Infy	CA	06064
Nickerson, Nehemiah	Surg. 21st KY Infy	NY	No Number
Niebuhr, Caleb E.	Capt. 1st Battn. MA H Arty	MA	04630
Niedecken, Henry	2nd Lt. 29th WI Infy	WI	04722
Nields, Benjamin	Capt. 1st Batt DE L Arty BvtLTC	PA	08755
Nields, Henry C.	Lt. Commander USN	PA	00548
Nigh, Elias	LTC QM USV	OH	11189
Niles, John W.	Capt. 9th IA Infy	IL	12272
Niles, Kossuth	Capt. USN	PA	06470
Nill, Thomas J.	Capt. 118th PA Infy	PA	02127
Nimocks, Charles A.	Capt. 7th MI Infy	MN	04588
Nims, Frederick A.	1st Lt. 1st NY Cav	MI	09921
Nininger, Alexander R.	Capt. 28th Infy BvtLTC USA	OH	08171
Nipp, James B.	Capt. 40th KY Infy	KS	05600
Nixon, Oliver W.	Surg. 39th OH Infy	IL	02183
Noble, Charles	Capt. 119th PA Infy	PA	01723
Noble, Charles H.	Col. 10th Infy USA	IN	05674
Noble, Edward A.	1st Lt. 77ith PA Infy	KS	15246
Noble, George M.	Capt. 31st IN Infy	KS	06794
Noble, Henry T.	Col. QM USV	IL	04702
Noble, Horace	Capt. 9th MD Infy	DC	07564
Noble, John W.	Col. 3rd IA Cav BvtBG	MO	05561
Noble, Joseph	LTC 9th ME Infy	DC	09214
Noel, Jacob E.	Lt. Commander USN	WA	04445
Nolan, Frank	BvtCapt. USV	DC	07565
Nones, Henry B.	Chief Eng. USN	PA	00429
Nones, Henry B.	3rd Class	PA	00519
Norcross, John E.	2nd Lt. 25th USCT BvtCapt.	NY	03021
Norcross, Pliny	Capt. 13th WI Infy	WI	14812
Norcross, Winfield S.	1st Lt. Adj. 148th IL Infy	ME	13616
Norred, Charles H.	1st Lt. 7th IL Cav	MN	16531
Norris, Albert L.	Asst Surg. 114th USCTMA	MA	05425
Norris, Basil	Col. Surg. USA	CA	02660
Norris, Charles C.	Capt. 132nd PA Infy	PA	16975
Norris, William	3rd Class (Gov RI)	CA	07852

Name	Rank	Commandery	Insignia No.
Norris, William E.	Maj Paymaster USA	CA	09583 (Dup)
Norris, William F.	Asst Surg. BvtCapt. USA	PA	02442
North, George H.	Capt. 14th PA Cav	NY	01102
North, James N.	1st Lt. RQM 24th MA Infy	MA	05101
North, Joseph W.	Act Ensign USN	NY	07866
Northrop, George J.	Asst Surg. 1st DC Cav	MI	05661
Northrop, Theodore F.	1st Lt. 2nd NY Cav	NY	10430
Northrup, Henry J.	1st Lt. RQM 118th NY Infy	MI	08937
Northrup, Jay H.	Maj 93rd NY Infy	OH	07414
Northrup, John P.	Capt. 2nd NJ Infy	KS	05695
Norton, Charles A.	1st Lt. Adj. 46th OH Infy	KS	04806
Norton, Charles B.	BvtBG USV	NY	00576
Norton, Charles F.	Lt. USN	NY	03620
Norton, Charles L.	Col. 78th USCT	NY	08658
Norton, Charles S.	RAdm USN	NY	00529
Norton, Hannibal D.	Capt. 32nd MA Infy BvtMaj	DC	04392
Norton, Henry A.	Capt. 12th USCT BvtMaj	MN	11792
Norton, Lewis A.	3rd Class (Capt. USV Mexican War)	CA	02544
Norton, Oliver W.	1st Lt. 8th USCT	IL	02321
Norton, Thomas	Maj USA	CA	08564
Norton, William H.	1st Lt. NY H Arty	DC	07184
Norvell, John M.	Maj AAG BvtLTC USV	CA	03552 (Dup)
Norvell, Stevens T.	Col. USA	DC	02636
Norwood, Frederick W.	Capt. 68th USCT	IL	11650
Nott, Charles C.	Col. 176th NY Infy	DC	04323
Nott, Hugh	Act Paymaster USN	PA	00361
Nourse, Henry S.	Capt. 55th IL Infy	MA	10048
Nowlan, Henry J.	Maj 7th Cav USA	IL	03727
Noyes, David K.	LTC 49th WI Infy	WI	11484
Noyes, Edward F.	Col. 39th OH Infy BvtBG	OH	02441
Noyes, Edward L.	Maj 3rd MA Cav	MA	06686
Noyes, Frank G.	LTC CS USV	NY	00574
Noyes, Henry E.	BG USA	CA	14203
Noyes, Henry T.	Col. 38th USCT	NY	04338
Noyes, John B.	Capt. 28th MA Infy BvtCol.	NY	03360
Noyes, Joshua C.	Surg. 32nd WI Infy	WI	08688
Noyes, Nicholas N.	1st Lt. 48th MA Infy	MA	01479
Nugent, Edward D.	Maj 3rd MI Cav	MI	05659
Nugent, John R.	1st Lt. 69th NY Infy	NY	12128
Nute, Alonzo	1st Lt. RQM 6th NH Infy	MA	07132
Nutt, Edmund E.	Capt. 20th OH Infy	OH	10014
Nutt, William	LTC 55th MA Infy BvtCol.	MA	13248 (Dup)
Nutting, Lee	Capt. 61st NY Infy	NY	09957
Nye, Chester T.	Capt. 10th VT Infy	NE	11354
Nye, George H.	Col. 29th ME Infy BvtMG	MA	01053
Nye, Ira P.	1st Lt. 22nd WI Infy	KS	16101
Nye, Reuben L.	Capt. 36th OH Infy BvtLTC	CA	07312
Nye, William H.	1st Lt. 7th MA Infy	CA	03342

The Roster 315

Name	Rank	Commandery	Insignia No.
Oakes, Benjamin F.	Capt. 1st ME H Arty	MI	14924
Oakes, James	Col. 6th Cav BvtBG USA	DC	02259
Oakey, Daniel	Capt. 2nd MA Infy	MA	01494
Oakford, Edward	Capt. Ind. Battn. MN Cav	CA	16284
Oakley, Franklin W.	Capt. AQM USV	WI	03682
Oakley, Lewis W.	Surg. 2nd NJ Infy	NY	03012
Oakley, Thomas B.	Maj Paymaster USV	PA	05993
Oakman, Hiram A.	LTC 30th USCT BvtCol.	MA	10122
Oakman, Thomas C.	Capt. 6th PA Cav	MA	13330
Oaks, George J.	Capt. 151st NY Infy BvtMaj	NY	09862
Oates, Patrick	Capt. 133rd NY Infy	NY	06627
Oatman, Harrison B.	1st Lt. 1st OR Infy	OR	06114
OBearne, James R.	BvtBG	NY	00943
OBeirne, Richard F.	Col. 21st Infy USA	NY	01488
OBrien, Albert H.	2nd Lt. USMC	PA	01577
OBrien, Daniel J.	Capt. 7th NY H Arty	NY	14337
OBrien, Henry D.	Capt. 1st MN Infy	MO	12902
OBrien, John J.	1st Lt. 4th Infy USA	CA	04082
OBrien, John McG.	1st Lt. 86th USCT	KS	15827
OBrien, Lester M.	Col. USA	MI	03589
OBrien, Nicholas J.	Capt. 7th IA Cav	CO	12051
OBrien, Russell G.	2nd Lt. 124th IL Infy	WA	06319
Ochiltree, Thomas J.	2nd Lt. 136th USCT	IA	17473
OConnell, John J.	BG USA	DC	07214
OConnor, Frederick A.	Act Master USN	MA	03276
OConnor, Henry	Maj 35th IA Infy	CA	02658
OConnor, Stephen	Capt. 23rd Infy USA	IL	07273
Odell, Thomas B.	Capt. 80th USCT BvtMaj	NY	04072
Oderfeld, Henry	Capt. 58th OH Infy	KS	04920
Odiorne, David W.	1st Lt. 97th PA Infy	NY	03023
Odiorne, Frederick	2nd Lt. 44th MA Infy	MA	06506
Odiorne, Walter C.	Act Ensign USN	PA	03218
ODonnell, Charles W.	2nd Lt. 5th MI Cav	MI	13105
ODriscoll, Benedict J.	Capt. 88th NY Infy	DC	11796
Oehler, Reuben	Capt. 176th OH Infy	CA	17618
Oertel, Edward	1st Lt. 72nd IL Infy	WI	07250
OFarrell, Gerald D.	Asst Surg. 215th PA Infy	PA	07334
OFarrell, Patrick	1st Lt. 82nd NY Infy	DC	11610
Officer, Harvey	Capt. 1st MN H Arty	MN	03828
Offley, Robert H.	Col. 10th Infy USA	OH	03552 (Dup)
Ogden William L.	1st Lt. Adj. 3rd NY Cav	IL	02323
Ogden, Joshua M.	Capt. 97th IN Infy	IN	12338
Ogden, William A.	1st Lt. 39th NJ Infy BvtCapt.	KS	06868
Ogilby, Frederick D.	Capt. 8th Infy BvtMaj USA	PA	00510
Oglevee, John F.	1st Lt. 98th OH Infy	OH	04229
Ohr, Martin L.	1st Lt. 70th IN Infy	DC	17376
Olcott, Dudley	Capt. 25th NY Infy BvtLTC	NY	02057
Oleson, Charles W.	Asst Surg. 14th USCT	IL	05133

Name	Rank	Commandery	Insignia No.
Olin, Luman, D.	Capt. 48th WI Infy	CA	09537
Olin, Rollin C.	Capt. AAG USV	MI	04592
Oliphant, S. Duncan	Col. VRC BvtBG	PA	00436
Olive, David H.	1st Lt. 86th IN Infy	IN	12759
Oliver, Joseph B.	Capt. 5th WI Infy	WI	01589
Oliver, Joseph C.	1st. Lt. 89th OH Infy	CA	07849
Oliver, Paul A.	Capt. 5th NY Infy BvtBG	PA	01988
Oliver, Robert Shaw	1st Lt. 8th Cav USA	DC	01241
Oliver, William H.	Capt. 4th NY Cav	NY	12135
Olmstead, Samuel H.	Surg. 170th NY NY Infy	NY	01440 (Dup)
Olmstead, William A.	Col. 59th NY Infy BvtBG	IN	00708
Olmsted, Frederick Law	3rd Class (Sec. US Sanitary Com.)	MA	06345
Olney, Henry C.	Capt. 52nd WI Infy	WA	07480
Olney, Warren	Capt. 65th USCT	CA	04862
ONeil, Charles	Act Lt. USN	PA	00907 (Dup)
ONeil, Charles	RAdm USN	DC	13034
ONeil, John O.	Capt. 116th PA Infy	DC	10812
Orahood, Harper M.	Capt. 3rd CO Cav	CO	05626
Orcutt, Frank E.	2nd Lt. 95th USCT	MA	06637
Ordway, Albert	Col. 24th MA Infy BvtBG	DC	00784
Ordway, David S.	1st Lt. QM 51st WI Infy	WI	06367 (Dup)
OReilly, Bernard	Capt. 164th NY Infy	WI	13503
OReilly, Robert M.	BG Surg. Gen. USA	DC	07182
OReilly, Thomas	2nd Lt. 5th NY Cav	NY	16088
Orleman, Louis H.	Capt. USA	PA	00804
Orme, George R.	Capt. AQM BvtCol. USV	PA	00194
Ormsbee, Ebenezer J.	Capt. 12th VT Infy	VT	05797
Ormsby, Salmon B.	Capt. 108th USCT	OR	13368
Orne, James D.	Capt. 18th MA Infy	PA	06267
Orr, George S.	Capt. 77th NY Infy	VT	14017
Orr, Robert L.	Col. 61st PA Infy	PA	01196
Orr, William P.	Capt. 152nd OH Infy	OH	10130
Orton, Herman M.	1st Lt. 41st USCT	NY	08111
Orton, Richard H.	Capt. 1st CA Cav	CA	02034
Orwig, Thomas G.	Capt. 1st PA L Arty	IA	13363
Osborn, Francis A.	Col. 24th MA Infy BvtBG	MA	00680
Osborn, Hartwell	Capt. 55th OH Infy	IL	03392
Osborn, Sylvester W.	Capt. 16th WI Infy	WI	11974
Osborn, Thomas H.	Capt. 4th OH Cav	OH	06832
Osborn, Thomas O.	BG BvtMG USV	CA	08869
Osborne, Edwin S.	Maj 149th PA Infy	PA	07867
Osborne, George S.	Surg. 5th MA Cav	MA	01287
Osborne, Harris B.	Surg. USV	MI	06033
Osborne, Nathan W.	Col. 5th Infy USA	CA	03641
Osborne, Thomas A.	3rd Class (Lt. Gov. KS)	KS	06307
Osbourn, Francis A.	1st Lt. V.R.C. BvtCapt.	PA	08985
Osbourne, Samuel	Capt. 46th IN Infy	CA	02537
Osburn, Arthur P.	Commander USN	OH	15813

Name	Rank	Commandery	Insignia No.
Osburn, Charles Y.	Capt. 5th MI Cav	MI	03752
Osgood, Charles E.	2nd Lt. 1st MA H Arty	MA	13747
Osgood, Henry B.	Col. Asst Comm. Gen. USA	DC	12058
Osgood, Josiah A.	Capt. 47th MA Infy	CA	01513
Osterhaus, Peter J.	MG USV	MO	14354
Osterstock, Joseph S.	2nd Lt. 214th PA Infy	PA	08228
Ostrander, James S.	1st Lt. 18th Infy USA	IN	03379
Otis, Elmer	Col. 8th Cav USA	CA	05668
Otis, Ephraim A.	Capt. AAG USV	IL	02172
Otis, Harrison G.	Capt. 23rd OH Infy BG USV	CA	05326
Otis, John L.	Col. 10th CT Infy BvtBG	MA	01313
Otis, Theodore C.	1st Lt. 3rd MA Cav	NY	00820
OToole, Patrick	Asst Surg. 3rd MI Cav	CA	08305
Ottile, Charles	Surg. 9th WI Infy	WI	07735
Ovenshine, Samuel	BG USA	DC	03997
Overton, Edward	LTC 50th PA Infy	PA	07348
Overton, Gilbert E.	Maj USA	CA	02650
Overturf, John W.	1st Lt. 91st OH Infy BvtMaj	OH	05663
Owen, Alfred D.	Col. 80th IN Infy	IN	09012
Owen, Charles D.	Capt. 1st RI L Arty	MA	02456
Owen, Charles H.	1st Lt. 1st CT H Arty BvtCapt.	PA	04171
Owen, Frederick W.	BvtMaj USV	NY	17339
Owen, Joshua T.	BG USV	PA	00143
Owen, Leander C.	Act Ensign USN	MA	07535
Owen, Manly P.	Capt. 18th USCT	MO	17604
Owen, Oscar D.	Act Ensign USN	MO	16658
Owen, Silas	Act Master USN	NY	09863
Owen, Thomas J.	1st Lt. 50th NY Eng.	WI	16785
Owen, William H.	Col. QM USV	DC	05128
Owens, Benjamin B.	1st Lt. 11th MD Infy	MD	10939
Owens, Thomas	Surg. USN	DC	09107
Pabst, Rudolph	Capt. 10th MI Infy	MI	12085
Pace, Lewis C.	LTC 25th MO Infy	NE	18125
Packard, Jasper	Col. 128th IN Infy BvtBG	IN	12681
Packard, Stephen B.	Capt. 12th ME Infy	IA	04973
Packer, Edward A.	2nd Lt. Batt "L" 1st MI L Arty	CA	15190
Packer, Warren W.	Col. 5th CT Infy	MA	14087
Packwood, George H.	1st Lt. 20th MA Infy	NY	13270
Paddock, Algernon S.	3rd Class (Gov. of NB, US Senator NB)	NE	07592
Paddock, Charles H.	1st Lt. 157th NY Infy	NY	09864
Paddock, George L.	Maj 11th USCT	IL	02016
Paddock, Joseph W.	Maj AAG USV	NE	05276
Paddock, Martin L.	1st Lt. Batt "M" 1st OH L Arty	IL	15134
Page, Charles	BG USA	MD	04791
Page, Charles E.	2nd Lt. 81st USCT	MA	17311
Page, Henry	Capt. AQM BvtCol. USV (MajUSV)	PA	00777
Page, Henry T.	Act Ensign USN	MA	03844
Page, John H.	BG USA	DC	09083

Name	Rank	Commandery	Insignia No.
Page, William R.	2nd Lt. Benton Cadets, MO Infy	IL	13177
Page, Zeno B.	1st Lt. 1st MN H Arty	MN	06355
Paige, Harlan P.	1st Lt. 4th VT Infy	MA	11364
Paine, A. Elliot	Asst Surg. 104th USCT	MA	02426
Paine, Charles J.	BG BvtMG USV	MA	00956
Paine, Franklin	Capt. 11th MN Infy	MN	06681
Paine, Halbert E.	BG BvtMG USV	DC	03085
Paine, James M.	Capt. 2nd MN Cav	MN	04931
Paine, Jedediah C.	Capt. Sig. Corps BvtLTC USV	NY	04689
Paine, John L.	1st Lt. 50th NY Eng.	Dc	12847
Paine, Samuel D.	1st Lt. 7th Batt ME L Arty	OH	10703
Palfrey, Francis W.	Col. 20th MA Infy BvtBG	MA	00927
Palfrey, John C.	Capt. Eng. BvtBG USA	MA	08339
Palmer, Alfred L.	1st Lt. 12th IA Infy	WA	14892
Palmer, Andrew J.	Capt. 2nd WI Cav	CA	17787
Palmer, Charles B.	2nd Lt. 1st WI H Arty	OH	09386
Palmer, David J.	LTC 25th IA Infy	IA	12756
Palmer, Elisha L.	2nd Lt. 61st NY Infy	NY	07614
Palmer, Franklin	LTC 16th NY Infy	NY	17439
Palmer, George H.	Maj 4th Infy USA	IL	10849
Palmer, George R.	1st Lt. 19th ME Infy	ME	17007
Palmer, Gideon S.	Surg. 3rd ME Infy BvtCol.	DC	00674
Palmer, Henry	Surg. 7th WI Infy BvtLTC	WI	04124
Palmer, Henry E.	Capt. 11th KS Cav	NE	03937
Palmer, Innis N.	BG BvtMG USV	DC	02518
Palmer, James S.	RAdm USN	PA	No Number
Palmer, John	1st Lt. 91st NY Infy	NY	09311
Palmer, John J.	Capt. AQM BvtMaj USV	IN	07818
Palmer, Lowell M.	1st Lt. 1st OH L Arty	NY	12555
Palmer, Moses P.	Capt. 13th MA Infy BvtMaj	MA	09994
Palmer, Theodore J.	1st Lt. Adj. 61st OH Infy	NY	06743
Palmer, William H.	Act Asst Paymaster USN	NY	16745
Palmer, William H.	Surg. 3rd NY Cav	MA	11208
Palmer, William L.	Capt. 19th MA Infy BvtCol.	MA	01596
Palmetier, Charles	1st Lt. 8th WI Infy	WI	03423
Pancoast, William H.	3rd Class	PA	01045
Pannes, John B.	Capt. ADC USV	NY	08357
Paramore, James W.	Col. 3rd OH Cav	MO	05092
Pardee, Ario, Jr.	Col. 147th PA Infy BvtBG	PA	04666
Pardee, Calvin	1st Lt. 147th PA Infy	PA	04667
Pardee, Charles I.	Asst Surg. 16th NY Infy	NY	05825
Pardee, Don A.	LTC 42nd OH Infy BvtBG	OH	07304
Parham, Charles	LTC 29th PA Infy	PA	00007
Park, William H.	Asst Surg. 110th OH Infy	OH	07419
Park, Harvey S.	Capt. 2nd KY Cav	IL	08614
Park, Horace	Col. 43rd OH Infy	OH	04197
Park, John G.	Act Asst Surg. USN	MA	10941
Park, William	2nd Lt. 9th Batt MA L Arty	MA	03508

The Roster

Name	Rank	Commandery	Insignia No.
Parke, Brinton J.	BvtCapt. USV	PA	00698
Parke, John B.	BvtLTC USA	PA	00448
Parke, John G.	BvtMG USA	DC	00121
Parke, William A.	1st Lt. 6th NY Cav	NY	14126
Parkell, Alonzo B.	Maj 4th IA Cav	MO	13905
Parker, Hilon A.	1st Lt. 10th NY H Arty	IL	06488
Parker, Alonzo H.	Capt. 19th IA Infy	CA	09836
Parker, Benjamin F.	1st Lt. 1st WI H Arty (LTC 3rd WI Infy)	WI	04975
Parker, Charles E.	Capt. 7th VT Infy	VT	09659
Parker, Charles H.	Maj 17th IL Cav	NE	04764
Parker, Daingerfield	BG USA	DC	02637
Parker, David B.	2nd Lt. 72nd NY Infy	DC	02976
Parker, Edgar	Asst Surg. 13th MA Infy	MA	02221
Parker, Ely S.	Col. ADC BvtBG USA	NY	05414
Parker, Foxhall A.	Commander USN	MA	00182
Parker, Francis B.	LTC Ordnance USA	NY	02139
Parker, Francis J.	Col. 32nd MA Infy	MA	01364
Parker, Francis W.	LTC 4th NH Infy	IL	11195
Parker, George W.	LTC 79th IN Infy	IN	06901
Parker, Gilbert L.	Capt. AQM BvtLTC USV	PA	12666
Parker, Isaac B.	Capt. ADC BvtLTC USV	PA	00462
Parker, Jabez P.	1st Lt. 16th ME Infy	MA	04346
Parker, James	Lt. Commander USN	NY	07083
Parker, Joel	3rd Class (Gov. NJ)	PA	04970
Parker, John B.	3rd Class	PA	00720
Parker, John C.	Act Vol. Lt. USN	MO	00511
Parker, John D., Jr.	Capt. 2nd MA H Arty	MA	01306
Parker, John L.	1st Lt. 11th MA Infy	MA	10841
Parker, John M.	1st Lt. 3rd NH Infy	MA	12670
Parker, Joseph B.	Med. Director USN	PA	01097
Parker, Leopold O.	LCT USA	CA	12583
Parker, Moses G.	Asst Surg. 2nd USC Cav	MA	05953
Parker, Richard C.	Capt. 12th Infy BvtMaj USA	DC	04253
Parker, Robert M.	2nd Lt. 5th MA Cav	IL	10443
Parker, Simon B.	1st Lt. 5th NY Infy	MA	05878
Parker, Theodore K.	Capt. 2nd MA Infy	MA	10512
Parker, Wallace H.	1st Lt. 122nd USCT	VT	14618
Parker, William H.	2nd Lt. 8th US Vol Infy Bvt1stLt	MA	08268
Parker, William S.	Surg. 192nd OH Infy	OH	07028
Parkhurst, Charles H.	LTC 3rd RI Cav	MA	03505
Parkhurst, John G.	Col. 9th MI Infy BvtBG	MI	03252
Parkhurst, Sherman W.	1st Lt. 2nd VT Infy	VT	09171
Parkhurst, Thomas C.	1st Lt. Adj. 4th NY H Arty BvtCapt.	NY	14417
Parkinson, Edward C.	Capt. 13th NY H Arty	NY	12319
Parkinson, John	2nd Lt. 44th MA Infy	MA	00985
Parks, John W.	Capt. 147th PA Infy	PA	16572
Parks, Warham	Maj 3rd WI Infy BvtLTC	WI	08955
Parlin, William D.	Capt. 1st USCT	MA	10316 (Dup)

Name	Rank	Commandery	Insignia No.
Parmalee, Benjamin F.	1st Lt. 108th OH Infy	MO	06416
Parmalee, William E.	1st Lt. Batt "H" 1st OH L Arty	OH	16369
Parmentier, William J.	Maj 23rd NJ Infy	PA	02938
Parnell, William R.	LTC 4th NY Cav BvtCol.	CA	03538
Parrott, Edwin A.	Col. 1st OH Infy	OH	03041
Parrott, Henry E.	1st Lt. Adj. 86th OH Infy	OH	03035
Parry, Edward H.	1st Lt. 1st NJ Cav	PA	07350
Parry, Thomas P.	Capt. 17th PA Infy	PA	01989
Parshall, John R.	1st Lt. 6th OH Cav	MN	05772
Parsons, Arthur T.	Act Ensign USN	PA	05894
Parsons, Byron	Maj 94th NY Infy	IN	11319
Parsons, Charles	Capt. AQM BvtCol. USV	MO	05205
Parsons, Charles B.	Capt. 4th MI Infy	MO	05897
Parsons, Charles B.	Capt. 1st NY Eng. BvtMaj	NY	07615
Parsons, David E.	Maj 19th ME Infy	ME	07229
Parsons, Edwin B.	Capt. 24th WI Infy	WI	05021
Parsons, Elias H.	Capt. 40th OH Infy	DC	08005
Parsons, Enos B.	Maj AAG BvtLTC USV	NY	07616
Parsons, Henry	Capt. 134th NY Infy	NY	12791
Parsons, Henry	Capt. 148th NY Infy	MA	09995
Parsons, Henry R.	Capt. 62nd USCT BvtMaj	MO	13915
Parsons, John	Asst Surg. BvtCapt. USV	NY	11246
Parsons, John E.	Col. 187th PA Infy	PA	00054
Parsons, John E.	Act Passed Asst Surg. USN	MA	12830
Parsons, John W.	Asst Surg. 24th MA Infy	MA	03275
Parsons, Joseph B.	LTC 10th MA Infy BvtCol.	MA	07773
Parsons, Lewis B.	BG BvtMG USV	IL	08615
Parsons, Oliver A.	Maj 61st PA Infy	PA	11018
Parsons, Theron E.	Capt. AAG BvtMaj USV	NY	08950
Partridge, Benjamin F.	Col. 16th MI Infy BvtBG	MI	06815
Partridge, Charles A.	1st Lt. 48th OH Infy	OH	03304
Partridge, John N.	Capt. 24th MA Infy	NY	00861
Partridge, Sylvester B.	1st Lt. Sig. Corps USV	ME	10474
Parvin, James D.	Capt. 149th IN Infy	IN	10673
Paschal, George W.	LTC 2nd TX Cav	DC	15627
Patch, Samuel	Capt. 35th MA Infy	MA	09475
Patier, Charles O.	Capt. 6th MO Infy	MO	06176
Patrick, George H.	1st Lt. Adj. 82nd USCT	OH	11101 (Dup)
Patrick, James P.	2nd Lt. 2nd USC H Arty	IA	13360
Patrick, John J. R.	Capt. 130th IL Infy	IL	08426
Patrick, John N.H.	1st Lt. 5th OH Cav	NE	06207
Patrick, Samuel L.	Capt. 34th IL Infy	KS	08531
Patten, George W.	LTC 2nd Infy USA	NY	00235
Patten, George W.	Capt. 73rd IL Infy BvtMaj	OH	08165
Patten, Zeboim C.	1st Lt. 149th NY Infy	OH	08166
Patterson, Alex V.	Surg. 102nd OH Infy	OH	09089
Patterson, DeWitt C.	Surg. 124th OH Infy	DC	03725
Patterson, Edward L.	Capt. 79th OH Infy	OH	04535

Name	Rank	Commandery	Insignia No.
Patterson, Frank G.	2nd Lt. 5th ME Infy	CO	06530
Patterson, George T.T.	1st Lt. 14th Infy USA	KS	06037
Patterson, Joab N.	Col. 2nd NH Infy BvtBG (Capt. 1st NH)	DC	01523
Patterson, John E.	Asst Surg. 118th OH Infy	OH	07026
Patterson, John H.	BG USA	NY	04665
Patterson, Marion	BvtLTC USV	KS	16003
Patterson, Robert	Capt. 82nd OH Infy	OH	11704
Patterson, Robert	MG PA Militia	PA	00094
Patterson, Robert E.	Col. 115th PA Infy BvtBG	PA	02260
Patterson, Robert F.	LTC 29th IA Infy BvtBG	OH	07719 (Dup)
Patterson, Samuel F.	1st Lt. 2nd NH Infy	MA	17313
Patterson, Theodore F.	1st Lt. Sig. Corps USV	PA	01161
Patterson, Theodore H.	Surg. 187th OH Infy	IL	03141
Patterson, Thomas H.	RAdm USN	PA	00611
Patterson, William J.	2nd Lt. 62nd PA Infy	PA	07349
Patterson, William W.	1st Lt. 12th Infy USA	NE	06699
Pattison, Everett W.	Capt. 2nd MA Infy	MO	04528 (Dup)
Pattison, Livander H.	1st Lt. 2nd IL Cav	KS	08414
Patton, Alexander G.	LTC 7th NY Cav	OH	04213
Patton, David H.	Col. 38th IN Infy	IN	09464
Patton, Frederick H.	Asst Surg. 12th WVA Infy	OH	08376
Patton, Jonathan N.	1st Lt. 36th OH Infy (Capt. AQM USV)	IA	09078
Patton, Joseph T.	Capt. 93rd OH Infy	MI	04590
Patton, William McI.	1st Lt. RQM 47th IL Infy	PA	14053
Patzki, Julius H.	LTC USA	DC	04358
Paul, Charles H.	Col. 30th Infy USA	CA	02342
Paul, Frank W.	1st Lt. 24th Infy BvtCapt. USA	PA	00689
Paulding, Samuel H.	1st Lt. 150th NY Infy	NY	05119
Paulding, Tatnall	Capt. 6th Cav BvtLTC USA	PA	00464
Paulen, Jacob W.	1st Lt. 130th IL Infy	KS	05355
Paulson, John	BvtMaj USV	MN	05870
Paver, John M.	1st Lt. 5th OH Infy	IN	07817
Pavey, Charles W.	2nd Lt. 80th IL Infy	IL	07584
Paxton, John R.	2nd Lt. 140th PA Infy	NY	02294
Paxton, Wilson N.	1st Lt. 140th PA Infy	DC	02875 (Dup)
Payne, C.M.	Capt. AQM USV	NY	00631
Payne, Eugene B.	LTC 37th IL Infy BvtBG	DC	06324
Payne, James G.	Capt. AQM BvtLTC USV	DC	02665
Payne, John	2nd Lt. 36th WI Infy	WI	18032
Payne, John A.	Maj 14th MO Cav	OR	14741
Payne, Walter S.	Capt. 2nd LA Infy	OH	04572
Payson, Charles	BvtCapt. USV	DC	15564
Peabody, James H.	Surg. BvtLTC USV	NE	04028
Peabody, Oliver W.	LTC 45th MA Infy	MA	00867
Peabody, William S.	Capt. 74th USCT	DC	03906
Peach, Benjamin F.	Col. 8th MA Infy	MA	02549
Peake, Ebenezer	Chap 28th WI Infy	MN	09933
Pealer, Russell R.	1st Lt. 16th PA Cav	MI	11122

Name	Rank	Commandery	Insignia No.
Pearce, Charles E.	Maj 16th NY H Arty	MO	04368
Pearce, Enoch	Surg. BvtLTC USV	OH	10677
Pearce, Henry	2nd Lt. 10th Batt RI L Arty	MA	04626
Pearce, John	1st Lt. 61st OH Infy	OH	13525
Pearce, Samuel A.	Maj Paymaster BvtLTC USA	MA	01763
Pearce, Walter	Act Master USN	MA	03053
Pearsall, Uri B.	Col. 48th WI Infy BvtBG	KS	06558
Pearson, Aven	1st Lt. Henshaw's Batt IL L Arty	Dc	10694
Pearson, Charles D.	Surg. 82nd IN Infy	IN	06605
Pearson, Edward P., Jr.	BvtLTC USA	PA	00567
Pearson, Henry C.	1st Lt. 21st PA Cav	DC	03723
Pearson, Robert N.	LTC 31st IL Infy BvtBG	IL	06315
Pearsons, Henry A.	1st Lt. 8th IL Cav	IL	02677
Pease, Charles E.	Capt. AAG BvtMaj USV	NY	02376
Pease, Edward	Capt. 2nd USCT	MA	13692
Pease, Giles M.	Asst Surg. 54th MA Infy	CA	02858
Pease, Henry C.	Capt. 86th USCT	MA	07230
Pease, Phineas	Col. 49th IL Infy BvtBG	IL	05767
Pease, William B.	Capt. 8th Infy USA	NY	03008
Peck, Benjamin B.	1st Lt. Adj. 27th MA Infy	IN	03058
Peck, Charles B.	1st Lt. RQM 36th WI Infy	MI	11066
Peck, David B.	LTC 7th VT Infy	DC	11569
Peck, Erastus J.	Maj 4th WI Cav	KS	05537
Peck, George	Med. Director USN	NY	00570
Peck, George B.	2nd Lt. 2nd RI Infy	MA	02551
Peck, George R.	Capt. 31st WI Infy	KS	04805
Peck, George W.	2nd Lt. 4th WI Cav	WI	02023
Peck, Henry T.	1st Lt. 118th PA Infy	PA	05734
Peck, Porter P.	1st Lt. 1st WI Cav	MN	07496
Peck, Samuel C., Jr.	Capt. 6th CT Infy	NY	05005
Peck, Theodore S.	Capt. AQM USV	VT	01397
Peck, William H. H.	Capt. 6th VT Infy	OH	04536
Peckham, Fenner H., Jr.	2nd Lt. 12th RI Infy	MA	10343
Peckham, G.W.	1st Lt. 1st WI H Arty	WI	01586-15251
Pedan, Milton	Col. 147th IN Infy	IN	10800
Peddle, William R.	Capt. 157th PA Infy	DC	07397
Pedigo, Joseph O.	Capt. 28th USCT	IN	07272
Pedrick, William E.	Capt. 2nd OH Cav	OH	09230
Peelle, Stanton J.	2nd Lt. 57th IN Infy	DC	03321
Peet, Frederick T.	1st Lt. USMC	NY	00218
Pegram, John C.	Ensign USN	MA	01423
Peirce, Elisha N.	2nd Lt. 5th MA Infy	MA	13131
Peirce, Henry B.	1st Lt. RQM 23rd MA Infy	MA	01747
Peironnet, Charles A.	Capt. 11th IL Infy	MO	05282
Peirson, Charles L.	LTC 39th MA Infy BvtBG	MA	01310
Pemberton, John	Passed Asst. Eng. USN	NY	05071
Pence, John B.	Capt. 40th IN Infy	IN	06606
Pendergast, Austin	Commander USN	PA	00911

Name	Rank	Commandery	Insignia No.
Pendergast, Richard	1st Lt. 2nd MA Infy	MA	10383
Pendleton, Edmund	2nd Lt. 4th NY H Arty	DC	10566
Pendleton, Edwin C.	RAdm USN	PA	16023
Penfield, James A.	Capt. 5th NY Cav	MA	09239
Penfield, James K.	2nd Lt. 144th NY Infy	NY	12957
Penfield, William H.	Act Ensign USN	CA	02136
Penn, William H.	2nd Lt. 13th IA Infy	IA	11443
Penney, Charles G.	BG USA	CA	03063
Penniman, Bethuel	1st Lt. RQM 3rd MA Infy	MA	05872
Pennington, Alex C.M.	BG USA	DC	10776
Pennington, Henry	1st Lt. Adj. 2nd US Vol. Infy	PA	04668
Pennock, Alexander M.	RAdm USN	NY	00236
Pennypacker, Galusha	BG BvtMG USA	PA	00382
Pennywit, William C.	Capt. 5th IA Infy	DC	14114
Penrose, Charles B.	Maj CS BvtLTC USA	PA	07869
Penrose, Thomas N.	Med. Director USN	PA	07870
Penrose, William H.	BG USV	KS	08081
Pentecost, Alexander J.	1st Lt. RQM 5th WVA Cav BvtCapt.	PA	14475
Pentecost, George F.	Chap 8th KY Cav	NY	12320
Perce, LeGrand W.	Capt. AQM BvtCol. USV	IL	10482
Percival, James R.	Capt. 19th OH Infy	OH	07944
Perin, Glover	Col. Asst Surg. General USA	MN	03825
Perine, John J.	1st Lt. 8th NJ Infy	NY	10763
Perkins, Albert A.	Capt. 25th IA Infy BvtMaj	CO	07139
Perkins, Bishop W.	Capt. 16th USCT	DC	04558
Perkins, Charles G.	Act Vol. Lt. USN	IN	09013
Perkins, Edwin S.	Act Asst Surg. USN	PA	10631
Perkins, George C.	3rd Class (Gov. of CA, US Senator CA)	CA	06335
Perkins, George H.	Commodore USN	MA	01130
Perkins, George T.	LTC 105th OH Infy BvtBG	OH	02966
Perkins, Henry C.	1st Lt. 53rd IN Infy	KS	17467
Perkins, Hiram E.	Maj 73rd USCT	VT	09184
Perkins, Norman	1st Lt. 56th NY Infy	MN	06754
Perkins, Simon, Jr.	Cap. AQM USV	OH	04999
Perkins, William E.	Capt. 2nd MA Infy	MA	00887
Perley, John K..	1st Lt. 9th NY Infy	NY	00418-841
Perot, James P.	LTC 49th Infy PA Militia	PA	00146
Perrin, William B.	1st Lt. 3rd Batt VT L Arty	IA	12192
Perrine, William W.	1st Lt. 13th Batt WI L Arty	NY	03764
Perry, Aaron F.	3rd Class	OH	07376
Perry, Alexander J.	BG USA	DC	02830
Perry, Clarence D.	Capt. 150th IL Infy	DC	15329
Perry, David	BG USA	DC	05843
Perry, Edward S.	Capt. 7th CT Infy	NY	08659
Perry, Henry F.	Maj 38th IN Infy	CA	14903
Perry, James H.	Capt. USN	PA	11943
Perry, John F.	2nd Lt. VRC	MN	10379
Perry, John L.	Asst Surg. 115th NY Infy	NY	01794 (Dup)

THE ROSTER

Name	Rank	Commandery	Insignia No.
Perry, Leonard B.	Capt. AAG USV	CA	16061
Perry, Oran	LTC 69th IN Infy BvtCol.	IN	02850
Perry, Robert C.	LTC USA	NY	00367
Peshine, John H.H.	Maj 11th Infy USA	DC	06471
Peters, Matthew H.	Capt. 74th OH Infy	IL	07556
Peters, Theodore H.	Capt. 82nd PA Infy	PA	00019
Petrie, James A.	Act Asst Surg. USN	NY	10166
Pettengill, Charles H.	2nd Lt. 29th ME Infy Bvt1stLT	NY	13759
Pettibone, Augustus H.	Maj 20th WI Infy	DC	03174
Pettibone, Heman D.	1st Lt. 3rd MN Infy BvtCapt.	MN	13483
Pettis, George H.	1st Lt. 1st CA Infy BvtCapt.	CA	05065
Pettit, Eleazer W.	Capt. 26th USCT	OH	08159
Pettit, James F.	2nd Lt. 6th NY Cav	NY	06629
Pettit, Silas W.	Capt. 213th PA Infy	PA	08756
Pettit, Stacy	1st Lt. 104th OH Infy	OH	04646
Pettit, Willis H.	2nd Lt. 4th Batt IN L Arty	CA	08304
Peugnet, Ernest H.	Capt. AQM USV	MO	04581
Pew, Alfred	Capt. 3rd MI Infy	DC	11668
Peyton, Isaac W.	2nd Lt. 135th IL Infy	CA	15419
Pfahler, William H.	1st Lt. RQM 45th PA Infy	PA	08229
Pfeiffer, John Q.	Capt. 202nd PA Infy	Dc	13035
Phair, James H.	1st Lt. 1st ME Infy	ME	16304
Phalen, Michael W.	1st Lt. Adj. 9th MA Infy	IL	10923
Phelen, Richard A.	LTC AAG USV	MO	08010
Phelps, Alfred C.	1st Lt. 93rd USCT	CO	08558
Phelps, Alonzo J.	Surg. BvtLTC USV	IL	09247
Phelps, Byron	1st Lt. 3rd IL Cav	WA	09718
Phelps, Charles E.	Col. 7th MD Infy BvtBG	MD	06568
Phelps, Dudley F.	1st Lt. Adj. 20th USCT	NY	12792
Phelps, Francis M.	1st Lt. 38th WI Infy	CA	16911
Phelps, John E.	Col. 2nd AR Cav BvtBG	MO	05395
Phelps, Thomas S.	RAdm USN	CA	03920
Phelps, Timothy G.	3rd Class (Representative CA)	CA	07853
Philbrick, Caleb	Capt. 33rd MA Infy	MA	14295
Philbrick, Chase	LTC 15th MA Infy	MA	10316 (Dup)
Philbrook, Hiram A.	Chap 8th ME Infy	ME	03475
Philip, John W.	RAdm USN	CA	04001
Philippi, Edwin T.	Passed Asst. Eng. USN	PA	06529
Philips, John F.	Col. 7th Cav MO State Militia	MO	14080
Philler, Hugo	Asst Surg. 45th NY Infy	WI	05267
Phillips, Albert W.	Asst Surg. 149th NY Infy	NY	10968
Phillips, Duncan C.	Maj 4th PA Cav	DC	05505
Phillips, George	Capt. 28th IA Infy	IA	11686
Phillips, George M.	1st Lt. 128th OH Infy	MN	05213
Phillips, Henry M.	2nd Lt. 4th MA Cav BvtCapt.	MA	00854
Phillips, John	Capt. 2nd MA Cav	MA	01744
Phillips, John W.	LTC 18th PA Cav	MO	04265
Phillips, Joseph A.	Surg. 38th PA Infy BvtLTC	PA	05503

Name	Rank	Commandery	Insignia No.
Phillips, Lionel D.	1st Lt. 6th USCT	CA	11975
Phillips, Robert E.	LTC 59th USCT	OH	06848
Phillips, Rolla O.	Capt. 85th PA Infy	NE	05363
Phillips, William A.	Act 1st Asst Eng. USN	CA	02158
Phillips, William W. L.	Surg. 1st NJ Cav	PA	02109
Phinney, William C.	1st Lt. 1st ME Infy	ME	15539
Phipps, Frank H.	Col. Ordnance USA	NY	03002
Phipps, Robert J.	Maj 4th PA Cav BvtLTC	PA	10875
Phisterer, Frederick	Capt. 18th Infy USA	NY	10969
Phillips, Charles O.	Capt. 6th Batt MA L Arty BvtMaj	MA	01244
Phoenix, Lloyd	Lt. USN	NY	00217
Piaget, Louis A.	1st Lt. 25th NJ Infy	NY	10431
Pickands, Henry S.	Maj 103rd OH Infy	IL	03132
Pickands, James	Col. 124th OH Infy	OH	02963
Pickering, Henry Y.	Capt. 104th PA Infy	PA	08986
Pickett, Josiah	Col. 25th MA Infy BvtBG	MA	00682
Picking, Henry F.	RAdm USN	PA	00459
Pickins, Francis M.	Capt. 31st IN Infy	IN	13236
Pickman, Benjamin	1st Lt. 1st Unattached Co. MA Cav	MA	01000
Pierce, Alfred C.	Capt. 11th KS Infy	KS	16985
Pierce, Byron R.	BG BvtMG USV	MI	03737
Pierce, Calvin	1st Lt. 42nd OH Infy	OH	07030
Pierce, Charles E.	1st Lt. 4th MA H Arty	MA	06108
Pierce, Charles W.	Capt. VRC BvtMaj	NE	04314
Pierce, Edward C.	Capt. 3rd ME Infy	MA	01125
Pierce, Edward W.	2nd Lt. 3rd MA Cav	KS	06157
Pierce, Edwin S.	LTC 2nd MI Infy	DC	03745
Pierce, Elihu P.	1st Lt. Asst Surg. 6th NH Infy	MA	15506
Pierce, Elliot C.	Maj 13th MA Infy	MA	02089
Pierce, Francis E.	Col. 8th US Vet.Vol. Infy BvtBG	MN	09146
Pierce, Gilbert A.	Col. QM USV	MN	04249
Pierce, Henry L.	3rd Class (Representative MA)	MA	02496
Pierce, James O.	Maj AAG USV	MN	00356
Pierce, Robert B.F.	2nd Lt. 135th IN Infy	IN	11518
Pierce, Samuel C.	LTC 3rd NY Cav	NY	10656
Pierce, Seymour	Capt. 27th NY Infy	NY	14831
Pierpont, William H.	Capt. 7th CT Infy	NY	04339
Pierson, George H.	Col. 5th MA Infy	MA	01137
Pierson, Hamilton W.	3rd Class (Sec. Christian Commission)	OH	03437
Pierson, Henry L.	Capt. AAG USV	NY	08499
Pierson, J. Frederick	Col. 1st NY Infy BvtBG	NY	02570
Pierson, John L.	Maj 2nd NJ Cav	OH	02586
Pierson, Stephen	1st Lt. Adj. 33rd NJ Infy BvtMaj	NY	02295
Piggott, Michael	Capt. 66th IL Infy	IL	08427
Pike, Robinson D.	1st Lt. 1st MI Cav	MN	04932
Pilcher, Lewis S.	Passed Asst Surg. USN	NY	10897
Pilkington, Hugh L.	2nd Asst Eng. (Master) USN	CA	15266
Pillsbury, John E.	RAdm USN	DC	16053

Name	Rank	Commandery	Insignia No.
Pillsbury, John S.	3rd Class (Gov. MN)	MN	06291
Pillsbury, William S.	1st Lt. 1st NH H Arty	MA	11987
Pilsbury, Samuel H.	Capt. 5th ME Infy	ME	11477
Pinder, Albert	Capt. 59th MA Infy	MA	11615
Pineo, Peter	LTC Med. Inspector USV	MA	01619
Pingree, George E.	Capt. 11th NH Infy	IA	13437
Pinkerton, John W.	Capt. 62nd OH Infy	OH	11705
Pinkham, Charles H.	Bvt 1st Lt. USV	MA	16125
Pinkham, George E.	Asst Surg. 3rd MA H Arty	MA	03250
Pinkney, Bertine	Col. 20th WI Infy	KS	05076
Pinkney, Howard	Asst Surg. 83rd NY Infy	NY	00739
Pinkney, Ninian	Med. Director USN	PA	00285
Pinto, Francis E.	Col. 32nd NY Infy BvtBG	NY	02040
Piper, Edgar W.	1st Lt. 114th USCT	CA	08129
Piper, Henry B.	Capt. 11th PA Infy	PA	08462
Piper, Horace L.	1st Lt. 4th USCT BvtMaj	DC	13151
Pirtle, Alfred	1st Lt. 10th OH Infy	OH	09644
Pitcher, Thomas G.	BG USV	DC	02207
Pitkin, Perley P.	Col. QM USV	MA	08738
Pitman, John	Col. Ordnance USA	MN	05156
Pitman, William G.	Capt. 23rd WI Infy	WI	07737
Pitt, William E.	Capt. 144th IL Infy	KS	16798
Pittman, James E.	3rd Class (Insp. Gen. MI)	MI	03868
Pittman, Samuel E.	Capt. AAG BvtLTC USV	MI	03740
Pitzman, Julius	Capt. 6th MO Infy	MO	06552
Place, Frank	LTC 157th NY Infy	NY	15797
Plaisted, Harris M.	BvtBG US	PA	00257
Platt, E.C.	Capt. 13th VRC	PA	00093
Platt, Edward R.	Maj AAG BvtLTC USA	CA	01314
Platt, James DeL.	LTC 10th OH Cav	OH	03079
Platt, James H.	Capt. 4th VT Infy	CO	05781
Platt, Robert	Commander USN	DC	07678
Platt, William H.	Asst Eng. USN	PA	16805
Pleasanton, Alfred	MG USV	NY	00237
Plimpton, Howard A.	Maj 39th IL Infy	CA	16253
Plowman, George	2nd Lt. 4th MN Infy BvtLTC	MN	13303
Plowman, George H.	Capt. 3rd MD Infy	MO	11033
Plumb, Henry C.	1st Lt. 59th NY Infy BvtCapt.	IA	06687
Plumb, Joseph W.	1st Lt. Adj. 2nd NJ Infy (BG USV)	NY	05012
Plumb, Preston B.	LTC 11th KS Cav	DC	01371 (Dup)
Plumer, Arnold A.	1st Lt. Battn. Adj. 4th PA Cav	PA	13822
Plumer, George W.	1st Lt. 121st PA Infy	OH	08286
Plummer, Samuel G.	Surg. 13th IL Infy	IL	07440
Plunkett, Francis C.	Asst Surg. 183rd OH Infy	MA	08857
Plunkett, George	Paymaster USN	PA	00607
Plunkett, Michael H.	Asst Eng. USN	MD	13582
Plunkett, William H.	Maj 17th WI Infy BvtLTC	DC	05467
Pocock, Edgar J.	1st Lt. 51st OH Infy	OH	09348

Name	Rank	Commandery	Insignia No.
Podrasnik, Alois	1st Lt. 156th IL Infy	IL	06709
Poe, Charles L.	Asst Surg.43rd OH Infy	OH	16637
Poe, Orlando M.	BG USV	MI	02697
Pogue, Joseph	Surg. 66th IL Infy	MO	05653
Poland, John S.	Col. 17th Infy USA BvtBG USV	OH	10277
Pollack, Bernard	1st Lt. 39th NY Infy	IL	16043
Pollard, Henry M.	Maj 5th VT Infy	MO	04288
Pollard, John K.	2nd Lt. 182nd OH Infy	OH	05819
Pollock, Alexander	Act 3rd Asst Eng. USN	NY	01785
Pollock, John	LTC 40th MA Infy	MA	11774
Pollock, Otis W.	LTC USA	CA	06060
Pollock, Robert	Col. 3rd CA Infy	OR	06321
Pomeroy, Edgar	1st Lt. 1st CA Infy	CA	14006
Pomeroy, John J.	Chaplin, 3rd Regt. PRVC	PA	00210
Pomeroy, John M.	Maj Paymaster USV	PA	00147
Pomutz, George	BvtBG USA	PA	01159
Pond, Cornelius V.R.	1st Lt. RQM 12th CT Infy	MI	03744
Pond, George E.	Col. Asst QM Gen. USA	DC	04619
Pond, Homer W.	1st Lt. 3rd WI Cav	KS	04441
Pond, James B.	Capt. 3rd WI Cav	NY	04912
Pond, Nathan P.	LTC 2nd USC Cav	NY	11339
Pond, Richard H.	Capt. 12th Infy BvtMaj USA	CA	03233
Pool, Joseph	Maj Paymaster BvtLTC USV	NY	05840
Pool, Theodore L.	Capt. 123rd NY Infy BvtMaj	NY	08500
Poole, DeWitt C.	LTC USA	DC	03441
Poole, Horace	Capt. AAG USV	IA	11440
Pooley, Samuel M.	Capt. 51st NY Infy	NY	16640
Poor, Frederick W.	1st Lt. 24th Batt OH L Arty	DC	02355
Poor, James W.	1st Lt. 1st ME Cav	CA	02870
Poor, Mark	Capt. 1st Vet. WVA Infy	OH	18074
Poore, Benjamin Perley	Maj 8th MA Infy	DC	01516
Pope, Albert A.	Capt. 35th MA Infy BvtLTC	MA	01428
Pope, Benjamin F.	LTC Dept. Surg. Gen. USA	CA	01190
Pope, Edmund M.	Col. 8th NY Cav BvtBG	MN	04244
Pope, George	LTC 54th MA Infy	NY	01420
Pope, Graham	1st Lt. 23rd MI Infy	MI	04261
Pope, Henry D.	1st Lt. 3rd MA Cav	MA	01399
Pope, James	Capt. 1st MA H Arty	MA	06638
Pope, James W.	Col. AQM Gen. USA	DC	17060
Pope, John	MG USA	MO	02807
Pope, Joseph P.	Capt. CS BvtMaj USV	IN	09208
Pope, Lemuel	Act Master USN	MA	01029
Pope, Percival C.	BG USMC	MA	07679
Pope, William S.	Maj Paymaster BvtLTC USV	MO	04371
Popham, Richard M.	1st Lt. 10th NJ Infy	PA	01273
Poree, Ferdinand C.	2nd Lt. 30th MA Infy	MA	07134
Porteous, James G.	Surg. 46th NY Infy	NY	07085
Porter, Andrew	BG USV	NY	00792

Name	Rank	Commandery	Insignia No.
Porter, Anthony B.	Capt. 134th IL Infy	NY	10794 (Dup)
Porter, Burr	Col. 3rd MA Cav	NY	00573
Porter, Charles	LTC 22nd Infy USA	DC	03448
Porter, Charles H.	1st Lt. 39th MA Infy	MA	01536
Porter, Charles L.	2nd Lt. 18th NH Infy	MA	09335
Porter, David Dixon	RAdm USN	PA	00029
Porter, David R.	Asst Surg. 5th KS Cav	MO	05046
Porter, George L.	Asst Surg. BvtMaj USA	NY	04064
Porter, Henry M.	LTC 7th VT Infy	NY	01086
Porter, Henry T.	1st Lt. Adj. 13th IL Infy	IL	01929
Porter, Horace	Col. ADC BvtBG USA	NY	02768
Porter, James W.	2nd Lt. 2nd USC L Arty	IL	07145
Porter, John R.	Capt. 48th PA Infy	PA	13291
Porter, Julius W.	Capt. 2nd LA Cav	NY	No Number
Porter, Robert P.	1st Lt. 8th VT Infy	VT	09661
Porter, Samuel A.	Col. 123rd USCT BvtBG	MA	01435
Porter, William A. Von V.	2nd Lt. 214th PA Infy	NY	18076
Porter, William C.	Chap 20th IN Infy	KS	14630
Porter, William L.	Capt. AAG	TN	00357
Post, Henry A.V.	Col. 2nd US Shpshtrs.	NY	04608
Post, Philip S.	Col. 59th IL Infy BvtBG	Il	08122
Post, Truman A.	1st Lt. Adj. 40th MO Infy	MO	05974
Postles, J. Parke	Capt. 1st DE Infy	PA	08230
Potter, Albert	Surg. 8th RI H Arty	MA	11675
Potter, Alvah K.	Maj 18th NH Infy	NY	15216
Potter, Andrew M.	1st Lt. Adj. 74th IL Infy BvtCapt.	PA	07868
Potter, Carroll H.	Col. 6th USV Infy BvtBG	KS	05077
Potter, Charles	Act Master USN	CA	07921
Potter, Edward E.	Commodore USN	PA	05504
Potter, Frederick E.	Surg. USN	MA	06185
Potter, Henry C.	Capt. 18th PA Cav	PA	01741
Potter, Henry L.	Col. 71st NY Infy	NY	08358
Potter, Isaac M.	Capt. 5th RI H Arty	MA	05426
Potter, James J.	2nd Lt. 22nd MI Infy	MI	16383
Potter, James M.	1st Lt. 117th USCT	OH	04223
Potter, John	Capt. 53rd IL Infy	CA	07212
Potter, John F. "Bowie Knife"	3rd Class (US Representative WI)	WI	06208
Potter, Joseph A.	Col. QM BvtBG USA	DC	02829
Potter, Joseph B.	Surg. 30th OH Infy	OH	02998
Potter, Joseph H.	BG USA	OH	03820
Potter, Samue O.L.	Surg. USV	CA	13606
Potter, Theodore E.	Capt. 11th MN Infy	MN	13711
Potter, William E.	Capt. 12th NJ Infy BvtMaj	PA	00812
Potter, William F.	Capt. 3rd PA Cav	PA	02108
Potter, William H.	Capt. 137th USCT	IN	12862
Potter, William H.	2nd Lt. 9th RI Infy	MA	11676
Potter, William W.	Surg. 57th NY Infy BvtLTC	NY	04062
Potts, Isaac B.	Capt. 95th OH Infy	OH	07034

The Roster

Name	Rank	Commandery	Insignia No.
Potts, J. Newport	Capt. CS USV	DC	04683
Potts, John T.	Capt. VRC	PA	02443
Potts, Joseph H.	Capt. 75th OH Infy	IN	17422
Potts, Robert	Chief Eng. USN	DC	13583
Potwin, George C.	1st Lt. 19th USCT BvtMaj	DC	07706
Poundstone, Alexander McC.	Capt. 5th USCT BvtMaj	OH	10461
Powell, Charles F.	LTC Eng. USA	DC	06450
Powell, E. Henry	LTC 10th USCT	VT	06109
Powell, Elias	Capt. 7th WVA Cav BvtMaj	CA	05208
Powell, Eugene	BvtBG USV	OH	05471
Powell, Isaac P.	Maj 146th NY Infy	MI	12448
Powell, J. Tyler	Capt. 1st DC Infy	DC	13036
Powell, James W.	Col. 17th Infy USA	NY	03542
Powell, John W.	Maj 2nd IL L Arty	DC	10374
Powell, Levin M.	RAdm USN	PA	00468
Powell, William H.	Col. 9th Infy USA	DC	03651
Powell, William H.	BG BvtMG USV	MO	04367
Powelson, Benjamin F.	1st Lt. 41st USCT	CO	15857
Power, John C.	Capt. 6th IA Cav	IA	11145
Power, William A.	1st Lt. 9th IL Cav	MN	08434
Powers, F. Frank	Capt. 16th MI Infy	NE	10060
Powers, George H.	Asst Surg. 60th MA Infy	CA	02155
Powers, William P.	1st Lt. 4th Batt WI L Arty	IL	10951
Powleson, Oliver C.	Capt. 80th OH Infy	OH	11706
Pratt, Calvin E.	BG USV	NY	11463
Pratt, Electus A.	Capt. 8th USCT	DC	05862
Pratt, Franklin A.	Capt. 1st CT H Arty	MO	04527
Pratt, Henry	Capt. 89th NY Infy	NY	06170
Pratt, Henry C.	Capt. 13th Infy USA	PA	00762
Pratt, James H.	Capt. AQM USV	NE	07544
Pratt, John	Capt. AAG USV	NY	02764
Pratt, John B.	Act Ensign USN	MO	08137
Pratt, Joseph T.	Maj 32nd USCT	PA	00109
Pratt, Leonard B.	1st Lt. RCS 1st RI Cav	MA	08858
Pratt, Nichols	Act Master USN	DC	05593
Pratt, Richard H.	BG USA	DC	04172
Pratt, Robert	Capt. 5th VT Infy	MN	06284
Pratt, Sedgwick	LTC Arty USA	CA	08501
Pratt, William	Capt. AAG USV	MA	00623
Pratt, William B.	Capt. ADC BvtMaj USV	DC	03822
Pratt, William F.	2nd Asst Eng. USN	PA	08987
Pratt, William H.	1st Lt. RQM 1st Battn CA Mountrs.	CA	09409
Pratt, William M.	LTC 8th CT Infy	DC	09367
Pray, Samuel M.	Capt. 4th IA Cav	IN	16757
Preble, George H.	RAdm USN	MA	00671
Prentice, Fowler	Surg. 73rd NY Infy	NY	00296
Prentice, Nathan B.	1st Lt. RQM 37th WI Infy	DC	12414
Prentice, Sartell	Capt. 12th Infy BvtMaj USA	IL	02000

Name	Rank	Commandery	Insignia No.
Prentice, William P.	LTC AAG USV	NY	03189
Prentiss, Jerome J.	1st Lt. MI Eng. Mechs.	NY	16689
Prescott, Calvin B.	1st Lt. 1st Battn. MA H Arty	MA	01427
Prescott, Royal B.	1st Lt. 13th NH Infy	MA	07403
Prescott, Thomas C.	Capt. 8th NH Infy	IA	08446
Pressnel, Thomas H.	Capt. 1st Battn. MN Infy	MN	07822
Preston, Albert W.	Col. USA	Ca	01579
Preston, Edward V.	Maj Paymaster USV	MA	10513
Preston, Everett B.	Capt. 22nd CT Infy	IL	04848
Preston, Noble D.	Capt. 10th NY Cav	PA	10632
Prevost, Charles M.	Col. 16th VRC BvtBG	PA	00145
Price, Butler D.	BG USA	IL	08920
Price, Curtis E.	Surg. USA	CA	03453
Price, Emmor H.	Capt. 11th OH Infy	OH	05476
Price, George F.	Capt. 5th Cav USA	CA	01481
Price, George T.	Capt. 1st DE Infy	DC	16712
Price, Isaiah	Maj 97th PA Infy	PA	00490
Price, John G.	Capt. 75th IL Infy	PA	00781
Price, Marshall F.	Surg. 1st PA L Arty	CA	04903
Price, Milton M.	LTC 13th IA Infy	IA	14899
Price, Samuel W.	Col. 21st KY Infy BvtBG	DC	13490
Prickett, William A.	Capt. 25th USCT	NY	15058
Prickett, William R.	Maj 150th IL Infy	MO	05703
Pride, John W.	1st Lt. 1st MN Infy	MN	13334
Prieson, Gustav A.	Asst Surg. 6th PA Cav	PA	10399
Priest, Charles N.	Capt. 155th NY Infy	PA	06268
Priest, George E.	1st Lt. RQM 57th MA Infy	MA	05096
Prime, Ebenezer G.	R Adm. USN	NY	16153
Prime, Ralph E.	LTC 6th NY H Arty	NY	02767
Prince, Frederick W.	LTC 16th NY H Arty BvtCol.	DC	10090
Prince, Howard L.	Capt. 20th ME Infy	DC	03811
Prindle, Franklin C.	Civil Eng. USN	DC	02894
Prindle, Harrison	1st Lt. 14th VT Infy	CA	12294
Prindle, John Adams	Capt. 7th VT Infy	OH	04745 (Dup)
Pringle, W. DeWolf	1st Lt. Adj. 9th Arty NY Vols.	MN	04033
Pritchard, Arthur J.	Pay Director USN	MD	01830
Pritchard, Jesse L.	Maj 2nd CA Cav	KS	15415
Pritchett, George E.	1st Lt. 126th NY Infy	NE	05108
Probasco, Jacob O.	Capt. 6th MI Cav	MI	13967
Probst, John D.	1st Lt. 21st NJ Infy	NY	02899
Proctor, David E.	Capt. 30th USCT BvtMaj	MA	10514
Proctor, Redfield	Col. 15th VT Infy	VT	04386
Proctor, Thomas R.	Admiral's Secretary USN	NY	11334
Prosser, William F.	Maj 2nd TN Cav	WA	03901
Proudfit, Alexander	Hospital Chap USV	OH	11480
Proudfit, James K.	Col. 12th WI Infy BvtBG	KS	11096
Prouty, Cheney	Capt. 33rd IA Infy	IA	12757
Provine, William M.	1st Lt. 84th IL Infy	IL	13338

Name	Rank	Commandery	Insignia No.
Provost, Norman	1st Lt. 6th CT Infy	NY	16087
Prudhomme, Lucien F.	1st Lt. 11th PA Cav (Professor USN)	PA	01255
Pruyn, Augustus	LTC 4th NY Cav	NY	12402
Pugh, Robert T.	LTC 53rd WI Infy	WI	07736
Pulcifer, Alfred H.	Capt. 2nd MA H Arty	NY	06231
Pulford, John	Col. BvtBG USA	MI	03419
Pumpelly, James K.	1st Lt. 32nd WI Infy	WI	16011 (Dup)
Purdy, Charles	1st Lt. 81st USCT	CA	17619
Purdy, William B.	Act Asst Paymaster USN	NY	14289
Purington, Dillwyn V.	Capt. AQM USV	IL	02790
Purington, George A.	LTC 3rd Cav USA	MO	02485
Purington, Robert H.	Capt. 54th ME Infy	CO	07905
Purviance, George	1st Lt. Adj.134th PA Infy	PA	08757
Puster, Louis	Capt. 21st MO Infy	IN	11230 (Dup)
Puterbaugh, George	Capt. 47th IL Infy	CA	05914
Puterbaugh, Sabin D.	Maj 11th IL Cav	IL	06524
Putnam, Arthur A.	Capt. 14th MA Infy	MA	12740
Putnam, Charles E.	Capt. 13th IA Infy	IA	04849
Putnam, David E.	Capt. 92nd OH Infy	OH	16065
Putnam, Douglas	LTC 92nd OH Infy	OH	05475
Putnam, Edgar P.	Capt. 9th NY Cav	NY	10537
Putnam, Edwin	Pay Director USN	DC	12103
Putnam, George H.	1st Lt. Adj. 176th NY Infy	NY	05837
Putnam, John C.	Capt. 20th MA Infy	MA	00989
Putnam, Joseph B.	LTC 42nd USCT BvtCol.	IL	04135
Putnam, Thomas C.	Capt. 15th NY Cav	CO	05965
Putnam, William	Chap 160th NY Infy	MI	13863
Putney, Frank H.	2nd Lt. 12th WI Infy	WI	04509
Pyne, Charles M.	Capt. 42nd Infy USA	NY	00844
Quackenbush, Jay L.	Capt. 8th MI Infy	WA	14016
Quackenbush, Stephen P.	RAdm USN	DC	03173
Quaiffe, Alfred R.	Capt. 152nd NY Infy	DC	10777
Quarles, Joseph V.	1st Lt. 39th WI Infy	W/I	02959
Quay, Matthew S.	Col. 134th PA Infy	PA	04669
Queen, Walter W.	RAdm USN	DC	00540
Quentin, Julius E.	Capt. 14th Infy USA	OR	06806
Quier, Levi	1st Lt. RQM 54th PA Infy	PA	07069
Quigg, Matthew	Capt. 10th KS Infy	KS	06487
Quimby, Stilman J.	Maj Surg. 61st USCT	PA	No Number
Quinby, Ira	LTC USA	DC	14408
Quincy, Samuel M.	Col. 2nd MA Infy BvtBG	MA	01302
Quinlan, James	LTC 88th NY Infy	NY	10432
Quinn, George F.	1st Lt. 155th NY Infy	CA	03636
Quinn, James	Capt. 15th PA Cav	PA	11712
Quinn, John	Capt. 2nd CA Cav	CA	17053
Quinn, John P.	Surg. USN	PA	00565
Quinn, Thomas F.	Maj USA	NY	04319
Quinn, Timothy	LTC 7th NY Cav	OH	03301

The Roster

Name	Rank	Commandery	Insignia No.
Quint, Alonzo H.	Chap 3rd MA Infy	MA	00983
Quinton, William	BG USA	CA	03655
Race, George A.	Maj 10th IL Infy	IL	09751
Race, George S.	1st Lt. 2nd WI Cav	WI	13278
Racey, William H.	1st Lt. 53rd NY Infy	NY	08145 (Dup)
Racklely, Benjamin F.	Capt. 1st NH Cav	MA	02164
Radcliff, William D.	Capt. 7th MD Infy	KS	05453
Radcliffe, Marcus B.	1st Lt. 114th OH Infy	OH	10126
Radcliffe, Samuel J.	LTC Med. Director USV	DC	08817
Radford, William	RAdm USN	PA	00174
Radinsky, Louis D.	Surg. 104th USCT	PA	02746
Rae, Thomas	Passed Asst. Eng. USN	NY	02378
Raefle, Max G.	Act Asst Eng. USN	NY	06229
Raffauf, Jacob	1st Lt. 8th NY Infy	WI	17018
Rafferty, Thomas	LTC 71st NY Infy	NY	02203
Ragan, Robert A.	Capt. 8th TN Infy	DC	15243
Ragan, William	Maj 18th IA Infy	MN	05864
Rahn, Charles F.	2nd Lt. Independent Co. PA Infy	PA	07874
Raines, John	Capt. 85th NY Infy	NY	02555
Rainey, John K.	Asst Surg. 11th IL Infy	OH	12918
Ralston, Robert S.	3rd Class	PA	00520
Ramsay, Alexander	3rd Class (Gov. MN)	MN	03887 (Dup)
Ramsay, George D., Jr.	Capt. Ordnance USA	PA	00410
Ramsay, John S.	Surg. 130th PA Infy	PA	09282
Ramsay, Robert H.	Maj AAG BvtLTC USV	PA	00122
Ramsey, Joseph G.	Capt. 2nd Arty USA	DC	No Number
Rand, Arnold A.	Col. 4th MA Cav	MA	01311
Rand, Charles F.	1st Lt. VRC Bvt Capt.	DC	07563
Rand, Edward M.	1st Lt. Adj. 27th ME Infy	ME	01750
Rand, Edwin D.	Capt. 7th NH Infy	MA	15201
Rand, Frederic H.	Capt. 26th NY Cav	MA	01451
Rand, George D.	Act Asst Paymaster USN	IA	11883
Rand, Philip C.	1st Lt. Adj. 15th CT Infy	NY	10433
Rand, Stephen	Pay Director USN	DC	03506
Rand, Thomas B.	LTC 9th NY Infy	NY	02137
Randall, Alpheus W.	BvtCapt. USV	CA	03339
Randall, Edmund	1st Lt. 116th PA Infy	PA	08231
Randall, Francis J.	Maj 95th PA Infy	PA	09505 (Dup)
Randall, George M.	MG USA	OR	13517
Randall, George W.	BvtMaj USA BvtLTC USV	PA	00654
Randall, John F.	2nd Lt. 21st CT Infy	MO	11425
Randall, Samuel C.	1st Lt. 23rd MI Infy	MI	07394
Randall, William P.	Commander USN	MA	06830
Randlett, James F.	Col. USA	CA	12581
Randol, Alanson M.	Maj 1st Arty BvtCol. USA	CA	02535
Randolph, George E.	Capt. 1st RI L Arty BvtCol.	CO	05627
Randolph, Wallace F.	MG USA	DC	05251
Rankin, John E.	2nd Lt. 2nd KS Cav	KS	04925

The Roster

Name	Rank	Commandery	Insignia No.
Rankin, Joseph	Capt. 27th WI Infy	WI	02086
Rankin, William H.	Capt. 104th PA Infy	NY	16006
Ranlett, Seth A.	1st Lt. Adj. 36th MA Infy	MA	01800
Rannells, William J.	Capt. 75th OH Infy	OH	04573
Ranney, George E.	Surg. 2nd MI Cav	MI	06817
Ranney, Henry C.	Capt. AAG USV	OH	03386
Ranney, Philip M.	1st Lt. 26th NY Cav	MN	07952
Ransom, George M.	Commodore USN	NY	00136
Ransom, John	Asst Surg. 19th USCT BvtCapt.	CA	05642
Ransom, John E.	1st Lt. 21st NY Infy	NY	14911
Ransom, Rastus S.	1st Lt. 50th NY Eng.	NY	01841
Raper, John T.	1st Lt. Adj. 26th OH Infy	OH	05753
Raphall, Alfred M.	Capt. 40th NY Infy BvtMaj	PA	03597
Rassieur, Leo	Capt. 30th MO Infy	MO	08903
Rastill, John E.	1st Lt. 1st MD Infy	DC	16945
Rath, Christian	Capt. 17th MI Infy BvtLTC	MI	08417
Rathbone, Clarence	Ensign USN	NY	01542
Ratliff, Robert W.	Col. 13th OH Cav BvtBG	OH	03263
Raub, Jacob F.	Asst Surg. 210th PA Infy	DC	06472
Rauch, John H.	Surg. BvtLTC USV	IL	08723
Raum, Green B.	BG USV	PA	02296
Rawle, William Brooke	Capt. 3rd PA Cav BvtLTC	PA	00173
Rawles, Jacob B.	BG USA	CA	01584
Rawlins, John W.	Surg. 88th PA Infy	DC	08319
Rawn, Charles C.	Maj 24th Infy USA	KS	04748
Rawolle, William C.	Capt. 2nd Cav USA BvtLTC	CA	03445
Ray, John M.	Capt. 140th PA Infy	PA	08758
Ray, P. Henry	Col. 4th Infy USA	DC	03522
Ray, Patrick H.	Capt. 6th VRC USA	PA	00082
Raymond, Albert C.	Capt. 17th VT Infy	VT	10070
Raymond, Charles H.	1st. Lt. 177th NY Infy	NY	01246
Raymond, Charles W.	BG USA	PA	02782-2803
Raymond, Edward T.	Capt. 36th MA Infy BvtMaj	MA	10748
Raymond, Francis, Jr.	Capt. 1st MI Infy	MO	04526
Raymond, Henry C.	Capt. 32nd IA Infy	IA	15346 (Dup)
Raymond, Henry S.	LTC 23rd MI Infy	MI	12449
Raymond, Israel W.	3rd Class (Pioneer settler)	CA	03249
Raymond, James W.	1st Lt. RQM 177th OH Infy	MN	08730
Raymond, John B.	Capt. 31st IL Infy	DC	02940
Raymond, Rossiter W.	Capt. ADC USV	NY	02868
Raynor, William H.	Col. 56th OH BvtBG	OH	04859
Rea, John P.	Capt. 1st OH Cav BvtMaj	MN	04236
Rea, Joseph N.	2nd LT 152nd IL Infy	CA	13420
Read, George H.	Commander USN	DC	18315
Read, Henry A.	Maj 99th PA Infy	CA	09832
Read, Ira B.	Capt. 101st OH Infy	NY	03763
Read, J. Meredith	3rd Class (Adj. Gen. NY)	NY	01023
Read, John	Act Asst Paymaster USN	MA	00869

Name	Rank	Commandery	Insignia No.
Read, John J.	RAdm USN	PA	00939
Read, Louis W.	Surg. Bvt LTC USV	PA	01951
Read, Walter A.	Capt. 4th RI Infy	MA	14215
Reagles, James	Asst Surg. 62nd NY Infy	OR	13369
Ream, Norman B.	1st Lt.85th Infy	IL	05546
Reamy, Thaddeus A.	Surg. 122nd OH Infy	OH	03202
Reany, Henry	Act Master USN	MI	10904
Reardon, John	Capt. 115th IL Infy	CA	10199
Reat, James L.	Surg. 21st IL Infy	IL	12392
Rector, John F.	2nd Lt. 29th IL Infy	MO	06727
Reddick, Noah W.	1st Lt.30th IL Infy	KS	08201
Redding, William F.	Capt. 24th MA Infy	MA	No Number
Redfield, George S.	Act Asst Paymaster USN	NY	01936
Redington, Edward D.	Maj Paymaster USV	IL	07759
Redlon, Benjamin M.	Capt. 29th ME Infy BvtMaj	ME	12020
Redlon, Cyrus F.	2nd Lt. 113th USCT	MN	12721
Redman, James C.	1st Lt. 79th OH Infy	OH	12348
Redman, William H.	Capt. 12th IL Cav	IA	06196
Reece, Alonzo N.	1st Lt. RQM 124th IL Infy	IL	02815
Reece, Jasper N.	Capt. 138th IL Infy	IL	11929
Reed, James McClure	1st Lt. Adj. 2nd PA Cav	NY	01545
Reed, Allen V.	RAdm USN	DC	15804
Reed, Axel H.	1st Lt. 2nd MN Infy	MN	06095
Reed, David W.	Capt. 12th IA Infy BvtMaj	IL	05431
Reed, Edmund W.	2nd Lt. 83rd PA Infy	DC	09529
Reed, Edward P.	Capt. 12th MA Infy	MA	01590
Reed, Henry A.	LTC Arty USA	DC	04117
Reed, Horace L.	1st Lt. 104th OH Infy	OH	09088
Reed, John A.	Capt. Ind. Co. MN Cav	MN	04035
Reed, John B.	Capt. 1st NC Infy	MA	09671
Reed, John H.	3rd Class (QM Gen. MA)	MA	00818
Reed, Joseph A.E.	Surg. 155th PA Infy	PA	08463
Reed, Joseph R.	Capt. 2nd Batt IA L Arty	IA	06198
Reed, Julius H.	2nd Lt. 37th MA Infy	IL	17603
Reed, Lewis	Capt. 54th MA Infy	MA	09336
Reed, Myron W.	Capt. 18th MI Infy	CO	05959
Reed, Nathan A., Jr.	1st Lt. 50th OH Infy	IL	10219
Reed, Thomas Baird	Surg. BvtLTC USV	PA	03229
Reed, Thomas Benton	Capt. 205th PA Infy BvtLTC	PA	07871
Reed, Thomas Brackett	Act Asst Paymaster USN	ME	02499
Reed, Thomas D.	Capt. 51st PA Infy	PA	10633
Reed, William B.	Capt. 50th WI Infy	WI	08759
Reed, William E.	Capt. 32nd MA Infy	MA	13049
Reed, William F.	1st Lt. Adj. 60th USCT	DC	12415
Reeder, Frank	LTC USV	PA	01304
Reeder, H. James	Capt. 153rd PA Infy	PA	01305
Rees, Corwin P.	Capt. USN	ME	14223
Rees, Jonathan	Capt. 27th OH Infy	OH	04393

Name	Rank	Commandery	Insignia No.
Rees, Morris	Capt. 72nd OH Infy	OH	11570
Reese, Henry B.	Maj Paymaster USA	OH	06430
Reeve, Felix A.	Col. 8th TN Infy	DC	06879
Reeve, Isaac V.D.	Col. 13th Infy BvtBG USA	NY	01225
Reeve, James H.	Capt. 3rd NY Infy BvtMaj	DC	13152
Reeve, James T.	Surg. 21st WI Infy	WI	06367 (Dup)
Reeve, John B.	Capt. 37ith IN Infy	IN	07158
Reeves, James F.	Act Asst Paymaster USN	IN	09014
Reeves, Patrick S.	Capt. 23rd KY Infy	OH	09647
Regan, James	Col. 9th Infy USA	NY	03895
Rehr, Lewis	Capt. 54th PA Infy	PA	08988
Reibling, Augustus J.	2nd Lt. 4th NY H Arty	NY	15059
Reichard, Adolph L.	2nd Lt. 98th PA Infy	CO	06533
Reichard, Francis H.	LTC 118th PA Infy	PA	00015
Reichard, George N.	LTC 143rd PA Infy	PA	11538
Reichelderfer, Levi	Capt. 96th OH Infy	OH	08907
Reichelm, Edward P.	Capt. 51st USCT	PA	11539
Reid, George C.	BG USMC	DC	00663
Reid, James B.	Capt. 10th Infy USA	NY	00666-11918
Reid, John B.	LTC 130th IL Infy	IL	13508
Reid, John G.	Capt. 5th US Vet.Vol.	IL	03697
Reid, Robert K.	Surg. 2nd CA Infy BvtLTC	CA	04617
Reiff, Josiah T.	1st Lt. 15th PA Cav	NY	No Number
Reilly, Bernard, Jr.	1st Lt. 5th Cav USA	PA	14196
Reilly, Francis W.	Surg. 26th IL Infy	IL	11601
Reilly, Henry J.	Capt. 5th Arty USA	CA	12584
Reilly, James	Capt. 91st NY Infy	CA	02304
Reilly, James W.	BG USA	DC	07873
Reilly, John E.	Capt. 187th PA Infy	PA	05254
Reilly, William W.	Capt. 30th OH Infy	OH	04227
Reimers, Augustus	1st Lt. 15th MO Infy	IA	04850
Reinhart, John D.	1st Lt. 39th KY Infy	OH	07945
Remey, George C.	RAdm USN	DC	07509
Remey, William B.	Col. USMC	Dc	06970
Remick, Otis	Maj 11th WI Infy	CO	07165
Remick, Royal A.	1st Lt. 23rd MI Infy	MI	03891
Remington, Jeremiah B.	Maj 89th NY Infy	KS	08695
Remington, Wagar H.	Capt. 111th NY Infy	NY	11919
Rennie, Zenas C.	Capt. 49th MA Infy	CA	01903
Rennyson, William M.	Capt. 10th NJ Infy	PA	04179
Reno, Henry C.	1st Lt. 128th OH Infy	CA	10612
Renshaw, James	1st Asst Eng. USN	CO	10100
Restieaux, Edward B.W.	Capt. AQM USV	MA	01202
Reuhle, John V.	Capt. 2nd MI Infy	MI	08714
Reutlinger, Adolph	2nd Lt. 5th KY Infy	OH	07310
Rex, George P.	Surg. 33rd IL Infy	PA	01530
Rex, Oliver P.	Asst Surg. 33rd IL Infy	PA	01406
Rexford, William H.	LTC USA	NY	06607

Name	Rank	Commandery	Insignia No.
Rexford, Willie M.	LTC 131st NY Infy BvtCol.	NY	02365
Reyburn, Robert	Surg. BvtLTC USV	DC	03977
Reynolds, Albert	Asst Surg. 88th USCT	IA	11548
Reynolds, Benoni O.	Surg. 3rd WI Cav	WI	03809
Reynolds, Charles	Capt. 12th WI Infy	WI	13887
Reynolds, Charles A.	LTC DQMG USA	DC	05165
Reynolds, Charles A.	2nd Lt. 2nd CT H Arty	NY	13453
Reynolds, Frank W.	Capt. 44th MA Infy	MA	00924
Reynolds, George D.	LTC 6th USC H Arty	MO	05915
Reynolds, George W.	Capt. 130th OH Infy	CA	08000
Reynolds, Herbert M.	1st Lt. 19th MI Infy	MI	10606
Reynolds, James K.	1st Lt. 6th OH Infy	OH	03042
Reynolds, John A.	Maj 1st NY L Arty BvtCol.	NY	09432
Reynolds, John P.	Capt. 19th MA Infy	MA	02689
Reynolds, Joseph J.	MG USV	DC	05941
Reynolds, Samuel W.	1st Lt. 4th USCT BvtCapt.	MO	06404
Reynolds, William	RAdm USN	PA	00137
Rhind, Alexander C.	Commander USN	NY	00208
Rhines, James	Capt. 88th IL Infy	MI	07574
Rhoades, Archibald C.	Med. Inspector USN	NY	05402
Rhoades, Charles W.C.	Capt. 26th NY Cav	MA	05159
Rhoades, Frank W.	1st Lt. 36th USCT	PA	13553
Rhoades, Henry E.	Asst Eng. USN	MA	04692
Rhoades, Lawrence	Capt. CS BvtCol. USV	MA	02459
Rhoades, William W.	Commander USN	OR	05943
Rhoads, Thomas J. B.	1st Lt. Surg. 169th PA Infy	PA	17036
Rhodes, Charles D.	Capt. AAG USV	IL	01940
Rhodes, Charles D.	Capt. 5th PA H Arty	PA	08464
Rhodes, Darius G.	Capt. 42nd PA Infy	NE	06696
Rhodes, Elisha Hunt	LTC 2nd RI Infy BvtCol.	MA	09476
Rhodes, Frank A.	1st Lt. 10th Batt RI L Arty	MA	02312
Rhodes, George H.	Capt. 1st NH Cav	NY	12403
Rhodes, James P.	2nd Lt. 1st RI L Arty	MA	11998
Rhodes, W.A.E.	2nd Lt. 6th IA Infy	CA	04908
Rhodes, William B.	Capt. 1st RI L Arty BvtMaj	MA	07404
Ribble, George T.	Asst Surg. 11th NJ Infy	DC	10375
Rice, Albert R.	Act Asst Surg. USN	MA	10196
Rice, Alexander A.	Capt. AAG USV	IN	07745
Rice, Alexander H.	3rd Class (US Representative MA)	MA	02464
Rice, Americus	BG USV	OH	03040
Rice, Archibald A.	1st Lt. 7th MN Infy	IL	09543
Rice, Charles E.	Maj 26th NY Cav	MA	01559
Rice, Charles S.	Capt. 17th Batt OH L Arty	OH	08036
Rice, Edmund	BG USA	MA	00960
Rice, Eugene W.	1st Lt. RQM 33rd IA Infy	IA	09685 (Dup)
Rice, Frank R.	Capt. USA	MO	04373
Rice, Franklin E.	1st Lt. RQM 9th VT Infy	MA	05236
Rice, Henry M.	3rd Class (US Senator MN)	MN	04234

Name	Rank	Commandery	Insignia No.
Rice, J. Marcus	Surg. 27th MA Infy	MA	00873
Rice, James	Capt. 1st VT H Arty	CA	06118
Rice, James H.	Capt. BvtLTC USA	MA	01383
Rice, John B.	Surg. USV	DC	02701
Rice, John L.	LTC 75th USCT	MA	05367
Rice, John McD.	Asst Surg. USN	PA	00171
Rice, John W.	1st Lt. 9th NY H Arty	NY	11751
Rice, L. Frederick	Capt. 31st MA Infy BvtMaj	MA	01463
Rice, Marshall N.	Capt. 35th USCT	MA	05162
Rice, Owen	Capt. 153rd PA Infy	OH	03157
Rice, Percy W.	Capt. 1st OH L Arty	OH	14249
Rice, Welcome	Capt. 48th IN Infy	IN	11055
Rice, William E.	Capt. 23rd OH Infy	CO	09635
Rice, William F.	Capt. 19th MA Infy	MA	01758
Rich, Giles H.	LTC 1st USCT	MA	04384
Rich, Joseph Smith	1st Lt. 5th IA Cav	MA	09672
Rich, Watson W.	Capt. 4th MN Infy	MN	04745 (Dup)
Richards, Alonzo V.N.	2nd Lt. Sig. Corps USV	IL	03731
Richards, Benjamin W.	Capt. ADC BvtLTC USV	PA	01993
Richards, Channing	Capt. 23rd OH Infy	OH	00590 (Dup)
Richards, Edward S.	Capt. AAG BvtLTC USV	IL	13165
Richards, Henry M.M.	Lt. USN	PA	17350
Richards, John T.	Maj 2nd MA Cav	ME	02620
Richards, Rees G..	Capt. 45th PA Infy	OH	10021
Richards, Sharp L.	Capt. 1st PA L Arty	CA	03463
Richards, Thomas M.	Capt. 128th PA Infy	PA	03798
Richards, William J.	Ma. 81st IN Infy	IN	07042
Richards, William V.	LTC AAG USA	MI	01116-5168
Richardson, Almyne H.G.	Capt. 114th PA Infy	DC	01749
Richardson, Charles A.	Maj 126th NY Infy	NY	05296
Richardson, Charles H.	2nd Lt. 26th MA Infy	MA	13331
Richardson, Edward B.	2nd Lt. 45th MA Infy	MA	01506
Richardson, Edward C.	Maj 24th MA Infy	MA	00832
Richardson, Edward F.	1st Lt. 16th NY H Arty	NY	04598
Richardson, George P.	1st Lt. 3rd MA H Arty	MA	12689
Richardson, George R.	Capt. 2nd IL L Arty	IL	10685
Richardson, George W.	Maj 11th NY Cav	NY	08660
Richardson, James M.	Maj 3rd MA H Arty BvtLTC	MA	01504
Richardson, James P.	LTC 38th MA Infy	MA	06507
Richardson, Jesse	Capt. 2nd MA Infy	OH	16925
Richardson, Lyman	Capt. 1st NE Infy	NE	05910
Richardson, R. Julian	Paymaster USN	MA	02066
Richardson, Spencer W.	Capt. 44th MA Infy	MA	01799
Richardson, William E.	1st Lt. RQM 33rd MA Infy	MA	12690
Richart, Robert S.	Capt. 12th IN Cav	WA	18047
Richart, David	Capt. 101st IN Infy	OH	12970
Richeson, William	1st Lt. Asst Surg. 73rd OH Infy	MN	06282
Richmond, Jacob L.	Capt. 1st MI L Arty	MN	15467

Name	Rank	Commandery	Insignia No.
Richmond, Silas P.	Col. 3rd MA Infy	MA	14088
Rick, Charles	1st Lt. 128th PA Infy	PA	06769
Rickell, Henry	2nd Lt. 6th IA Cav	IA	07142
Ricker, James W.	1st Lt. 2nd WVA Cav	OH	04749
Ricker, Oliver P.	2nd Lt. 39th MA Infy	MA	16113
Rickert, Thomas H.	1st Lt. RQM 7th PA Cav	PA	07875
Ricketts, James B.	MG USV	DC	04772
Ricks, Augustus J.	1st Lt. 104th OH Infy	OH	03205
Riddle, Daniel W.	Act Asst Paymaster USN	NY	16445
Riddle, Francis A.	1st Lt. 93rd USCT	IL	04142
Riddle, Matthew B.	Chap 2nd NJ Infy	PA	08233
Ridgely, Daniel B.	Commodore USN	PA	No Number
Ridgely, Franklin L.	2nd Lt. 6th Infy USA	MO	04530
Ridgeway, Henry	1st Lt. 11th NJ Infy	NY	16401
Ridgway, Barzillai	LTC 4th NJ Infy	PA	08760
Ridgway, Frank	Maj Surg. 74th NY Infy	NY	15710
Ridgway, Joseph T.	Act Ensign USN	PA	06770
Riebsame, Christian	Capt. 116th IL Infy	IL	05932
Ries, Florian J.	1st Lt. 17th WI Infy	WI	14689
Rife, Jacob M.	Capt. 7th WVA Cav	OH	18344
Riffenberick, Richard P.	Capt. 4th OH Cav	OH	02787
Rigby, William T.	Capt. 24th IA Infy	IA	04851 (Dup)
Riggen, John A.	1st Lt. 18th MO Infy	IA	07141
Riggs, William H.	1st Lt. 1st WVA Infy	NE	11960
Riley, Charles T.	1st Lt. 71st OH Infy	OH	05318
Riley, Daniel A.L.	Capt. 2nd WI Cav	MN	08283
Riley, Francis M.	Capt. 12th NJ Infy	PA	12112
Riley, Reuben	Act 2nd Asst Eng. USN	NY	08801
Rinaker, John I.	Col. 122nd IL Infy BvtBG	IL	07698
Rinehart, William V.	Maj 1st OR Infy	WA	09400
Ring, George W.	Capt. 2nd WI Cav USV	NY	01050
Ringgold, Cadwalader	RAdm USN	NY	00365
Ringland, George S.	Capt. 11th PA Cav	IA	11075
Ripka, Andrew A.	Capt. 119th PA Infy	PA	00036
Ripley, Edward H.	Col. 9th VT Infy BvtBG	NY	03013
Ripley, Lauren H.	1st Lt. 4th MI Cav	MI	04010
Ripley, Lyman B.	1st Lt. RQM 33rd MO Infy	MO	04372
Ripley, Robert A.	1st Lt. 13th CT Infy	NY	00219
Ripley, William Y.W.	LTC 1st US Shpshtrs.	VT	07092
Rippey, Charles H.	Col. 90th OH Infy	CA	12197
Risser, Abraham F.	Capt. 106th IL Infy	IL	05134
Ristine, Henry	Surg. 20th IA Infy	IA	06195
Risum, Otto A.	1st Lt. 15th WI Infy	WI	09095
Ritner, Isaac N.	Post Chap USA BvtCapt.	PA	08989
Rittenhouse, Benjamin F.	Maj USA	DC	01412
Rittenhouse, Henry N.	Capt. Med. Storekpr. USA	PA	04417
Ritter, Charles H.	1st Lt. Adj. 5th MI Infy	MI	11008
Ritter, Eli T.	Capt. 79th IN Infy	IN	14982

The Roster

Name	Rank	Commandery	Insignia No.
Ritter, Martin Van B.	2nd Lt. 23rd OH Infy	CA	03913
Ritzius, Henry P.	Maj USA	NY	11220
Rives, Wright	Maj USA	DC	12705
Rizer, Henry C.	Col. 3rd MD Infy	DC	16054
Rizer, Robert O'Neil	1st Lt. 2nd CA Cav	KS	16244
Roach, George H.	LTC 20th Infy USA	MO	05212
Roath, Warrington D.	Act Vol. Lt. USN	CA	11663
Robbins, Ambrose M.	1st Lt. Adj. 105th OH Infy	OH	09646
Robbins, Charles A.	Act Asst Paymaster USN	NY	04599
Robbins, Irvin	Maj 123rd IN Infy	IN	07043
Robbins, Nathaniel A.	1st Lt. RQM 4th ME Infy	DC	12256
Robbins, Walter R.	LTC 1st NJ Cav BvtBG	IL	05768
Robe, Charles F.	BG USA	CA	12290
Roberson, Theodore M.	Capt. 124th NY Infy	NY	16083
Robert, Henry M.	BG Chief Eng. USA	PA	05994
Robert, Hugh O.	Maj 95th PA Infy	PA	00478
Roberts, Benjamin K.	BG USA	NY	01683
Roberts, Cassius C.	1st Lt. 1st ME H Arty BvtCapt.	IL	14444
Roberts, Charles	2nd Lt. Sig. Corps USV	NY	08112
Roberts, Charles W.	Col. 2nd ME Infy BvtBG	ME	00453
Roberts, Charles W.	1st Lt. Adj. 17th ME Infy	ME	03010
Roberts, Charles W.	Capt. 124th PA Infy	PA	08234
Roberts, Cyrus S.	BG USA	OH	05390
Roberts, Edward E.	2nd Asst Eng. USN	NY	09312
Roberts, George H.	1st Lt. 9th ME Infy	ME	13615
Roberts, George M.	2nd Lt. 60th MA Infy	MA	11989
Roberts, Horatio	1st Lt. 1st MA Infy	MA	08340
Roberts, Jacob	Asst Surg. 23rd MA Infy	PA	04173
Roberts, James D.	1st Lt. Adj. 53rd OH Infy	OH	05748
Roberts, John	Capt. 3rd NJ Infy	PA	07649
Roberts, John H.	Capt. 2nd ME Cav	MA	01396
Roberts, John J.	1st Lt. 48th WI Infy	WI	11118
Roberts, John N.	Maj 6th OH Cav	KS	06363
Roberts, Joseph	Col. 4th Arty BvtBG USA	PA	04958
Roberts, Nathan B.	2nd Lt. Sig. Corps USV	NY	10765
Roberts, Robert B.	Col. 30th PA Infy	PA	00152
Roberts, Robert N.	Maj 38th WI Infy	WI	04297
Roberts, Thomas A.	2nd Lt. 53rd PA Infy	PA	05735
Roberts, Thomas B.	1st Lt. 1st WI Cav	NY	12556
Roberts, Thomas R.	Capt. 12th OH Infy	MI	08825
Roberts, William	Chief Eng. USN	MA	00594
Roberts, William H.	Act Ensign USN	CA	11664
Roberts, William P.	1st Lt. 45th USCT	MN	07702
Robertson, Gilbert A.	Passed Asst Paymaster USN	NY	02763
Robertson, James P.	Lt. Commander USN	PA	00906
Robertson, John	3rd Class (Adj. Gen. MI)	MI	05176
Robertson, Robert S.	1st Lt. 93rd NY Infy BvtCol.	IN	03059
Robertson, William S.	Maj 5th IA Infy	IA	04150

Name	Rank	Commandery	Insignia No.
Robeson, Andrew	Capt. 1st NY Eng. BvtMaj	MA	00874
Robeson, John T.	Capt. 7th TN Cav	NY	02051
Robie, Edward D.	Chief Eng. USN	DC	09215
Robie, Frederick	Maj Paymaster BvtLTC USV	ME	02394
Robins, Edward B.	1st Lt. 20th MA Infy BvtCapt.	MA	01145
Robins, Richard	Capt. 39th Infy USA	IL	01185
Robinson, Abram W.	Capt. 118th IL Infy	KS	15828
Robinson, Alfred N.	1st. Lt. RQM 5th OH Cav	DC	12104
Robinson, Augustus G.	LTC DQMG USA	MA	01809
Robinson, Charles	3rd Class (Gov. KS)	KS	06560
Robinson, Charles A.	Capt. 114th PA Infy	PA	00074
Robinson, Charles D.	Col. 50th WI Infy	WI	01554
Robinson, Charles H.	2nd Lt. 136th IL Infy	DC	11686
Robinson, Charles T.	1st Lt. 5th MA V.M.	MA	17150
Robinson, Daniel	Maj USA	IA	03670
Robinson, Edward M.	Capt. 12th ME Infy	ME	10616
Robinson, Erastus R.	Capt. USMC	NY	08359
Robinson, Frank U.	BG USA	CA	14756
Robinson, George	LTC Chap USA	DC	05283
Robinson, George F.	Capt. 80th OH Infy	OH	13962
Robinson, George F.	Capt. 89th IL Infy	IL	12998
Robinson, George F.	LTC USA	CA	10741
Robinson, George H.	2nd Lt. 2nd CA Cav	CA	11526
Robinson, George I.	Capt. Chi. Bd. of Trade Batt IL L Arty	IL	02777
Robinson, George T.	Capt. 10th Cav USA	PA	01347
Robinson, Gilbert P.	LTC 3rd MD Infy BvtCol.	NY	13220
Robinson, Henry S.	1st Lt. 36th MA Infy	MA	13169
Robinson, James B.	Act Ensign USN	MA	13471
Robinson, James S.	BG BvtMG USV	OH	05193
Robinson, John A.	1st Lt. 70th IL Infy	CA	02474
Robinson, John C.	MG USA	NY	01340
Robinson, John C.	2nd Lt. 104th PA Infy	PA	08761
Robinson, John H.	1st Lt. 45th MA Infy	MA	01390
Robinson, John L.	Surg. 8th MA Infy	MA	06996
Robinson, Lewis W.	RAdm USN	PA	02112
Robinson, Myron W.	Surg. 6th CT Infy	NY	12793
Robinson, Oscar D.	Capt. 9th NH Infy	NY	05834
Robinson, Richard W.E.	2nd Lt. 2nd NH Infy	CA	03914
Robinson, Robert K.	Surg. 7th MD Infy	DC	13037
Robinson, William A.	LTC 77th PA Infy BvtBG	PA	07872
Robinson, William A.	1st Lt. 2nd MA Cav	CA	02475
Robinson, William M.	Capt. 26th MO Infy	MI	06809
Robinson, William W.	Col. 7th WI Infy	WA	11734
Robinson, William W., Jr.	LTC DQMG USA	WA	10349
Robison, Andrew R.	Capt. 39th OH Infy	OH	04399
Roby, William	Capt. 58th OH Infy	OH	14512
Rochester, Montgomery	LTC AAG USV	NY	04402
Rochester, William B.	BG Paymaster Gen. USA	DC	02610

The Roster

Name	Rank	Commandery	Insignia No.
Rockafeller, Henry	Capt. 21st VRC BvtLTC	NY	00530
Rockafellow, Benjamin F.	Capt. 6th MI Cav	CO	13519
Rockefeller, Charles M.	Maj 6th Infy USA	CA	03896
Rockwell, Alfred P.	Col. 6th CT Infy BvtBG	MA	01033
Rockwell, Almon F.	LTC DQMG USA	PA	02348
Rockwell, Alphonso D.	Surg. 6th OH Cav	NY	06633
Rockwell, Bertrand	Capt. 34th IA Infy	KS	04753
Rockwell, Charles H.	RAdm USN	MA	05004
Rockwell, Charles H.	Capt. AQM USV	CA	06929
Rockwell, Cleveland	Capt. Vol. ADC	OR	01894
Rockwell, Joseph P.	Capt. 18th CT Infy	MA	03679
Rockwell, Justus O.	1st Lt. 97th OH Infy	WA	14694
Rockwood, Aaron L.	Capt. 4th IL Cav	CA	09834
Rockwood, William T.	Capt. 8th MN Infy	NY	06224
Rodenbough, Theoph. F.	BG USA	NY	10657
Rodger, John A.	RAdm USN	MD	18000
Rodgers, Andrew D.	Maj Paymaster USV	OH	07840
Rodgers, C.R.P.	RAdm USN	NY	00571
Rodgers, Frederick	RAdm USN	NY	00690
Rodgers, James B.	1st Lt. RQM 109th PA Infy	PA	00017
Rodgers, John F.	Capt. USA	DC	04475
Rodgers, John H.	Surg. 104th OH Infy	OH	04568
Rodgers, John L.	BG USA	DC	12379
Rodgers, Theopolis P.	1st Lt. 46th IN Infy	KS	05059
Rodgers, Thomas B.	LTC 104th PA Infy	MO	07808
Rodman, Charles W.	1st Lt. 4th NY Infy	NY	08360
Rodman, Thomas R.	Capt. 38th MA Infy	MA	06916
Rodney, George B.	BG USA	PA	00970
Roe, Francis A.	Commodore USN	NY	00330
Roe, John H.	Capt. 104th USCT	NE	06698
Roe, Robert S.	1st Lt. Adj. 2nd CO Cav	CO	05628
Roebling, Washington A.	Maj ADC BvtCol. USV	PA	08762
Roehr, Henry E.	1st Lt. 20th NY Infy	NY	10970
Roemer, Paul	Capt. 5th Arty USA	PA	02111
Roeschlaub, Robert S.	Capt. 84th IL Infy	CO	07487
Rogers, Andrew J.	Capt. 25th NJ Infy	NY	14522
Rogers, Charles D.	Capt. 24th WI Infy	WI	03685
Rogers, Earl M.	1st Lt. 6th WI Infy BvtMaj	WI	04451
Rogers, Edward W.	Capt. 19th Batt NY L Arty BvtLTC	NY	11752
Rogers, Elisha T.	1st Lt. Cass Co. Home Guard MO Cav	MO	05970
Rogers, Fordyce H.	1st Lt. 1st MI Cav	MI	03421
Rogers, George D.	LTC 31st WI Infy	MN	12089
Rogers, George W.	1st Lt. 3rd NY Infy	NY	11109
Rogers, George W.	Act Vol. Lt. USN	PA	00596
Rogers, H. C.	BvtBG USV	NY	01048
Rogers, Henry G.	2nd Lt. 24th WI Infy	WI	14021
Rogers, Henry M.	Act Asst Paymaster USN	MA	00853
Rogers, Horace B.	2nd LT VRC	MI	04006

Name	Rank	Commandery	Insignia No.
Rogers, Horatio	Col. 2nd RI Infy BvtBG	MA	05369
Rogers, Isaac N.	Capt. 177th OH Infy	CO	06945
Rogers, J. Sumner	Capt. 31st ME Infy BvtMaj	MI	03742
Rogers, James H.	Act Ensign USN	MA	11419
Rogers, James S.	Capt. 1st SC Volunteers	MA	06186
Rogers, Orville F.	Asst Surg. 117th USCT	MA	05567
Rogers, Robert M.	Maj USA	ME	03083
Rogers, Theodore S.	Capt. 105th IL Infy	IL	05554
Rogers, William	Act Ensign USN	ME	11772
Rogers, William F.	Col. 21st NY Infy BvtBG	NY	01051
Rogers, William P.	BG USA	DC	02941
Rogers, William W.	Capt. 14th Infy BvtLTC USA	CA	03660
Rohrbacher, Paul F.	Capt. 77th PA Infy	PA	09777
Roler, Edward G.F.	Surg. 51st IL Infy	IL	01950
Roller, William C.	Maj 23rd PA Infy	PA	01405
Roller, William W.	Capt. 64th NY Infy	CO	05782
Rollins, Henry G.	1st Lt. 48th MA Infy	CA	06933
Rollins, Nathaniel	Capt. 2nd WI Infy	CO	09444
Rolls, William H.	Capt. 5th MI Cav BvtMaj	MI	11880
Rolph, Albert H.	Capt. 14th USCT	MI	14825
Romeyn, Henry	Maj USA	DC	04231
Roney, J. W.	1st Lt. 1st US Vet. Vol. Infy	PA	00085
Rood, Henry H.	1st Lt. Adj. 13th IA Infy	IA	04852
Roome, Charles	Col. 37th Infy NY St. Milita BvtBG	NY	01834
Roome, William P.	Capt. AAG BvtMaj USV	NY	05303
Rooney, Charles A.	1st Lt. 1st NY L Arty	MI	08597
Roosevelt, Nicholas L.	Lt. USN	NY	01840
Roosevelt, Theodore, Sr.	3rd Class (Soldiers sending pay home)	PA	00166
Root, George F.	3rd Class (Composer, Civil War Songs)	IL	06213 (Dup)
Roots, Logan H.	Capt. CS BvtLTC USV	MO	05319
Roper, George S.	Capt. CS BvtMaj USV	IL	03142
Roper, John L.	Capt. CS BvtMaj USV	DC	08006
Ropes, James M.	Capt. 8th Cav BvtMaj USA	CA	08878
Ropes, John C.	3rd Class (Founder Mil. Hist. Soc. MA)	MA	01134
Rorick, Dave	1st Lt. 31st IA Infy	MO	04021
Rose, Elisha D.	1st Lt. 8th KS Infy	KS	06358
Rose, Francis M.	Surg. 43rd OH Infy	MN	07106
Rose, Stephen C.	Capt. 40th MA Infy	MA	04468
Rose, Thomas E.	Col. 77th PA Infy BvtBG	CA	05389
Rose, William H.	1st Lt. Adj. 54th PA Infy	PA	10876
Rosecrans, William S.	MG USV	Dc	01804
Rosencranz, Albert C.	Maj 4th IN Cav	IN	13893
Rosenmiller, David P.	Act Master USN	PA	05506
Ross, Charles H.	1st Lt. Adj. 13th IN Infy BvtMaj	WI	03190
Ross, Fred A.	Capt. 133rd IN Infy	IN	11804
Ross, H.E.	BvtBG USV	DC	02681
Ross, Henry S.	Capt. USN	NY	11340
Ross, James R.	Maj ADC BvtLTC USV	IN	06608

Name	Rank	Commandery	Insignia No.
Ross, John	Act Ensign USN	CA	02921
Ross, John W.	2nd Lt. 23rd Batt IN L Arty	IN	12536
Ross, John W.	Act Ensign USN	IA	06860
Ross, Leonard F.	BG USV	IL	11977
Ross, Levi A.	Capt. 86th IL Infy	CA	13836
Ross, Orlando H.	Capt. ADC USV	DC	05944
Ross, William L.	1st Lt. 64th NY Infy	MA	08550
Rosseter, Lemuel	Capt. 6th US Vet. Vol. Infy	CA	00086
Rossing, Torkild A.	Capt. 15th WI Infy	IA	10294
Rost, Charles	1st Lt. RQM 20th MA Infy	IL	11282
Rothrock, Joseph T.	Capt. 20th PA Cav	PA	14265
Round, George C.	2nd Lt. Sig. Corps. USA	DC	15839
Roundy, Daniel C.	Surg. 37th WI Infy	IL	08561
Rourke, Patrick F.	Capt. 28th PA Infy	PA	13125
Rouse, Gaylor	2nd Lt. 10th NY H Arty	CA	14605
Rouse, John D.	Capt. 130th IL Infy	OH	15709
Rousseau, Charles D.	Capt. 7th NY Cav	NY	05820
Routt, John L.	Capt. AQM USV	CA	07491
Rouzer, John R.	Capt. 6th MD Infy BvtLTC	Dc	14259
Row, Samuel H.	1st Lt. 20th MI Infy	MI	09480
Rowan, Stephen C.	V Adm. USN	DC	00329-2510
Rowe, David W.	LTC 126th PA Infy	PA	16455
Rowe, George Max.	Capt. 5th MI Infy	OR	04855
Rowell, Edward T.	Maj 2nd Shpshtrs. USA	MA	01814
Rowell, Eliphalet	Maj Paymaster USV	ME	10473
Rowland, John H.	Commander USN	PA	00502
Rowland, Joseph G.	Maj 10th IL Infy	KS	12621
Rowley, George A.	1st Lt. 2nd Infy BvtCapt. USA	MO	07384
Rowley, James B.	1st Lt. 17th IL Infy	KS	05362
Rowley, Manley S.	1st Lt. Adj. 11th MI Cav	WI	13688
Rowley, Thomas A.	BG USV	PA	02343
Rowley, William W.	Capt. 28th NY Infy	WI	07437
Roy, James	1st Lt. Adj. 152nd IL Infy	DC	13075
Roy, William	LTC 1st IN H Arty	CA	11062
Royal, Andrew	Capt. 32nd MO Infy	CO	08023
Royal, William	Capt. 9th USCT BvtMaj	CA	02865
Royall, William B.	Col. 4th Cav BvtBG USA	PA	00191
Royce, Alfred L.	Chap USN	PA	09281
Royce, Charles H.	1st Lt. 57th MA Infy BvtMaj	NY	11464
Royce, Clark E.	Col. 29th USCT	CA	02531
Royce, Harrison A.	Capt. AQM BvtCol. USV	MA	06508
Royer, Henry	Col. 53rd Infy PA Militia	PA	07650
Roys, Cyrus D.	1st Lt. 1st MI L Arty	IL	05608
Roys, Lester W.	1st Lt. 1st MI L Arty	WA	14840
Royse, Isaac H.C.	2nd Lt. 115th IL Infy	IN	06609
Rubey, Charles W.	Capt. 16th MO Cav	MO	05562
Ruby, William F.	1st Lt. RQM 154th IN Infy	IN	13706
Rucker, Daniel H.	BG QMG BvtMG USA	DC	13378

The Roster

Name	Rank	Commandery	Insignia No.
Rucker, Louis H.	BG USA	MO	04986
Rucker, William A.	Col. Asst Paymaster Gen. USA	MO	04810
Ruckle, Nicolas R.	Col. 148th IN Infy	IN	06610
Ruddock, William	1st Lt. 1st MI Shpshtrs.	MI	07576
Rudrauff, W.N.	2nd Lt. 82nd PA Infy	CA	15420
Ruff, Charles F.	LTC 3rd Cav BvtBG USA	PA	00688
Ruffner, Ernest H.	Col. Eng. USA	OH	16491
Ruger, Thomas H.	MG USA	NY	05584
Ruger, William	BvtMaj USV	WI	10508
Rugg, DeWitt C.	LTC 48th IN Infy	MO	08616
Ruggles, George D.	BG AdjG USA	DC	02398
Ruggles, James D.	1st Lt. 2nd WI Infy	CA	03340
Rugh, Jacob W.	1st Lt. 37th PA Infy	PA	12983
Ruhm, John	1st Lt. 15th USCT	PA	02590
Rule, William	1st Lt. Adj. 6th TN Infy	OH	04533
Rumford, Charles G.	1st Lt. 1st Batt DE L Arty	PA	07651
Rummell, Joseph P.	Capt. 120th OH Infy	OH	09087
Rumrill, Calvin H.	Maj 1st WA Infy	CA	01625
Rumsey, Henry D.	Lt. Commander USN	NE	04086
Rumsey, Israel P.	Capt. 1st IL L Arty	IL	02176
Rumsey, John W.	1st. Lt. 1st IL L Arty	IL	01995
Rumsey, William	Maj AAG BvtLTC USV	NY	00580
Rundell, Frank	LTC 100th OH Infy	OH	08838
Rundlet, Taylor P.	Capt. 38th MA Infy BvtMaj	IL	01631-1639
Rundlett, James C.	Capt. 128th USCT	ME	09378
Runkle, Benjamin P.	Col. 45th OH Infy BvtMG	OH	13173
Runyan, John N.	1st Lt. 74th IN Infy	IN	06611
Runyan, Theodore	BG NJ Militia	PA	05253
Ruple, George H.	2nd Lt. 13th IA Infy	CO	08959
Ruschenberger, William S.W.	Med. Director USN	PA	04957
Rusk, Jeremiah M.	LTC 25th WI Infy BvtBG	WI	02388
Rusling, James F.	Col. QM BvtBG USV	PA	02110
Russ, Edward K.	Capt. 1st & 2nd LA Cav	OH	17347
Russell, Alexander W.	Pay Director USN	PA	00313
Russell, Anthony O.	Maj 6th OH Infy	OH	10943
Russell, Charles B.	Capt. 6th OH Infy	OH	07431
Russell, Charles P.	Capt. 3rd MI Infy	MI	11299
Russell, Edmund K.	Maj 1st Arty USA	PA	01861
Russell, Edward J.	Capt. 3rd MA H Arty	MA	03501
Russell, George A.	2nd Lt. 21st ME Infy	ME	10743
Russell, George B.	LTC 14th Infy USA	MA	01007
Russell, Gerald	LTC USA	CO	08555
Russell, Henry C.	Act Asst Paymaster USN	IL	13702
Russell, Henry S.	Col. 5th MA Cav BvtBG	MA	01321
Russell, Horace A.	2nd Lt. 63rd NY Infy	CA	12276
Russell, Ira	Surg. BvtLTC USV	MA	02734
Russell, James M.	1st Lt. Adj.118th OH Infy	OH	07205
Russell, John H.	RAdm USN	DC	03596

THE ROSTER 345

Name	Rank	Commandery	Insignia No.
Russell, John H.	1st Lt. 38th USCT	CA	03910
Russell, John K.	Capt. AQM USV	NY	08661
Russell, Martin J.	1st Lt. Adj. 23rd IL Infy	IA	02189
Russell, Milton	Capt. 51st IN Infy	IA	05433
Russell, Roswell M.	LTC 9th PA Cav	PA	08990
Russell, Thomas P.	Asst Surg. 1st WI Infy	WI	04453
Russell, William H.	1st Lt. 17th MI Infy	NE	12921
Russell, William H.H.	LTC 4th WVA Infy	CA	02532
Rust, Henry	Col. 15th ME Infy BvtBG	MA	01708
Rust, Henry A.	Maj 27th IL Infy	IL	02011
Ruth, James	Capt. 6th IA Cav	IA	09684
Ruth, Melancthon L.	Surg. USN	DC	03812
Rutherford, Joseph C.	Surg. 17th VT Infy	DC	08320
Rutherford, Robert G.	Capt. BvtLTC USA	DC	10339
Rutherford, William H.	Chief Eng. USN	DC	10340
Ryan, Abraham H.	Col. 3rd AR Cav	NY	00775
Ryan, David	Capt. 8th IA Infy	IA	11144
Ryan, George	Capt. 47th IL Infy	CO	07669
Ryan, John R.T.	2nd Lt. 10th NJ Infy	PA	06771
Ryan, John W.	1st Lt. 34th IN Infy	IN	06612
Ryan, Thomas	Capt. 141st PA Infy	DC	12706
Ryan, William	1st Lt. 99th NY Infy	CA	05678
Ryder, Seth B.	Capt. 5th NY Cav	NY	07091
Rynearson, Sylvester	Capt. 15th IA Infy	OH	16235
Rynex, Richard C.	1st Lt. RQM 23rd MO Infy	Dc	13685
Sabin, Albert R.	Capt. 9th VT Infy	IL	08294
Sabin, Alvin N.	Capt. 5th MI Cav BvtMaj	MI	07575
Sabin, George M.	1st Lt. Adj. 5th WI Infy	CA	03334
Sabin, John A.	Maj Paymaster BvtLTC USV	MN	04232
Sabin, Marden	Capt. 100th IN Infy	MI	14555
Sacket, Delos B.	BG BvtMG Ins. Gen. USA	DC	01526
Sackett, Augustine	2nd Asst Eng. USN	NY	11852
Sackett, Frederic M.	1st Lt. 1st RI L Arty	MA	01538
Safford, Benjamin D.	Capt. 17th MI Infy BvtMaj	MI	14185
Safford, Charles H.	Capt. 5th MI Cav BvtMaj	MI	07395
Safford, Darius J.	LTC 1st VT H Arty	DC	07903
Safford, James B.	1st Lt. 10th IN Cav	IN	06903
Sage, Clinton H.	Col. 110th NY Infy	NY	14832
Sage, Wilbur H.	1st Lt. Adj. 3rd OH Infy	OH	07529
Sahm, Siegfried	1st Lt. 119th IN Infy	WA	08624
Sailer, John	2nd Lt. Keystone Batt PA L Arty	PA	04959
Saint, Albert W.	1st Lt. 36th IN Infy	IN	16452
SaintAlbe, Gustavus A.F.	Capt. ADC USV	NY	12728
SaintJohn, Herman D.	2nd Lt. 46th IA Infy	IA	13908 (Dup)
Sale, John W.	2nd Lt. 24th IN Infy	IN	15623
Salomon, Edward S.	Col. 82nd IL Infy BvtBG	CA	03332
Saltonstall, William G.	Act Vol. Lt. Commander USN	MA	01902
Sample, Nathaniel W.	1st Lt. 15th PA Cav	PA	06939

The Roster

Name	Rank	Commandery	Insignia No.
Sampson, Archibald J.	1st Lt. 27th USCT BvtCapt.	CO	05630
Sampson, Augustus N.	1st Lt. 13th MA Infy	MA	01670
Sampson, Charles M.	BvtMaj AQM USV	CA	17083
Sampson, Ira B.	Capt. 2nd MA H Arty	NY	02377
Sampson, John B.	2nd Lt. 194th OH Infy	OH	12917
Sampson, William A.	Capt. 66th OH Infy	IN	11646
Sampson, William T.	RAdm USN	DC	08387
Sanborn, Augustus D.	Capt. 5th NH Infy	NY	06233
Sanborn, James A.	Capt. 10th NH Infy	MA	13748
Sanborn, John B.	BG BvtMG USV	MN	03493
Sanborn, Peter B.	1st Lt. 1st US Shpshtrs.	MI	06535
Sanborn, Washngton I.	Maj 35th Infy USA	CA	00763
Sanders, Charles	1st Lt. 48th MA Infy	MA	08859
Sanders, Henry P.	Capt. 151st NY Infy	DC	13379
Sanders, Wilbur F.	1st Lt. Adj. 64th OH Infy	DC	08516
Sanders, William H.	1st Lt. 4th USC H Arty	CA	17255
Sanders, William N.S.	Capt. 3rd NY Infy	NY	12321
Sanderson, Edward	3rd Class	WI	05573
Sanderson, Frederick M.	Capt. 21st MA Infy	OH	06078
Sanderson, Ira L.	1st Lt. 31st NJ Infy	NE	07546
Sanderson, James W.	Capt. 189th OH Infy	IN	13813
Sanderson, John W.	Act Ensign USN	DC	16620
Sanderson, Joseph W.	Capt. 3rd PA H Arty	WI	03191
Sanderson, Thomas W.	Col. 10th OH Cav BvtBG	OH	04391
Sandes, Henry R.	1st Lt. Adj. 3rd WI Cav	IL	09084
Sands, Charles J.	Capt. 6th NY H Arty	NY	08361
Sands, Francis P.B.	Act Master USN	DC	05333
Sands, James H.	RAdm USN	DC	15892
Sands, Louis J.	Act Asst Paymaster USN	MA	06007
Sanford, George B.	Col. 6th Cav USA	NY	02922
Sanford, George P.	Maj Paymaster BvtLTC USV	MI	04717
Sanford, Hugh S.	Capt. 115th NY Infy BvtMaj	MI	09967
Sanford, Joseph P.	Capt. USN	NY	01020
Sanford, Oliver S.	Maj 7th CT Infy	DC	07680
Sanger, Eugene F.	Surg. BvtLTC USV	ME	01700
Sanger, Joseph P.	MG USA	DC	00226
Sankey, John G.	Act Asst Paymaster USN	PA	07652
Sanno, James M.J.	BG USA	KS	03546
Sansoni, Anthony J.	1st Lt. 8th CA Infy	KS	13888
Sappington, Nicholas J.	Capt. CS BvtMaj USV	MD	12031
Sargent, Bailey	1st. Lt. 2nd MA H Arty	MA	14183
Sargent, Charles S.	Capt. ADC BvtMaj USV	MA	02118
Sargent, Daniel	1st Lt. 24th MA Infy	MA	01382
Sargent, Edward P.	1st Lt. 26th IA Infy	MA	07687
Sargent, Horace Binney	Col. 1st MA Cav BvtBG	MA	00676
Sargent, Hosea Q.	Capt. 12th NH Infy	OH	05671
Sargent, John	Capt. 51st OH Infy	IL	09204
Sarratt, James F.	Maj 2nd OH Infy	OH	10678

Name	Rank	Commandery	Insignia No.
Sarson, Horace B.	Capt. 2nd Infy USA	NE	05107
Satterfield, John	1st Lt. 140th PA Infy	NY	07087
Satterlee, Dwight	Asst Surg. 11th CT Infy	CA	14617
Satterthwaite, J. Fisher	1st Lt. Adj. 22nd NJ Infy	NY	09433
Saunders, Alvin	3rd Class (Gov. NB)	NE	04828
Saunders, Caleb	1st Lt. 1st MA H Arty	MA	13084
Saunders, Edwin	Capt. 29th MI Infy	MI	10594
Savage, Edward G.	LTC 9th PA Cav	KS	06788
Savage, Egbert B.	LTC 13th Infy USA	CA	02911
Savage, James W.	Col. 12th NY Cav	NE	03923
Savage, Robert H.	1st Lt. 72nd NY Infy	PA	09286
Savage, William R.	1st Lt. 1st CA Cav	CA	12590
Savery, John E.	Capt. 75th NY Infy	NY	12136
Saville, James R.	1st Lt. 3rd MI Infy	CO	02775
Sawtelle, Arthur M.	Act Asst Eng. USN	CA	17816
Sawtelle, Charles G.	BG QMG USA	PA	01276
Sawyer, Charles H.	Act Ensign USN	CA	04695
Sawyer, Charles H.	Act Ensign USN	ME	09098
Sawyer, Charles. F.	Capt. 20th ME Infy	DC	02827
Sawyer, Frederic A.	Surg. 52nd MA Infy	MA	01633
Sawyer, Horatio B.	1st Lt. 8th ME Infy	ME	09702
Sawyer, Hudson	Capt. 1st ME H Arty BvtMaj	ME	13639
Sawyer, Iram A.	2nd Lt. 60th USCT	IA	11376
Sawyer, J. Estcourt	LTC DQMG USA	NY	00744
Sawyer, James	Capt. CS BvtMaj USV	WI	01555
Sawyer, Nathaniel C.	Maj Paymaster BvtLTC USV	DC	08064
Sawyer, Wesley C.	Capt. 23rd MA Infy	CA	09837
Sawyer, William H.	Capt. 36th MA Infy	MA	15002
Saxton, Rufus	BG BvtMG USV	DC	02467
Saxton, S. Willard	Capt. ADC BvtMaj USV	DC	09216
Saxton, William	Capt. 157th NY Infy	CA	17265
Sayer, Daniel	1st Lt. 7th OH Cav	CA	15188
Sayler, Henry B.	Maj 118th IN Infy	IN	07694
Sayles, Thomas W.	Capt. 3rd RI Cav	CA	17621
Saylor, Benjamin	Capt. CS BvtMaj USV	PA	06772
Saylor, John A.	2nd Lt. 95th PA Infy	PA	13667
Sayre, Hal	Maj 3rd CO Cav	CO	07738
Scantling, John C.	LTC USA	DC	03518
Scarborough	Maj 104th PA Infy	PA	08763
Scarlett, Joseph A.	Ensign USN	OH	04191
Schaefer, Christian H.	Capt. 56th OH Infy	OH	10462
Schaff, Morris	Capt. Ordnance USA	MA	04385
Schaffnit, Henry	2nd Lt. 10th IL Infy	CO	15856
Schall, George	1st Lt. 51st PA Infy	PA	08235
Schall, John W.	Col. 87th PA Infy (Col. 6th PA Infy)	PA	04181
Schauffler, Edward W.	Capt. 127th NY Infy	MO	05050
Schaurte, Frederick W.	LTC 2nd Indian Home Guard KS Infy	MO	04990
Schayer, George F.	Capt. VRC BvtLTC	DC	00974

Name	Rank	Commandery	Insignia No.
Scheffer, Albert	1st Lt. 43rd WI Infy	MN	03497
Schefler, William	Capt. ADC USV	CA	03239
Schell, Henry S.	Capt. Asst Surg. BvtLTC USA	PA	01954
Schenck, Alexander D.	LTC Arty USA	IL	04326
Schenck, Caspar	Pay Director USN	CA	00660
Schenck, Peter V.	Capt. Asst Surg. BvtMaj USA	PA	00463
Schenck, Robert C.	MG USV	DC	02661
Schenck, Washington L.	Surg. 17th OH Infy	KS	14082
Schenck, William T. Y.	Capt. 110th USCT	CA	02914
Schenk, John	Capt. AQM USV	MO	03800
Schenkelberger, Jacob	2nd Lt. 1st NY L Arty	NY	09958
Schermerhorn, E. Nott	1st Lt. Adj. 18th NY Infy	NY	10658
Schermerhorn, F. Aug.	1st Lt. 185th NY Infy BvtCapt.	NY	09434
Schieffelin, Willilam H.	Maj 1st NY Mounted Rifles	NY	00735
Schindler, William F.B.	1st Lt. 2nd CA Infy	CA	03116
Schlaudecker, Matthew	Col. 111th PA Infy	CA	10302
Schley, John	Capt. 4th MD Infy	IN	13624
Schley, Winfield Scott	RAdm USN	NY	09233
Schmitt, Carl	Maj 22nd IN Infy	KS	06362
Schmucker, Francis R.	Capt. 128th PA Infy	PA	10401
Schneider, Frederick	LTC 2nd MI Infy	MI	12922
Schneider, William	LTC 13th OH Infy	OH	10023
Schnitger, Gustave	Maj 2nd IA Cav	CO	09885
Schoales, Joseph D.	Surg. 12th PA Cav	PA	04175
Schober, Frederick	2nd Asst Eng. USN	PA	01853
Schoch, Martin L.	1st Lt. Adj. 51st PA Infy	PA	08764
Schofield, James	Hosp. Chap USA	CA	05327
Schofield, John M.	LTG USA	DC	01274
Schofield, Robert	Col. USV	WI	17513
Schoonmaker, Cornelius M.	Capt. USN	DC	03220 (Dup)
Schoonmaker, James M.	Col. 14th PA Cav	PA	05737
Schoonmaker, Joseph S.	Capt. 14th PA Cav	PA	07653
Schoonover, John	LTC 11th PA Infy BvtCol.	PA	09285 (Dup)
Schouler, James	2nd Lt. 43rd MA Infy	MA	09605
Schoyer, Samuel C.	Capt. 139th PA Infy	PA	07070
Schreiner, Herman	Maj BvtLTC USA	DC	13790
Schroeder, Edward L.	Capt. 5th MD Infy	PA	09284
Schultze, John G.	BvtCol. USV	PA	00200
Schuster, George	Col. ADC MO State Militia	MO	07747
Schuyler, Herman P.	1st Lt. 1st WI Infy	NY	01914
Schuyler, Philip	Capt. 14th Infy BvtMaj USA	NY	01249
Schwan, Theodore	BG USA	DC	04888
Schwartz, Edward	Maj 9th NY Cav	CA	09692
Schwartz, James E.	2nd Lt. 22nd USCT	PA	05995
Schwarz, George W.	Capt. 2nd PA Cav	OH	04996
Schwarz, Julius	2nd Lt. 2nd PA Cav	PA	06269
Scofield, Edward	Capt. 40th PA Infy BvtMaj	WI	05470
Scofield, James K.	Capt. CS BvtMaj USV	PA	03799

Name	Rank	Commandery	Insignia No.
Scofield, Levi T.	Capt. 103rd OH Infy	OH	02886
Scofield, Walter K.	Med. Director USN	NY	11450
Scot, John A.	Chief Engineer USN	PA	11021
Scott, Alexander H.	1st Lt. 12th MI Infy	MI	16854
Scott, Alexander M.	1st Lt. 43rd IN Infy	IN	08144
Scott, Anthony W.	1st Lt. 42nd USCT BvtMaj	KS	12329
Scott, David I.	1st Lt. 10th Infy USA	PA	00606
Scott, Douglas M.	Maj USA	DC	00900
Scott, Eben G.	1st Lt. 5th Arty USA	NY	01635
Scott, Gustavus H.	RAdm USN	PA	00539
Scott, Henry B.	LTC 4th MA Cav	IA	09969
Scott, John	Act Vol. Lt. USN	OH	09090
Scott, John N.	Maj Paymaster USV	WA	07753
Scott, John W.	Capt. 157th PA Infy BvtMaj	PA	13441
Scott, Joseph A.	Capt. 18th IN L Arty	KS	18004
Scott, Lemuel L.	Capt. 84th IL Infy	IL	07699
Scott, Robert N.	LTC 3rd Arty USA	DC	02346
Scott, Thomas R.	Capt. 174th NY Infy	DC	13957
Scott, Thomas W.	Capt. 98th IL Infy BvtMaj	IL	07557
Scott, William F.	1st Lt. Adj. 4th IA Cav	NY	09959
Scott, William M.	1st Lt. Adj. 13th WI Infy	OH	08906
Scott, Winfield	Maj Chap USA	CA	04621
Scott, Winfield	MG BvtLG USA	PA	00027
Scovill, Edward A.	LTC 128th OH Infy	OH	03065
Scoville, Frederick	Capt. 8th NY Cav	KS	05948
Scranton, Edwin E.	Capt. 65th OH Infy	OH	05675
Scribner, Benjamin F.	Col. 38th IN Infy BvtBG	IN	08395
Scribner, Wiley Smith	1st. Lt. RQM 16th WI Infy	IL	No Number
Scrymser, James A.	Capt. ADC USV	NY	03615
Scudder, Thomas W.	LTC 5th KS Cav	KS	16861
Scudder, William V.D.	Capt. 2nd NJ Cav	PA	03801
Sculley, James	1st Lt. 43rd USCT	PA	09505 (Dup)
Scully, James W.	BG USA	OH	07413
Scully, Thomas	Chap 9th MA Infy	MA	11618
Scupham, John R.	1st Lt. 1st MO Eng	CA	02154
Seagrave, Charles S.	1st Lt. 25th MA Infy	MA	11744
Seaman, Marinus W.	Surg. 122nd IL Infy	CO	07002
Seamans, William H.	Capt. 3rd MA Cav	CA	01613
Searle, Charles P.	Capt. 8th IA Infy	IA	08868
Searle, Daniel W.	1st Lt. Adj. 141st PA Infy	PA	07352
Searles, James M.	Capt. 38th WI Infy	IA	07447
Searles, Joseph N.	Capt. 1st MN Infy	MN	05429
Sears, Alfred F.	Maj 1st NY Eng.	OR	06192
Sears, Clinton B.	LTC Eng. USA	NY	01843
Sears, Cyrus	LTC 49th USCT	OH	15456
Sears, Edward H.	Capt. 2nd RI Infy	MA	01520
Sears, George C.	2nd Lt. 8th CA Infy	OR	04188
Sears, Joseph A.	1st Lt. RQM 147th IL Infy	IL	07390

Name	Rank	Commandery	Insignia No.
Sears, Robert B.	Capt. 43rd IN Infy	IN	13625
Sears, William B.	Capt. 2nd RI Infy	MA	01510
Seaton, John	Capt. 22nd IL Infy	KS	08530
Seaver, James E.	1st Lt. 7th MA Infy	MA	11588
Seaverns, Joel	Surg. BvtLTC USV	MA	02599
Seavey, Webber S.	Capt. 5th IA Cav	WA	14485
Seaward, Benjamin	1st Lt. Adj. 48th NY Infy BvtCapt.	NY	04058
Seawell, Washington	Col. 6th Infy BvtBG USA	CA	03096
Seay, Abraham J.	LTC 32nd MO Infy	MO	05209
Sebree, Uriel	RAdm USN	CA	16252
Sechler, Thomas M.	1st Lt. 2nd OH H Arty	OH	03253
Secord, James K.	Capt. 77th IL Infy	CA	06932 (Dup)
Sedam, Walker Y.	Act 1st Asst Eng. USN	CO	06526
See, John J.	1st Lt. 8th MO Cav	WA	17959
Seeley, Francis W.	Capt. 4th Arty USA	MN	05264
Seeley, Thomas	Capt. 4th IA Infy	IA	11507
Seely, Franklin A.	Capt. AQM BvtLTC USV	DC	05898
Seely, Henry B.	Capt. USN	PA	05738
Seesholtz, Isaac H.	Capt. 118th PA Infy	PA	11329
Seibert, Charles	2nd Lt. 62nd PA Infy	MO	10930
Seibert, Jacob M.	1st Lt. 93rd PA Infy	CA	12604
Seibold, Louis P.	2nd Lt. "Pernell Legion" MD Infy	DC	15527
Selbert, Albert	Capt. 183rd OH Infy	OH	05667
Selfridge, James L.	BvtBG USV	PA	00282
Selfridge, Thomas O.	RAdm USN	DC	00610-6854
Selkirk, George H.	LTC 49th NY Infy	NY	14912
Sellers, Alfred J.	Maj 90th PA Infy BvtCol.	PA	00918
Sellers, Edwin E.	Capt. 10th US Infy	PA	00066
Sellers, Henry E.	1st Lt. 18th ME Infy	ME	10934
Sellew, George E.	1st Lt. 6th USCT Infy	NY	14913
Sellmer, Charles	Capt. 11th ME Infy BvtLTC	DC	03667
Sells, Elijah	Act Vol. Lt. USN	CA	04868
Sells, Michael	1st Lt. 59th OH Infy	DC	09217
Sells, William H.	Asst Paymaster USN	CA	04760
Selvage, Henry C.	2nd Lt. 87th NY Infy	NY	08802
Semple, Alexander C.	Capt. AAG USV	OH	12421
Senat, George L.	2nd Lt. 17th PA Infy	PA	08236
Sensner, George W.	Chief Eng. USN	DC	13513
Seran, William L.	Capt. 125th USCT	CA	17817
Serrill, Edward W.	BvtBG USV	NY	06228
Sessions, John Q.A.	1st Lt. 7th MI Cav	MI	11877
Seton, William	Capt. 4th NY Infy	NY	10659
Severance, LaGrange	1st Lt. Adj. 12th ME Infy	IN	07695
Severance, Martin J.	Capt. 10th MN Infy	MN	05929
Seville, William P.	Capt. 1st DE Infy	DC	14534
Sewall, Frederick D.	Col. 19th ME Infy BvtBG	ME	04730
Sewall, John S.	Chap 8th MA Infy	ME	08083 (Dup)
Sewall, Thomas	Capt. 127th IL Infy	NE	05646

Name	Rank	Commandery	Insignia No.
Seward, Samuel H.	1st Lt. 14th CT Infy	NY	11633
Seward, William H.	BG USV	NY	04696
Seward, William H.	3rd Class (Secretary of State)	PA	00050
Seward, William T.	Capt. CS BvtMaj USV	DC	06668
Sewell, George	Chief Eng. USN	NY	01155
Sewell, William J.	Col. 38th NJ Infy BvtMG	PA	00811
Sexton, James A.	Capt. 72nd IL Infy	IL	02792
Sexton, Marshall	Surg. 52nd IN Infy	IN	07931
Sexton, Samuel	Asst Surg. 8th OH Infy	NY	06167
Sexton, William H.	1st Lt. RQM 83rd IL Infy	IL	13985
Seyburn, Isaac D.	Act Master USN	DC	03587
Seymour, Elisha W.	Capt. 116th NY Infy	NY	13760
Seymour, Frederick S.	1st Lt. 14th CT Infy	IL	08865
Seymour, Isaac	1st Lt. 2nd NY Cav	MN	04935
Seymour, William C.	Act Ensign USN	CA	09696
Seys, Henry H.	Surg. 15th OH Infy	OH	14272
Shackford, William G.	Act Ensign USN	NY	07471
Shaffer, A. Webster	Capt. 44th NY Infy BvtLTC	DC	08818
Shaffer, Onesimus P.	2nd Lt. 19th OH Infy	OH	10704
Shaffer, William F.	LTC 2nd MO Cav	DC	03817
Shafter, John N.	Capt. 19th MI Infy	MI	16560
Shafter, William R.	MG USA	CA	05178
Shaler, Alexander	BG BvtMG USV	NY	00641
Shaler, Charles	Col. Ordnance USA	IN	02226
Shallenberger, George A.	LTC QM USV	DC	09938
Shallenberger, William S.	1st Lt. Adj. 140th PA Infy	DC	12181
Shanbacher, Jacob H.	1st Lt. 207th PA Infy	PA	12775
Shanks, Thomas P.	1st Lt. 9th KY Cav	OH	04538
Shannon, James H.	Capt. 1st AL & TN Indpt. Vol. Cav	ME	16188
Shannon, Richard C.	Capt. AAG BvtLTC USV	NY	04911
Sharman, Charles H.	1st Lt. Adj. 33rd IA Infy	MO	06418
Sharp, Alonzo G.	Capt. 46th OH Infy	OH	09454
Sharp, Thomas	Maj 17th Infy USA	PA	04418
Sharpe, Alexander B.	Capt. ADC BvtCol. USV	PA	04670
Sharpe, George H.	Col. 120th NY Infy BvtMG	NY	01077
Sharpe, Jacob	Col. 156th NY Infy BvtBG	NY	00741
Shatswell, Nathaniel	LTC 1st MA H Arty BvtCol.	DC	12827
Shattuc, William B.	1st Lt. 2nd OH Cav	OH	04746
Shattuck, Charles C.	Capt. 1st NH H Arty	CA	03464
Shattuck, Lorenzo B.	Capt. 35th NY Infy	IL	03703
Shattuck, Samuel W.	Capt. 6th VT Infy	IL	10999
Shaughnessey, Michael	1st Lt. 47th IL Infy	CA	05067
Shaum, Benjamin F.	Bvt Capt. USV	MO	16968
Shaut, William B.	LTC 131st PA Infy	CA	04898
Shaw, Abner O.	Surg. 20th ME Infy	ME	00669
Shaw, Charles F.	2nd Lt. 38th ME Infy	MA	05801
Shaw, Elijah M.	Capt. 10th ME Infy	ME	02618
Shaw, George K.	Capt. 43rd WI Infy	MN	06349

The Roster

Name	Rank	Commandery	Insignia No.
Shaw, George R.	Capt. 75th IL Infy	IL	08428
Shaw, Henry G.	1st Lt. 125th OH Infy	CA	01628
Shaw, Horace H.	1st Lt. 1st ME H Arty	ME	10744
Shaw, James	Col. 7th USCT BvtBG	MA	01598
Shaw, John M.	Capt. 25th WI Infy	MN	05861
Shaw, John O.	Act Ensign USN	ME	10247
Shaw, John W.	1st Lt. 46th OH Infy	DC	09034
Shaw, William L.	Capt. 110th OH Infy BvtMaj	OH	04195
Shaw, William T.	Col. 14th IA Infy	IA	05480
Sheafer, Henry J.	Maj 107th PA Infy BvtCol.	PA	10400
Sheafer, James	Col. 101st PA Infy	PA	07351
Shedd, Lorenzo W.	1st Lt. 9th USCT	VT	09193
Sheen, William G.	Capt. 39th MA Infy BvtMaj	MA	01467
Sheets, John C.	1st Lt. 10th OH Cav	OH	16443
Sheets, Levi D.	Asst Surg. BvtCapt. USV	NY	10546
Sheldon, Alvanus W.	Capt. CS BvtLTC USV	NY	01634
Sheldon, George C.	Capt. 16th MI Infy	MI	05660
Sheldon, Harley G.	2nd Lt. 14th VT Infy	VT	14104
Sheldon, Henry N.	1st Lt. 55th MA Infy	MA	12070
Sheldon, John A.	Capt. CS USV	VT	09190
Sheldon, William A.	Capt. 6th NY Cav	NY	09435
Sheley, George A.	2nd Lt. Batt M. MI L Arty	MI	03872
Shellenberger, John K.	Capt. 64th OH Infy	MN	04540
Shelley, William F.	Capt. 147th IN Infy	IN	07273
Shelly, Thomas C.	1st Lt. 15th IL Infy	NE	12190
Shelton, Eugene E.	Capt. CS BvtMaj USV	MA	01070
Shelton, William H.	1st Lt. 1st NY L Arty	NY	16007
Shepard, Charles O.	1st Lt. 82nd NY Infy	NY	01787
Shepard, Edward O.	Maj 32nd MA Infy BvtLTC	MA	01034
Shepard, Edwin M.	RAdm USN	DC	06473
Shepard, James E.	1st Lt. Adj. 9th ME Infy	MA	05028
Shepherd, Charles H.	1st Lt. 9th Infy USA	PA	01042
Shepley, George F.	BG USV	MA	00281
Sheppard, Lewis D.	Capt. 9th NJ Infy	IA	09686
Sheppard, Morris F.	Capt. 16th NY H Arty	NY	05821
Sherburne, John H.	1st. Lt. USMC	MA	01560
Sherer, Edward	1st Lt. Adj. 159th NY Infy	NY	13454
Sherer, Samuel B.	Maj 15th IL Cav	IL	02319
Sheridan, Michael V.	BG USA	DC	02796
Sheridan, Millard J.	Capt. 65th USCT	IL	07146
Sheridan, Philip H.	General USA	DC	00750
Sherlock, Samuel H.	Capt. 94th OH Infy	OH	09818
Sherman, Buren R.	Capt. 13th IA Infy	IA	05437
Sherman, Charles L.	1st Lt. USMC	PA	00695
Sherman, Duncan	1st Lt. 1st Cav USA	PA	01044
Sherman, Edgar J.	Capt. 48th MA Infy BvtMaj	MA	01184
Sherman, Elijah B.	2nd Lt. 9th VT Infy	IL	04637
Sherman, Francis T.	BG USV	IL	05555

The Roster   353

Name	Rank	Commandery	Insignia No.
Sherman, Henry S.	1st Lt. Adj. 120th OH Infy	OH	03156
Sherman, Hoyt	Maj Paymaster USV	IA	04136
Sherman, James L.	1st Lt. 33rd MA Infy	MA	17992
Sherman, John	3rd Class (US Senator OH)	DC	04177 (Dup)
Sherman, Linus E.	Capt. 9th VT Infy	CO	10561
Sherman, Matthew	Capt. 4th CA Infy	CA	08879
Sherman, Thomas W.	MG USA	PA	00643
Sherman, William Tecumseh	General USA	OH	04567
Sherratt, John H.	Capt. 42nd USCT	IL	04505
Sherwin, Edward	Passed Asst Paymaster USN	MA	01687
Sherwin, Thomas	LTC 22nd MA Infy BvtBG	MA	01705
Sherwood, Isaac R.	Col. 111th OH Infy BvtBG	OH	08175
Sherwood, James E.	1st Lt. Adj. 34th IN Infy	OH	08178
Sherwood, Thomas H.	Surg. 27th PA Infy	DC	06694
Shields, David	Capt. 63rd PA Infy	PA	14373
Shields, John	Capt. 53rd PA Infy	PA	06474
Shields, Joseph C.	Capt. 19th Batt OH L Arty	OH	03197
Shields, William	Capt. VRC	PA	00277
Shimmel, August	Capt. AQM USV	NY	09313
Shipley, Howard W.	1st Lt. 91st PA Infy	PA	05996
Shipley, William J.	1st Lt. 1st OR Infy	OR	04778
Shipman, Stephen V.	Maj 1st WI Cav BvtCol.	IL	07391
Shippen, Edward	Med. Director USN	PA	00937
Shippen, Edward	Col. Med. Director USV	PA	01605
Shipton, James P.	1st Lt. Batt B VA L Arty	OH	12349
Shively, Joseph W.	Surg. USN	DC	03578
Shock, William H.	Chief Eng. USN	DC	00659-6376
Shockley, William B.	Maj 54th KY Infy	KS	04095
Shoemaker, Francis B.	2nd Lt. 150th OH Infy	OH	15887 (Dup)
Shoemaker, Michael	Col. 13th MI Infy	MI	04263
Shoemaker, William M.	1st Lt. 9th PA Cav	PA	11330
Shoenberger, John H.	3rd Class	PA	00609
Sholl, Alexander	Capt. 118th IL Infy	IL	09658
Shonnard, Frederic	Maj 6th NY H Arty	NY	07785
Shook, Edgar H.	Maj 5th MI Infy	MI	07742
Shoop, Samuel J.	Capt. 31st USCT	CO	14211
Shorkley, George	Maj BvtCol. USA	PA	00896
Short, Joseph C.	Asst Surg. USA	CA	05328
Shoup, George L.	Col. 3rd CO Cav	CA	04896
Showalter, John T.	Bvt 1st Lt. USV	KS	09323
Shrader, John C.	Surg. 22nd IA Infy	IA	07166
Shrady, John	Surg. 2nd TN Infy	NY	05408
Shreve, Jonathan R.	Maj 90th PA Infy	PA	00116
Shreve, William P.	1st Lt. 2nd US Shpshtrs. BvtMaj	MA	01208 (Dup)
Shryer, John G.	1st Lt. RQM 97th IN Infy	IN	13237
Shufeldt, Robert W.	RAdm USN	DC	02666
Shuler, Benjamin P.	Capt. 9th MN Infy	CA	05341
Shuman, George W.	Capt. 2nd MN Infy	MN	10009

Name	Rank	Commandery	Insignia No.
Shurly, Edmund R. P.	Capt. 26th NY Infy BvtLTC	IL	01998
Shurtleff, Giles W.	Col. 5th USCT BvtBG	OH	10017
Shurtleff, Hiram S.	Capt. 56th MA Infy	MA	00825
Shurtz, Elias W.	Capt. 196th PA Infy	PA	00018
Shute, Charles H.	1st Lt. RQM 2nd NH Infy	MA	06692
Shute, George M.	1st Lt. 2nd NH Infy	CO	10645
Sibley, Arthur	Act Asst Paymaster USN	MA	04260
Sibley, Ebenezer K.	Capt. 1st VT Cav BvtMaj	NY	06739
Sibley, Henry H.	BG BvtMG USV	MN	03498
Sibley, Hiram L.	1st Lt. 116th OH Infy	OH	08839
Sicard, Montgomery	RAdm USN	NY	01760
Sickel, Horatio G.	Col. 108th PA Infy BvtMG	PA	00012
Siddall, Joseph J.	1st Lt. Adj. 6th IN Infy	IL	01997
Sides, George E.	Capt. 2nd NH Infy	CA	08921
Sides, Robert C., Jr.	1st Lt. Adj. 2nd NH Infy	NY	10329
Siebert, John	Capt. 13th OH Infy	OH	05666
Siebert, Louis P.	Capt. AAG USV	DC	11372
Siefert, Joseph	1st Lt. 37th OH Infy	OH	12971
Sigler, David G.	2nd Lt. 6th IA Infy	IA	06690
Siglin, Jacob M.	2nd Lt. 8th IL Cav	OR	05166
Sigsbee, Charles D.	RAdm USN	DC	15391
Sill, Edward E.	Capt. AAG BvtMaj USV	NY	07978
Silloway, Jacob	1st Lt. 6th NY Infy	MA	01810
Silsby, Horace	1st Lt. 75th NY Infy	MI	04706
Silva, Valentine M.C.	Capt. 21st Infy USA	WA	14984
Simmons, George	1st Lt. 11th IN Infy	DC	17550
Simmons, Samuel	LTC CS USV	MO	07812
Simmons, William E.	1st Lt. 13th ME Infy	NY	15955
Simmons, William T.	1st Lt. 11th MO Infy	CA	12912
Simms, Joseph M.	Act Ensign USN	DC	13491
Simms, William T.	Maj 59th NY Infy	NY	01084
Simon, Frederick W.	Capt. 8th MD Infy BvtMaj	DC	06028
Simonds, William E.	2nd Lt. 25th CT Infy	NY	07681
Simonton, Edward	Capt. 1st USCT BvtLTC	MN	03823
Simpson, John	BG USA	DC	13123
Simpson, John H.	Capt. 4th MI Cav	CA	01695
Simpson, Matthew	3rd Class (elected 3/7/1866)	PA	No Number
Simpson, Samuel P.	LTC 31st MO Infy BvtBG	MO	04742 (Dup)
Simpson, Thomas McC.	2nd Lt. 1st VA Infy	OH	17131
Sims, Clifford S.	Act Asst Paymaster USV	PA	00040
Sinclair, Edward W.	2nd Lt. 18th MI Infy	MO	05091
Sinclair, William	BG USA	DC	12137
Sinclair, William H.	Maj AAG BvtCol. USV	MO	06415
Sinclair, William T.	2nd Lt. 165th NY Infy	KS	07172
Sine, John B.	Maj 35th NJ Infy	IL	14572
Singiser, Theodore F.	Capt. 20th PA Cav	DC	03724
Sinnott, Martin N.	1st Lt. 21st MO Infy	KS	18016
Siskron, Samuel F.	2nd Lt. 30th USC MA H Arty	MA	17241

Name	Rank	Commandery	Insignia No.
Sisson, John F.	Capt. 143rd IL Infy	CA	17789
Skelding, Henry T.	Paymaster USN	NY	01374
Skerrett, Joseph S.	RAdm USN	DC	10063
Skerrett, William H.	1st Lt. 72nd OH Infy	CA	09839
Skilton, DeWitt C.	1st Lt. 22nd CT Infy	NY	03614
Skinner, Benjamin M.	Maj 9th WVA Infy	OH	05314
Skinner, Calvin	Surg. 106th NY Infy	NY	11753
Skinner, Edward A.	1st Lt. RQM 9th NY Cav	NY	09960
Skinner, Eugene C.	1st Lt. 117th NY Infy BvtCapt.	MI	04710
Skinner, George R.	1st Lt. 92nd IL Infy BvtMaj	IA	07295
Skinner, George W.	Capt. 77th PA Infy	PA	09283
Skinner, James A.	2nd Lt. 1st NY L Arty	CO	12217
Skinner, James R.	Maj Jdge Adv USV	OH	08537
Skinner, Jeffrey	LTC 2nd CT H Arty	NY	13455
Skinner, Mark	3rd Class (Pres. NW Sanitary Com.)	IL	05141
Slack, Charles B.	1st Lt. 13th Batt MA L Arty	OH	07844
Slack, Charles H.	Act 1st Asst Eng. USN	IL	11000
Slack, William B.	Maj USMC	DC	00470
Sladden, Sidney P.	Capt. 3rd IA Infy	OR	04463
Slade Jonathan	1st Lt. Battn Adj. 12th IL Cav	IL	12224
Slade, Samuel	Capt. 51st OH Infy	OH	07311
Sladen, Joseph A.	Capt. 14th Infy USA	OR	03942
Slagle, Jacob F.	Maj Jdge Adv USV	PA	02638
Slamm, Jefferson A.	Act Ensign USN	WA	11534
Slater, Luther W.	1st Lt. Indpt Battn WVA Cav	DC	09848
Slater, Thomas O.	Capt. 12th NJ Infy	PA	08237
Slater, William H.	Capt. 15th NJ Infy	DC	12549
Sleeper, J. Henry	Capt. 10th Batt MA L Arty BvtMaj	MA	00786
Slevin, Patrick S.	Col. 100th OH Infy BvtBG	OH	08285
Slipper, Joseph A.	Maj AAG BvtCol. USV	NY	00133
Sloan, Alexander C.	1st Lt. 148th PA Infy	OR	17434
Sloan, George W.	1st Lt. 132nd IN Infy	IN	10205
Sloan, Hannibal K.	Capt. 40th PA Infy BvtMaj	PA	08765
Sloane, John L.	2nd Lt. 2nd CA Cav	CA	07850
Sloat, Frank D.	Capt. 27th CT Infy	DC	03358
Slocum, Henry W.	MG USV	NY	00949
Slocum, Joseph J.	Col. CS USV	NY	02370
Sloggy, Charles P.	Capt. 18th WI Infy	WA	12304
Slorah, Andrew	1st Lt. 16th NY Cav	CA	02241
Sloss, Louis	3rd Class (Financial advisor to US Gov)	CA	06336
Slosson, Henry L.	Passed Asst. Eng. USN	NY	13114
Smails, John D.	1st Lt. 9th MI Cav	CO	07485
Small, Abner R.	Maj 16th ME Infy	ME	09704
Small, Eldridge F.	Act Ensign USN	MA	11616
Small, Emilius N.	2nd Lt. 2nd ME Cav	ME	13743
Small, Horatio N.	Surg. 10th NH Infy	ME	02503
Small, Michael P.	LTC ACGS BvtBG USA	DC	04884
Small, Sylvanus C.	1st Lt. RQM 3rd ME Cav	MA	06145

Name	Rank	Commandery	Insignia No.
Smallwood, W. H.	Capt. 79th USCT	MN	15342
Smart, Charles	Col. Asst Surg. Gen USA	DC	06573
Smart, David	1st Lt. 110th USCT	CA	17786
Smead, Daniel W.	1st Lt. 1st USC H Arty	VT	09660
Smedberg, William R.	Maj BvtLTC USA	CA	01315
Smiley, Charles E.	1st Lt. 43rd IL Infy	IL	08123
Smith, Albert E.	Capt. 8th WI Infy	WI	12207
Smith, Alfred B.	Col. 150th NY Infy BvtBG	NY	05006
Smith, Alfred T.	BG USA	IL	10386
Smith, Alva J.	Capt. 4th NY H Arty BvtMaj	OH	03305
Smith, Andrew H.	Surg. 94th NY Infy	NY	00883
Smith, Andrew J.	MG USV	MO	05391
Smith, Andrew J.	Maj AAG BvtCol. USV	NY	01359
Smith, Andrew K.	Col. Surg. USA	CA	04897
Smith, Andrew R.G.	Asst Surg. 2nd ME Cav	ME	10352
Smith, Arthur A.	Col. 83rd IL Infy BvtBG	IL	08429
Smith, Ben L.	Capt. 67th IN Infy	IN	06902
Smith, Benjamin	2nd Lt. 5th WI Infy	WI	13886
Smith, Bradley	1st Lt. 9th ME Infy	CA	12200
Smith, Brewer	Capt. 65th OH Infy BvtMaj	OH	02992
Smith, Charles A.	Capt. 5th CA Infy	IL	00494
Smith, Charles H.	Col. 19th Infy BvtMG USA	DC	00254
Smith, Charles H.	2nd Lt. 4th IA Cav	IA	05791
Smith, Charles H.	Maj 27th OH Infy	OH	04748
Smith, Charles M.	Capt. 55th OH Infy	OH	14027
Smith, Charles W.	1st Lt. 109th USCT	IN	06613
Smith, Cornel	Capt. 19th OH Infy	PA	00497
Smith, Cyrus	Surg. 9th MI Infy	MI	08938
Smith, Dallas B.	2nd Lt. 1st AL Cav	OH	15395
Smith, Daniel A.	Pay Director USN	CA	11382
Smith, David	Chief Eng. USN	CA	10727
Smith, Dexter A.	1st Lt. 193rd NY Infy	NY	08662
Smith, E. Howard	Maj 13th USC H Arty	IA	08182
Smith, Edmund L.	Capt. 19th Infy BvtMaj USA	CO	08709
Smith, Edward W.	LTC AAG BvtBG USV	NY	01112
Smith, Elvin H.	1st Lt. 31st WI Infy	WI	05469
Smith, Erskine D.	1st Lt. Adj. 49th PA Infy	PA	06757
Smith, Francis A.	2nd Lt. 3rd NY Infy	NY	12794
Smith, Francis G.	1st Asst Eng. USN	PA	00809
Smith, Francis M.	1st Lt. Adj. 1st MD Infy BvtCapt.	MD	12887
Smith, Frank G.	BG USA	DC	08600
Smith, Frederick E.	1st Lt. RQM 8th VT Infy	VT	05880
Smith, Gad N.	Capt. 2nd CT H Arty BvtMaj	MI	04364
Smith, George A.	Capt. 2nd RI Cav	MA	11719
Smith, George F.	Col. 61st PA Infy	PA	00457
Smith, George G.	2nd Lt. 29th USCT	DC	15565
Smith, George M.	Act Ensign USN	MA	13472
Smith, George S.	Capt. 8th OH Infy BvtMaj	CO	08828

Name	Rank	Commandery	Insignia No.
Smith, George W.	LTC 88th IL Infy BvtBG	IL	02798
Smith, George W.	1st Lt. Adj. 13th KS Infy	NY	11557
Smith, George Williamson	Chap USN	NY	11634
Smith, Gilbert C.	LTC DQMG USA	MO	01327
Smith, Gustave F.	1st Lt. 111th OH Infy	MI	07284
Smith, Hamilton E.	Surg. 27th MI Infy	MI	03735
Smith, Harry M.	Capt. 21st Infy USA	CA	01234
Smith, Henry A.	Capt. 128th OH Infy	OH	09895
Smith, Henry E.	2nd Lt. 193rd NY Infy	MA	11483
Smith, Henry Eagle	Capt. 12th Infy BvtMaj USA	NY	02133
Smith, Henry I.	Capt. 7th IA Infy	IA	10804
Smith, Herman P.	2nd Lt. 1st ME H Arty	NY	15381
Smith, Hermon J.	Asst Surg. 5th USC Cav	MA	10913
Smith, Hillman	Capt. 8th ME Infy	ME	11241
Smith, Hiram	Maj QM USV	NY	11465
Smith, Horace J.	Capt. 92nd IL Infy	KS	06866
Smith, Howard M.	1st. Lt. 184th NY Infy	NY	04491
Smith, Israel C.	Col. 10th MI Cav BvtBG	MI	04073
Smith, Jacob H.	BG USA	MI	09073
Smith, James B.	LTC 36th MA Infy	IL	03864
Smith, James E.	Capt. 4th Batt NY L Arty	DC	06245
Smith, James H.	2nd Lt. 121st NY Infy	IL	11679
Smith, James H.	1st Lt. 43rd NY Infy	CA	17818
Smith, James J.	LTC 69th NY Infy BvtCol.	OH	13315
Smith, James T.	Capt. 54th IL Infy	DC	03316
Smith, Jared A.	BG USA	OH	05342
Smith, John A.	Capt. 7th IL Infy	IL	05135
Smith, John A.B.	RAdm USN	PA	08465
Smith, John B.	1st Lt. 72nd OH Infy	OH	07803
Smith, John C.	LTC 96th IL Infy BvtBG	IL	04140
Smith, John C.	1st Lt. 33rd NJ Infy	NY	11754
Smith, John D. K.	2nd Lt. 92nd OH Infy	OH	09734
Smith, John E.	BG USV BvtMG USA	IL	02420
Smith, John H.	1st Lt. 2nd Arty BvtCapt. USA	CA	03105
Smith, John H.	Capt. 13th IN Infy	KS	04787
Smith, John S.	Capt. 3rd US Vet Infy	MN	07224
Smith, John T.	Passed Asst. Eng. USN	DC	13154
Smith, John W.	Paymaster USA	PA	00783
Smith, John W.	Capt. 7th CA Infy	Ca	07515
Smith, John W.	2nd Lt. 2nd OH H Arty	IN	06614
Smith, John Y.T.	1st Lt. 4th CA Infy	CA	10613
Smith, Joseph A.	Pay Director USN	PA	01549
Smith, Joseph H.	Capt. 97th NY Infy	CA	16283
Smith, Joseph K.	1st Lt. 12th USCT	WI	17079
Smith, Joseph O.	2nd Lt. 11th ME Infy	ME	02783
Smith, Joseph P.	BvtMaj USA	PA	00252
Smith, Joseph R.	Maj 7th Infy BvtBG USA	NY	00742
Smith, Joseph R.	BG USA	PA	00612

Name	Rank	Commandery	Insignia No.
Smith, Joseph S.	1st Lt. 122nd NY Infy	IL	12157
Smith, Joseph S.	LTC CS BvtBG USV	MA	01729
Smith, Leonard T.	3rd Class	KS	04880
Smith, Leslie	Col. USA	NY	03535
Smith, Levi H.	LTC 128th PA Infy	PA	06003
Smith, Lewis	LTC USA	DC	11661
Smith, Linton	Surg. 4th DE Infy BvtLTC	PA	07654
Smith, Lionel J.	Surg. 33rd OH Infy	WI	10590
Smith, Louis McD.	Capt. 5th VT Infy	VT	09175
Smith, Lucien A.	1st Lt. 136th NY Infy	MI	04005
Smith, Luther R.	Capt. 1st MI L Arty	DC	13076
Smith, Lyman B.	1st Lt. 2nd MN Infy	MI	08824
Smith, Martin G.	2nd Lt. 11th H Arty USA	MA	16359
Smith, Martin H.	Capt. 123rd OH Infy	MO	06550
Smith, Martin V.B.	2nd Lt. 5th PA Cav	PA	07655
Smith, Melancthon	RAdm USN	NY	00276 (Dup)
Smith, Melvin	1st Lt. 105th IL Infy	IA	08447
Smith, Melvin S.	1st Lt. 13th MA Infy	ME	17379
Smith, Michael E.	Capt. 40th NY Infy	CO	06943
Smith, Milton H.	2nd Lt. 3rd NY Cav	NY	00996
Smith, Nathan G.	Capt. 75th USCT	MA	02310
Smith, Nicholas	Capt. 19th Infy USA	NY	01828
Smith, Nicholas	Capt. 33rd WI Infy	WI	12208
Smith, Norman M.	Capt. 19th PA Cav BvtLTC	PA	08466
Smith, Orland	Col. 73rd OH Infy BvtBG	OH	02715
Smith, Orlando J.	Maj 6th IN Cav	NY	11341
Smith, Oskaloosa M.	Maj CS USA (LTC CS USV)	IN	04215
Smith, Peter D.	2nd Lt. 1st MA H Arty	MA	03532
Smith, Philip	1st Lt. 4th MA H Arty	MA	12741
Smith, Richard Penn	Col. 71st PA Infy	NY	03621
Smith, Robert Burnett	1st Lt. 11th Infy BvtCapt. USA	NY	04605
Smith, Robert M.	Maj 78th PA Infy	IA	11881
Smith, Rodney	BG USA	MN	02956
Smith, Samuel B.	Capt. 93rd OH Infy	OH	02444
Smith, Samuel R.	1st Lt. 6th Infy BvtMaj USA	PA	01662
Smith, Sidney L.	1st Asst Eng. USN	MA	15815
Smith, Solomon P.	Capt. 115th NY Infy	CA	15535
Smith, Stephen B.	1st Lt. Adj. 26th MA Infy	NY	12557
Smith, Sylvester T.	Capt. 1st KS Infy	IL	04765
Smith, Theodore E.	Act Asst Paymaster USN	NY	05112
Smith, Thomas B.	1st Lt. Adj. 13th NJ Infy	MO	12598
Smith, Thomas C.	2nd Lt. 170th NY Infy	OR	10184
Smith, Thomas C.R.	BG USV	CA	02648
Smith, Thomas Kilby	BG BvtMG USV	PA	00376
Smith, William	BG Paymaster Gen. USA	MN	03492
Smith, William	Capt. 2nd OH Cav	OH	03375
Smith, William A.	Capt. 40th MA Infy	MA	13929
Smith, William B.	1st Lt. 2nd DE Infy	DC	09459

The Roster

Name	Rank	Commandery	Insignia No.
Smith, William French	BvtMG USA	NY	00878
Smith, William H.H.	1st Lt. 21st Batt OH L Arty	OH	03262
Smith, William J.	Col. 6th TN Cav BvtBG	OH	07203
Smith, William M.	Surg. 85th NY Infy	NY	03128
Smith, William M.	2nd Lt. 5th CA Infy	PA	12233
Smith, William Niles	Capt. 9th NY Cav	NY	08799
Smith, William O.	Maj 7th KY Cav	OH	07233
Smith, William Penn	Capt. 5th CT Infy	MA	12025
Smith, William S.	Chief Eng. USN	PA	08874
Smith, William Sooy	BG USV	IL	08295
Smith, William W.	Maj 17th MA Infy	KS	06869
Smith, Wilson C.	3rd Class	NY	00743
Smith, Woodbury C.	Capt. 35th USCT	MA	14814
Smith, Zemro A.	LTC 1st ME H Arty BvtCol.	IN	03055
Smithe, J. Curtiss	2nd Lt. 150th NY Infy	DC	06385
Smither, Robert G.	Maj USA	CO	11487
Smolinski, Joseph	2nd Lt. 9th NY Cav	DC	13213
Smyser, Eugene M.	Asst Surg. 48th PA Infy	PA	00480
Smyth, Newman	1st Lt. 16th ME Infy	NY	13115
Smythe, Samuel S.	Capt. 1st IL L Arty	CA	07793
Snell, Alfred T.	Commander USN	CA	01279
Snell, William B.	Capt. 13th ME Infy	DC	05124
Snelling, Frederick G.	Surg. USV	NY	01019
Snider, Gustavus	Col. 185th NY Infy BvtBG	NY	09120
Snider, Samuel P.	Capt. 13th USCT	MN	06073
Snider, William H.	Maj 94th OH Infy	IN	08145 (Dup)
Snodgrass, Jesse	Asst Surg. 8th TN Infy	OH	09746
Snook, George S.	Capt. 10th IN Cav	CA	06136
Snow, Albert S.	RAdm USN	ME	16628
Snow, George W.	Surg. 35th MA Infy	MA	03680
Snow, Norman L.	Surg. 153rd NY Infy	NY	03015
Snow, Samuel W.	Bvt Maj USV	DC	15840
Snow, William A.	Capt. 1st LA Cav	MA	09811
Snow, William M.	Capt. 3rd WI Infy	MA	11268
Snowden, George O.	Capt. 39th IL Infy	IA	11932
Snowden, George R.	Capt. 142nd PA Infy	PA	16573
Snowwhite, E.H.A.	Bvt Capt. USV	OH	10024
Snyder, Charles W.	1st Lt. Adj. 49th USCT BvtMaj	WA	11996
Snyder, Edward	1st Lt. 178th NY Infy	CA	06710
Snyder, Henry J.	Maj 192nd PA Infy	PA	16804
Snyder, Henry N.	Capt. 59th IL Infy	DC	05334
Snyder, James A.	Capt. 3rd Infy USA	DC	03650
Snyder, John W.O.	Asst Surg. 2nd MO Cav	CO	07906
Soest, Konrad E.C.F.	1st Lt. 82nd USCT	MO	08017
Somers, Thomas H.	Capt. 41st OH Infy	MI	15998
Somerville, William	Capt. 16th IL Infy	IL	07424
Sonnanstine, Joseph F.	Capt. 65th OH Infy	OH	08040
Soper, Erastus B.	Capt. 13th IA Infy	IA	06406

Name	Rank	Commandery	Insignia No.
Soule, Charles C.	Capt. 55th MA Infy	MA	00833
Soule, Charles E.	1st Lt. 10th MI Cav	MI	16903
Soule, Frank	2nd Lt. USA	CA	16380
Soule, Harrison	Maj 6th MI Infy	MI	05346
Southworth, Edward	1st Lt. 2nd USCT	MA	16114
Southworth, Malek A.	Surg. 1st TX Cav	CA	10570
Soward, Tom H.	1st Lt. 2nd KY Cav	KS	05097
Sowers, Isaac M.	1st Lt. 9th PA Reserves	CA	18009
Sowle, Luther T.	2nd Lt. 98th NY Infy	MN	15237
Sowle, Orlando T.	2nd Lt. 51st WI Infy	WI	06449
Spaeth, Henry P.	1st Lt. 9th OH Infy	OH	06844
Spafford, Henry W.	1st Lt. RQM 4th VT Infy	VT	14101
Spahr, Joel R.	2nd Lt. 42nd PA Infy	IN	13312
Spain, David F.	Capt. 48th IN Infy	IN	11964
Spalding, Edgar G.	1st Lt. 22nd MI Infy	MI	04589
Spalding, George	Col. 12th TN Cav BvtBG	MI	09224
Sparks, Rufus T.	1st Lt. 64th IL Infy	MA	01457
Sparling, Frederic W.	Surg. 10th MI Infy	WA	00321
Spaulding, Edward B.	1st Lt. 52nd IL Infy	IA	08448
Spaulding, Edward J.	Maj 4th Cav USA	CA	04860
Spaulding, Joseph W.	LTC 19th ME Infy	ME	02386
Spaulding, Oliver L.	Col. 23rd MI Infy BvtBG	MI	04591
Spaulding, Rufus C.	Paymaster USN	NY	00533
Speakman, Franklin B.	Col. 133rd PA Infy	PA	09287
Spear, Ellis	Col. 20th ME Infy BvtBG	DC	03814
Spear, George G.	Capt. 30th MA Infy	MA	10318
Spear, John C.	Med. Inspector USN	PA	07353
Spear, Vivian K.	1st Lt. 38th MA Infy BvtCapt.	NY	09303
Spear, Wallace M.	Capt. 1st WI H Arty	PA	01101
Speed, George K.	Capt. 4th KY Cav	OH	03308
Speed, James	3rd Class (Attorney General US)	OH	05384
Speed, James B.	1st Lt. Adj. 27th KY Infy	OH	06189
Speed, Thomas	1st Lt. Adj. 12th KY Infy	OH	04193
Speer, Alexander M.	Surg. BvtLTC USV	PA	07072
Speer, James P.	Maj 40th PA Infy BvtLTC	PA	07354
Speer, William F.	Capt. 22nd PA Cav BvtLTC	PA	07071
Spellman, Oscar M.	1st Lt. 1st MO Cav	MO	10896
Spence, John	Capt. 75th OH Infy	WI	04112
Spencer, Albert N.	Capt. 103rd OH Infy	MA	16666
Spencer, Charles A.	Capt. 47th WI Infy	WI	04126
Spencer, Frederick A.	1st Lt. 2nd CO Cav	NY	01489
Spencer, George K.	Capt. USA	KS	14631
Spencer, Gideon	1st Lt. 1st RI L Arty	MA	11209
Spencer, James H.	1st Lt. 20th MA Infy (Capt. USA)	PA	00967
Spencer, T. Rush	Surg. Bvt LTC USV	NY	00297-845
Spencer, William A.	Chap 8th IL Cav	PA	13198
Spencer, William H.	Maj 61st NY Infy	MA	11409
Spencer, William T.	Capt. 2nd CT H Arty	DC	09917

The Roster 361

Name	Rank	Commandery	Insignia No.
Spencer, William V.	1st Lt. 13th Infy USA	PA	00559
Sperry, Anson	Maj Paymaster BvtLTC USV	IL	05547
Spicer, Simeon	Capt. AQM USV	MD	13179
Spicer, William F.	Commodore USN	MA	01126
Spiegelhalter, Joseph	Surg. 12th MO Infy	MO	05656
Spielman, John A.	2nd Lt. 17th IA Infy	IA	13679
Splaine, Henry	LTC 17th MA Infy	MA	13861
Sponable, Wells	Maj 34th NY Infy	NY	07472
Spooner, Charles W.	Act Ensign USN	NY	06173
Spooner, Henry J.	1st Lt. Adj. 4th RI Infy	MA	02822
Spooner, John A.	Hospital Chap USV	PA	07656
Spooner, John C.	Bvt Maj USV	WI	15458
Spooner, Samuel B.	Maj 46th MA Infy	MA	02552
Sprague, Augustus B.R.	Col. 51st MA Infy BvtBG	MA	00683
Sprague, Charles J.	Maj Paymaster BvtLTC USA	CA	01341
Sprague, DeWitt C.	1st Lt. 27th CT Infy	DC	14488
Sprague, Ezra	Capt. 20th CT Infy	NY	01826
Sprague, Homer B.	LTC 13th CT Infy	CA	05180
Sprague, John W.	BG BvtMG USV	WA	05901
Sprague, Waldo	1st Lt. 17th NY Infy	NY	06632
Sprague, William	3rd Class (Gov. RI)	PA	00095
Springer, James D.	1st Lt. 55th USCT	MN	06097
Springer, Thomas B.	Capt. 11th IN Cav	IN	15325
Spurgin, William F.	BG USA	DC	04070
Spurling, Andrew B.	BvtBG USV	IL	15105
Spurrier, John H.	Surg. 123rd IN Infy	IN	08146
Squire, Watson C.	Capt. 7th Co. OH Shpshtrs. BvtCol.	DC	01910
Squires, Charles E.	Capt. 20th IA Infy	CA	04081
Sry, Randolph	Capt. 4th IA Infy	OH	15885
Stacey, May H.	Capt. 12th Infy BvtLTC USA	CA	03550
Stackhouse, Powell	Maj 198th PA Infy	PA	00202
Stackpole, J. Lewis	Maj Jdge Adv BvtLTC USV	MA	00988
Stafford, John A.	1st Lt. 19th MI Infy	VT	10079
Stafford, Stephen B.	Maj USA	IL	03967
Stagg, John	1st Lt. 1st MI Cav	NY	15171
Stahel, Julius	MG USV	NY	01491
Stahl, Wilson O.	1st Lt. 94th IL Infy	IL	13509
Stahler, Enoch	1st Lt. 3rd NY Cav	Dc	14793
Stalder, Frederick	1st Lt. 53rd OH Infy	OH	07764
Staley, Gideon	1st Lt. 1st Regt. Potomac R. Brig. MD Infy	MD	13514
Stallman, Charles H.	1st Lt. 87th PA Infy PA	PA	12985
Stambaugh, Danield B.	Capt. 105th OH Infy	OH	07031
Stamm, Charles W.	Paymaster	PA	01012
Stamm, William S.	Chief Eng. USN	PA	02231
Stamp, H.M.F.V.	BvtCapt. USV	PA	00998
Stancliff, Henry T.	Paymaster USN	DC	09108
Stanfield, Edward P.	1st Lt. Adj. 48th IN Infy	IN	11576
Stanford, Leland	3rd Class (Gov. CA)	CA	03993

Name	Rank	Commandery	Insignia No.
Stanhope, Philip W.	Maj BvtLTC USA	IN	10220
Staniels, Rufus P.	Capt. 13th NH Infy	MA	02335
Stanley, David S.	MG USV	DC	03158
Stanley, Frederic N.	2nd Lt. 13th CT Infy	NY	09865
Stanley, James R.	2nd Lt. 147th PA Infy	CA	16305
Stanley, William S.	1st Lt. 6th NY H Arty BvtCapt.	WI	02096
Stannard, George J.	BG BvtMG USV	MA	01324
Stanton, Byron	Surg. 120th OH Infy	OH	12350
Stanton, Clark	Capt. 1st NY Cav	DC	13077
Stanton, Cornelius A.	Maj 3rd IA Cav	MO	05648
Stanton, Edwin M.	3rd Class (Secretary of War)	PA	00044
Stanton, Irving W.	1st Lt. Adj. 2nd CO Cav	CO	06528
Stanton, Joshua O.	Surg. US Vet. Vols.	DC	03729
Stanton, Oscar F.	RAdm USN	NY	11110
Stanton, Thaddeus H.	BG Paymaster Gen. USA	NE	00855
Stanwood, Eben P.	LTC 48th MA Infy	MA	02626
Staples, David J.	3rd Class (Pioneer settler)	CA	03245
Staples, Frank	2nd Lt. 4th NY Cav	CA	00531
Staples, Henry G.	Col. 3rd ME Infy	ME	09377
Staples, Horatio	1st Lt. 2nd ME Infy	ME	12938
Staples, James W.	Capt. 78th NY Infy	CA	01696
Staples, Samuel C.	Maj Paymaster USV	NY	01104 (Dup)
Starack, Frederick E.	1st Lt. 20th IA Infy BvtMaj	CA	09072
Starbird, Isaac W.	Col. 19th ME Infy BvtBG	MA	11365
Stark, Denton D.	Capt. 1st AR L Arty	CA	15723
Starkey, Henry	1st Lt. 5th MI Cav	MI	04713
Starkey, James	Capt. 1st MN Mounted Rangers	MN	07705
Starkey, Robert A.	Capt. 53rd OH Infy	OH	06842
Starkloff, Hugo M.	Surg. 40th IL Infy	MO	04783
Starkweather, Archibald	1st Lt. 26th MA Infy	MA	12165
Starkweather, Colum C.	Capt. 9th MI Infy	MI	11696
Starling, William	Maj 9th KY Infy	OH	09588
Starr, Augustus W.	BvtMaj USV	CA	05183
Starr, George H.	Capt. 104th NY Infy	NY	08663
Starr, James	Maj 6th PA Cav BvtCol.	PA	02128
Starr, Pierre S.	1st Lt. 39th OH Infy	NY	16402
Starr, Samuel Henry	Col. USA	PA	03598
Starr, William C.	LTC 9th WVA Cav	IN	05815
Starring, Frederick C.	Col. 72nd IL Infy BvtBG	NY	01163
Stauffer, David McN.	Act Ensign USN	NY	01854
Stauffer, William DeS.	Capt. 195th PA Infy	PA	05507
Stavey, Nicholas H.	Passed Asst Paymaster USN	NY	17571
Stawitz, Christian	1st Lt. Adj. 32nd IN Infy	MO	04271
Stearns, Henry P.	Surg. BvtLTC USV	MA	02227
Stearns, James P.	1st Lt. 22nd MA Infy	MA	01707
Stearns, John C.	1st Lt. Adj. 9th VT Infy	VT	09161
Stearns, Ozora P.	Col. 39th USCT	MN	05428
Stearns, Riley B.	Capt. 7th VT Infy	VT	08502

Name	Rank	Commandery	Insignia No.
Stearns, Solomon S.	1st Lt. 4th ME Infy	DC	10556
Stearns, Daniel E.	1st. Lt. Adj. 3rd MI Cav	MI	13104
Stebbins, Asa H.	2nd Lt. 44th MA Infy	MA	00858
Stebbins, DeWayne	Act Master USN	WI	04115
Stedman, C. Ellery	Asst Surg. USN	MA	01459
Stedman, Joseph	LTC 42nd MA Infy	MA	02331
Stedman, William A.	1st Lt. 1st RI Infy	MA	05102
Steedman, Charles	RAdm USN	DC	00589
Steel, John A.	1st Lt. Adj. 106th PA Infy	PA	10634
Steele, Aaron J.	Surg. 13th NY H Arty	MO	08276
Steele, Daniel W.	1st Lt. 22nd KY Infy	OH	08698
Steele, George W.	Maj 101st IN Infy	IN	02629
Steele, Henry K.	Surg. 44th OH Infy	CO	05812
Steele, Hiram R.	Capt. CS BvtMaj USV	NY	08503
Steele, James M.	LTC 118th USCT	KS	06360
Steelhammer, Charles	Maj USA	CA	16315
Stegeman, John H.	1st Lt. 5th Batt OH L Arty	OH	05909
Steger, James H.	Maj AAG MO State Militia	MO	07910
Steiner, Lewis H.	3rd Class (Chief Inspr. US San. Com.)	NY	00881
Steinmetz, William R.	Maj USA	MD	10858
Steinmeyer, William	Capt. 26th WI Infy	WI	08590
Stellwagen, Henry S.	Capt. USN	PA	No Number
Stellwagen, Thomas C.	Act Asst Paymaster USN	PA	01658
Stembel, Roger M.	RAdm USN	PA	00568
Stephenson, Ferdinand D.	Col. 153rd IL Infy	DC	13155
Stephenson, James	1st Lt. Batt PA L Arty	PA	10879
Stephenson, Luther	LTC 32nd MA Infy BvtBG	MA	05954
Stephenson, William W.	Capt. 105th NY Infy	NY	04055
Sterling, Alexander F.	Asst Surg. USV	NY	01654
Sterling, Edward L.	2nd Lt. 2nd ME Infy	MA	16070
Sterling, James T.	LTC 103rd OH Infy BvtCol.	MI	03575
Sterling, William H.	Capt. 1st US Infy	PA	00557-1791
Sternberg, Francis C.	1st Lt. 20th KY Infy	NY	10971
Sternberg, George M.	BG Surg. Gen. USA	DC	02723
Sternberg, Theodore	Maj USA	CA	12306
Stetson, Prince R.	Capt. 15th Infy USA	PA	00560
Stevens, Asa B.	1st Lt. 203rd PA Infy	PA	12113
Stevens, Charles A.	1st Lt. 1st US Shpshtrs.	DC	12032
Stevens, Charles B.	1st Lt. 47th MA Infy	MA	01801
Stevens, Charles N.	1st Lt. 128th OH Infy	MO	04851 (Dup)
Stevens, Danville B.	2nd Lt. 17th ME Infy	ME	12811
Stevens, Frank D.	2nd Lt. 190th PA Infy	CA	17819
Stevens, George A.	Capt. USN	DC	06243
Stevens, George H.	Capt. 48th USCT	CA	05641
Stevens, Greenlief T.	Capt. 5th Batt ME L Arty BvtMaj	ME	14224
Stevens, Hazard	Maj AAG BvtBG USV	MA	01746
Stevens, Sylvanus H.	1st Lt. Chic. Bd of Trade Batt IL L Arty	IL	09615
Stevens, Thomas H.	RAdm USN	Dc	01072

The Roster

Name	Rank	Commandery	Insignia No.
Stevens, Thomas H.	RAdm USN	DC	16055
Stevens, Thomas N.	Capt. 28th WI Infy	MI	02810 (Dup)
Stevens, William C.	Maj 9th MI Infy	MI	03874
Stevenson, Alex. F.	Capt. 42nd IL Infy BvtCol.	IL	02187
Stevenson, Benjamin F.	Surg. 22nd KY Infy	OH	03486
Stevenson, John D.	BG BvtMG USV	MO	05280
Stevenson, John H.	Pay Inspector USN	NY	01188
Stevenson, Robert E.	Asst Surg. 75th IL Infy	KS	05215
Stevenson, Robert H.	LTC 24th MA Infy BvtBG	MA	00752
Steward, Ira W.	1st Lt. 28th Batt NY L Arty	NY	08504
Steward, Thomas L.	1st Lt. 11th OH Infy	OH	03968
Stewart, C. Seaforth	BG USA	NY	06741
Stewart, Charles	RAdm USN	PA	01119
Stewart, Charles	Capt. CS BvtMaj USV	MO	06309
Stewart, Edwn	Paymaster Gen. USN	NY	05827
Stewart, Francis R.	Capt. 49th OH Infy	OH	14176
Stewart, Henry H.	Chief Eng. USN	PA	00402
Stewart, Jacob R.	Capt. 17th IN Infy	OH	03484
Stewart, James	Capt. 17th USCT BvtMaj	NY	03606
Stewart, James	Maj USA	OH	08032
Stewart, James E.	Capt. 167th OH Infy BvtCol.	OH	04993
Stewart, James, Jr.	Col. 9th NJ Infy BvtBG	PA	03599
Stewart, John E.	1st Lt. Adj. 9th USCT	NY	06227
Stewart, Malcolm N.	Capt. 100th IL Infy BvtMaj	IL	12270
Stewart, Milton	LTC 13th WVA Infy	KS	04089
Stewart, Robert E.	Maj 24th USCT	PA	07073
Stewart, Thomas S.	BvtMaj USV	MA	16207
Stewart, William S.	Asst Surg. 83rd PA Infy	PA	01990
Stibbs, John H.	Col. 12th IA Infy BvtBG	IL	05807
Stickel, Joseph H.	1st Lt. 35th WI Infy	NE	08693
Stickney, Amos	Col. Eng. USA	MO	11807
Stickney, Horatio G.	Surg. 3rd RI H Arty	MA	01811
Stidger, John S.	Capt. 3rd IA Cav	CO	14646
Stifel, Charles G.	Col. 5th US Reserve Corps MO Infy	MO	10689
Stiles, Albert W.	Capt. 6th OH Cav	OH	09642
Stiles, Charles D.	1st Lt. 2nd Co. MA Shpshtrs.	MA	14241
Stiles, Israel N.	Col. 63rd IN Infy BvtBG	IL	01945
Stillman, Charles A.	Capt. USMC	MA	08362
Stillwell, Leander	1st Lt. 61st IL Infy	KS	04174
Stimson, Earl W.	1st Lt. 137th OH Infy	OH	10016
Stimson, Lewis A.	Capt. Vol. Aide-de-Camp	NY	10698
Stirling, Yates	RAdm USN	MD	05889
Stitt, William S.	1st Lt. 75th IN Infy	IN	06932 (Dup)
Stitzer, Frank A.	Capt. 48th PA Infy BvtMaj	CO	07806
Stivers, Charles E.	1st Lt. 18th OH Infy	OH	14931
Stivers, Edwin J.	Maj USA	NY	06353
Stockbridge, Virgil D.	1st Lt. Adj. 2nd DC Infy	DC	10986
Stocker, Anthony E.	Surg. Bvt LTC USV	PA	06475

Name	Rank	Commandery	Insignia No.
Stocker, John W.	1st Lt. 29th IA Infy	IA	08284
Stocking, Hobart M.	Capt. 48th WI Infy	MN	10271
Stockman, George H.	1st Lt. 6th MO Infy	PA	11164
Stockton, Charles H.	RAdm USN	DC	16168
Stockton, Howard	Capt. ADC USV	MA	06111
Stockton, Joseph	LTC 72nd IL Infy BvtBG	IL	02191
Stockton, Robert F.	3rd Class (Adj. Gen. NJ)	PA	00481
Stockton, William S.	1st Lt. 71st PA Infy	PA	08238
Stockwell, Levi S.	Paymaster USN	NY	01644
Stoddard, Enoch V.	Surg. 65th NY Infy	NY	05526
Stoddard, Joseph C.	1st Lt. 8th IA Infy	IA	05908
Stokeley, Samuel B.	1st Lt. Adj. 40th IL Infy	MO	07807
Stolbrand, Carlos J.	BG USV	NY	07481
Stoltze, Frank A.	2nd Lt. 23rd WI Infy	WI	12968
Stoms, Horace G.	Capt. 39th OH Infy	OH	03208
Stone, Andrew L.	Chap 45th MA Infy	CA	04096
Stone, Benjamin F.	Capt. 73rd OH Infy	OH	04401
Stone, Eben F.	Col. 48th MA Infy	MA	02114
Stone, Ebenezer W.	LTC 61st MA Infy BvtCol.	DC	03231 (Dup)
Stone, Frank F.	2nd Lt. 3rd MA Cav	CA	02081 (Dup)
Stone, Frederick P.	Capt. 1st NH Cav	CA	11779
Stone, George	Capt. 18th NY Cav	CA	10467
Stone, George A.	Col. 25th IA Infy BvtBG	IA	06197
Stone, George H.	Maj 1st MO L Arty	DC	14160
Stone, George N.	Capt. 7th RI Infy	OH	07320
Stone, George W.	Capt. 12th NY Infy	MA	05508
Stone, Henry	LTC 100th USCT BvtCol.	MA	01032
Stone, John Y.	2nd Lt. 5th IA Infy	IA	09890
Stone, Lauriston L.	1st Lt. RQM 2nd VT Infy	NY	12558
Stone, Lincoln R.	Surg. BvtLTC USV	MA	05161
Stone, Mason A.	Capt. 1st VT Cav BvtCol.	NY	06734
Stone, Michael	Capt. 31st OH Infy	OH	08532
Stone, Roy	Col. 149th PA Infy BvtBG USV	DC	11669
Stone, Thomas J.	2nd Lt. 12th VRC	MO	04295
Stone, William A.	2nd Lt. 187th PA Infy	PA	10878
Stone, William B.	1st Lt. 10th KS Infy	KS	04440
Stoneman, George	MG USV	CA	00030
Stoodley, Nathan D.	Maj 13th NH Infy	MA	06917
Storer, James B.	Capt. 29th OH Infy	OH	02968
Storer, Newman W.	Capt. 7th Batt MA L Arty	MA	14393
Storer, William Brandt	1st Lt. RQM 15th MA Infy	MA	01026 (Dup)
Storey, James H.	1st Lt. RQM 87th USCT	NY	08664
Storey, Joseph M.	Capt. 26th IN Infy	IN	07274
Stork, William L.	Capt. 29th PA Infy	MD	12707
Storke, Jay E.	1st Lt. Adj. 3rd NY L Arty	NY	07473
Storrow, Charles	Capt. 44th MA Infy	MA	00959
Storrs, Charles E.	Maj 6th MI Cav	MI	11494
Storrs, Lucius C.	Capt. 12th NY Infy	MI	04363

Name	Rank	Commandery	Insignia No.
Storrs, Samuel J.	LTC 52nd MA Infy	NY	05518
Story, John P.	MG USA	CA	16377 (Dup)
Stott, Charles A.	Maj 6th MA Infy	MA	08739
Stott, William T.	Capt. 18th IN Infy	IN	14208
Stouch, George W.H.	LTC USA	CO	12332
Stoughton, Charles B.	Col. 4th VT Infy BvtBG	NY	00848
Stoughton, Edwin H.	BG USV	NY	00839
Stout, Abraham	Asst Surg. 153rd PA Infy	PA	09775
Stout, Alexander M.	Col. 17th KY Infy BvtBG	IL	02414
Stowe, William P.	Chap 27th WI Infy	IL	07920
Stradling, James M.	2nd Lt. 1st NJ Cav	PA	13554
Strain, Alexander	LTC 153rd NY Infy	NY	05418
Stranahan, F. Stewart	1st Lt. 1st VT Cav	VT	03878
Stranahan, James A.	1st Lt. 3rd Battn PA Infy	PA	13195
Strang, John R.	LTC 104th NY Infy	NY	10434
Stratton, Joel A.	Capt. 53rd MA Infy	KS	17029
Straw, Cyrus W.	Capt. 81st PA Infy	PA	11019
Streeter, Buell G.	Surg. 4th NY Cav	NY	10252
Streeter, John W.	1st Lt. 1st MI L Arty	IL	02015
Strickland, David H.	Surg. 111th PA Infy	PA	11944
Strickland, Dudley W.	LTC 48th NY Infy	CO	04742 (Dup)
Strickland, Isaac	1st Lt. 6th ME Infy	ME	12890
Strong, Colin G.	Surg. 36th IA Infy	CA	09258
Strong, Edgar E.	1st Lt. 16th CT Infy	OH	03260
Strong, Edward T.	RAdm USN	PA	11161
Strong, Frank L.	Passed Asst. Eng. USN	NY	16892
Strong, Frank P.	Maj 1st AR Cav	DC	07186
Strong, Henry C.	1st Lt. RQM 128th OH Infy	OH	03960
Strong, Richard P.	LTC Arty USA	DC	02350
Strong, Rollin M.	LTC 19th WI Infy	NE	07590
Strong, William E.	LTC 12th WI Infy BvtBG	IL	01915
Stroud, George D.	Capt. 20th PA Cav	PA	00073
Stroup, Lawrence K.	Capt. 91st OH Infy	OH	06849
Stryker, William S.	Maj Paymaster BvtLTC USV	PA	02113
Stuart, Daniel D.V.	RAdm USN	DC	16345
Stuart, James E.	Capt. 21st WI Infy, Maj 2nd IL Infy	IL	04146
Stuart, John	Capt. 51st NY Infy	NY	01344
Stubbins, Benjamin A.	Surg. 14th KY Infy	OH	06433
Stubbs, George E.	Asst Surg. BvtCapt. USV	PA	05736
Studer, Adolphus G.	Capt. 15th IA Infy BvtMaj	IA	11623
Studley, John M.	LTC 51st MA Infy	MA	07569
Stueven, Charles E.	1st Lt. 82nd IL Infy BvtMaj	KS	05694
Sturdevant, Samuel H.	Col. CS USV	PA	09774
Sturdy, Albert W.	2nd Lt. 18th MA Infy	MA	06112
Sturgeon, William R.	Capt. 107th PA Infy	DC	06569
Sturges, Edwin C.	Capt. 101st NY Infy	NY	05292
Sturgis, Henry H.	1st Lt. 20th MA Infy	MA	00817
Sturgis, Russell	Maj 45th MA Infy	MA	01146

Name	Rank	Commandery	Insignia No.
Sturgis, Samuel D.	BG USV BvtMG USA	DC	02606
Sturgis, Thomas	1st Lt. 57th MA Infy	NY	04768
Sturm, Herman	LTC 54th IN Infy	CO	09445
Sturtevant, John W.	Capt. 14th NH Infy	MA	02090
Stuyvesant, Moses S.	Lt. Commander USN	MO	04685
Sudborough, Joseph A.	Capt. 17th MI Infy	MO	08369
Suddards, James	Med. Director USN	PA	00427
Suess, Henry	Maj 7th MO Cav	CO	05629
Sullivan, Henry D.	Capt. 44th MA Infy	MA	03886
Sullivan, John	Asst Surg. 13th NH Infy	MA	01461
Sullivan, John S.	1st Lt. 14th IN Infy	MO	16716
Sullivan, Thomas C.	BG USA	DC	01887-2721
Sullivant, Lyne S.	Maj 113th OH Infy	OH	04998
Sumbardo, Charles L.	Capt. 12th IA Infy	WA	07254
Summerhayes, John W.	LTC USA	DC	03456
Summers, John E.	BG USA	DC	05756
Sumner, Alexander B.	Maj 1st ME Ve. Infy BvtLTC	ME	04132
Sumner, Charles A.	Capt. AQM USV	CA	05064
Sumner, Edward A.	1st Lt. 43rd MA Infy	MI	03761
Sumner, Edwin Vose	BG USA	DC	08132
Sumner, John H.	Capt. 3rd MI Infy	DC	14440
Sumner, Samuel S.	MG USA	DC	03645
Sumner, William P.	1st Lt. 27th MI Infy	MI	06812
Sutcliffe, Hamer	1st Lt. 4th US Vol. Infy	OR	13367
Sutermeister, Arnold	Capt. 11th Batt IN L Arty	MO	08963
Sutherland, Charles	BG Surg. Gen. USA	DC	02729
Sutherland, George E.	Capt. 13th USC H Arty	WI	05766
Sutorius, Alexander	Capt. 3rd Cav USA	PA	00495
Sutter, John J.	Capt. 2nd MO Arty	MO	06723
Sutton, Joseph F.	Chap 102nd NY Infy	NY	14454
Sutton, Joshua P.	Capt. 7th MI Infy	MI	04707
Sutton, Rhoades S.	Asst Surg. 9th PA Cav	PA	12647
Suydam, Charles C.	LTC 3rd NJ Cav	NY	03349
Swaim, David G.	BG Jdge Adv Gen. USA	DC	02359
Swain, Abram O.	1st Lt. 1st MA Cav	MA	15007
Swain, Edgar D.	LTC 43rd IL Infy BvtCol.	IL	02184
Swain, James A.	Capt. AQM BvtLTC USV	TN	00273
Swain, Julius M.	2nd Lt. Sig. Corps BvtCapt. USV	MA	09606
Swain, William C.	Capt. 93rd NY Infy	WI	06289
Swaine, Peter T.	Col. 22nd Infy USA	CA	06322
Swallow, Benjamin	Hospital Chap USV	DC	03979
Swallow, George R.	Col. 10th IN Cav	CO	09586
Swalm, William F.	Asst Surg. 15th NY Eng.	NY	08113
Swan, Francis H.	Pay Inspector USN	PA	00615
Swan, Joseph H.	Capt. 3rd MN Infy	IA	07300
Swan, William W.	Capt. 17th Infy BvtLTC USA	PA	00901
Swart, Menzo	2nd Lt. 16th MI Infy	MI	12853
Swartout, William	1st Lt. 169th NY Infy	NY	15444

Name	Rank	Commandery	Insignia No.
Swartzlander, Frank	Asst Surg. 74th PA Infy	PA	04671
Swasey, John	1st Lt. Benton Cadets, MO Infy	OH	11970
Swayne, Wager	MG USV	NY	02893
Swearingen, Thomas B.	Capt. AAG BvtMaj USV	PA	07657
Sweeney, Alexander	1st Lt. 140th PA Infy BvtCapt.	OH	08840
Sweeney, Charles H.	Capt. 19th IL Infy	IA	11442
Sweeny, Henry	Capt. 4th Cav BvtMaj USA	CA	00761
Sweeny, Thomas W.	BG USA	NY	02210
Sweet, Franklin	Capt. 63rd PA Infy	NE	05278
Sweet, Owen J.	Col. 28th Infy USA	MN	04934
Sweet, William E.	Capt. 23rd OH Infy BvtMaj	CO	07492
Sweitzer, Jacob B.	Col. 62nd PA Infy BvtBG	PA	00475
Sweitzer, Nelson B.	Col. 2nd Cav BvtBG USA	DC	05063
Swem, Edward L.	2nd Lt. 59th USCT	IA	17242
Swett, Atwell W.	Asst Surg. 29th ME Infy	ME	11410
Swett, Frank H.	1st Lt. 10th NH Infy	CA	03243
Swift, Charles N.	Capt. 30th USCT BvtLTC	NY	01335
Swift, Elijah	1st Lt. RQM 38th MA Infy	MA	10272
Swift, Frederic W.	Col. 17th MI Infy BvtBG	MI	04264
Swift, Harlan J.	Capt. 2nd NY Mounted Rifles	NY	09131
Swift, John L.	Capt. 3rd MA Cav	MA	08065
Swift, William	RAdm USN	DC	16169
Swigart, Frank	Capt. 46th IN Infy	IN	13991
Swiggett, William Y.	Maj 9th DE Infy	DC	02609
Swinburne, William L.	RAdm USN	CA	15949
Swing, Peter F.	Capt. 9th OH Cav	OH	02837
Swingley, Oliver H.	2nd Lt. 4th & 12th IL Cav	NE	16463
Swobe, Thomas	1st Lt. 12th MI Infy	NE	04303
Swords, Henry L.	Capt. 59th MA Infy BvtMaj	NY	01517
Sylvis, George W.	1st Lt. 47th OH Infy	OH	07425
Symes, George G.	Col. 44th WI Infy	CO	05710
Symonds, Frederick M.	RAdm USN	CA	16314
Symonds, Henry C.	Maj CS BvtCol. USA	CA	04607
Taber, Benjamin C.	1st Lt. RQM 55th OH Infy	OH	06836
Taber, Freeman A.	1st Lt. 20th MA Infy	CA	01813
Tabor, Orin	Capt. 1st NH H Arty	CA	02538
Tabor, Rufus K.	Capt. 10th VT Infy	IL	06304
Tafel, Gustav	LTC 106th OH Infy	OH	06846
Taft, Roscoe C.	1st Lt. 49th MA Infy	MA	14460
Taggart, Francis H.	1st Lt. 8th USCT	PA	11451
Taggart, Grantham I.	LTC CS USV	PA	02262
Taggart, Joseph	1st Lt. 30th PA Infy BvtCapt.	PA	12234
Taggart, Robert J.	Capt. 116th PA Infy	PA	14266
Taggart, William H.	Maj 2nd PA Cav	PA	00291
Tailof, Ivan	Maj 2nd US Vet Vol Infy	NY	01189
Taintor, Henry E.	2nd Lt. 1st CT H Arty	MA	10842
Tait, George F.	Capt. 10th NY Infy	NY	13829
Talbot, Thomas H.	LTC 1st ME H Arty BvtBG	MA	01860

Name	Rank	Commandery	Insignia No.
Talbot, Zephaniah	1st Asst Eng. USN	MA	11210
Talcott, E.V.K.	1st Lt. NY Eng.	IL	02173
Talcott, Harvey D.	1st Lt. 110th NY Infy	CA	02153
Talley, J. Smith	2nd Lt. 1st Batt DE L Arty	IN	09015
Tallman, Edward A.	Capt. 24th NY Cav	NY	01770
Tallman, Henry C.	Lt. Commander USN	NY	06234
Tannatt, Thomas R.	Col. 16th MA Infy BvtBG	OR	02157
Tanner, Zera L.	Commander USN	DC	06715
Tappan, Lewis W., Jr.	Capt. 45th MA Infy	MA	00865
Tappen, T.T.B.	Col. 30th PA Infy (4th Reserves)	PA	00107
Tarbell, George G.	Asst Surg. 3rd MA Cav	MA	02687
Tarbell, John F.	Paymaster USN	MA	00619
Tarbox, Henry F.	2nd Lt. 108th NY Infy	NY	12322
Tarkington, John S.	Capt. 132nd IN Infy	IN	10577
Tarr, Frederick C.	Maj Paymaster USV	MD	15168
Tarr, Horace G. H.	Capt. 20th CT Infy	NY	06171
Tassin, Augustus G.	Col. 35th IN Infy	NY	01109
Tate, James H.	1st Lt. 2nd RI Infy	WI	04456
Tatem, Henry H.	Capt. 137th OH Infy	OH	10481
Tatlock, Erasmus W.	2nd Lt. 3rd IA Cav	CA	14149
Taussig, Edward D.	RAdm USN	DC	16056
Taylor, Alexander A.	Capt. 122nd OH Infy	OH	12836
Taylor, Alfred B.	Capt. 5th Cav BvtMaj USA	DC	10341
Taylor, Alfred K.	Capt. 3rd OH Infy	MO	07287
Taylor, Anthony	1st Lt. 15th PA Cav	PA	03601
Taylor, Asher C.	BG USA	DC	08300
Taylor, Benjamin F.	BvtCol. USV	MD	14871
Taylor, Charles A.	Capt. 24th NY Cav	NY	12008
Taylor, David A.	Capt. 111th NY Infy	NY	11046
Taylor, Edward L.	Capt. 95th OH Infy	OH	14663
Taylor, Franck E.	Capt. 1st Arty BvtMaj USA	OR	01808
Taylor, Frank	BG USA	WA	10250
Taylor, Henry C.	RAdm USN	CA	08919
Taylor, Henry G.	Asst Surg. 8th NJ Infy	PA	05997
Taylor, Isaac A.	Capt. 13th TN Cav	KS	06863
Taylor, James E.	Capt. 5th OH Cav	IN	09016
Taylor, Jeremiah G.	Capt. ADC USV	OH	03487
Taylor, John	1st Lt. 31st PA Infy BvtCapt.	PA	04176
Taylor, John	2nd Lt. 70th OH Infy	WA	06079
Taylor, John N.	2nd Lt. 143rd OH Infy	OH	06187
Taylor, John P.	Col. 1st PA Cav BvtBG	PA	02942
Taylor, John T.	Capt. ADC USV	KS	08928
Taylor, John T.	2nd Lt. 147th IL Infy	DC	17377
Taylor, John Y.	Med. Director USN	PA	00426
Taylor, Joseph D.	Capt. 88th OH Infy BvtLTC	DC	12182
Taylor, Joseph H.	BvtCol. USV	PA	00244
Taylor, Oscar	Capt. 1st MN Mounted Rangers	MN	09145
Taylor, Robert D.	Passed Asst. Eng. USN	PA	07658

Name	Rank	Commandery	Insignia No.
Taylor, Robert R.	Surg. BvtLTC USV	PA	05739
Taylor, Silas E.	Capt. 50th NY Eng.	IN	17248
Taylor, Stuart M.	Capt. AAG BvtLTC USV	CA	00390-444
Taylor, Thomas T.	BvtBG USV	KS	06483
Taylor, Virgil C.	1st Lt. 84th OH Infy	OH	04741
Taylor, William E.	Med. Inspector USN	CA	02906
Taylor, William H.	1st Lt. RQM 113th IL Infy	IL	05609
Taylor, William H.	Capt. 118th OH Infy	OH	09816
Tayor, Gamaliel S.	1st Lt. Adj. 3rd IN Cav	IN	12682
Tebbetts, Albion W.	Maj 33rd MA Infy	DC	08007
Teeple, Addison V.	1st Lt. 8th IL Cav	MN	04049
Teetor, Henry B.	BvtLTC USV	CA	09633
Teller, David A.	2nd Lt. 177th NY Infy	NY	10330
Temple, David J.	Capt. 52nd IN Infy	MO	06728
Temple, Henry F.	Capt. 21st KY Infy	OH	07032
Temple, Jesse J.	Surg. 2nd KY Infy	DC	12040
Tencate, Frederick A.	Capt. 124th USCT	PA	10137
Ten-Eyck, Jacob H.	Maj 154th NY Infy	NY	02042
Ten-Eyck, Jerome B.	Capt. 5th MI Infy BvtMaj	DC	09109
Tennant, Richard S.	1st Lt. 133rd IN Infy	IN	13086
Terhune, Henry C.	1st Lt. 26th NJ Infy	NY	11920
Terrell, Charles M.	BG USA	NE	04026
Terrell, Lynch M.	1st Lt. 14th IN Infy	OH	06168
Terry, Alfred H.	MG USA	NY	01148
Terry, Edward	Commander USN	PA	00661
Terry, Ira C.	BvtLTC USV	MO	15905
Terry, J. Wadsworth	Surg. 20th CT Infy	NY	08951
Terry, John H.	Capt. 127th NY Infy	MO	08962
Terry, Silas W.	RAdm USN	DC	12505
Teters, Wilbur B.	LTC 116th OH Infy	CA	10644
Tevis, Edwin L.	1st Lt. 6th PA Cav	PA	00830
Thacher, Luin K.	Maj 9th KS Cav	MO	05085
Tharp, Joseph L.	Capt. 126th IL Infy	CA	02150
Thatcher, Henry K.	RAdm USN	PA	00700
Thatcher, Isaac B.	Capt. 45th IA Infy	CA	17481
Thaxter, Samuel	1st Lt. 45th MA Infy	NY	10498
Thaxter, Sidney W.	Maj 1st ME Cav	ME	02545
Thayer, Abel H.	Surg. 6th WVA Cav	DC	12492
Thayer, Amos M.	1st Lt. Sig. Corps BvtMaj USV	MO	04276
Thayer, Charles H.	Capt. 1st RI Cav	IL	07392
Thayer, George A.	Capt. 2nd MA Infy	OH	03200
Thayer, George D.	1st Lt. 2nd AR Infy	CO	11432
Thayer, Harry G.	Act Asst Paymaster USN	PA	08766
Thayer, Stephen A.	1st Lt. 17th OH Infy	IL	16738
Thayer, Theodore A.	1st Lt. 45th MA Infy	MA	03000
Theune, Roderick	Capt. 16th US VRC	PA	00083
Thibaut, Frederick W.	Capt. 6th Infy USA	OH	03560
Thiel, Charles A.	Capt. 4th MO Cav	OH	08034

The Roster

Name	Rank	Commandery	Insignia No.
Thistlewood, Napoleon B.	Capt. 98th IL Infy	IL	15653
Thoeny, Mathias	Capt. 2nd MN Infy	MN	16352
Thom, George	Col. Eng. BvtBG USA	ME	02384
Thoma, George H.	Asst Surg. 2nd NY H Arty	CA	13825
Thomas, Abner D.	Surg. 3rd AR Cav	MO	11424
Thomas, Benjamin	1st Lt. 4th MA Cav	MA	01434
Thomas, Benjamin A.	Capt. 62nd OH Infy	OH	09758
Thomas, Chalkley	Capt. 98th OH Infy	IA	13908 (Dup)
Thomas, Charles L.	Surg. 25th IN Infy	IA	07044
Thomas, Charles W.	BvtCol. USA	PA	00379
Thomas, Charles W.	2nd Lt. 2nd MA Infy	MO	09325
Thomas, Charles W.	1st Lt. 3rd IL L Arty	MO	14356
Thomas, David W.	Capt. 29th OH Infy	MD	02965
Thomas, Dexter L.	Capt. 88th IN Infy	NE	05757
Thomas, E. Darwin	1st Lt. Adj. 86th IN Infy	MN	13516
Thomas, Earl D.	Col. 11th Cav USA	IA	05080
Thomas, Findlay I.	Maj 87th PA Infy	PA	07659
Thomas, George H.	MG USA (Elected 3/6/1870)	PA	No Number
Thomas, George W.	1st Lt. 3rd NY L Arty	OH	15887 (Dup)
Thomas, Hampton S.	Maj 1st PA Cav BvtCOL.	PA	00384
Thomas, Henry G.	BG BvtMG USV	ME	00256
Thomas, Horace H.	Capt. AAG USV	IL	02185
Thomas, James B.	Capt. 107th PA Infy BvtMaj	PA	10264
Thomas, James P.	1st Lt. 94th NY Infy	PA	13196
Thomas, Jerome B.	Asst Surg. 24th IL Infy	OH	08577
Thomas, John J.	2nd Lt. 118th PA Infy	PA	03600
Thomas, John R.	Capt. 120th IN Infy	DC	03026
Thomas, Joseph	Surg. 118th PA Infy	PA	00077
Thomas, Joseph B.	3rd Class (Com. of Safety CA)	MA	02461
Thomas, Joseph H.	2nd Asst Eng. USN	PA	08239
Thomas, Nelson C.	Capt. 6th MI Cav	MI	13232
Thomas, Rhys M.	LTC 14th KY Infy	MO	09324
Thomas, Richard P.	1st Lt. 1st NY Cav	CA	03341
Thomas, Samuel	Col. 64th USCT BvtBG	OH	05199
Thomas, Samuel B., Jr.	3rd Class	PA	00362
Thomas, Stephen	BG USV	VT	09174
Thomas, William H.	Chap 4th NH Inf	NY	01105
Thomason, Samuel E.	Capt. 176th NY Infy	DC	09340
Thomasson, Nelson	Capt. 5th Infy USA	IL	05136
Thombs, Pembroke R. D.	Asst Surg. 89th IL Infy	CO	07484
Thompson, Al B.	Capt. 18th Infy BvtMaj USA	MA	02064
Thompson, Albert C.	Capt. 105th PA Infy	OH	03963
Thompson, Almon A.	Asst Surg. 11th MI Cav	MI	08528
Thompson, Alonzo J.	Capt. 2nd OH H Arty	PA	10138
Thompson, Archibald H.	Capt. 12th OH Cav	OH	12528
Thompson, Bradley M.	BvtLTC USV	MI	14923
Thompson, Charles	1st Lt. 7th MI Infy	MI	13797
Thompson, Charles H.	Capt. 1st USC H Arty	CA	07820

Name	Rank	Commandery	Insignia No.
Thompson, Charles P.	Paymaster USN	PA	01710
Thompson, Charles R.	Col. 12th USCT BvtBG	CA	02646
Thompson, Charles W.	1st Lt. 39th MA Infy	DC	02874
Thompson, DeWitt C.	Maj 2nd MA Cav	CA	01580
Thompson, Edward D.	1st Lt. Adj. 2nd KS Infy	KS	14629
Thompson, Elbridge A.	Surg. 12th ME Infy	ME	07902
Thompson, George J.	Capt. 2nd MA Infy	MA	02327
Thompson, George W.	LTC 152nd NY Infy	NY	08505
Thompson, George W.	2nd Lt. 25th USCT	WA	06320
Thompson, Heber S.	Capt. 7th PA Cav	PA	06774
Thompson, Hugh S.	Capt. 9th USCT	CA	05640
Thompson, J. Dixwell	1st Lt. 45th MA Infy	MA	00749
Thompson, J. Milton	BG USA	PA	04419
Thompson, James	1st Lt. RQM 24th MA Infy	MA	01470
Thompson, James A.	1st Lt. 12th OH Cav	CA	14847
Thompson, James L.	Surg. 2nd TN H Arty	IN	06826
Thompson, James M.	Capt. 12th ME Infy	ME	10567
Thompson, John A., Jr.	1st Lt. 4th MD Infy	MD	13958
Thompson, John H.	1st Lt. 192nd NY Infy	CA	01737
Thompson, John L.	Col. 1st NH Cav BvtBG	IL	01921
Thompson, John McC.	Maj 134th PA Infy	PA	09781
Thompson, John P.	Maj USA	CA	06062
Thompson, John R.	1st Lt. 15th VT Infy	DC	03165
Thompson, John W.	2nd Lt. 43rd OH Infy	IL	05808
Thompson, John W.	2nd Lt. 48th NY Infy	NY	14455
Thompson, Joseph W.	Capt. 12th Battn ME Infy	ME	08328
Thompson, Richard S.	LTC 12th NJ Infy	IL	10850
Thompson, Robert M.	Master USN	NY	01599
Thompson, S. Millett	2nd Lt. 13th NH Infy	MA	01753
Thompson, Seymour D.	Capt. 3rd USC H Arty	MO	06547
Thompson, Theodore S.	Pay Director USN	NY	01099
Thompson, Thomas H.	Capt. 52nd IL Infy	CA	09538
Thompson, William	Col. 1st IA Cav BvtBG	WA	10152
Thompson, William A.	Maj 17th PA Cav BvtLTC	PA	11540
Thompson, William B.	2nd Lt. 11th MI Cav	DC	02826
Thompson, William B.	2nd Lt. 24th NJ Infy	DC	12183
Thompson, William G.	Maj 20th IA Infy	IA	10391
Thompson, William G.	1st Lt. 6th NJ Infy	MI	03762
Thompson, William J.	Pay Director USN	WA	03673
Thoms, Joseph C.	1st Lt. 35th OH Infy	OH	13778
Thomson, Chester G.	LTC 72nd IN Infy	IN	09462
Thomson, Clifford	Maj 5th USC Cav	NY	03022
Thomson, Frank M.	1st Lt. 14th NY H Arty	IL	08047
Thomson, James W.	Chief Eng. USN	PA	06775
Thomson, Mark L.	Capt. 20th IA Infy BvtMaj	IA	10806
Thomson, William	Asst Surg. BvtMaj USA	PA	02297
Thornburgh, John	1st Lt. RQM 4th IN Cav	IN	08612
Thorndike, Albert	1st Lt. 19th MA Infy	MA	01462

Name	Rank	Commandery	Insignia No.
Thorndike, William	Surg. 39th MA Infy	WI	02455
Thorne, Rufus F.	2nd Lt. 5th KY Cav	KS	06490
Thorne, Thomas W.	Capt. 83rd Ny Infy	NY	12480
Thornton, Frank M.	Capt. 18th USCT BvtMaj	MN	05558
Thornton, Gardiner P.	1st Lt. 14th USCT	OH	08383
Thornton, Gilbert E.	Pay Director USN	NY	06878
Thornton, James M.	1st Lt. 13th MO Infy	KS	17030
Thornton, James S.	Capt. USN	PA	00590 (Dup)
Thornton, Joseph H.	LTC 49th IN Infy	OH	09385
Thorp, Abner	Act Asst Surg. USN	OH	12351
Thorp, Darius D.	2nd Lt. 25th MI Infy	MI	06923
Thorp, Frank	Col. Arty USA	DC	06020
Thorp, Martin R.	1st Lt. 2nd US Vet Vol Infy Bvt Capt.	DC	12059
Thorp, Thomas J.	BvtBG USV	MI	07894
Thrall, William R.	Surg. 27th OH Infy	OH	06325
Thrift, Robert W.	Surg. 49th OH Infy	OH	04743
Throckmorton, Charles B.	Maj 2nd Arty USA	CA	01622
Throop, Charles B.	2nd Lt. 4th IL Cav	IL	01440 (Dup)
Thruston, Gates P.	LTC AAG BvtBG USV	OH	06431
Thurber, Charles DeF.	1st Lt. RDQM 77th NY Infy	NY	09314
Thurber, James D.	Capt. 55th MA Infy BvtMaj	MA	01319
Thurstin, Wesley S.	Capt. 111th OH Infy	OH	03477
Thurston, Charles S.	Lt. USN	MA	16410
Thurston, James S.	Maj Paymaster BvtLTC USV	NY	04336
Thurston, Robert H.	1st Asst Eng. USN	NY	03613
Thwing, Franklin J.	1st Lt. 36th IL Infy	IL	13547
Tibbits, William B.	BG BvtMG USV	NY	01296
Tice, William W.	2nd Lt. 12th Ind. Batt NY L Arty	IL	16041
Tichenor, George C.	Maj ADC BvtCol. USV	DC	04727
Tichenor, Isaac S.	Capt. 105th NY Infy BvtCol.	DC	02489
Tichenor, Willis V.	Capt. 28th WI Infy	WI	04455
Ticknor, Benjamin H.	Capt. 2nd MA H Arty	MA	00857
Tidball, John C.	Col. 1st Arty BvtMG USA	DC	02354
Tidball, Zan L.	1st Lt. RQM 59th NY Infy	IL	07760
Tidd, John E.	Capt. 32nd MA Infy	MA	09673
Tiedemann, Frederick	Capt. 75th PA Infy	NY	00206
Tiemann, William F.	Capt. 159th NY Infy	NY	00227-5403
Tiernon, John L.	BG USA	NY	12852
Tiers, Edmund T.	LTC 157th PA Infy	PA	10402
Tiffany, Charles C.	Chap 6th CT Infy	MA	01648 (Dup)
Tiffany, Otis H.	3rd Class (VP NW Sanitary Com.)	MN	07825
Tifft, Lewis A.	Capt. 8th MA Infy	MA	01173 (Dup)
Tilden, Charles W.	Col. 16th ME Infy BvtBG	ME	02502
Tilden, John G.	Chief Carpenter USN	MA	13882
Tilden, Joseph	Capt. 55th MA Infy	CA	03633
Tileston, Thomas	Capt. 131st NY Infy	NY	00951
Tilford, Joseph G.	BG USA	DC	08095
Tillman, Walter P.	Capt. 30th NY Infy	NY	05015

Name	Rank	Commandery	Insignia No.
Tillman, William	BvtLTC USV	OH	04224
Tillotson, Ephraim	1st Lt. 27th Infy USA	OH	04858
Tillson, Davis	BG BvtMG USV	ME	08334
Tillson, George M.	Capt. 161st NY Infy	NY	08665
Tilson, John	1st Lt. 18th IN Infy	IN	13814
Tilton, Albert K.	1st Lt. 4th NH Infy	CO	05631
Tilton, Henry R.	Col. USA	DC	11061
Tilton, McLane	LTC USMC	CA	12927
Tilton, William S.	Col. 22nd MA Infy BvtBG	MA	01060
Timoney, Edward McB.	Capt. 15th Infy USA	CA	12587
Tingley, Clement, Jr.	1st Lt. Batt E, PA L Arty	PA	01474
Tinney, Henry C.	Capt. AAG USV	IN	13313
Tirrell, Chesley B.	1st Lt. 1st Battn. MN Infy	MN	07953
Tisdall, James M.	Capt. 95th IL Infy	NE	06697
Tisdall, William N.	Capt. 1st Infy USA	PA	02261
Titcomb, John S.	Capt. 88th USCT	CO	08187
Titcomb, Joseph A.	Act Master USN	ME	10353
Titus, Daniel	1st Lt. 5th Batt WI L Arty	CA	03911
Titus, Uriel B.	1st Lt. 11th NJ Infy BvtCapt.	PA	11541
Tobey, John F.	1st Lt. Adj. 10th RI Infy	MA	02062
Tobey, Thomas F.	Maj USA	MA	01066
Tobias, Joseph F.	Maj Volunteer ADC	PA	00997
Tobie, Edward P.	2nd Lt. 1st ME Cav	MA	10843
Tobin, John M.	Capt. 9th MA Infy	MA	09996
Todd, Henry D.	Lt. Commander USN	NY	No Number
Todd, Henry H.	Capt. 8th NJ Infy	CA	09838
Todd, Samuel A.	1st Lt. 8th OH Cav	OH	05388
Todd, Simeon S.	Surg. 4th CA Infy	MO	06050
Todd, William	Capt. 8th NJ Infy	IL	07441
Todd, William C.	Surg. 5th PA Cav	PA	01926
Toffey, John J.	1st Lt. 33rd NJ Infy	NY	04960
Toland, Harford	1st Lt. 154th OH Infy	OH	16066
Tomlinson, Abia A.	Col. 5th WVA Infy	MO	05086
Tomlinson, Joseph M.	Capt. 5th US Vol Infy	CA	17783
Tompkins, Charles H.	Col. 1st RI L Arty BvtBG	NY	04056-6022
Tompkins, John A.	LTC 1st RI L Arty	PA	02591
Tompkins, John W.	2nd Lt. 123rd IN Infy	IN	14155
Toppin, John D.	Passed Asst. Eng. USN	NY	05710
Torbert, Alfred T.A.	BG USV BvtMG USA	PA	00052
Torbert, George L.	Maj 46th IA Infy	IA	05430
Torbert, William F. A.	Paymaster USN	PA	00430
Torrance, Ell	2nd Lt. 97th PA Infy	MN	06098
Torrence, Thomas R.	1st Lt. 14th PA Cav	PA	11718
Torrey, Dolphus	Capt. 20th IA Infy	MO	08595
Torrington, John E.	1st Lt. 1st MD Cav	KS	15493
Totten, Enoch	Maj 5th WI Infy	DC	04774
Tourgee, Albion W.	1st Lt. 105th OH Infy	NY	13949
Tourtelotte, John E.	Col. 4th MN Infy BvtBG	DC	04471

The Roster 375

Name	Rank	Commandery	Insignia No.
Tower, Angelo E.	Capt. 6th MI Cav	MI	05575
Tower, Charlemange	Capt. 6th PA Infy	PA	06270
Tower, George E.	Chief Eng. USN	DC	12212
Tower, Morton	Capt. 13th MA Infy	OR	11875
Tower, Osmond S.	Capt. 6th MI Cav	MI	11493
Towers, Michael	1st Lt. 6th PA Cav	PA	13555
Towle, George F.	LTC AIG USV	MA	08048
Towle, Phineas S.	Act Asst Paymaster USN	IA	11074
Towle, Samuel K.	Surg. 30th MA Infy	MA	08321
Towler, Silas H.	1st Lt. 22nd Batt OH L Arty	MN	13485
Town, Francis L.	Col. Asst Surg. Gen. USA	PA	00485
Town, Thomas J.	Col. 95th PA Infy	PA	01484
Towne, Heraim McC.	1st Lt. Batt C 1st MI Arty	MI	16514
Towne, Nathan P.	Chief Eng. USN	PA	10880
Towne, Orin C.	1st Lt. 11th IL Infy	IL	10309
Townsend, Amos	1st Lt. 1st Batt OH L Arty	OH	03568
Townsend, Charles	Maj 30th OH Infy	OH	11707
Townsend, Charles C.	1st Lt. Adj. 1st PA Cav	PA	07355
Townsend, Charles H.	2nd Lt. 29th WI Infy	NE	03988
Townsend, Cyrus	1st Lt. RQM 211th PA Infy	KS	04922
Townsend, Eddy B.	2nd Lt. 80th NY Infy	DC	04554 (Dup)
Townsend, Edward D.	BG, Adj. Gen. BvtMG USA	DC	04881
Townsend, Edwin F.	BG USA	DC	02121
Townsend, Franklin	3rd Class	NY	00945
Townsend, Frederick	LTC 9th Infy BvtBG USA	NY	00799
Townsend, George M.	2nd Lt. 10th Batt MA L Arty	MA	01477
Townsend, Hosea	2nd Lt. 2nd OH Cav	CO	12331
Townsend, Luther T.	1st Lt. Adj. 16th NH Infy	MA	08066
Townsend, Oliver C.	1st Lt. 21st MI Infy	MI	13357
Townsend, Thomas G.	Capt. USA	KS	04891 (Dup)
Townshend, Smith	Maj 32nd IL Infy	DC	03527
Tracy, Albert	Maj 15th Infy BvtCol. USA	ME	09376
Tracy, Amasa S.	Col. 2nd VT Infy	VT	10072
Tracy, Benjamin F.	Col. 100th NY Infy BvtBG	NY	08008
Tracy, Charles W.	Lt. Commander USN	MA	00914
Tracy, D. Burnham	Chap 1st MI Eng.	MI	06412
Tracy, John	BvtCol.	NY	01261
Tracy, John P.	1st Lt. 8th Cav MO State Militia	MO	07911
Tracy, Osgood V.	Capt. 122nd NY Infy BvtLTC	NY	06235
Tracy, William G.	Capt. ADC BvtMaj USV	NY	06230
Tracy, William W.	Capt. 26th USCT	NY	04063
Train, Charles B.	Capt. AQM USV	MA	03161
Trask, Henry D.	1st Lt. 2nd USC Cav BvtCapt.	MA	13332
Trask, Lafayette L.	2nd Lt. 176th OH Infy	WA	14110
Trau, Adam	Asst Surg. USN	PA	00412
Traver, Lorenzo	Act Asst Surg. USN	PA	00597
Travis, Henry F.	Capt. 124th NY Infy	KS	15245
Travis, Robert A.	Capt. 8th USCT	PA	16802

Name	Rank	Commandery	Insignia No.
Treadwell, George H.	Capt. 7th NY H Arty BvtMaj	NY	02268
Treadwell, William A.	Capt. 14th NY H Arty	CA	14848
Treat, Nathaniel B.	Capt. 31st WI Infy	WI	12472
Treat, Richard B.	Col. CS USV	CA	16281
Tredway, Dwight	Capt. AQM BvtMaj USV	MO	04293
Treichel, Charles	Maj 3rd PA Cav BvtLTC	CA	02052
Tremain, Henry E.	Maj ADC BvtBG USV	NY	11561
Tremaine, William S.	Maj Surg. USA	NY	02142
Trenchard, Stephen D.	RAdm USN	NY	00239
Trescott, Benjamin F.	Capt. 65th OH Infy	OH	13777
Tricker, John A.	Capt. 114th PA Infy	PA	14476
Trickey, William H.	Maj 3rd NH Infy	MA	02162
Trilley, Joseph	RAdm USN	CA	02161
Trimble, Harvey M.	1st Lt. Adj. 93rd IL Infy	IL	12893
Trimble, Joel G.	Maj USA	CA	00946
Tripler, Charles S.	Maj Surg. BvtBG USA	NY	00227-1325
Tripler, Thomas C.	1st Lt. 39th MO Infy	PA	00056
Tripp, Stephen S.	Capt. 11th IL Infy	IL	09489
Tripp, Willard D.	LTC 29th MA Infy	MA	09674
Trounstine, Philip	Capt. 5th OH Cav	CO	05632
Trowbridge, Charles T.	LTC 33rd USCT	MN	14164
Trowbridge, Luther S.	Col. 10th MI Cav BvtMG	MI	03513
Trowbridge, William E.	2nd Lt. 16th WI Infy	WI	10893
Troxel, Thomas G.	Maj USA	IL	03556
Troy, Lewis L.	1st Lt. Adj. 9th IL Infy	IL	07700
True, Edward A.	LTC 8th ME Infy BvtCol.	MA	08860
True, James B.	1st Lt. Adj. 40th KY Infy	CA	14205
True, Theodore E.	BG USA	DC	07719 (Dup)
Truesdell, George	Maj Paymaster BvtLTC USV	DC	02513
Truesdell, Samuel	Capt. 65th NY Infy	NY	01206
Trufant, William B.	Act Ensign USN	CO	09739
Trull, Ezra J.	Capt. 39th MA Infy	MA	01595
Truman, Benjamin C.	3rd Class (Aide to Andrew Johnson)	CA	03954
Trumbull, H. Clay	Chap 10th CT Infy	PA	01001
Trumbull, James L.	Capt. AQM BvtLTC USV	IL	06316
Trush, Jacob	Asst Surg. 16th IL Infy	OH	03151
Truxton, William T.	Commodore USN	PA	00309
Tryon, James R.	Surg. Gen. USN	PA	00339
Tucker, Alba M.	Capt. AQM BvtCol. USV	OH	07528
Tucker, James	LTC 25th MA Infy BvtCol.	MA	09675
Tucker, James M.	1st Lt. 2nd USC Cav	MN	08994
Tucker, Joseph	1st Lt. 49th MA Infy	MA	01088
Tucker, Louis N.	Capt. 18th MA Infy BvtMaj	MA	00684
Tucker, Payson E.	2nd Lt. 16th MA Infy	MA	01031
Tucker, William P.	Capt. 1st IN Cav	CA	13135
Tuckerman, S. Cary	2nd Lt. Sig. Corps USV	MA	00961
Tuerk, Herman	2nd Lt. 12th MO Infy	MO	08275
Tufts, Gardner	3rd Class (Inspector of Prisons & Hosp.)	MA	07137

Name	Rank	Commandery	Insignia No.
Tufts, William F.	2nd Lt. 32nd MA Infy	MO	16948
Tuller, Loren W.	Capt. 60th NY Infy	NY	12795
Tullidge, Frank G.	Capt. 57th IN Infy	OH	05809
Tully, David	Chap 77th NY Infy	PA	06773
Tully, Redmond	1st Lt. 1st Art. BvtCapt. USA	MN	04930
Tupper, Francis W.	1st Lt. 1st AL Cav	CO	06693
Tupper, John S.	1st Lt. 3rd VT Infy	VT	10071
Tupper, Tullius C.	Maj 6th Cav BvtLTC USA	OH	04516
Turck, William S.	Capt. 26th MI Infy	MI	11496
Turley, John A.	Col. 91st OH Infy BvtBG	OH	07123
Turnbull, Charles N.	Capt. Eng. BvtCol. USA	MA	00687
Turnbull, John G.	Maj 1st Arty USA	DC	00982
Turner, Alfred L.	Capt. 29th ME Infy	ME	08332
Turner, Emory S.	2nd Lt. 120th NY Infy	NY	03019
Turner, George	Capt. 1st US Vet. Vol Eng.	MI	07741
Turner, George H.	Capt. 9th MI Cav	MI	13796
Turner, Henry A.	1st Lt. RQM 43rd MA Infy	MA	05025
Turner, Henry L.	1st Lt. 5th USCT (Col.1st IL Infy)	IL	05607
Turner, J. Thomas	Capt. 3rd MD Cav	DC	13038
Turner, John W.	BG BvtMG USV	MO	04282
Turner, Thomas	RAdm USN	PA	00175
Turner, Thomas McM.	1st Lt. RQM 36th OH Infy BvtMaj	IL	07014
Turner, Timothy G.	1st Lt. RQM 19th MI Infy	MI	10595
Turner, William H.	Maj 1st RI Cav	MA	07405
Turnley, Parmenas T.	Capt. AQM USA	IL	09827
Turrill, Henry S.	LTC Dept. Surg. Gen. USA	NY	03454
Tutein, Edward G.	Capt. 61st MA Infy	MA	05163
Tutewiler, Henry W.	1st Lt. RQM 17th IN Infy	IN	13006
Tuthill, Richard S.	1st Lt. 1st MI L Arty	IL	02003
Tuthill, Robert K.	Surg. 145th NY Infy	NY	07474
Tuttle, Benjamin B.	Capt. 1st CT Cav	OR	02152
Tuttle, Benton	Capt. 108th USCT	MO	04316
Tuttle, Francis	Act Ensign USN	WA	11112
Tuttle, Horace P.	Paymaster USN	PA	00503
Tuttle, James M.	BG USV	IA	05434
Tuttle, Jonathan B.	Capt. 102nd USCT	CA	10918
Tuttle, Joseph	Capt. AQM USV	CA	04019
Tweedale, John	LTC AAG USA	DC	12522
Twichell, Joseph H.	Chap 71st NY Infy	NY	12559
Twining, Edward H.	Capt. ADC USV	NY	04694
Twitchell, Adelbert B.	Capt. 1st ME L Arty BvtMaj	NY	09436
Twitchell, George B.	Surg. USV	MA	01385
Twitchell, Marshall H.	Capt. 109th USCT	VT	10381
Twombly, Voltaire P.	Capt. 2nd IA Infy	IA	05788
Twyeffort, Louis P.	2nd Lt. 72nd IL Infy	NY	12323
Tyler, Charles M.	Chap 22nd MA Infy	NY	09569
Tyler, Francis E.	Capt. 74th NY Infy BvtLTC	OH	03958
Tyler, George O.	Capt. 43rd MA Infy	VT	01802

Name	Rank	Commandery	Insignia No.
Tyler, Ira	1st Lt. 6th MD Infy	DC	07566
Tyler, John	Capt. 17th MI BvtMaj	MI	06091
Tyler, Mason W.	Maj 37th MA Infy	NY	05407
Tyler, Richard W.	Maj USA	DC	02507
Tyler, Robert O.	BG USV BvtMG USA	NY	00535-850
Tyndale, Hector	BG BvtMG USV	PA	00917
Tyner, Noah N.	BvtCapt. USV	OR	07150
Tyner, Richard H. H.	1st Lt. 9th IN Infy	IN	17600
Tyson, Carroll S.	1st Lt. Adj. 20th PA Cav	PA	12114
Udall, Franklin Oliver	1st Lt. 6th IA Cav	IA	11375
Ulio, James	Maj USA	NE	04988
Ullman, Frederic	1st Lt. 1st WI H Arty	IL	05610
Ulmer, Albert F.	Act Ensign USN	PA	08767
Ulrich, Charles P.	Capt. 31st USCT BvtMaj	NY	01832
Underhill, Andrew M.	1st Lt. 11th NY Infy	NY	05290
Underhill, Henry P.	LTC 160th NY Infy	DC	03986
Underwood, Adin B.	BG BvtMG USV	MA	00987
Underwood, Benjamin W.	1st Lt. Adj. 72nd IL Infy	IL	02181
Underwood, W. S.	Capt. 97th PA Infy	PA	16935-602
Updike, Edward	2nd Lt. 14th NJ Infy	NE	13370
Upham, Charles L.	Col. 15th CT Infy	NY	10435
Upham, Frank K.	Capt. 1st Cav USA	CA	02753
Upham, John H.	Capt. 107th USCT	MN	04550
Upham, John J.	Col. 8th Cav USA	WI	02302
Upham, Nathaniel L.	Chap 35th NJ Infy	MN	15151
Upham, William H.	1st Lt. 4th Arty USA	WI	03214
Upshur, John H.	RAdm USN	DC	02406
Upton, Albert F.	1st Lt. RQM 35th MA Infy	MA	01733
Upton, William B.	Capt. 1st US Vols.	CO	01676
Urell, M. Emmet	2nd Lt. 82nd NY Infy BvtMaj	DC	12431
Urwiler, George C.	Capt. 67th PA Infy	PA	00479
Usher, John P.	3rd Class (Sec. of the Interior)	KS	06308
Vail, David F.	2nd Lt. 16th WI Infy	MN	06555
Vale, Josiah M.	2nd Lt. 47th IA Infy	DC	06803
Valentin, Harry A.	1st Lt. 14th OH Infy	WI	08519
Valentine, Alonzo B.	Capt. CS BvtMaj USV	VT	03017
Valier, Charles	2nd Lt. 7th IL Cav	MO	11400
Vallette, Henry F.	LTC 105th IL Infy	CA	15722
VanAllen, James H.	BG USV	NY	00228
VanAntwerp, William W.	Capt. 4th MI Cav BvtMaj	MI	02059
VanArman, Hiram M.	2nd Lt. 58th IL Infy	CA	06332
VanArsdale, Nathaniel H.	1st Lt. 1st NJ Infy	NY	08506
VanBoyer, Samuel	2nd Lt. 40th IL Infy	MN	09227
VanBrimmer, Joshua	BvtCol. USV	NY	05830
VanBrunt, Henry	RAdm Secy. USN	MO	00977
VanBrunt, Ralph	BvtMaj USV	MN	07703
VanBuren, Daniel T.	Col. ADC BvtBG USV	NY	00126
VanBuren, John D.	1st Asst Eng. USN	PA	00704

Name	Rank	Commandery	Insignia No.
VanBuren, Thomas B.	Col. 102nd NY Infy BvtBG	CA	04006
VanBuskirk, Joseph	Capt. 2nd MI Infy	MI	05578
Vance, Alex F., Jr.	Maj Paymaster USV	OH	05316
Vance, John L.	LTC 4th WVA Infy	OH	07200
Vance, Joseph W.	1st Lt. 21st IL Infy	CA	17820
Vance, Lewis R.	Act Ensign USN	CA	10730
Vance, William H.	1st Lt. 165th NY Infy	NY	03616
Vance, Wilson J.	BvtCapt. USV	DC	02517
VanCise, Edwin	2nd Lt. 45th IA Infy	CO	13324
VanCleef, Augustus	Asst Surg. USV	PA	09978
VanCleve, Alfred A.	Capt. 20th MI Infy	MI	10235
VanCleve, Horatio P.	BG BvtMG USV	MN	04732
VanDeman, John D.	2nd Lt. 145th OH Infy	KS	10602
VanDeMan, Joseph H.	Capt. 66th OH Infy	OH	04744
VandeMark, William N.	Chap 92nd USCT	CA	17054
Vanderbilt, Aaron	Act Ensign USN	NY	02274
VanDerBurgh, David W.	Asst Surg. 10th MI Infy	MA	13385
Vandergrift, George A.	Maj 137th OH Infy (Maj Paymaster USV)	OH	02987
VanderHorck, John	Capt. 8th Vet. Res. Corps.	MN	03829
Vanderlip, William L.	Capt. 44th NY Infy BvtMaj	DC	05127
Vanderpoel, Samuel O.	3rd Class (Surg. Gen. NY)	NY	02146
Vanderslice, Thaddeus L.	2nd Asst Eng. USN	PA	08240
VanDerVeen, Arend	Asst Surg. 8th MI Infy	MI	10945
VanDerVeer, Albert	Surg. 6th NY Infy	NY	02374
VanDerveer, Ferdinand	BG USV	NY	06833
VanDeusen, Albert H.	Capt. 97th NY Infy	DC	03980
VanDeventer, James	Capt. CS BvtCol. USV	OH	07418
Vandever, William	BG BvtMG USV	CA	02814
Vandewater, William C.	2nd Lt. 22nd NJ Infy	NY	11853
VanDuyn, Augustus C.	Surg. BvtLTC USV	KS	04432
VanDuyn, John	Asst Surg. BvtCapt. USV	NY	07084
VanDuzee, Alonzo J.	1st Lt. RQM 44th IA Infy	IA	13907
VanDuzee, Edward M.	Maj 12th IA Infy	MN	05016-5150
VanDyke, Benjamin G.	Act Ensign USN	OH	17209
VanElls, John	1st Lt. 9th WI Infy	WI	08691
VanEtten, Edgar	2nd Lt. 2nd NJ Infy	NY	14288
VanGiesen, Henry C.	Act Asst Surg. USN	NE	13103
VanHoff, Henry L.	1st Lt. Adj. 114th IL Infy	IN	13993
VanHorn, James J.	Col. 8th Infy USA	CA	09043
VanHorn, Marian D.	Capt. 42nd USCT BvtMaj	CO	05960
VanHorn, Robert T.	LTC 25th MO Infy	MO	05971
VanHorne, William M.	BG USA	IL	06701
VanLeuvin, George M., Jr.	2nd Lt. 72nd USCT	IA	09074
VanNatta, Job H.	LTC 10th IN Infy	IN	11054
Vannort, William J.	1st Lt. 11th MD Infy	MD	13214
VanOsdel, Angus D.	Capt. 3rd IN Cav	CA	04906
VanOsdel, John M.	Capt. 59th IL Infy	IL	04143
VanPelt, Corwin R.	1st Lt. 81st OH Infy	IN	12944

Name	Rank	Commandery	Insignia No.
VanPelt, Francis M.	1st Lt. 17th IN Infy	IN	17778
VanReed, William E.	Capt. 5th Arty USA	CA	00022
VanRensselaer, Killlaen	1st Lt. 30th NY Infy	NY	01777
VanReypen, William K.	Surg. Gen. USN	DC	04357
VanSandford, Abram P.	1st Lt. 93rd NY Infy	CA	17815
VanSellar, Henry	LTC 12th IL Infy	IL	13629
VanSlyck, David B.	Maj 22nd NY Cav	CA	15639
VanSlyck, Nicholas	Capt. 1st RI Infy	MA	02063
VanSlyke, Napoleon B.	Capt. AQM BvtLTC USV	WI	05225
VanSteenburg, Linas	Capt. 57th IL Infy	MO	11789
VanValzah, David D.	Col. 18th Infy USA	MN	07749
VanVliet, Frederick	Maj 10th Cav BvtLTC USA	PA	02639
VanVliet, Stewart	BG USV BvtMG USA	DC	00745
VanVoast, James	Col. USA	OH	02988
VanWinkle, Edgar B.	Capt. 102nd USCT	NY	00441
Varney, Almon L.	Col. USA	IN	07774
Varney, George	Col. 2nd ME Infy BvtBG	ME	00263
Varney, James A.	Chap 7th ME Infy	OR	05672 (Dup)
Varnum, John	Capt. 82nd USCT BvtMaj	CO	11582
Vaughan, Charles E.	Act Asst Surg USN	CA	06340
Vaughan, Hiram C.	Capt. 24th ME Infy	ME	06160
Veale, Moses	Maj 109th PA Infy	PA	02075
Veazey, Wheelock G.	Col. 16th VT Infy	DC	07406
Vedder, R. C.	1st Lt. USV	CA	01333
Veil, Charles H.	1st Lt. 1st Cav BvtCapt. USA	PA	11836
Veitch, William	2nd Asst Eng. USN	WI	04300
Venable, Charles H.	Lt. USN	DC	18459
Verdier, John A.S.	Capt. 27th WI Infy	MI	12263
VerMeulen, Edmund C.	Surg. USN	PA	07876
Vernon, George R.	Capt. 14th US Infy	CA	01624
Vernon, George W.F.	LTC 1st Regt. Potomac Home Brig. MD Cav	DC	07181
Vernon, Maris R.	LTC 78th IL Infy	CA	05324
Vernor, Benjamin	3rd Class	MI	06369
Vernor, James	2nd Lt. 4th MI Cav	MI	04714
Vernou, Charles A.	Maj 17th Infy USA	MI	00115
Verrill, George W.	Capt. 17th ME Infy	ME	09846
Vezin, Henry A.	Capt. 5th PA Cav BvtLTC	PA	00292
Vickers, David	BvtBG USV	PA	00117
Vickery, Richard S.	LTC USA	DC	12033
Vidal, Theodore C.	1st Lt. Sig. Corps USV	NY	00626
Viele, Charles D.	BG USA	CA	12205
Viele, Egbert L.	BG USV	NY	00129
Vifquain, Victor	Col. 97th IL Infy BvtBG	NE	08522
Vignos, Augustus	Maj 107th OH Infy	OH	07415
Villeplait, A. Beaufort	1st Lt. RQM 182nd NY Infy	NY	10766
Vincent, Thomas M.	BG USA	DC	06149
Vincent, Walter S.	Surg. 9th VT Infy	VT	10075
Vinton, Francis L.	GB USV	NY	00843

Name	Rank	Commandery	Insignia No.
Vinton, Warren G.	Capt. 24th MI Infy	MI	04009
Virgin, William W.	Col. 22nd ME Infy	ME	08329
Viven, John L.	Capt. 12th Infy USA	CA	03451
Vliet, John B.	LTC 51st WI Infy	WI	05765
Vocke, William	Capt. 24th IL Infy	IL	06133
Vogdes, Anthony W.	BG USA	CA	06733
Vogdes, Israel	BG USV	NY	00122
Vogel, Theodore K.	Capt. 198th PA Infy	PA	02943
Volkmar, William J.	Col. AAG USA	CO	02679
Vollor, Joseph	1st Lt. RQM 42nd IL Infy	IL	11765
Vollum, Edward P.	Col. Chief Med. Purveyor USA	NY	08114
VonBaumbach, Frederick	Capt. 35th WI Infy	MN	03851
VonBraida, Sigmund C.	2nd Lt. 2nd NJ Cav	DC	09035
VonFritsch, Frederick O.	Capt. 68th NY Infy	DC	05677
VonHaake, Adolph	Maj 68th NY Infy	DC	06877
VonKoenig, Robert	Capt. 68th NY Infy	DC	12548
VonKolkrow, Edwin R.	1st Lt. 12th IL Cav	IL	16042
VonLeliwa, Carl E.W.P.	Capt. 58th NY Infy	NY	11247
VonLuttwitz, Adolph H.	Capt. 54th NY Infy	NY	01094
VonMitzel, Alexander T.	LTC 74th PA Infy	PA	01195
VonSchirach, Frederick C.	Maj USA	NY	00877
VonSeldeneck, Leopold	1st Lt. 103rd NY Infy	PA	14634
VonSteinwehr, Adolph	BG USV	NY	00388
Voorhees, Jacob E.	Capt. 58th Ind Batt Arty	IN	11805
Voorhees, Philip R.	1st Asst Eng. USN	NY	07786
Voorhees, Richard M.	Capt. 65th OH Infy	OH	12499
Voris, Alvin C.	Col. 67th OH Infy BvtMG	OH	05313
Voris, Archibald C.	Capt. CS BvtLTC USV	IN	10288
Vose, Rufus C.	Capt. 1st CA Cav	CA	07213
Vose, William P.	BG USA	DC	08683
Votteler, Henry J.	2nd Lt. 37th OH Infy	OH	15454
Vought, John E.	1st Lt. 103rd OH Infy	IN	06615
Vredenburgh, John S.	Capt. 10th IL Infy	IL	07833
Vroom, Peter D.	BG Inspector Gen. USA	PA	01093
Waddell, Lloyd D.	LTC 11th IL Infy	NY	05839
Wade, Henry P.	BvtMaj USA	OH	09743
Wade, James F.	MG USA	OH	00445
Wade, William H.	LTC 40th USCT	MO	06525
Wadhams, Albion V.	Commodore USN	DC	17297
Wadleigh, George H.	RAdm USN	MA	06831
Wadsworth, Charles F.	Capt. 116th NY Infy	DC	10419
Wadsworth, James W.	Capt. ADC BvtMaj USV	DC	03217
Wagenhalls, Samuel	1st Lt. 114th OH Infy	IN	16045
Wagner, Clinton	BvtLTC USA	NY	03350
Wagner, George E.	LTC 9th USCT BvtCol.	PA	04964
Wagner, Henry	Col. USA	NY	02867
Wagner, Henry C.	Capt. 54sth PA Infy	PA	02641
Wagner, Jacob	BvtCapt. USA	PA	02946

Name	Rank	Commandery	Insignia No.
Wagner, John B.	Capt. 135th IN Infy	IN	08141
Wagner, Samuel C.	1st Lt. 3rd PA Cav	PA	15860
Wagner, William	Maj 15th PA Cav	OH	05117
Wagoner, Aaron	2nd Lt. 6th OH Cav	OH	04203
Wagoner, Martin V.B.	Capt. 118th USCT	NY	13116
Wagstaff, Alfred	Maj 91st NY Infy	NY	00240
Wainwright, John	Col. 97th PA Infy	DC	02607
Wainwright, Richard	RAdm USN	DC	18342
Wainwright, William A.	Capt. AQM BvtMaj USA	IN	13057
Wait, Horation L.	Paymaster USN	IL	02005
Waite, Charles	Col. 27th MI Infy BvtBG	IL	04110
Waite, Jasper H.	Capt. 17th IL Cav	MO	05047
Waite, Lyman C.	1st Lt. 21st WI Infy	CA	12929
Waite, Norman	Maj 189th OH Infy	OH	03037
Waite, Richard	Capt. 84th OH Infy	OH	03044
Walbridge, Charles E.	LTC QM USV	NY	07475
Walbridge, James H.	Col. 2nd VT Infy	VT	09182
Walcott, Aaron F.	1st Lt. 3rd Batt MA L Arty	MA	12108
Walcott, Alfred F.	Capt. 21st MA Infy	NY	02035
Walcott, Charles F.	Col. 61st MA Infy BvtBG	MA	01293
Walcott, William Stuart	2nd Lt. 76th NY Infy	NY	09617 (Dup)
Walcutt, Charles C.	BG BvtMG USV	OH	02449
Walden, William A.	Capt. 36th OH Infy	OH	04194
Waldron, George W.	Capt. CS BvtMaj USV	TN	00358
Waldron, Stephen G.	2nd Lt. ME H Arty	ME	15991
Wales, B. Read	Capt. 42nd MA Infy	MA	12539
Wales, John P.	Capt. 17th Infy BvtMaj USA	PA	01740-2640
Wales, Nathaniel	Maj 35th MA Infy BvtCol.	MA	01685
Wales, Sigourney	Maj 55th MA Infy	IN	03120
Wales, Thomas B.	Capt. 45th MA Infy	MA	06948
Walke, Henry	RAdm USN	NY	00300
Walker, Aldace F.	LTC 1st VT H Arty	NY	05409
Walker, August C.	Surg. 18th NY Cav	NY	03124
Walker, Charles	Maj 10th ME Infy	ME	08335
Walker, Charles A.	Capt. 165th NY Infy	NY	10901
Walker, Charles B.	1st Lt. RQM 33rd MA Infy	MA	09066
Walker, Charles H.	1st Lt. 45th MA Infy	MA	00757
Walker, Edward A.	Commander USN	MA	01270-1286
Walker, Edwin P.	Capt. 89th IL Infy BvtMaj	DC	07296
Walker, Francis A.	LTC AAG BvtBG USV	MA	02330
Walker, George J.	1st Lt. 9th WVA Infy	OH	09384
Walker, George M.	Capt. 33rd MA Infy	MA	04469
Walker, George M.	2nd Lt. 11th KS Infy	IA	11882
Walker, George S.	Surg. 6th MO Infy	MO	04577
Walker, Ivan N.	Col. 73rd IN Infy	IN	10245
Walker, James	Capt. 15th ME Infy	ME	14277
Walker, John	1st Lt. 132nd NY Infy	NY	06628
Walker, John C.	1st Lt. 63rd USCT	IL	12391

Name	Rank	Commandery	Insignia No.
Walker, John G.	RAdm USN	DC	02356
Walker, John H.	BvtMaj USA	NY	No Number
Walker, Leicester	Capt. USA	NE	15718
Walker, Peleg R.	1st Lt. 92nd IL Infy	IL	12382
Walker, Richard L.	Capt. 19th OH Infy	KS	06486
Walker, Robert C.	Maj Paymaster USA	CA	03996
Walker, Robert W.	2nd Lt. 34th MA Infy	MA	11269
Walker, Thomas McC.	Col. 111th PA Infy BvtBG	PA	11835
Walker, William D.	Act Asst Paymaster USN	PA	12356
Walker, William J.	1st Lt. 165th NY Infy	DC	03585
Walker, William R.	1st Lt. 1st RI Infy	MA	05881
Walker, William T.	3rd Class	OH	03272
Walkinshaw, Joseph C.	1st Lt. 38th PA Infy	KS	13223
Walkley, Charles S.	Chap USA	VT	13866
Wallace, Frederick S.	Maj 82nd OH Infy (Capt. 61st OH Infy)	OH	05754
Wallace, George W.	LTC USA	PA	00758
Wallace, Henry C.	1st Lt. 12th WVA Infy	CA	04759
Wallace, John S.	Chap USN	CA	08861
Wallace, Jonathan C.	Capt. 12th OH Infy	MO	05365
Wallace, Lew	MG USV	IN	05194
Wallace, Robert C.	Maj 5th MI Cav BvtLTC	CA	03927
Wallace, Rush R.	Commodore USN	DC	06380
Wallace, Thomas	Capt. 12th MI Infy	IL	07006
Wallace, William	Capt. 105th OH Infy	OH	05934
Wallace, William	1st Lt. Adj. 4th OH Infy	NE	04084
Wallace, William M.	Col. 15th Cav USA	DC	13039
Wallace, William W.	Capt. 20th PA Infy	PA	04672
Wallace, Wilson DeWitt	Capt. 40th IN Infy	IN	08771
Wallber, Albert	1st Lt. 26th WI Infy	WI	15249
Walling, Julius M.	1st Lt. 61st USCT	CA	04866
Wallingford, John N.	1st Lt. Adj. 10th KY Cav	IN	08147
Wallis, George H.W.	1st Lt. 3rd Infy USA	CA	02472
Wallis, Obed W.	1st Lt. 1st WI H Arty	IL	09352
Walsh, Patrick F.	Capt. 84th PA Infy	CA	11229
Walters, Albert H.	Capt. 118th PA Infy BvtMaj	PA	03413
Walton, Henry H.	2nd Lt. 16th NY H Arty	IL	11794
Walton, Thomas C.	Med. Director USN	NY	08666
Walworth, Nathan H.	Col. 42nd IL Infy	IL	02171
Wanner, Leonard F.	2nd Lt. 23rd WI Infy	WI	14429
Wappenhaus, Charles F.R.	Act Master USN	IN	08727
Ward, Alanson H.	Capt. 61st MA Infy	MA	00753
Ward, Andrew J.	Surg. 2nd WI Infy	WI	08689
Ward, Augustus H.	1st Lt. 90th NY Infy	CA	09121
Ward, Byron C.	1st Lt. Adj. 2nd VT Infy	IA	12755
Ward, Edward F.	Maj Surg. 38th MA Infy	NY	15577
Ward, George S. L.	Capt. 22nd Infy USA	PA	00106
Ward, George W.	2nd Lt. 137th OH Infy	OH	08039
Ward, Granville B.	Capt. 14th IN Infy	IN	16240

Name	Rank	Commandery	Insignia No.
Ward, Henry C.	BG USA	CA	00834
Ward, J. Langdon	Maj 75th USCT	NY	04603
Ward, Jasper D.	1st Lt. 1st MO Eng.	CO	11115
Ward, John H.	LTC 27th KY Infy	OH	03395
Ward, Samuel B.	Asst Surg. USV	NY	01222
Ward, Thomas	BG USA	DC	03362
Ward, Thomas	1st Lt. Adj. 9th MO Cav	CO	10782
Ward, William C.	LTC 115th PA Infy	PA	02232
Ward, William D.	LTC 37th IN Infy	IN	08148
Wardner, Horace	Surg. BvtLTC USV	IL	06938
Wardwell, Edward H.	2nd Lt. Sig. Corps BvtCapt. USV	NY	03123
Ware, Elton W.	1st Lt. 9th ME Infy	ME	08585
Ware, Eugene F.	Capt. 7th IA Cav	KS	04795
Ware, Joseph	Act Ensign USN	NY	10086
Ware, M. Everett	Capt. 6th MA Infy	MA	01681
Ware, William E.	Capt. 27th MO Infy	MO	04018
Warfield, Richard H.	1st Lt. 50th NY Eng.	CA	02240
Waring, George E., Jr.	Col. 4th MO Cav	MA	05031
Warmoth, Henry C.	LTC 32nd MO Infy	OH	06509
Warner, Alexander	LTC 13th CT Infy	NY	05032
Warner, Charles G.	Capt. 32nd MO Infy	MO	04287
Warner, Clermont E.	LTC 36th WI Infy	WI	15573
Warner, Darius B.	LTC 133rd OH Infy BvtBG	MI	01136
Warner, Edgar W.	2nd Lt. 74th IL Infy	KS	05217
Warner, Edward R.	Maj 1st Art USA BvtBG	DC	04728
Warner, Frederick L.	Capt. 7th WI Infy	WI	04976
Warner, Frederick R.	1st Lt. 50th PA Infy	IL	09205
Warner, George E.	Capt. 10th USC H Arty BvtMaj	NE	14305
Warner, Henry	2nd Lt. Batt "G" PA L Arty	PA	08241
Warner, James M.	BG USV	NY	01908
Warner, Rodolphus G.	2nd Lt. 44th NY Infy	OH	11571
Warner, Vespasian	Capt. CS BvtMaj USV	IL	11766
Warner, Wallace B.	Capt. 111th PA Infy	PA	09289
Warner, Willard	Col. 180th OH Infy BvtMG	OH	03299
Warner, William	Maj 44th WI Infy	MO	03819
Warner, William H.	1st Lt. 101st NY Infy	NY	10767
Warner, William R.	2nd Lt. 13th MA Infy	MA	09240
Warnock, William R.	Maj 95th OH Infy BvtLTC	OH	06127
Warren, Charles E.	1st Lt. 184th OH Infy	CO	13476
Warren, Charles S.	Act Asst Paymaster USN	IL	12746
Warren, Daniel L.	2nd Lt. 10th ME Infy	ME	10354
Warren, Dwight	1st Lt. 189th NY Infy	MI	14344
Warren, Elisha W.	1st Lt. 3rd PA Cav	PA	12235
Warren, George L.	Capt. 157th NY Infy	NY	16008
Warren, Henry	2nd Lt. 1st CA Cav	MA	01762
Warren, Henry E.	Capt. 9th TN Cav	MO	15156
Warren, Lucius H.	LTC 38th USCT BvtBG	PA	01712
Warren, Robert L.	2nd Lt. 27th MI Infy	MI	15698

The Roster

Name	Rank	Commandery	Insignia No.
Warren, Selleck B.	Capt. 23rd OH Infy	KS	06361
Warrens, Charles H.	Maj 5th MO Cav	CA	05900
Warson, Martin L.	1st Lt. 45th USCT	MO	05044
Warwick, Newton R.	2nd Lt. 91st OH Infy	OH	04219
Washburn, Andrew	Maj 1st MA H Arty	MA	09443
Washburn, George A.	Capt. 22nd MA Infy	MA	10344
Washburn, Zadeck	Capt. 10th USC H Arty	MA	09676
Washburne, Elihu B.	3rd Class (US Representative IL)	IL	02001
Washer, Solomon R.	1st Lt. Adj. 8th KS Infy BvtMaj	KS	09388
Wasson, Alonzo M. L.	Act 3rd Asst Eng. USN	OH	06081
Wasson, William H.H.	1st Lt. 6th PA H Arty	PA	13127
Waterhouse, Allen C.	LTC 1st IL L Arty BvtCol.	IL	08403
Waterhouse, Eben W.	1st Lt. 3rd RI H Arty	PA	04673
Waterman, Arba N.	LTC 100th IL Infy	IL	02174
Waterman, Harrison L.	1st Lt. 1st NY Eng	IA	15367
Waterman, Luther D.	Maj 39th IN Infy	IN	12683
Waterman, Richard	Capt. 1st RI L Arty	MA	01612
Waterman, Richard	1st Lt. 1st RI Cav	IL	05137
Waterman, Robert H.	Capt. 31st IN Infy	KS	12502
Waterman, Rufus	Lt. USN	MA	01701
Waters, Charles C.	Capt. 56th USCT	MO	07378
Waters, David R.	Capt. 10th IL Infy	MI	13794
Waters, Joseph G.	BvtCapt. USA	KS	17354
Waters, William E.	LTC Dept. Surg. Gen. USA	DC	01213
Waters, William G.	1st Lt. 15th MA Infy	CA	14005
Watkins, Charles W.	1st Lt. Adj. 10th MI Cav BvtCapt.	MI	08198
Watkins, Erwin C.	Capt. AAG USV	MI	08194
Watkins, Frederick W.	Capt. 107th USCT BvtMaj	NY	14624
Watkins, George R.	Paymaster USA	PA	00431
Watkins, William H.	Surg. 1st OR Cav	OR	04856
Watkins, William W.	1st Lt. Adj. 1st WI Infy	WI	11186
Watmough, James H.	Paymaster Gen. USN	PA	00334
Watmough, Pendleton G.	Lt. Commander USN	PA	14474
Watmough, William N.	Paymaster USN	PA	00938
Watrous, Charles L.	Capt. 76th NY Infy	IA	05432
Watrous, Jerome A.	Maj Paymaster USA	WI	03221
Watson, Adolphus E.	Pay Director USN	PA	00311
Watson, Alexander T.	Surg. BvtLTC USV	NY	05838
Watson, Amasa B.	Maj 8th MI Infy	MI	05173
Watson, Benjamin F.	LTC 6th MA Infy BvtCol.	NY	05014
Watson, Beriah A.	Surg. 4th NJ Infy	NY	06731
Watson, Charles T.	Capt. AQM BvtMaj USV	OH	04204
Watson, Eugene W.	RAdm USN	PA	00504
Watson, George W.	Capt. 90th PA Infy	DC	07682
Watson, Henry B.	2nd Lt. 11th USC H Arty	IL	13166
Watson, James L.	Surg. 17th NY Infy	NY	08115
Watson, John G.	RAdm USN	DC	08871
Watson, William L.	Capt. 21st WI Infy	NY	04057

Name	Rank	Commandery	Insignia No.
Watt, David M.	Capt. 74th NY Infy	PA	06271
Watters, John	Commander USN	PA	00141
Wattles, Washington W.	1st Lt. 28th PA Infy	PA	07356
Watts, Arthur H.	BvtCapt. USV	OH	15455
Watts, Charles	1st Lt. 1st NJ Cav	PA	08768
Watts, Elijah S.	LTC 2nd KY Cav	IL	08124
Watts, George H.	1st Lt. 4th RI Infy	PA	08467
Watts, Richard A.	Capt. 17th MI Infy BvtLTC	MI	13390
Watts, Robert	Surg. 133rd NY Infy	NY	01078
Way, David L.	1st Lt. 127t OH Infy BvtCapt.	OH	10679
Way, John A.	1st Lt. 10th CT Infy	MA	13333
Wayland, Heman L.	Chap 7th CT Infy	PA	08769
Wayne, William	Capt. 97th PA Infy	PA	00491
Weakley, Thomas J.	Capt. 110th OH Infy	OH	09759
Weand, Henry K.	Capt. 15th PA Cav	PA	04674
Weare, John F.	Capt. 40th MA Infy	IL	05145
Weatherwax, Jacob	2nd Lt. 10th MI Cav	MI	04012
Weaver, Aaron W.	RAdm USN	DC	00936
Weaver, Francis H.	Maj USA	PA	16132
Weaver, Henry C.	Capt. 16th KY Infy	OH	07938
Weaver, James B.	Col. 2nd IA Infy BvtBG	IA	11624
Weaver, Joseph K.	Capt. Indpt Co. PA Mounted Infy	PA	04961
Weaver, Joseph S.	1st Lt. Adj. 11th PA Cav	KS	04919
Weaver, Stanton	Capt. 62nd USCT BvtLTC	OH	14513
Weaver, Thomas R.	LTC 119th USCT	CA	18294
Webb, Alexander S.	BG USV BvMG USA	NY	00302
Webb, Edward C.	Surg. 24th NY Infy	CA	02863
Webb, Elias H.	2nd Lt. 51st WI Infy	CO	06120
Webb, Henry P.	1st Lt. 111th USCT	PA	17285
Webb, Lewis H.	1st Lt. 38th IN Infy	CA	15881
Webb, Melville E.	Asst Surg. 33rd MA Infy	MA	02711
Webb, Robert S.	Maj Paymaster BvtLTC USV	NY	01297
Webb, Watson	Capt. 3rd Arty USA	CA	01342
Webb, William C.	Col. 53rd WI Infy	KS	05539
Webb, William H.	Lt. Commander USN	NY	10972
Weber, Daniel	Col. 39th OH Infy	OH	05198
Weber, Gustav C.E.	Surg. 129th OH Infy	OH	10285
Weber, John B.	Col. 89th USCT	NY	12729
Webster, Almar P.	Capt. 9th NY Infy	NY	00585
Webster, Daniel	Capt. 1st WI L Arty	OR	15745
Webster, Edward	Capt. 4th USC H Arty	DC	09939
Webster, Edward F.	1st Lt. 25th Batt OH L Arty	OH	04210
Webster, George P.	Capt. AQM BvtCol. USV	NY	09866
Webster, George P.	Capt. AQM BvtCol. USV	NY	09866
Webster, Harrie	RAdm USN	DC	08308
Webster, John C.	2nd Lt. 40th IN Infy	IN	07743
Webster, John McA.	Capt. 22nd Infy USA	DC	13791
Webster, Joseph R.	LTC 44th USCT	NE	07548

The Roster

Name	Rank	Commandery	Insignia No.
Webster, Ralph C.	Col. QM USV	CO	11605
Webster, William H.	1st Lt. 5th CT Infy	DC	02683
Wedemeyer, William G.	Maj USA	CA	03579
Wedge, Albert C.	Surg. 3rd MN Infy	MN	07104
Weed, Theodore J.	Maj ADC BvtLTC USV	CA	04815
Weeden, Elnathan S.	1st Lt. 68th USCT	IL	07442
Weeden, William B.	Capt. 1st RI L Arty	MA	02625
Weeks, Benjamin F.	Capt. CS BvtMaj USV	MA	01309
Weeks, Charles B.	2nd Lt. 9th USC H Arty	CA	09410
Weeks, Edgar	Capt. 22nd MI Infy	MI	12578
Weeks, George H.	BG QM Gen. USA	DC	02722
Weeks, George W.	1st Lt. 51st USCT	IA	09075
Weeks, Henry A.	Col. 12th NY Infy	NY	04341
Weeks, John H.	Capt. 91st PA Infy	PA	02445
Wehrle, Joseph C.	Capt. 76th OH Infy BvtLTC	OH	05473
Wehrum, Charles C.	Capt. 12th MA Infy	NY	10973
Weid, Ivar A.	Capt. 82nd IL Infy	CA	13610
Weidman, Grant	Maj 173rd PA Infy	PA	01118
Weidman, William M.	Surg. 2nd PA Cav	PA	02130
Weidner, Peter	Capt. 106th OH Infy	OH	07843
Weigel, Eugene F.	Capt. 82nd IL Infy BvtMaj	MO	04277
Weir, Henry C.	Maj AAG BvtLTC USV	NY	05302
Weir, Robert F.	1st Lt. Asst Surg. USA	NY	16085
Weir, Robert McQ.	Act 2nd Asst Eng. USN	CA	13636
Weir, Thomas B.	LTC 3rd MI Cav	PA	00556
Weirick, John H.	1st Lt. 57th IL Infy	PA	11542
Weirick, Samuel T.	Capt. USA	DC	16170
Weist, Jacob R.	Surg. 1st USCT	IN	03390
Weitzell, Philip	1st Lt. 54th OH Infy	OH	10283
Welch, David E.	LTC 2nd OH Cav	DC	13584
Welch, Deming N.	Capt. AQM BvtCol. USV	IL	01917
Welch, George P.	1st Lt. Adj. 10th VT Infy	OH	03036
Welch, James G.	2nd Lt. 10th NY L Arty	KS	18448
Welch, John F.	Capt. 116th OH Infy	OH	09748
Welch, Johnson M.	Maj 18th OH Infy	OH	04208
Weld, Francis M.	Surg. 27th USCT	MA	01228
Weld, Richard H.	Capt. 44th MA Infy	MA	02686
Weld, Stephen M.	Col. 56th MA Infy BvtBG	MA	00785
Welker, Frederick	Maj 1st MO Arty BvtCol.	CA	09209
Welles, George E.	BvtBG USV	MN	08924
Welles, Gideon	3rd Class (Secretary of the Navy)	PA	00045
Welling, Joseph	Col. 9th NY H Arty	NY	09132
Wellington, Edward W.	2nd Lt. 2nd MA Cav	MA	01177
Wellman, David W.	Capt. 9th MN Infy	CA	04291
Wells, Almond B.	BG USA	NE	07545
Wells, Andrew B.	Capt. 8th PA Cav	PA	05509
Wells, Charles A.	LTC 1st NY Cav	NY	07787
Wells, Charles W.	Capt. 118th NY Infy BvtMaj	MI	05902

Name	Rank	Commandery	Insignia No.
Wells, Daniel T.	Capt. 8th Infy BvtMaj USA	MI	02756
Wells, David W.	1st Lt. 10th MA Infy	IL	09248
Wells, Ebenezer T.	Capt. 89th IL Infy BvtCol.	CO	05961
Wells, Edwin	Chief Eng. USN	PA	02944
Wells, Frank	Capt. 13th CT Infy BvtMaj	NY	06748
Wells, Frank S.	1st Lt. 1st US Shpshtrs.	NY	06223
Wells, G. Wiley	Capt. 19th NY Infy	CA	06063
Wells, Gideon	1st Lt. 6th MA Infy	MA	03677
Wells, Henry M.	Med. Director USN	NY	00885
Wells, James M.	Capt. 8th MI Cav	CA	09539
Wells, John L.	2nd Lt. 111th PA Infy	PA	11543
Wells, Lemuel H.	1st Lt. 32nd WI Infy	WA	08630
Wells, Levi	Capt. CS BvtMaj USV	PA	11453
Wells, William	BG BvtMG USV	VT	03897 (Dup)
Wells, William S.	2nd Asst Eng. USN	NY	03130
Welsh, Edward H.	1st Lt. 65th NY Infy	DC	12708
Welsh, Osgood	2nd Lt. 6th PA Cav	NY	05521
Welton, Everard B.	1st Lt. 24th MI Infy	MI	05576
Welton, Henry S.	Capt. 19th Infy USA	CA	06928
Welty, Charles C.	1st Lt. 51st OH Infy	OH	09899
Wenckebach, Enno F.	Capt. USA	PA	00711
Wentworth, Mark F.	Col. 32nd ME Infy BvtBG	ME	09553
Werden, Reed	RAdm USN	NY	00738
Werneck, Francis J.	Capt. 54th NY Infy	NY	09867
Werner, Frederick J.	1st Lt. 106th OH Infy	OH	05202
Werth, Gotthold J.	Capt. 1st MO Eng.	MO	10598
Werth, John E.	Chap 75th NY Infy	MO	04269 (Dup)
Wesendorff, Maximilian	Maj USA	NY	05182
Wessells, Leverette W.	Col. 19th CT Infy	NY	06225
Wessels, Francis	LTC 106th PA Infy	PA	00600
West, Arnold J.	1st Lt. 16th MI Infy	WA	12625
West, Charles	1st Lt. 14th IL Cav	CO	04984 (Dup)
West, Charles W.	1st Lt. Adj. 72nd PA Infy	PA	01953
West, Francis H.	Col. 31st WI Infy BvtBG	WI	05022
West, George W.	Col. 17th ME Infy BvtBG	DC	01724
West, Granville C.	1st Lt. 4th KY Infy	DC	06030
West, Joseph R.	BvtMG USV	DC	02615
West, Theodore	LTC 24th WI Infy	DC	04360
West, William	Capt. 118th PA Infy	MA	02081 (Dup)
West, William C.	Commander USN	PA	00501
West, William C.	2nd Lt. 1st Louisiana Cav	MA	17075
West, William H.G.	1st Asst Eng. USN	PA	00405
Weston, Byron	Capt. 49th MA Infy	MA	02225
Weston, Charles B.	BvtLTC	NY	01192
Weston, John F.	MG USA	DC	08322
Weston, Thomas	Maj 18th MA Infy BvtLTC	MA	08551
Wetherbee, George C.	Capt. CS BvtMaj USV	MI	06092
Wetherill, Alexander M.	Capt. 6th Infy USA	OH	03669

The Roster

Name	Rank	Commandery	Insignia No.
Wetherill, Francis D.	Capt. 3rd PA Cav	PA	02129
Wetherill, John M.	LTC 82nd PA Infy	PA	04178
Wetherill, Samuel	Maj 11th PA Cav BvtLTC	PA	02588
Wettstein, Andrew	LTC 103rd NY Infy	CA	10569
Wever, Joseph L.	Surg. 7th KS Cav	KS	04794
Wexel, Henry	2nd Lt. 45th NY Infy	MA	11617
Weyland, Jacob	Capt. 126th OH Infy BvtLTC	PA	14635
Weymouth, Harrison G.O.	Maj 1st US Vol. Infy	MA	01564
Whaley, Alvin M.	Capt. 17th NY Infy	IA	06442
Wham, Joseph W.	Maj Paymaster USA	IL	05297
Wharton, John S.	Capt. 14th Infy USA	CA	03661
Wharton, Robert S.	2nd Lt. 2nd PA H Arty	PA	02589
Whaton, Benjamin B. H.	Chief Eng. USN	PA	06778
Wheat, James L.	Capt. 5th MA Cav	CA	06209
Wheatland, George	Maj 48th MA Infy	MA	14089
Wheaton, Frank	MG USA	DC	02147
Wheaton, George H.	Capt. 131st NY Infy	CA	01627
Wheaton, Lloyd	MG USA	KS	06279
Whedon, Americus	Capt. 82nd IN Infy	OH	14070
Wheelan, James N.	BG USA	NY	01114
Wheeler, Charles	1st Lt. 1st CO Cav	VT	05633
Wheeler, Charles A.	Asst Surg. 12th MA Infy	MA	07688
Wheeler, Cornelius	1st Lt. 2nd WI Infy	WI	02084
Wheeler, Daniel D.	BG USA	CA	03998
Wheeler, Edmund S.	Act Asst Paymaster USN	NY	00705-7618
Wheeler, Edward	Capt. 56th NY Infy	WA	07220
Wheeler, Edward R.	Surg. 24th MA Infy	MA	04554 (Dup)
Wheeler, George A.	Surg. BvtLTC USV	ME	12714
Wheeler, George F.	Capt. 7th IL Infy	MD	07180
Wheeler, Gideon	Capt. 32nd IA Infy	DC	13156
Wheeler, Harrison H.	Capt. 10th MI Infy	MI	10917
Wheeler, Henry	Chap 17th PA Cav	PA	10403
Wheeler, Henry O.	1st Lt. 1st VT Cav BvtCapt.	VT	09162
Wheeler, Jerome B.	Capt. 6th NY Cav	NY	08667
Wheeler, John D.	Capt. 15th CT Infy	NY	16746
Wheeler, John R.	Maj 16th WI Infy	IA	11380
Wheeler, Obed	Capt. 150th NY Infy	NY	02375
Wheeler, Stephen	Capt. 113th USCT	MO	07912 (Dup)
Wheeler, Willard D.	Maj Paymaster USV	MA	00866
Wheeler, William L.	Act Passed Asst Surg. USN	MA	03052
Wheeler, Xenophon	Capt. 129th OH Infy	OH	05673
Wheelock, Joseph A.	3rd Class	MN	06292
Wheelock, Lewis L.	Capt. 160th NY Infy	MN	04733
When, George	1st Lt. 12th PA Cav	PA	11452
Wherry, William M.	BG USA	OH	03444
Whipple, George M.	Capt. 23rd MA Infy	MA	01291
Whipple, Steven G.	LTC 1st Batt CA Infy BvtCol.	CA	02726
Whipple, William D.	BG USV BvtMG USA	PA	00031

Name	Rank	Commandery	Insignia No.
Whisson, Amos A.	Maj 182nd OH Infy	MO	16015
Whistler, Charles W.	Capt. 2nd Batt PA Infy	PA	16131
Whistler, Joseph N.G.	Col. 13th Infy USA BvtBG	WI	05832
Whitaker, Edward W.	LTC 1st CT Cav BvtBG	DC	12416
Whitaker, Ezra J.	Chief Eng. USN	NY	08116
Whitall, Samuel R.	Col. 27th Infy USA	CA	13634
Whitbeck, Horatio N.	BvtBG USV	OH	03070
White, Amos H.	Col. 5th NY Cav	MI	05577
White, Andrew G.	1st Lt. 3rd NY Infy	NY	07619
White, Ansel L.	Capt. 19th ME Infy BvtMaj	NY	03018
White, Charles A.	Capt. 3rd NH Infy BvtLTC	CO	05968
White, Charles H.	1st Lt. 14th NJ Infy	DC	06871
White, Charles H.	Med. Director USN	MA	01152
White, Clement A.	1st Lt. 8th PA Cav	IL	04141
White, David	Chap USA	KS	09622
White, Edward P.	1st Lt. 2nd MA H Arty	MA	01353
White, Elisha M.	Surg. 37th MA Infy	MA	07974
White, Francis E.	1st Lt. RCS 4th NY Cav	MA	07959
White, Frank	1st Lt. RQM 9th KY Infy	OH	07377
White, Frank H.	1st Lt. RQM 14th MI Infy	IL	07225
White, George B.	Capt. USN	PA	00971
White, George H.	Chief Eng. USN	PA	05998
White, George Q.	Capt. 44th Infy BvtMaj USA	MN	02750
White, George S.	BvtCapt. USV	MI	15430
White, Harrison	LTC 6th NY Cav BvtCol.	MN	14649
White, Henry C.	Lt. Commander USN	PA	02233
White, James C.	Capt. 2nd MA H Arty	IL	00822
White, James E.	Capt. 13th IA Infy	DC	07921
White, James E.	Capt. 12th Batt IN L Arty	IN	09093
White, James H.	1st Lt. Adj. 165th PA Infy	PA	12986
White, Jarvis	Capt. 24th MA Infy	IL	04853
White, John C.	Maj USA	MA	02706
White, John E.	Capt. 90th NY Infy	MA	01422
White, John I.	1st Lt. Adj. 105th NY Infy	IN	07277
White, John L.	2nd Lt. 22nd CT Infy	IL	13701
White, John P.	Capt. 10th NY Cav	NE	13143
White, John P.P.	Surg. 10th NY Infy	NY	00230
White, John Robert	Capt. 118th PA Infy USV	PA	02447
White, Julius	BG BvtMG USV	IL	01942
White, Rufus A.	Capt. 11th MA Infy	MA	01478
White, Schubael F.	Capt. 28th MI Infy	MN	05930
White, Truman C.	1st Lt. 10th NY Cav	NY	13572
White, William B.	LTC 10th MA Infy	MA	02314
White, William H.	Maj Surg. 79th PA Infy	PA	00496
White, William H.	1st Lt. 1st Batt MA H Arty	KS	15968
White, William Henry	1st Lt. 68th PA Infy	NY	02674
White, William J.	Capt. 5th USC H Arty BvtMaj	OH	04388
White, William V.	Surg. 57th MA Infy	NY	02202

Name	Rank	Commandery	Insignia No.
Whitehead, Gerrard I.	Maj Jdge Adv USV	NY	05517
Whitehead, Ira C.	Act Asst Surg. USN	NY	06272
Whitehead, W.H.	1st Lt. 124th PA Infy	CO	15402
Whitehead, William	Capt. USN	PA	00061
Whitehouse, Edward N.	Paymaster USN	NY	00545
Whiteside, Samuel M.	BG USA	DC	02616
Whitesides, Edward G.	Capt. 125th OH Infy BvtMaj	PA	05740
Whitfield, Smith A.	LTC 123rd USCT	OH	03203
Whiting, Fred S.	Capt. 4th IA Cav	IA	05444
Whiting, James H.	1st Lt. Adj. 23rd CT Infy	MI	12498
Whiting, Joseph B.	Surg. 33rd WI Infy	WI	05266
Whiting, Webster A.	Capt. 88th IL Infy	CA	17623
Whiting, William H.	RAdm USN	CA	12042
Whitley, Hiram C.	Maj 7th LA Colored Infy	KS	06977
Whitman, Frank	Surg. 58th MA Infy	MA	03525
Whitman, Royal E.	Col. 30th ME Infy	DC	02559
Whitmarsh, William W.	Capt. 29th ME Infy	ME	09375
Whitmore, William T.	Act Asst Paymaster USN	NY	12730
Whitney, Allston W.	Surg. 13th MA Infy BvtLTC	MA	01460
Whitney, Benjamin F.	1st Lt. 10th ME Infy	ME	18126
Whitney, Edward J.	Surg. BvtLTC USV	NY	09315
Whitney, Folliot A.	Maj 6th Infy USA	DC	10859
Whitney, Henry A.	Maj 33rd Infy USA	CA	17622
Whitney, Jophanus H.	Col. 5th MA Infy	MA	13523
Whitney, Joseph C.	1st Lt. 11th USC H Arty	CA	04863
Whitney, Joseph N.	1st Lt. 2nd RI Cav	DC	06874
Whitney, Stephen	1st Lt. 4th Arty USA	NY	09868
Whitney, Walter R.	Chap 101st PA Infy	DC	12105
Whitney, William C.	Capt. 11th USCT	KS	06978
Whitney, William H.	Capt. 38th MA Infy BvtMaj	MA	04330
Whitney, William L.	1st Lt. 54th MA Infy	MA	07135
Whiton, John C.	LTC 58th MA Infy BvtCol.	MA	05024
Whitsit, Courtland E.	Capt. 26th IN Infy	IN	06616
Whitsit, John A.	1st Lt. 26th IN Infy	IN	07159
Whittaker, James T.	Act Asst Surg. USN	OH	11708
Whittaker, James W.	Chief Eng. USN	PA	00403
Whittelsey, Charles H.	Maj AAG BvtBG USV	PA	00647
Whittelsey, Henry M.	Col. QM BvtBG USV	PA	01036
Whittemore, Edward W.	LTC 12th Infy USA	DC	02453
Whittemore, James B.	1st Lt. 1st CA Infy	CA	03240
Whittemore, James M.	BG USA	PA	01991
Whittemore, Walter H.	Maj 136th USCT	MI	08891
Whitten, James C.	Capt. 14th KY Infy	OH	09822 (Dup)
Whittier, Charles A.	BvtBG	MA	01307
Whittier, Edward N.	1st Lt. 5th Batt ME L Arty BvtCapt.	MA	02160
Whittier, John Greenleaf	3rd Class Poet	MA	07969
Whittlesey, Edward L.	Capt. 85th PA Infy	PA	16674
Whittlesey, Elephalet	Col. 46th USCT BvtBG	DC	09940

Name	Rank	Commandery	Insignia No.
Whittlesey, Robert D.	1st Lt. 1st OH L Arty	OH	03368
Whittleton, Robert J.	Capt. 25th WI Infy	DC	09446
Wickersham, Charles J.	BvtMaj AAG	PA	00021
Wickersham, Morris D.	Col. QM USV	OH	10298
Wickham, Charles P.	LTC 55th OH Infy	OH	07710
Widdicomb, William	1st Lt. Adj. 1st MI Infy	MI	08893
Widdicombe, Albert C.	Capt. 16th WVA Infy	CO	05973
Widdiefield, Henry A.	1st Lt. Adj. 104th PA Infy	PA	01122
Widdis, Cornelius C.	LTC 150th PA Infy	PA	04177 (Dup)
Widmer, John H.	Maj 104th IL Infy	IL	10580
Widvey, Theodore J.	Capt. 3rd WI Infy	WI	05023
Wiedersheim, William A.	Capt. 119th PA Infy BvtMaj	PA	02446
Wiegand, Eugene	1st Lt. 75th PA Infy	CA	08882
Wiehl, Frederick F.	2nd Lt. 78th PA Infy	OH	07823 (Dup)
Wiestling, Joshua M.	1st Lt. 127th PA Infy	WA	08468
Wiggin, Francis	1st Lt. 16th ME Infy	ME	14997
Wight, Edwin B.	Maj 24th MI Infy	OR	04534
Wight, Frederick D.	1st Lt. 1st Batt ME Shpshtrs.	CO	05964
Wight, George B.	1st Lt. 1st NJ Infy	PA	03228
Wikoff, Charles A.	Col. 23rd Infy USA	DC	02698
Wilber, Eugene	Capt. 106th NY Infy	MI	11879
Wilber, Mark D.	1st Lt. RQM 159th NY Infy	NY	10902
Wilbur, Charles T.	Surg. USV	MI	05479
Wilbur, George H.	2nd Lt. 9th IN Infy	WI	12832
Wilbur, John W.	2nd Lt. 47th OH Infy	CA	15583
Wilbur, Joshua G.	Asst Surg. 18th MA Infy	NY	07983
Wilcox, Aaron M.	Capt. CS BvtMaj USV	NY	03306
Wilcox, Alfred F.	1st Lt. 11th MI Infy	MI	16855
Wilcox, Alfred G.	Capt. 105th OH Infy	MN	08543
Wilcox, Charles W.	2nd Lt. 9th NH Infy	MA	09607
Wilcox, Edward S.	1st Lt. Adj. 52nd IL Infy	IL	13545
Wilcox, John S.	Col. 52nd IL Infy BvtBG	IL	08915
Wilcox, Lyman G.	Maj 3rd MI Cav	MI	08596
Wilcox, Minot L.	1st Lt. RQM 130th OH Infy	OH	14661
Wilcox, Timothy E.	BG USA	OR	14165
Wilcox, Vincent M.	Col. 132nd PA Infy	NY	06957
Wilcox, William H.	Capt. 52nd IL Infy	IL	08916
Wild, John L.	1st Lt. 10th MI Cav	MI	14073
Wild, Theodore	Asst Surg. 36th USCT BvtMaj	IL	09616
Wilde, Ferdinand A.	2nd Lt. 27th USCT	WI	13687
Wilde, George F.F.	RAdm USN	DC	12060
Wilde, James B.	2nd Lt. 61st NY Infy	MO	04781
Wilder, Abraham M.	Surg. BvtLTC USV	CA	02149
Wilder, Frank	RAdm USN	ME	07901
Wilder, John T.	Col. 17th IN Infy BvtBG	OH	06845
Wilder, William F.	Capt. 46th IL Infy	CA	12994
Wildman, John F.	Maj 153rd IN Infy	IN	11647
Wildman, William D.	Capt. 88th IN Infy	NE	06702

The Roster

Name	Rank	Commandery	Insignia No.
Wildrick, John A.	LTC 28th NJ Infy	NY	14169
Wiles, William D.	Capt. 36th IN Infy	IN	06617
Wiley, Aquila	Col. 41st OH Infy	OH	15752
Wiley, John A.	BG USV	PA	14054
Wiley, William F.	Capt. 24th MA Infy	MA	03051
Wiley, William H.	Capt. Indpt. Corps NY Infy	NY	02566
Wilhelm, Charles	LTC 23rd PA Infy	PA	00057
Wilhelm, Thomas	Col. 2nd PA H Arty	CA	02855
Wilkeson, Frank	2nd Lt. 4th Art. BvtCapt. USA	KS	10491
Wilkin, Eli	Capt. 31st OH Infy BvtMaj	IA	04854
Wilkin, Jacob W.	Capt. 130th IL Infy	IL	06405
Wilkins, Hartwell A.	1st Lt. 88th USCT	NY	06017
Wilkins, James E.	Capt. 112th IL Infy	IA	09685 (Dup)
Wilkins, James E.	1st Lt. 1st MI Cav	CA	17791
Wilkinson, Charles R.	1st Lt. 8th OH Infy	MN	17259
Wilkinson, Francis M.	Capt. 68th IN Infy	OH	07232
Wilkinson, Melville C.	Capt. 3rd Infy BvtMaj USA	MN	06456
Wilkinson, Robert F.	Maj 128th NY Infy BvtCol.	NY	03348
Wilkinson, Thomas B.	1st Lt. 3rd IN Cav	IN	12339
Wilkinson, Webb G.	1st Lt. Adj. 5th IL Cav	DC	No Number
Willard, Charles D.	Capt. 19th WI Infy	NY	17506
Willard, Edward N.	Capt. 127th USCT	PA	11834
Willard, Erastus W.	1st Lt. 138th IL Infy	IL	14571
Willard, Eugene B.	2nd Lt. 91st OH Infy	OH	07207 (Dup)
Willard, John P.	Maj Paymaster BvtLTC USA	DC	02087
Willard, Lewis H.	Act Asst Surg. USN	PA	13668
Willard, Lot S.	Maj ADC USV	WA	14841
Willard, Robert	Asst Surg. USN	MA	01503
Willard, Samuel	Surg. 97th IL Infy	IL	11101 (Dup)
Willard, Wells	Col. USA	DC	03978
Willaur Senaca G.	Capt. VRC BvtMaj	PA	14197 (Dup)
Willcox, Orlando B.	BG BvtMG USA	DC	02817
Willett, James R.	BvtLTC USA	IL	02013
Willetts, Isaiah W.	Cap. 30th PA Mil. Infy	PA	15120
Williams, Abram	1st Lt. RQM 6th IA Cav	IL	06216
Williams, Alpheus S.	BG BvtMG USV	PA	01181
Williams, Andrew G.	2nd Lt. 63rd PA Infy	PA	13292
Williams, Andrew J.	2nd Lt. 7th OH Infy	OH	03367
Williams, Augustus H.D.	1st Lt. 5th Cav BvtCapt. USA	PA	00450
Williams, Augustus P.	Asst Surg. BvtMaj USV	NY	06029
Williams, Carlos D.	1st Lt. 12th VT Infy	VT	12172
Williams, Charles	Capt. 82nd PA Infy	PA	04963
Williams, Charles F.	Col. USMC	CA	02981
Williams, Charles H.	2nd Lt. 3rd RI H Arty	MA	09608
Williams, Columbus L.	Capt. 31st OH Infy	OH	15394
Williams, Constant	BG USA	CA	03547
Williams, Edward E.	Capt. 114th PA Infy	PA	06776
Williams, Edward P.	Capt. CS USV	NY	06434

Name	Rank	Commandery	Insignia No.
Williams, Elihu S.	Capt. 71st OH Infy	OH	05665
Williams, Ethan C.	Act Ensign USN	OH	02882
Williams, George	BvtCapt. USA	OR	06807
Williams, George N.	Capt. 98th NY Infy	NY	08803
Williams, Henry G.	1st Lt. 1st USCT	PA	04962
Williams, Henry M.	1st Lt. 11th Batt IN L Arty	IN	05814
Williams, Horace P.	Capt. 22nd MA Infy	MA	10319
Williams, James M.	Col. 79th USCT BvtBG	DC	11670
Williams, Jeremiah	LTC 25th OH Infy	DC	13078
Williams, John A.P.	Capt. 28th WI Infy	MO	08273
Williams, John B.	Capt. 96th OH Infy	OH	10015
Williams, John F.	Asst Surg. 2nd US Vol. Infy	IL	08125
Williams, John H.	Asst Surg. 5th Cav MO State Militia	PA	08992
Williams, John M.	Capt. 122nd OH Infy	MO	14822
Williams, John R.	1st Lt. 13th NJ Infy	NY	06219
Williams, John S.	Col. 62nd IN Infy	IN	04473
Williams, John W.	Surg. USA	CA	03099
Williams, Leander P.	1st Lt. 73rd IN Infy BvtMaj	DC	04726
Williams, Lyman S.	Capt. 6th VT Infy	IA	11138
Williams, Oliver W.	1st Lt. 25th OH Infy	OH	08030
Williams, Rees	1st Lt. 116th OH Infy	NE	07835
Williams, Robert	BG USA	DC	09941
Williams, Robert	2nd Lt. 39th MA Infy	MA	08067
Williams, Robert, Jr.	LC 54th OH Infy	OH	09449
Williams, Rudolph	2nd Lt. 111th OH Infy	IL	03855
Williams, Samuel B.	2nd Lt. 50th NY Eng.	CA	03989
Williams, Samuel K.	Maj 8th VRC	MA	11745
Williams, Thomas J.	1st Lt. 56th OH Infy	OH	10463
Williams, Thomas, Jr.	1st Lt. 5th Arty BvtMaj USA	PA	05255
Williams, Vinson V.	LTC 145th IN Infy	IN	17599
Williams, William C.	Col. 44th IN Infy	IN	13088
Williams, William H.	Maj 42nd OH Infy	OH	04226
Williams, William H.	1st Lt. 60th USCT	IL	12747
Williams, William H.H.	Paymaster USN	NY	09962
Williams, William N.	1st Lt. USA	IN	15762
Williams, William S.	Capt. 3rd Batt Ohio L Arty	OH	03154
Williams, William W.	Pay Director USN	CA	03265
Williamson, Henry V.	Maj 83rd NY Infy	NY	11635
Williamson, James A.	BG BvtMG USV	NY	02526
Williamson, John D.	Act Chief Eng. USN	PA	02749
Williamson, John E.	Cap. 12th KY Cav	MO	09841
Williamson, John E.	1st Lt. 37th WI Infy	WI	07895
Williamson, Thom	Chief Eng. USN	CA	04002
Williamson, William C.	1st Asst Eng. USN	PA	02748
Willis, Henry A.	1st Lt. Adj. 53rd MA Infy	MA	01735
Williston, Edward B.	BG USA	CA	08297
Willoughby, Aurelius M.	1st Lt. 8th IN Cav	IN	10206
Wills, Andrew W.	Capt. AQM BvtLTC USV	OH	02842

Name	Rank	Commandery	Insignia No.
Willson, Hugh McG.	Asst Surg. 2nd NY Mounted Rifles	CA	13740
Willson, James C.	Surg. 8th MI Infy	MI	06539
Willson, Lester S.	LTC 60th NY Infy BvtBG	NY	06644
Willson, William H.	Surg. 179th NY Infy	OH	04570
Wilmington, Oscar N.	1st Lt. 57th IN Infy	IN	19405
Wilshire, Joseph W.	Capt. 45th OH Infy	OH	03056
Wilshire, William W.	Maj 136th IL Infy	PA	00778
Wilson, Albert	Surg. 113th OH Infy	OH	05386
Wilson, Albion P.	Capt. 2nd ME Infy	CA	09822 (Dup)
Wilson, Arthur H.	Asst Surg. 7th US Vet. Vols.	MA	02197
Wilson, Benjamin B.	Surg. BvtLTC USV	PA	13293
Wilson, Benjamin F.	Act Asst Surg. USN	DC	08413
Wilson, Benjamin H.	Capt. 7th MO Cav	CO	07673
Wilson, Bluford	Capt. AAG BvtMaj USV	IL	11680
Wilson, Byron	Capt. USN	CA	02448
Wilson, C. Webster	Act Vol. Lt. USN	MA	05798
Wilson, Charles B.	1st Lt. 19th USCT	IL	11283
Wilson, Charles H.	Surg. 49th PA Infy	PA	04421
Wilson, Charles I.	BG USA	NE	01356
Wilson, Charles L.	Capt. 3rd NJ Infy	NY	02049
Wilson, Charles L.	Surg. 75th OH Infy	IN	04352
Wilson, Charles P.	Maj Surg. 138th OH Infy	OH	05937
Wilson, Christopher W.	1st Lt. 73rd NY Infy	NY	09570
Wilson, David	1st Lt. 11th IN Infy	IN	06904
Wilson, David B.	Col. USA	NE	13102
Wilson, Downs L.	Lt. Commander USN	DC	16057
Wilson, Edward S.	1st Lt. 91st OH Infy	OH	09346
Wilson, Eugene M.	Capt. 1st MN Mtd. Rangers	MN	03887 (Dup)
Wilson, Fletcher A.	Chief Eng. USN	MA	12490
Wilson, Francis H.	Bvt Capt. USA	PA	00994
Wilson, Frank	Capt. 19th Batt OH L Arty	OH	13846
Wilson, Frank C.	1st Lt. Chicago Bd. of Trade IL L Arty	IL	03134
Wilson, George	Act Asst Paymaster USN	NY	10422
Wilson, George E.	Capt. 6th NJ Infy	PA	05741
Wilson, George S.	Capt. 12th Infy USA	KS	03626 (Dup)
Wilson, George W.	1st Lt. Adj. 54th OH Infy	OH	02989
Wilson, Harrison	Col. 20th OH Infy	OH	02996
Wilson, Henry	Col. 22nd MA Infy (Vice Pres US)	PA	00028
Wilson, Henry H.	Capt. 28th & 147th PA Infy	PA	No number
Wilson, Henry W.	Capt. 6th MA Infy	MA	12568
Wilson, Horace	2nd Lt. 12th ME Infy	CA	02728
Wilson, James Grant	Col. 4th USC Cav BvtBG	NY	04340
Wilson, James Harrison	MG USV BG USA	DC	12106
Wilson, James L.	Capt. 6th Arty USA	CA	02239
Wilson, Joel	Capt. 1st ME Cav	NY	04078
Wilson, John M.	BG Chief of Eng. USA	DC	09571
Wilson, John R.	1st Lt. 11th VT Infy	VT	17435
Wilson, Joseph	2nd Lt. 39th NY Infy	CA	04832

Name	Rank	Commandery	Insignia No.
Wilson, Joseph F.	Capt. CS BvtMaj USV	DC	07802
Wilson, Lewis P.	Capt. 13th NH Infy	MA	07689
Wilson, Milton H.	1st Lt. Adj. 11th OH Infy	IL	12823
Wilson, Oliver M.	Capt. 54th IN Infy	MO	03220 (Dup)
Wilson, Percival C.	1st Lt. 2nd OH H Arty	OH	14664
Wilson, Philip L.	2nd Lt. VRC	NY	02053
Wilson, Robert	Capt. 12th OH Infy	OH	03969
Wilson, Robert B.	1st Lt. 194th OH Infy	OH	03046
Wilson, Robert P.	Capt. AAG USV	NY	01771
Wilson, Samuel J.	Maj 10th IL Infy	MO	07001
Wilson, Samuel L.	1st Lt. 16th OH Infy	KS	06980
Wilson, Theodore D.	Naval Constructor USN	DC	02663
Wilson, Thomas	Capt. 44th IA Infy	DC	06662
Wilson, Thomas	Col. Asst Com. Gen. BvtBG USA	NY	00514
Wilson, Thomas P.	Capt. AQM BvtMaj USV	MN	04038
Wilson, William	Capt. 124th OH Infy	OH	07935
Wilson, William C.	Col. 135th IN Infy	IN	03080
Wilson, William G.	Capt. 71st OH Infy	OH	16010
Wilson, William L.	1st Lt. 142nd PA Infy	NE	05277
Wilson, William M.	Capt. 122nd OH Infy	OH	06076
Wilson, William P.	Capt. 21st Infy BvtLTC USA	PA	00962
Wilson, William Stockton	Surg. 210th PA Infy	NY	12324
Wilson, William W.	1st Lt. RQM 29th IA Infy	NE	11103
Wilson, William, Jr.	Capt. 33rd NJ Infy	NY	10087
Wiltbank, William W.	Capt. CS BvtMaj USV	PA	07358
Wiltse, Gilbert C.	Capt. USN	NY	03020
Wiltsee, William P.	Capt. Benton Cadets MO Infy	OH	03062
Winas, William G.	1st Lt. 23rd NJ Infy	NY	07620
Winder, William A.	Capt. 3rd Arty USA	CA	09690
Wines, Frederick H.	Hospital Chap USV	DC	13157
Wing, Charles T.	Capt. AQM BvtCol. USV	NY	03359
Wing, Heman R.	1st Lt. 12th VT Infy	VT	09181
Wing, Isaac H.	1st Lt. 4th WI Infy	MN	04047
Wing, Joseph K.	Capt. AQM BvtLTC USV	OH	11783
Wing, Lucius M.	1st Lt. 19th MI Infy	MI	03746
Wingate, Edwin R.	Capt. 77th USCT	ME	09551
Wingate, George E.	Commander USN	MA	02428
Winger, Amaziah	Capt. 94th OH Infy	OH	09017
Winger, Benjamin F.	LTC 2nd PA H Arty	PA	00203
Winkler, Frederick C.	LTC 26th WI Infy BvtBG	WI	01857
Winn, Charles A.	LTC 58th PA Infy	IL	15919
Winn, John K.	Commander USN	MA	13170
Winne, Archibald	1st Lt. 8th NY H Arty	IL	02413
Winne, Charles K.	Col. USA	NY	02041
Winship, Theron S.	1st Lt. Adj. 29th OH Infy	OH	08604
Winslow, Edward F.	Col. 4th IA Cav BvtBG	NY	05008
Winslow, George F.	Med. Director USN	MA	08440
Winslow, Gordon	Cap. 8th Infy BvtMaj USA	CA	03107

Name	Rank	Commandery	Insignia No.
Winslow, William H.	Act Master USN	MA	07877
Winsor, Alfred	1st Lt. 45th MA Infy	MA	00981
Winsor, Henry, Jr.	Capt. 6th PA Cav	MA	00870
Wint, Theodore	BG USA	MO	02945
Winterbotham, John R.	1st Lt. Adj. 155th NY Infy BvtLTC	IL	05556
Wirsing, James J.	Capt. 84th PA Infy	PA	14636
Wise, George D.	BvtBG USV	PA	00345
Wise, Henry A.	Capt. USN	PA	00159
Wise, John	1st Lt. 12th OH Infy	OH	07024
Wise, Pembroke V.	Capt. 31st USCT	CA	03466
Wise, William	1st Lt. 2nd CO Cav	CO	07486
Wise, William C.	RAdm USN	ME	07898
Wise, William G.	1st Lt. 6th MA Infy	NY	01632
Wishart, John W.	Surg. 140th PA Infy	PA	07357
Wisner, James W.	Capt. 97th IL Infy	DC	14489
Wisnewski, John F.	Capt. 2nd KY Infy	NY	15522
Wistar, Joseph W.	Maj 8th PA Cav	PA	00005
Wister, Francis	Col. 215th PA Infy	PA	02587
Wister, Langhorne	Col. 150th PA Infy BvtBG	PA	02344
Wister, William R.	LTC 20th PA Cav	PA	11945
Witcher, John S.	LTC USA BvtBG	DC	02724
Witherell, Charles S.T.	BvtMaj USA	KS	04923
Withers, Frederick C.	1st Lt. 1st NY Eng.	NY	03361
Withington, James H.	Capt. 198th PA Infy	NY	01332 (Dup)
Withington, William H.	Col. 17th MI Infy BvtBG	MI	03738
Witt, Thomas D.	1st Lt. 1st MO L Arty	MO	08136
Woddward, David M.	LTC 60th MA Infy	MA	01132
Wolcott, Francis E.	Maj 20th KY Infy	NE	06148
Wolcott, Henry K.	Maj 42nd IL Infy	IL	06711
Wolcott, John W.	Capt. Batt "A" MD L Arty	MA	01537
Wolcott, Joseph L.	2nd Lt. 67th OH Infy	OH	03388
Wolcott, Laurens W.	1st Lt. 52nd IL Infy	MI	05269
Wolf, Joseph A.	Surg. 29th PA Infy	PA	04675
Wolf, William P.	Capt. 46th IA Infy	IA	09482
Wolfe, Solomon B.	Surg. 181st OH Infy	NY	12009
Wolfkill, Robert F.	2nd Lt. 13th OH Infy	OH	13592
Wolfley, Lewis	Maj 3rd KY Cav	OH	05317
Wolverton, Theron	Med. Inspector USN	NY	01151
Wood, Abram E.	Capt. 4th Cav USA	CA	07512
Wood, Adolph	1st Lt. 137th OH Infy	CA	11503
Wood, Albert	Surg. 1st MA Cav	MA	01243
Wood, Andrew G.	1st Lt. 123rd IN Infy	IN	09909
Wood, Andrew G.	2nd Lt. 51st OH Infy	PA	10881
Wood, Benjamin F.	Chief Eng. USN	NY	09316
Wood, Bradford R.	Capt. 44th NY Infy BvtMaj	NY	09869
Wood, Charles A.	LTC 11th WI Infy	CA	03630
Wood, Charles O.	LTC 8th CA Infy BvtCol.	OH	03581
Wood, Edmund E.	1st Lt. Adj. 108th OH Infy	OH	14310

Name	Rank	Commandery	Insignia No.
Wood, Edward E.	1st Lt. 17th PA Cav (Prof. USMA)	NY	01913
Wood, Ephriam M.	Capt. 15th Infy USA	OH	02841
Wood, Henry C.	BG USA	NY	00947
Wood, Horatio D.	Capt. CS BvtMaj USV	MO	05888
Wood, James	BvtMG	NY	01232
Wood, James R.	1st Lt. Adj. 11th NY Cav	PA	06777
Wood, James W.	Capt. 2nd MN Infy	MI	06984
Wood, John S.	Maj 7th IA Cav	IA	12573
Wood, Joseph H.	LTC 2nd NY Mtd Rifles	IL	02676
Wood, Marshall W.	LTC USA	OR	05590
Wood, Nathan S.	Capt. 4th NY H Arty BvtMaj	MI	11878
Wood, Oliver E.	LTC Arty USA	CA	08301
Wood, Palmer G.	LTC 11th Infy USA	CA	03897 (Dup)
Wood, Preston	Chap 38th IL Infy	IL	13175
Wood, Robert W.	Capt. 10th KS Infy	MO	04877
Wood, Samuel E.	1st Lt. 86th OH Infy	IL	13164
Wood, Thomas B.	1st Lt. 11th IN Infy	IN	12110
Wood, Thomas D.	1st Lt. 2nd OH H Arty	DC	15766
Wood, Thomas J.	MG USA	OH	02961
Wood, William M.	Med. Director USN	NY	01442
Wood, William W.W.	Chief Eng. USN	DC	00270
Wood, Zeno K.	1st Lt. Adj. 1st New Orleans Infy	IL	13402
Woodbridge, Timothy	Surg. 128th OH Infy	OH	06843
Woodbridge, William S.	2nd Lt. 1st AR Cav	MN	15413
Woodburn, Matthew A.	2nd Lt. 27th PA Infy	NY	16089
Woodburn, Robert H.	Capt. 123rd PA Infy	PA	13823
Woodbury, George E.	Asst Surg. 2nd DC Infy	MA	13473
Woodbury, George T.	Capt. Batt "D" NJ L Arty	MA	04151
Woodbury, Roger W.	Capt. 3rd NH Infy	CO	10032
Woodbury, Urban A.	Capt. 1st VT H Arty	VT	05799
Woodfin, Philip T., Jr.	1st Lt. 16th Batt MA L Arty	DC	06383
Woodford, Stewart L.	Col. 103rd USCT BvtBG	NY	00536
Woodhull, Alfred A.	BG USA	NY	04060
Woodhull, Maxwell V.Z.	LTC AAG BvtBG USV	DC	01006
Woodhull, William W.	Pay Inspector USN	PA	04420
Woodman, Andrew J.	1st Lt. 2nd ME Cav	PA	05510
Woodman, Edwn E.	Capt. 13th WI Infy	MN	06152
Woodman, George F.	2nd Lt. 1st NC Infy	MA	01673
Woodman, Joseph H.	Capt. 27th MI Infy	MI	15875
Woodruff, Charle A.	BG USA	OH	02953
Woodruff, Charles A.	BG USA	CA	05448
Woodruff, Edward C.	LTC 11th Infy USA	CA	03551
Woodruff, Elias B.	1st Lt. 4th IA Cav	IA	10931
Woodruff, Ezra	Col. USA	NY	11248
Woodruff, Henry W.	BvtCol. USV	PA	00250
Woodruff, Lafayette	Asst Surg. 57th OH Infy	OH	11102
Woods, George W.	Med. Director USN	CA	01350
Woods, Robert M.	1st Lt. Adj. 64th IL Infy BvtMaj	IL	12160

The Roster

Name	Rank	Commandery	Insignia No.
Woods. Charles H.	Capt. 16th NH Infy	MN	05868
Woodson, Albert E.	BG USA	MO	05088
Woodward, Adrian T.	Surg. 14th VT Infy	VT	09187
Woodward, Edwin T.	Commander USN	VT	01825
Woodward, Edwin W.	Capt. 25th NY Cav	CA	10198
Woodward, George A.	BG USA	DC	00614
Woodward, Gilbert M.	1st Lt. Adj. 2nd WI Infy	WI	07626
Woodward, James H.	LTC 1st TN L Arty	CA	03902
Woodward, John B	3rd Class (Col. 13th NY St. Militia)	NY	00625
Woodward, John H.	Capt. CS BvtMaj USV	OR	05899
Woodward, John W.	1st Lt. 26th PA Infy BvtLTC	PA	02744 (Dup)
Woodward, Joseph J.	BvtLTC USA	PA	00247
Woodward, Joseph T.	1st Lt. Adj. 21st ME Infy	ME	03003
Woodward, Llewellyn D.	1st Lt. 26th ME Infy	OR	06705
Woodward, Orpheus S.	Col. 83rd PA Infy BvtBG	KS	13774
Woodward, Philip G.	Capt. 36th MA Infy	MN	12751
Woodward, Samuel L.	BG USA	MO	01472
Woodward, Thomas J.	Act Vol. Lt. USN	ME	06862
Woodward, William R.	Act Asst Paymaster USN	NY	07788
Woodward, William W.	Col. 116th USCT	OH	10925
Woodworth, Albert L.	2nd Lt. 29th CT Infy	DC	07798
Woodworth, John M.	Surg. 1st IL L Arty BvtLTC	PA	01714
Woolen, Green V.	Asst Surg. 27th IN Infy	IN	07275
Wooley, George C.	Capt. 9th NY Cav	DC	13380
Woolsey, Charles W.	1st Lt. 164th NY Infy BvtLTC	NY	05835
Woolsey, Melancthon B.	Commodore USN	PA	00304
Woolsey, Richard D.	1st Lt. 12th USCT	IL	12999
Woolson, John S.	Asst Paymaster USN	IA	05783
Wooster, Samuel R.	Surg. 1st MI Cav	MI	08200
Wooster, William B.	Col. 29th CT Infy	NY	10768
Wooster, William H.H.	1st Lt. RQM 6th CT Infy	NY	08068
Worcester, George S.	Maj 3rd MA H Arty	MA	02627
Worden, James A.	2nd Lt. 74th OH Infy	PA	08991
Worden, John L.	RAdm USN	NY	00220
Worden, William W.	1st Lt. 77th NY Infy	NY	03182
Work, William G.	2nd Lt. 60th USCT	IA	13361
Workizer, Charles J.G.	2nd Lt. 8th IN Cav	MO	12637
Worman, Charles H.	Maj 2nd PA Infy	PA	16675
Wormer, Grover S.	Col. 30th MI Infy BvtBG	MI	05685
Worth, John C.	1st Lt. Adj. 124th PA Infy	PA	13126
Worth, John W.	Capt. 5th MD Infy	DC	12888
Worth, William S.	BG USA	NY	02757
Worthington, Chester B.	Capt. AQM USV	IA	13281
Worthington, Lewis N.	2nd Lt. 6th OH Infy	NY	09317
Worthington, Thomas	1st Lt. 106th OH Infy	OH	05664
Worthman, James S.	1st Lt. 28th WI Infy	WI	16662
Wortley, Clark S.	1st Lt. RQM 20th MI Infy	MI	10237
Worts, George	2nd Lt. 67th OH Infy	OH	07033

Name	Rank	Commandery	Insignia No.
Wren, James	Maj 48th PA Infy	PA	09288
Wright, Albert D.	Capt. 43rd USCT	DC	17587
Wright, Albert J.	Act Asst Paymaster USN	MA	02328
Wright, Benjamin	1st Lt. 10th CT Infy	NY	09122
Wright, Benjamin F.	Capt. 146th NY Infy BvtMaj	MN	05339
Wright, Benjamin F.	2nd Lt. 137th OH Infy	OH	13549
Wright, Carroll D.	Col. 14th NH Infy	DC	12213
Wright, Charles J.	LTC 39th USCT BvtCol.	NY	10167
Wright, Edward B.	Capt. 1st MI Arty	MI	15821
Wright, Edward H.	Col. ADC USA	NY	01784
Wright, Edward S.	Capt. 62nd PA Infy	PA	07074
Wright, Elias	Col. 10th USCT BvtBG	PA	09776
Wright, Francis M.	2nd Lt. 39th OH Infy	IL	09617 (Dup)
Wright, George B.	Col. 106th OH Infy	OH	02973
Wright, George G.	3rd Class	IA	06691
Wright, Henry T.	Pay Director USN	NY	05592
Wright, Horatio G.	MG USV	DC	09341
Wright, J. Montgomery	Maj AAG USV	DC	06130
Wright, John E.H.	Act Ensign USN	CA	13689
Wright, John G.	Col. 51st NY Infy BvtBG	MO	04269 (Dup)
Wright, John H.	Med. Director USN	MA	00734
Wright, John K.	Capt. 16th KS Cav	KS	04754
Wright, Joseph P.	Col. Asst Surg. Gen. USA	KS	07234
Wright, Joseph W.B.	Capt. 24th Batt MA L Arty	MA	12071
Wright, Julian P.	Capt. 34th NJ Infy	PA	10404
Wright, Levi P.	LTC 1st MA H Arty	DC	06070
Wright, Marshall B.	Capt. 46th OH Infy	MO	05043
Wright, Marshall W.	1st Lt. RQM 105th OH Infy	OH	11481
Wright, Nathaniel A.	Capt. 147th NY Infy BvtMaj	NY	11466
Wright, Samuel	Capt. AAG BvtLTC USV	PA	05999
Wright, Samuel H.	1st Lt. 31st MO Infy	IL	12271
Wright, Thomas	Maj 31st USCT BvtLTC	MO	03699
Wright, Thomas B.	1st Lt. 21st NY Infy	PA	07075
Wright, Thomas S.	1st Lt. Adj. 3rd IA Cav	IL	05447
Wright, William	Act Master USN	NY	07359
Wright, William	Capt. 9th CT Infy	OH	08535
Wright, William	1st Lt. 150th PA Infy	PA	16976
Wright, William B.	LTC 27th MI Infy	MI	09142
Wright, William P.	Capt. 156th IL Infy	IL	10240
Wrigley, William	Capt. 197th PA Infy	PA	15664
Wrotnowski, Arthur F.	LTC 95th USCT	CA	14318
Wuerz, William	Capt. 86th USCT	NY	No Number
Wurtzebach, John F.	Capt. 2nd DC Infy	CO	05634
Wyckof, Ambrose B.	Lt. USN	WA	16840
Wyckoff, James S.	1st Lt. 39th NY Infy	DC	12736
Wyckoff, William O.	Capt. 32nd NY Infy	NY	05011
Wyer, Edwn F.	1st Lt. Adj. 5th MA Infy	MA	14090
Wyman, John C.	Capt. 3rd MA Cav	MA	05964

The Roster

Name	Rank	Commandery	Insignia No.
Wyman, Luther B.	3rd Class	NY	No Number
Wyman, Robert H.	RAdm USN	DC	02516
Yale, Thomas B.	Capt. 108th NY Infy	NY	09437
Yard, James S.	Maj 3rd NJ Infy	PA	06476
Yard, John E.	Col. 18th Infy USA	KS	00651
Yarrow, Henry C.	Asst Surg. 5th PA Cav	DC	09942
Yaryan, John L.	1st Lt. Adj. 58th IN Infy	IN	06827
Yates, Arthur R.	Capt. USN	PA	00541
Yates, Henry J.	1st Lt. Adj. 72nd NY Infy	NY	11249
Yates, Theodore	Col. USA	DC	05230
Yeager, Frederick M.	Capt. 128th PA Infy	PA	09780
Yeatman, James E.	3rd Class (Pres. West. Sanitary Com.)	MO	07814
Yelton, John W.	1st Lt. 38th IL Infy	CO	07672
Yemens, Charles C.	2nd Lt. 24th MI Infy	MI	03758
Yeo, Joshua M.	1st Lt. Adj. 196th OH Infy	OH	12899
Yeoman, Joseph A.O.	Capt. 1st OH Cav	IA	12388
Yeoman, Samuel N.	LTC 90th OH Infy	OH	05000
Yeomans, Stephen B.	Col. 43rd USCT BvtBG	CO	08191
Yerkes, Krewson	Maj 5th OH Infy	PA	08242
Yerkes, William H.	Maj 179th PA Infy	PA	02131
Yingling, George S.	Asst Surg. 164th OH Infy	OH	14213
Yoder, Charles T.	Maj Paymaster, USV	DC	08517
Yoder, Samuel S.	2nd Lt. 178th OH Infy	DC	08375
York, Alexander M.	LTC 15th USCT	CA	16389
Yorke, Patton J.	LTC 2nd NJ Cav BvtCol.	NY	03365
Yost, Daniel M.	LTC 179th PA Infy	PA	08770
Youmans, Morris	LTC 70th USCT	OH	15020
Young, Andrew H.	Maj Paymaster BvtLTC USV	OH	02336
Young, Charles L.	Capt. 70th NY Infy BvtLTC	OH	02135
Young, Christian	1st Lt. 186th PA Infy	PA	07660
Young, George W.	2nd Lt. NY L Arty	PA	01129
Young, Hugh	Capt. 79th NY Infy	NY	14418
Young, James	Chap 81st OH Infy	MO	11353
Young, James B.	1st Lt. USMC	PA	01852
Young, Jesse B.	1st Lt. 84th PA Infy	OH	14535
Young, John	1st Lt. 19th IL Infy	IL	11928
Young, Richard	1st Lt. 109th PA Infy	PA	00208
Young, Samuel B.M.	LTG USA	DC	06477
Young, Stephen J.	Surg. 79th IL Infy	IN	07276
Young, Thomas	Maj 127th USCT	NY	12404
Young, Thomas L.	LTC 118th OH Infy BvtBG	DC	02979
Young, Thomas M.	2nd Lt. 4th MN Infy	WA	09625
Young, William H.H.	1st Lt. 13th NH Infy	MA	02525
Youtsey, Thomas B.	1st Lt. 37th KY Infy	OH	04230
Yule, George	2nd Lt. 40th IA Infy	CO	09232
Zabriskie, Elias B.	Capt. 1st NV Cav	CA	09991
Zabriskie, James A.	1st Lt. 5th CA Cav	CA	02862
Zalinski, Edmund L.	Maj USA	NY	01454

Name	Rank	Commandery	Insignia No.
Zarracher, Benjamin F.	Capt. 29th PA Infy	MN	12835
Zehn, George	BvtBG USV	PA	00605
Zeigler, Edwin E.	Maj 107th PA Infy	PA	11716
Zeilin, Jacob	BG USMC	PA	00482
Zell, T. Elwood	LTC 3rd Batt PA Infy	PA	00002
Zeller, Theodore	Chief Eng. USN	PA	00592 (Dup)
Zerega, Alfred L.B.	Act Master USN	DC	10420
Zick, Bernard	1st Lt. 8th IL Infy	MO	08015
Ziegler, Philip M.	Asst Surg. 62nd PA Infy	PA	15040
Zimmerman, Edward O.	2nd Lt. 6th MN Infy	MN	05585
Zimmerman, Eugene	Act Master USN	OH	10228
Zimmerman, John	2nd Lt. 3rd IL Cav	IL	10222
Zimmerman, Lewis M.	Capt. 1st Regt. Potomac Home Brig. MD Cav	MD	12184
Zollars, Thomas J.	Capt. 4th IA Cav	CO	11488
Zollinger, Charles A.	Col. 129th IN Infy	IN	06619
Zulavsky, Ladistas L.	Col. 82nd USCT	NY	01167

BIBLIOGRAPHY

Manuscript Collections

The Membership Records of the Pennsylvania Commandery and the Commandery-in-Chief of the Military Order of the Loyal Legion of the United States, 35 cubic feet, 1865–2000, War Library and Museum of the Military Order of the Loyal Legion of the United States, aka the Pennsylvania Civil War Library and Museum, Philadelphia.

The Photographic Collection of the Massachusetts Commandery of the Military Order of the Loyal Legion of the United States, Photographic Division, United States Military History Institute, Carlisle, Pennsylvania.

The Records of the Commandery-in-Chief, Military Order of the Loyal Legion of the United States and the Several State Commanderies, 112 cubic feet, 1865–1998, United States Military History Institute, Carlisle, Pennsylvania.

Reference Works

Annual Report of the Adjutant General of Kentucky, 1861–1866, 2 vols., 2,144 pages. Frankfort, Ky.: John H. Harney, Public Printer, 1866–1867.

Aubin, J. Harris. *Register of the Military Order of the Loyal Legion of the United States, Compiled from the Registers and Circulars of the Various Commanderies*, 574 pages, with manuscript annotations. Boston, Mass.: Commandery of the State of Massachusetts, 1906.

Bates, Samuel P. *History of Pennsylvania Volunteers, 1861–65, Prepared in Compliance with Acts of the Legislature*, 5 vols., 6,722 pages. Harrisburg, Pa.: B. Singerly, State Printer, 1869–1871.

Benedict, G. G. *Vermont in the Civil War: A History of the Part Taken by Vermont Soldiers and Sailors in the War for the Union, 1861–65*, 2 vols., 1,428 pages. Burlington, Vt.: Free Press Association, 1886–1888.

Bowman, John S., ed. *Who Was Who in the Civil War,* 224 pages. New York: Crescent Books, 1994.

Breithaupt, Richard H., Jr. *Aztec Club of 1847: Military Society of the Mexican War,* 1,494 pages. Los Angeles, Calif.: Walika Publishing Co., 1998.

Callahan, Edward W. *List of Officers of the Navy of the U.S. and of the Marine Corps from 1775–1900,* 750 pages. Philadelphia, Pa.: L.R. Hammersly and Co., 1901.

Cogar, Willam B. *Dictionary of Admirals of the U.S. Navy, Vol. 1: 1862–1900,* 217 pages. Annapolis, Md.: Naval Institute Press, 1989.

Dyer, Elisha, ed. *Annual Report of the Adjutant General of the State of Rhode Island and Providence Plantations for the Year 1865,* 2 vols., 2,301 pages. Providence, R.I.: E. L. Freeman and Sons, Printers to the State, 1893–1895.

Heitman, Francis B. *Historical Register and Dictionary of the United States Army, from its Organization, September 29, 1789 to March 2, 1903,* 2 vols., 1,695 pages. Washington, D.C.: U.S. Government Printing Office, 1903.

Hunt, Roger D., and Jack R. Brown. *Brevet Brigadier Generals in Blue,* 700 pages. Gaithersburg, Md.: Olde Soldier Books, 1990.

Johnson, Robert Underwood, and Clarence Clough Buel, ed. *Battles and Leaders of the Civil War, Being for the Most Part Contributions by Union and Confederate Officers: Based upon "The Century" War Series,* 4 vols., 3,091 pages. New York: Century Co., 1887–1888.

Lang, Theodore F. *Loyal West Virginia from 1861 to 1865, with an Introductory Chapter on the Status of Virginia for Thirty Years Prior to the War,* 382 pages. Baltimore, Md.: Deutsch Publishing Co., 1895.

Love, William DeLoss. *Wisconsin in the War of the Rebellion: A History of All Regiments and Batteries the State Has Sent to the Field, and Deeds of Her Citizens, Governors and Other Military Officers, and State and National Legislators to Suppress the Rebellion,* 1,140 pages. Chicago, Ill.: Church and Goodman, 1866.

Massachusetts Soldiers, Sailors, and Marines in the Civil War, 9 vols., 7,459 pages. Brookline, Mass.: Riverdale Press, 1931–1935.

McClure, Alexander K., ed. *The Annals of the War Written by Leading Participants North and South.* Originally published by the *Philadelphia Weekly Times*, 800 pages. Philadelphia, Pa.: Times Publishing Co., 1879. Reprint, with introduction by Gary W. Gallagher, New York: Da Capo Press, 1994.

Minnesota in the Civil and Indian Wars, 1861–1865: Prepared and Published under the Supervision of the Board of Commissioners, Appointed by the Act of the Legislature of Minnesota of April 6, 1889, 2 vols., 1,496 pages. St. Paul, Minn.: Pioneer Press Co., 1890–1893.

Official Army Register, 1861–1866, 9 vols., 1,150 pages. Washington, D.C.: U.S. War Department, U.S. Government Printing Office, 1861–1866.

Official Army Register of the Volunteer Force of the United States Army: For the Years 1861, 1862, 1863, 1864, 1865, 8 vols., 3,822 pages. Washington, D.C.: U.S. Government Printing Office, 1865.

Official Records of the Union and Confederate Navies in the War of the Rebellion, 31 vols., 28,330 pages. Washington, D.C., U.S. Government Printing Office, 1894–1927.

Official Roster of the Soldiers of the State of Ohio in the War of the Rebellion, 1861–1866, 12 vols., 9,369 pages. Akron, Ohio: Werner Printing and Lithography Co., vols. 1, 4–6, and 11; Cincinnati, Ohio: Wilstach, Baldwin and Co., vol. 2; Cincinnati, Ohio: Ohio Valley Co., vols. 3 and 7–10; and Norwalk, Ohio: Laning Co., vol. 12; 1886–1895.

Orton, Richard H. *Records of California Men in the War of the Rebellion, 1861 to 1867,* 887 pages. Sacramento, Calif: J. D. Young, State Printers, 1890.

Peck, Theodore S., ed. *Revised Roster of Vermont Volunteers and Lists of Vermonters Who Served in the Army and Navy of the United States during the War of the Rebellion, 1861–66,* 863 pages. Montpelier, Vt.: Press of the Watchman Publishing Co., 1892.

Phisterer, Frederick. *New York in the War of the Rebellion,* third ed., 6 vols., 4,871 pages. Albany, N.Y.: J. B. Lyon and Co. State Printers, 1912.

Record of Service of Connecticut Men in the Army and Navy of the United States, during the War of the Rebellion, 1,071 pages. Hartford, Conn.: Press of the Case, Lockwood and Brainard Co., 1889.

Record of Service Michigan Volunteers in the Civil War, 1861–1865, 45 vols., 6,783 pages. Kalamazoo, Mich.: Ihling Bros. and Everard, Printers, 1905.

Register of the Commandery of the State of Massachusetts, 522 pages. Cambridge, Mass.: University Press, 1912.

Reid, Whitelaw. *Ohio in the War: Her Statesmen, Her Generals, and Soldiers,* 2 vols., 1,999 pages. Cincinnati, Ohio: More, Wilstach and Baldwin, 1868.

Report of the Adjutant General of Illinois Containing Reports for the Years 1861–66, 8 vols., 5,674 pages. H. W. Springfield, Ill.: Rokker, State Printer, 1886.

Report of the Adjutant General of the State of Indiana, 8 vols., 5,904 pages. Indianapolis, Ind.: Alexander H. Conner, State Printer, 1865–1869.

Report of the Adjutant General of the State of Kansas, 1861–65, 2 vols., 984 pages. Topeka, Kans.: Kansas State Printing Co., 1896.

Roster and Record of Iowa Soldiers in the War of the Rebellion, Together with Historical Sketches of Volunteer Organizations, 1861–1866, 6 vols., 8,977 pages. Des Moines, Iowa: Emory H. English, State Priner, 1908–1911.

Roster of Nebraska Volunteers, from 1861 to 1869. Compiled from Books, Records and Documents on File of the Office of the Adjutant General of State, 236 pages. Hastings, Nebr.: Wigton and Evans, State Printers, 1888.

Roster of Wisconsin Volunteers, War of the Rebellion, 1861–1865, 2 vols., 1,808 pages. Madison, Wisc.: Democrat Printing Co., 1886.

Tennesseans in the Civil War: A Military History of Confederate and Union Units with Available Rosters of Personnel, 2 vols., 179 pages. Nashville, Tenn.: Tennessee Civil War Centennial Commission, 1964–1965.

Stryker, William S., ed. *Record of Officers and Men of New Jersey in the Civil War, 1861–1865,* 2 vols., 1,934 pages. Trenton, N.J.: John L. Murphy, Printer, 1876.

War of the Rebellion: A Compilation of the Official Records of the Union and Confederate Armies, 70 vols., in 128 serials, 138,579 pages. Washington, D.C.: U.S. Government Printing Office, 1880–1901.

War Papers of the Military Order of the Loyal Legion of the United States, 1887–1915, 66 vols., 29,215 pages. Wilmington, N.C.: Broadfoot, 1991–1996.

Waite, Otis F. R. *New Hampshire in the Great Rebellion, Containing Histories of the Several New Hampshire Regiments, and Biographical Notices of Many of the Prominent Actors in the Civil War of 1861–65,* 608 pages. Claremont, N.H.: Tracy, Chase and Co., 1870.

Warner, Ezra J. *Generals in Blue: Lives of the Union Commanders,* 680 pages. Baton Rouge, La.: Louisiana State University Press, 1964.

Whiteman, William E. S., and Charles H. True. *Maine in the War for the Union: A History of the Part Borne by Maine Troops in the Suppression of the American Rebellion,* 637 pages. Lewiston, Me.: Nelson Dingley, Jr., and Co., 1865.

Wilmer, L. Allison, J. H. Jarrett, and George W. F. Vernon. *History and Roster of Maryland Volunteers, War of 1861–65, Prepared under Authority of the General Assembly of Maryland,* 2 vols., 119 pages. Baltimore, Md.: Press of Gugenheimer, Weil and Co., 1898–1899.

Biographical and Historical Works

Adams, Charles Francis, Jr. *Charles Francis Adams, 1835–1915: An Autobiography,* 224 pages. Boston, Mass.: Houghton Mifflin Co., 1916.

Acken, J. Gregory. *Inside the Army of the Potomac: The Civil War Experiences of Captain Francis Adams Donaldson,* 500 pages. Mechanicsburg, Pa.: Stackpole Books, 1998.

Agassiz, George R., ed. *Meade's Headquarters, 1863–1865: Letters of Colonel Theodore Lyman from the Wilderness to Appomattox,* 371 pages. Boston, Mass.: Atlantic Monthly Press, 1922.

Ames, Blanche. *Adelbert Ames, 1835–1933: General, Senator, Governor: The Story of His Life and Times and His Integrity as a Soldier and Statesman in the Service of the United States of America throughout the Civil War and in Mississippi in the Years of Reconstruction,* 625 pages. North Easton, Mass.: Privately Published, 1964.

Anderson, Isabel, ed. *The Letters and Journals of General Nicholas Longworth Anderson: Harvard, Civil War, Washington, 1854–1892,* 320 pages. New York: Fleming H. Revel Co., 1942.

Armstrong, William H. *Warrior in Two Camps: Ely S. Parker, Union General and Seneca Chief,* 244 pages. Syracuse, N.Y.: Syracuse University Press, 1978.

Baker, Lafayette C. *History of the United States Secret Service,* 704 pages. Philadelphia, Pa.: Privately Published, 1867.

Beatty, John. *The Citizen-Soldier; or, Memoirs of a Volunteer,* 401 pages. Cincinnati, Ohio: Wilstach, Baldwin and Co., 1879.

Blair, William A., ed. *A Politician Goes to War: The Civil War Letters of John White Geary.* University Park, Pa.: Pennsylvania State University Press, 1995.

Brinton, John H. *Personal Memoirs of John H. Brinton, Major and Surgeon U.S.V., 1861–1865,* 361 pages. New York: Neale Publishing Co., 1914.

Butler, Benjamin F. *Autobiography and Personal Reminiscences of Major-General Benj. F. Butler: Butler's Book,* 1,154 pages. Boston, Mass.: A. M. Thayer and Co., 1892.

Butterfield, Julia L. S., ed. *A Biographical Memorial of General Daniel Butterfield, Including Many Addresses and Military Writings,* 379 pages. New York: Grafton Press, 1904.

Byrne, Frank L., ed. *The View from Headquarters: Civil War Letters of Harvey Reid,* 257 pages. Madison, Wisc.: State Historical Society of Wisconsin, 1965.

Cain, Marvin R. *Lincoln's Attorney General: Edward Bates of Missouri,* 361 pages. Columbia, Mo.: University of Missouri Press, 1965.

Carroon, Robert G., ed. *From Freeman's Ford to Bentonville: The 61st Ohio Volunteer Infantry,* 70 pages, Shippensburg, Pa.: Burd Street Press, 1998.

Carter, Robert Goldthwaite. *Four Brothers in Blue; or, Sunshine and Shadows of the War of the Rebellion: A Story of the Great Civil War from Bull Run to Appomattox,* 509 pages. Washington, D.C.: Gibson Brother's Press, 1913.

Censer, Jane Turner, ed. *Defending the Union: The Civil War and the U.S. Sanitary Commission 1861–1863: The Papers of Frederick Law Olmsted.* Vol. 4, 757 pages. Baltimore, Md., The Johns Hopkins University Press, 1986.

Chamberlain, Joshua Lawrence. *The Passing of the Armies.* Reprint, 405 pages. Chicago, Ill.: Press of Morningside Bookshop, 1991.

Corby, William. *Memoirs of Chaplain Life by Very Rev. W. Corby: Three Years Chaplain in the Famous Irish Brigade,* "Army of the Potomac," 391 pages. La Monte, O'Donnell and Co., Chicago, 1893.

Cozzens, Peter, and Robert I. Girardi, ed. *The Military Memoirs of General John Pope,* 285 pages. Chapel Hill, N.C.: University of North Carolina Press, 1998.

Cox, Jacob D. *Military Reminiscences of the Civil War,* 2 vols., 1,145 pages. New York: Charles Scribner's Sons, 1900.

Cresap, Bernarr. *Appomattox Commander: The Story of General E.O.C. Ord,* 418 pages. San Diego, Calif.: A. S. Barnes and Co., 1981.

Dana, Charles A. *Recollections of the Civil War: With the Leaders at Washington and in the Field in the Sixties,* 296 pages. New York: D. Appleton and Co., 1898.

DeMontravel, Peter R. *A Hero to His Fighting Men: Nelson A. Miles, 1839–1925,* 463 pages. Kent, Ohio: Kent State University Press, 1998.

Dennett, Tyler, ed. *Lincoln and the Civil War in the Diaries and Letters of John Hay,* 348 pages. New York: Dodd, Mead and Co., 1939.

De Trobriand, Regis. *Four Years with the Army of the Potomac,* 757 pages. Boston, Mass.: Ticknor and Co., 1889.

Dodge, Grenville M. *Personal Recollections of President Abraham Lincoln, General Ulysses S. Grant, and General William T. Sherman,* 237 pages. Council Bluffs, Iowa: Monarch Printing Co., 1914.

Donald, David Herbert. *Lincoln,* 660 pages. New York: Simon and Schuster, 1995.

Eckert, Edward K., and Nicholas J. Amato, ed. *Ten Years in the Saddle: The Memoir of William Woods Averell, 1851–1862,* 443 pages. San Rafael, Calif.: Presidio Press, 1978.

Eisenhower, John S. D. *Agent of Destiny: The Life and Times of General Winfield Scott.* Reprint, 496 pages. Norman, Okla.: University of Oklahoma Press, 1999.

Eisenschiml, Otto, ed. *Vermont General: The Unusual War Experiences of Edward Hastings Ripley, 1862–1864,* 340 pages. New York: Devin-Adair Co., 1960.

Farragut, Loyall. *The Life of David Glasgow Farragut, First Admiral of the United States Navy, Embodying His Journal and Letters,* 586 pages. New York: D. Appleton and Co., 1879.

Fitch, Michael H. *Echoes of the Civil War as I Hear Them,* 368 pages. New York: R. F. Fenno and Co., 1905.

Ford, Worthington Chauncey, ed. *War Letters, 1862–1865, of John Chipman Gray and John Codman Ropes,* 532 pages. Boston: Houghton Mifflin Co., 1927.

Gibbon, John. *Personal Recollections of the Civil War,* 426 pages. New York: G. P. Putnam's Sons, 1928.

Glatthaar, Joseph T. *Forged in Battle: The Civil War Alliance of Black Soldiers and White Officers,* 370 pages. New York: Free Press, 1990.

Grant, Ulysses S. *Personal Memoirs of U.S. Grant,* 2 vols., 1,231 pages. New York: Charles L. Webster and Co., 1885–1886.

Harrington, Fred Harvey. *Fighting Politician, Major General N.P. Banks,* 301 pages. Philadelphia, Pa.: University of Pennsylvania Press, 1948.

Hazen, William B. *A Narrative of Military Service,* 450 pages, Boston: Ticknor and Co., 1885.

Heyman, Max L. *Prudent Soldier: A Biography of Major General E.R.S. Canby 1817–1873,* 418 pages. Glendale, Calif.: Arthur H. Clark Co., 1959.

Higginson, Thomas Wentworth. *Army Life in a Black Regiment,* 296 pages. Boston, Mass.: Fields, Osgood and Co., 1870.

Hoogenboom, Ari. *Rutherford B. Hayes: Warrior and President,* 626 pages. Lawrence, Kans.: University Press of Kansas, 1995.

Howard, Oliver Otis. *Autobiography of Oliver Otis Howard,* 2 vols., 1,220 pages. New York: Baker and Taylor Co., 1907.

Howe. M. A. Dewolfe, ed. *Marching with Sherman: Passages from Letters and Campaign Diaries of Henry Hitchcock, Major and Assistant Adjutant of Volunteers, November 1864–May 1865,* 332 pages. New Haven, Conn.: Yale University Press, 1927.

Howe, M. A. Dewolfe, ed. *Touched with Fire: Civil War Letters and Diary of Oliver Wendell Holmes, Jr., 1861–1864,* 158 pages. Cambridge, Mass.: Harvard University Press, 1946.

Huebner, Richard A., ed. *Meserve Civil War Record: With the Intriguing War Story by Major William N. Meserve, to Amass the Great "Meserve Collection" of Over 200,000 Lincoln and Civil War Era Photographs and Negatives,* 290 pages. Oak Park, Ill.: RAH Publications, 1987.

Johnson, Richard W. *A Soldier's Reminiscences in Peace and War,* 428 pages. Philadelphia, Pa.: J.B. Lippincott and Co., 1886.

Jones, James Pickett. *Black Jack: John A. Logan and Southern Illinois in the Civil War Era,* 314 pages. Carbondale, Ill.: Southern Illinois University Press, 1995.

Jordan, David M. *Winfield Scott Hancock: A Soldier's Life,* 393 pages. Bloomington, Ind.: Indiana University Press, 1988.

Keyes, Erasmus D. *Fifty Years' Observations of Men and Events, Civil and Military,* 515 pages. New York: Charles Scribner's Sons, 1884.

Kiper, Richard L. *Major General John Alexander McClernand: Politician in Uniform,* 386 pages. Kent, Ohio: Kent State University Press, 1999.

Laidlaw, Christine Wallace, ed. *Charles Appleton Longfellow: Twenty Months in Japan, 1871–1873,* 208 pages. Cambridge, Mass.: Friends of Longfellow House, 1998.

Lamers, William M. *The Edge of Glory: A Biography of General William S. Rosecrans, U.S.A.,* 499 pages. New York: Harcourt, Brace, and World, 1961.

Leckie, William H., and Shirley A. Leckie. *Unlikely Warriors: General Benjamin Grierson and His Family,* 368 pages. Norman, Okla.: University of Oklahoma Press, 1984.

Letterman, Jonathan. *Medical Recollections of the Army of the Potomac,* 194 pages. New York: D. Appleton and Co., 1866.

Livermore, Thomas L. *Days and Events, 1860–1866,* 485 pages. Boston, Mass.: Houghton, Mifflin Co., 1920.

Longacre, Edward G. *The Man behind the Guns: A Biography of General Henry J. Hunt, Commander of Artillery, Army of the Potomac,* 294 pages. South Brunswick, N.J.: A. S. Barnes Co., 1977.

Martin, Samuel J. *Kill-Cavalry: The Life of Union General Hugh Judson Kilpatrick,* 325 pages. Mechanicsburg, Pa.: Stackpole Books, 2000.

Marvel, William. *Burnside,* 504 pages. Chapel Hill, N.C.: University of North Carolina Press, 1991.

McClellan, George B. *McClellan's Own Story: The War for the Union, the Soldier's Who Fought It, the Civilians Who Directed It, and His Relations to It and to Them,* 677 pages. New York: Charles L. Webster and Co., 1887.

McKinney, Francis F. *Education in Violence: The Life of George H. Thomas and the History of the Army of the Cumberland,* 530 pages. Detroit, Mich.: Wayne State University Press, 1961.

McPherson, James M., and Patricia R. McPherson, ed. *Lamson of the Gettysburg: The Civil War Letters of Lieutenant Roswell H. Lamson, U.S. Navy,* 240 pages. New York: Oxford University Press, 1997.

Meade, George G., III, ed. *The Life and Letters of George Gordon Meade, Major General United States Army,* 2 vols., 821 pages. New York: Charles Scribner's Sons, 1913.

Meketa, Jacqueline Dorgan. *Legacy of Honor: The Life of Rafael Chacon, a Nineteenth Century New Mexican.* Reprint, 439 pages. Las Cruces, N.Mex.: University of New Mexico Press, 1986. Albuquerque, N.Mex.: Yucca Tree Press, 2000.

Merington, Marguerite, ed. *The Custer Story: The Life and Intimate Letters of General George A. Custer and His Wife Elizabeth,* 339 pages. New York: Devin-Adair Co., 1950.

Miers, Earl Schenck, ed. *Lincoln Day by Day: A Chronology, 1809–1865,* 3 vols., 1,119 pages. Washington, D.C.: Lincoln Sesquicentennial Commission, 1960.

Miles, Nelson A. *Serving the Republic: Memoirs of the Civil and Military Life of Nelson A. Miles.* Reprint 1971, 339 pages. Freeport: Books for Libraries Press, 1911.

Miller, Edward A., Jr. *Lincoln's Abolitionist General: The Biography of David Hunter,* 293 pages. Columbia S.C.: University of South Carolina Press, 1997.

Moynihan, James H. *The Life of Archbishop John Ireland.* New York: Harper and Brothers, 1953. Reprint, New York: Arno Press, 1976, 441 pages.

Nicolay, John G., and John Hay. *Abraham Lincoln: A History,* 10 vols., 4,706 pages. New York: Century Co., 1890.

Nicholson, John Page, and Henry Coppee, ed. *History of the Civil War in America* [by Louis Phillipe Albert d' Orleans, Comte de Paris], 4 vols., 3,003 pages. Philadelphia, Pa.: Porter and Coates, 1876–1888.

Niven, John. *Salmon P. Chase: A Biography,* 546 pages. New York, Oxford University Press, 1995.

Palfrey, Francis Winthrop, ed. *Memoir of William Francis Bartlett*, 309 pages. Boston, Mass.: Houghton, Osgood and Co., 1878.

Perkins, J. R. *Trails, Rails and War: The Life of General G. M. Dodge*, 371 pages. Indianapolis, Ind.: Bobbs-Merrill Co., 1929.

Porter, David Dixon. *Incidents and Anecdotes of the Civil War*, 357 pages. New York: D. Appleton and Co., 1885.

Pula, James S. *For Liberty and Justice: The Life and Times of Wladimir Krzyzanowski*, 288 pages. Chicago, Ill.: Polish American Charitable Foundation, 1978.

Quaife, Milo M., ed. *From the Cannon's Mouth: The Civil War Letters of General Alpheus S. Williams*, 405 pages. Detroit, Mich.: Wayne State University Press, 1959.

Racine, Philip N., ed. *Unspoiled Heart: The Journal of Charles Mattocks of the 17th Maine*, 446 pages. Knoxville, Tenn.: University of Tennessee Press, 1994.

Reeves, Thomas C. *Gentleman Boss: The Life and Times of Chester Alan Arthur*, 512 pages. Newtown, Conn.: American Political Biography Press, 1975.

Ross, Sam. *The Empty Sleeve: A Biography of Lucius Fairchild*, 291 pages. Madison, Wisc.: State Historical Society of Wisconsin, 1964.

Schley, Winfield Scott. *Forty-five Years Under the Flag*, 440 pages. D. Appleton and Co., 1904.

Schmitt, Martin F., ed. *General George Crook: His Autobiography*, 326 pages. Norman, Okla.: University of Oklahoma Press, 1946.

Schofield, John M. *Forty-six Years in the Army*, 577 pages. New York: Century Co., 1897.

Scott, Robert Gareth, ed. *Forgotten Valor: The Memoirs, Journals and Letters of Orlando B. Wilcox*, 720 pages. Kent, Ohio: Kent State University Press, 1999.

Selfridge, Thomas O., Jr. *Memoirs of Thomas O. Selfridge, Jr., Rear Admiral, U.S.N.*, 288 pages. New York: G. P. Putnam's Sons, 1924.

Sheridan, Philip H. *Personal Memoirs of P. H. Sheridan*, 2 vols., 986 pages. New York: D. Appleton and Co., 1888.

Sherman, William Tecumseh. *Memoirs of General W. T. Sherman: Written by Himself*, 2 vols., 814 pages. New York: D. Appleton and Co., 1875.

Sievers, Harry J. *Benjamin Harrison: Hoosier Warrior,* 374 pages. New York: University Publishers, 1960.

Slade, A. D. *A.T.A. Torbert: Southern Gentleman in Union Blue,* 230 pages. Dayton, Ohio: Press of Morningside Bookship, 1992.

Slocum, Charles Elihu. *The Life and Services of Major General Henry Warner Slocum,* 391 pages. Toledo, Ohio: Slocum Publishing Co., 1913.

Smith, Walter George, ed. *Life and Letters of Thomas Kilby Smith, Brevet Major General, United States Volunteers, 1820–1887,* 487 pages. New York: G. P. Putnam's Sons, 1898.

Spector, Ronald. *Admiral of the New Empire: The Life and Career of George Dewey,* 220 pages. Columbia, S.C.: University of South Carolina Press, 1988.

Steiner, Paul E. *Physician-Generals of the Civil War: A Study in Nineteenth Mid-Century American Medicine,* 194 pages. Springfield, Ill.: Charles C. Thomas, 1966.

Stilwell, Leander. *The Story of a Common Soldier of Army Life in the Civil War, 1861–1865,* 278 pages. Kansas City, Mo.: Franklin Hudson Publishing Co., 1920.

Sumner, Merlin E., ed. *The Diary of Cyrus R. Comstock,* 408 pages. Dayton, Ohio: Morningside, 1987.

Thomas, Benjamin P., and Harold M. Hyman. *Stanton: The Life and Times of Lincoln's Secretary of War,* 642 pages. New York: Alfred A. Knopf, 1962.

Thompson, Robert Means, and Richard Wainwright. *Confidential Correspondence of Gustavus Vasa Fox, Assistant Secretary of the Navy, 1861–1865,* 5 vols., 932 pages. Washington, D.C.: Naval History Society, 1918.

Townsend, E. D. *Anecdotes of the Civil War in the United States,* 287 pages. New York: D. Appleton and Co., 1884.

Trulock, Alice R. *In the Hands of Providence: Joshua Lawrence Chamberlain and the American Civil War,* 569 pages. Chapel Hill, N.C.: University of North Carolina Press, 1992.

Tyler, William S., ed. *Recollections of the Civil War: With Many Original Diary Entries and Letters Written from the Seat of War, and with Annotated References,* 379 pages. New York: G. P. Putnam's Sons, 1912.

Van Deusen, Glyndon G. *William Henry Seward,* 666 pages. New York: Oxford University Press, 1967.

Wallace, Susan Elston, and Mary H. Krout, ed. *Lew Wallace: An Autobiography,* 2 vols., 1,028 pages. New York: Harper and Bros., 1906.

Weigley, Russell F. *Quartermaster General of the Union Army: A Biography of M. C. Meigs,* 396 pages. New York: Columbia University Press, 1959.

Weld, Stephen Minot, Jr. *War Diary and Letters of Stephen Minot Weld, 1861–1865,* 428 pages. Cambridge, Mass.: Riverside Press, 1912.

Welles, Gideon. *The Diary of Gideon Welles.* 3 vols., 1,943 pages. Boston, Mass.: Houghton Mifflin Co., 1911.

Williams, T. Harry. *Hayes of the Twenty-third: The Civil War Volunteer Officer,* 324 pages. New York: Alfred A. Knopf, 1965.

Wilson, James Harrison. *Under the Old Flag: Recollections of Military Operations in the War for the Union, the Spanish War, the Boxer Rebellion, etc.,* 2 vols., 1,162 pages. New York: D. Appleton and Co., 1912.

Young, Kenneth Ray. *The General's General: The Life and Times of Arthur MacArthur,* 400 pages. Boulder, Colo.: Westview Press, 1994.